Structures of capital

Structures of capital

The social organization of the economy

Edited by

SHARON ZUKIN AND PAUL DIMAGGIO

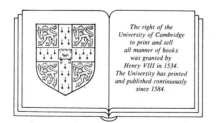

The right of the
University of Cambridge
to print and sell
all manner of books
was granted by
Henry VIII in 1534.
The University has printed
and published continuously
since 1584.

CAMBRIDGE UNIVERSITY PRESS

Cambridge

New York   Port Chester   Melbourne   Sydney

Published by the Press Syndicate of the University of Cambridge
The Pitt Building, Trumpington Street, Cambridge CB2 1RP
40 West 20th Street, New York, NY 10011, USA
10 Stamford Road, Oakleigh, Melbourne 3166, Australia

First published 1990

Printed in the United States of America

Library of Congress Cataloging-in-Publication Data
Structures of capital : the social organization of the economy /
edited by Sharon Zukin and Paul DiMaggio.
  p. cm.
ISBN 0-521-37523-1. – ISBN 0-521-37678-5 (pbk.)
1. Economics – Sociological aspects.   2. Capital.   3. Capitalism.
I. Zukin, Sharon.   II. DiMaggio, Paul.
HM35.S77   1990
306.3–dc20
                                                  89-70798
                                                      CIP

British Library Cataloguing in Publication Data
Structures of capital : the social organization of the economy.
1. Economics. Social aspects.
I. Zukin, Sharon   II. DiMaggio, Paul
330

ISBN 0-521-37523-1 hard covers
ISBN 0-521-37678-5 paperback

Contents

vi   STRUCTURES OF CAPITAL

Preface

The chapters in this volume represent a wide range of perspectives on the sociology of economic life, but not an exhaustive selection. We have tried to create a user-friendly volume, one that can be read profitably by sociologists and other scholars approaching the topic for the first time and by students in graduate and advanced undergraduate courses in economic sociology, socioeconomics, political sociology, social stratification, political economy, and the sociology of organization. Thus for the book's first section we have favored papers that provide a broad overview of economic sociology; and for the latter sections we have sought lucid, empirically based accounts of significant aspects of economic organization, behavior, or change. (Almost half of the chapters represent article-length summaries of significant books that together would otherwise require a semester's syllabus of their own.) We have not included papers relying on complex mathematical models or statistical analyses that would be inaccessible to many readers; and we have excluded work on topics that, like the economics of labor markets, have been thoroughly covered in other texts.

This project and our collaboration have their roots in a special issue of the journal *Theory and Society* from 1986, in which a number of the following chapters originally appeared. The special issue was initiated by Sharon Zukin, who was studying the economic process called deindustrialization; she was joined almost immediately by Paul DiMaggio, who brought to the editorial process an interest in organizational aspects of economic phenomena. From the outset, the co-editors shared more or less equally in the chapter-editing and writing chores, often editing the same papers and rewriting the same material so many times that they effectively blurred the idiosyncrasies of individual authorship. Throughout the process the senior editor carried the major share of manuscript preparation, communication with authors, and similar duties.

To the extent that there has been an intellectual division of labor, it has reflected the co-editors' rather different backgrounds. One of us, Zukin, was steeped in political economy; the other, DiMaggio, comes out of what we call the social-organizational approach. One of the pleasures of collaboration has been our mutual exposure to the perspective of the other, and a growing appreciation of the synergistic relevance of the political-economy and social-organization perspectives to the problems that economic sociology addresses. Because these two perspectives have ordinarily operated in casual mutual disregard, we view the attempt to combine them, in the chapters that follow and especially our introduction, as a notable innovation. At the same time, we have no illusion of having reached closure on this point. We believe that we have succeeded in bringing the two traditions to the altar; subsequent scholarship will be required to consummate the marriage.

Many people deserve our thanks. Most deserving are our authors, almost all of whom went through two or more exhausting rounds of revision with enthusiasm and good cheer. If all productive workers displayed so little shirking and so much other-regarding behavior, there would be no need for agency theory.

We are indebted, further, to our colleagues on the *Theory and Society* editorial board for their support, patience, and enthusiasm. In particular, we are grateful to Janet W. Gouldner, the journal's executive editor, who deftly interceded in complicated publishers' negotiations; and Karen Lucas, whose special role is inadequately captured by the title of managing editor.

We also express appreciation to the Center for Advanced Study in the Behavioral Sciences and Yale's Program on Non-Profit Organizations and Sociology Department, which facilitated DiMaggio's work.

Finally, we thank our three fine editors at Cambridge: Sue Allen-Mills, who launched the project; Emily Loose, who saw it into port; and, especially, Penny Carter, without whose effective ministrations it would have sunk in mid-voyage.

S.Z.
P.J.D.

New York City
Rowayton, Conn.

Contributors

FRED BLOCK is professor of sociology at the University of Pennsylvania. A co-author of *The Mean Season: The Attack on the Welfare State*, he is completing *Beyond the Economic Paradigm: Postindustrialism and Economic Sociology*.

LUC BOLTANSKI, author of *Les Cadres: La Formation d'un Groupe Social* (published in English by Cambridge University Press), is a directeur d'etudes at the École des Hautes Études en Sciences Sociales in Paris, where he heads the research group in political and moral sociology. He is collaborating with an economist on studies of the social construction of a legitimate order.

GÖRAN BRULIN is a researcher at the Center for the Study of Working Life in Stockholm. He has just completed a work on managerial ideologies in Sweden, *Från den 'suenska modellen' till företagskorporatism?*

PAUL DIMAGGIO, co-editor of this volume, is associate professor of sociology at Yale University. He is the editor of *Nonprofit Enterprise in the Arts: Studies in Mission and Constraint*, and is currently completing a book on the social organization of the arts in the United States. He is a senior editor of the journal *Theory and Society* and a 1990 John Simon Guggenheim Memorial Foundation Fellow.

JON ELSTER is professor of political science at the University of Chicago and research director of the Institute for Social Research in Oslo. His recent publications include *The Cement of Society, Solomonic Judgments*, and *Nuts and Bolts for the Social Sciences*.

ROGER FRIEDLAND is professor of sociology at the University of California at Santa Barbara, where he coordinated an interdisciplinary faculty group that examined approaches to the social organization of the economy. Co-editor of *Beyond the Marketplace: Rethinking Economy and Society*, he has recently written about the integration of interpretive and

ix

materialist approaches to institutional analysis, and the relations between corporate and urban systems.

RAY FRIEDMAN is an assistant professor at Harvard Business School.

ULF HIMMELSTRAND, professor of sociology at the University of Uppsala, has been on leave since 1988 as a visiting professor at the University of Nairobi. Together with economists and other social scientists, he has produced a volume on the notion of exogenous factors in economic analysis for the IDEA Project (Interdisciplinary Dimensions of Economic Analysis). The co-editor and joint author of a text on *Sweden: Social Structure and Everyday Life*, Himmelstrand is working in Kenya on problems of African development.

PAUL M. HIRSCH is The Allen Professor of Strategy, Organizational Behavior, and Sociology at the Kellogg Graduate School of Management at Northwestern University. He is the author of a book on executive displacement in corporate restructuring.

MARSHALL W. MEYER is professor of management and Anheuser-Busch Term Professor in the Wharton School and professor of sociology at the University of Pennsylvania. His books include *Environments and Organizations* (with several co-authors), *Change in Public Bureaucracies, Limits to Bureaucratic Growth, Bureaucracy in Modern Society* (with Peter Blau), and *Permanently Failing Organizations* (with Lynne Zucker).

STUART MICHAELS is a research associate in the Department of Sociology at the University of Chicago.

BETH MINTZ, associate professor of sociology at the University of Vermont, is co-author (with Michael Schwartz) of *The Power Structure of American Business*. With recent publications on social class and organization among U.S. corporate capitalists, she is now doing research on the changing structure of the medical industry.

PAUL MONTAGNA, professor of sociology at Brooklyn College and the Graduate School of City University of New York, has written about the accounting field and its cultural context. He is now tracing the history of the tobacco industry in the Connecticut Valley from merchant capitalism to full-scale capitalist industrialization.

CHARLES PERROW, who has prepared new editions of both *Complex Organizations: A Critical Essay* and *Normal Accidents*, is professor of sociology at Yale University. He has turned his attention to organizational analysis of the industrial revolution, on the one hand, and the AIDS crisis, on the other.

JIMY SANDERS is assistant professor of sociology at the University of South Carolina. He has published several articles on the welfare state; and is now studying the political character of the business cycle, state policies of redistribution, and alternative modes of socioeconomic mobility among contemporary immigrant groups.

MICHAEL SCHWARTZ is professor of sociology at the State University of New York, Stony Brook. The co-author (with Beth Mintz) of *The Power Structure of American Business*, he has also recently been co-editor of *Structural Analysis of Business* and *The Corporate Elite as a Ruling Class*. He is engaged in longterm research on the causes and consequences of plant closings, and mathematical analysis of corporate networks.

LINDA BREWSTER STEARNS is associate professor of sociology at the University of California, Riverside. She has recently been a Russell Sage Foundation Scholar and a Howard Foundation Fellow. Co-author of articles on interlocking directorates and occupational segregation by sex, she is working on a book that investigates the relation between capital markets, corporate capital structures, and corporate behavior.

RICHARD SWEDBERG, assistant professor of sociology at the University of Stockholm, is author of *Economic Sociology: Past and Present* and *Economics and Sociology: Redefining Their Boundaries – Conversations with Economists and Sociologists*. He is currently editing Joseph A. Schumpeter's writings and studying Swedish exports.

MICHAEL USEEM is professor of sociology at Boston University. In addition to *The Inner Circle: Large Corporations and the Rise of Business Political Activity in the U.S. and U.K.*, his publications focus on corporate political and social outreach, and the relations between corporate restructuring, educational cultures in company management, and the organization of professional and managerial work.

ROGER WALDINGER is associate professor of sociology at The City College and Graduate School, City University of New York. He is the author of *Through the Eye of the Needle: Immigrants and Enterprise in New York Garment Trades* and a co-author of *Immigrant Entrepreneurs: Immigrant Business in Europe and the United States*. He is doing research on immigration, the economic aspects of ethnicity, and urban change.

PETER WHALLEY is associate professor of sociology at Loyola University. Having written *The Social Production of Technical Work*, he is now doing research on the social organization of independent inventing and technical entrepreneurship.

SHARON ZUKIN, co-editor of this volume, is professor of sociology at Brooklyn College and the Graduate School, City University of New York. Author of *Loft Living: Culture and Capital in Urban Change* and the forthcoming *American Market/Place: Landscapes of Economic Power*, she has spent 1989-90 at the Russell Sage Foundation, working on a book on Jewish-Americans and African-Americans. She is a senior editor of the journal *Theory and Society*.

1

Introduction

SHARON ZUKIN AND PAUL DIMAGGIO

Today, more than at any time since the Great Depression, economic phenomena command our interest. Structural changes in both the domestic and world economies affect the way we live and work. Political reaction to the consequences of these changes has moved the "neoclassical" tradition within economic theory to the forefront of social analysis.

The influence of neoclassical economics mounted during the political attack on liberalism that began around 1968 and was reinforced by the oil "shocks" and economic crises of the 1970s. Neoclassical perspectives grew in popularity as corporations in the United States, Britain, and elsewhere edged away from historical compromises with labor and the welfare state. This shift directed attention to individual rather than collective welfare, and private rather than public obligation. Embracing neoclassical models and metaphors enabled conservative leaders and political parties in many nations to identify themselves with a "hardnosed" realism that became more attractive to voters in a time of global economic competition.

During the 1980s, political power in many countries shifted to regimes that followed the lead of Ronald Reagan and Margaret Thatcher, who offered to restrict the social orientation of many government activities. At the same time, cultural power celebrated the individualistic, profit-oriented "yuppies." Paradoxically, the "party of order" sanctioned change in many institutional values, rejecting the language of moral imperatives for that of utility maximization and cost-benefit analysis. For this project, neoclassical economics provided both the tools and a "scientific" justification.

Like everyone else, sociologists have been influenced both by the scale and complexity of economic change. But, while neoclassical thought has asserted itself as the mainstream and dominant paradigm in economics and has even vied for hegemony in other social sciences, sociology has resisted. As Hirsch et al. note in this volume, most sociologists, whatever their paradigm, exhibit a visceral distaste for the principles and procedures of the neoclassical model. They find it difficult to conceive of a social world in which abstract norms (such as "maximizing") count for more than power, group membership, or patterned interactions. They also emphasize the usefulness of real-world observation. Sociologists are more inclined than orthodox economists to accept the fallibility and flexibility of human action; to view social causation as contingent, path-dependent, and, except at microscopic levels, irreducible to simple models of high generality; and to value carefully designed empirical research over ingenious mathematical models based on untested assumptions.

The press of economic events, the implausibility of the dominant neoclassical paradigm in economics, and the failures of work in that paradigm to explain a wide range of crucial problems – structural change, the origins of individual preferences, collective economic action, nonmarket allocation mechanisms – have led many sociologists to the conclusion that it is time to undertake a new analysis of the relation between economy and society. This aspiration recalls sociology's classical tradition. For all their differences, Marx and Weber took as their starting point the centrality of the institutional order that comprises a society's cultural and economic infrastructures. Some sociologists, following Marx, use the concept of capital as both substance and metaphor; others, following Weber, focus on broader aspects of the interpenetration of economic organization and social institutions.

On the one hand, the re-emergence of the classical tradition has led to the revitalization of the study of political economy. On the other hand, it has inspired attempts by students of social organization to develop sociological models of economic phenomena. Authors in the political economy tradition have tended to focus on issues at the societal or "macro" level of analysis. Those in the social organizational tradition have concentrated on the "meso" level of firms and markets.

This volume represents an effort to combine work in each of these two lines of inquiry. Its title, *Structures of Capital*, bears a loose double meaning. First, it refers to *capital*, by which we mean the economic and social resources that dominant groups use to maintain their control (and with which subordinate groups contest it). Several of the contributions, for example, focus on the use of investment capital to exercise control over economic actors in market situations, while others analyze the role of nonmarket forces – both state policy and informal relations among economic elites – in channeling investment. The reference to *structure* also invokes the notion of social organization, by which we mean the ways in which formal and informal social relations mediate or constitute the operation of markets for goods and services. Thus several chapters analyze the ways in which owners of firms control, or fail to control, subordinates, and the influence of such efforts on organizational structures and behavior.

We believe that these two traditions in economic sociology – the political economic and the social organizational – need one another. The social-organizational approach depends upon political economy to explain the frameworks in which economic action proceeds, the rules and legal systems that constitute such objects as firms and markets, and the pressures to which the accumulation process subjects owners and managers. At the same time, political-economic analysis requires models of the forms of social organization that mediate the effects of macroscopic processes, and cause variation in their consequences at the level of industries and national economies.

This essay introduces the chapters of *Structures of Capital* in four stages. First, we describe the paradigm crisis of neoclassical economics that creates a gap for economic sociology to fill, emphasizing the notion of rationality, the theory of the firm, and macroeconomic theory. Second, we suggest that the major themes employed by sociologists who criticize neoclassical models (and by unorthodox economists and political scientists as well) reflect a conviction that economic action is characterized by four kinds of "embeddedness" – cognitive, cultural, social, and political – that neoclassical economics tends to ignore. Third, using illustrations at three levels of analysis (rationality, control, and intercorporate coordination), we point to ways in which both social organizational and political economic perspectives shape satisfactory sociological accounts of economic processes. Finally, we indicate how the perspective of economic sociology applies to several examples of contemporary change.

The crisis of confidence in neoclassical economics

The resurgence of economic sociology in the 1980s reflects a growing recognition, both within and outside of economics, that the discipline's dominant neoclassical paradigm suffers from serious limitations.[1] Few regions of economic orthodoxy have been untouched by this critical reassessment. It has extended from microeconomics and the notion of individual rationality, to the theory of the firm and models of collective rationality and control, and to macroeconomics and the failures of both Keynesian and monetarist theory.

The crisis of individual rationality
According to neoclassical economics, individuals allocate scarce resources according to a utility function of ranked preferences

for goods, services, or, in some versions, commodities for which goods
or services are inputs. To do this, they must behave rationally, that is,
in a manner that is calculating and self-interested. But economic orthodoxy does not merely hold (as most social scientists would agree) that
it is useful in theory-building to assume that people generally pursue
what they believe to be their self-interest. Rather, it entails a system of
assumptions including, in strict versions, that people have only one stable ranking of preferences, that they have reasonably full information
about alternatives, that they behave individualistically in terms of both
ends and means; and that, because these conditions are satisfied, their
choices, *in toto*, yield an equilibrium characterized by "Pareto optimality," whereby no one can do better without making someone else worse
off.

Recent work has assailed this notion of rationality on numerous
grounds. The most radical critics suggest that human behavior is so far
from calculatingly rational as to make models based on this assumption
fundamentally misguided. Many have argued that interests and modes
of pursuing them (including economic rationality itself) are broadly cultural and encoded in institutions. A related line of attack draws on eth-
nomethodology to characterize human behavior as largely scripted and
conventional, based on taken-for-granted assumptions and an inherent
human urge to establish institutions and confirm mutual definitions of
reality. Thus in real societies the "free market" is always bounded by
sets of mutual assumptions and obligations and guaranteed by the
state. And in real life we "economic" men and women are surrounded
by a-rational but thoughtful behavior, epitomized by the legendary
economist who leaves a tip at a restaurant to which she knows she will
never return.[2]

Even if we grant that people are fundamentally rational in their orientations toward economic action, critics dispute the notion that individuals have but one utility function, as implied by the assumption that
they make trade-offs among various objects of desire. In this view, individuals often face decisions between incommensurate goods that
must be decided on the basis of custom or, as Amitai Etzioni has argued, moral imperatives in the form of values or norms that cannot be
reduced to utilities on a single hierarchy.[3]

Let us pretend for a moment that people both behave rationally and
possess a single utility function. A problem still remains in the assumption that individuals' choices are independent of one another. Four
kinds of interdependence challenge models built on this assumption.
First, our utility may be a function not only of our own welfare but of
the welfare of those we care about; if by maximizing our personal welfare we cause theirs to decline, we shall be less well off. Second, the
value to us of a given good or service (for example, a status symbol) may

depend on the extent to which others consume it. Third, our ability to act may be constrained by the fact that others will respond to our actions; if we maximize ruthlessly, for example, we may be subject to reprisals from our peers. Fourth, we may only be able to enhance our own welfare by cooperating with others, i.e., by acting collectively; this will require integrating different utility functions in one way or another. (In his chapter, Elster argues that game theoretic approaches are useful in understanding how this might be done.)[4]

If we drop all these objections, the neoclassical paradigm remains vulnerable on still another count because individuals rarely have the information required to engage in synoptic decision-making. Some critics have pointed to behavioral research showing that consumers rarely acquire very complete information before making even relatively important decisions. Others contend on theoretical grounds that gathering and processing full information is so costly that only a fool would try to do it. Because we do not have full information about alternatives and cannot predict fully the results of our decisions, these will be suboptimal unless we consult complex payoff matrices. This makes no sense as an assumption about behavior, however; and, as theory, it suggests that choices may depend not only on preferences but also on such things as one's capacity to tolerate risk.[5]

Imagine, however, that people do have all the information they need, that they act without regard to the preferences of others, that they are unambivalently committed to a single set of preferences, and that they enter into every choice with the sole intention of maximizing utility. Even these assumptions run aground on cognitive evidence. Psychologists' studies of what they call "decision heuristics" reveal that error is embedded in the very cognitive structure of decision. Researchers have found that, holding constant the utility to be lost or gained, people are more likely to accept a risky option that is framed in terms of gains than losses; they are more likely to place a high value on a human cost if they can visualize those who will incur it; and they are more likely to estimate a high probability for a random event if they are given an arbitrarily high baseline than if they are given an equally arbitrary low one. In other words, even when we try to make rational decisions, we often cannot do so.[6]

Economics is far from defenseless against these charges. Analyses of information, interdependent decision processes, and decision-making under uncertainty are all growing topics of inquiry aimed at rescuing the neoclassical model. Taken together, however, the criticisms we have reviewed cast a long shadow over it.

Crisis in the theory of the firm

The conventional economic theory of the firm conceives of the business corporation as a unitary rational actor just like the natural person. We might imagine that the case for rationality would be easier to make for firms than for people. For one thing, while people have many preferences to juggle, firms are supposed to concentrate on one: maximizing profit. For another, natural selection in the marketplace more plausibly enforces optimizing behavior on firms. It is easier to imagine that inefficient companies in a market economy eventually go out of business than to believe that inefficient people have fewer children.

Yet the economic theory of the firm has also come under a dark cloud of suspicion in recent years, due to three prominent lines of attack by outside critics and dissidents within economics. One set of criticisms concerns *complexity*: firms are so complex, it is argued, that they cannot be very rational. Because firms are composed of many individuals and departments that cannot easily coordinate their activities, information is hard to obtain and aggregate; firms, moreover, face uncertain environments about which they can predict relatively little. A second set of criticisms has to do with *control*: the people who work in firms have so many diverse motivations that they cannot be guided toward a single coherent goal. Even if firms possessed the technical means of synoptic rationality, they could not use them because the people who work for business corporations – from top management to men and women on the shop floor – try to enhance their own well-being rather than the profitability of the firm as a whole. A third and final set of criticisms has to do with *selection*: all firms are not equally constrained by economic discipline. If the economy generates large oligopolies that, within broad bounds, are invulnerable to market competition, such firms can get away with a great deal of submaximizing behavior.

Let us turn first to complexity. Landmark studies of decision-making within corporations were undertaken by behavioral scientists of the "Carnegie School," notably Nobel laureate Herbert Simon and James G. March. Simon, March, and colleagues noted that the firms they observed *rarely* maximized in making decisions; to do so would have been too costly or awkward. Instead, companies relied on organizational routines: experience-based formulas for such tasks as setting prices, maintaining inventories, and making budgets. Such routines were questioned only when key indicators (e.g., profits or sales) strayed outside of given parameters. Even then, decisions were not made after gathering complete information but by considering alternatives one at a time until an acceptable one was found. Big problems were "factored" into little ones and assigned to specialized departments, each of which favored solutions that maximized its own priorities rather than the welfare of the firm as a whole. Real firms, according to the Carnegie researchers, are far from being the omniscient maximizers of economic texts. Rather, they use "bounded rationality" and "satisfice" in search of merely adequate solutions.[7]

Other researchers, especially sociologists, have argued that corporate rationality is limited not just by complexity but by the ubiquity of self-interested behavior on the part of the firm's employees. As Charles Perrow has put it: "Organizations are tools . . . that people inside and outside . . . make use of and try to control." Studies of firms show constant political conflict between top and middle managers, among middle managers and between them and staff, and between managers and workers. Top managers are said to put sales and growth above profitability; middle managers strive to boost their department budgets; professional staff care more about their reputations outside the firm than about their contributions to it; and workers combine to resist every attempt by management to boost productivity. If such self-seeking is rampant, how can owners ever establish enough control to maximize profits?[8]

The classic response of economic orthodoxy is on a "higher level": the invisible hand of the market will reward efficient firms with survival, while inefficient firms that resist control will fail. A more recent development in this tradition, agency theory, goes inside the black box of the firm to specify both the nature of market discipline and techniques for minimizing "agency costs," i.e., the costs of self-serving actions by nonowners and of means used to limit them. The invisible hand is replaced by the action of capital markets; we are told that the quality of a firm's management will be reflected in its equity prices. Inside the firm, control is facilitated by such tangible devices as bonus systems that link managerial rewards to firm profitability. (The long-term interests of the firm may, however, be threatened by other devices, such as stock options, that link managerial rewards to short-term changes in equity prices.)[9]

Perrow notes, in his chapter, that agency theory rests on a Hobbesian creation myth. Just as a social contract creates the state, firms are supposed to be dense patches in networks of relations among economic free agents. As this perspective suggests, the major insights of agency theory concern capitalists' control of top management. Agency theory has nonetheless been applied more generally to employment relations throughout the firm. Perrow criticizes the assumptions of agency theory as unrealistic and ideologically tinged. He finds that it embodies a view of humans as undersocialized and greed-driven, denies inequality of power within the employment relationship, and is obsessively concerned with the potential malfeasance of employees to the exclusion of that of employers.

Although Perrow does not make this point, agency arguments are limited as explanations of firm efficiency as well. The use of bonuses and similar motivational techniques is restricted to agency problems concerning top managers and to employees whose outputs are easily monitored. Further, even if outsiders can monitor the efficiency of team production within the firm (and this is a big "if"), capital markets will *not* discipline firms that fail to meet an abstract ideal of maximizing efficiency, but only firms that are noticeably *less* efficient than their competitors. This seems a weak as well as an indirect means of control. No wonder that, as Marshall Meyer and Lynne Zucker have pointed out, firm age is poorly correlated with performance and many organizations limp along as semi-permanent invalids.[10]

The most devastating critique of natural-selection metaphors for firms' efficiency comes from within economics. Richard Nelson and Sidney Winter have taken evolutionary arguments seriously and developed models of selection based on behaviorally sound assumptions similar to those of the Carnegie School. The organizational counterpart to genes, they argue, are routines, or standardized decision rules. "But whereas in orthodox theory . . . decision rules are assumed to be the consequence of maximization," in the Nelson and Winter formulation such rules only reflect "at any moment . . . the historically given routines governing the actions of a business firm." Because Nelson and Winter's firms are bound by precedent, they emphasize a slow process of organizational learning in place of strict selection of "the best" structures and forms. Similarly, firms are satisficers, not maximizers. Instead of strict determinism and equilibrium, they emphasize chance ("stochastic") effects and constant change. At best, Nelson and Winter note, competition can only select those firms best adapted to past environments. Such firms may not be the best equipped to deal with present conditions.[11]

An important contribution of the "new organizational economics," especially the work of Oliver Williamson, has been to bring firms and markets within a single analytic compass as alternative structures of allocation and choice. Williamson argues that bureaucracy grows in response to conditions that make the *transaction costs* of market exchange unacceptably high. (By contrast, Marshall Meyer, in this volume, contends that bureaucracy grows not because it is efficient but because it is rational: that is, because organizations face endemically uncertain environments and creating bureaucracy is the only way they know how to deal with them.) Williamson's framework is like agency theory in that it preserves the classical assumption that firms are efficient maximizers while entering the black box of the firm to discover fresh problems that drive managers' choices. But, while agency theory considers bureaucracy as a site of connivance, Williamson views bureaucracy as an efficient solution to situations in which market exchange is too risky or imposes too many costs. As Perrow and Meyer point out, this rather naive view of formal organization as an unproblematic source of control runs counter to the evidence from organizational ethnographies that transaction costs in bureaucracies are often exceptionally high.[12]

Organizations, as Perrow points out, increasingly acknowledge the futility of erecting strong boundaries between markets and bureaucracies as decision structures. Firms incorporate markets as means of control, establishing shadow prices for transfers of goods between divisions (see, e.g., Peter Whalley's "Metalco," this volume) and using divisional profits as criteria for internal investment. (As Robert Eccles has shown, these processes are themselves highly political ones.) Large firms maintain stables of dependent suppliers through market ties so intrusive as to approximate hierarchical control. Small firms establish ongoing relations at numerous levels to capture the benefits of integration without sacrificing autonomy. Many of these methods rely on "relational contracting," the economists' term for ongoing relationships of trust and mutual dependency, suggesting a need for a third ideal-type decision structure, based on informal social relations, parallel to markets and firms.[13]

Agency theorists place firms and markets within a common framework to analyze the former as versions of the latter. Williamson goes further, treating markets and hierarchy as parallel solutions to similar problems. Once so much is granted, it is a natural step to reverse the agency theorists' strategy and, in Harrison White's apt phrase, regard "markets as social structures." Increasingly, sociologists have viewed markets as constituted by ongoing relationships among concrete actors rather than by the maximizing responses of atomistic sellers to impersonal market signals. It is no accident that the brand of economics used in business schools to train managers – the industrial organization approach associated with Michael Porter – does not emphasize abstract models of homogeneous sellers in competitive markets but rather concrete accounts of highly differentiated firms communicating with one another through tacit signals in order to limit competition.[14]

Orthodox economists have attempted to salvage the neoclassical model of the firm. But the challenges have been so numerous as to call the paradigm into question. Once opened to empirical scrutiny, the black box of the organization has been a Pandora's box of findings that challenge the very categories of orthodox thought.

Crisis in macroeconomic theory

Many social scientists and policymakers have also questioned the adequacy of macroeconomic theory derived from the neoclassical model. This inadequacy stems in part from the long predominance of Keynesianism itself. But with the breakdown of the Keynesian mode of macroeconomic regulation, with its expansionary economy, consensus ideology, and tolerance for mass consumption even at public expense, attention is forcibly directed to the social and political context of growth. Those who believe the major benefits of a market economy – growth and relatively equitable allocation – are seriously threatened by individualistic economic decisions show skepticism toward orthodox claims about the invisible hand. They also find it problematic to apply microeconomic models that are themselves flawed to analysis of a dynamic national or global economy. On the one hand, neither macroeconomic models nor the microeconomic models on which they are based take important noneconomic factors from climate to politics into account. On the other hand, such models cannot predict change over time. In general, moreover, it is implausibly simplistic to generalize (or aggregate) microeconomic decisions into a large picture of the whole economy. As Lester Thurow has argued, real macroeconomic situations confront disequilibria, social agreements, and comparisons between social groups; these factors are all ignored by orthodox macroeconomic theory.[15]

Political economists have always taken a holistic view of growth and decline, examining interconnections that both orthodox economists and organizational theorists tended to avoid (as "exogenous factors") or leave implicit in their assumptions. Thus while others wanted to redesign the firm, or realign the relation between quantitative parameters (such as factor prices and interest rates) and individual action, political economists focused on the societal causes and effects of large-scale economic changes. They were especially drawn to the mutual influences on growth and allocation of economic actors (e.g., industrialists and financiers) as well as noneconomic actors such as social classes and the state. Thus political economy oriented macroeconomic theory to the social functions of capital and the state's economic roles.

Many studies in the new political economy after 1973 concentrated on the state's responsibilities in providing a material basis of support for capitalist profit-making, i.e., the state's accumulation function, and its provision of a moral education that legitimized the motivations of leading capitalists over time. If these capitalists were able to overcome the resistance of the work force and manipulate the levers of the state, their triumphs were always imposed against the form of collective action known as "class struggle" on the one hand and the "relative autonomy" of the state on the other. Such a compromised result was Keynesianism itself. But, as Fred Block argues in this volume, *post facto* explanations that reduce economic outcomes to the "logic of capital" are flawed by functionalism. They ignore the complexity and variability of economic systems, as well as the necessity of explaining system failure instead of adjustment. The economic crises of the 1970s and the consequent search by capital for new strategic models of capital accumulation shaped three more subtle orientations in the political economy approach that would relate the macroeconomic and social functions of investment, employment, and production.[16]

First, the rebirth of crisis theory directed attention to long-term cycles in such economic processes as the falling rate of profit and the rise and decline of entire systems of capitalist domination. To some degree, periodic crisis was seen as an inevitable product of capitalism's "contradictions." But crisis was also portrayed as reflecting the increasing efficacy of political and social constraints on capital accumulation. Crisis, therefore, could be examined as a socially constructed response to a shift in power relations between basic groups, especially social classes and the state.[17]

The second new orientation in political economy directed attention to the specific conditions in which power relations among social groups produce systemic crisis. In James O'Connor's influential formulation, the state's efforts to balance coercion and compliance at some point impose economic costs in the form of "fiscal crisis." Capitalists who initially support government social expenditures turn against them when the costs of government become too high. At the same time, both capital and labor press the state to increase expenditures on their behalf. Capitalists push for social investment and social consumption, which lower the wage bill and make private investment more productive; and labor demands social expenditures, mainly in the welfare system, that enhance the quality of life and ultimately make workers, in the capitalists' view, less compliant.[18]

O'Connor's theory just barely pre-dated the real fiscal crises that emerged after 1975 in the United States, Britain, France, and numerous cities, beginning with New York. Rather than explain these crises in terms of either rising interest rates or the self-serving actions of individual politicians, political economic analysis sought *political* reasons for reducing social expenditures, in terms of either raising profits for capital or "disciplining" labor. Just as fiscal crisis was subjected to such inquiry, so were the major phases of the business cycle: depression and inflation. The assumption that such crises were autonomous or predetermined yielded to questions about the conditions under which capital (or labor) was willing to instigate a crisis and tip the balance of public policy. Numerous historical analyses focused on the development of the welfare state. A smaller number of studies have presented research on specific areas such as inflation, regulation, and industrial policy.[19]

A third new orientation emerged with the recognition that the crisis that began in many economic systems after 1973 was brought on by accelerated capital mobility, which was seen as the unconstrained result of numerous individualistic decisions. Facilitated to a great degree by technological advances in automation and transportation, capital investment moved rapidly from one geographical region to another and from "declining" to "advancing" sectors of the economy (e.g., Sunbelt vs. Frostbelt, steel and autos vs. computers and silicon chips, large bureaucratic businesses vs. small dynamic firms). The "hypermobility" of capital, as Barry Bluestone and Bennett Harrison termed it, did not result in even economic growth or equitable allocation. On the one hand, regional and sectoral disparities in capital investment exacerbated differences in labor markets and public and private resources. On the other hand, the inability to control capital by existing forms of political and social mediation made such institutions as the local community and the nation-state increasingly irrelevant. Political economists like Lester Thurow, Robert Reich, and Bluestone and Harrison were also concerned that a capitalist class oriented to short-term profit would fail to invest in modernization, long-term research and development, and organizational renewal in older industries and industrial areas. This concern shaped an attempt to reformulate macroeconomic policy in order to make the market economy more competitive and its system of social rewards more fair.[20]

In the United States and Western Europe, the major stimulus that has made both nonorthodox economists and sociologists more attentive to macrolevel forces has been the rise of a global economy and the recognition that these regions have lost their hegemonic position within it. Japan has served both as a screen upon which the discontents of American managers have been projected and a laboratory for students of the role of state and social structure in encouraging economic growth. Japan's development of an automobile industry as prime engine of the economy after World War II, and the rise of its integrated-circuit sector after 1970, to take two prominent examples, would have been inconceivable without a web of cooperative relations among producers, the government, and finance capital, as well as national and firm-level cultures that shift the balance between investment and consumption.

Management theorists reacted initially to the "Japanese miracle" by urging Americans to emulate Japanese methods and structures, in effect replacing the assumptions of the self-regulating competitive market with an equally stylized model of internal labor markets, state-guided investment, and intercorporate consultation. But the *japonisme* of the 1970s and 1980s has been succeeded by a recognition that there exist a variety of institutional paths to economic success. In contrast to the orderly collectivism of Japan's largest enterprises, in the newly industrializing countries of Southeast Asia, the behavior of extremely competitive firms and entrepreneurs is structured by government policy that stops just short of public control. Also unlike Japan's coalition of primary sector and state, Italy's prosperity has been fueled by the ability of small firms to develop new forms of regional cooperation without initial state intervention.

Just as the macroeconomic sources of success in global competition show great variability, so do conjectures about decline. In Western Europe, not only must such factors as wages and currency values be taken into account, but also the closeness of relations between industrial and financial capital, and the degree of cooperation among big business, small business, labor unions, and the state. If "dual" structures, moreover, appear to be a constant of most advanced industrial economies – with a competitive and a monopoly sector, and "core" and "peripheral" workers – the way those dualities are managed by macro-level institutions has important consequences for overall economic performance.

In sum, macroeconomic explanation has accorded a new prominence to institutional and structural factors. Recognizing the heterogeneity of successful models has interred the faith in a "one best system" and, with this, raised grave doubts about the imagery of single-equilibrium analyses.[21]

Not only the state, but transnational actors have been accorded new importance as determinants of macroeconomic performance. From the 1970s transnational corporations have grown more influential in shaping policies of the nation-state, as well as imposing their own quasi-governmental rules of global exchange. The debt crisis, mediated by policies of the International Monetary Fund and the World Bank, has altered the direction of state economic policy in the economically less developed nations of Latin America, Africa, and Eastern Europe, and shifted long-standing preferences of many governments (Mexico, Ghana, China) from public to private ownership. Moreover, integration of financial markets in the United States, Britain, and the European Community has opened these markets to greater influence by both the state and financial investors.[22]

In general, the efforts of neoclassical economics to turn tenets about the economic behavior of individuals and firms into explanatory principles to guide the economic performance of national economies have been swamped by failure in much of the world. The neoclassical model has been rejected due to a growing awareness that macro-level institutional structures may play the crucial role in shaping macroeconomic outcomes. Neoclassical economics has, moreover, been challenged by the recognition that institutional variation among successful national economies calls for complex and contingent explanatory models. Such developments open the way for new work on the economy that gives full recognition to its noneconomic sources and boundaries.

Four kinds of embeddedness of economic action

It is not very difficult to identify the failures of the neoclassical tradition. A greater challenge is to develop an alternative scenario, one in which economic institutions are thoroughly integrated with social relations. It must be noted, as a methodological starting point, that economic sociologists vary widely in their posture toward economics. While some are content to criticize, others try to improve economic models by incorporating more realistic (and more sociological) behavioral assumptions. Still others prefer to ignore economics, either because they regard its assumptions and modes of operation as preposterous or because they are interested in different issues.

The authors of the chapters in the first part of this volume take on the relationship between economics and sociology explicitly. Hirsch et al. regard neoclassical economists with the wonder of anthropologists encountering an isolated tribe: they emphasize the positivistic goals of that discipline and its totalizing imperative, the focus of neoclassicists upon models and their distaste for data, and their limited appetite for ambiguity. In other words, Hirsch and his colleagues suggest that neoclassical economists have a distinctive project that has little to do with sociology. Were it not for an often open competition between the disciplines for influence on public policy and a share of public funds, we could live and let live. Yet Hirsch et al. leave us with a sense of relief that sociology has not abandoned its generalist's curiosity, nor its concern about problems that cannot be definitively resolved.

Swedberg and colleagues also review a number of dimensions on which (neoclassical) economics and (mainstream) sociology differ, but focus less on method and more on assumptions about the nature of the world. Sociologists, they observe, have a wider view of actors (one that includes groups, classes and institutions as well as persons and firms), a different notion of economic action (as part of a social economy), and a dislike of equilibrium analysis. Theirs is not a policy of isolation, however. Sociologists, they argue, must read and learn from economics so as to challenge it on its own terrain.

Elster's contribution, by contrast, strikes out in a different direction, urging Marxist social theorists to forsake sociological functionalism and adopt both a principle, methodological individualism, and a method, game theoretic analysis, more commonly associated with economics. To be sure, Elster only uses individualism as a means toward the analysis of collective rationality, and his most glaring cases of functionalist folly come from neoclassical economics. By the same token, the economists who use game theory have been anything but orthodox. Yet, while Elster's voice has been influential, the approach he describes is mainly a matter of abstract rational modeling; it thus contrasts with the emphasis of much economic sociology on "dirty hands." Moreover, although Elster's criticism of functionalism is well taken, it does not speak to nonfunctionalist kinds of institutionalism that account for individual action in ways that are to some extent inconsistent with models of strategic rationality. Descriptions of individual action as conventional or very boundedly rational, for example, do not correspond to a game theoretic model.

But Elster is not alone in bringing work by nonorthodox economists to bear on sociological problems. Roger Waldinger's chapter on immigrant enterprise, which draws on industrial-organization economics and dual-labor-market theory, also illustrates how sociology can benefit from economists' behavioral and institutional observations.

If there is a core principle that unites most, if not all, of the contributions to this volume, it is a belief in the *embeddedness* of economic action. The notion of embeddedness is derived from the economic anthropology of Karl Polanyi, who claimed in his landmark study *The Great Transformation* that the self-regulating market of eighteenth-century England cast economic exchange adrift from the social relations to which it had until then been moored. Although all previous societies conducted exchange according to such *social* principles as reciprocity, redistribution, householding, and autarchy, Polanyi wrote, the self-regulating market subordinated society to the economy. To be sure, this subordination was not complete: the ravages of the market were unacceptable even to capitalist elites, and the state responded by limiting the market's scope. But the rise of the self-regulating market and the ideology that sustained it marked a watershed in human history.[23]

Contemporary scholars, while acknowledging the brilliance of Polanyi's contribution, have been skeptical about the starkness of his model (see Block's chapter in this volume). Mark Granovetter, whose recent essay has restored the concept of embeddedness to center stage, has argued that economic action in nonmarket societies is more calculating and strategic than Polanyi implied, and economic behavior in market societies is more embedded. But the notion of embeddedness represents a convenient framework for considering the implications of this volume's contents for each of the crises we noted in the previous section.[24]

We use "embeddedness" broadly to refer to the contingent nature of economic action with respect to cognition, culture, social structure, and political institutions. After briefly discussing cognitive and cultural embeddedness, we highlight the social and political embeddedness of economic action, as emphasized by the chapters in this volume.

Cognitive embeddedness

By "cognitive embeddedness," we refer to the ways in which the structured regularities of mental processes limit the exercise of economic reasoning. Such limitations have for the most part been revealed by research in cognitive psychology and decision theory. Although none of the contributions to this volume emphasize this theme, most of them share, along with most work in sociology, a keen sense of the limits to rationality posed by uncertainty, complexity, and the costs of information.

At the organizational level, the notion of bounded rationality is central to Perrow's argument that transaction costs of bureaucracy are much greater than Williamson acknowledges. At excessive scale, Perrow suggests, "firms probably lose control over some of their subsidiaries and the complex, internal interactions, and the ability to respond to external shocks, and lose out." Bounded rationality is also central to Meyer's contention that complex organizations expand bureaucracy as a ritualistic but inefficient means of achieving rationality. Two aspects of Meyer's argument deserve emphasis in this respect. First, he diverges from the neoclassical tradition by distinguishing between formal rationality (i.e., structured pursuit of given ends) and efficiency (i.e., success in that pursuit). Second, Meyer's suggestion that bureaucracies expand almost indefinitely in a feckless quest for rationality seems at odds with Perrow's contention that bureaucracy contains the seeds of its own destruction. These somewhat different theoretical tones may reflect the different contexts in which Perrow and Meyer have done empirical research. Perrow has worked on elaborate technological systems where the complexity-multiplying features of formal controls may result in devastating "normal accidents"; Meyer has studied public bureaucracies where expanding complexity is more likely to lead to "permanent failure."[25]

Paul Montagna's description of the ways in which accountants deal with risk and uncertainty illustrates the ongoing tension between formal rationality and the synoptic rationality of economic models. Yet the difficulty of establishing firm criteria of valuation has not prevented accounting as an intellectual discipline from claiming to develop objective decision-making standards (e.g., cost-benefit analysis). At the individual level, moreover, Peter Whalley demonstrates that organizational parameters have great influence over whether individual workers resist or reify market constraints. Whalley also suggests that such policies are less the result of conscious management strategy – and still less of "natural selection" – than of company-wide routines.

The notion of cognitive embeddedness is useful in calling attention to the limited ability of both human and corporate actors to employ the synoptic rationality required by neoclassical approaches. On the other hand, as Elster points out, there are analytic advantages to assuming that people do know ordinarily what is good for them and try to achieve it. To what extent (and under what conditions) are actors sufficiently aware of both their interests and means-ends relationships that we can realistically assume rationality instead of acknowledging cognitive limitations? Certainly, although they diverge from neoclassical notions in numerous other respects, many of the authors in this volume – Friedland and Sanders, Mintz and Schwartz, Useem, and Waldinger, for example – find it useful to assume that individuals, firms, and even classes are purposeful and reasonably clear-headed in their pursuit of self-interest.

Cultural embeddedness

When we say that economic behavior is "culturally" embedded, we refer to the role of shared collective understandings in shaping economic strategies and goals. Culture sets limits to economic rationality: it proscribes or limits market exchange in sacred objects and relations (e.g., human beings, body organs, physical intimacy) or between ritually classified groups. Moreover, as Viviana Zelizer has argued, culture may shape terms of trade, placing the insurance value of a child's life, for example, well above the price that could be justified on the basis of sheer economic calculation. Culture, in the form of beliefs and ideologies, taken for granted assumptions, or formal rule systems, also prescribes strategies of self-interested action (e.g., individualistic market exchange or political mobilization) and defines the actors who may legitimately engage in them (e.g., self-interested individuals, families, classes, formal organizations, ethnic groups). Culture provides scripts for applying different strategies to different classes of exchange. Finally, norms and constitutive understandings regulate market exchange, causing persons to behave with institutionalized and culturally specific definitions of integrity even when they could get away with cheating. Thus culture has a dual effect on economic institutions. On the one hand, it constitutes the structures in which economic self-interest is played out; on the other, it constrains the free play of market forces.[26]

Cultural analysis has a distinguished history in economic sociology, going back to Marx's analysis of fetishism and reification and Durkheim's observations on the noncontractual elements of contracts. Yet, in recent years, much sociology has deemphasized cultural aspects of economic action in favor of either a "structural" or "political" approach (see below). This may be appropriate for very specific investigations, when well-bounded groups share cultural understandings of the economy. But cultural embeddedness is important to take into account in cross-national comparisons, analysis of transnational processes, and studies of long-term or dramatic historical change.

Thus, in his chapter, Luc Boltanski interprets the modern management movement in postwar France as an effort by a coalition of American economists and French conservative politicians and industrialists to transform the "mentality" of French society and the "spirit" and "way of being" of French managers. Boltanski portrays "rationality" as a profoundly cultural construct, tied to human-relations psychology and a credentialist view of expertise. Management training and ideas were related to alternative conceptions of France and the future. Boltanski shows that the very language of economic discourse – e.g., the term *cadres* – was derived from a larger cultural and political project.[27]

Just as postwar French management training reflects a cultural image borrowed selectively from U.S. models, so do contemporary accounting concepts reflect cultural models of economic actors. In his chapter, Paul Montagna demonstrates that such formal categories of the accounting profession as value, risk, and uncertainty implicitly derive from an entrepreneurial or even a speculative model of the capitalist firm.

Structural embeddedness

More important than either cognitive or cultural embeddedness is what Mark Granovetter has called "structural embeddedness": the contextualization of economic exchange in patterns of ongoing interpersonal relations. The term "structure" refers to the manner in which dyadic relations are articulated with one another – for example, whether relations are bundled up in densely connected but mutually segregated cliques as opposed to scattered diffusely throughout a population. From this point of view, Granovetter contends that "the anonymous market of neoclassical models is virtually nonexistent in economic life and . . . transactions of all kinds are rife with" social connections.[28]

Social embeddedness is central to, or implicit in, most chapters in this volume. In some cases, social networks dramatically shape the operation of economic markets. Beth Mintz and Michael Schwartz, for example, note that ongoing relations among financial institutions serve to create pack behavior suggestive of a collective decision process, as when finance capitalists stopped investing in nuclear-power plants.

In his chapter, Roger Waldinger describes how tightly knit immigrant social networks enable ethnic entrepreneurs to solve the problem of recruiting a labor force, arguably more cheaply than their nonimmigrant counterparts. Although word-of-mouth recruitment is typical of many kinds of labor markets, immigrant networks are particularly likely to be characterized by redundant and consequential relations that are useful in keeping bosses and workers mutually accountable. (This viewpoint contrasts, of course, with a more conflictual perspective that would emphasize opposition between employers and workers on the basis of social class.) Less contestably, Waldinger's immigrant entrepreneurs also use ethnic networks to recruit consumers, in some cases providing numerous services in addition to those conventionally offered. With both consumers and employees, entrepreneurs draw from their shared community a "repertoire of symbols and customs that can be invoked to underline cultural interests and similarities in the face of a potentially conflictual situation." Waldinger does not exaggerate the importance of ethnic ties. Once established in suitable economic niches, however, the embeddedness of immigrant enterprise in ethnic networks provides entrepreneurs with strong competitive advantages.

The structure of ongoing social relations is crucial as well in economic actors' efforts at self-regulation, or policing markets by their own means. Mintz and Schwartz describe how silver traders and bankers combined to quash the efforts of the Hunt brothers to corner the world silver market in the 1970s. When the invisible hand failed to provide market discipline, it was effectively replaced by the mailed fist of coordinated action.

Similarly, Michael Useem analyzes the structure of relations that permitted what he calls the "inner group" of the American and British capitalist classes to play significant roles in the rise of the political right in both countries during the late 1970s. Several of Useem's points deserve emphasis. First, cohesive networks enable substantial sets of actors to behave with a rationality that reflects the interests not of their firms, but of the capitalist class as a whole. Such collective action requires only the participation of a critical mass – an elite – not all large business enterprises. Collective capitalist rationality is apparently motivated by some combination of political conviction and self-preservation. Useem reports that the institutional mechanisms of elite solidarity are somewhat different in the U.K. and U.S., reflecting different historical trajectories. But in both countries, political-economic and social-organizational forces combined to yield the changes Useem describes. The informal organization of business leaders enabled them to shape state economic policy, and their capacity to act was enhanced by a secular trend toward the concentration of capital. As Fred Block's chapter also suggests, the political response of capital was neither automatic nor necessarily successful.[29]

Other authors demonstrate that the social embeddedness of economic action is crucial in a wide range of contexts. Boltanski, for example, contends that the harshness of the isolation to which France's Jewish bourgeoisie were subject before World War II (as well as the experience of the Holocaust) engendered both particularly close and multifaceted networks and an aversion to the ethos of the *patronat*. From this experience they derived both the capacity and inclination to support postwar efforts to emulate U.S. models of management. In their chapter on public policy in the United States and Western Europe since 1960, Roger Friedland and Jimy Sanders argue that the social experience of workers conditions their response to economic change. In countries where unions are strong, state social investments result in greater willingness on the part of labor to permit management to adopt productivity-enhancing technologies. If atomistic models were more correct than social embeddedness, labor unions would simply demand higher wages.

Taken together, the contributions to this volume demonstrate that the social embeddedness of economic action leads to numerous outcomes that neoclassical models would not anticipate. Networks serve as templates that channel market exchange; and they facilitate collective action both within and outside market contexts. The significance of informal social structure as a component of and context for economic action should play a central role in formulating economic sociologists' research agenda. The time is ripe, we think, to begin to compare, classify, and develop analytic theories about varieties of informal social structures just as scholars have theorized about the structure of states and industries.

Political embeddedness

By "political embeddedness" we refer to the manner in which economic institutions and decisions are shaped by a struggle for power that involves economic actors and nonmarket institutions, particularly the state and social classes. Certainly the legal framework of any society (especially the tax code) and the accepted system of collective bargaining are universally acknowledged as having direct influence on economic strategies. But the political context of economic action is made up of a complex web of interrelations and expectations. The formation of strategies within industrial sectors, for example, takes account not only of prices, wages, demand, and competition, but also policies of the national and local state, the social balance between regional employers, and the willingness of a local labor force to tolerate change.[30]

Thus we have relegated to "political embeddedness" the sources and means of economic action that reflect inequalities of power. This has long been the terrain of scholars in the political-economy tradition and some political sociologists. But, unlike the traditional approach which emphasized strictly determined dichotomies (e.g., economic base and social, political, or cultural infrastructure; capitalists and working class), new research explores historically contingent asymmetries of power.

Political embeddedness is illustrated most clearly when power relations among economic actors are inscribed in, or prescribed by, the legal framework of the state. Although Perrow, Stearns, and Mintz and Schwartz are not directly concerned with legislation, laws help provide the capacity for organized economic action that each of their chapters examines. Toward the end of Perrow's critique of transaction-cost analysis, he suggests that observations of firm behavior must not lose sight of the organizational environment. Patent and tax laws, government procurement policies, and governmental regulation all influence the structure of markets.

Similarly, Linda Stearns's research focuses on private sources of investment capital rather than the law. Yet the lending patterns she describes are contingent on such governmental action as decisions of the Federal Reserve Board, increase in the federal debt, laws regulating insurance companies and banks, and tax policy that permits deduction of interest payments. Another influence on capital markets from the 1960s was the decision by various governments to expand the use of Eurocurrency and Eurobonds. In their chapter, Mintz and Schwartz emphasize the quasi-governmental role of finance capital, especially in imposing loan conditions on Third World countries. The uncertainty such lenders encounter, however, is both mediated and to some degree created by state action.

Political values and institutions also have an impact on the behavior of professional accountants. Montagna shows that, in a liberal market economy, accepted notions of political and democratic accountability shape the hegemony of "objective" accounting procedures. A more direct influence on accounting firms is exercised by governmental regulation. The significance of the SEC (Securities and Exchange Commission) in the United States is slowly being emulated by various laws adopted within the European Community.

Recent work in political economy has confirmed that public policy is structured by the distribution of power between social groups that are likely to be affected. Just as the state's historical capacity to take effective action determines the shape of macroeconomic policy, so do immediate pressures that are exercised by domestic (and increasingly foreign) interests. In their chapters, Block and Friedland and Sanders emphasize these sources of variability in governmental policy. Most explicitly in France and Britain, and implicitly in other advanced market economies, lobbying by organized interests as well as market pressures have forced government to retreat from – or embark upon – audacious shifts in policy. Useem's chapter suggests, moreover, that we may trace such recent shifts as privatization, i.e., the sale by government of equity in nationalized firms or governmental insistence that firms follow more stringent market criteria, to decisions taken in private elite organizations, rather than to a rational consideration of various alternatives within the public sector.

Shifts in investment and production by both public and private actors take concrete form on the shop floor, in the production process and labor relations. Though the European concept of "accumulation regimes" has not made much headway in English social-science usage, researchers in political economy have used it to describe the political embeddedness of economic decisions based on employers' power over labor. By making detailed analyses of the strategic and normative linkages between production processes, labor control, and managerial behavior, research shows that industrial performance is linked to mechanisms of social compliance.[31] Whalley's and Boltanski's chapters in this volume follow a related approach. While Whalley provides an ethnography of how technical staff absorb new behavioral criteria within two British firms, Boltanski uses historical documents to trace the development of the new managerial regime in postwar France.

By the same token, social compliance within capitalists' ranks is also linked to regimes of power, especially those founded on control of capital. Stearns's research as well as that of Mintz and Schwartz fills a gap that had existed since Hilferding's publication of *Finance Capital* (in German) in 1910. But in contrast to the earlier political-economy approach, which emphasized the power of finance capital over society, current work is infused by a sociological examination of how power is wielded by different groups of capitalists over time. Stearns and Mintz and Schwartz explicitly relate their work to earlier American inquiries into managerial power.[32]

Political embeddedness in the largest sense refers to the global context of investment flows and shifts in the sites of production. Some researchers see a narrow tie between the political micro-climate in specific countries and regions and new "spatial divisions of labor." A broader influence can, however, be attributed to the global political-economic shifts that generate transnational migration of economic resources and actors. Waldinger's research on new immigrant entrepreneurs would be unthinkable without the new political context in which the countries of the Pacific Rim become exporters of both capital and labor. Similarly, the military policy of the United States in Central America and its government's steps toward economic integration with Mexico have done much to create an immigrant labor supply.[33]

By focusing on all these questions of political embeddedness, economic sociology has broadened its canonical influences from the opus of Marx to the works of Schumpeter, Veblen, and Polanyi. On the one hand, economic sociologists adhere to Schumpeter's call to study change rather than the status quo in capitalist institutions. On the other, they follow Polanyi's idea that all economic action (from markets to hegemony) occurs in socially constructed frameworks. Perhaps most politically embedded is the expectation of some economic sociologists that their research will lead to structural reform. To a far greater extent than orthodox economics but quite similar to classical political economy, economic sociology can include equity and justice in the research agenda.

Integrating political-economic and social-organizational themes in economic sociology

While the political-economy approach has always accepted *structure* as the expression of determination by forces that are larger-than-life and outside any individual's control, the social-organizational approach emphasizes the *variability* of institutions that are formed by conscious action or historical accretion. Though *capital*, moreover, is the *driving force and major resource* of the economy in the political-economy view, capital ordinarily remains *implicitly embedded* in the social-organizational approach to the economy. Inquiry that combines these approaches pursues two objectives.

On the one hand, it studies the macroeconomic, cultural, and societal *frameworks* in which people act; on the other hand, it studies the organizational variables that enhance their *capacity* to produce different outcomes. The distinctive contribution of the new studies in economic sociology is their emphasis on the interconnectedness of structures and capital – in other words, of power, culture, and organization.

Melding the perspectives of political economy and the study of social organization is beyond the scope of a single introductory essay. Yet, insofar as the contributors to this volume have already embarked on this task, we may suggest the form that such mutual influence may take. We do this with reference to three different analytic problems, each related to one of the crises of neoclassical theory identified in the first part of this essay. The first is the nature of rationality; the second, related to the crisis of the theory of the firm, is the control of economic agents; the third, related to the crisis of macroeconomic theory, has to do with the coordination of capital.

Varieties of rationality
The responsiveness of economic agents to sociocultural and political constraints casts doubt on the one-dimensional rationality described by neoclassical economics. Indeed, it might be more appropriate to speak of *rationalities*, varying with respect to the criteria and

formulations used to confront decisions and the extent to which such decisions invoke individual versus collective logics of action. As Charles Perrow argues, the extent to which employees are individualistic, self-regarding, utility-maximizing creatures is shaped by the structure and culture of firms. These tendencies are fostered more where structures are hierarchical and task performance is independent, than where leaders like to delegate authority and teamwork is rewarded. As Paul Montagna demonstrates, a form of rationality may be inscribed in intellectual paradigms, such as those of professional accounting, which reflect the power of centralized financial agents in large multinational accounting firms. Organizationally or intellectually, then, rationality is a conditioned response to dominant forms.

Political economy confirms that dominant forms of rationality are not pre-determined by an abstract logic. Roger Friedland and Jimy Sanders' research on private and social wage expansion in the advanced market economies during the 1970s shows no necessary relation between lower wages, unemployment, and capital accumulation. If Friedland and Sanders are correct, then governments enjoy a much wider range of policy alternatives than conservative politicians have thus far allowed in the larger capitalist states. Instead of arguing for welfare *or* profits, or restoring markets to preeminence over the state, politicians can devise broader frameworks for government action. Sweden's Meidner Plan, for example, includes labor's organized participation in capital investment, whereas France's socialist government encourages managers to develop corporate strategy without consulting other groups.

In his paper, Fred Block takes aim at both conservatives and radical political economists. Unlike those who believe in either a logic of accumulation or a logic of legitimation, Block suggests that economic expansion – for greater accumulation – could result in the institutional reforms that socialists want. He implicitly places his confidence in the variability of organizational forms that can be devised on the basis of growth. Just as automation may make possible a more skilled, more participatory work force in the firm, so the production of more services may facilitate an easier life. Like Friedman and Sanders, Block does not believe that capital accumulation is seriously obstructed by the state's redistributive policies or support of full employment.

Because such studies in political economy deny the validity of general models of economic rationality of both right and left, we are left with a need for middle-range explanations of the form that rationality will take in concrete instances. As the discussion of political embeddedness suggests, it may be that the institutional outcomes of the state's economic policies are a two-step result of, first, patterns of social relations influencing the capacity of both capital and labor to employ collective as opposed to individual forms of rationality; and, second, historical relations between labor and capital and the state's capacity to serve in a mediating role. Comparative research on patterns of interest aggregation and intermediation has been helpful in clarifying the focus on both class interest and organizational capacity as they interact with social structure.[34]

Such a grounded view of rationality also affects how we think about collective action in social class organizations. Most political economists posit a predetermined sequence of organizational development in which "class consciousness" leads to "class organization." By contrast, Jon Elster rejects the notion that solidarity automatically yields class action in favor of a view that working-class collective action represents a form of rational choice. Elster does not give up the notion of the basic asymmetry of power between capitalists and other economic actors, but transforms this structural asymmetry into a dynamic process that shapes contrary formulations of collective interest on the parts of capitalists and labor.

Such a view is similar in some respects to Claus Offe's concept of "two logics of collective action" for labor and capital.[35] But, just as the aggregate outcomes of rational action may vary with the institutional channels through which such outcomes are aggregated, so the capacity of both labor and capital to organize according to their respective logics may hinge to a degree on the kinds of macro-dynamics analyzed by political economists. Holding social structure constant, for example, workers have been more successful in achieving collective action when the economy produces slack resources that the state can use for side-payments to capital than they have been under conditions of acute fiscal crisis. Under the latter conditions, even workers may be tempted to pursue a narrower and more individualistic form of rationality than would otherwise be the case.

Control

The political-economy tradition's emphasis on domination by social class agents of capital does not promote a subtle understanding of social control. Though such concepts as "hegemony" suggest historical variability among different modes of establishing and exercising control, economic capital remains the underlying source of power. By contrast, work in the social-organizational tradition views the establishment of control as highly problematic. Overall hegemony has little everyday meaning when organizations are complex, environmental conditions uncertain, and information in short supply. Thus a central task for economic sociology is the understanding of how and why control is institutionalized in specific patterns. As institutional economics has recognized, organizational forms result not from an implicit logic of economic domination but as pragmatic solutions to problems of control that may vary considerably within a single political-economic regime. Perrow's essay on "Economic Theories of Organization" suggests that forms of control are limited by "technologies, capital requirements, and the shape of the market"; and these are in turn affected by government control.

By the same token, the exercise of control is also conditioned by problem-solving in the face of sociocultural, political, and economic constraints. Capitalists may gain control of their work force by selective recruitment, as described in Waldinger's chapter on "Immigrant Enterprise." Alternatively, ensuring the adherence of agents to organizational norms, especially in a time of innovation, may require managers to retrain workers comprehensively and rechannel the flow of information within the firm. We are familiar with the thought-control practiced by forcible resocialization to the collective economy in the Soviet Union or China, and the obstacles to changing organizational norms in those countries toward those of a market economy. But in capitalist economies, too, behavior modification is practiced on economic agents, albeit ordinarily by subtler means.

In the early 1950s, as Boltanski describes, French industrial managers and labor union leaders were flown to the United States, given management courses, and imbued with organizational perspectives associated with U.S. management science. The objective defined by the French government and the Marshall Plan was not only to make the French economy better and more productive, but also to make French managers think like American businessmen. Revitalizing French capitalism after the war demanded institutionalizing new strategies for exercising power: these strategies were supposed to be more competitive *and* more democratic, less collectivistic *and* less patriarchal. Postwar France provides a good illustration of the variability Perrow describes.

Similarly, the intense global competition that began in the 1970s shaped new management training strategies. In Britain, as Peter Whalley shows, firms reacted differently. Some placed technical staff in direct contact with sales data and consumers in an effort to internalize market forces as a means of control; others sought to buffer professionals from the market, relying instead on direct bureaucratic command.

If Boltanski's chapter portrays the link between movement in the international political economy and ideologies of control within national firms, Whalley's account indicates the range of means by which firms may cope with a similar political-economic context. Once again, both political-economic and social-organizational perspectives are required to understand the origins of innovation in economic behavior.

The coordination of capital

Though capital is central to the political-economic approach, political economists often reify it. They do not have much to say about capital's role in constituting power relations, or about how that role may be modified by sociocultural and political constraints. Students of social organization, by contrast, have exhibited a keen interest in the informal social organization of business leadership, but have rarely made clear connections between political-economic processes, social organization, and economic capacity. Several contributors to this volume point the way to an integration of these approaches.

Linda Brewster Stearns describes how shortages of capital since 1945 led U.S. corporations (and households) to increase their indebtedness. To manage their debt and increase their access to capital, corporations had to defer to financial agents such as commercial banks and investment banks. Under these conditions, the old debate on the separation of corporate ownership and control is redefined. It requires, on the one hand, an empirical investigation of how corporate reliance on external capital varies over time; and, on the other hand, how corporate indebtedness affects the relative autonomy of both owners and professional managers.

Beth Mintz and Michael Schwartz expand on this issue. Tracing collective cohesion to the centralized control of investment capital, they survey stock trading, loans to industrial sectors and individual firms, and loans to underdeveloped countries, to show that the exercise of financial control in capital markets has decisive effects on nonfinancial corporations. Just as political economy often interprets the exercise of power by industrial capitalists as labor discipline, so Mintz and Schwartz view the exercise of power by finance capitalists as disciplining the managers of individual firms and even entire industrial sectors. By relating this ability to exert discipline to a particular form of social organization, the authors pave the way for a comparative analysis of how such processes may differ in capitalist polities that do not, as does the United States, prohibit bank ownership of nonfinancial firms, and in which the state takes a more direct role in economic decision-making.

Michael Useem's chapter uses a comparative perspective to demonstrate that capitalists' attacks on the welfare state and preparation for industrial restructuring relied on new modes of intraclass organization. On the one hand, social and economic power at the micro-level are exercised under the hierarchical control of large, bureaucratic corporations. On the other hand, social and economic power on the macro-level are exercised under the control of classwide political associations. The capitalist hegemony that might be taken for granted in the political-economic approach is thus described in social-organizational terms as socially constituted on different levels and in different but related forms. Just as the state historically expands its capacity to rule, so do capitalists devise new organizational responses to changes in markets, technology, and government.[36]

Economic sociology and the study of economic change

The roster of contemporary economic changes around the world offers economic sociology a boundless research agenda. Because many developments involve highly contingent political decisions – on free trade, for example, or other market parameters – they are not reducible to neoclassical models. Those models, in any case, have never offered much insight into discontinuous or structural change. Economic sociologists drawing on a combination of political-economic and social-organizational concepts and methods have a much better chance of explaining and theorizing systemic shifts in economic organization.

The rise of markets in planned economies

In socialist economies, to take a noted example, political leaders have embarked on an ambitious program of organizational reform. Moving a command economy toward a market economy confronts all three areas of economic sociology that we have outlined: the control of economic agents, the coordination of capital, and the nature of rationality. Socialist leaders face a historically new problem of instituting the social controls over economic agents associated with markets without reconstituting the hegemony of either an administrative class (e.g., managers or party bureaucrats) or finance capitalists (e.g., banking organizations). This problem requires them to devise new organizational forms sanctioned neither by official Marxist ideology nor by Soviet authority. (In the Soviet Union and China, of course, the problem is both compounded and eased by being "first among equals" in the socialist world.) Though socialist economies have always vacillated between organizational norms of coercion, moral example, and financial incentives, the comprehensive reforms now envisaged demand a coherent and consistent rationality that is quite different from prior experience. Similarly, the notion of permitting inefficient firms to go bankrupt conflicts with hallmark socialist norms of both central planning and political allocation of economic goods.

The perspective of economic sociology can help analysis of changing socialist economies in two ways. First, it can examine the mutual effects of political articulation of interests (e.g., sectoral, regional, class) in state and party institutions and different forms of organizational control in the economy; such research may explore the highly speculative relation between market-oriented firms and political democracy. Second, economic sociology can analyze emerging forms of organizational control within firms and economic sectors (e.g., subcontracting among corporate divisions) and their impact on existing forms of allocating capital; this research has implications for developing entrepreneurship in socialist societies.[37]

Change in the structure of states and firms

Global competition has inspired significant changes in the scope and scale of both government agencies and firms in the advanced capitalist economies. On the one hand, the state has shifted from overseeing relations among different producers in different sectors of the national economy, to representing domestic producers in their relations with foreign competitors, often by means of new organizational forms of interstate coordination. On the other hand, firms have outlined new organizational alternatives that fall between markets and hierarchies. As the northern Italian example has shown, small firms may be more dynamic and more flexible than branches of large corporations; and as the Japanese have demonstrated, job security – in core economic firms and sectors – does not impede the use of technological goads to labor productivity.

By the same token, "marketizing" organizational relations does not necessarily result in more job security, higher income, or a more enjoyable pace of work. Although globalization has created niches for small firms that can produce in small batches and rapidly respond to changes in demand, the labor practices of these subcontractors and their ability to evade governmental regulation do not suggest an advance over bureaucratic organizational controls. Economic sociology faces a dual research challenge in this regard. On the one hand, it must analyze how an increasingly centralized allocation of capital (in different firms and sectors, regions, and technologies) by large transnational firms and banks generates more decentralized forms of control. On the other hand, it should explore how the relation between investment, employment, and production on a global level affects the formation and expression of collective interests (e.g., on the part of a transnational capitalist class and new categories of core and peripheral labor) in cities and nation-states.[38]

From manufacturing to service economies

Another area of global change concerns the shift in the advanced economies from basic manufacturing to the services. Macro-level discussions of this transformation (e.g., the work of Daniel Bell) have mainly concentrated on the shift in relatively high-level jobs from producing material goods to manipulating intangible "information." Such a shift is said to have an impact on social structure, increasing situs rather than class identification, as well as on the articulation of demands on the public sector. Unlike future-oriented literature, discussion of the service-sector transformation that focuses on current conditions tends to emphasize low-level service jobs (e.g., cooks, clerks, security guards) and the lowering of average wages their growth portends, leading to a "K-marting of the labor force" even in growth regions and a general social "polarization."[39]

Here economic sociology can draw on the full variety of social embeddedness that we have described. Culture and cognitive processes both frame the transformation of production from manufacturing to services and are affected by it, creating new social values for old as well as new production roles. Economic sociology could examine, for example, the changing status and significance of basic industry in the advanced industrial societies, or the increasing abstraction of economic value in image-creation in consumer-goods sectors like entertainment and advertising. Social structure as well as market competition shape the response to this transformation in industrial sectors and elite groups. Economic sociology could explore the conditions under which firms and sectors shift from producing a good (such as computer hardware) to a service (such as information services). Political embeddedness applies to the changes in social arrangements – from labor contracts to government subsidies – that facilitate or impede the service-sector transformation. In this area, economic sociology could analyze the weakness of traditional labor unions and the emergence of new forms of labor mobilization and control; the lobbying by firms in the services to be included in intergovernmental industrial negotiations such as GATT; and the difference in demands on the public sector imposed by manufacturers and, say, business services.[40]

Though at this time economic sociology cannot offer any dramatic new paradigm of socialist economic transformation, change in firm and state organization, and the shift to the services, these areas indicate a need for the multidimensional analysis of change that economic sociology provides.

Organization of this volume

This volume is divided into two introductory parts – on theory-building and organizations – and three empirical parts on major institutional arenas of capital: finance, the state, and entrepreneurship.

The first part, on theory-building, develops the differences between economics and sociology, outlines the classical sources of economic sociology's emerging paradigm, and suggests how far that paradigm may be stretched by offering a rigorous, individualistic discussion of collective rationality. The second part presents two in-depth discussions of organizational variability that criticize both the neoclassical model and recent reformulations that pit markets against hierarchies, and rationality against efficiency.

The remaining parts present empirical research in three major institutional arenas in which structures of capital are formed. Part III, on finance capital, discusses capital markets, banks and corporate autonomy, and professional (especially multinational) accounting. Part IV, on the state and public policy, relates historical forms of corporate, class, and elite organization to public-policy choices. Part V, on management and entrepreneurship, offers studies of three different social contexts in which entrepreneurship has recently been fostered: postwar France, British factories in the 1970s, and contemporary urban immigrant communities in the United States.

We are confident that readers will be inspired by this variety of topics and methods to design their own studies, demonstrating that all economic processes must be understood as socially embedded. The distinctive contribution of economic sociology should inform case studies as well as general theory, connecting power, values, and organization in economic change.

Notes

1. See, for example, Kenneth Arrow, "Gifts and Exchanges," in *Altruism, Morality, and Economic Theory*, edited by Edmund S. Phelps (New York: Russell Sage Foundation, 1975); Amartya K. Sen, "Rational Fools: A Critique of the Behavioral Foundations of Economic Theory," *Philosophy and Public Affairs* 6 (1977): 317–44; Robert E. Lane, "Markets and the Satisfaction of Human Wants," *Journal of Economic Issues* 12 (1978): 799–827; Richard R. Nelson and Sidney G. Winter, *An Evolutionary Theory of Economic Change* (Cambridge, Mass.: Harvard University Press, 1982); Peter E. Earl, *The Economic Imagination: Towards a Behavioural Analysis of Choice* (Armonk, New York: M. E. Sharpe, 1983); Robert H. Frank, *Choosing the Right Pond: Human Behavior and the Quest for Status* (New York: Oxford University Press, 1985); and "If Homo Economicus Could Choose His Own Utility Function Would He Want One with A Conscience?" *American Economic Review* 77 (1987): 593–604; and Mark Granovetter, "Economic Action and Social Structure: The Problem of Embeddedness," *American Journal of Sociology* 91 (1985): 481–501. For an indispensable review of this literature and challenge to the assumptions of economic orthodoxy, see Amitai Etzioni, *The Moral Dimension: Toward a New Economics* (New York: The Free Press, 1988).

2. Marshall Sahlins, *Culture and Practical Reason* (Chicago: University of Chicago, 1976); Anthony Giddens, *The Constitution of Society* (Berkeley: University of California

Press, 1985); Mary Douglas, *Risk Acceptability According to the Social Sciences* (New York: Russell Sage Foundation, 1986); Stephen Gudeman, *Economics As Culture: Models and Metaphors of Livelihood* (Boston: Routledge & Kegan Paul, 1986); Etzioni, *Moral Dimension*; Harvey Molotch, "Sociology and the Economy," manuscript, University of California, Santa Barbara, Department of Sociology, 1988; Roger Friedland and Robert Alford, "Bringing Society Back In: Symbols, Practices, and Institutional Contradictions," in *The New Institutionalism in Organizational Analysis*, edited by Walter W. Powell and Paul DiMaggio (Chicago: University of Chicago Press, 1990); Ronald L. Jepperson and John W. Meyer, "The Public Order and the Construction of Formal Organizations," in *The New Institutionalism in Organizational Analysis*.

3. Neil J. Smelser, *The Sociology of Economic Life* (Englewood Cliffs, N.J.: Prentice-Hall, 1963); Sen, "Rational"; Etzioni, *Moral Dimension*.

4. See Paul DiMaggio, "Cultural Aspects of Economic Action," in Roger Friedland and A. F. Robertson, eds., *Beyond the Marketplace: Rethinking Models of Economy and Society* (Chicago: Aldine, 1990); and Mark Granovetter and Roland Soong, "Threshold Models of Interpersonal Effects on Consumer Demand," *Journal of Economic Behavior and Organization* 7 (1986): 83–99.

5. Etzioni, *Moral Dimension*, 158–59; Charles E. Lindblom, "The Science of Muddling Through," *Public Administration Review* 19 (1959): 79–88; Jon Elster, *Ulysses and the Sirens: Studies in Rationality and Irrationality* (New York: Cambridge University Press, 1984); Joseph E. Stiglitz, "Information and Economic Analysis: A Perspective," Working Papers in Economics, No. E-84-16, The Hoover Institution, Stanford University, December 1984.

6. Amos Tversky and Daniel Kahneman, "Judgment Under Uncertainty," *Science* 185 (1974): 1124–31; Etzioni, *Moral Dimension*, chap. 7; Robert H. Frank, "Patching Up the Rational Choice Model," in *Beyond the Marketplace: Rethinking Models of Economy and Society*.

7. James G. March and Herbert Simon, *Organizations* (New York: Wiley, 1958); Richard M. Cyert and James G. March, *A Behavioral Theory of the Firm* (Englewood Cliffs, N.J.: Prentice-Hall, 1963).

8. The quote is from Charles Perrow, *Complex Organizations: A Critical Essay*, 3d ed. (New York: Random House, 1986), 11. Numerous studies have documented such instances. See, for example, Donald Roy, "Quota Restriction and Goldbricking in a Machine Shop," *American Journal of Sociology* 57 (1952): 427–42; Alvin W. Gouldner, *Patterns of Industrial Bureaucracy* (New York: The Free Press, 1954); Melville Dalton, *Men Who Manage* (New York: John Wiley, 1959); Michel Crozier, *The Bureaucratic Phenomenon* (Chicago: University of Chicago Press, 1964); Michael Burawoy, *Manufacturing Consent: Changes in the Labor Process under Monopoly Capitalism* (Chicago: University of Chicago Press, 1979); and Jeffrey Pfeffer, *Power in Organizations* (Marshfield, Mass.: Pitman, 1981).

9. Among the key readings in agency theory are Armen A. Alchian and Harold Demsetz, "Production, Information Cost, and Economic Organization," *American Economic Review* 62 (1972): 777–95; Michael C. Jensen and William H. Meckling, "Theory of the Firm: Managerial Behavior, Agency Costs, and Ownership Structure," *Journal of Financial Economics* 3 (1976): 305–60; Eugene F. Fama, "Agency Problems and the Theory of the Firm, *Journal of Political Economy* 88 (1980): 288–305; and Eugene Fama and Michael Jensen, "Separation of Ownership and Control," *Journal of Law and Economics* 26 (1983): 301–25. Several of these are reprinted, along with thoughtful if somewhat uncritical commentary, in *Organizational Economics*, edited by Jay B. Barney and William G. Ouchi (San Francisco: Jossey-Bass, 1986).

10. Marshall Meyer and Lynne G. Zucker, *Permanently Failing Organizations* (Beverly Hills: Sage Publications, 1989).

11. The quotation is from p. 17 of Richard R. Nelson and Sidney G. Winter, *An Evolutionary Theory of Economic Change* (Cambridge, Mass.: Harvard University Press, 1982); for a withering critique of the orthodox model, see Sidney G. Winter, "Economic 'Natural Selection' and the Theory of the Firm," *Yale Economic Essays* 4 (1964): 225–72.

12. R. H. Coase, "The Nature of the Firm," *Economica* 4 (1937): 386–405; Oliver Williamson, *Markets and Hierarchies: Analysis and Antitrust Applications* (New York: The Free Press, 1975); and *The Economic Institutions of Capitalism* (New York: The Free Press, 1985). Granovetter criticizes the assumption that bureaucratic transaction costs are low in "Economic Action and Social Structure: The Problem of Embeddedness," *American Journal of Sociology* 91 (1985): 481–510.

13. William G. Ouchi, "Markets, Bureaucracies, and Clans," *Administrative Science Quarterly* 25 (1980): 124–41; Michael Porter, *Competitive Strategy: Techniques for Analyzing Industries and Competitors* (New York: The Free Press, 1980); Michael Piore and Charles Sabel, *The Second Industrial Divide: Possibilities for Prosperity* (New York: Basic Books, 1984); M. Y. Yoshino and Thomas B. Lifson, *The Invisible Link* (Cambridge, Mass.: MIT Press, 1986); Robert Eccles and Dwight B. Crane, "Managing through Networks in Investment Banking," *California Management Review* 30 (1987): 176–95; Robert Eccles and Harrison White, "Price and Authority in Inter-Profit-Center Transactions," *American Journal of Sociology* 94 (1988): 517–51; Mark Lazerson, "Organizational Growth of Small Firms: An Outcome of Markets and Hierarchies?" *American Sociological Review* 53 (1988): 330–43; Walter W. Powell, "Neither Market nor Hierarchy: Network Forms of Social Organization," in *Research in Organizational Behavior*, vol. 12, edited by Barry Staw and Lawrence L. Cummings (Greenwich, Conn.: JAI Press, 1989); Walter W. Powell, "The Transformation of Organizational Forms: How Useful is Organization Theory in Accounting for Social Change?" in *Beyond the Marketplace: Rethinking Models of Economy and Society.*

14. Porter, *Competitive Strategy*; Harrison White, "Where Do Markets Come From?" *American Journal of Sociology* 87 (1981): 517–47; Ronald S. Burt, *Corporate Profits and Cooptation: Networks of Market Constraints and Directorate Ties in the American Economy* (New York: Academic Press, 1983); Wayne Baker, "The Social Structure of a National Securities Market," *American Journal of Sociology* 90 (1984): 777–811; Mitchel Abolafia, "Structured Anarchy: Formal Organization in the Commodity Futures Industry," in *The Social Dynamics of Financial Markets*, edited by Peter Adler and Patricia Adler (Greenwich, Conn.: JAI Press, 1984). See also game theoretic approaches to the analysis of oligopolistic behavior, e. g., Jacob Marschak and Roy Radner, *Economic Theory of Teams* (New Haven: Yale University Press, 1972); and Martin Shubik, *A Game Theoretical Approach to Political Economy* (Cambridge, Mass.: MIT Press, 1985).

15. Lester Thurow, *Dangerous Currents* (New York: Random House, 1983).

16. See, for example, the approach outlined in Michel Aglietta, *A Theory of Capitalist Regulation* (London: New Left Books, 1979 [Paris, 1976]); and Scott Lash and John Urry, *The End of Organized Capitalism* (Cambridge, Eng.: Polity Press, 1987).

17. For the resurgence of Kondratiev cycles and long-term structural analysis, see Ernst Mandel, *Late Capitalism* (London: New Left Books, 1975 [Paris, 1972]), and R. B. Day, "The Theory of the Long Cycle: Kondratiev, Trotsky, Mandel," *New Left Review* 99 (1976): 67–82; for the development of capitalism in terms of world-system analysis, see Immanuel Wallerstein, *The Modern World System*, vols. 1–3 (New York: Academic Press, 1974, 1988); for a summary, see James O'Connor, *The Meaning of Crisis* (New York: Basil Blackwell, 1987).

18. James O'Connor, *The Fiscal Crisis of the State* (New York: St. Martin's Press, 1973). Note that O'Connor later specified, in contrast to other post-Keynesian economists, that the current crisis of capitalism reflected underproduction (rather than overproduction) and too much desire to consume (instead of underconsumption). *Accumulation Crisis* (New York: Basil Blackwell, 1984).

19. See, for example, Fred Hirsch and John H. Goldthorpe, eds., *The Political Economy of Inflation* (Cambridge, Mass.: Harvard University Press, 1978); Claus Offe, *Contradictions of the Welfare State* (Cambridge, Mass.: MIT Press, 1984); Jill Quadagno, "Welfare Capitalism and the Social Security Act of 1935," *American Sociological Review* 49 (1984): 632–47; Theda Skocpol and Edwin Amenta, "Did Capitalists Shape Social Policy?" *American Sociological Review* 50 (1985): 572–75; Jill Quadagno, "Two Models of Welfare State Development: Reply to Skocpol and Amenta," *American Sociological Review* 50 (1985): 575–77; and Edwin Amenta and Theda Skocpol, "States and Social Policies," *Annual Review of Sociology* 12 (1986): 131–57. On nineteenth-century industrial policy, see Stephen Skowronek, *Building a New American State* (Cambridge, Eng.: Cambridge University Press, 1982), and on the 1980s, see Sharon Zukin, ed., *Industrial Policy: Business and Politics in the United States and France* (New York: Praeger, 1985).

20. Barry Bluestone and Bennett Harrison, *The Deindustrialization of America* (New York: Basic Books, 1982); Robert B. Reich and Ira Magaziner, *Minding America's Business* (New York: Harcourt Brace Jovanovich, 1982); Lester Thurow, *The Zero-Sum Society* (New York: Simon and Schuster, 1985).

21. Ezra F. Vogel, *Japan as Number One: Lessons for America* (Cambridge, Mass.: Harvard University Press, 1979); William Ouchi, *Theory Z: How American Business Can Meet the Japanese Challenge* (Reading, Mass.: Addison-Wesley, 1981); Chalmers Johnson, *MITI and the Japanese Miracle: The Growth of Industrial Policy* (Stanford, Calif.: Stanford University Press, 1982); Robert E. Cole, *Work, Mobility, and Participation: A Comparative Study of American and Japanese Industry* (Berkeley: University of California Press, 1979); Piore and Sabel, *The Second Industrial Divide*; Ronald Dore, *Structural Adjustment in Japan, 1970–82* (Geneva: International Labour Office, 1986); Thomas B. Gold, *State and Society in the Taiwan Miracle* (New York: M. E. Sharpe, 1986); Gary G. Hamilton and Nicole Woolsey Biggart, "Market, Culture, and Authority: A Comparative Analysis," *American Journal of Sociology* 94 (1988): S52–S94; Lazerson, "Organizational"; Marco Orrù, Gary Hamilton and Nicole Biggart, "Organizational Isomorphism in East Asia: Broadening the New Institutionalism," in *The New Institutionalism in Organizational Analysis*, edited by Walter Powell and Paul DiMaggio (Chicago: University of Chicago Press, 1990); Peter Hall, *Governing the Economy: The Politics of State Intervention in Britain and France* (New York: Oxford University Press, 1986); and for a plea to take account of multiple industrial systems, see the critique by Michael Rose, "Universalism, Culturalism, and the Aix Group: Promise and Problems of a Societal Approach to Economic Institutions," *European Sociological Review* 1, no. 1 (May 1985): 65–83.

22. Peter Evans, *Dependent Development* (Princeton, N.J.: Princeton University Press, 1979); Barbara Stallings, *Banker to the Third World: U.S. Portfolio Investment in Latin America, 1900–1986* (Berkeley and Los Angeles: University of California Press, 1987); Stephen Krasner, *Structural Conflict: The Third World against Global Liberalism* (Berkeley and Los Angeles: University of California Press, 1985). There is a surprising lack of analysis of social and political mediation of global financial markets. See, however, Michael Clarke, *Regulating the City: Competition, Scandal, and Reform* (Milton Keynes: Open University Press, 1986) and Geoffrey Ingham, *Capitalism Divided?* (New York: Schocken, 1984).

23. Karl Polanyi, *The Great Transformation* (Boston: Beacon Press, 1957).

24. Granovetter, "Embeddedness" and "The Old and the New Economic Sociology: A History and an Agenda," in *Beyond the Marketplace: Rethinking Models of Economy and Society*.

25. See Charles Perrow, *Normal Accidents: Living With High Risk Technologies* (New York: Basic Books, 1984); Marshall Meyer, William Stevenson, and Stephen Webster, *Limits to Bureaucratic Growth* (New York: de Gruyter, 1985); and Meyer and Zucker, 1989, *op. cit.*

26. For a fuller development of these ideas, see DiMaggio, "Cultural Aspects of Economic Action." See also Sahlins, *Culture and Practical Reason*; Fred Hirsch, *Social Limits to Growth* (London: Routledge & Kegan Paul, 1977); Viviana Zelizer, *Morals and Markets: The Development of Life Insurance in the United States* (New York: Columbia University Press, 1979); Mary Douglas and Baron Isherwood, *The World of Goods: Towards an Anthropology of Consumption* (New York: Norton, 1982); Chandra Mukerji, *From Graven Images: Patterns of Modern Materialism* (New York: Columbia University Press, 1983); Pierre Bourdieu, *Distinction: A Social Critique of the Judgement of Taste*, translated by Richard Nice (Cambridge, Mass.: Harvard University Press, 1984); Viviana Zelizer, *Pricing the Priceless Child: The Changing Social Value of Children* (New York: Basic Books, 1985); Arjun Appadurai, ed., *The Social Life of Things* (New York: Cambridge University Press, 1986); Stephen Gudeman, *Economics As Culture: Models and Metaphors of Livelihood* (Boston: Routledge & Kegan Paul, 1986); Ann Swidler, "Culture in Action," *American Sociological Review* 51 (1986): 273–86; Friedland and Alford, "Bringing Society Back In"; and Ronald L. Jepperson and John W. Meyer, "The Public Order and the Construction of Formal Organizations," in *The New Institutionalism in Organizational Analysis*.

27. See also Luc Boltanski, *The Making of a Class: Cadres in French Society* (New York: Cambridge University Press, 1987).

28. Granovetter, 1985, *op. cit.*, 495.

29. See also Michael Useem, *The Inner Circle: Large Corporations and the Rise of Business Political Activity in the U.S. and the U.K.* (New York: Oxford University Press, 1984); for a more abstract formulation of the free-rider problem consistent with Useem's findings, see Pamela Oliver and Gerald Marwell, "The Paradox of Group Size in Collective Action: A Theory of the Critical Mass, II," *American Sociological Review* 53 (1988): 1–8.

30. See, for example, Folker Frobel et al., *The New International Division of Labor* (Cambridge, Eng.,: Cambridge University Press, 1980); Doreen Massey, *Spatial Divisions of Labor* (New York: Methuen, 1984); Bryan Roberts, Ruth Finnegan, and Duncan Gallie, eds., *New Approaches to Economic Life* (Manchester, Eng.: Manchester University Press, 1985); and Allen J. Scott and Michael Storper, eds., *Production, Work, Territory* (Boston: Allen and Unwin, 1986).

31. For a historical study, see Richard Edwards, *Contested Terrain: The Transformation of the Workplace in the Twentieth Century* (New York: Basic Books, 1979), or Andrew L. Friedman, *Industry and Labor* [a study of the British automobile industry] (London: Macmillan, 1977). A radical view insists on the specificity of sociocultural, i.e., national, production regimes; for an insightful critique along these lines, see Rose, 1985, *op. cit.*, 65–83. On contemporary production regimes in cross-national perspective, see Michael Burawoy, *The Politics of Production* (London: Verso, 1981).

32. See Rudolf Hilferding, *Finance Capital* (London: Routledge & Kegan Paul, 1985 [1910]; and Adolph Berle and Gardiner Means, *The Modern Corporation and Private Property* (New York: Harcourt, Brace and World, 1932). For recent economic sociology on intraclass regimes of power based on control of capital, see Maurice Zeitlin, "Corporate Ownership and Control: The Large Corporation and the Capitalist Class," *American Journal of Sociology* 79 (1974): 1073–1119; Michael Soref and Maurice Zeitlin, "Finance Capital and the Internal Structure of the Capitalist Class in the United States," in *Intercorporate Relations: The Structural Analysis of Business*, edited by Mark S. Mizruchi and Michael Schwartz (Cambridge, Eng.: Cambridge University Press, 1987); Maurice

Zeitlin, ed., *Classes, Class Conflict, and the State* (Cambridge, Mass.: Winthrop, 1980); Richard Ratcliff, "Banks and Corporate Lending: An Analysis of the Impact of the Internal Structure of the Capitalist Class," *American Sociological Review* 45 (1980): 553–70; Beth Mintz and Michael Schwartz, *The Power Structure of American Business* (Chicago: University of Chicago Press, 1985); and Davita Silfen Glasberg, "Control of Capital Flows and Class Relations," *Social Science Quarterly* 68 (Mar. 1987): 51–69.

33. See Alejandro Portes and John Walton, *Labor, Class, and the International System* (New York: Academic Press, 1981) and Saskia Sassen, *The Mobility of Labor and Capital* (Cambridge, Eng.: Cambridge University Press, 1987).

34. See Hall, *Governing the Economy*; John H. Goldthorpe, ed., *Order and Conflict in Contemporary Capitalism: Studies in the Political Economy of Western European Nations* (New York: Oxford University Press, 1984); Gerhard Lehmbruch and Philippe Schmitter, eds., *Patterns of Corporatist Policy-Making* (Beverly Hills: Sage, 1982), and Philippe Schmitter and Gerhard Lehmbruch, eds., *Trends Toward Capitalist Intermediation* (Beverly Hills: Sage, 1979).

35. Claus Offe, "Two Logics of Collective Action," in *Disorganized Capitalism* (Cambridge, Mass.: MIT Press, 1985).

36. For an introduction to additional comparative materials, see John Scott, "Intercorporate Structures in Western Europe: A Comparative Historical Analysis," in *Intercorporate Relations*; Enrique Ogliastri and Carlos Davila, "The Articulation of Power and Business Structures: A Study of Colombia," in *Intercorporate Relations*; and Koji Taira and Teiichi Wada, "Business-Government Relations in Modern Japan: A Todai-Yakkai-Zaikai Complex?" in *Intercorporate Relations*.

37. An interesting preliminary series of questions is posed in David Stark and Victor Nee, eds., *Remaking the Economic Institutions of Socialism* (Stanford: Stanford University Press, 1989).

38. See, for example, June Nash and Patricia Fernandez-Kelly, eds. *Women, Men, and the International Division of Labor* (Albany, N.Y.: State University of New York, 1983); and Michael Peter Smith and Joe R. Feagin, eds., *The Capitalist City* (New York: Basil Blackwell, 1987).

39. See Daniel Bell, *The Coming of Post-Industrial Society* (New York: Basic Books, 1973); cf. Bennett Harrison and Barry Bluestone, *The Great U-Turn* (New York: Basic Books, 1988). "K-marting" from Edward W. Soja et al., "Urban Restructuring: An Analysis of Social and Spatial Change in Los Angeles," *Economic Geography* 59 (1983): 195–230.

40. For preliminary conceptualization of some sorts of cultural embeddedness and contemporary economic change, see Sharon Zukin, *American Market/Place: Landscapes of Economic Power* (Berkeley and Los Angeles: University of California Press, forthcoming).

Part I
Theory-building in economic sociology

2

Clean models vs. dirty hands: why economics is different from sociology

PAUL HIRSCH, STUART MICHAELS, AND
RAY FRIEDMAN

When you dig deep down, economists are scared to death of being sociologists. The one great thing we have going for us is the premise that individuals act rationally in trying to satisfy their preferences. That is an incredibly powerful tool, because you can model it.

(*Charles Schultze, former president of the
American Economic Association, 1985; quoted in Kuttner 1985*)

The problem is that the assumptions underlying the economic model are not only very simple, they are also very strong and wildly unrealistic. . . . The cost is that economic policy premised on [such] simple assumptions often leads to unintended – and dysfunctional – consequences.

(*Bower, 1983, p. 181*)

Those who prefer to conduct inquiry into the relationships among classes, states, and other organizations as such, and without attempts to *reduce analysis to the individuals* who participate, do not, in my view, pass muster as social scientists in any useful sense of the term.

(*James Buchanan, from remarks made at the conference
"Symposium on Social Science Paradigms," the University of Chicago,
November 15, 1985, emphasis added*)

Introduction

During the last decade, sociologists and economists have both shown increasing interest in substantive and methodological problems that, until recently, were recognized as each other's intellectual territory. Population ecology, as developed by sociologists (Hannan and Freeman 1977; Aldrich 1979), is a perspective with marked similarities to economic models; human capital theory, as developed by Gary Becker (1975), treats issues long examined in sociological studies of status attainment, stratification, and the family. Similarly, sociologists concerned with issues in ownership and control (Perrow, 1981 and 1986) have begun to examine economic work in agency theory, incentives, and transaction costs (Jensen and Meckling, 1976; Williamson, 1975;

Williamson and Ouchi, 1981). Sociologist James Coleman was invited to address the 1984 meeting of the American Economic Association. Harrison White (1981) has written about the sociology of economic markets. And Herbert Simon (a psychologist by training) has been awarded a Nobel prize in economics.

In this article we propose that these movements toward a convergence of interests between the "sister disciplines" may be more apparent than real; that the commonality of interests shown so far is largely substantive, more so than an indication of growth in shared analytic perspectives, theory and concepts, first principles and paradigms. We argue that a serious convergence of perspectives will (and should) be restrained by each discipline's fundamentally different world-views and intellectual traditions. Our analysis will focus on methodological and meta-theoretical differences between the disciplines.

Economics has a more unified core model and approach than sociology. The marginalist revolution allowed economics to redefine itself on a much more streamlined basis. Microeconomics became the paradigm for the discipline as a whole. Thus, contemporary economics exemplifies a highly abstract, deductive approach to social science. Its style is characterized by the development of models based on deliberately, vigorously, and rigidly simplified assumptions. The *elegance* of the models, especially their "parsimony," is prized and the intent is that they be predictive. The individual level of analysis is taken to be real, and higher (macro) levels of analysis are derived and built from the individual level via aggregation. A series of heuristic assumptions about human nature, taking the existence and pre-eminence of markets as a given, and other related principles such as fixed preferences are assumed and generally unquestioned. The claim that these are all exogenously determined factors lying outside the realm of economics has a certain disingenuous quality.

Sociology on the other hand tends to value description or explanation over prediction. That is, the *realism* of the concepts and proposition used, their resemblance to the perceptions and meanings of the participants, is highly valued. There are few if any fundamental notions, such as rational action, that cut across and deeply into the discipline. Indeed, sociology often takes these very assumptions as problematic.

Since there is no single widely accepted paradigm in sociology either theoretically or methodologically, there is much fiercer debate about conceptual frameworks, theories, and concepts. Sociology tends to be much more "data-driven." While there are traditions and schools of "grand theory," most sociologists spend their time developing original data and interpretations of data. Instead of neat theory, they tend to be more involved in the complexities of the phenomenon under scrutiny.

Even grand theory itself tends to be more closely "grounded" by empirical phenomena, whether or not the data were generated by the theorist.

A critical question at this point is: *Given such differences, what are the limits to fruitful dialogue and collaboration between the two fields?* The concept of rational action and a related set of assumptions about human nature, the acceptance of the individual level as the "real" level of analysis, and the deductive (and often highly mathematical) style of theorizing based on the operation of these rational atoms under conditions of scarcity are currently influencing a substantial body of work in sociology. Sociologists seem increasingly enamored of economic theory and methods. Economics is being taken as the model for what a science or social science is supposed to be in a way that certain natural sciences – such as physics and biology – were in the past.

This is occurring at a number of levels: theoretical, methodological, and in terms of fundamental assumptions. Besides the continuing and increasing emphasis on quantification and mathematical models in sociology, several of the hottest new methodological developments – structural equations and longitudinal data analysis – are derived from economics. More generally, economics (econometrics) has replaced psychology as the main influence on sociological statistical methodology. This is most clearly evidenced by the decline and practical disappearance of the Analysis of Variance paradigm and its replacement by the multiple regression approach to the General Linear Model. Charles Schultze need no longer fear being a sociologist so much, especially to the extent that more and more sociological concepts and methods are being derived from economics.

Ironically, even as many sociologists are turning to economics as a guide, there is much fundamental questioning and soul-searching within our sister discipline, so much so that it appears to be undergoing a crisis of its own (see e.g., Wilbur and Jameson 1983; Kuttner 1985). In particular the keystone of rationality is being questioned within economics itself (see e.g., Field 1979 and 1981). Economists' modeling of human behavior, deduced from that core assumption about human nature, is elegant, thoroughly consistent, and recently and increasingly claims universal applicability. But, *despite the stability and power of economists' core assumptions and the logical consistency they allow, there is a fatal flaw for sociologists in their deductive modeling: it leads them to ignore the empirical world around them.*

Before swallowing whole these assumptions, we should first seriously consider economists' own advice to consumers: *caveat emptor* (let the buyer beware). Even in the study of economic exchange, there are many factors of great importance that lie outside the realm of economists' strictly "rational" action. By precluding attention to nonrational elements of human behavior, economists leave themselves no mechanism for *learning* about the crude and messy empirical world that so defies their models. Economists pay a heavy price for the very simplicity and elegance of their models: empirical ignorance, misunderstanding, and, relatedly unrealistic and bizarre policy recommendations.

Sociologists need to be reminded of these costs, lest we succeed in turning ourselves into second-rate versions of what economists already do so well! The discipline, it is true, has a long and hallowed tradition that argues effectively against leaving the study of economic phenomena solely to economists. But the issue now is much more fundamental. Sociologists must be cautious not to let the attraction of elegant models lead us into the thicket of economists' overly rationalistic world-view, especially in our research into noneconomic aspects of human experience, but also in our studies of the economic domain. While sociologists should not deny the possibility of rational action nor preclude its study, our "comparative advantage" – an openness to culture and an interest in values and social structure – must not be traded in for a simple rational-action theory. Our penchant for and emphasis on empirical research also must not be abandoned for deductive modeling.

"Clean models" vs. "dirty hands": a road-map comparison of the two disciplines

Table 2.1 contrasts the fundamentally different intellectual bases and traditions of economics and sociology, and shows how these two disciplines embody such opposing perspectives and world-views. Any comparison of sociology and economics is bound to oversimplify. Neither field is unitary. In each there are a variety of styles and schools, mainstream scholars and mavericks. Economics is the older of the two disciplines. Marx Weber himself, perhaps the preeminent sociological theorist of the twentieth century, held academic positions as an economist. It is also the more developed, more mature of the two disciplines, especially "scientifically." In comparison, sociology appears proudly diverse, even if almost adolescent and continually suffering mini-identity crises. At the risk of overemphasizing their differences, we now compare both disciplines' essential characteristics.

Economics and sociology, in broad brush strokes, differ fundamentally at each of three distinct levels: assumptions, theory and research, and policy implications. We will discuss each of these in turn.

Assumptions

The most basic difference between economics and sociology concerns their assumptions about human nature. The famous *homo*

Table 2.1. *Economics and sociology: ideal type contrasts*

Item	Economics	Sociology
Assumptions		
Assumptions about human nature	Rational Greedy (Maximizers) Self-interested Instrumental Fixed preferences	Complex Variable Cultural Expressive Fluid preferences
Main unit of analysis	Individual	Collectivities
Concept of society	Nominal Aggregates of individuals Hobbesian	Real Sui generis Rousseau
Philosophical stance	Behaviorist Materialist	Interpretive (verstehen) Idealist
Theory and Research		
Mode of theorizing	Deductive Axiomatic	Inductive Data-driven
Method	Analytic theoretical modeling Quantitative mathematical Abstracted Secondary data	Inductive, grounded theory-building Qualitative and quantitative Ask people (surveys) Primary data-collection
Model characteristics	Few variables Elegant	Many variables Messy
Criteria for validity	Predictive	Realistic Explanatory
Policy Implications		
Orientation to market	Pro Independent variable Market > firm	Neutral Intervening or dependent variable Firm > market
Policy stance	Normative Solution-oriented Treatment Status quo Free market	Value neutral Problem-defining Diagnosis Debunking Regulation
In Sum	Clean models	Dirty hands

Source: See text.

economicus is a rational, self-interested, instrumental maximizer with fixed preferences. *Homo sociologicus*, by contrast, is much harder to define. Closer to a *tabula rasa* upon which historically developed institutions, societies, and cultures write, the sociological "model of man," rather than assuming fixed preferences, treats values, attitudes, and behavior as fluid and changeable. Actions follow from culturally given values, not just some pure (culture-free) calculation of individual self-interest. And action may be expressive rather than purely instrumental. This distinction is not new. It underlies one of the standard sociological criticisms of economics and constitutes one basis for sociology's claims as a contributor to the larger social scientific enterprise.

Sociology also diverges from economics by taking collectivities seriously. It is, after all, society that defines values, and collectivities that influence preferences. This assumption of societal influence on values and preferences permeates the entire discipline: Weber's "Protestant Ethic," Durkheim's "*conscience collective*," Marx's "class consciousness," Goffman's "interaction rituals," Gramsci's "hegemony," Merton's "reference groups." Society is not derived *de novo* each day from individual choice, à la Hobbes; rather, individual choice presumes the prior existence of society for sociologists. While economists build up to higher levels of analysis by aggregating individual level rational decisions, Parsons and Smelser (1965), expressing a general sociological perspective, argued that "the basic structures of institutionalized motivation are *learned* in the course of social experience (p. 182)" not given *a priori*; and that norms, by definition, are social conventions. Applying this perspective to their consideration of economics, they argued: "The central fallacy in much of economic thought is to postulate some single motivational entity as an explanation of all economic behavior (p. 182). . . . The meaning of "rationality" is . . . limited to the orientation of action toward maximal conformity with a norm (p. 176)."

Thus, strictly materialist behavior is not the sole force motivating human behavior for sociologists. Rather, they see whatever motivations are in place as socially learned and changeable, not atomistically and permanently chosen by individuals. Preferences and actions are influenced by the ways people come to understand and value – through socialization and enculturation – different aspects of their world. Therefore, action is understood by looking at the institutional structures, social norms, and cultural values that determine preferences.

Sociologists consider it a valid project to *interpret* others' understanding of their world. They are concerned that their concepts and propositions be consistent with the perceptions and meanings of the participants; perceptions and meanings are taken to influence action, and inconsistencies between the two are therefore problematic. Thus, the question is not – *"given* the utility function we assume, what can we predict" – but rather "how can we *locate and interpret* people's utility functions, and how do we track their formation and measure their change over time."

Theory and Research

Moving to the next level of analysis, theory and research, we find economists deducing axioms from their assumptions, while sociologists (having minimal assumptions to begin with), must investigate, empirically, the nature of preferences, values, behavior, and motivation. This need for grounded empirical research is obviated for economists. Rather, highly abstracted secondary data are used along with elegant models to predict, demonstrate, and "explain" human behavior. Until recently this research was deliberately restricted to economic areas that can be so analyzed.

But *sociology takes economics' rationality assumptions themselves as problematic.* Rather than any widespread agreement on human nature within sociology, it is likely to be either investigated or defined anew in every research undertaking. Indeed, since Weber, rationalization itself has been a major subject of theory and research for sociology, both as an orientation of individuals and as a historic process in the development of organizations and institutions.

For most sociologists, research even more than theory is where the action is. They are most likely to gather data first and then build their theories from the data. Often the results are too contingent to fit into neat formulas. They are also messy and tentative. But *many sociologists genuinely revel in the intellectual ferment this produces;* for where the answers are not assumed already, there are always more questions to be asked. Methodological issues also become crucial here for sociologists since *the truth-value of these theories depends on empirical support, not logical connections* with core assumptions.

For example, an economist, extrapolating from the rationality assumption might flatly *predict* that, if legal abortions paid for by welfare were not available, the aggregate level of teen-age pregnancies would decrease. But most sociologists would be more concerned with explaining why teenage pregnancies occur so frequently among lower-income girls, and why they so often prefer (as a result of their presumably rational decision-making) delivering illegitimate children to abortions.

Policy

Sociologists seek to be realistic; economists seek to be predictive, above and even in spite of reality, when necessary. *To be "right for the wrong reasons" is of little concern to the economist, whereas for sociologists it is terribly embarrassing and often would not even be considered correct.* At the policy level, economics, with its assumptions about individual choice and free-market options, can always provide an answer. Sociologists are ambivalent about the free market (their judgments are based more on how they value the policy implications than on ideology about free market vs. regulatory choices). They are more likely to hedge about answers and less likely to confidently offer predictions based on simplified assumptions, few variables, and elegant models. Sociologists often are policy outsiders, preferring to define the problems and debunk nearly all solutions! (See Gusfield [1976 and 1981] for two excellent examples concerning the rhetoric of research design and drunk [or "drinking"] driving.)

In the end what we have is a contrast between unrealistic but clean models in economics and "verstehen"-oriented dirty hands in sociology.

Economic imperialism

Too many scholars prefer clean models to dirty hands. There is certainly an attraction to elegant models, and some discomfort with sloppy reality. We strongly caution against imposing surgical elegance on messy problems for the illusory value of clean but unrealistic (even sociologically boring) models. Such moves require abandoning assumptions that have been basic to the discipline, and turn out to involve no reciprocity from economics. In fact, as Gary Becker (1981, p. iv) tells us:

The economic approach is not restricted to material goods and wants or to markets with monetary transactions, and *conceptually* does not distinguish between major and minor decisions or between "emotional" or other decisions. Indeed . . . the economic approach provides a framework applicable to all human behavior – to all types of decisions and to persons from all walks of life.

(See also Becker and Stigler [1977] for an even stronger statement of this imperialistic stance.) Economics is a well-elaborated and established perspective, with its assumptions embodied at its very core. It is

basically a way of thinking. The theories of economists, with surprisingly few exceptions, are simply extensions of the assumption that individuals choose those options which seem to them most likely to secure their largest net advantage. Everyone, it is assumed, acts in accordance with that rule: miser or spendthrift, saint or sinner, consumer or seller, politician or business executive, cautious calculator or spontaneous improvisor. (Heyne, 1976, p. 1)

From such a perspective we are denied the possibility of asking many sociologically important questions such as "why do preferences *change?*" and are forced to ignore important "sociological" problems.

When notable economists such as Becker and Stigler (1977) and Williamson (1981) present economic formulations of "sociological" problems, they impose the definitional assumptions noted above about instrumental motivation and self-interested rational actors, along with the methodological preference for aggregated data and deductive modeling. These moves do not represent humble contributions by outsiders to add a new perspective on familiar sociological questions. Rather, they effectively redefine a whole field and supplant previous work with economists' articulate and well-developed theoretical apparatus (Granovetter, 1985; Maitland, Bryson, and Van de Ven, 1985). In sociology, these same characteristics are seconded and reinforced (nonsociologically) by many studies in the subfields of population ecology, labor markets, and collective action. In terms of Parsons' distinctions, these studies focus on his A and G cells and essentially ignore or assume away integration and pattern-maintenance (i.e., questions about meaning, perception, legitimacy, influence, and subjective interpretation by participants).

What implications would the unqualified adoption of economists' assumptions have for sociology, and what dangers do they entail? We next propose that moves which uncritically imitate economics risk making sociologists: too far removed from the empirical world we want to know about; incompetent to address the cultural side of life in society; and too limited to take account of the richness and variety of social life – all factors that are clearly strengths of our discipline which should not be abandoned for fool's gold.

A cautionary tale

Economics does not question whether its assumptions fit reality in different historical, cultural, or institutional circumstances. It defines these as external to its models and deliberately avoids asking questions crucial to sociologists. Instead, economists seek to derive "universally applicable hypotheses . . . which transcend institutional, systematic, and historical variations (Wilbur and Jameson 1983:32)." Economists treat such variations as "noise" to be eliminated by theoretical generalization or filtered out in empirical work. To the degree sociologists take up the assumptions and methods of the economic perspective, we too will be unable to see historical and cultural variations when they occur. An interesting illustration of the type of problems this overeconomizing of the world creates can be seen in the debate surrounding the "moral economy" view of peasant politics.

In 1976 James Scott published *The Moral Economy of the Peasant*. It created quite a stir by arguing that, for peasants who live close to the level of subsistence, there is "little scope for the profit maximizing calculus of neo-classical economics (p. 4)." Concerned with survival, not profits, peasants, says Scott, must forego risky experiments with new technologies even though they could increase crop yields; they operate according to a "safety-first principle." Also, knowing that help from neighbors is likely to be needed at any time, even poor peasants will share their resources with others as needed; this type of behavior is enforced through socially institutionalized "norms of reciprocity" and social sanctions. Finally, high tax rates are accepted so long as they are structured to allow peasants to survive in bad years; it is within the framework of such a "subsistence ethic" that peasants evaluate the legitimacy of claims upon their resources. Thus Scott argues that particular "nonmaximizing" patterns of action in poor peasant communities are reinforced by diffuse social sanctions, norms of behavior, and concepts of legitimacy.

In response to Scott's analysis, Samuel Popkin wrote his book *The Rational Peasant* (1979), arguing that such "irrational" behavior could not be rational. Beginning from the assumption that peasants, *like everybody else*, act to maximize profits, Popkin argued that peasants would chafe under the pressure of collective restraints, and social norms would be of little use given free rider problems and the lure of profits. "Rational" peasants will ensure their security through personal savings and farming innovations, giving little to their less well-off counterparts and preferring tax structures that enhance their ability to hold onto extra profits.

While the arguments on both sides are complex, the crux of the debate centers around the issue: Is a universal notion of individual self-interest sufficient for understanding political behavior? While both Scott and Popkin recognize that peasants have interests, Scott allows that these interests can become institutionalized as a set of ethical norms and values, that the content of the interests they represent are affected by structural conditions, and that these norms and values serve as a guide for social action. People protect their interests, but not only in the form of short-term, individual income maximization.

What is interesting about this debate is the various levels at which economic rationality is purported to show up and what room is left (or not left) for values depending on where rationality is placed. Scott's explanation of peasant culture is, in fact, also based on a theory of individual rational calculations. These values developed, he suggested, because poor peasants realized that their situation was so precarious that it was essential they cooperate: thus the norm of reciprocity. The odds were that if they did not help each other out, there would be no long run. Likewise, they believed the most important thing about taxes was not how much was taken but how much was left: thus the "subsistence ethic." Individual calculation would, in terms very similar to Hobbes, lead any rational peasant to submit to these shared cultural norms rather than always look out for "number one." This view is essentially sociological in that (in Parsonian terms) values and norms exist to help support goal attainment and adaptation.

Popkin, by contrast, contends that peasant behavior can be fully understood in terms of "universal" standards of economic rationality, i.e., individual profit maximization. Beginning with an "economic" assumption about human nature, normative, cultural, and structural factors of the type analyzed by Scott are precluded. To claim that alternative "rationalities" or nonindividualistic forces may be at play, as Scott does, is equivalent to calling people "irrational" from Popkin's perspective. Economically speaking, only peasants who are individual profit maximizers are "rational."

What is distinctive about this "economic" reaction to Scott's book is its unwillingness to consider "nonrational" behavior, the importance of social relations, the influence of another culture's norms and values, or the influence of particular historical circumstances. Popkin's approach is typical of analyses based on the economic paradigm. The wholehearted incorporation of such an elegant and "universal" theory of human action (i.e., economics) would blind sociology to important historical, cultural, and institutional variations in social organization.

Trade-offs between economic theorizing and sociological research

Economic theory, with its foundation in an unquestioned (and in some forms tautological) proposition that humans act as rational, individual utility maximizers, is comprehensive, all-inclusive, and powerful. But the very *strength* of that theory is also the source of its major weaknesses. For example, economics increasingly claims universality, but it remains static and unable to incorporate major social changes into its models. Two serious problems discussed up to now only in passing are: (1) the lack of diversity in economics' approach to problems; and (2) its ignoring or discounting of data.

Lack of diversity

The Scott-Popkin debate points to economics' narrow and self-imposed rejection of alternatives, to its studied incapacity to see more than a single dimension of most phenomena. In contrast, sociology is a multiparadigmed field that affords its practitioners more conceptual freedom but at the cost of less aggregated data and therefore lower R^2s. Sociology attends to many more dimensions of complex realities, whereas economics generally restricts itself to only one way of approaching problems. A good example is the study of corporate directors, and theories of agency, ownership, and control – all substantive topics of recent and overlapping concern in both disciplines.

While sociology and economics have long held a common interest in these topics, there has been little convergence, historically, because the core problems posed by each discipline were either of little interest to the other, or based on entirely different assumptions. For example, whereas economic models take the market as an unchallengeable independent force beyond the control of individual investors and corporate actors, sociology has been very receptive to conceiving the market as easily manipulated by corporations and commercial banks. More recently, the two fields have drawn closer together: economists have expanded agency theory and the theory of the firm to pose questions about organizations and managers; sociologists, extending the study of organizations, have focused increasingly on environments and markets. Substantive topics like executive compensation, managerial incentives, and inter- and intra-organizational problems like transfer pricing are being examined by both fields now, but through their respective disciplinary lenses (cf. Van de Ven and Joyce, 1981).

While these substantive areas show some movement toward convergence, here too there remain respective core assumptions separating the disciplines. In its interpretation of interlocking directorate data, for example, economics is, once again, more homogenous than sociology. Its general conclusion is that interlocking directorates are a non-issue. But Table 2.2 summarizing four possible approaches to the study of corporate directors, includes three *additional* interpretations commonly found in the literatures of sociology and organization theory.

The two columns in this table dichotomize the amount of power each theory sees exercised by "inside" directors (i.e. management). The two rows similarly dichotomize the degree of control exercised by "outside" board members. Despite the broad range of possibilities this yields, we see economic theory begins and ends with Cell 4. In that cell, *both* inside and outside directors are seen to exert low levels of control because they, in turn, are controlled by the discipline of the marketplace. These actors are merely epiphenomenal agents of market forces. The same view is congruent with population ecology in sociology, i.e., functional organizations are merely selected out (rewarded) by the (all-knowing) "environment." Executives and board members, therefore, have little, if any, power to exert. For Cell 4, accordingly, the composition of corporate boards is irrelevant.

While there certainly is empirical support for this view some of the time, it hardly presents a complete or accurate picture of reality. In fact it represents an idealized image of market (or environmental) forces

Table 2.2. *Alternative theories of power and influence over corporate policy exercised by individual board members*

		Degree of control by top management's inside directors	
		High	Low
Degree of control by outside directors	High	"Hegemonists" (e.g., Domhoff) (1)	"External Control Theory" (e.g., Zeitlin; U.S. House, Patman Committee) (2)
	Low	"Organization Theory" (e.g., Pfeffer; Gordon) (3)	"Corporate Actor" and "Population Ecology" Theories (e.g., Coleman; Manne; Hannan and Freeman) (4)

Source: See text.

that is questionable at best (Perrow, 1986). Indeed, in other historical periods, it is the reality idealized in Cell 1 – in which the large corporation and its directors jointly dominate the market – that is just as real as in Cell 4's. Alternatively, where conflict, rather than cooperation or conspiracy, *within* the director elite, is adduced (Cells 2 and 3), it is sociology and organization theory which generate models of which subgroup dominates the other.

If we view all of these perspectives as partially correct – usually at different points in time or in varying circumstances – we see that, taken as a whole, sociology's multiple paradigms are better able to interpret and explain these multiple realities. While economists could criticize the discipline for being undirected because it accommodates each of these multiple perspectives, *we believe this is a strength of sociology which should be nurtured and maintained.* Sociology is more attentive to the empirical variety of conditions in the real world. In contrast, economics presents the more unified and simpler model, which can be more relied upon to always predict the same results.

Ignoring data

For the most part, the clean models of economics are deductive and do not even rely on data. A study of the articles in *The American Economic Review* from 1977 to 1981 by Nobel-prize-winning economist

Wassily Leontief (reported in Kuttner 1985) found that 54 percent of the articles used mathematical models without data; only one half of 1 percent of the articles were empirical analyses of original data generated by their authors. In describing subsequent issues of the journal, Leontief is quoted as saying he "found exactly one piece of empirical research, and it was about the utility maximization of pigeons (Kuttner 1985:78)." However, even in cases where data are generated to test economic models, they are usually ignored when they run counter to economists' assumptions. The question becomes not *whether* the data fit their assumptions, but how they can be *made* to fit the model.

This is not to say there is no empirical work in and around economics. There is another side to the empirically based debate of the fundamental tenets and assumptions of economics. In fact, the rationalistic assumptions of microeconomics have been attacked head-on by empirical research in cognitive psychology. Tversky and Kahneman (1981) showed that, if choice situations are "framed" differently, then preferences differ; Svenson (1979) showed that most decision-making problems are solved without a complete search of information; Einhorn and Hogarth (1985) have shown that ambiguity and attitudes toward ambiguity affect the differential weighing of imagined probabilities; and Kahneman, Knetsch, and Thaler (1985) have shown that consumers' concern for "fairness" may slow down the process of reaching equilibrium, or prevent the market from clearing. Economists' rationalistic assumptions, including those of continuity, transitivity, and independence in decision-making, are challenged by these and other authors.

In response to the work just cited, economists can respond that parameters were improperly set in these experiments, that other rationalistic factors can explain these results, or that economic models should only be tested in "real" economic settings, not experimental ones. Indeed, when queried by reporters, several economists explained: "Having a consistent and well-reasoned point of view is more important than being right all of the time. 'Both your successes and your failures' have to be explicable, says [economist] Kudlow. 'People have to know where you stand and what you believe in (*Newsweek*, Feb. 4, 1985).' "

When the data do not fit, many economists too often and too easily revert to what empirical researchers often see as the security of tautology and the reassertion of core assumptions. On the micro level, economists' assumption of rationality can be restated as psychological hedonism, at which point the proposition becomes irrefutable. If a person chooses a job with lower pay, the economist will add that his or her utility function must include variables besides pay – you just have to include them in the formulas to show that utility was maximized. If a *samurai* in feudal Japan commits *hara-kiri*, the economist can argue that, if you add the cost of shame to the man's utility function, it is obvious that his choice maximized his utility. Made irrefutable in this way, economists' proposition of utility maximization is at the same time rendered useless for nonbelievers.

On the macro level, Wilbur and Jameson (1983:85) suggest another example of this problem:

The structure of laissez faire theory makes it particularly difficult to verify any of its constituent propositions. Its survival and attractiveness derive from the theory's tendency to shift from interesting empirical, though false or misleading, propositions to true, though empty, tautologies. For example, from the *truism* that people seek their economic advantage, [economists] deduce the *empirical proposition* that productive investment and work effort are reduced by taxes and similar government measures that reduce the rate of return. However, when confronted with evidence that investment rates over the period 1948 to 1980 *actually* were stable or even increased slightly in the face of escalating tax rates and government regulations, they retreat to a comparison of *potential* effects: in the long run if tax rates and other burdens were increased enough, eventually productive investment and work effort should fall.

Such arguments remind us of the religious doomsday movements' reinterpretation of their situation after the world did not end on the day they had proclaimed it would, in Festinger et al.'s (1956) study *When Prophesy Fails*.

Conclusion: on bridging the gap between sociology and economics

In contrast to economics, the discipline of sociology seems a tower of Babel. Each substantive area has its own traditions of theory and research. Attempts at unification are mainly the specialty of a minority of theorists ("grand theorists" as they are derisively known to most of the rest of the discipline) and at their best provide fodder for graduate courses and other grand theorists, but in practice are ignored by most sociologists. It is therefore not surprising that sociologists are prone to periodic infatuations with external models of scientific rigor and grace and that economics should serve as such a model.

The contrast we have drawn between the disciplines is dramatic. We have argued that many characteristics of sociology that make its own practitioners uncomfortable are in fact strengths rather than weaknesses – assets to be cherished and developed. Sociology's very lack of definition, its broad substantive claims, its theoretical cacophony, its strong empirical bent, and its perennial identity crisis can be viewed as selective *advantages*. Economics which is continuously being narrowed and refined theoretically (while making exaggerated claims empirically) is a specialist style of adaptation; sociology is ever the generalist.

The question of the respective scientific achievement and perhaps even nature of the two disciplines is not to be dismissed lightly. On the one hand, science is the broader ground and set of values on which any sort of joint appeal or venture is likely to be based. The commitment to the norms of science is the value most widely shared by sociologists and economists. However, on the other hand, it may well be argued that it is exactly on the very definition of the nature of the social scientific enterprise that sociology and economics part company.

What this means for productive dialogue and collaboration between the two fields is that it cannot be managed via a simple transformation of one or another aspect of one field or the other. To be sure, it is useful to imagine (if not try out) economic models in which the assumption of fixed preferences for consumers is relaxed, or to conceive of sociological studies in which the number of variables is halved. For the already ongoing dialogue between fields to either continue expanding, or stop, however, it is equally, if not more, important for each to develop greater understanding of how differently the other poses questions, defines problems, evaluates results, and designs research. While each field may learn from the other, progress cannot occur through simple imitation. There is too much to be lost in each field.

Sociology and economics tend, at least in their cores, to be extremist. True scientific progress may in fact be based on a combination of, or dialectic between, "clean models" and "dirty hands," not either one or the other. *Pure elegance of models leads to sterility; unwillingness to abstract from and go beyond one's data leads to pure narrative. Our bias, if forced to choose, however, is that we already have too much of the former and not enough "dirty hands."*

Given the losses inherent in any efforts to appear more like economists, why, we may ask, are sociologists in such hot pursuit of the magic of economics and the economists' grail? One answer may be that it is the economic framework which has the larger impact on social policy. Government officials are truly taken by "clean models." As we noted earlier, "having a clear argument" is often more important than being "right." Consistency, purity, and elegance are themselves of high value. To have a "complete" explanation, and a core theory, is very convincing, rhetorically.

More important, perhaps, is the comfortable fit between economic theory and American culture. To trace all action back to individual rational behavior is to make it understandable within our peculiarly individualistic and rationalistic culture. The individual rationality assumption has its basis in Locke and Hobbes and the very idea of a social "contract." The cultural project of economists is to interpret the world in such a way that even the grandest of phenomenon – e.g., the existence of society – can be traced back to free individual choice and utility maximization.

Economics also succeeds, even more deliberately and effectively than sociology, in avoiding all consideration of ethical claims by the very groups and individuals whose behavior it claims to predict and explain. Instead, economics upholds its *own* implicit moral order, or ideology, while it eschews cultural and historical variation and claims universal validity for its axioms. That moral order is a (naturally) elegant restatement of utilitarianism. In economists' language, this means moving to the Pareto frontier. This, of course, fits very well with the folklore and rhetoric of American capitalism and its current incarnation in conservative government and policy circles.

Acknowledgment

We are grateful to Diane Binson, Paul DiMaggio, Wendy Espeland, Jonathan Frenzen, and Sharon Zukin for their helpful comments and criticism.

Bibliography

Aldrich, Howard. *Organizations and Environments.* Englewood Cliffs, N.J.: Prentice-Hall, 1979.

Becker, Gary. *A Treatise on the Family.* Cambridge, Mass.: Harvard University Press, 1981.

———. *Human Capital.* New York: National Bureau of Economic Research, 1975.

Becker, Gary, and George Stigler. "De Gustibus Non Est Disputandum." *American Economic Review* (Mar. 1977): 76–90.

Bower, Joseph L. *The Two Faces of Management.* Boston: Houghton Mifflin, 1983.

Coleman, James S. *Power and the Structure of Society.* New York: Norton, 1974.

Domhoff, G. William. *The Powers That Be: Processes of Ruling Class Domination in America.* New York: Vintage Press, 1978.

Einhorn, Hillel J., and Robin M. Hogarth, "Ambiguity and Uncertainty in Probabilistic Inference." *Psychological Review* 92, no. 4 (Oct. 1985): 433–61.

Festinger, L., H. W. Riecken, and S. Schachter. *When Prophesy Fails.* Minneapolis: University of Minnesota Press, 1956.

Field, Alexander J. "The Problem with Neoclassical Institutional Economics: A Critique with Special Reference to North/Thomas Model of Pre-1500 Europe." *Explorations in Economic History* 18 (1981): 174–98.

———. "On the Explanation of Rules Using Rational Choice Models." *Journal of Economic Issues* 13, no. 1 (Mar. 1979): 49–72.

Gordon, Robert. *Business Leadership in the Large Corporation.* New York: Harper, 1945.

Granovetter, Mark. "Economic Action and Social Structure: The Problem of Embeddedness. *American Journal of Sociology* 91 (1985): 481–510.

Gusfield, Joseph R. *The Culture of Public Problems: Drinking-Driving and the Symbolic Order.* University of Chicago Press, Chicago, 1981.

————. "The Literary Rhetoric of Science: Comedy and Pathos in Drinking Driving Research." *American Sociological Review* 41 (1976): 16–34.

Hannan, M. T., and J. H. Freeman. "The Population Ecology of Organizations." *American Journal of Sociology* 88(1977): 1116–45.

Heyne, Paul. *The Economic Way of Thinking*, 2d ed. Chicago: Science Research Associates, Inc., 1976.

Jensen, Michael C., and William H. Meckling. "Theory of the Firm: Managerial Behavior, Agency Costs, and Ownership Structures." *Journal of Financial Economics* 3 (Oct. 1976): 306–60.

Kahneman, David, Jack Knetsch, and Richard Thaler. "Perceptions of Unfairness: Constraints on Wealth Seeking." Presented at "Behavioral Foundations of Economic Theory," University of Chicago Graduate School of Business, Oct. 1985.

Kuttner, Robert. "The Poverty of Economics." *Atlantic Monthly* (Feb. 1985): 74–84.

Maitland, I., J. Bryson, and A. Van de Ven. "Sociologists, Economists, and Opportunism." *Academy of Management Review*, 20 (1985): 59–65.

Manne, Henry. "Mergers and the Market for Corporate Control." *Journal of Political Economy* 73 (Apr. 1965): 110–20.

Parsons, Talcott, and Neil J. Smelser. *Economy and Society*. New York: The Free Press, 1965.

Perrow, Charles. *Complex Organizations: A Critical Essay*, 3d ed. New York: Random House, 1986.

————. "Markets, Hierarchies, and Hegemony," pp. 371–406 in *Perspectives on Organization Design and Behavior*, edited by A. Van de Ven and W. F. Joyce. New York: Wiley, 1981.

Pfeffer, Jeffrey. "Size and Composition of Corporate Boards of Directors: The Organization and Its Environment." *Administrative Science Quarterly* 17 (1972): 218–28.

Popkin, Samuel. *The Rational Peasant*. Berkeley: University of California Press, 1979.

Scott, James. *The Moral Economy of the Peasant*. New Haven: Yale University Press, 1976.

Svenson, Ola. "Process Descriptions of Decision Making." *Organizational Behavior and Human Performance* 23 (1979): 86–112.

Tversky, Amos, and David Kahneman. "The Framing of Decisions and the Psychology of Choice." *Science* 211 (Jan. 30, 1981): 453–58.

U.S. Congress. House. Committee on Banking and Currency, Domestic Finance Subcommittee. "Commercial Banks and Their Trust Activities: Emerging Influence on the American Economy." 90th Congress, 2nd Session. Washington, D.C.: U.S. Government Printing Office, 1968.

Van de Ven, A., and W. F. Joyce, eds. *Perspectives on Organization Design and Behavior*. New York: Wiley, 1981.

White, Harrison C. "Where Do Markets Come From?" *American Journal of Sociology* 87 (1981): 517–47.

Wilbur, Charles K., and Kenneth P. Jameson. *An Inquiry into the Poverty of Economics*. Univ. of Notre Dame Press, Notre Dame, Ind.: University of Notre Dame Press, 1983.

Williamson, Oliver E. "The Economics of Organization: The Transaction Cost Approach." *American Journal of Sociology* 87 (Nov. 1981): 548–77.

————. *Markets and Hierarchies*. New York: Free Press, 1975.

Williamson, Oliver E., and William G. Ouchi. "The Markets and Hierarchies Program of Research: Origins, Implications, and Prospects" pp. 247–370 in *Perspectives on Organization Design and Behavior* edited by A. Van de Ven and W. F. Joyce. New York: Wiley, 1981.

Zeitlin, Maurice. "Corporate Ownership and Control: The Large Corporation and the Capitalist Class." *American Journal of Sociology* 79, no. 5 (Mar. 1974): 1073–1119.

3
The paradigm of economic sociology

RICHARD SWEDBERG, ULF HIMMELSTRAND, AND
GÖRAN BRULIN

Economic sociology today lacks clear status as a specific field of sociological inquiry. This, like everything else, has its specific history. One
can thus look at U.S. sociology and note that neither the Chicago School
nor the "golden fifties" of American sociology resulted in the kind of
sustained analysis of the economy that came to characterize, say, urban
problems or the family. The same, on the whole, is true for European
sociology before and after World War II. Economics was left to the economists, and sociologists shied away from the topic. Sociologists might
have thought that they studied all of society, but what they looked at
was, in Smelser's poignant formulation, more of "a grab-bag of left-
overs"[1] from economics and political science.

Even if one grants that economic sociology has been slow in acquiring
its own identity as a distinct field of sociological inquiry during the
twentieth century, two things should be noted. First, economic sociology has a very strong theoretical tradition – from the classics onward –
to lean on. And, second, there exists a growing interest in the topic today that has resulted in a series of excellent studies. Add to this that the
economy in contemporary society is going through radical changes that
baffle the economists[2] and that the economists are increasingly invad-
ing the domain of sociology,[3] and it will be clear that there are plenty of
reasons today to revive what the classical sociologists called "economic
sociology."[4]

In the last analysis, however, the study of economic sociology derives
its raison d'etre from the fact that the economy constitutes a very important area in society and that sociology over the years has developed
a series of theories and techniques that are well suited to the study of
economics. We hope the time has now come when sociologists will decide to give economics their sustained attention. If they so do, it is our
conviction that they will be amply rewarded because, even if economic

sociology is in need of reconstruction, it also holds the promise of becoming one of the most exciting areas of sociology in the near future.

Economic sociology: today and yesterday

If we now turn to the intellectual history of economic sociology, it should be stressed that Marx's *Das Kapital* and Weber's *Wirtschaft und Gesellschaft* are, first and foremost, sociological studies of the economy. For Marx, the economy is the central aspect of society around which all the others turn. Labor is the existential condition and the one that is ultimately responsible for the shape our lives assume. Weber was nearly as obsessed as Marx with economic questions but assigned a more independent status to other forces in society. As a consequence, he was able to perceive with more clarity the sociological limits of the economy as is evident from his succinct outline for what economic sociology should look like in chapter two of *Wirtschaft und Gesellschaft*, "Sociological Categories of Economic Action."[5] If we add to Marx's and Weber's writings *De la division du travail social* by Durkheim, *Philosophie des Geldes* by Simmel, and *Economy and Society* by Parsons and Smelser, it should be obvious that economic sociology has as good a theoretical foundation as it is possible for any field of sociological inquiry to have in the twentieth century.

As noted earlier, economic sociology did not develop very forcefully during the time after the classics. This is true also, despite interesting exceptions, for the period of the structural-functionalists. Talcott Parsons, Neil Smelser, and Wilbert E. Moore did indeed try to launch the topic, but the opposing forces were too strong and instead the topic fragmented into fields such as stratification analysis, industrial sociology, and the like.[6]

During the paradigm crisis of the 1960s and early 1970s, a great variety of sociological studies appeared that insisted on the centrality of economics in society's "totality." These were mainly written from the perspectives of women's studies, neo-Marxism, and Third World theories.[7] Simultaneously, however, important theoretical developments were made by economists, political scientists, and organization theorists. The various impulses came together in the mid-seventies and resulted in a number of excellent studies in economic sociology. To mention just a few: Fred Block, *The Origin of International Economic Disorder* (1977); Rosabeth Moss Kanter, *Men and Women of the Corporation* (1977); Gudmund Hernes, *Forhandlingsøkonomi og blandingsadministrasjon* (1978); Louise A. Tilly and Joan W. Scott, *Women, Work, and Family* (1978); Ivar Berg (editor), *Sociological Perspectives on the Labor Market* (1981); Harry Makler, Alberto Martinelli, and Neil Smelser (editors),

The New International Economy (1982); and Arthur Stinchcombe, *Economic Sociology* (1983). Though it might well be true that economic sociology is in need of a general theoretical reconstruction to deal with today's economic realities, the works since the mid-seventies must nevertheless be credited on several accounts. New topics have thus been introduced into economic sociology: the international economy,[8] the role of women in the economy,[9] the existence of labor markets as well as financial markets,[10] and the interaction between political and economic steering systems.[11] Sophisticated mathematical models for use in economic sociology have been constructed; and general sociological theories, such as network analysis, have been successfully introduced into economic sociology.[12]

A comparison of two paradigms: neoclassical theory and economic sociology

Despite the progress during the last years, there is still reason to look at the basic principles of economic sociology. This is necessitated, first and foremost, by the fact that not enough sustained theoretical attention has been paid to economic sociology as a whole since the 1950s when Parsons and Smelser's *Economy and Society* appeared.

In this chapter, we outline the paradigm of economic sociology by contrasting it to microeconomic theory. There are several advantages to looking simultaneously at the basic principles of microeconomics and of economic sociology. For one thing, it quickly brings out what is distinctive about economic sociology in relation to economic theory. It should also help to open a fruitful dialogue between economists and sociologists by showing that they after all are struggling with related problems. And finally, it highlights the kind of arguments that economic sociology will have to face if it is to gain acceptance, since neoclassical orthodoxy today has something of a monopoly on how to analyze economic problems.[13]

Microeconomics, it has been argued, is the closest that the social sciences have to a paradigm in Kuhn's sense.[14] It thus has a distinct research program that defines which problems to look at and how to go about analyzing them. The microeconomic paradigm has its origin in the new developments that took place in economic science in the 1870s when the labor theory of value was challenged and eventually replaced by marginal utility analysis.[15] Save for a decade or so when Keynesian macroeconomics attracted the most attention, neoclassical economics has dominated twentieth-century economics,[16] "The last decade," one can read in a recent issue of *American Economic Review*, "has seen an almost complete victory for the neoclassical school."[17]

Over the years, neoclassical economics has developed a very impressive body of scientific theories and come to regard itself, in Paul Samuelson's words, as "indeed the queen of the social sciences."[18] The high quality of the work produced by economists is generally acknowledged in other social sciences, but doubts have also been raised as to microeconomics' capacity to connect with empirical reality.[19] The mixture of enthusiasm, awe, and hesitation that microeconomics can inspire, is well reflected in the following quote by Gudmund Hernes:

> If I, in all friendliness, were to allow myself a frivolous analogy, I would liken neo-classical theory to a gothic cathedral. People have worked at it during many ages. Parts are romanesque, gothic, renaissance and baroque. The great spirits have constructed whole naves and channels on the cathedral. The lesser spirits have built towers and spires. Great processions of people have come to chisel out a beautiful inscription and to build an arch, a theorem which unites a tower with a sideship. Some have left behind gargoyles and some have only marked a stone with their name. All the energy expanded and all the individualistic labor are marked by the totality. The overarching structure is clear but no-one can grasp or really encompass all the details. People from distant disciplines travel like pilgrims to the cathedral, speak with a hushed voice once inside and usually kneel down in religious awe even if one or two scoundrels may break something off as a souvenir, which can be used to acquire status in some other discipline. Many a person is steadfast at work in the cathedral: Leontief has thus taken over Walras' old workroom and looks after the cross-vaults. Frisch has left behind a workshop filled with half-finished figures, which seven little dwarfs are busily working on. As in the period of the late renaissance there is also a Milton who detests everything which is not classically pure. But most eyes are directed at the tower: there Arrow is working away and, yes, he seems to want to build another tower. But one is tempted to ask a silent question: Should we be building the Gothic way today?[20]

Economic sociology is decidedly a less imposing edifice than microeconomic theory. And when we talk about it here in the sense of a "paradigm," we do this not so much in the sense that Kuhn has given the term but rather in that of Robert Merton in his well-known essay "The Sociology of Knowledge."[21] Like Merton, we shall thus use "paradigm" mainly to indicate the basic principles and problem-solving approaches that characterize economic sociology as a special field of sociological inquiry.

Points of divergence between the paradigms of neoclassical theory and economic sociology

To catch most of the significant differences between the way microeconomic theory and economic sociology look at economic reality, we have outlined seven points of divergence between the two (see Table 3.1). In the presentation of the basic principles of economic sociology, an effort

Table 3.1. *The paradigms of neoclassical theory and economic sociology: a comparison*

Items	Neoclassical theory	Economic sociology
Concept of the actor	Individuals, households, and firms (*separate utility maximizer*)	Individuals, groups, classes, institutions (*social actor*)
Arena of action	Any situation where choice and scarcity of resources are present; by preference the market (*separate economy*)	The economic system as part of society (*social economy*)
Types of economic action	Exclusively rational actions with emphasis on choice and maximization (*formal rationality*)	Rational actions as well as other forms of economic action (*social rationality and social economic actions in general*)
Result of economic actions	Tendency to equilibrium (*equilibrated harmony*)	Tendency to more or less institutionalized yet tension-filled interest struggles (*tension-filled interest struggles*)
View of the analyst	Producer of scientific results (*objective outsider*)	Producer of scientific results and member of society (*objective insider*)
Concept of time	Stylized and stationary time concept; identical to action that is analyzed (*stationary and adaptive time concept*)	Extended and variable time concept: goes beyond the action that is the focus of the analysis (*sociohistorical time concept*)
General scientific method	Predictions and explanations based on radical abstractions	Descriptions and explanations based on empirically adjusted abstractions

Source: See text.

has been made to draw on the more programmatic statements in economic sociology, among which we include not only the major works by Marx and Weber but also certain key texts by Thorstein Veblen, Talcott Parsons, Neil Smelser, Karl Polanyi, Gudmund Hernes, and Mark Granovetter.[22] When differences of opinion exist in these writings, we have chosen to highlight these as well as to indicate our own preferences. Little is to be gained by denying that economic sociology still faces, in Smelser's formulation, "many unsolved mysteries."[23]

The Concept of the Actor: The Separate Utility Maximizer versus the Social Actor. Microeconomic theory uses three kinds of actors: individuals, households, and firms. The two latter are often assumed, for purposes of analysis, to act like individuals, which means that they are unitary or unstructured ("black boxes").[24] The activities of households and firms are stylized and few in number because the scarcity of resources in combination with the maximization principle limit the spectrum of possible types of actions. The households and the firms are fundamentally separate from one another and mainly interact through the market mechanism in acts of buying and selling.

Many economists agree that the notion of separate utility maximizers presents serious problems of analysis. In a well-known article in the *Journal of Economic Literature*, Lee E. Preston has noted that "very few of the interactions between real firms and their host environments can be usefully formulated within the conventional (that is, neoclassical) framework."[25] To counteract problems of this type, economists have developed concepts such as that of "externalities," and also glanced at "generalized morality," "custom," and the like.[26]

Problems of this type are to a large extent avoided in economic sociology because it conceptualizes the actor as a social agent. In general, the assumption that the actor is social has several important consequences for the way economic sociology views economic processes. Here we shall discuss three of these: (1) that the actor is always connected to other actors and to the social environment; (2) that a broad spectrum of actors and actions must be taken into account; and (3) that contradictions in the behavior of the actors are to be expected. (Other implications of the social-actor assumption will be discussed below.)

That there exist complicated links between an economic actor and other actors as well as the social environment in general is something that all strands of economic sociology agree upon. The idea has received its most succinct expression in the work of Karl Polanyi with its notion of "embeddedness." According to Polanyi, economic action without the "societal element" would be "bare bones;" it would have no "unity" or "stability" whatsoever.[27] In *The Great Transformation*, Polanyi has attempted to show the terrible anarchy that developed in nineteenth-century England when the social foundations of the economy for a brief period crumbled. For Polanyi and for economic sociology, the idea that the economic actors are separate from society is unrealistic and the cause of many misunderstandings in neoclassical economics.

Because economic sociology in the words of Marx "set out from real, active men" in their concrete social surroundings, it by necessity encompasses a much broader set of actions and actors than mainstream economic theory.[28] Where, for instance, neoclassical theory has had to develop such forced concepts as "endogenous politicians"[29] to account for the economic actions by the state, economic sociology has from its beginnings included the state among the economic actors.[30] The same goes for actors such as trade unions, employers' organizations, and similar organizations.[31] Neither do there exist any good reasons for economic sociology not to acknowledge women as distinct economic actors, something that is more difficult to do in orthodox economic theory.[32] The only bottom line that economic sociology has to stick to is that it studies economic action that is social, that is, the actor "takes account of the behavior of others."[33]

By opening up the analysis to a greater variety of economic actors than neoclassical theory, economic sociology is forced to acknowledge that the behavior of the actors is exceedingly complex and often contradictory. In economic sociology, it is usually not enough to see households and firms as just two economic actors and nothing else. There also exist actors within these actors and this has to be explicitly taken into account when the actions of households and firms are analyzed. The very multiplicity of actors on the same and different levels of social reality forces economic sociology to face the issue of contradictory behavior. "Role conflict," "class struggle," "negotiated order," and "relative deprivation" are a few examples of the kind of concepts economic sociology necessarily must use in the analysis to handle problems of this type.

It can finally be noted that it is of course not only economic sociology but sociology in general that utilizes the concept of social actors. The specific task of economic sociology is thus to construct successful hypotheses about the different ways economic actors are embedded in social reality. Here much work still remains to be done even if one can point to the accomplishments in the classic tradition as well as to some recent contributions, such as Granovetter's attempt to flesh out the notion of embeddedness with the help of network analysis.[34] What is especially needed, in our opinion, is more imaginative models of a middle-range type that can ground economic sociology in concrete reality.

To give an example of such a model, we shall briefly present Fredrik Barth's conceptual scheme in *The Role of the Entrepreneur in Social Change in Northern Norway*.[35] What Barth here tries to do is to construct a theory of how a local entrepreneur acts in a small community in an industrialized country with the help of concepts such as "niche," "resources," "restrictions," and "social costs." In order to exploit the "niche" – defined as the source of exploitation in relation to clients and competitors – the entrepreneur must have enough "resources," among which are included not only the conventional items but also contacts with bureaucrats, politicians, and the like. The "niche" and the "resources" together impose certain "restrictions" on the entrepreneur's behavior. The entrepreneur's choice of actions and general strategy are, in the final analysis, also determined by their "social cost," by which is meant various moral and social restraints such as, for instance, goodwill in the community. Barth's model, in conclusion, is a nice example of economic sociology because it cuts across the conventional borders in microeconomic analysis but retains the focus on the entrepreneur as an economic actor.

The Arena of Action: The Separate Economy versus the Social Economy. Economic action, according to neoclassical economics, takes place in its own separate space. Compared to the classical economists, who paid much attention to institutions and "disturbing causes," neoclassical thinkers have shown little interest in what lies outside the economic system and in how this can be "endogenized." In *Economic Theory in Retrospect*, Mark Blaug thus notes that, "having marked the boundaries of economics, neoclassical writers openly confessed noncompetence outside that boundary and were satisfied to throw out a few common sense conclusions and occasionally a suggestive insight."[36] It is also assumed in mainstream economics that the economic system is sufficient to itself. Present in the microeconomic paradigm is thus the notion that, because a kind of "supreme autonomy" characterizes the economic system, society should adjust itself to what the economy demands and not vice versa.

Mainstream economics tends to identify the economy with the market or, more correctly, with what has been called "the hypothetical market."[37] The last decades have, however, also witnessed several attempts by economists to broaden considerably the traditional perspective by, for instance, looking at different economic systems.[38] Oliver Williamson has also succeeded in linking up the concept of the market to that of the firm through the notion of "transaction costs."[39] Williamson's analysis is reminiscent of the public-choice approach in the sense that both attempt to analyze social structures with the help of the microeconomic concept of rationality. In contrast to the latter approach, Williamson has, however, succeeded in extending the traditional concept of the economy by introducing the idea that markets and hierarchies are functional alternatives.

Economic sociology, in contrast to microeconomic theory, conceptualizes the economy as a *social economy*. Several implications follow from this approach that are worth mentioning. For one thing, the economy is seen as part of society and subordinate to the social system. There also exist distinct boundaries between the economy and the other parts of society. And finally, the economic system must be assumed to have its own distinct autonomy.

The assumption that the economy is part of society is basic to economic sociology. If one, like Polanyi once did, divides economic thinkers into those who see the economy as a "separate system" and those who view it as "one aspect of society," it would soon become evident that economic sociologists belong to the latter category.[40]

If economic sociologists agree that the economy is a part of society, the situation is different when it comes to conceptualizing the exact link between the economy and society. Weber is characteristically cautious on this point and is only wiling to concede, for instance, that there exists an "elective affinity" between cultural values such as religion and the economy. Marx's position is difficult to nail down because his theory, as Schumpeter has stressed, is simultaneously economic and sociological; the key concepts and the major propositions are "both economic and sociological and carry the same meaning on both planes."[41] To summarize Marx's position, one could say that his view of the relation between the economy and the rest of society is profoundly historical, dialectical, and always insists on the centrality of labor.

Of all the works in the field, *Economy and Society*, by Parsons and Smelser, is the one that contains the most extensive discussion of how the economy is related to the rest of society. It is here assumed that any society must successfully address four problems. These are adaptation (A), goal-attainment (G), integration (I), and latency or pattern-maintenance (L). The social system, the authors argue, is made up of four analytical subsystems of which the economy is one. The main task of the economy is to take care of society's need to adapt (A).

Another difficult question in economic sociology – and one which needs more discussion – concerns the autonomy of the economic system. Weber did see the economy as a fairly autonomous system of economic action, but was vague on the topic. Marx, Veblen, and Polanyi were all involved in polemics with mainstream economic thought and probably spent more energy on the futility of sharply separating the economy from society than on outlining a stringent alternative to this view. It was really first with Parsons-Smelser, as Niklas Luhmann has noted, that a theoretical effort was made to outline a sociological concept of the economy as a totality.[42] The main idea in *Economy and Society*, as mentioned earlier, is that the economy can be conceptualized as a distinct subsystem that addresses the problem of adaptation. The economic system is subordinate to the social system as a whole and interacts with the three other subsystems through various input-output exchanges. The adaptive system, finally, can itself be subdivided according to the AGIL schema.

Parsons and Smelser's theory of how to conceptualize the autonomy of the economy is very formal and not really discussed enough to warrant either a firm approval or disapproval.[43] It must however be said that economic sociology stands to benefit very much from a renewed interest in the concept of the economic system and its autonomy. Such a concept would, for instance, be able to throw new light on topics such as stratification analysis, industrial sociology, and labor-market sociology by integrating these into a new and meaningful totality. Exactly how a reconstructed concept of the economic system would look is, to repeat, unclear today. A few comments, however, can be made. First, it is clear that the concept of the economic system must be quite different from the one used in neoclassical economics. Clear lines also need to be drawn between the economy and the other subsystems in order to avoid having a concept of the economic system where the economy just fades into the rest of society at some undetermined point, as in Polanyi's notion of "embeddedness." In addition to outlining clearly the parameters of economic action and the interaction between the economy and the other subsystems of society, it might also be worthwhile to center the new concept of the economy around the notion of actors' limited choices as, for instance, Luhmann[44] has suggested. This way the concept of the economic system would become truly dynamic and a healthy balance could be struck between "the undersocialized concept of man" in economic theory and "the oversocialized concept of man" that one frequently finds in the sociological literature, according to Granovetter.[45] Other building stones in a theory of a social economy might be the notion of social actors, the concept of social rationality, and the sociohistorical time concept (discussed elsewhere).

The Concept of Rationality: Formal Rationality versus Social Rationality. If one, with Smelser,[46] distinguishes between "formal rationality" and "social rationality," it is clear that the microeconomic concept of rationality belongs to the former category. In its most elementary formulation, the rationality concept means that firms and households choose the kind of action that maximizes their own self-interest; firms seek to maximize profits, and households, utility. "More advanced treatments," one can read in an overview of the literature, "note that the ability to detect indifference between market baskets of goods and the ability to chose consistently given a well-ordered preference function defines rationality in consumer theory, while rational firms must operate on their production function, choose least-cost combinations of inputs for each possible level of output, and choose the level of output which maximizes profits."[47]

The key elements in the microeconomic concept of rationality are few – correct *choice* based on *full information* in a situation of *scarce re-*

sources – and this has led critics to argue that the neoclassical concept of rationality is empty. In an article with the telling title "Rational Fools," Amartya Sen has claimed that "traditional theory has *too little* structure."[48] In a recent issue of *American Economic Review*, Albert O. Hirschman concurs with Sen and argues that if economic theory is to be able to capture more of reality, it will have to invest its basic concept with a more complex structure.[49] In this context, it should finally be mentioned that some economists have tried to remedy the deficiencies in the microeconomic concept of rationality through notions such as "bounded rationality," "satisficing," and "x-efficiency."[50]

In a famous quote from *Foundations of Economic Action*, Paul Samuelson says that "many economists would separate economics from sociology upon the basis of rational or irrational behavior."[51] This opinion, however, shows at the most that many economists have read Pareto and little else in sociology. Closer to the truth is that most sociologists have not looked twice at the concept of rationality and do not find the distinction between rational and irrational behavior particularly relevant to their work. If we turn to economic sociology, the situation is somewhat different. Here, discussions of the notion of rationality are common but the opinions about its usefulness are sharply divided.

Among the opponents to the formal concept of rationality in economic sociology are, first and foremost, many institutionalists and people like Polanyi and his followers. The attitude of Marx is more ambiguous. On the one hand, it is clear that Marx in his own work used a very rational method of analysis and that followers like Oskar Lange were positive to a modified concept of rationality.[52] On the other hand, one can also easily imagine Marx's sardonic comments if he had lived long enough to read the kind of definitions of the economy that one can find in works such as, for instance, that of Lord Robbins.[53]

Among the sociologists who have had a positive attitude to the concept of rationality (including the one used by the economists) are Max Weber, Talcott Parsons, and Neil Smelser. Weber's analysis of the notion of rationality constitutes more or less a chapter of its own in the history of the social sciences. To give a quick hint of the complexity as well as the scope of Weber's analysis, we have reproduced below an illustration from Habermas that tries to capture the manifold manifestations of Weber's notion of "occidental rationalism"[54] (see Table 3.2). Parsons and Smelser have followed in the Weberian tradition, but do not center their whole analyses around the concept of rationality. For them, it is just an important concept in the analysis of the economy.

Our own opinion in the debate about rationality is that economic sociology definitely needs to discuss the concept of rationality and try to reach a new assessment of its value. Mark Granovetter's statement that

Table 3.2. *Forms of manifestation of occidental rationalism in the emergence of modernity according to Max Weber*

General manifestation	Cognitive elements	Evaluative elements		Expressive elements
Culture	Modern natural science	Rational natural law	Protestant ethic	Autonomous art
Society	Scientific enterprise (universities, academies, laboratories)	University-based jurisprudence, specialized legal training	Religious associations	Artistic enterprise (production, trade, reception, art criticism)
	Capitalist economy	Modern governmental institutions	Bourgeois nuclear family	
		Behavioral dispositions and value orientations		
Personality		of the methodical conduct of life		of the countercultural life-style

Source: Jürgen Habermas, *The Theory of Communicative Action*, Vol. 1. *Reason and The Rationalization of Society*, p. 167.

rational choice constitutes "a good working hypothesis" that always will be "problematical"[55] pretty much sums up our attitude.

The main point, however, is that a sustained debate about rationality is needed today among economic sociologists. Some of the questions that need to be discussed are the following: Which are the more practical or methodological advantages to using the concept of rationality? How does rationality look from an empirical point of view? And can the concept of rationality be used to improve sociological theory construction? When questions of this type have been discussed more fully, economic sociology will be in a better position to pass final judgment on the usefulness of the concept of rationality.

As to the practical advantages to using the concept of rationality, there is for example the idea of Oskar Lange that assumptions of rationality lead to quicker discoveries in the social sciences. In describing the use of rationality as a "short-cut," Lange writes:

The postulate of rationality . . . provides us with a most powerful tool for simplification of theoretical analysis. For, if a unit of decision acts rationally, its decision in any given situation can be predicted by mere application of the rules of logic (and of mathematics). In absence of rational action such prediction could be made only after painstaking empirical study of uniformities in the decision patterns of the unit. . . . Thus, the postulate of rationality is a short-cut to the discovery of laws governing the decisions of units and to the prediction of their actions under given circumstances.[56]

Weber uses a different argument from Lange's to show that it is useful from a methodological standpoint to begin the analysis with the assumption of rationality. The main idea here is that the structure of *any* social behavior is most conveniently analyzed if one (1) first decides what the rational course of action would have been; (2) then compares the actual course of action to the rational action; and (3) finally, focuses on why the deviation from the rational course of action took place. To illustrate with an example from *Wirtschaft und Gesellschaft*: " . . . a panic on the stock exchange can be most conveniently analyzed by attempting to determine first what the course of action would have been if it had not been influenced by irrational effects; it is then possible to introduce the irrational components as accounting for the deviation from this hypothetical course."[57] As opposed to Lange's idea of using rationality as a "short-cut" for the discovery of rational patterns of action, Weber is thus interested in the "gap" between the rational and the actual course of events. Both Lange's and Weber's suggestions for how the concept of rationality can be used for "methodological convenience," as Weber puts it, are in our opinion well worth exploring.[58]

The second question about the concept of rationality that needs to be discussed concerns the empirical existence of rational action. On this point, Weber's work is of course very important even if it is clear that one should be wary of his tendency to expand the analysis of rationality into a kind of philosophy of history. His distinction between "formal" and "substantive" rationality in economic action is, on the other hand, evocative for a variety of reasons.[59] One of these is that moral values play an important role in any economy. Another is that the distinction between "formal" and "substantive" rationality points to the existence of different types of rationality as opposed to a single one as in economic theory. Especially Smelser has picked up on Weber's idea that there exist several kinds of rationalities in society and that these might very well be in conflict with one another. In "Reexamining the Parameters of Economic Activity," these themes are well developed, and the article contains an interesting attempt by Smelser to reconstruct a conflict in

Wirtschaft und Gesellschaft between two different types of rationality: that of the official economy ("economic rationality") and that of communally based associations ("communal rationality").[60]

Maybe the most exciting aspect of the rationality concept concerns its possible use as a tool in sociological theory construction. A major reason for this is that the notion of rationality, if handled correctly, might provide a solution to the old problem in sociology of simultaneously accounting for the autonomy of the actor and the influence of the social surroundings on his or her actions. The concept of rationality safeguards the notion of the actor's autonomy through its stress on the importance of choice. If this choice plus its parameters could be properly accounted for in sociological terms, the ship so to speak would be in harbor. The problem, of course, is more complex than that, but theories like Hernes's, which define institutions as *"rationality contexts"* (which "include" as well as "exclude" certain actions), seem quite promising.[61] One possibility would be to combine the idea that rationality is socially determined with the insights of game theory. An interesting attempt in this direction can be found in the work of Jon Elster.[62] He proposes that many important forms of social action can be analyzed according to a "two-step model" of rationality. One first has to determine which actions are at all possible. This first "filtering device" he labels "parametric rationality." Game theory can then be used to analyze which of the possible actions are most likely to be chosen ("strategic rationality"). According to Elster, "the two main theorists of rationality . . . are Max Weber and John von Neumann."[63]

In conclusion, it can be said that the concept of rationality deserves to become a key concept in economic sociology and to be discussed properly. Until now it has mainly been economists, political scientists, and philosophers of science such as Jon Elster who have carried on the debate. If economic sociologists got into the discussion, they could probably contribute quite a bit to it because economic sociology as a field is extremely well situated for testing the usefulness of the notion of social rationality.

The Result of Individual Economic Actions: General Equilibrium versus Tension-Filled Interest Struggles. In the classics of economic theory, ground rent was conceived in terms of marginal utility. The first great discovery of the 1870s was the idea that one could extend the notion of marginality to the demand side and thereby be in a position to tie together demand and supply into one single theoretical system, which could account for the formation of prices. Exactly how this was done – through the notion of "equilibrium" – was the second great discovery of modern economics.[64]

From its very beginnings, it was really the Anglo-American branch of marginalism – as opposed to the Austrian branch – that subscribed to the idea of equilibrium. Over the years, a series of arguments about market imperfections, disequilibrium, monopolistic competition, and so on have also been advanced that either modify or outright question the idea that a general equilibrium can automatically be reached.

Of the various criticisms that have been leveled at equilibrium theory, two quite general ones carry the most weight in our opinion. According to the first one, the ingenious models that have been proposed by Arrow et al. are unrealistic because they depict the workings of the economic system in such an incredibly smooth and idealized way:

The "general equilibrium" model, as perfected by Arrow, Debreu, Koopmans et al., is a jewelled set of movements, a celestial clockwork, to use an old image of Laplace, in which perfect competition and optimal allocations operate as an Invisible Hand, except that the invisible hand is neither God, the principle of benevolence, nor the spontaneous adaptations of Nature, but a mathematical theorem. . . . It is a work of art, so compelling that one thinks of the celebrated pictures of Apelles who painted a cluster of grapes so realistic that the birds would come and pick at them. But is the model "real"?[65]

The second major argument in our opinion against equilibrium theory is that it totally excludes the concept of "power." In *Power in Economics*, one of the few books that raises questions of this type, K. W. Rothschild stresses that during the twentieth century economic theory has chosen to exclude power from the analysis:

. . . a traditional way of economic thinking and theorizing evolved, which rapidly advanced in explaining the mechanics of market adjustment and "equilibrium" under the impact of competitive forces, but which had little room for such factors as power, non-pecuniary motives, group behavior and the like. Qualms about the neglect of these "non-economic" factors were increasingly suppressed in view of the rapid specialization of science. Economics could be regarded as being responsible only for the "purely" economic phenomena while other influences – such as power – should be taken care of by sociologists or political scientists.[66]

From the viewpoint of economic sociology, it is clear that no general equilibrium even vaguely reminiscent of the type that mainstream economics talks about exists in the economic system. Instead, the individual interactions in the economy lead to tensions and various forms of interest struggle. The way these struggles have been conceptualized in economic sociology varies quite a bit, and we shall quickly outline some of the main positions.

In Marx, the idea that a power struggle is going on in the economy has received its most forceful expression. As Marx saw it, the major struggles in the whole of society have their roots in the way the forces of production are operated and controlled by different groups and classes. The order that rules in the economic sphere – as well as in society as a whole – periodically breaks down, when the contradictory interests no longer can be reconciled.

Weber separates the spheres of economics and politics much more sharply than Marx; violence is thus by definition excluded from the concept of "economic action."[67] Yet, Weber's notion of the economic order differs markedly on two points from that of neoclassical economists. First, it is clear that in his *Wirtschaftssoziologie* the consumers are "price takers" and not "price givers."[68] And second, according to Weber, "it is essential to include the criterion of power of control and disposal (*Verfügungsgewalt*) in the sociological conception of economic action, for no other reason than that at least a modern market economy (*Erwerbwirtschaft*) essentially consists in a complete network of exchange contracts, that is, in deliberate planned acquisitions of powers of control and disposal."[69] It can finally be said that the notion of the economy as a general system of exclusively rational actions is alien to Weber's universe, where rational actions always coexist uneasily with irrational, traditional, and affectual forms of action.

Thorstein Veblen felt that neoclassical economists were totally wrong in the assumption that "harmony" always tends to be established in the economy; this, he felt, was a very artificial assumption and he sarcastically labeled it "the standpoint of ceremonial adequacy."[70] Like the institutionalists that came after him, Veblen replaced the idea of harmonious balance with a much more dynamic concept, that of "cumulative causation." Veblen's keen sense for the element of power struggle in the economy has also been kept alive in the institutionalist tradition. In his presidential address in 1972 to the American Economic Association, John Kenneth Galbraith thus made the neglect of the concept of power in economic theory his major focus. Mainstream economic theory, he argued, is built on principles that lead to analyses in which "power . . . is excluded from the subject."[71]

In *Economy and Society*, by Parsons and Smelser, the emphasis on struggle of interests plays a much more subdued role than in the other major works in economic sociology. Two points, however, need to be made. Parsons and Smelser, for one thing, always stress that tensions are inherent in the functioning of the social system as well as in its subsystems. And, when Parsons and Smelser talk of the equilibrium of the social system, it is clear that they "emphasiz(e) the priority of a state of equilibrium for the society as a whole over that of the economy considered in isolation."[72]

From this account of the way the concepts of tension and power have been treated in the various brands of economic sociology, it is clear that a consensus does not exist on the question of how one is to characterize the general state of the economic system. In our opinion, no single one of the various theorists in economic sociology has been able to advance successfully a theory of how the economic system operates. (See also in this context our discussion of the autonomy of the economic system above.) If one were allowed an eclectic solution, our choice would be (1) to follow Marx in his great realism as to the brutality and ruthlessness or sheer inefficiency with which the economic system works; (2) to pick up on Weber's ideas that the rationality of an economic system is historically determined and that there exists a specific form of power in the economic system that is not to be confused theoretically with those that exist in other areas of society; and (3) to follow Parsons and Smelser in their effort to construct specific theories for how the economic system interacts with the other subsystems of society.

Eclectic solutions, however, are usually bad because they rest on the illusion that a few good parts add up to a satisfactory whole. In addition, economic realities have changed so drastically since World War II both on the national and the international level that it is doubtful that an adequate solution to our problem can be found in the older works in economic sociology. One would probably do better to keep one's eyes glued on present-day work, such as Lindblom's and Hernes's imaginative theories of how economics and politics have come to meld into one another.[73]

The View of the Analyst: The Objective Outsider versus the Objective Insider. Paul Samuelson has emphasized that "the fact must be faced that economic issues are close to everybody emotionally. Blood pressures rise and voices become shrill whenever deep-seated beliefs and prejudices are involved, and some of these are thinly veiled rationalizations of special economic interests."[74] One can, however, ask the question whether economics as a science is equipped to handle the problem of veiled rationalizations and rising blood pressures. The answer must be that twentieth-century economics has had great difficulties in dealing with such questions as ideology and value judgments. Its problems, to no small extent, are due to its view of the economist as an "objective outsider," that is, as a person who is separate from the reality he or she is studying.

It would seem in retrospect that many nineteenth-century economists dealt more successfully with the issue of the researcher as an objective outsider than is the case with their twentieth-century colleagues. The generation of British economists who were the first to lay down the basic methodological principles of economics thus accepted a firm distinction between economics as a "science" and as an "art" and also demanded that the economist should not confuse his or her roles as "a pure economist" and as "a social philosopher."[75] Mark Blaug, writing from the perspective of a century later, notes with raised eyebrows that Nassau Senior and John Stuart Mill "held the now surprising view that the economist cannot advise qua economist, not even if the science of economics is supplemented by appropriate value judgments, and Senior went so far at one point in his life as to deny that economists should ever give advice."[76]

During the twentieth century, however, neoclassical economists have set aside the cautious attitude of the British economists, and Senior's opinion that economists should never give advice would probably seem quite bizarre to many of today's economists. Calls from within the profession to take a closer look at the way value judgments and science are mixed together have usually been ignored and are definitely not popular. A case in point is Myrdal's *The Political Element in the Development of Economic Theory*, a book that is rarely referred to in mainstream economics, and when quoted is usually accompanied by disparaging remarks.[77] Schumpeter's call in *History of Economic Analysis* for economists to develop "a set of rules by which to locate, diagnose and eliminate ideological delusion"[78] has also largely gone unheeded.[79] The result is that economics has become more politicized – and hence unscientific – than it needs to be.

Sociology has a considerably more realistic self-image than economics, something that is connected to its view of the researcher as part of the reality he or she studies. There also exists a much stronger tradition in sociology than in economics to take a critical view of what is being produced in the profession. While, for instance, "the very notion of ideology is threatening (to economists),"[80] it is an accepted concept in sociology and very much used.[81]

Given that the sociological tradition is more congenial than the economic tradition to understanding the social dimensions of economic theories and the economic tradition, one would expect economic sociology to have produced quite a number of studies on the role of economists in politics, on the formation of different kind of economic ideologies, and so on. This, however, is not the case. There exists of course an awareness in the standard works in economic sociology that the economist and economic theories are products of their social surroundings and also some brief sections to that effect – but that is about all.

To initiate critical studies of this type is an urgent concern for today's economic sociology. Good research could probably be produced fairly quickly because such fields as political sociology, the sociology of knowledge, and the sociology of science have developed a number of concepts and middle-range theories that can probably be used without too many modifications in economic sociology.[82] It is also an area of research where economic sociology is in a position to influence economics in a positive way by helping it turn a more self-critical eye on its own activities. The present confusion in the economic profession about economics as a "science" and as an "art" will only damage it in the long run.

The Concept of Time: Stationary-Adaptive Time versus Sociohistorical Time. The time concept constitutes one of the most difficult and also most neglected issues in the social sciences. When we venture to discuss it here, it is simply to bring out a few more important differences between the paradigms of microeconomics and of economic sociology. The labels we have chosen for the respective approaches – "stationary-adaptive time" and "sociohistorical time" – are descriptive in a general sense and nothing else.

There are two aspects of the microeconomic concept of time that are relevant for our purposes. The first concerns the way the temporal dimension of the very unit of analysis is constructed; the second relates to how the same unit of analysis is isolated from what lies before it in time. The former aspect of the neoclassical concept of time has been called "operational" by Mark Blaug and basically denotes an adaptive movement within the framework of a stationary analysis.[83] "Although the terminology employed conveys an air of clock time," Blaug notes apropos of Marshall who initiated this concept of time in modern economics, "the impression is deceiving: periods are short or long, not according to the revolving hands of the clock, but according to the partial or the complete adaptions of producers to changing circumstances."[84]

The second aspect of the microeconomic concept of time involves the fact that the unit of analysis is seen as perfectly sufficient to itself and is usually so narrowly constructed that "the passage of time itself . . . (is) placed in the pound of *ceteris paribus.*"[85] To analyze a problem it is hence not necessary to trace the "history" of the economic actions in question; a kind of flashlight picture, which is then manipulated in the darkroom, is seen as perfectly sufficient.

In economic sociology, as in sociology in general, the analysis of time has played an important role in so far as *the past* has been stressed. Veblen thus emphasizes the "genetic" and "cumulative" dimensions of economic life. So does Weber and maybe even more so Marx. Schumpeter has admiringly compared Marx's way of simultaneously handling the diachronic and synchronic dimensions of economic analysis to that of mainstream economists: "Economists always have either done work in economic history or else used the historical works of others. But the facts of economic history were assigned in a separate compartment. They entered, if at all, merely in the role of illustrations. They mixed with it only mechanically. Now Marx' mixture is a chemical one; that is to say, he introduced them into the very argument that produces results."[86]

Less attention has been paid in economic sociology to the way *the future* influences decisions in economic life. An exception or two, however, exist, such as Niklas Luhmann's brilliant essay "The Economy as a Social System." It is here suggested that it is "time" rather than "need" that characterizes the economy as such because economic actions consist of decisions to defer satisfaction and simultaneously make sure that it will take place in the future.[87] An empirical illustration of how the future informs the present can also be found in Sverre Lysgaard's *Arbeiderkollektivet*, a very interesting work whose translation is long overdue. The author here shows that what ties a worker to the collective on the factory level is not his or her past in a union or roots in a specific locality as much as the perspective on the future; the longer an employer expects to stay in a job, the more willing he or she is to join and support the workers' collective.[88]

It should finally be noted that economic sociology needs to pay more attention to the notion of time, especially to the way uncertainty about the future structures many economic decisions. One angle, which could be pursued, would be to look at time in relation to *trust*. That trust is very important in economic life, as well as in social life in general, is today being increasingly realized in sociology.[89]

General Scientific Method: Predictions Based on Radical Abstractions versus Descriptions and Explanations Based on Empirically Adjusted Abstractions. We shall conclude our comparison of the two paradigms by contrasting their general modes of analysis.[90] Since they belong to two different traditions in the social sciences, microeconomic theory and economic sociology have quite divergent views on several important points when it comes to general methodology. Two of the more substantive issues concern the role abstractions should play in the analysis and what constitutes a good analysis in general. Economic sociology, for its part, makes use of abstractions mainly to ground the analysis better in empirical reality and to produce solid descriptions and explanations. Microeconomic theory, on the other hand, is characterized by a more analytical and radical approach to abstractions and holds that a good analysis is one that makes correct predictions.

The sharply different attitudes to abstractions that can be found in microeconomic theory and economic sociology became apparent during the so-called *Methodenstreit*, which took place in Germany but which in one form or another also was played out in England, France, and the United States.[91] The position that Carl Menger and some other economists took was that economic theory must be constructed on the basis of analytical abstractions and has little to gain from an analysis of historical facts. This methodological stance is still very much alive in microeconomic theory and is reflected, among other things, in a hostility to the institutionalists who are seen as unable to explain anything at all and only interested in unscientific descriptions.[92]

The sociological response to the *Methodenstreit* was formulated by Weber.[93] His position can be summarized as a kind of compromise, whose main point was that analytical abstractions must be used during the initial stage of the sociological analysis and then be adjusted to fit empirical reality better. In broad lines, Weber's argument is not too different from that of Marx. In the latter's method of "successive concretization," as outlined most clearly in the *Grundrisse*, one also starts out with analytical abstractions that are then gradually adjusted and expanded to fit concrete facts.[94] Of the economic sociologists who came after Marx and Weber, it is especially Parsons who has insisted on the need for sociology to use analytical abstractions.[95] Parson's hostility to the institutionalist kind of analysis is undisguised and to him it tends, like much of economic history, directly to "theoretical nihilism."[96]

As already indicated, some economic sociologists – Veblen for one – have doubted the usefulness of the more radical kind of abstractions. In this they are not alone; many contemporary sociologists probably feel that analytical abstractions are something to stay away from and that the analysis should stick close to the empirical facts from the beginning. This attitude is partly based on a misunderstanding of the way analytical abstractions are to be used in sociology according to Marx, Weber, and Parsons. The point is that the initial analytical abstraction must be followed by a series of steps that brings the analysis close to the empirical and historical reality. We shall not speculate if sociology in general will change its opinion on this issue. In economic sociology, however, the more analytical approach already has a fairly strong tradition, which in our opinion is well worth defending and expanding upon.

A second point on which mainstream economics and economic sociology part company, concerns the role description, explanation, and prediction should play in the analysis. "Since the days of Adam Smith," we can read in Blaug's *Economic Theory in Retrospect*, "economics has consisted of the manipulation of a priori assumptions, derived either from introspection or from causal empirical observations, in the production of theories or hypotheses yielding predictions about events in the real world."[97] The concept of explanation is closely connected to that of prediction in economic theory even if the exact link between the two is a much debated question.[98] The notion of description has, on the other hand, received very little attention by economists.[99] In sociology, the emphasis has by tradition been on description and explanation; prediction has played little, if any, role.[100] Much ingenuity has been used to develop rigorous methods for data collection and to gather empirical facts about various aspects of society. The explanations that have been advanced have, however, often been of the kind that Robert Merton calls "*post factum* sociological interpretations."[101] By this he means the kind of explanations that are produced *after* the facts have been collected. Merton is critical of this way of doing sociology because he feels that a "disarming feature of this procedure is that the explanations are indeed consistent with the given set of observations."[102] If the first explanation that is advanced turns out to be wrong, another one that "fits the facts" can easily be found. Merton suggests an alternative model of explanation, where the concept of prediction plays more of a role: "The more precise the inferences (predictions) that can be drawn from a theory, the less likelihood of *alternative* hypotheses which will be adequate to these. In other words, precise predictions and data serve to restore the *empirical* bearing upon research of the *logical* fallacy of affirming the consequent."[103]

Merton's reasoning is interesting because it raises the question of whether the concept of explanation that is often used in sociology is rather weak and should be strengthened by bringing in the notion of prediction. Economic sociology, with its interest in the idea of rationality and economic methodology in general, is ideally suited to take up a discussion of this type. We therefore end with a few general comments on what an adequate concept of prediction could look like in economic sociology.

Our first point is that a discussion is needed of the various ways in which the notion of prediction has been conceptualized in economic theory. In mainstream economics, prediction has been used to do "prognoses" as well as "real predictions." In econometrics, for instance, one is basically interested in prognoses. The difference between the two approaches is that prognoses only say "what" will happen while real predictions also answer "why." This is analogous to the way the notion of description has been handled in sociology (see Table 3.3).

A second point to discuss would be whether economic theory has succeeded in striking a proper balance between what could be called "general predictions" and "exact predictions." The distinction between the two is well brought out by Morgenstern in his article "Description, Prediction, and Normative Theory": "(1) Prediction is possible 'in the large' on the basis of *general theorems*; that is the implied essence of a theorem; (2) Historical concrete-prognosis 'in the small' is in general impossible in economics."[104]

It is clear that sociology as little as economics or any other social science can predict what will happen with great precision ("exact prediction").

Table 3.3. *Description, prediction, and explanation*

Item	Nonexplanatory	Explanatory
Description	1	2
Prediction	3	4

Note: 3 would be a "prognosis" while 4 is a "real prediction." Merton's "*post factum* sociological interpretations*"* are close to 1 while 2 is a sociological explanation more in tune with Merton's alternative.

Source: See text.

But maybe economic sociology could develop a more adequate concept of "general prediction" than microeconomic theory by trying to combine analytical assumptions with generalizations based on historical evidence. By omitting practically all social influences, it should be noted, microeconomic theory is forced to make exceedingly abstract and general predictions; economic sociology, if handled properly, might do better because it is based on a social concept of the economy.

The concept of prediction is complex and not really suited for a discussion on a few pages together with a host of other questions. We have, however, wanted to raise the question of prediction in order to point out that it is an interesting topic, which deserves to be on the agenda of economic sociology when it today is trying to regain momentum.

Concluding remarks: toward a new economic sociology

Economic sociology, as noted above, has gone through various stages in its development. During the formative years of sociology there emerged what was to become a "classical economic sociology" with Marx, Weber, and Veblen as three of the main theorists. The emphasis was on producing sociological alternatives to mainstream economic theory. Marx and Veblen wanted to replace the orthodox economic theories of their days with an economic theory that was more sociologically oriented ("historical materialism" and "evolutionary economics"), whereas Weber felt that his *Wirtschaftssoziologie* and neoclassical economics could very well coexist within the framework of a broad *Sozialökonomik* even if the topics that were analyzed would overlap.

Little happened during the 1930s in economic sociology, and the next major attempt by sociologists to grapple with economic topics had to wait until the 1950s. The structural-functionalist school in economic sociology differed from classical economic sociology in that it wanted to *complement* mainstream economic theory rather than produce *alternatives* to it. The emphasis during these years was on analyzing the sociological dimension of economic phenomena and the links among the economy and the other "subsystems" of society.

Since the mid-70s a series of works have appeared which signal a new attitude among sociologists to the study of the economy. Sociologists today are thus more willing to trespass on the economists' domain and ask questions that formerly only the economists did. This is a very exciting development that bodes well for economic sociology. Which exact direction this "new economic sociology" will be taking in the near future, is hard to say. Some lessons can however be learned from the more interesting works that have appeared during the last few years. *First, sociologists must become more familiar with the literature in economics. Second, sociologists should try to address boldly key problems in economic life – the structure of markets, price formation, productivity, etc. – and not only aim at "complementing" the economists' analyses. And third, economic sociology should try to stick to that nonideological and creative mixture of theoretical and empirical research that has been called "middle-range sociology."* An economic sociology conceived along these lines, we think, would stand the best chance to pick up where the classical economic sociologists left off and to improve the social scientific understanding of the economy.

Acknowledgment

This essay was presented in a somewhat different and considerably longer version at a workshop in economic sociology at the Nordic Sociology Conference, June 14–16, 1985, in Gothenburg.

Notes

1. N. J. Smelser, *The Sociology of Economic Life,* (Englewood Cliffs, N.J.: Prentice-Hall, 1963), 22.

2. See, for example, A. Lindbeck, "The Changing Role of the National State," *Kyklos* 28 (1975): 23–46; and J. I. Gershuny, "The Informal Economy: Its Role in Post-Industrial Society," *Futures* 11 (Feb. 1979): 3–15.

3. See, for example, G. J. Stigler, "Economics – The Imperial Science?" *Scandinavian Journal of Economics* 86 (1984): 301–13.

4. "Economic sociology" is the term used by sociologists such as Max Weber, Emile Durkheim, and Karl Mannheim as well as by Joseph Schumpeter. See, for example, Weber, *Wirtschaft und Gesellschaft: Grundriss der verstehenden Soziologie,* (Tubingen: J.C.B. Mohr, 1976) 34, 41; Durkheim, "Review of Georg Simmel, *Philosophie des Geldes,*" *L'Année Sociologique* (1900/1901): 141; Schumpeter, "Gustav v. Schmoller und die Probleme von heute," *Schmollers Jahrbuch* 50 (1926): 34–35, and *History of Economic*

Thought, (London: Allen & Unwin, 1954) 20–21, 537; and K. Mannheim, "Uber das Wesen und die Bedeutung des wirtschaftlichen Erfolgsstreben. Ein Beitrag zur Wirtschaftssoziologie," *Archiv für Sozialwissenschaft und Sozialpolitik* 63 (1930): 449–512. "Economic sociology" is the term often used in Europe, according to R. Swedberg, "Economic Sociology," *Current Sociology* 35, 1 (1987): 51–52, 138. In the United States the term "economy and society" seems to be the accepted one and "economic sociology" is more sparingly used. For an exception, see A. Stinchcome, *Economic Sociology*, (New York: Academic Press, 1983). About one out of four graduate departments of sociology thus offer courses in "economy and society," and this is also the term preferred by the ASA; see on this point ASA, *Guide to Graduate Departments of Sociology* (Washington, D.C.: ASA, 1984). The term "socio-economics" has recently begun to be used; see, for example, A. Etzioni, "Toward Socio-Economics," *Contemporary Sociology* 14 (1985): 178–79; and T. Baumgartner, T. Burns, and P. DeVille, *The Shaping of Socio-Economic Systems*, (New York: Gordon and Breach, 1985). Our own preference for the term "economic sociology" comes from the fact that it clearly indicates that economic phenomena are here analyzed from the viewpoint of *sociology*.

5. Weber, *Economy and Society: An Outline of Interpretive Sociology* (Berkeley: University of California Press, 1978 [1922]), 63–211.

6. T. Parsons, "Weber's 'Economic Sociology,' " in "Introduction" to Max Weber, *The Theory of Social and Economic Organizations* (New York: Oxford University Press, 1947), 31–35; Parsons, "The Rise and Fall of Economic Man," *Journal of General Education* 4 (1949): 47–53; Parsons and Smelser, *Economy and Society: A Study in the Integration of Economics and Social Theory* (London: Routledge & Kegan Paul, 1956); Parsons, "On Building Social System Theory: A Personal History," *Daedalus* (Fall 1970): 826–81; Smelser, *The Sociology of Economic Life*; Smelser, ed. *Readings on Economic Sociology*, (Englewood Cliffs, N.J.: Prentice-Hall, 1965); Smelser, "On Collaborating with Talcott Parsons: Some Intellectual and Personal Notes," *Sociological Inquiry* 51 (1981): 143–54; W. E. Moore, *Economy and Society* (New York: Doubleday & Company, Inc., 1955).

7. R. Swedberg, "The Critique of the 'Economy and Society' Perspective during the Paradigm Crisis: From the United States to Sweden," *Acta Sociologica* 29 (1986): 91–112.

8. See, for example, F. L. Block, *The Origins of International Economic Disorder: A Study of United States International Monetary Policy from World War II to the Present* (Berkeley: University of California Press, 1977); H. Makler, A. Martinelli, and N. Smelser, eds., *The New International Economy* (Beverly Hills: Sage Publications, 1982).

9. See, for example, R. Moss Kanter, *Men and Women of the Corporation*, (New York: Basic Books, 1977); and L. A. Tilly and J. W. Scott, *Women, Work, and Family*, (New York: Holt, Rinehart and Winston, 1978).

10. See, for example, I. Berg, ed. *Sociological Perspectives on Labor Markets*, (New York: Academic Press, 1981); and Patricia A. Adler and Peter Adler, eds., *The Social Dynamics of Financial Markets* (Greenwich, Conn.: JAI Press, 1984).

11. See, for example, G. Hernes, *Forhandlingsøkonomi og blandingsadministrasjon* (Bergen: Universitetsforlaget, 1978).

12. R. S. Burt, *Toward A Structural Theory of Action*, (New York: Academic Press, 1982); H. C. White, "Where Do Markets Come From?" *American Journal of Sociology* 87 (1983): 517–47; M. Granovetter, "Economic Action and Social Structure: The Problem of Embeddedness," *American Journal of Sociology* 91 (1985): 481–510.

13. Economic sociology has, as mentioned earlier, tended to shy away from the topics analyzed by economists. According to Granovetter, "Economic Action and Social Structure," 504, " . . . with few exceptions, sociologists have refrained from serious study of any subject already claimed by neoclassical economics."

14. T. Kuhn, *The Structure of Scientific Revolutions*, 2d ed. (Chicago: University of Chicago Press, 1970), 119.

15. An interesting comparison between "the classical paradigm" and "the neoclassical paradigm" can be found in M. De Vroey, "The Transition from Classical to Neoclassical Economics: A Scientific Revolution," *Journal of Economic Issues* 9 (1975): 430.

16. See M. Blaug, *Economic Theory in Retrospect*, 3d ed. (Cambridge, Eng.: Cambridge University Press, 1983), 4.

17. R. Startz, "Prelude to Macroeconomics," *American Economic Review* 74 (1984): 881–92.

18. P. Samuelson, *Economics*, 8th ed. (New York: McGraw-Hill, 1970), 5–6.

19. See, for example, D. Bell, "Models and Reality in Economic Discourse," in D. Bell and I. Kristol, eds., *The Crisis in Economic Theory* (New York: Basic Books, 1981), 46–80.

20. Hernes, "Mot en institusjonell okonomi," in Hernes, *Forhandlingsøkonomi*, 201–02 (our translation).

21. R. Merton, "Sociology of Knowledge," in *Social Theory and Social Structure*, enlarged ed. (New York: The Free Press, 1968), 510–42.

22. T. Veblen, "Why is Economics not an Evolutionary Science?" in M. Lerner, ed., *The Portable Veblen* (New York: The Viking Press, 1948 [1898]), 215–40; Parsons and Smelser, *Economy and Society*; Polanyi, *The Great Transformation* (Boston: Beacon Press, 1957 [1944]); Hernes, "Mot en institusjonell okonomi"; Smelser, "Re-examining the Parameters of Economic Activity," in E. M. Epstein and D. Votaw, eds., *Rationality, Legitimacy, and Responsibility* (Santa Monica: Goodyear Publishing Co., 1978), 48; Granovetter, "Economic Action and Social Structure."

23. Smelser, "Re-examining the Parameters of Economic Activity," 48.

24. For attempts within the neoclassical tradition to overcome these and similar weaknesses, see the longer version of this chapter in *Theory and Society*, 16 (1985): 193–97.

25. L. E. Preston, "Corporation and Society: The Search for a Paradigm," *Journal of Economic Literature* 13 (1975): 434.

26. See, for example, E. J. Mishan, "The Postwar Literature on Externalities: An Interpretive Essay," *Journal of Economic Literature* 9 (Mar. 1971): 1–28; K. Arrow, *The Limits of Organization* (New York: Norton, 1974); and G. Akerlof, "A Theory of Social Custom, of Which Unemployment May Be One Consequence," *Quarterly Journal of Economics* 95 (1980): 746–75.

27. Polanyi, "The Economy As an Instituted Process," in Polanyi, C. M. Arensberg, and H. W. Pearson, eds., *Trade and Markets in the Early Empires: Economies in History and Theory* (Chicago: Henry Regnery Company, 1971 [1957]), 249.

28. R. Freedman, ed., *Marx on Economics* (Harmondsworth, Eng.: Penguin Books, 1962), 4.

29. A. Lindbeck, "Endogenous Politicians and the Theory of Economic Policy," paper no. 35, Institute of International Economic Studies, University of Stockholm, (1978).

30. See, for example, Weber, *Economy and Society*, 74–75.

31. See, for example, Hernes, *Forhandlingsøkonomi*; and J. Goldthorpe, *Order and Conflict in Contemporary Capitalism* (New York: Oxford University Press, 1984).

32. See, for example, D. Greenwood, "The Economic Significance of 'Women's Place' in Society: A New-Institutionalist View," *Journal of Economic Issues* 18 (1984): 663–80.

33. Weber, *Economy and Society*, 4.

34. Granovetter, "Economic Action and Social Structure."

35. F. Barth, "Introduktion till 'Entreprenörens roll i social förändring i norra Norge (1963)," in *Socialantropologiska problem* (Vänersborg, Sweden: Prisma/Verdandi, 1971).

36. Blaug, *Economic Theory*, 701.

37. J. N. Keynes, *The Scope and Method of Political Economy*, 4th ed. (New York: Kelley & Millman, 1955 [1891]), 247–48.

38. See, for example, G. Grossman, *Economic Systems* (Englewood Cliffs, N.J.: Prentice-Hall, 1974).

39. O. E. Williamson, *Markets and Hierarchies: Analysis and Antitrust Implications* (New York: The Free Press, 1975).

40. See especially K. Polanyi, "Appendix," in G. Dalton, ed., *Primitive, Archaic, and Modern Economies: Essays of Karl Polanyi* (New York: Anchor Books, 1968), 13.

41. Schumpeter, *Capitalism, Socialism, and Democracy,* (New York: Harper & Row, 1975 [1942]), 45.

42. N. Luhmann, "The Economy as a Social System," in *The Differentiation of Society* (New York: Columbia University Press, 1982), 190.

43. For some literature on *Economy and Society,* see, for example, S. Kuznets, "Review of Parsons-Smelser, *Economy and Society,*" *Annals of the American Academy of Political and Social Science* 312 (1957) 175–76; H. W. Pearson, "Parsons and Smelser on the Economy," in Polanyi, C. M. Arensberg, and H. W. Pearson eds., *Trade and Market*, 307–319; and S. P. Savage, *The Theories of Talcott Parsons* (London: Macmillan, 1981).

44. Luhmann, "The Economy."

45. Granovetter, "Economic Action and Social Structure," 483–87.

46. Smelser, "Re-examining the Parameters," 37.

47. B. C. Caldwell, *Beyond Positivism: Economic Methodology in the Twentieth Century* (London: Allen & Unwin, 1982), 146.

48. A. Sen, "Rational Fools: A Critique of the Behavioural Foundation of Economic Theory," in F. Hahn and M. Hollis, eds., *Philosophy and Economic Theory* (Oxford, Eng.: Oxford University Press, 1979), 87–109.

49. A. O. Hirschman, "Against Parsimony: Three Ways of Complicating Some Categories of Economic Discourse," *American Economic Review* 74 (May 1984): 89.

50. H. A. Simon, *Administrative Behaviour: A Study of Decision-Making Processes in Administrative Organization,* (New York: The Free Press, 1965); H. Leibenstein, *General X-Efficiency Theory & Economic Development,* (New York: Oxford University Press, 1978).

51. Samuelson, *Foundations of Economic Analysis,* (Cambridge, Mass.: Harvard University Press, 1947), 90.

52. K. Marx, *Grundrisse: Foundations of the Critique of Political Economy* (New York: Vintage Books, 1973 [1953]), 100–108; O. Lange, *Political Economy. Volume 1. General Problems* (Oxford, Eng.: Pergamon Press, 1963), 148–225.

53. L. Robbins, *The Nature and Significance of Economic Science,* 3d ed. (London: Macmillan, 1984 [1932]).

54. J. Habermas, *The Theory of Communicative Action,* Volume 1, *Reason and the Rationalization of Society* (Boston: Beacon Press, 1984), 167.

55. Granovetter, "Economic Action and Social Structure," 506.

56. O. Lange, "The Scope and Method of Economics," *Review of Economic Studies* 13 (1945): 30.

57. Weber, *Economy and Society*, 6.

58. Ibid., 6.

59. Ibid., 85–86.

60. Smelser, "Re-examining."

61. Hernes, "Mot en institusjonell økonomi," 213.

62. See, Chapter 4 in this book and J. Elster, *Ulysses and the Sirens: Studies in Rationality and Irrationality,* (Cambridge, Eng.: Cambridge University Press, 1979).

63. Elster, "Some Unresolved Problems in the Theory of Rational Behavior," in L. Lévy-Garboua, ed., *Sociological Economics* (London: Sage Publications, 1979), 68.

64. G. Myrdal, *The Political Element in the Development of Economic Theory* (London: Routledge & Kegan Paul, 1961 [1930]), 63.

65. Bell, "Models and Reality," 57–58.

66. K. W. Rothschild, "Introduction," in *Power in Economics: Selected Readings* (Harmondsworth, Eng.: Penguin Books, 1971), 10–11.

67. Weber, *Economy and Society,* 64–65.

68. Ibid., 97, 99.

69. Ibid., 67.

70. Veblen, "Why is Economics not an Evolutionary Science?" 224.

71. J. K. Galbraith, "Power and the Useful Economist," *American Economic Review* 63 (Mar. 1973): 2.

72. Pearson, "Parsons and Smelser," 316.

73. C. E. Lindblom, *Politics and Markets: The World's Political-Economic Systems* (New York: Basic Books, 1977), Hernes, *Forhandlingsøkonomi.*

74. Samuelson, *Economics,* 6.

75. For example, Keynes, *Scope and Method,* 13.

76. Marc Blaug, *The Methodology of Economics – Or How Economists Explain* (Cambridge, Eng.: Cambridge University Press, 1980), 141.

77. See in this context, for example, G. Brulin, "Gunnar Myrdal i ett ekonomisk-sociologiskt perspektiv" (unpublished paper, Uppsala University, 1984).

78. Schumpeter, *History of Economic Thought,* 44.

79. See W. Samuels, "Ideology in Economics," in S. Weintraub, ed., *Modern Economic Thought* (Oxford: Blackwell, 1977), 467–84.

80. Ibid., 469.

81. See, for example, J. Larrain, *The Concept of Ideology,* (Athens, Ga.: Georgia University Press, 1980).

82. Some efforts in this direction already exist, such as A. W. Coats, "The Sociology of Knowledge and the History of Economics," in vol. 2 of W. Samuels, ed., *Research in the History of Economic Thought and Methodology* (Greenwich, Conn.: JAI Press, 1985), 211–34; and F. Block, "Postindustrial Development and the Obsolescence of Economic Categories," *Politics and Society* 14, no. 1 (1985): 71–104. See in this context also Axel Leijonhufvud's wonderful satire "Life among the Econ," *Western Economic Journal* 11 (1973): 327–37.

83. Blaug, *Economic Theory,* 391.

84. Ibid., 391.

85. Ibid., 700.

86. Schumpeter, *History,* 44.

87. Luhmann, "The Economy," 194.

88. S. Lysgaard, *Arbeiderkollektivet* (Oslo: Universitetsforlaget, 1961), 191–93.

89. Simmel was probably the first sociologist to realize the centrality of trust in economic life. See, for example, G. Simmel, *Philosophy of Money* (London: Routledge & Kegan Paul, 1978 [1907]), 178–79. For contemporary general discussions of trust, see specially N. Luhmann, *Trust and Power* (New York: John Wiley, 1979); B. Barber, *The Logic and Limit of Trust,* (New Brunswick: Rutgers University Press, 1983); and J. D. Lewis and A. Weigert, "Trust as a Social Reality," *Social Forces* 63 (1985) 967–85. Two case studies of the role of trust in financial institutions are S. P. Shapiro, *Wayward Capitalists: Target of the Securities and Exchange Commission* (New Haven: Yale University

Press, 1984); and R. Swedberg, "Bankernas Roll i Skuldkrisen, 1974–1982. En Ekonomisk-sociologisk Förklaringsmodell," *Sociologisk Forskning* 23 no. 1 (1986): 65–82.

90. Many of the arguments in this section are based on discussions with Peter Hedström (Harvard University and the Institute for Social Research, in Stockholm).

91. The *Methodenstreit* has been much discussed in sociology. Less known is the interesting British debate triggered off by Comte's critique of political economy and in which John Stuart Mill, Alfred Marshall, John Neville Keynes, and others took part. See Swedberg, "Economic Sociology."

92. As the reader by now is aware, we have chosen in this essay not to equate "economic sociology" with "institutionalism." One reason for this is that "neo-institutionalism" differs on too many points from economic sociology. The former paradigm has been described in the following way by A. G. Gruchy, "Institutional Economics: Its Influence and Prospects," *American Journal of Economics and Sociology* 37 (1978): 276–77: "The present-day mainstream institutionalists have a scientific research paradigm that revolves around the concept of the evolving economic process which is a subprocess of the larger social or cultural process. This process is at bottom a disequilibrium process that is influenced by a wide variety of noneconomic and economic factors. The dynamics of technological change at work within this process brings about an evolution of the economic system through a process of circular and cumulative causation that alters the system's structure and functioning. Inherent in the economic process is a logic or pattern of industrialization that gives shape or form to the course of industrial evolution with the result that mature economies like those of the United States, the United Kingdom, France, and West Germany have the common pattern of a triplistic industrial system. This system has a large-scale private oligopolistic sector, a small-scale private competitive sector, and a large public sector. The analytical norm used by the mainstream institutionalists in their interpretation of the functioning of the mature triplistic industrial economy is the large-scale corporate enterprise in the economy's industrial heartland and not the small-scale competitive norm of conventional economics. . . . It is the view of the mainstream institutionalists that the malfunctioning of the triplistic industrial economy will eventually lead to a postindustrial system in which democratic national planning will be substituted for the uncoordinated interventionism of regulated capitalism."

93. See, for example, Weber, " 'Objectivity' in Social Science and Social Policy," in *The Methodology of Social Sciences* (New York: The Free Press, 1949 [1904]), 49–112, and Weber, *Economy and Society; Weber, Rosher, and Knies: The Logical Problems of Historical Economics* (New York: The Free Press, 1975 [1922]).

94. Marx, *Grundrisse*, 100–108.

95. See, for example, T. Burger, "Talcott Parsons, the Problem of Order in Society, and the Program of an Analytical Sociology," *American Journal of Sociology* 83 (1977): 320–34; and Parsons, "Comment on Burger's Critique," *American Journal of Sociology* 83 (1977): 335–39.

96. Parsons and Smelser, *Economy and Society*, 306.

97. Blaug, *Economic Theory*, 697.

98. See, for example, Caldwell, *Beyond Positivism*, 199.

99. See, for example, Sen, "Description as Choice," *Oxford Economic Papers* 32 (1980): 353–69.

100. See, for example, T. Burns, "Sociological Explanation," in D. Emmet and A. MacIntyre, eds., *Sociological Theory and Philosophical Analyses* (London: Macmillan, 1970), 55–75.

101. Merton, "The Bearings of Sociological Theory on Empirical Research," in *Social Theory and Social Structure*, enlarged ed. (New York: The Free Press, 1968), 139–71.

102. Ibid., 147.
103. Ibid., 152.
104. O. Morgenstern, "Descriptive, Predictive, and Normative Theory," *Kyklos* 25 (1972): 705.

4
Marxism, functionalism, and game theory

JON ELSTER

How should Marxist social analysis relate to bourgeois social science? The obvious answer is: retain and develop what is valuable, criticize and reject what is worthless. Marxist social science has followed the opposite course, however. By assimilating the principles of functionalist sociology, reinforced by the Hegelian tradition, Marxist social analysis has acquired an apparently powerful theory that in fact encourages lazy and frictionless thinking. By contrast, virtually all Marxists have rejected rational-choice theory in general and game theory in particular. Yet game theory is invaluable to any analysis of the historical process that centers on exploitation, struggle, alliances, and revolution.

This issue is related to the conflict over methodological individualism, rejected by many Marxists who wrongly link it with individualism in the ethical or political sense. By methodological individualism I mean the doctrine that all social phenomena (their structure and their change) are in principle explicable only in terms of individuals – their properties, goals, and beliefs. This doctrine is not incompatible with any of the following true statements: (a) Individuals often have goals that involve the welfare of other individuals. (b) They often have beliefs about supra-individual entities that are not reducible to beliefs about individuals. "The capitalists fear the working class" cannot be reduced to the feelings of capitalists concerning individual workers. By contrast, "The capitalists' profit is threatened by the working class" can be reduced to a complex statement about the consequences of the actions taken by individual workers.[1] (c) Many properties of individuals, such as "powerful," are irreducibly relational, so that accurate description of one individual may require reference to other individuals.[2]

The insistence on methodological individualism leads to a search for microfoundations of Marxist social theory. The need for such foundations is by now widely, but far from universally, appreciated by writers on Marxist economic theory.[3] The Marxist theory of the state or of ide-

87

ologies is, by contrast, in a lamentable state. In particular, Marxists have not taken up the challenge of showing how ideological hegemony is created and entrenched at the level of the individual. What microeconomics is for Marxist economic theory, social psychology should be for the Marxist theory of ideology.[4] Without a firm knowledge about the mechanisms that operate at the individual level, the grand Marxist claims about macro-structures and long-term change are condemned to remain at the level of speculation.

The poverty of functionalist Marxism

Functional analysis[5] in sociology has a long history. The origin of functionalist explanation is probably the Christian theodicies, which reach their summit in Leibniz: all is for the best in the best of all possible worlds; each apparent evil has good consequences in the larger view, and is to be explained by these consequences. The first secular proponent perhaps was Mandeville, whose slogan "Private Vices, Public Benefits" foreshadows Merton's concept of latent function. To Mandeville we owe the Weak Functional Paradigm: an institution or behavioral pattern often has consequences that are (a) beneficial for some dominant economic or political structure; (b) unintended by the actors; and (c) not recognized by the beneficiaries as owing to that behavior. This paradigm, which we may also call the invisible-hand paradigm, is ubiquitous in the social sciences. Observe that it provides no explanation of the institution or behavior that has these consequences. If we use "function" for consequences that satisfy condition (a) and "latent function" for consequences that satisfy all three conditions, we can go on to state the Main Functional Paradigm: the latent functions (if any) of an institution or behavior explain the presence of that institution or behavior. Finally, there is the Strong Functional Paradigm: all institutions or behavioral patterns have a function that explains their presence.

Leibniz invoked the Strong Paradigm on a cosmic scale; Hegel applied it to society and history, but without the theological underpinning that alone could justify it. Althusser sees merit in Hegel's recognition that history is a "process without a subject," though for Hegel the process still has a goal. Indeed, this is a characteristic feature of both the Main and Strong paradigms: *to postulate a purpose without a purposive actor* or, in grammatical terms, a predicate without a subject. (Functionalist thinkers characteristically use the passive voice.) I shall refer to such processes guided by a purpose without an intentional subject *objective teleology*. They should be distinguished from both *subjective teleology* (intentional acts with an intentional subject) and *teleonomy* (adaptive behavior fashioned by natural selection). The main difference between subjective teleology and teleonomy is that the former, but not the latter, is capable of waiting and of using indirect strategies, of the form "one step backward, two steps forwards."[6] To the extent that the Main Functional Paradigm invokes teleonomy, as in the explanation of market behavior through a natural-selection model of competition between firms, there can be no objection to it. In the many more numerous cases where no analogy with natural selection obtains, latent functions cannot explain their causes.[7] In particular, long-term positive, unintended, and unrecognized consequences of a phenomenon cannot explain it when its short-term consequences are negative.[8]

Turning to examples of functional analysis in non-Marxist social science, consider this statement by Lewis Coser: "Conflict within and between bureaucratic structures provides the means for avoiding the ossification and ritualism which threatens their form of organization."[9] If instead of "provides the means for avoiding," Coser had written "has the consequence of reducing," there could be no methodological quarrel with him. But his phrasing implies objective teleology, a simulation of human intentional adaptation without specification of a simulating mechanism. Alexander J. Field has observed that a similar functional explanation lies behind the Chicago School of "economic interpretation of the law."[10] For a somewhat grotesque example, consider a statement by Richard Posner:

The economic case for forbidding marital dissolution out of concern for the children of the marriage is weakened if the parents love the child, for then the costs to the child of dissolution will be weighed by the parents in deciding whether to divorce, and they will divorce only if the gains to them from the divorce exceed the costs to the child, in which event the divorce will be welfare maximizing. If, as suggested earlier, love is a factor of growing importance in the production of children, this might help to *explain* why the law is moving toward easier standards for divorce.[11]

Posner and his school actually tend toward the Strong Functional Paradigm, which most sociologists have abandoned for the more subtle Main Paradigm. Merton, the leading exponent of the Main Paradigm, is also an acute critic of the Strong Paradigm.[12] In Radical and Marxist social science, however, both the crude Strong Paradigm and the less crude (but equally fallacious) Main Paradigm are flourishing. Although my main concern is with Marxism, a few comments on the closely related Radical approach may be in order. As exemplified in the work of Michel Foucault and Pierre Bourdieu, this tends to see every minute detail of social action as part of a vast design for oppression. For an example, we may take Bourdieu's assertion that when intellectuals play around with language and even deliberately violate the rules of grammar, this is a strategy designed to exclude the petty-bourgeois would-be intellectuals, who believe that culture can be assimilated by learning rules and who loose their footing when they see that it is rather a matter of knowing when to break them.[13] This sounds like a conspiratorial view, but actually is closer to functionalism, as can be seen from Bourdieu's incessant use of the phrase *"tout se passe comme si."*[14] If everything happens as if intellectuals thought of nothing but retaining their monopoly, then objectively this must be what explains their behavior. This argument is a theoretical analogue of envy – arising when "our factual inability to acquire a good is wrongly interpreted as a positive action against our desire."[15]

Marx recognized the Weak Functional Paradigm, but argued that what Sartre calls "counterfinality" – the systematic production of consequences that are harmful, unintended, and unrecognized – was equally important. In addition one can certainly trace to him the Main Functional Paradigm and in at least one passage the Strong Paradigm as well. In the *Theories of Surplus-Value*, Marx reconstructs the rational core of an adversary's argument:

1 . . . the various functions in bourgeois society mutually presuppose each other;

2 . . . the contradictions in material production make necessary a superstructure of ideological strata, whose activity – whether good or bad – is good, because it is necessary;

3 . . . all functions are in the service of the capitalist, and work out to his "benefit";

4 . . . even the most sublime spiritual productions should merely be granted recognition, and *apologies* for them made to the bourgeoisie, that they are presented as, and falsely proved to be, direct producers of material wealth.[16]

Although the context is ambiguous and the text far from clear, a plausible reading suggests the Strong Paradigm. All activities benefit the capitalist class, and these benefits explain their presence. This conspiratorial world-view, in which all apparently innocent activities, from Sunday picnics to health care for the elderly, are explained through their function for capitalism, is not, however, pervasive in Marx's work. Much more deeply entrenched, from the level of the philosophy of history to the details of the class struggle, is the Main Paradigm.

Marx had a theory of history, embedded in a philosophy of history: an empirical theory of the four modes of production based on class division; and a speculative notion that before and after the division there was, and will be, unity. In the latter idea, clearly, there is also present the Hegelian or Leibnizian[17] notion that the division is necessary to bring about the unity, and can be explained through this latent function. Marx's objective teleology is especially prominent in the 1862–63 notebooks, of which the middle third was published as the *Theories of Surplus-Value*, while the remaining parts are only now becoming available.[18] Consider in particular the argument that

The original unity between the workers and the conditions of production . . . has two main forms. . . . Both are embryonic forms and both are equally unfitted to develop labour as *social* labour and the productive power of social labour. Hence the necessity for the separation, for the rupture, for the antithesis of labour and property. . . . The most extreme form of this rupture, and the one in which the productive forces of social labour are also most fully developed, is capital. The original unity can be reestablished only on the material foundations which capital creates and by means of the revolutions which, in the process of this creation, the working class and the whole society undergoes.[19]

Elsewhere Marx states that "insofar as it is the coercion of capital which forces the great mass of society to this [surplus labour] beyond its immediate needs, capital creates culture and exercises an historical and social function."[20] He also quotes one of his favorite verses from Goethe:

> Sollte diese Qual uns quälen,
> Da sie unsre Lust vermehrt,
> Hat nicht Myriaden Seelen
> Timur's Herrschaft aufgezehrt?[21]

It is difficult, although perhaps not impossible, to read these passages otherwise than as statements of an objective teleology. Marx, as all Hegelians, was obsessed with *meaning*. If class society and exploitation are necessary for the creation of communism, this lends them a significance that also has explanatory power. In direct continuation, Marx can also argue that various institutions of the capitalist era can be explained by their functions for capitalism, as in this analysis of social mobility:

The circumstance that a man without fortune but possessing energy, solidity, ability and business acumen may become a capitalist in this manner [i.e., by receiving credit] – and the commercial value of each individual is pretty accurately estimated under the capitalist mode of production – is greatly admired by the apologists of the capitalist system. Although this circumstance continually brings an unwelcome number of new soldiers of fortune into the field and into competition with the already existing individual capitalists, it also reinforces the supremacy of capital itself, expands its base and enables it to recruit ever new forces for itself out of the substratum of society. In a similar way, the circumstance that the Catholic Church in the Middle Ages formed its hierarchy out of the best brains in the land, regardless of their estate, birth or fortune, was one of the principal means of consolidating ecclesiastical rule and suppressing the laity. The more a ruling class is able to assimilate the foremost minds of a ruled class, the more stable and dangerous becomes its rule.[22]

By using the word "means" in the penultimate sentence, Marx suggests that the beneficial effects of mobility also explain it. In this case the explanatory assertion, although unsubstantiated, might be true, because the Catholic Church was in fact a corporate body, able to promote its interests by deliberate action. This cannot be true of social mobility under capitalism, however, because the capitalist class is not in this sense a corporate body, shaping and channeling everything for its own benefit. That mobility may have favorable consequences for "capital" is neither here nor there, as capital has no eyes that see or hands that move. Indeed, the German "capital logic" school represents a flagrant violation of the principle of methodological individualism, when it asserts or suggests that the needs of capital somehow bring about their own fulfillment.[23]

There is, however, one way in which the capitalist class may promote its collective interests: through the state. Here we confront the difficulty of specifying the capitalist character of the state in a capitalist society. Marx did not believe that the concrete states of the nineteenth century were a direct outgrowth and instrument of capitalist class rule. On the contrary, he argued that it was in the interest of the capitalist class to have a noncapitalist government – rule by the aristocracy in England, by the emperor and his bureaucracy in France. It was useful for the English capitalists to let the aristocracy remain in power, so that the political struggle between rulers and ruled would blur the lines of economic struggle between exploiters and exploited.[24] Similarly, capitalism on the European continent could only survive with a state that apparently stood above the classes. In these analyses Marx asserts that the noncapitalist state was beneficial for capitalism. He never states or implies that this benefit was deliberately brought about by the capitalist class, and yet he strongly suggests that it explains the presence of the noncapitalist state:

The bourgeoisie confesses that its own interests dictate that it should be delivered from the danger of its *own rule*; that in order to restore the tranquillity in the country its bourgeois Parliament must, first of all, be given its quietus; that in order to preserve its social power intact its political power must be broken; that the individual bourgeois can continue to exploit the other classes and enjoy undisturbed property, family, religion and order only on condition that his class be condemned along with the other classes to like political nullity; that in order to save its purse it must forfeit the crown, and the sword that is to safeguard it must at the same time be hung over its own head as the sword of Damocles.[25]

I defy anyone to read this text without understanding it as an *explanation* of the Bonapartist régime. What else is it but a functional explanation? The anti-capitalist state is the indirect strategy whereby the capitalists retain their economic dominance: one step backward, two steps forward. But an explanation in terms of latent functions can never invoke strategic considerations of this kind. "Long-term functionalism" suffers from all the defects of ordinary functional explanations, notably the problem of a purpose in search of a purposive actor. Moreover, it is *arbitrary*, because the manipulation of the time dimension nearly always lets us find a way in which a given pattern is good for capitalism; *ambiguous*, because the distinction between the short and the long term may be read either as a distinction between transitional effects and steady-state effects, or as a distinction between two kinds of steady-state effects,[26] and *inconsistent*, because positive long-term effects could never dominate negative short-term effects in the absence of an intentional actor. It is not possible, then, to identify the state in a capitalist society as a capitalist state simply by virtue of its favorable consequences for bourgeois economic dominance.

From Marx, I now turn to some recent Marxist writings. Consider first some writings by Marxist historians. In an otherwise important study, John Foster makes the following argument: "The basic function of feudal social organization was, therefore, to maintain just that balance between population and land which (given technological conditions) would produce the biggest possible feudal surplus. . . . It was enough to ensure that [peasant] marriage and childrearing were strictly tied (by customary practice and religion) to the inheritance of land, and rely on peasant self-interest to do the rest."[27] But what is the subject of the verbs "ensure" and "rely" in the last sentence? This is clearly a case of objective teleology, of an action in search of an actor.

E. P. Thompson writes that in pre-industrial England there were recurring revolts which, although usually unsuccessful in achieving their immediate objectives, had long-term success in making the propertied classes behave more moderately than they would have otherwise. He also seems to conclude that long-term success provides an (intentional or functional) explanation of the revolts. This, at any rate, is how I interpret his rhetorical question of whether the revolts "would have continued over so many scores, indeed hundreds of years, if they had consistently failed to achieve their objective."[28] If functional, the explanation fails for reasons by now familiar. If intentional, it fails for reasons related to a crucial difference between individual and collective action. If an individual acts in a way that he knows to be in his interest, we may conclude that he acted for the sake of that interest. But, when a group of individuals act in a way that is to their collective benefit, we cannot conclude that they did so to bring about that benefit.[29]

The attempt to read meaning into behavior that benefits the actors can take one of three distinct forms. First, the functionalist, discussed above. Second, the consequences can be transformed into motives, as in the example from Thompson. This inference, although not always incorrect, is unwarranted in the cases where the benefits emerge only if the actions are performed by *all* the actors concerned, yet the *individual* has no incentive to perform them. For instance, it is beneficial for the capitalist class as a whole if all capitalists search for labor-saving inventions, for then the aggregate demand for labor and hence the wage rate will fall. And it may well be true that historically there has been a trend to labor-saving inventions. Yet the collective benefits cannot explain the trend, for they could never motivate the individual capitalist who, under conditions of perfect competition, is unable to influence the overall wage level. The trend, if there is one, must be explained by some other mechanism, of which the collective benefits are accidental by-products. Third, one may invoke a conspiratorial design and seek one unifying but hidden intention behind the structure to be explained. Thus, if a pattern such as social mobility benefits the capitalist class as a whole, but not the "already existing individual capitalists," the conspiratorial explanation postulates a secret executive committee of the bourgeoisie. I do not deny that conspiracies occur, or that their existence may be asserted on indirect evidence. I simply argue the need for evidence – preferably direct or, if this is not available, as in the nature of the case it may not be, indirect – pointing to some hidden coordinating hand. Simply to invoke beneficial consequences supplies no such evidence.

Turning now from Marxist history to Marxist social science proper, we find that functionalism is rampant. Functional explanations pervade the theory of crime and punishment,[30] the analysis of education,[31] the study of racial discrimination,[32] and (most important) the analysis of the capitalist state, a Marxist growth industry during the last decades. Not all Marxist studies fall victim to the functionalist fallacies identified above, but most Marxist authors seem to believe that "everything that happens in a capitalist society necessarily corresponds to the needs of capital accumulation,"[33] so that the "correspondence between the actions (and structure) of the state and the requirements of capital accumulation [is] taken for granted."[34] Alternately, the "assumption is made that the capitalist state is universally functional for reproducing the dominance of the capitalist class."[35] These neo-Marxist works appear to be guided by the following principles: (i) All actions of the state serve the collective interest of the capitalist class. (ii) Any action that would serve the collective interest of the capitalist class is in fact undertaken by the state. (iii) Exceptions to the first principle are explained by "the relative autonomy of the state." (iv) Exceptions to the second principle are explained along the lines of Marx in the *Eighteenth Brumaire*: It is in the political interest of the bourgeoisie that the state should not always act in the economic interest of the bourgeoisie. Needless to say, the effect of the last two clauses is to render the first two virtually vacuous. In a seminal article, Michal Kalecki[36] raised some of the issues that came to the forefront in recent debates, particularly concerning the limits of state intervention to save capitalism from itself. To the question of why industrial leaders should oppose government spending to achieve full employment, he offers three answers, the two most important of which are these. First,

under a *laisser-faire* system the level of employment depends to a great extent on the so-called state of confidence. . . . This gives to the capitalists a powerful indirect control over Government policy: everything which may shake the state of confidence must be carefully avoided because it would cause an economic crisis. But once the Government learns the trick of increasing employment by its own purchases, this powerful controlling device loses its effectiveness. Hence budget deficits necessary to carry out the Government intervention must be regarded as perilous. The social function of the doctrine of "sound finance" is to make the level of employment dependent on the "state of confidence."

Second, Kalecki argues that capitalists not only oppose this way of overcoming the crisis, but actually need the crisis itself:

[Under] a regime of permanent full employment, "the sack" would cease to play its role as a disciplinary measure. The social position of the boss would be undermined and the self-assurance and class consciousness of the working class would grow. Strikes for wage increases and improvements in conditions of work would create political tension. It is true that profits would be higher under a regime of full employment than they are on the average under *laisser-faire*; and even the rise in wage rates resulting from the stronger bargaining power of the workers is less likely to reduce profits than to increase prices, and thus affects adversely only the rentier interests. But "discipline in the factories" and "political stability" are more appreciated by business leaders than profits. Their class instinct tells them that lasting full employment is unsound from their point of view and that unemployment is an integral part of the normal capitalist system.

In conclusion, Kalecki states that "one of the important functions of fascism, as typified by the Nazi system, was to remove the capitalist objection to full employment." To the extent that this thesis is only a variation on the inherent dilemma of the capitalist class – *Et propter vitam vivendi perdere causas*[37] – there can be no objection to it. As admirably explained in the work of Amid Bhaduri,[38] the ruling class often faces a change that gives short-term economic profit but has adverse long-term political (and hence economic) effects. But Kalecki never says whether his analysis is intentional or functional, in addition to being causal. He does make the case for a causal relation between unemployment and the interests of capital, but how does the latter explain the former? As any serious historian can imagine, a mass of detailed evidence is required to make an intentional explanation credible – hence the strong temptation to take the functionalist short-cut.

Many contemporary Marxists think the state has three main functions: repression, legitimation, and creating the conditions for accumulation. Whereas traditional Marxists stress the first function, their modern counterparts assert the importance of the second. Indeed, legitimation is viewed as "symbolic violence" that in modern societies is the functional equivalent of repression. The state exerts its legitimating function through "ideological apparatuses" (e.g., education) and the provision of social welfare. The state's function for capital accumulation is mainly to help the capitalist class overcome the particular interests of individual capitalists. In fact, the state is sometimes said to represent "capital in general," which is (logically) prior to the many individual capitals.[39] This of course is a drastic violation of the tenet of methodological individualism defended here. True, there is often a need for concerted capitalist action, but the need does not create its own fulfillment. The necessary collective action may fail to materialize even if seen as possible and desirable, because of the free-rider problem, and *a fortiori* if the need and possibility go unperceived. Failures of cartelization, of standardization, of wage coordination take place all the time in capitalist societies. Moreover, even when the actions of the state serve the interests of capital against those of individual capitalists, evidence must be given to show that this consequence has explanatory power – i.e., that there exists a mechanism by which state policy is shaped by the collective interest of the capitalist class. The mechanism need not be intentional design[40] – but *some* mechanism must be provided if the explanation is to be taken seriously.

Examples of the Marxist-functionalist analysis of the state abound in the German tradition of Altvater or the French manner of Poulantzas. In the United States, Marxist functionalism is best represented by James O'Connor's influential *The Fiscal Crisis of the State*, from which the following passage is taken:

The need to develop and maintain a "responsible" social order also has led to the creation of agencies and programs designed to control the surplus population politically and to fend off the tendency toward a legitimization crisis. The government attempts to administer and bureaucratize (encapsulate) not only monopoly sector labor-management conflict, but also social-political conflict emerging from competitive sector workers and the surplus population. The specific agencies for regulating the relations between capital and organized labor and unorganized workers are many and varied. . . . Some of these agencies were established primarily to maintain social control of the surplus population (e.g. HEW's Bureau of Family Services); others serve mainly to attempt to maintain harmony between labor and capital within the monopoly sector (e.g., the Bureau of Old Age and Survivors Insurance). In both cases the state must remain independent or "distant" from the particular interests of capital (which are very different from the politically organized interests of capital as the ruling class). The basic problem is to win mass loyalty to insure legitimacy; too intimate a relation between capital and state normally is unacceptable or inadmissible to the ordinary person.[41]

Note the implicit three-tier structure of capital interests: (1) the interest of the individual capitalist out to maximize profits come what may; (2) the interest of the capitalist class, which may have to curb the individual's greed; and (3) the interest of Capital, which may have to dissociate itself from class interests to ensure legitimacy. It is not surprising that *any* given state action can be viewed from one of these perspectives. O'Connor's scheme suggests the following methodological principle: If crude class interests will not do the explanatory job, then – but only then – invoke subtle class interests. This makes Marxism invulnerable to empirical disconfirmation, and nullifies its scientific interest.

Obviously, an alternative approach is required. Having given my views elsewhere,[42] let me summarize them briefly. (1) There are three main types of scientific explanation: the *causal*, the *functional*, and the *intentional*. (2) All sciences use causal analysis. The physical sciences use causal analysis exclusively. (3) The biological sciences also use functional analysis, when explaining the structure or behavior of organisms through the benefits for reproduction. This procedure is justified by the theory of natural selection, according to which such beneficial effects tend to maintain their own causes. Intentional analysis, on the other hand, is not justified in biology – because natural selection is basically myopic, opportunistic, and impatient, as opposed to the capacity for strategic and patient action inherent in intentional actors. (4) The social sciences make extensive use of intentional analysis, at the level of individual actions. Functional analysis, however, has no place in the social sciences because there is no sociological analogy to the theory of natural selection. (5) The proper paradigm for the social sciences is a mixed causal-intentional explanation – *intentional understanding* of the individual *actions*, and *causal explanation* of their *interaction*. (6) Individuals also interact intentionally. And here – in the study of the intentional interaction between intentional individuals – is where game theory comes in. The need for game theory arises as soon as individual actors cease to regard each other as given constraints on their actions, and instead regard each other as intentional beings. In parametric rationality each person looks at himself as a variable and at all others as constants, whereas in strategic rationality all look upon each other as variables. The essence of strategic thought is that no one can regard himself as privileged compared to the others: each has to decide on the assumption that the others are rational to the same extent as himself.

The uses of game theory in Marxist analysis

The basic premises of rational-choice theory[33] are (1) that structural constraints do not completely determine the actions taken by individuals in a society; and (2) that within the feasible set of actions compatible with all the constraints, individuals choose those they believe will bring the best results. If the first premise is denied, we are left with some variety of structuralism – an element of which reasoning is present in Marx, and is most fully developed in French Structuralism. Although it may occasionally be true that the feasible set shrinks to a single point, a general theory to this effect cannot be defended – unless by the ptolemaic twist of counting preferences or ideologies among the constraints. True, the ruling class often manipulates the constraints facing the ruled class so as to leave it no choice, but this very manipulation itself presupposes some scope of choice for the rulers. If the second premise is denied, we are left with some variety of role theory, according to which individuals behave as they do because they have been socialized to, rather than because they try to realize some goal: causality vs. intentionality. Against this I would argue that what people acquire by socialization is not quasi-compulsive tendencies to act in specific ways, but preference structures that – jointly with the feasible set – bring it about that some specific action is chosen. If the role theory was correct, it would be impossible to induce behavior modification by changing the feasible set (e.g., the reward structure), but clearly such manipulation is an omnipresent fact of social life.[44]

Game theory is a recent and increasingly important branch of rational-choice theory, stressing the *interdependence of decisions*. If all violence were structural, class interests purely objective, and class conflict nothing but incompatible class interests, then game theory would have nothing to offer to Marxism. But because classes crystallize into collective actors that confront each other over the distribution of income and power, as well as over the nature of property relations, and as there are also strategic relations between members of a given class, game theory is needed to explain these complex interdependencies. In a "game" there are several players or actors. Each actor must adopt an action or a strategy. When all actors have chosen strategies, each obtains a reward that depends on the strategies chosen by him *and* by the others. *The reward of each depends on the choice of all*. The notion of a reward can be understood narrowly or broadly. In the narrow interpretation, it signifies the material benefit received by each actor. In the broad interpretation, it covers everything in the situation of value to the actor, including (possibly) the rewards to other actors. *The reward of each depends on the reward of all*.[45] It is assumed that the actors strive to maximize their reward – to bring about a situation they prefer to other situations. When an actor chooses a strategy, he must take account of what the others will do. A strategy that is optimal against one set of strategies on the part of the others is not necessarily optimal against another set. To arrive at his decision, therefore, he has to *foresee their decisions*, knowing that they are trying to foresee his. *The choice of each depends on the choice of all.* The triumph of game theory is its ability to embrace simultaneously the three sets of interdependencies stated in the italicized sentences.[46] Nothing could be further from the truth, then, than the allegation that game theory portrays the individual as an isolated and egoistic atom.

An essential element of the situation is the *information* that the actors possess about each other. In games with perfect information, each individual has complete information about all relevant aspects of the situation. These include the capabilities of the other actors, their preferences, their information, and the payoff structure that maps sets of individual strategies into outcomes. The condition of perfect information is likely to be realized only in small and stable groups, or in groups with a coordinating instance. Also crucial is the notion of an *equilibrium point* – a set of strategies in which the strategy of each actor is optimal vis-à-vis those of the others. It is thanks to this notion that game theory can avoid the infinite regress of "I think that he thinks that I think . . . " which plagued early attempts to understand the logic of interdependency. The notion of a *solution* can be defined through that of an equilibrium point. Informally, the solution to a game is the set of strategies toward which rational actors with perfect information will tacitly converge. If there is only one equilibrium point, it will automatically emerge as the solution – it is the only stable outcome, in the sense that no one gains from defection. If there are several such equilibria, the solution will be the one that is collectively optimal – the equilibrium point preferred by all to all the others. Not all games have solutions in this sense.

A brief typology of games may be useful. One basic distinction is between two-person and n-person games, both of which are important for Marxism. The struggle between capital and labor is a two-person game; the struggle between members of the capitalist class an n-person game. Often, however, complicated n-person games can be reduced without too much loss of generality to simpler two-person games – as games played between "me" and "everybody else."[47] The simplest two-person games are zero-sum games, in which the loss of one player exactly equals the gain of the other. This is the only category of games that always have a solution. The conceptual breakthrough that made proof of this proposition possible was the introduction of *mixed strate-*

gies, i.e., the choice of a strategy according to some (optimal) probability distribution. In poker, for instance, a player may decide to bluff in one half of the cases, a policy implemented by tossing a coin in each case. Here the opponent may calculate how often the player will bluff, but not whether he will do so in any particular case. In variable-sum games not only the distribution of the rewards, but also the size of the total to be distributed, depends on the strategies chosen. These games can be further divided into games of pure cooperation and games of mixed conflict and cooperation (whereas zero-sum games are games of pure conflict). Not all variable-sum games have a solution in the sense indicated above. They can, however, have a solution once we take the step from noncooperative to cooperative games. In cooperative games – which should not be confused with the (noncooperative) games of pure cooperation – there is joint rather than individual choice of strategies. The actors can coordinate their choices so as to avoid certain disastrous combinations of individual strategies. If there is a choice between left-hand and right-hand driving, the actors may agree to toss a coin between both driving on the right and both driving on the left – a *jointly mixed strategy*. If they toss a coin individually, the chances are 50 percent that they will end up on on collision course.

The value of the cooperative approach to game theory is contested because it appears to beg the question by assuming that agreements to cooperate will be enforced. On general grounds of methodological individualism, noncooperative games are prior to cooperative games. Assuming that the actors will arrive at a cooperative solution is much like assuming that a functional need will create its own fulfillment. For this reason, and also because there are so many solution concepts for cooperative games, one will have to tread carefully when explaining the emergence of cooperative behavior in terms of cooperative games. Properly used, however, the method can yield important results, and in any case is fruitful for the purpose of normative analysis. For n-person games, the cooperative approach does not involve universal cooperation, but rather the cooperation of some actors against the others. The theory of coalitions in n-person game theory is an increasingly important branch of game theory for economic, political, and normative analysis.[48] The simplest solution concept for such games is that of the "core" – the set of all reward distributions in which no coalition of individuals can improve their lot by breaking out and acting on their own. Once again, the cooperative approach begs the question by assuming that coalitions can be formed and maintained whenever needed. And, once again, this is more an objection to the analytical-explanatory than to the normative use of the theory.

Turning now from exposition to applications, I discuss in turn the logic of solidarity and cooperation within classes, the problem of worker-capitalist coalitions, and some static and dynamic aspects of the class struggle. These applications all presuppose that we have left behind us – if it ever existed – the capitalism of perfect competition, unorganized capital and unorganized labor. The income distribution that would emerge under perfect competition can serve as a baseline for comparison with the distributions that result when one or both of the main classes behave in an organized and strategic manner. Whether the classes will so behave is itself a question to be decided by game theoretic analysis. I define class consciousness as the capacity of a class to behave as a collective actor. Operationally, this means the capacity to overcome the free-rider problem. This problem arises within both the capitalist and the working classes. As well explained by Mancur Olson,[49] each worker is tempted by the prospect of a free ride, of benefitting from the strikes fought by the other workers without taking part in the action himself. Similarly, capitalists face the same difficulty with regard to cartelization, wage policy, etc. If, however, we want to penetrate past these generalities to the fine grain of the problem, some distinctions must be made. I assume that each actor within the class has a choice between a *solidary strategy* (S) and an *egoist strategy* (E). In the artificial two-person game between "me" and "everybody else," four possibilities can be distinguished:

A. Universal cooperation: everybody uses S.
B. Universal egoism: everybody uses E.
C. The free rider: "I" use E, "everybody else" uses S.
D. The sucker: "I" use S, "everybody else" uses E.

Every individual in the society will rank these outcomes in a particular order, according to what he – in the role of "I" – would prefer. Excluding ties, there are twenty-four possible rankings of these four alternatives.[50] If we disregard all that rank B before A, as we are permitted to do by the very nature of the problem under discussion, we are left with twelve cases. If we then exclude the "masochistic" cases that have D ranked above A, we are left with eight alternatives. I shall limit myself to four cases that have a central place in the literature on collective action. I shall also limit myself to the hypothesis that each "I" views the situation in the same way. Although mixed cases will be the rule in actual situations, the assumption of homogeneity makes for a more tractable analysis.[51]

The first case is the well-known Prisoners' Dilemma, defined by the ranking CABD and characterized by the following features: (1) Strategy E is dominant, i.e., for each actor it is the best choice regardless of what the others will do. Here, then, we need not impose any stringent information requirement for the solution to be realized. Also, it is not true here that "the choice of each depends on the choice of all." In a sense, therefore, it is a rather trivial game. (2) The solution to the game is universal egoism, which everybody ranks below universal cooperation. Individual rationality leads to collective disaster. (3) Universal cooperation is neither individually stable nor individually accessible: everybody will take the first step away from it, and no one the first step toward it. We can apply this to the workers' predicament. For the individual there is no point in going on strike if his fellow workers do so, for by remaining at work he can derive the benefit from their action *and* be (highly) paid during the strike – and, if they do not strike, he has nothing to gain and much to lose by unilateral action.

Is there a "way out" of the Prisoners' Dilemma? Can individuals caught in this situation overcome the dilemma and behave cooperatively? No consensus has emerged from the extensive literature, but I believe that in the present context two approaches stand out as the most promising. In the case of working-class cooperation, the most plausible explanation is by change of the preference structure. Through continued interaction the workers become both concerned and informed about each other. Concern for others changes the ranking of the alternatives, and information about others enables the actors to realize the solution of the ensuing game. This is the "Assurance Game," defined by the ranking ACBD and possessing the following features: (1) There is no dominant strategy in this game. Egoism is "my" best reply to egoism; solidarity the best reply to solidarity. (2) The optimum of universal cooperation is individually stable, but not individually accessible. (3) Universal egoism and universal solidarity are both, therefore, equilibrium points in the game. Because universal cooperation is preferred by all to universal egoism, the former emerges as the solution to the game. (4) Because there is no dominant strategy, the solution will be realized only if there is perfect information. Imperfect information – about preferences or information – easily leads to uncertainty, suspicion, and play-safe behavior. Amartya Sen has argued that Marx's *Critique of the Gotha Programme* can be interpreted in terms of the Assurance Game.[52] Solidarity can substitute for material incentives. I would tend to believe that quite generally working-class solidarity and collective action can be understood in these terms, although I shall later point to an alternative explanation.

Although the Prisoners' Dilemma and the Assurance Game differ profoundly in their structure, behavior – in cases of incomplete information — may occur *as if* the preferences were a Prisoner's Dilemma when in fact they form an Assurance Game. In tax evasion or suboptimal use of public transportation, for instance, the observed outcome may be the result of lack of information rather than of free-rider egoism. Likewise, the Assurance Game preferences should be distinguished from those of the Categorical Imperative, although behaviorally they may be indistinguishable. The Categorical Imperative is defined by the ranking ADBC, with solidarity as a dominant strategy. The history of the working class shows, in my opinion, that cooperative behavior typically is conditional rather than unconditional — motivated by the concern for doing one's share of a common task rather than by the spirit of sacrifice or disregard for actual consequences characteristic of the Categorical Imperative. Indeed, more harm than good sometimes ensues from heroic individual acts of revolt or disobedience, if the others are not willing to follow suit, because such acts may provide the authorities or the employers the excuse they need to crack down further on the workers. This, I believe, shows that Kant's individualistic ethic is not appropriate for collective action.[53]

The Assurance Game also provides an interpretation of Charles Taylor's notion of *common meaning*, designed to elucidate the meaning of consensus. In his polemic against methodological individualism, Taylor asserts there are two forms of meaning that are irreducibly nonsubjective: the intersubjective meanings and the common meanings. Intersubjective meanings are, roughly, rules for social behavior whose negation cannot be generalized without contradiction. Thus promises should be kept because the notion of a society in which promises are never kept is logically contradictory. Common meanings illustrate the Assurance Game. Taylor distinguishes common meanings from shared subjective meanings by saying that "what is required for common meanings is that this shared value be part of the common world, that *this sharing itself be shared*."[54] The phrase I have italicized amounts to a condition of perfect information. For a consensus to be a living force, it must be known to exist. Everybody acts in a solidary manner because of knowing that the others are going to do so as well. This way of looking at consensus enables us to refute the following claim made by Taylor:

Common meanings, as well as intersubjective meanings, fall through the net of mainstream social science. They can find no place in its categories. For they are not simply a converging set of subjective reactions, but part of the common world. What the ontology of mainstream social science lacks is the notion of meaning as not simply for an individual subject; of a subject who can be a 'we' as well as an 'I.'[55]

Game theory provides what Taylor claims is lacking – the notion of a subject that can be a "we" as well as an "I." Through the triple interdependence that game theory analyzes – between rewards, between choices, and between rewards and choices – the individual emerges as a microcosm epitomizing the whole network of social relations. A similar demystification makes good sense of Sartre's notion of the "group," even though he claims it cannot be rendered in the "neo-positivist" language of "analytical reason."[56]

Arthur Stinchcombe analyzes Trotsky's account of the October Revolution in terms that fit this analysis of solidarity. The key idea in Stinchcombe's explanation is the breakdown of authority in the prerevolutionary situation. The old authority breaks down when new social orders become thinkable, i.e., real possibilities. The "Revolution grows by the exploration of these possibilities, and by the communication of there being possibilities to those who would support them, 'if only they knew they were really Bolsheviks.' "[57] When the workers and the soldiers, especially, come to believe that change is possible, change becomes possible:

The fickleness of the masses during a revolution thus takes on a completely different interpretation. Trotsky's sarcasm about spontaneity as an explanation of the movements is essentially an assertion that the explanations of the masses about why they are doing what they are doing are going to be reasonable, but that reasonableness is going to be based on their estimates of the probabilities that (a) this institution or authority will pursue my goals; or (b) this institution or authority is the best I am likely to find, because no alternatives are possible or because the alternatives are in the hand of the enemy. And it is these probabilities that fluctuate wildly during a revolution but are reasonably stable during times of governmental quiescence.[58]

Revolutions succeed when these probabilities cease to fluctuate wildly and settle into some new and stable pattern because uncertainty, suspicion, and play-safe thinking no longer are predominant. Tacit coordination that becomes possible when people come to trust each other is the essential condition for successful collective action. The role of the revolutionary leader is to provide the information that makes this tacit coordination possible, rather than to be a center of command and authority. This view constitutes an alternative to the Leninist theory of revolutionary leadership. Mancur Olson,[59] following Lenin, assumes that the only possible motivational structures are the free-rider egoism of the Prisoners' Dilemma and the unconditional altruism of the Categorical Imperative. Rightly rejecting the latter as wishful thinking, and observing that the former can never bring about collective action, he concludes that strikes or revolutions can only be brought about from above, through discipline verging on coercion. But the conditional altruism of the Assurance Game is also a possible motivational structure, which may lead to collective action by tacit coordination, given information provided by the leaders.

The problem of capitalist class solidarity requires different tools. We can hardly assume that interaction between capitalists will make them care about each other and change their motivations. Nor can we assume that the structure of their coordination problems invariably is that of a Prisoners' Dilemma. As to the last question, we can return to the issue of labor-saving inventions, which illustrates the ranking CADB.[60] This game has the paradoxical feature that the optimum is individually accessible, but not individually stable. When everyone uses E, it is in the interest of each actor to use S, but, when everyone uses S, it is in the interest of each to switch to E. The game, in fact, has no solution. If no other capitalists seek labor-saving inventions, wages can be expected to rise, which makes it rational for the individual capitalist to preempt the wage rise by saving on labor – but if all capitalists do this, the individual capitalist has no incentive to do so. Clearly, this inherent contradiction sets up a pressure for concerted action,[61] which may or may not be realized.

I have assumed that for the individual capitalists there are costs associated with the search for labor-saving inventions, as distinct from the search for inventions in general. If we drop this assumption, the resulting interaction structure takes the following form. Each capitalist is different between A and C, but prefers both to B and D, between which he is also indifferent. This, again, offers a crucial scope for the exercise of leadership. The task of the business leaders will be to persuade the individual entrepreneurs to act in a way that is neither harmful nor beneficial from their private viewpoint, but which brings about collective benefits when adopted by all. Leadership, then, is to make use of the "zone of indifference" of the individuals.[62]

These problems are hardly discussed in the literature. By contrast, there are many discussions of capitalist Prisoners' Dilemmas, mainly in the context of cartelization. For each firm the best option is to have a high output at the high prices made possible by the cartel restrictions on the output, but such free-rider behavior will of course make the cartel break up, or its anticipation prevent the cartel from forming. Yet cartels sometimes do form without immediately breaking up. This often happens because of asymmetries among the firms. A large firm will be strongly motivated to adopt the cartel policy even if the others do not follow suit because it can internalize more of the benefits.[63] Moreover, it will typically possess the economic power to retaliate against firms that do not follow suit. But, even in competitive markets with many identical firms, cartelization may occur by voluntary and selfish action. This may be explained by the theory of "supergames," or repeated Prisoners' Dilemmas.[64] When the same actors play a Prisoners' Dilemma over and over again, the possibility of retaliation against free riders may make it rational to cooperate. It is easy to see that this will occur only if the number of iterations is indefinite. If the actors know when the games come to an end, there will be no reason for cooperation in the very last game because no retaliation can take place afterwards if they defect. But this means that for the purposes of decision the penultimate game can be treated as the last, to which the same reasoning applies, and so on in argument that inexorably zips back to the first game. According to John Bowman, this explains the failure of Roosevelt's National Recovery Act: "Voluntary cooperation in the Prisoners' Dilemma is possible only when the supergame is of indefinite length. The N.R.A. had a terminal date. Thus it was in the best interests of every conditional cooperator to break the code provisions before his competitors did."[65]

Explanations in terms of supergames may also apply to working-class cooperation, though less plausibly. I believe anyone familiar with the history of the working class will agree that solidarity is not merely enlightened long-term selfishness. Operationally, the issue could be decided by looking at cases in which the working-class interaction was known to have a terminal date, as in the National Recovery Act, and see whether this had any stifling effects on cooperation and solidarity. For solidarity among the workers to emerge, it is crucial that they interact for some time because otherwise the mutual concern and knowledge will not have time to be shaped. But there should be no reason to believe that solidarity requires a cooperation of indefinite length, if my account is correct. In perfectly competitive capitalism, as I have argued elsewhere, workers are doubly alienated – from the means of production and from the products of their labor.[66] Alienation from the means of production stems from the alienation of the workers from their own history, i.e., from past generations of workers who produced the means of production currently used. The alienation from the products stems from their alienation from the class to which they belong, and permits the capitalist to treat each worker as if he were "the marginal worker," in the economic sense of that term, and to pay him according to marginal productivity. Only by overcoming this double alienation, by taking possession of their past history and by acting jointly as a class, can the workers achieve class consciousness that goes beyond wage claims to make a radical rupture with capitalist relations.

What happens if the workers overcome the alienation from their class, but not that from their history – if they see through the "marginalist illusion," but not the "presentist illusion"? This partial liberation distinguishes the modern capitalist societies of the social democratic variety, in which working-class organizations negotiate with employer associations over the division of the net product. Because the basic assumption behind this bargaining is that capital, as a "factor of production" on a par with labor, has a right to some part of the product, the only issue of the class struggle becomes the *size* of that part, not its existence. Take first the simplest case, in which we disregard the question of reinvestment out of profits. In this purely static setting, workers do not ask what use is made of the surplus value extracted from them. If they could get the whole net product and spend it immediately, they would. But they cannot. The problem, then, is one of dividing a jointly made product between the producers. It is, clearly, a mixed conflict-cooperation game, in which the strategies determine both the total product and how it is to be divided. Both parties have threats – strikes and lockouts – that are characteristically double-edged: they enhance the probability of getting a large share of the total, but reduce the total to be shared. In such bargaining each side has a lower limit beneath which it cannot go, e.g., subsistence for the workers and a minimal profit for the capitalists. And the sum of these limits is smaller than the total to be shared. In other words, there is a set of possible divisions that are compatible with the last-ditch demands of both classes, and over which the bargaining takes place.

There is no way the two groups can converge tacitly in a pair of demands that exactly exhaust the total product. The game has no noncooperative solution. Considerations other than purely rational calculation must, therefore, decide the outcome. Bargaining theory addresses this problem. Its general assumption is that the actors must form some psychological hypotheses about each other, even if these cannot be rationally justified. Indeed, according to some bargaining models, each actor at each step of the process believes himself to be one step ahead of the other.[67] The mutual inconsistency of these beliefs does not, however, necessarily prevent the sequence of demands and counterdemands from converging toward some division of the product, which is then the outcome of the bargaining process.

Of the many varieties of bargaining theory,[68] one has received general attention and is uniquely interesting from the methodological point of view. This is the Zeuthen-Nash theory, named after the authors who proposed two radically different versions, which John Harsanyi later proved to be mathematically equivalent.[69] The Nash version offers an axiomatic method of finding the normatively justified outcome for two-person cooperative games, whereas the Zeuthen method offers a step-by-step method, taking us through claims and counterclaims to a uniquely determined outcome. Because both versions lead to the same result, we can use cooperative game theory without coming into conflict with methodological individualism. We do not, that is, simply *assume* that the cooperative outcome will be realized simply because there is a *need* for it; rather we exhibit *a causal mechanism whereby it will be achieved*. The Nash solution is determined by assuming that a certain number of conditions are fulfilled. First, it should not make any difference to the outcome whether the rewards are measured on one particular utility scale among the many scales that are positive linear transformations of each other. To explain the last expression, it should suffice to point out that the Celsius and Fahrenheit temperature scales are positive linear transformations of each other, differing only in the choice of zero and in the unit of measurement. Secondly, the outcome should be Pareto-optimal, so that it is impossible to improve the situation of one actor without harming that of another. Thirdly, it should be symmetrical, in the sense that equally powerful actors should get equal rewards. Lastly, it should satisfy the "condition of the independence of irrelevant alternatives," stipulating that adding new alternatives to the bargaining situation can only change the outcome if the new outcome is one of the new options. The addition of a new alternative, that is, can never make a different old alternative emerge as the outcome.

Nash's theorem states there is only one division of the product that satisfies these conditions – viz., the division that maximizes the mathematical product of the rewards. From the way these rewards are measured,[70] a further feature of the solution follows: it typically accords the largest portion of the jointly made product to the most powerful actor. This is the "Matthew effect" in bargaining theory: to him that hath, shall be given. For a poor actor, even a small gain is so important that he can be made to be content with it, whereas the more affluent can say with equanimity, "Take it or leave it." The Matthew effect may itself be seen as a form of exploitation,[71] or at least as contrary to distributive justice, which rather demands that the least advantaged person should be given more.[72] This inequity, however, is secondary because there is no normative basis for the capitalist class to get anything at all. In any case, the model may be behaviorally attractive even if its normative appeal is weak. Zeuthen's argument shows that it is plausible to believe that this outcome will in fact be the result of bargaining, if at each step the player whose relative loss is smaller makes a concession to the opponent.[73] This approach is important in bargaining cases that involve a once-and-for-all confrontation that does not have consequences beyond the present. If, however, the bargaining parties know they will have to bargain again later, and that the outcome of present bargaining will affect future welfare, it will not do. Wage bargaining, in fact, tends to be regular, institutionalized, sometimes even continuous. Also, the current division of the net product between wages and profit makes a big difference to the future welfare of both classes because part of the profit is reinvested. The less the capitalist class has left in profits, the smaller the prospects for economic growth and future increases in consumption.

Kelvin Lancaster proposes a model that captures this double time-dependence of bargaining.[74] He views the wage struggle between capital and labor as a "differential game," i.e., as a continuous strategic interaction. The model, and even more the general theory behind it, constitutes an important conceptual breakthrough, with many consequences for the way in which we think about exploitation, power, and capitalism. The theory does for social democracy what Marx did for classical capitalism: it explains how class struggle evolves when the workers overcome the synchronic alienation, but not the diachronic one. Lancaster assumes that workers and capitalists confront each other as organized groups, and that there are no other social classes. He assumes, moreover, that each of the two classes controls an essential economic variable. The workers can, within certain limits,[75] determine the rate of working-class consumption out of the current net product, whereas the capitalists can control the rate of investment out of profits. The assumption regarding the capitalists' control variable is simply part of the definition of capitalism, whereas the assumption regarding the workers' control over current consumption reflects the development of capitalism since Marx. In modern capitalist economies, especially the social democratic variety prominent in north-western Europe, the workers have the power – either directly through unions or indirectly through profit taxation – to retain for themselves virtually all of the net product, should they so desire. This statement is not easily substantiated, being counterfactual, yet it is defensible. Under early capitalism, working-class consumption was kept down to subsistence for many reasons, including low productivity, weak working-class organizations, a high degree of capitalist cohesion, rapid population growth, and a state that championed the capitalist class. In modern capitalist economies of the social democratic variety, none of these conditions obtains. True, the capitalist class remains strong, in that it is able to discipline its own members. But its capacity for subjugating the workers has been drastically reduced, for if the workers are denied in direct wage bargaining, they can retaliate with state intervention and heavy taxation on profits.

Yet the workers do not use their power. Lancaster suggests, correctly, that this hesitancy owes to certain strategic facts of the situation and to the interest of both classes in present and future consumption. Hence the workers must leave some profit to the capitalists for reinvestment and increased future consumption. Finn Kydland and Edward Prescott suggest that the workers, therefore, should bind themselves – that the "workers, who control the policy, might rationally choose to have a constitution which limits their power, say, to expropriate the wealth of the capitalist class."[76] This is a new twist on the theme of abdication, performed here by the workers instead of the capitalists, as in Marx's *Eighteenth Brumaire*. Their analysis is incomplete, however, as it does not take the strategic nature of the situation into account, as Lancaster does when he observes that both the workers and the capitalists are in a dilemma. To be precise, we have:

The Workers' Dilemma: If they consume everything now, nothing will be left for investment and future increases in consumption, but if they leave something for profits, they have no guarantee that the capitalists will use this for investment rather than for their own consumption.

The Capitalists' Dilemma: If they consume the entire profits now, nothing will be left for investment and future increases in consumption, but if they invest out of profits, they have no guarantee that the workers will not retain for themselves the increase in consumption thereby generated.

Observe the assumption that capitalists desire consumption rather than profits. The rate of profit is fixed by the working class, hence it cannot also be maximized by the capitalists. This argument does not deny the importance of profit maximization, for if capitalists can do even better than the rate fixed for them, they will also benefit in consumption terms. Observe, too, that the model has potential applications in many settings. Consider, for instance, the relation between a multinational firm that controls the rate of local reinvestment out of locally created profits, and the local government that controls the tax rate on profits.

A strategy, in the game set up by these dilemmas, is a time profile of values of the control variable, i.e., a continuous sequence of rates of consumption out of the net product for the workers, and a sequence of rates of investment out of profits for the capitalists. A solution, here as in general, consists of two strategies that are optimal against each other. Lancaster shows that, if the two classes are assumed to maximize their consumption over some finite time period, the game has a solution. He also shows that the solution is suboptimal, in the sense of implying a smaller total consumption for each class than would be possible with different time profiles. It is also discontinuous: at one point in time, both classes switch from minimal to maximal consumption. In my view these results depend too heavily on the specific assumptions of the model to be of great interest. The importance of the model is above all conceptual. It shows how the workers can hold political power, yet be powerless if the capitalists retain economic power; how the workers may control consumption, yet be powerless if the capitalists control investment; how the workers can determine the present, yet be powerless if the capitalists determine the future. The exploitation of the working class, then, does not consist only in the capitalists' appropriation of surplus-value, but also in the workers' exclusion from decisive investment choices that shape the future. Or, alternatively, the workers suffer not only exploitation, but also lack of self-determination.[77] In the capitalist countries where social democracy is most advanced, one may argue with Ralf Dahrendorf that power rather than wealth is the crux of the class struggle.[78]

Cooperative n-person game theory has been usefully applied to the study of exploitation. In John Roemer's *General Theory of Exploitation and Class*, it is shown that the feudal, capitalist, and socialist modes of exploitation can be characterized by means of notions from this theory.[79] A group of individuals are said to be exploited if, were they to withdraw from society according to certain withdrawal rules, they could improve their situation. Different forms of exploitation correspond to different withdrawal rules. Thus the serfs were exploited in the feudal sense because they could have done better for themselves had they withdrawn from society with their own land. Workers are capitalistically exploited because they could have done better were they to withdraw with their per capita share of society's tangible assets, i.e., capital goods. And under socialism a group is exploited if it could do better were it to withdraw with its per capita share of the intangible assets, i.e., skills and talents. Whereas the last notion is somewhat hazy, the characterizations of feudal and capitalist exploitation are very valuable, as is also the observation that the neoclassical view, that workers are not exploited under capitalism, really amounts to a denial of feudal exploitation in capitalist societies. It is also possible to arrive at specific statements about the intensity of exploitation, by using the framework of cooperative game theory. Consider a case discussed by Lloyd Shapley and Martin Shubik,[80] agricultural production where one capitalist owns the land and the workers own only their labor power. How will the product the divided between landowner and workers if coalitions can be formed between the owner and some of the peasants? Shapley and Shubik show that the outcome is worse for the workers than it is under perfect competition where no coalitions of any kind are allowed. Worker-landowner coalitions conform to a "divide and rule" principle: the workers are weakened by landowner inducements that lead them to betray their class. Even if the workers are too weak to agree on concerted action, they may be strong enough to prevent such partial accommodations with the capitalist. Compared to collective bargaining, individual wage negotiations betray weakness; but, opposed to coalition bargaining, they betoken incipient class consciousness. Coalition theory thus embraces simultaneously the problems of class solidarity and of class struggle.

The weakness of game theory, in its present state, is the lack of testable hypotheses. There are many experimental studies of gaming, within the noncooperative and the cooperative framework, but few applications to nonexperimental settings. The value of the theory, therefore, is mainly in illuminating the nature of social interaction and in creating more discriminating categories of sociological analysis. Yet I am confident that this is a transitory situation only, and that game theory will increasingly help us understand social and historical problems. My reasons for this belief are somewhat *a priori*. If one accepts that interaction is the essence of social life, then I submit that the three, interlocking sets of interdependencies set out above capture interaction better than does any alternative. Game theory provides solid microfoundations for any study of social structure and social change. Yet the problems of aggregation and statistical analysis still confound us when it comes to complex real life cases. This is not an argument for abandoning the search for micro-foundations, but a compelling reason for forging better links between aggregate analysis and the study of individual behavior.

For Marxism, game theory is useful as a tool for understanding cases of mixed conflict and cooperation: cooperation in producing as much as possible, conflict over dividing up the product. Game theory can help understand the mechanics of solidarity and class struggle, without assuming that workers and capitalists have a common interest and need for cooperation. They do not. The interest of the working class is to suppress the capitalist class – and itself qua wage-earners – not to cooperate with it. Within the alienated framework of capitalism, however, this interest is easily misperceived. For there is the appearance of a common interest, such that working-class action will follow lines like those sketched here. Only through proper analysis of the mechanism of this reformist class struggle can one understand how to transform it into one that aims at abolishing the capitalist system.

Notes

1. The philosophical point invoked here is that in contexts of belief, desire, etc. it is not in general possible to substitute for each other expressions with the same reference, without change of truth value. We fear an object as described in a certain way, and we may not fear it under a different description.

2. For an analysis of this idea, see my *Logic and Society* (Chichester, Eng.: Wiley, 1978), 20 ff.

3. A forceful statement of the need for micro-foundations is in John Roemer, *Analytical Foundations of Marxian Economic Theory* (Cambridge, Eng.: Cambridge University Press, 1981), chap. 1 and *passim*.

4. I argue in more detail for this claim in chap. 5 of my *Sour Grapes* (Cambridge, Eng.: Cambridge University Press, 1985).

5. For a fuller statement of my views on functional explanation, see chap. 2 of my *Explaining Technical Change*, (Cambridge, Eng.: Cambridge University Press, 1983); see also my exchange with G. A. Cohen in *Political Studies* 28 (1980), my exchange with Arthur Stinchcombe in *Inquiry* 23 (1980), and my review of P. van Parijs, *Evolutionary Explanation in the Social Sciences* (Totowa, N.J.: Rowman and Littlefield, 1981), *Inquiry* 3 (1981) 378–85.

6. For a fuller statement, see chap. 1 of my *Ulysses and the Sirens* (Cambridge, Eng.: Cambridge University Press, 1979).

7. Natural selection invokes competition between co-existing individuals. Arthur Stinchcombe (in his contribution to *The Idea of Social Structure: Papers in Honor of Robert K. Merton*, edited by Lewis A. Coser [New York: Harcourt, Brace, Jovanovich, 1975]) points to an analogous model involving selection among successive social states. The model pictures social change as an absorbing Markov process – which for the present purposes may be summarized by saying that institutions undergo continuous change until they arrive in a state in which there is no pressure for further change (the "absorbing state"). This view could be used as a basis for functional explanation, with the modification that it would explain social states in terms of the absence of destabilizing consequences rather than through the presence of stabilizing ones. I would argue, however, that – unlike the biological case – there are no reasons for thinking that this adaptive process would ever catch up with the changing social environment.

8. A radically different account of functional explanation is offered by G. A. Cohen, *Karl Marx's Theory of History* (Oxford, Eng.: Oxford University Press, 1978). He argues that functional explanations can be sustained by *consequence laws*, of the form "Whenever x would have favorable consequences for y, then x appears." If a law of this form is established, we may affirm that x is explained by its favorable consequences for y, even if no mechanism is indicated (although Cohen asserts that some mechanism must indeed exist). To the (partially misguided) objections to this idea stated in my review of his book in *Political Studies* (note 5 above), I now would like to add the following. First, x and the y-enhancing effect of x might both be effects of some third factor z, and thus related by spurious correlation. Second, the definition of a consequence law is vitiated by the imprecise way in which the time dimension is brought in. The law could in fact be vacuously confirmed by suitably ignoring short-term in favor of long-term consequences.

9. "Social Conflict and the Theory of Social Change," in *Conflict Resolution: Contributions of the Behavioral Sciences*, edited by C. G. Smith (Notre Dame, Ind.: University of Notre Dame Press, 1971), 60.

10. "What's Wrong with the New Institutional Economics" (Mimeograph, Department of Economics, Stanford University, 1979).

11. *Economic Analysis of the Law* (Boston: Little, Brown, 1977), 106, italics added, parentheses deleted.

12. R. K. Merton, *Social Theory and Social Structure*, rev. ed. (New York: Free Press, 1957), 30 ff.

13. P. Bourdieu, *La Distinction* (Paris: Editions de Minuit, 1979), 285. For a critical discussion of this inverted sociodicy, which proceeds from the assumption that all is for the worst in the worst of all possible worlds, see my review in *London Review of Books*, 5–18 Nov. 1981.

14. I counted 15 occurrences of this phrase in *La Distinction*.

15. Scheler, *Ressentiment* (New York: Schocken, 1972), 52.

16. *Theories of Surplus-Value*, 3 vols. (Moscow: Progress, 1963–71), vol. 1, 287.

17. "You know my admiration for Leibniz" (Marx to Engels, 10 May 1870). For the structure of Leibniz's philosophy of history, see chap. 6 of my *Leibniz et la Formation de l'Esprit Capitaliste* (Paris: Aubier-Montaigne, 1975).

18. The manuscript consists of 23 notebooks, of which books 6 to 15 were published by Kautsky as *Theories of Surplus-Value*, Books 1 to 5 and 16 to 18 have recently been published in the new *Marx-Engels Gesamt-Ausgabe*, and the remaining will soon be available in the same edition. Just as Marx's *Grundrisse* testify to the influence of Hegel's *Logic*, these manuscripts bear witness to the influence of Hegel's philosophy of history.

19. *Theories of Surplus-Value*, vol. 3, 422–23.

20. *Marx-Engels Gesamt-Ausgabe*, Zweite Abteilung, Band 3, Teil 1 (Berlin: Dietz, 1976), 173.

21. Ibid., 327. The verse is also quoted in Marx's article on "The British Rule in India" (*New York Daily Tribune*, 25 June 1853) and, in a more ironic vein, in *Neue Oder Zeitung*, 20 Jan. 1855.

22. *Capital*, 3 vols. (New York: International Publishers, 1967), vol. 3, 600–1. For the distinction between short-term and long-term functionalism in Marxism, see also Roemer, *Analytical Foundations*, 9.

23. For surveys, see B. Jessop, "Recent Theories of the Capitalist State," *Cambridge Journal of Economics* 1 (1977): 353–74, and the Introduction to J. Holloway and S. Picciotta, eds., *State and Capital* (London: Edward Arnold, 1978). I should mention here that by "corporate body" I mean something different from what is later referred to as a "collective actor." The former refers to a juristic person, or more broadly to any kind of formal organization with a single decision-making center. The latter is defined below as any group of individuals who are able, by solidarity or enlightened self-interest, to overcome the free-rider problem. Another way of overcoming it is to create a corporate body with legal or effective power to keep individual members in line, but in the discussion below I mostly limit myself to cooperation emerging by tacit coordination.

24. *New York Daily Tribune*, 25 Aug. 1852.

25. "The Eighteenth Brumaire of Louis Bonaparte," in Marx and Engels, *Collected Works* (London: Lawrence and Wishart, 1979), 143.

26. De Tocqueville, in *Democracy in America*, distinguishes both between the transitional effects of democratization and the steady-state effects of democracy; and between the inefficient use of resources and the efficient creation of resources that are both inherent in democracy as a going concern. For details, see chap. 1 of my *Explaining Technical Change*.

27. *Class Struggle and the Industrial Revolution* (London: Methuen, 1974), 15. Thus Marxist functionalism explains the institutional arrangements of feudalism in terms of their favorable consequences for the surplus product, whereas non-Marxist functionalists such as D. North and R. P. Thomas (*The Rise of the Western World* [Cambridge, Eng.: Cambridge University Press, 1973]) explain the same arrangements in terms of their favorable consequences for total product.

28. "The Moral Economy of the English Crowd in the Eighteenth Century," *Past and Present* 50 (1971): 120.

29. For an analysis of this fallacy, see my *Logic and Society*, 118 ff.

30. Stark examples include W. J. Chambliss, "The Political Economy of Crime: A Comparative Study of Nigeria and the USA," in *Critical Criminology*, edited by I. Taylor et al. (London: Routledge & Kegan Paul, 1975), and W. J. Chambliss and T. E. Ryther, *Sociology: The Discipline and Its Direction* (New York: McGraw-Hill, 1975), 348. The closely related Radical approach is exemplified by M. Foucault, *Surveiller et Punir* (Paris: Gallimard, 1975), 277 and passim.

31. S. Bowles and H. Gintis, *Schooling in Capitalist America* (London: Routledge & Kegan Paul, 1976), e.g., 103, 114, and 130 features many such examples. In the same vein is also M. Levitas, *Marxist Perspectives in the Sociology of Education* (London: Routledge & Kegan Paul, 1974). A Radical version is that of P. Bourdieu and J.-C. Passeron, *La Reproduction* (Paris: Editions de Minuit, 1970), e.g., 159.

32. S. Bowles and H. Gintis, "The Marxian Theory of Value and Heterogeneous Labour: A Critique and Reformulation," *Cambridge Journal of Economics* 1 (1977): 173–92; J. Roemer, "Divide and Conquer: Microfoundations of a Marxian Theory of Wage Discrimination," *Bell Journal of Economics* 10 (1979): 695–705. The fallacy involved in both these articles is the belief that because internal cleavages in the working class benefit capitalist class domination, they are to be explained in terms of this benefit. This, however, is to confuse what Simmel (*Soziologie* [Berlin: Dunker und Humblot, 1908], 76 ff.) referred to as, respectively, *tertius gaudens* and *divide et impera*. Third parties may benefit from a struggle even when they have not been instrumental in setting it up.

33. As Jessop, "Recent Theories," 364, characterizes the "capital logic" school.

34. Introduction to Holloway and Picciotta, 12, characterizing Yaffe's work.

35. E. O. Wright, *Class, Crisis, and the State* (London: New Left Books, 1978), 231.

36. M. Kalecki, "Political Aspects of Full Employment," in *Selected Essays on the Dynamics of the Capitalist Economy* (Cambridge, Eng.: Cambridge University Press, 1971), 139–41.

37. "And for the sake of life to sacrifice life's only end" (Juvenal), quoted by Marx in *Neue Oder Zeitung*, 12 June 1855.

38. A. Bhaduri, "A Study in Agricultural Backwardness under Semi-Feudalism," *Economic Journal* 83 (1973): 120–37, and "On the Formation of Usurious Interest Rates in Backward Agriculture," *Cambridge Journal of Economics* 1 (1977): 341–52.

39. R. Rosdolsky, *Zur Entstehungsgeschichte des Marxschen "Kapital"* (Frankfurt: Europäische Verlagsanstalt, 1968, 61–71), refers to the passages (mainly in the *Grundrisse*) where Marx develops the concept of "capital in general."

40. For a survey of alternatives to intentional design, see P. Van Parijs.

41. *The Fiscal Crisis of the State* (London: St. Martin's 1973), 69–70. Closely related explanations of the welfare state are given in J. Hirsch, *Staatsapparat und Reproduktion des Kapitals* (Frankfurt: Suhrkamp, 1974), 54; and N. Poulantzas, *Pouvoir Politique et Classes Sociales* (Paris: Maspero, 1968), 310.

42. Van Parijs, passim; also *Ulysses and the Sirens*, chap. 1.

43. A standard treatment is R. D. Luce and H. Raiffa, *Games and Decisions* (New York: Wiley, 1957). Some nonstandard problems are raised in *Ulysses and the Sirens*, especially chap. 3.

44. For an elaboration of my critique of structuralism and role theory, see *Ulysses and the Sirens*, chaps. 3.1 and 3.6.

45. This could be part of what Marx meant by his statement in the *Communist Manifesto*: "In place of the old bourgeois society, with its classes and class antagonism, we shall have an association in which the free development of each is the condition for the free development of all." (Another possible reading is indicated in the next note.) If "each" and "all" are transposed in this passage, a more adequate expression occurs. Proper understanding of the philosophical anthropology behind this statement presupposes the idea that, even for the single individual, the free development of all faculties is the condition for the free development of each faculty (*The German Ideology*, in Marx and Engels, *Collected Works* [London: Lawrence and Wishart, 1976], vol. 5, 262). The freely developed person is both a totality of freely developed faculties and part of a totality of freely developed persons. Hypertrophy is atrophy, in the individual and in society.

46. A fourth kind of independence falls outside game theory, however. It can be summed up by saying that the *preferences of each depend on the actions of all*, by sociali-

Game theory takes preferences as given, and has nothing to offer concerning preference formation. The transformation of a Prisoners' Dilemma into an Assurance Game (see below) must be explained by social psychology, not by game theory. We can explain behavior intentionally in terms of preferences, but the latter themselves are to be explained causally.

47. For n-person versions of some of the games discussed here, see A. Sen, "Isolation, Assurance and the Social Rate of Discount," *Quarterly Journal of Economics* 80 (1967) 112–24. For a treatment of heterogeneous preferences in n-person games, see the brilliant framework developed by T. S. Schelling, *Micromotives and Macrobehavior* (New York: Norton, 1978).

48. The most general analysis, permitting overlapping coalitions, is J. Harsanyi, *Rational Behavior and Bargaining Equilibrium in Games and Social Situations* (Cambridge, Eng.: Cambridge University Press, 1977). The economic theory of the core is made easily accessible by W. Hildebrand and A. P. Kirman, *Introduction to Equilibrium Theory* (Amsterdam: North-Holland, 1976). Applications to ethics include John Roemer, *A General Theory of Exploitation and Class,* (Cambridge, Mass.: Harvard University Press, 1982); and Roger Howe and John Roemer, "Rawlsian Justice as the Core of a Game," *American Economic Review* 71, (1981): 880–90.

49. *The Logic of Collective Action* (Cambridge, Mass.: Harvard University Press, 1965), chap. 4.

50. For a more fine-grained typology, see A. Rapoport, M. J. Guyer, and D. G. Gordon, *The 2 × 2 Game* (Ann Arbor, Mich.: University of Michigan Press, 1976). For other discussions of the relation among the preference structures analyzed here, see S. C. Kolm, "Altruismes et Efficacités," *Social Science Information* 20 (1981): 293–344; and R. van der Veen, "Meta-Rankings and Collective Optimality," *Social Science Information* 20 (1981): 345–74.

51. For a brief discussion of some mixed cases, see my introduction to the articles by Kolm and van der Veen cited in the preceding note. See also Schelling, *Micromotives and Macrobehavior.*

52. A. Sen, *On Economic Inequality* (London: Oxford University Press, 1973), chap. 4.

53. The point is that acting unilaterally on the Categorical Imperative may be downright unethical. A striking example could be unilateral disarmament, if the situation is such that other countries will rush in to fill the power vacuum. Instead of acting in a way that would lead to good results *if* everyone else did the same, one should act to promote the good on realistic assumptions about what others are likely to do. A little morality, like a little rationality, may be a dangerous thing. There is room and need for a "moral theory of the second best," corresponding to the economic theory of the second best which shows that if out of n conditions for an economic optimum, one is not fulfilled, the optimum may be more closely approached if additional conditions are violated. R. G. Lipset and K. Lancaster, "The Economic Theory of Second Best," *Review of Economic Studies,* 24 (1957–8): 133–62.

54. C. Taylor, "Interpretation and the Sciences of Man," *Review of Metaphysics* 25 (1971): 31.

55. Ibid., 31–32.

56. J.-P. Sartre, *Critique de la Raison Dialectique* (Paris: Gallimard, 1960), 417, 404 ff.

57. A. Stinchcombe, *Theoretical Methods in Social History* (New York: Academic Press, 1978), 54.

58. Ibid., 41.

59. Olson, *Logic of Collective Action* 106.

60. For details about this game (often called "Chicken" after a well-known ritual of American juvenile culture), see A. Rapoport, *Two-Person Game Theory* (Ann Arbor: University of Michigan Press, 1966), 140 ff.

61. Luce and Raiffa, *Games and Decisions* 107.

62. I am indebted to Ulf Torgersen for this observation. See also A. Stinchcombe, *Constructing Social Theories* (New York: Harcourt, Brace and World, 1968), 157, for a discussion and some further references.

63. Olson, *Logic of Collective Action* 29–30.

64. For the general theory of supergames, see M. Taylor, *Anarchy and Cooperation* (New York: Wiley, 1976). For applications to competition and cooperation among firms, see M. Friedman, *Oligopoly and the Theory of Games* (Amsterdam: North-Holland, 1977).

65. "New Deal, Old Game: Competition and Collective Action among American Capitalists, 1925–1934" (unpublished manuscript, University of Chicago, Department of Political Science, 1979).

66. "The Labor Theory of Value," *Marxist Perspectives* 3 (1978): 70–101.

67. A. Coddington, *Theories of the Bargaining Process* (London: Allen and Unwin, 1968), 58 ff.

68. For surveys, see ibid., and the articles collected in *Bargaining*, edited by O. Young (Urbana: University of Illinois Press, 1975).

69. For a full explanation, see Harsanyi, *Rational Behavior*.

70. The rewards are measured in cardinal utilities, which are constructed from the individual's preferences over alternatives, some of which may be lotteries (Luce and Raiffa, *Games and Decisions*, chap. 2). This lends great importance to the attitude toward risk-taking; and typically the rich will be less risk-averse than the poor.

71. Perhaps Marx had something like this in mind when he wrote that, in some forms of international trade, the "richer country exploits the poorer one, even where the latter gains by the exchange" (*Theories of Surplus-Value*, vol. 3, 106).

72. This requirement could be defended either on utilitarian grounds, because the poor generally will get more utility out of a given increase in income, or on the grounds of the "difference principle" (J. Rawls, *A Theory of Justice* [Cambridge, Mass.: Harvard University Press, 1971]), stating that one should maximize the welfare of the least-advantaged.

73. "Relative loss" means the difference between demand and offer, divided by the demand. "Concession" means making a new demand that gives one's opponent the smallest relative loss.

74. K. Lancaster, "The Dynamic Inefficiency of Capitalism," *Journal of Political Economy* 81 (1973): 1092–1109. Further developments of the model include M. Hoel, "Distribution and Growth as a Differential Game between Workers and Capitalists," *International Economic Review* 19 (1978): 335–50; and, importantly, A. Przeworski and M. Wallerstein, "The Structure of Class Conflict in Democratic Capitalist Societies," *American Political Science Review* 76 (1982): 215–38.

75. These limits are required for the game to have a solution, but they may be arbitrarily close to = and 100% respectively, and hence do not restrict the model in any substantial manner.

76. "Rules Rather than Discretion: The Inconsistency of Optimal Plans," *Journal of Political Economy* 85 (1977): 473–92.

77. L. Kolakowski (*Main Currents of Marxism* [Oxford, Eng.: Oxford University Press, 1978], 3 vols., vol. 1, 333) defines exploitation in terms of the "exclusive powers of decision held by the capitalist. Similarly, E. O. Wright in various works (e.g., *Class Structure and Income Determination* [New York: Academic Press, 1979], 14 ff.) adds authority to surplus extraction as a component of exploitation and class. John Roemer (*A*

78. It should be observed at this point that even the Marxists who accept that authority relations are a component of class restrict themselves to intrafirm relations of command and subordination, whereas Dahrendorf extends the notion to include authority relations in any organization.

79. Roemer also argues, more ambitiously, that exploitation can be *defined* in terms of hypothetical alternatives. In my "Roemer vs. Roemer: A Comment on New Directions in the Marxian Theory of Exploitation and Class," *Politics and Society* 11 (1982): 363–73, I argue that this proposal has counterintuitive consequences. It remains true that important cases of exploitation can be (nondefinitionally) characterized in the way he proposes.

80. "Ownership and the Production Function," *Quarterly Journal of Economics* 80 (1967): 88–111.

Part II
Forms of organization

5
Economic theories of organization

CHARLES PERROW

Until the last ten years or so the relationship between economics and organizational analysis has been a quite distant one. Most economic theorists treated the organization as an entrepreneur in a field of entrepreneurs, and saw little need to inquire into the nature of the organization itself. On the other hand, organizational analysts paid relatively little attention to the interaction of organizations, even less to industry characteristics, and virtually none to the role of organizations in the economy as a whole. The organization responded to an environment, and its response was the focus of interest, not the environment. This has changed. Two closely related bodies of theory in economics – agency theory and transaction-cost analysis – have taken the internal operation of the firm as problematical and have investigated it. Agency theory has focused upon the problem the "principal" has in controlling the employee ("agent"), and transaction-cost analysis has focused upon the advantages of eliminating market contracts by incorporating suppliers and distributers into one's own firm – the replacement of the market by hierarchy. Organizational analysts, on the other hand, have begun to develop the notion of the environment in a variety of ways, some of which involve networks of organizations; others take account of industry characteristics (but as yet none has studied the dynamics of the economy as a whole).

These ventures by the two disciplines, if I may speak of organizational analysis as a discipline, are, of course, to be welcomed for a variety of obvious reasons. The two disciplines have much to learn from each other. A less obvious reason for welcoming the developments will concern me in this article, and it is a somewhat perverse one. I find the formulations regarding human behavior and organizations by the economists to be not only wrong but dangerous. However, I find my own field of organizational analysis, and sociology in general, to be insuffi-

121

ciently developed to convincingly demonstrate the full measure of error. Therein resides the danger. But it is also an opportunity.

We are forced to develop an adequate answer to the characterization of human behavior as preeminently the self-interested maximization of utilities, and forced to make a discriminating analysis of the rise of large corporations. The first, self-interested behavior, has been a controversial view of human nature since the first marginalist doctrines two centuries ago, and our contribution to that intractable debate will be largely to try to keep alive alternative notions of human nature. The second, the rise of giant bureaucracies, is of more recent origin; and we have a chance of making a somewhat larger contribution there. I will start with agency theory, but spend most of this essay on transaction-cost analysis.

Agency theory

Agency theory refers to a contract in which one party is designated as the principal, and the other, the agent. The agent contracts to carry out certain activities for the principal, and the principal contracts to reward the agent accordingly.[1] Three assumptions are at the core of agency theory. The first is the one common to most economists: individuals maximize their own self-interest. The second is more specific to agency theory: social life is a series of contracts, or exchanges, governed by competitive self-interest. The third applies to internal organizational analysis: monitoring contracts is costly and somewhat ineffective, especially in organizations, thus encouraging self-interested behavior, shirking, and especially opportunism with guile, or to put it more simply – cheating. Contracts *will* be violated because of self-interest, and *can* be violated because of the costs and ineffectiveness of surveillance. The theory then attempts to build models, almost always without empirical data, regarding the most effective ways to write and monitor contracts to minimize their violations.

If these assumptions sound extreme, note that they are widely shared. We invoke them when we blame unpleasant results on others, rather than ourselves or the situation. We say "he was supposed to do that and didn't," or "she should have known," or "he works for me and I told him not to do that." All assume either the difficulty of controlling subordinates or agents, or the opportunism of subordinates, or both when dealing with team efforts. We all invoke agency theory. We can all point to people who did not do their share and thus got more rewards than they deserved – the "free-rider" problem celebrated by Mancur Olsen.[2]

For agency theorists, even if the deception that occurs is unintended, without guile, and merely due to the slippage that occurs in social life, such as in missed signals, forgetfulness, or chance serendipity, the rational individual will turn it to his or her self-interest if that is possible. There is no occasion when behavior will intendedly be other-regarding, rather than self-regarding, on any predictable basis or to any significant degree. Presumably there might be behavior that is neither self- or other-regarding, but is neutral in its consequences, but this is never discussed and would probably be regarded as unmotivated or even non-rational behavior. Agency theory, along with transaction-cost analysis, assumes that "human nature as we know it," as Oliver Williamson puts it, is prone to opportunism with guile.

This condition accounts for capitalism. Alchian and Demsetz give us the scenario.[3] Four people performing a cooperative task, say loading trucks, find that the risk of any one of them slacking is such that they hire a fifth to monitor their work. The monitor has to have the power to hire and fire, thus we have a manager. She also appropriates a part of the income of the group, in the form of a salary. In order to motivate her to do the difficult job of watching the others work, she also gets any residual income or profit left over after paying the wages and her salary. (Measuring the work of others and watching them is universally regarded by these theorists as requiring more rewards than doing the work itself.) If she or the team decide to purchase equipment to increase their performance, say a fork-lift truck, they go to the money lenders. The level of trust being what it is, the money lenders set up a monitor to monitor the manager so as to assure them that their investment is protected. *They* then appropriate the residual income or profit. We now have stockholders, a board of directors, a CEO, management, workers, and capital equipment – in short, capitalism. It all started because four workers could not trust one another.

At least one heroic assumption is at work in agency theory: that human nature as we know it is ruled only or primarily by self-interest. Combined with the problems and costs of monitoring it means that people, being prone to cheating, will get the chance to do so. But human nature as I know it signifies primarily a *lack of instinctual responses*, compared to nonhuman nature, and this means humans are highly adaptive (as well as inventive and variable and so on). If so, the setting in which interactions or contracts occur is the most important thing to consider in explaining behavior. Some settings, or organizational structures, as I shall argue shortly, will promote self-interested behavior; others will promote other-regarding behavior; and still others will be neutral. Furthermore, I follow Herbert Simon[4] and assume that rationality is bounded, or limited. If so, even where self-interest is encouraged by the context of behavior, humans (1) do not have clear utilities to maximize; (2) do not have much of the information needed to maximize utilities; and (3) do not know of cause-effect relations regarding maximization. Agency theorists do not model the context of behavior, nor the slippage occasioned by limited rationality, even though both of these should account for most of any observed variance in behavior.

A second problem is less with the model than its applications, though I believe the model builders nearly intend a biased application. When dealing with principal-agent relationships within organizations, they almost invariably assume that it is the agent that is opportunistic, even to the point of cheating, rather than the principal. This may stem from unrealistic assumptions about an unimpacted (i.e., highly fluid) market for labor: the assumption that there is no authority relationship within firms, but only a series of contracts, because if the principal cheats, the agent is free to go elsewhere. Because agents (employees) generally don't go elsewhere, theorists assume any contract violations must be on their part rather than the principal's part. Were an authority relationship admitted (even the simple one that suggests the boss is free to fire employees, and maintain the firm by hiring others, while employees are not free to fire the boss and maintain the firm[5]), then the unequal power of the parties to the contract would have to be admitted. Once unequal power is entertained, it becomes obvious that, given self-interested behavior, the boss has more occasions for cheating on employees than the reverse. He may exploit them, either by breaking the contract, or not including in the contract matters that violate their self-interest.

This focus upon agent opportunism to the exclusion of principal opportunism extends to the agency theory work on "adverse selection" – hiring a poorly qualified agent. The principal has a problem, they say: the agent may misrepresent her "type," that is, her training, skills, and character, when seeking employment. Elaborate models deal with this form of cheating.[6] But I could find no model in the literature that considered that the principal also has a "type" and might misrepresent it to the prospective agent, e.g., in terms of hazardous working conditions, production pressures, adequacy of equipment, fairness of supervision, advancement possibilities, amount of compulsory overtime, etc. Agency theorists might argue that the principal who misrepresents himself will suffer a loss of reputation and thus not get agents, but prospective agents probably cannot determine the reputation accurately beforehand, will bear the costs of seeking a new job and perhaps relocation, and may simply find that "elsewhere" also exploits. The employment relationship is an asymmetrical one; this is neglected by the theory, just as is the possibility that the principal's type may be misrepresented. Agency theory appears to be ideologically incapable of keeping an eye on both ends of the contract, and incapable of noting any permanent asymmetry of resources and power stemming from the context.

Why, then, bother with it? First, because it, along with transaction-cost economics, is experiencing an amazing growth in popularity among organizational theorists,[7] possibly because it is so simple as to promise to cut through the complexities most of us are entangled in, and because it touches upon something we all like to do: blame our fellow workers or particularly our subordinates for failures that may well be a result of the situation or even our own behavior. It is also in keeping with a recent presidential campaign theme of self-interest: are *you* better off today, not your community, city or nation, and not the less fortunate members of the community, city, or nation, and not the prospects for the next generation – just you. There appears to be a basic cultural shift over the last two hundred or so years toward the celebration of self-interest.

The second reason we should bother with it is that it highlights the varying degree to which the major organizational theories recognize the asymmetry of power in organizations. Briefly, agency theory comes close to zero in this respect; in fact, I suspect it may be designed to distract us from the existence of power differences. Human-relations theory does better; it recognizes the responsibility of masters to use their power wisely and humanely.[8] As such, it recognizes, to at least a limited extent, that behavior is structurally determined and leaders are responsible for that structure. Classical bureaucratic theory pursues power and structure further, finding that power operates through such structural devices as specialization, formalization, centralization, and hierarchy. It assumes that, while shirking and deceptive representation of one's type will be problems, employment status is evidence that employees accept the necessity of unequal power relations, and can do little, other than shirk, to maximize their utilities at the expense of owners. The major problems of organization with both the human relations and bureaucratic model are not shirking by agents, but establishing routines, innovation when needed, and the coordination of the output of diverse units. Under the conditions of wage dependency and profit maximization, employee utilities are likely to be limited to continual employment, interesting work, opportunity to use and develop skills, safe work, some autonomy, and some influence in decisions that affect the efficiency of the organization.

The neo-Weberian model goes even further in recognizing power differences and undercutting agency theory. It makes a central point of the fact that groups legitimately vie for power, as in the contest of sales and production; they seek to use the organization for their own ends, but these are rarely maximizing leisure or even income; because of bounded rationality one's interests are problematical at best, and the role of premise-setting and unobtrusive controls in capitalist societies overrides the simple determination of interest. Thus, agency theory, by anchoring extreme assumptions about power and preferences, gives us a scale for judging theories.

But the best reason to pay attention to agency theory is that it forces us to consider the conditions under which organizations may promote competitive self-interested behavior, and when they will promote other-regarding behavior. I will consider only short-run consequences of behavior where some immediate self-interest such as status, power, or income appears to be sacrificed in order to either not harm another, or to actually help another. In the world of organizations competitive self-regarding behavior appears to be favored by such conditions as the following:

1. *Self-interested behavior is favored when continuing interactions are minimized.* Some examples: a highly fluid ("unimpacted") labor market where job seekers are not constrained by personal or family ties to friends and the community when they seek work locations; "spot contracting" in a labor market as with migrant workers, temporary help, high turnover fast-food franchises, all of which maximize free movement of labor; heavy emphasis upon individual promotions or individual, rather than group, job rotations; rewarding loyalty to the firm rather than more proximate groups such as your own group and the other groups it interacts with.

2. *Self-interested behavior is favored where storage of rewards and surpluses by individuals is encouraged.* The tax structure favors individual rather than group rewards; organizational hierarchy promotes it, steep salary structures reinforce it; a stable class system (minimal redistribution of wealth) provides the context for it.

3. *Self-interested behavior is favored where the measurement of individual effort or contribution is encouraged.* This is done through personnel evaluations, promotions, piece rates, and the celebration of leadership; it is a continuing legacy of nineteenth-century individualism, celebrating individual rather than cooperative effort.

4. *Self-interested behavior is favored where we minimize interdependent effort through design of work flow and equipment.* Work flow and equipment can minimize cooperative effort and responsibility by breaking up tasks and favoring assembly lines; precise contractual relationships promote this; so does the presumption that shirking is potentially rampant and that installing surveillance systems thwarts it.

5. *Self-interested behavior is favored where there is a preference for leadership stability and generalized authority.* This occurs when leaders are held to be all-competent and the position held continuously. Instead, we

could alternate leadership tasks according to the skills of the individuals, thus avoiding stable patterns of dependency in subordinates and self-fulfilling assumptions of expertise in leaders. This is possibly a legacy of individualism and private ownership rights.

6. *Self-interested behavior is favored where tall hierarchies are favored.* These are based upon unequal rewards and notions that coordination must be imperatively achieved.

It might be argued that I have just described capitalist organizations in the United States, and thus agency theory is appropriate. There are several responses. First, while capitalist organizations do encourage self-interested behavior, this does not mean that human nature is self-interested; it may be the situation or context, that is, the organizational structures fostered by capitalism, that encourages it. The counterargument then would be that public organizations also have these characteristics, and even most organizations in the so-called socialist states. I would still resist the agency-theory formulation on the grounds that once what I call "factory bureaucracy" (specialization, formalization, centralization, and hierarchy) is made possible by creating a wage-dependent population, only extraordinary resistance to economic and political elites will prevent factory bureaucracy from spreading to noneconomic organizations and to other nations. Next I would note that even in factory bureaucracy the overwhelming preponderance of behavior is cooperative and "neutral-regarding," and some is even other-regarding. Many have argued that social life would be impossible without other-regarding and neutral forms of behavior.

Finally, I would argue that the task is to create structures that minimize self-regarding behavior, and there is evidence that organizations vary considerably in this respect. Indeed, there are some recognized firms which appear to minimize self-interested behavior. Joyce Rothschilde-Whitt describes many in her work, though they are small and unstable; Rosabeth Kanter and others argue that large ones can be designed in this way; Japanese firms, while far from ideal in many respects, do minimize some of the six characteristics that encourage self-interested behavior. It may be that some small, innovative, high-technology firms require some to be successful; and Scandinavian societies, in particular Sweden, have successfully developed some alternative structures, and in a shorter period than it took most Western countries to develop capitalist structures.[9]

Agency theory, then, forces us to recognize the extent to which we are all agency theorists in our worse moments, blaming others when the structure or ourselves should be blamed; forces us to examine the structures that evoke different kinds of behavior; reminds us that, easy as it is to say so, human behavior is not rooted in some vague notion of "human nature as we find it," but depends upon the contexts that we create. Each generation of organizational analysts should be reminded of these key points, and be forced to continually explore them. For this, we might be grateful for agency theory, despite its very conservative political bias.

Transaction-cost economics

Transaction-cost economics (TCE), largely the creation of economist Oliver Williamson following early work of John Commons and Ronald Coase, is less politically conservative than agency theory.[10] In contrast to most agency theory, it recognizes authority relations, denies that it is useful to consider the organization as nothing more than a series of contracts between parties, and recognizes some of the societal problems associated with giant corporations. It is also far more attentive to bounded rationality and sociological and structural variables. It has received much acclaim in the organizational literature, and indeed it claims to supplant most existing organizational theories. Like agency theory, however, it is based upon a self-interest model of human behavior, and is relentlessly and explicitly an efficiency argument. Its appearance should prompt organization theorists, especially left-leaning ones, into some vigorous work; and for this reason we should welcome it.

The theory raises many issues that need discussion by organizational analysts. I will make the following arguments: we need a better formulation of some of our fuzzy notions of trust, and it provides one; we need more awareness of the economic concepts regarding industries and market characteristics, and TCE provides this; we have not explored issues of mergers sufficiently, such as the effect upon complexity and tight coupling, and a critique of TCE will encourage this; discussion of market concentration, monopoly power, and the growth of huge organizations needs to include standard economic concepts more than has been the practice; TCE concepts provide a way of bridging inter- and intra-organizational analysis more than has been our practice; the issue of markets versus hierarchies is falsely posed by this theory and we can use this opportunity to reconceptualize an important area of interorganizational analysis; and, perhaps most important, Williamson does not ask simply why there are so many big firms, but asks where will big firms fail to appear, a question even left-leaning organizational theorists have failed to ask. Thus, though I think TCE is a wrong theory, it forces us to address questions we have tended to neglect or improperly pose. This part of my essay will range widely and necessarily briefly over these several issues; each could be an essay in its own right. I hope it will stimulate more searching essays by others.

The theory

Transaction-cost economics is an efficiency argument for the present state of affairs, as most mainstream economic theories are, arguing that the appearance of giant organizations in some industries represents the most efficient way of producing goods for an industrial society. Distortions are acknowledged, and that the government should get out of this or that, but in general capitalism and the free market produce the most efficient economic system, apparently despite the fact that the market is supplanted by hierarchies. Williamson is explicit regarding efficiency, by which he means the efficiency of organizational forms, not the efficiency of specific practices or machines or sales techniques or transportation devices, though the efficiently run organization will seek out these other operating efficiencies. Discussing the shift from many organizations to a few large ones over the century, he says, "I argue that efficiency is the main and only systematic factor responsible for the organizational changes that have occurred."[11]

There are four components in his theory: uncertainty, small-numbers bargaining, bounded rationality, and opportunism. Bounded rationality and opportunism are ever present, but will only result in large firms where there is uncertainty and small-numbers bargaining.

Uncertainty refers to changes in the environment that the owner cannot foresee or control; it provides the dynamic element that makes equilibrium of the market unstable.

Small-numbers bargaining means that once a long-term contract has been signed, with suppliers or workers or customers, the normal market situation is disturbed. The parties to the contract have privileged positions because they have more experience with the other party, and more specialized resources to serve it, than those in the market that sought but did not get the contract.

For example, if you find that your supplier's quality is slipping, you may be reluctant to break the contract and find another because you are set up to deal with that supplier; you have made an investment in routines and have experience with that firm's supplies and procedures and idiosyncrasies, and that investment will be lost. Or, within the firm, after employees have worked for you for awhile, they gain experience and skills; and, if they threaten to quit or strike, you cannot simply hire others that will immediately be as productive.

A related concept is *asset specificity*. If, by working for a firm at a specialized job, one develops specific skills that job seekers outside the organization don't have, one has specific assets, and this gives one some bargaining power. The employer has to think twice about firing the person, or about refusing a demand for a raise. While I think this concept is useful, the bilateral nature of exchange renders it opaque: because these assets are specific to this firm, it gives the boss some power, too – the employee's specific skills will give him or her no bargaining advantage over another potential employer because the skills are specific to this one organization. This is rarely acknowledged by Williamson. A similar bilateral relationship occurs between supplier and customer, which Williamson does acknowledge.

Bounded rationality creates a problem because of *opportunism*. Lacking perfect information about suppliers or workers allows them to behave opportunistically. You cannot judge the claim of the supplier that labor problems or raw-material problems delay deliveries, and you cannot costlessly turn to another supplier. Similarly, the customer may misrepresent his problems to the supplier, and fail to honor the contract. But an alternative customer is not always available. Such situations are called "market failures"; uncertainty about labor or supplies or demand, when combined with small-numbers bargaining, and the lack of adequate information and the chance of opportunism all disrupt the normal market relationships. In the normal, neoclassical market, a large number of suppliers and producers bargain daily over prices. The market assures the lowest possible prices; adjusts to changes in demand immediately, and discourages opportunism because opportunists will not find people to trade with the next day. Instead, we find uncertainty, small numbers, bounded rationality, and opportunism, that is, a failure to achieve the classical market.

Well, that's serious. (It is also the rule in our economy; the markets of neoclassical theory are few in number and small in impact.) What is to be done? Williamson and capitalists have the solution: vertical integration. One can integrate forward by buying out the person one sells to (or setting up one's own distribution services) or integrate backward by buying out one's supplier (or building one's own source of supply). If the supplier is part of your firm, you can control her. It eliminates the leverage she had as one of a handful of suppliers that you had to depend upon. She won't dare lie about labor problems or raw-material problems because you can check the books (controlling opportunism). And you will not have to write all those contracts with her, trying to specify complex future contingencies, and have your people checking to see that all the promises are fulfilled. This way you reduce the costs of transacting business, hence the term transaction-cost economics. There will be other economies, such as economies of scale, though they are not stressed by Williamson, but these economies are likely to be quite small. For Williamson, minimizing transaction costs is the key to efficiency; and it explains concentration of production in large firms better than several competing theories, including Marxist and other power theories, historian Alfred Chandler's theory of coordination and throughput speed, technological arguments, and those that deal with the strategic use of finance.[12]

The development of large firms, so evident in our twentieth-century economic history, does not occur in all areas, however, and the ability to explain why markets will persist in some areas while they disappear in others would indicate the power of his theory. The question has often been asked: Why, if giant firms are more efficient, do we not have just one giant firm? Here the potential payoff of TCE becomes apparent.

Markets, argues Williamson, will continue to exist if spot contracts will do the job efficiently. The market for supplies is cleared each day, so to speak, if transactions are one-shot, so no long-term contacts need to be written. The firm that wishes to buy some furniture asks for bids and selects the lowest, just as a person shops for a television. There is no opportunity for cheating on long-term delivery contracts, no "first-mover advantages" (where the first firm to get the contract has an inside track on all future contracts because of small-numbers bargaining). Markets can also survive if there is little uncertainty in price, volume, production costs, labor relations, and the like, even if the market is not a spot one. Standard supplies (toilet paper, business forms, batteries, picks and shovels) are available from many sources, have clear prices, and the quality is readily judged. Markets will also survive if the costs of entry (starting up a production facility) are low; entrepreneurs will see that existing producers are making a lot of money and so they will come in and thus bring the price down because of competition. The cost of entry will be more likely to be low if the technology is well known. Predictable high-volume demand also reduces uncertainty and favors market transactions instead of vertical integration. Thus, hierarchy replaces markets when there are long-term contracts in an uncertain environment and the barriers to entry are reasonably high because the costs of opportunism are reduced by substituting an authority relationship ("You now work for me") for a contractual one.

The value of the theory

Williamson's work highlights a number of variables that organizational theorists unfortunately neglect. Take the notion of "asset specificity." We are wont to invoke vague terms such as tradition, or trust, when we encounter long-term relationships between firms and suppliers, or firms and customers, or even a supervisor and workers. A good part of that tradition or trust may lie in the bilateral dependency of each of the parties. The supplier is as dependent upon the customer as he is upon her because of asset specificity. The assets of the supplier are highly specific in order to meet the specific demands of the customer, and the customer's products are made more specific or inflexible because of the specificity of the supplier's components. (Note, though, that using this concept with its clear bilateral implications reduces any efficiency difference between markets and hierarchies because relationships in both will tend toward an equilibrium. Because hierarchies have replaced some markets, Williamson must explain the disappearance of bilaterality and the trust it implies on other than efficiency grounds.)

A similar argument can be made regarding the tasks the supervisor wants done, and the skills the workers have developed. Asset specificity, in a sense, demands the continuity that we call tradition, and produces the repeated interactions that we call trust. Locating the source of tradition and trust in an economic relationship need not remove the sociological concern with the social and cultural content of these transactions. One reason trust may appear in bilateral exchanges is that the parties get to know crucial noneconomic aspects of each other and of their interdependency. Political, ethical, and cultural values are exchanged and modified. The economic relationship becomes "embedded" (as Granovetter terms it, in his important essays on economics and sociology)[13] in social and cultural exchanges; and the strictly economic and strictly self-interested nature of the exchange is modified and over-laid. But Williamson reminds us that it cannot be ignored, and economic concepts help us to see it.

The bilateral relationship may not be equal, we should note. Generally, the larger firm has the greatest leverage. If the larger firm is the buyer, its purchasing power allows it to find another source of supply, and probably do it more readily than the supplier can develop another customer. Similarly, the employer would prefer to retain the experienced employee, but can replace her, while she will have more trouble finding another employer, unless unusual skills or an unusual labor market exists. But any analysis of the concepts of trust and tradition had best be aware of Williamson's discussion of small-numbers bargaining and asset specificity.

Nor have organizational theorists paid much attention to the characteristics of market transactions. Distinguishing spot from long-term contracts, many bargainers from small numbers of them, degrees of substitutability of goods or services, and stability and instability of demand, technologies, and so on may not appear to be a signal contribution. In one form or another these ideas are used by many theorists. But

Williamson links them together, makes them explicit, and demands that issues of market concentration, monopoly power, the growth of huge organizations, and the like be addressed with these considerations in mind. In particular, formalizing the argument about transactions allows us to focus on the important question of why hierarchies replace markets.

Furthermore, because the concepts can be applied both to the relations between organizations and to relationships within organizations, we get a fruitful link between the nature of markets (interorganizational relationships) and the nature of firms (intraorganizational relationships). By allowing us to make the link, Williamson also brings into organizational analysis a field that it has neglected – industrial economics, which deals with the characteristics of industries (concentration, size, rates of change, characteristics of customers, and so on), though the literature has left the firms themselves as empty shells. Williamson provides us with some of the most relevant aspects of industrial economics, packaged for organizational theory.

Finally, Williamson restates the problem "Why so many big firms?" as: Why do we get big firms (hierarchies) in some areas and not in others? This is a more interesting and more tractable problem. (The historian Alfred DuPont Chandler also raises it in this form and treats it as the main question a historian of business organizations should answer.[14]) Marxists have an answer of a sort for the first question: the disappearance of small firms and the growth of big ones is the product of the dynamics of capitalism – a ceaseless search for ever more profits, wherein the big fish gobble up the small. But they have no answer for the second question: when will markets (small firms) persist, despite the existence of powerful organizations nearby that seek ever more profits? These are questions that an organizational theory that has finally met the environment should be preoccupied with; we deal with them at the margins of our work, but we have not directly confronted them. Williamson has.

The criticisms

An extended example will illustrate some major criticisms one can make of TCE, and then we will review the criticisms of other scholars. My example is intended to explore a variety of issues regarding the costs of integration; I argue that the costs are born because the advantages are not efficiency, but appropriating profitable businesses and establishing market control. I do not believe that the costs of vertical integration have been systematically assessed in the literature; if not, and if my fictional example rings true, we owe this assessment to the challenge of Williamson's argument. In general, the criticisms of Williamson are likely to enrich the field more than his theory has.

TCE would have us explain why firms are not engaged in only one single function, such as grinding valves, which are sent to another firm that puts them in an engine block that a third has made, and so on. But systems with that much specialization disappeared one or two centuries ago, for the most part. The real question is: Why does a firm that is *already* large, buy up another good sized firm? Why merge *two hierarchies*, rather than why move from a bunch of tiny firms to a few big ones?

Consider this hypothetical account of a firm called Engines, Inc. It has about a thousand employees producing engines for air conditioning systems. It then buys out a firm, Radiators, Inc., with three hundred employees, that supplies radiators for these engines. Engines, reflecting its new acquisition, renames itself the ACE Company (for air conditioning equipment). TCE would have us believe that the costs of long-term contracts between Engines and Radiators were too high, so Engines bought Radiators in 1980. ACE now controls all the people that were owners and employees of Radiators and can reduce opportunism on the part of these people and save on lawyers who write contracts and accountants who monitor them. But is there really a saving?

Prior to 1980, there were two sets of transaction costs: writing and monitoring the contracts between Radiators and Engines, and the costs that each of the firms had in dealing with other parts of its environment. The second costs are not reduced. When Engines buys Radiators out, it must continue to deal with the environment that Radiators had to deal with, for example, buying metal and other supplies, dealing with the government, with labor, the community, and so on. As we shall see, these costs may actually rise because the form of transactions will change somewhat under the new ownership. The transaction costs associated with the Radiators-Engines relationship will certainly change, but I will argue that they are actually likely to rise, rather than fall, as far as Engines is concerned.

If the market for air conditioning equipment declines, the new firm, ACE, cannot simply tell its supplier of radiators that it is canceling its order (with due notice, or even a penalty), or cutting the size of a new one, thus making Radiators suffer all or most of the loss. ACE itself has to absorb the loss of business (fixed capital lying idle, layoffs with unemployment insurance costs, excess managerial staff, and loss of profit-generating activity). The sum total of transaction costs remain; their location is different. (One of the problems with TCE is that the definition of a transaction cost is altogether too flexible for a convincing test of the theory; but shutting down facilities and laying off experienced employees seem to qualify as transaction costs.)

Suppose the opposite happened, and the demand for its product soared. The radiator division within ACE can build new facilities to expand its production no faster than Radiators could (though it might get capital a bit faster if ACE had some lying around); there is no saving here. In fact, there might be a loss. Radiators might have added facilities to meet the new demand, calculating that if the rise in demand by Engines turned out to be temporary, they still might be able to sell their excess to other engine companies. But ACE might find it awkward to become a supplier to its own competitors (though it happens regularly in a few industries such as electronics); and the competitors would probably prefer to buy from suppliers they can control rather than from a competitor. Thus ACE is less likely to risk an expansion of facilities. Some flexibility is lost in the acquisition.

Well, what about opportunism? Ms. Radoe, once the head of Radiators, is now the general manager of the Radiator division of ACE. According to TCE, she can now be watched much more carefully (ACE has the information on her behavior); and any disputes between her and, say, the chief operating officer, Mr. Enginee (the former head of Engines who now oversees the radiator and engines divisions) can be settled "by fiat," that is, a direct order. Before, there were transaction costs: contract writing, bargaining, legal actions, and so on. If Mr. Enginee needs support for disciplining Ms. Radoe if fiat is resisted, he can turn to the chief executive officer of ACE, Mr. Banke, Mr. Banke was an officer of the bank that provided the loan for buying up the radiator company. As a condition of that loan, he was made CEO of the company. (He need not know anything about air conditioning, but he must know about transaction costs, according to TCE, because these efficiencies count the most. He does, as a finance man and banker.)

But what is Ms. Radoe likely to be doing in her new position? Here we will use the assumptions about opportunism and competitive self-interest that Williamson shares with agency theory. We will assume that the firm is structured, as most are, to encourage competitive self-interest. When Ms. Radoe headed up Radiators she worked extremely hard because she owned the company and got the profits from it. No motivation to shirk or slack on her part. But at ACE she gets a salary (and perhaps a bonus) rather than direct profits. She has less incentive to work hard, and indeed, more to shirk, or even steal. Reflecting the incentives problem, ACE may develop an elaborate bonus plan based in part on the performance of Ms. Radoe's division and in part on the performance of the firm as a whole, as other companies have done. Such plans have led to fierce controversy over internal pricing decisions within firms – a substantial transaction cost. Is the radiator division being charged more than its share of the overhead, and thus its internal profits are set lower than they would be if it were independent? Robert Eccles details the extensive transaction costs and political problems of internal pricing schemes, necessary once the market no longer exists. He concludes from extensive research that firms perceive the costs of *internal* transactions to be higher than external ones, and did not find TCE useful in understanding the transfer pricing problem.[15]

No doubt, given the emphasis upon opportunism in TCE, Ms. Radoe will also be required to monitor it in her subordinates, just as she did when she owned the firm. But if there is no bonus plan she has less incentive to do so; their slacking or stealing will have a trivial effect upon her income, though it should not become so gross as to invite an inspection from Mr. Enginee or Mr. Banke. If there is a bonus plan, she will take up her superior's time by arguing about internal pricing, as Eccles documents.

Furthermore, Mr. Enginee, who used to watch her intermittently from a distance when she was his supplier, now has to watch her continually as her superior. Her division draws upon the resources of ACE and affects its accounting and personnel practices. Another set of transaction costs have increased. If she allowed rampant opportunism on the part of her employees when she headed up Radiator, it was of no concern to Mr. Enginee. It just meant she got less out of them and thus less profits; perhaps, if she treated them well and they worked hard, she made more profits, though we could have reservations about that. But the price to Mr. Enginee was not affected, so he did not need to bother about it. He was only concerned with the contract, not her whole firm. Now he is held accountable for the whole division; if they slacken, the profits to ACE are reduced. (Setting the radiator division up as a "profit center" is of little help. Contracts must still be written. If it is made maximally independent, with no more interactions than when it was a supplier of radiators to Engines, it may as well have remained a separate firm because there are no transaction-cost savings – with one very important difference: as a separate firm, ACE would not "appropriate its profit stream," as economists put it. That is, the profits now go to ACE, not to Ms. Radoe. We will later count this as possibly the primary motive for acquisitions.)

One can imagine Mr. Enginee going home one night and telling his wife:

What a mistake. I read Oliver Williamson and it looked as if Engines was ripe for savings on transaction costs. You know, he is the one who called Perrow's theory "bankrupt" in that book where Perrow criticized Williamson.[16] Well, we had this small-numbers bargaining situation with big Ms. Radoe, and long-term contracts, uncertainty about product demand, and all the rest including opportunism on her part – she claimed those leaky radiators were the result of poor handling by us and threatened to sue us if we refused to pay. So I decided to buy her out. She was working eighty hours a week and she didn't like her reputation for driving her employees, so she was willing to come to work for us.

But I had to let Mr. Banke come in as CEO in order to get capital for the buyout. Williamson never mentioned that there are large costs in acquiring even small firms. It was profitable, so we could raise the money, and it should increase our profits – Mr. Banke and the stockholders will get them and not Ms. Radoe. But it saddled us with three hundred employees and all kinds of commitments at a time when sales were falling. We are losing money, not her. (Or, "Now that sales are booming it is we that have to pay for the increase in overtime and other special production costs, whereas before she would have had to take less profit on each item because of the contract, at no cost to us.") [TCE neglects to consider all transaction costs. Flexibility in response to changes is reduced.]

"Furthermore," he continues, turning up his custom-built air-conditioner as he gets more heated:

I have had a hell of a time getting their accounting and information-management system to link up with ours. Theirs was fine for their product and volume, while ours doesn't work well for them. But we have to have an integrated financial statement by law and the bankers demand certain kinds of reports, personnel needed to standardize and so on. So I had to hire more accountants, and Ms. Radoe complains that she can't watch performances and budgets as closely now. [Internal coordinating costs rise when different operations must be combined. Accounting and surveillance systems must be standardized while variable, tailor-made systems would be more effective: there are costs to decentralizing large, complex systems that do not appear in smaller, simpler ones.]

It's even worse. In 1979, before we bought them, I used to call up two or three other radiator firms and find out what they were charging for various models, and she knew it, so she kept her prices in line. Now I don't have a good idea of the costs of our radiators because of internal pricing problems. The accountants say the radiator division is a profit center, but it has to contribute to the firm's overhead and advertising costs, some personnel costs, a lot of staff running back and forth to her city, and we just don't know if the prices they charge us for radiators are fair or not. It would cost us a lot to find out if they are fair. [Internal pricing and internal cost systems are unreliable and expensive; the market provides comparatively cheap and reliable information.]

When Radoe had labor trouble before the merger, we just invoked the contract and it cost her plenty to fight that union, but it was her money (and her temper). We gave a little, of course, we couldn't hang a good supplier, and buying elsewhere was expensive. But all in all it only cost us about 10 percent in profits for the quarter. But now we have to bear the total cost. Our industrial relations manager doesn't know that union. The union is mad because of the strike two years ago. (It's very hard to put a price on the quality of labor relations when you buy a firm. Those agency theorists call it reputation and think that it can be priced like radiators, but it is hard to verify and easy for a firm to exaggerate with a bit of strategic public relations, classy accounting, and mimicry of leading firms in the field. The people at Radiators mislead us and I think we should have paid less because of the labor problem.) Any settlement they get will rev up our other union. And, while Radoe was willing to do battle with the union and take the losses when she headed the firm, now I don't really think she sees the urgency of the labor problem as much as when she owned Radiators. [Costs of acquisitions are poorly estimated and subject to opportunism. Reputation is subject to "isomorphic pressures," that is, firms come to look alike by imitating superficial attributes of leading firms.[17] Unexpected interactions are increased in large systems.]

We are still having problems with leaky radiators and the squabbling and charges between the radiator division and the engine division is worse than before the acquisition because personality clashes now make it more difficult. Not only are there problems with getting information about who is really responsible in the market [Williamson calls the problem "information impactedness"], but it can be worse in your own firm, especially when you try to do two different things, such as making stationary engines *and* radiators; the two processes, and the organizations and the personnel are just different." [Information and control within the firm is subject to political and personality problems that may make it more expensive and less reliable than in the market. Coordination of diverse activities within a firm is expensive; such coordination is not needed in the market.]

I would like to sell the division, but the transaction cost of selling it, after all those of buying it [which Williamson never mentioned], would just be too great. I agree with Perrow. You only should integrate forward or backward when it means you can get more market control, or get your hands on a very profitable piece of property and keep those profits for yourself.[18]

Mrs. Enginee's only comment was: "Dear, you read too many books."

As lighthearted as this vignette may sound, it contains some important points. As Williamson himself notes in one chapter of his book on TCE, there are transaction costs within the firm as well as between firms, and his examples suggest that some are higher in hierarchies than in markets.[19] We should also note that markets can be efficient in establishing prices, whereas firms find "internal pricing" (the allocation of costs to various units) difficult and a highly politicized process. The incentive structure is artificial and politicized in hierarchies as compared to markets. Settling disputes by "fiat" is difficult because of the very things Williamson has made us aware of: asset specificity and small-numbers bargaining *within* the firm. Not all transaction costs are counted in Williamson's argument. Uncertainty affects internalized units as severely as it affects independent firms in the market; fluctuation in demand and supplies, labor problems, problems with competitors, and so on do not disappear, and their resolution may be more difficult in a large firm. Opportunism, to the extent that it is a problem, will accompany the acquired firm because it is a hierarchy itself, and persist within the acquiring firm. Costs that could be externalized and risks that could be borne by the independent firm must be internalized by the acquiring firm, and it may have less flexibility in dealing with them because of long-term commitments and the power of groups with specific assets within the firm. Finally, while my account at several points favors markets over hierarchy, it does not assume a neoclassical perfect market. These rarely exist. Markets tend to be concentrated, rigged, protected, and inefficient. However, I would still give two cheers for markets, and only one for hierarchies, if only because of the power of giant firms to shape our premises to their own ends. (Three cheers for the market socialism described by Branko Horvat.[20]) But in any case the TCE argument is markets versus hierarchies, so the comparison has to be in these terms.

Lying behind my fiction is a more general point that goes beyond the critique of TCE: there is an advantage to decoupled units in a system, and a disadvantage to tight coupling. For instances, Radiators devised accounting and information management systems that were tailored to its specific operations; integrating it with the systems that were good for Engines entailed changes that made the new systems less efficient. The labor relations of Radiators may have been bad from some points of view, but they were not entangled with those of Engines. In the combined firm, ACE, any settlement for the radiator division will have an impact upon the engine division. Engines was buffered from changes in demand by Radiators, which absorbed some of the shock; ACE had to absorb all the shock.

Furthermore, Engines had the people and offices that knew how to deal with large suppliers, and thus could move quickly if demand was up; ACE lost some of that expertise, raising its transaction costs. When demand was down, Radiators suffered, but at least it could look for other customers, lowering its price (and profits). But, as a division of ACE, it will find it more difficult to sell radiators to ACE's competitors. As a division, it probably can't trim its overhead during slack times as well as it could as an independent firm; some of the overhead costs assigned to it in ACE are "lumpy," that is, not divisible; overhead is a difficult thing to cut in large firms during retrenchment because of structural problems; it impacts all divisions regardless of their individual needs.

Finally, it is possible (though hardly inevitable) that Radiators could more easily change its production methods and incorporate new technologies than the division within ACE. As an independent firm, it can do what it wants with production as long as it meets the quality standards of the customer, Engines. As a division, it interfaces with the rest of the organization at many points, and changes may be resisted by people at some of those points who see disadvantages in the changes.

(Were ACE to provide significant research and development services for the division, this might change, but there is evidence to suggest that smaller firms are the more innovative.)

These are arguments for loosely linked components of a system where there are likely to be uncertainties or shocks from the environment or from within. Tightly coupled systems have advantages, certainly; resources can often be more efficiently used, there is less redundancy and waste, and the processes are faster. But these advantages only appear if there is little uncertainty in the system – few "exogenous" shocks (those coming from without the system); few endogenous shocks (those coming from within), plenty of time to recover from shocks, and many different paths to recovery. Most industries do not have these luxuries, and thus loose coupling is likely to be a more efficient system property than tight coupling. Loose coupling is associated with a large number of small units engaged in straightforward bilateral exchanges.[21]

Causes of hierarchy

Efficiency, as realized by the reduction of transaction costs, is thus an uncertain accompaniment of vertical integration, and some flexibility and buffering may be lost in the process. Clearly, in a comparison of two firms in the same industry with the same market power, political ties, etc., the more efficient will prosper and survive; and reducing transaction costs will make some unknown contribution to efficiency. But comparing firms with efficient and inefficient internal operations is not the issue; it is the grounds for vertical and horizontal integration in parts of the economy that must be explained. I will sketch a possible explanation that relies primarily on the gross size of potential profits as realized through three factors: appropriation of "profit streams" of other companies, market control, and government tolerance or support.

A firm requires various "factors of production" such as land, labor, capital, supplies, technologies, and outlets. Advantages in any of these by one firm will lead to its growth relative to its competitors. Growth also requires at least tolerance on the part of the government, though the firm will benefit from a variety of state enabling factors (anti-union legislation, limits on liabilities, tax policies, tariffs) and from state resources (contracts, loans, access to minerals on public property). Many of these will favor a whole industry, allowing it to prosper and grow, and thus provide an incentive for some in the industry to take over other firms. There is little incentive for absorbing enterprises in a low-profit or low-growth industry; while the purchase price will reflect the stock market's evaluation of the industry and the firm, to the extent that future growth possibilities are good and greater market control over pricing and competitive products is possible, firms will reap advantages from attractive industries net of the existing stock price.

For the firm to grow there must be market growth, through the discovery or creation of new markets or expanding existing ones. Because firm growth will be challenged by the growth of other firms, and markets are not infinite, it must keep competitors out entirely, or failing that, limit or reduce the number of competitors. An illustration in the music recording industry provides an example of the *growth* of transaction costs with concentration, and their probable decline with competition.[22] Under oligopolistic conditions prevailing until the 1950s, transaction costs for the major firms were high, not low, because they had to maintain stables of recording stars on long-term contracts, control all outlets, and keep producers and manufacturing units on their payrolls. When intense competition set in because of technological changes that lowered entry costs and allowed numerous small firms to enter the market and expand it (by catering to untapped tastes for unconventional popular music), the transaction costs were probably greatly reduced. Companies established spot contracts with producers, stars, and manufacturers, and let them bear the risks of market uncertainty. But this also meant that the small firms could reap the profits when they were lucky, so the concentration ratio plummeted, and the profits of the majors did not grow as fast as the industry profits. The major firms managed to get control of the market again through various devices, appropriating the industry profit streams, but incurring the increased costs of internalizing risks and market fluctuations, controlling outlets, financing "payola," and standardizing tastes once more.

Another example provides specific evidence of the irrelevancy of narrow efficiency, and a critique of both Williamson and Alfred DuPont Chandler's "visible hand" theory.[23] At the end of the nineteenth century, the iron and steel company of Andrew Carnegie grew phenomenally (and later became the basis of U.S. Steel). An associate of Carnegie, James Howard Bridges, addressed the issue of transaction costs. It is particularly relevant because Carnegie was a fanatic on cost-cutting in production areas and developed sophisticated bookkeeping devices to keep his transaction and production costs low. However, Bridges stated that "it was other considerations than increased efficiency and economy that promoted the first and perfect combination of the Carnegie properties," that is, the growth of his empire. There was no plan to the acquisitions, he flatly states. Instead, as Bridges details, there was the coveting of the high profits of other corporations; maneuvering to get rid of an officer; eliminating a competitor by getting the railroad pool to cut it out of the deals to provide cheap freight, until he could buy the competitor at distress prices (Carnegie was paying dividends of 40 percent at the time); and so on. He found the profits of the ore companies to be very large, so he moved in and through a combination of financial power and threats acquired a good bit of the Mesabi range; and, when the ore boat companies would not reduce their prices, set up his own. His company was immensely rich and powerful. He did not have to worry about transaction costs, and they did not motivate his actions.[24]

Because of the factors of production, it is unwise to consider strategies of market growth and competition only in terms of the firm; other organizations in the environment are crucial. Perhaps of most importance is the source of investment capital, a competitive but still concentrated system of banks, insurance companies, investment houses, and venture capital firms. Holding liquid (readily available) assets, they can provide the means for one firm to buy out competitors (with no efficiency gain), to finance price wars that force out competition, to buy up and destroy competitive goods or services (as the DuPont and General Motors interests were able to destroy much of public city transport in the United States in order to increase the demand for cars, and force the construction, through taxes, of roadways for them to run on),[25] or for firms to move to low-wage areas. Banks, insurance companies, and investment firms can make legal or illegal donations to politicians and political parties here and abroad to influence government actions that will tend to increase concentration in industries and reduce competition. They are not particularly concerned with the efficiency of a loan applicant, but with the opportunities the industry provides and the applicant's ability to exploit opportunities in it.

Firms, generally with resources from the financial community, may also use the patent system and other devices, legal and illegal, to gain control of new technologies and in some cases perhaps restrict their development in order to increase market control, and thus size. (Charges of suppressing innovations are common, but hard to prove. Industrial espionage is widespread and acknowledged, however.) Firms may conspire with suppliers or customers to undercut competitors and drive them out with illegal rebates, espionage, and defamation; concentrated industries can benefit all concerned: suppliers, producers, and distributors. Of course, fraud and force can be used to gain market control or other advantages, and our industrial history right up to the present is replete with examples. Some of our largest firms have fraud and force as active ingredients in their early history, quite possibly contributing significantly to their present dominance. The age of the "robber barons" coincided with the great vertical and horizontal concentrations of industrial power.

As a few firms eliminate the competition and as they integrate vertically, many opportunities for exercising power appear. Prices can be increased, and thus profits. With larger and fewer firms, the cost of entry for potential competitors goes up even though there is the attraction of large profits; new firms must start large. Market domination also slows the rate of innovation, limiting expensive changes and prolonging the returns on expensive capital investments. Fewer producers can also mean more coordinated lobbying activity regarding tariff protection, subsidized research, investment tax credits, and so on; more concentrated economic power with regard to labor; more plant location incentives from local government; and local tax abatements. These are a few of the benefits of size in our economy. Thus, even if the acquired facility is not highly profitable in itself, it may add to the power and thus the profits of the acquiring firm.

I apologize for an account that will be obvious to many readers, but the above account is necessary to raise the more difficult question: Why do we not have a few large firms dominating each industry? Why is steel concentrated but furniture not? Traditionally, factors such as size of capital investment, transportation costs, perishability of goods, and so forth have explained the differences in concentration rates. (A high concentration ratio is equivalent to the degree of hierarchy; technically, hierarchy is a feature of organizational forms, not of industries, but if a decent-sized industry has over, say, 50 percent of its capacity in the hands of four firms, the firms will be very large and in almost all cases hierarchical firms). I would like to put these explanations in a somewhat different light and argue that markets persist where large profits are not available, and in some cases where government policy prevents concentration.

Until recently, when financial considerations prompted the growth of conglomerates – firms that incorporated unrelated activities – most profit-seeking acquisitions were in closely related fields, such as suppliers, competitors, or distributors. The acquiring firm simply had more information about these types of firms, and had experience with the product. There may be economies of scale and benefits from smoother coordination of the enlarged input-throughput-output cycle achieved by acquisitions of closely related firms, but I believe these were secondary motives. Firms with resources will attempt to buy firms that are making good profits; transaction-cost savings or scale economies are of little importance if the profits to be gained are small. The purchase price will reflect the profitability of the firm, of course; profitable firms will have high stock values and cost more. But future profits are to be realized by the market power and political power that comes with increased size; neither unprofitable firms nor unprofitable industries favor the realization of such power.

Of course, the target firm must have sufficient amounts of profits (regardless of the rate of profits) to offset the costs of acquisition and integration. A very large firm will not usually be very interested in a tiny one no matter how profitable, though it does happen. A moderate-sized firm, however, would be interested. Note that the increased profits of the acquiring firm do not mean that the acquisition is more profitably run, or that transaction costs have been saved, only that its profits have been appropriated, that is, assumed by the acquiring firm. (This is important in judging efficiency questions; increased profits or rates of profit after acquisition do not necessarily mean more efficiency; they can mean less competitive pricing and tax advantages.)

There are many highly profitable small firms that are not targets for acquisition. They can exist where there are small or localized markets. For example, the market for specialized luxury goods is small. The market for ethnic goods or foods is generally localized. Some items have small markets because they are unique or idiosyncratic. We speak of such markets as "niches," small crevices in the economy where a few producers can make a lot of money, but the demand is fairly inelastic (it won't grow much because it is so specialized), thus there is no possibility for increased market control (too small a market) or expanding the market. The large firm has no interest in such firms; though the rate of profit in some niches is large, its absolute amount can be small; additionally, its absolute amount must be great enough to offset the substantial costs of integrating small, diverse businesses into a large firm. Acquisitions are not costless; there are transaction costs and organizational redesign costs, as illustrated in the case of the ACE firm.

Industries need not be forever unprofitable or fragmented into niches. In the nineteenth century the modest profits of the hundreds of small flour mills hardly made them a target for acquisitions, because they sold to middlemen and grocers who dumped the flour into a bin labeled "flour." By promoting branded flour through advertising ("as pure as the drifted snow"), market control was achieved and a few large milling companies soon dominated the industry and still do. Much the same thing has happened with restaurants serving limited, quickly prepared meals, though there we must admit the importance of organizational efficiencies, including reduced transaction costs. Small restaurants always existed, and were mom-and-pop operations requiring long hours and generating low profits. As the demand for quick meals out increased, heavily advertised chains moved in and took over the market. By combining the advantages of centralized control with nominal local ownership, they have been able to reap the advantages of low-paid local labor with high turnover, and nominal owners who work the long hours of mom and pop. Centralized buying, heavy advertising, and rigid procedures have no doubt contributed to the profitability of these chains, so in this one case we might say that profits may stem from efficiencies, including centralized control of transaction costs.

In addition to market control and acquiring profitable investments, financial "manipulation" plays a role in mergers. In some cases, the profit rate of acquired subsidiaries will actually decline after the merger, but capital accumulation by investors and officers through financial manipulations, rather than firm profit, is then the goal. This occurred when U.S. Steel was formed by buying up many steel firms. Much money was made through issues of watered stock, making it a very profitable move for the investors, even though operating efficiencies declined. The decline was offset by enormous market power by the new combine. Today, stock manipulation, appropriation of cash flows (milking the profitable acquisition without reinvestment), and buying footholds in new markets figure prominently in merger and acquisition strategies – so prominently that it has become a national scandal. Lower transaction costs presumably play no role in these manipulations; indeed, transaction costs are greatly increased, but fortunes are made anyway.[26]

Though it is somewhat less apparent today because of the weakness of unions, control of labor has also been a motivation for acquisitions, resulting in increased profits though no increase in production efficiency. Acquiring facilities in low-wage areas, acquiring nonunion facilities and using this as a means of attacking the unions in the existing facilities, and absorbing a sufficient proportion of the local work force to be able to control local wage rates are some of the tactics.

The creation of large, market-dominating firms also requires the acquiescence of the federal government. Large firms flourish in the national defense industry because the government favors them for military defense reasons. In fact, such firms are occasionally "bailed out" by awarding handsome government contracts because letting them go under would remove resources the government feels we need. One does not start up a giant aircraft and missile firm easily or quickly. Their "efficiency" is of secondary importance.[27] State banking laws have restricted the centralization of banking in the United States; a change in laws could produce a movement toward "hierarchy" that would not be caused by transaction-cost efficiencies, but rather, market control and the acquisition of profitable properties. Thus, the absence of federal enabling actions will help account for the persistence of markets.

A final concern that can lead to the persistence of at least some degree of market phenomena rather than very high concentration ratios in an industry is a recognition that some degree of loose coupling is efficient. This appears to be the reason why the Big Three automobile companies control, but do not own, their distributors.[28] Though the manufacturing of autos is highly concentrated, the distribution system appears to be a market with many small dealers. But I would count this as a "controlled market"; the manufacturers exercise great control over it. The retail dealers sign long-term contracts that govern the number and type of cars they are *allowed* to receive (a problem when a model turns out to be a "hot" seller and the contract cannot be revised), and the number and type of cars they *must receive* (a problem for disposing of the poor sellers, the "dogs"). These long-term contracts favor the seller. Contracts also cover how much of the cost of failures the dealer must bear under the warranty, how much they can charge for repairs in some cases, how much advertising they must do, and so on. The dealer has discretion only on trade-in prices or preparation prices or other deals that make the final selling price somewhat flexible. Otherwise, the dealer is quite constrained; indeed, the manufacturers may unilaterally and without warning raise the wholesale price to the dealer without posting a higher retail price, thus cutting the dealer's rate of profit. The argument is sometimes made that car dealers represent flexible adaptations to local markets, and thus are more efficient than if owned and controlled outright by the manufacturers. This does not appear to be so; they cannot order just the makes and volume they wish, the prices can be changed, warranty work is tightly regulated by complex contracts written by the manufacturer, and advertising is regulated. They can be flexible and adaptive only in their used-car line.

The effect of this is to require the dealers to absorb the market declines (they have to cut their profit to get rid of the quota of cars they must buy) even though they cannot fully participate in market rises (they cannot get all the hot-selling models they want). Cost of entry is not large for them, but as small businesspeople they do invest their own capital. They are forced to ride out poor times making little or no profit. A few dealerships do very well indeed, but most do not. Yet there are always small businesspeople willing to take the risk. Thus, the manufacturers are buffered from fluctuations in the market for cars and from the yearly gamble on model changes and new models. Because the profitability of dealerships overall is only modest and subject to much uncertainty, it is not worthwhile for the manufacturers to integrate forward into a business over which they already have considerable control.

While we have many dealer firms, we really have a controlled market with many small firms rather than either a hierarchy or a market. Most franchises, as in fast foods, are devices to spread risks and buffer the headquarters from uncertainties. Given the limited occasions for entrepreneurship in our economy for people without wealth or highly unique skills, there are always many who are willing to work very hard for low and risky returns. Though controlled, they have more autonomy than employees of large corporations.

Thus, we would expect to find small firms persisting in areas of the economy that show low overall industry profitability (unless the industry can be restructured to promote branded products or other forms of market control – there is always a drive to do that); where there are idiosyncratic factors despite high profits (local markets, niches); where the market cannot grow despite profitability (inelastic demand); or where government restrictions obtain. Finally, hierarchies are probably self-limiting; at some point, which varies according to technologies, capital requirements, and the shape of the market, firms probably lose control over some of their subsidiaries and the complex, internal interactions, and the ability to respond to external shocks, and lose out. The subsidiaries are sold off, or their efficiency declines to the point where they lose money despite substantial market control and other advantages of size, and someone else moves in. Some minimal efficiency *is* necessary, of course, but transaction costs rarely play a significant role.

This brief sketch of some of the forces contributing to hierarchy and economic concentration in our society stands in marked contrast to economic motives of efficiency in the face of opportunism and transaction costs. It is neither original or novel, but suggests the range of structural variables that are neglected by economic interpretations of organizational behavior.[29]

Beyond markets and hierarchy

The distinction between markets and hierarchies is an old one in economics, though Williamson has given it new life. It is a useful one because it frames questions we might not otherwise ask. But there is increasing evidence that this formulation hides as much as it reveals. Scholars are beginning to note that some markets are quite hierarchically organized, and that some hierarchies have many phenomena associated with markets. This suggests that we might abandon the distinction for some purposes and seek other ways to characterize interdependent behavior within and between organizations, or even to attack, once again, the recalcitrant conceptual problem of boundaries: what is the boundary between a supplier and a customer, the government and a firm, or between two industries. Rapid industrial change since the 1950s has made these questions pressing. I cannot even suggest answers to the problem of characterizing interdependencies and questioning formal definitions of boundaries here, but only conclude by mentioning some of the more interesting research that raises these questions. To a considerable degree, this research and theorizing has either been stimulated by Williamson's work, or at least posed as a critique of it. It is one of the reasons we should be thankful for TCE. The general point is that large firms may be so large as to operate like markets, and markets appear to be hierarchically, diagonally and horizontally so organized as to make the notion of independent, autonomous price givers and takers questionable. These "markets" may be governed by forces that most economists would not recognize as plausible.

A striking piece by Ronald Dore, a British sociologist familiar with Japanese history and industry, argues that Japanese industry is more efficient, overall, because the contracting involves a significant degree of goodwill, give-and-take, long-term horizons, and in general, an avoidance of opportunism. The classical market of economists is only efficient in allocating goods (if that). Citing the work of renegade economist Harvey Liebenstein for support, Dore argues that there are a number of efficiencies other than allocating goods that are more important; and they are realized by trust, noncompetitive relations, and mutual assistance in time of need. These other efficiencies include rapid spread of innovation; shared information on changing market situations and consumer choices; aggressive search for new uses of labor and capital if old markets decline; flexibility in task assignments; and the disaggregation of industry when desirable (for example, he cites the move from hierarchy to small firms in the textile industry in Japan). Finally, he questions whether this is necessarily a product of Japanese culture; much more cut-throat, self-interested practices prevailed *in Japan* during the 1920s and again immediately after World War II. He also finds evidence for goodwill and suspension of self-interest in the United States and England, especially in industries or in firms noted for their emphasis upon quality, rather than quantity. There is a mine of research projects in this attractive essay.[30]

Arthur Stinchcombe considers several industries such as defense contracting, large civil engineering firms, and franchise networks, noting how their relations with their customers tend to be hierarchically organized, even though these would seem to be examples of markets.[31] In defense contracting, the Department of Defense is very intimate with the contractors, putting inspectors and accountants in their firms, much as a multidivisional corporation puts inspectors and accountants into each of its divisions. This is true of consumer-goods industries too. Chevrolet treats its supposedly independent suppliers almost as profit centers and risk bearers, controlling much of what they do. On the other hand, hierarchies develop profit centers and divisions that bargain with each other and the main office in a market-like arrangement, encountering the large costs of simulating a market with "shadow prices" and numerous complex accounting practices that simulate a market relationship.

Harrison White argues, in a suggestive paper that blurs the distinction between markets and hierarchy, that the principal-agent model is misleading. He describes the principal-agent relationship as a reflexive one that oscillates, dissolves, and is born again, making it difficult and arbitrary to designate who is agent and who is principal. Ranging from the ancient Roman empire to high-technology industries, it is an effective though not very explicit criticism of TCE.[32] More generally, I think the interdependencies among economic units and among principals and agents should be analyzed in terms of such contextual influences that I argued will influence the degree of self-regarding and other-regarding behavior that is encouraged – such contexts as the length and durability of relationships, the distribution or centralized storage of surpluses, calculation of group efforts, rotation of authority, and extent of surveillance.

Sociologists and other organizational theorists are positioned to explore these problems because they embrace a more system-wide viewpoint than economists, with attendant developments in network theory, evolutionary models, and attention to the environment in general. Their work is not disabled by assumptions of rational or primarily self-interested behavior, but looks at the contexts that call out rational, non-rational, self-regarding, and other-regarding behavior. This broader inquiry is in part occasioned by the challenge that economists have presented by their foray into the world of organizations, a challenge that resembles the theme of the novel and movie *The Invasion of the Body-Snatchers*, where human forms are retained but all that we value about human behavior – its spontaneity, unpredictability, selflessness, plurality of values, reciprocal influence, and resentment of domination – has disappeared.

Acknowledgment

This article draws heavily on Chapter 7 of the third edition of my book *Complex Organizations: A Critical Essay* (New York: Random House, 1986), where the issues are discussed at somewhat greater length.

Notes

1. My primary sources for agency theory are Armen A. Alchian and Harold Demsetz, "Production, Information Cost, and Economic Organization," *American Economic Review* (1972): 777–95; Eugene F. Fama, "Agency Problems and the Theory of the Firm," *Journal of Political Economy* 88 (1980): 288–305; Eugene Fama and Michael Jensen, "Separation of Ownership and Control," *Journal of Law and Economics* 26 (June 1983): 301–25; and Michael Jensen and William Meckling, "Theory of the Firm: Managerial Behavior, Agency Costs, and Ownership Structure," *Journal of Financial Economics* 3 (Oct. 1976): 305–60. The best exposition of the theory I have seen is by political scientist Terry Moe, "The New Economics of Organization," *American Journal of Political Science* 28, no. 4 (Nov. 1984): 739–77.

2. Mancur Olson Jr., *The Logic of Collective Action*, rev. ed. (New York: Schocken Books, 1971).

3. Alcian and Demsetz, "Production." I have elaborated their example.

4. James March and Herbert Simon, *Organizations*, (New York: Wiley, 1958). I have discussed bounded rationality and its link to domination in Charles Perrow, *Complex Organizations: A Critical Essay*, 3d ed. (New York: Random House, 1986), chap. 4.

5. See the review in Terry Moe, "The New Economics."

6. Louis Putterman "On Some Recent Explanations of Why Capital Hires Labor," *Economic Inquiry* 33 (Apr. 1984): 171–87.

7. For the popularity of agency theory, see Moe, "The New Economics;" for the popularity of closely related transaction-cost economics see William Ouchi, "Markets, Bureaucracies, and Clans," *Administrative Science Quarterly* 25 (Mar. 1980): 129–41. Citations to both theories are mounting in the journals, such as *Administrative Science Quarterly*, and books discussing them are appearing, e.g., Arthur Francis, Jeremy Turk, and Paul Willman, eds., *Power, Efficiency and Institutions* (London: Heinemann, 1983).

8. For a discussion of human relations, bureaucratic, and neo-Weberian theories, see chaps. 1, 3, and 4 of Perrow, *Complex Organizations*.

9. Joyce Rothschild-Whitt, "The Collectivist Organization: An Alternative to Rational Bureaucratic Models," *American Sociological Review* 44 (1979): 509–27; Rosabeth Kanter, *The Change Masters* (New York: Simon and Schuster, 1983); Branko Horvat, *The Political Economy of Socialism* (Armonk, N.Y.: M. E. Sharpe, 1982).

10. The basic works are Oliver Williamson, *Markets and Hierarchies: Analysis and Antitrust Implications* (New York: The Free Press, 1975) and *The Economic Institutions of Capitalism* (New York: The Free Press, 1985). The latter incorporates more organizational and sociological variables, and attacks a wide range of problems from the markets and hierarchies viewpoint.

11. Oliver Williamson, "Organizational Innovation: The Transaction-cost Approach," in J. Ronen, ed., *Entrepreneurship*, (Lexington, Mass.: Heath Lexington, 1983), 101–34. Quote from 125.

12. Ibid., 125.

13. Mark Granovetter, "Economic Action and Social Structure" and "Labor Mobility, Internal Markets and Job Matching: A Comparison of the Sociological and Economic Approaches," both unpublished manuscripts, (Department of Sociology, State University of New York at Stony Brook, n.d.). The first was published in a shorter version that suffers from strict copy-editing in *American Journal of Sociology* (Nov. 1985): 481–510.

14. Alfred D. Chandler, *The Visible Hand: The Managerial Revolution in American Business* (Cambridge, Mass.: Harvard University Press, 1977).

15. Robert G. Eccles, "Control with Fairness in Transfer Pricing," *Harvard Business Review* (Nov.-Dec. 1983): 149–61, and "Transfer Pricing as a Problem of Agency," unpublished manuscript, (Harvard Business School, Feb. 1984), and *The Transfer Pricing Problem: A Theory for Practice*, (Boston: Lexington Books, 1984).

16. Oliver Williamson and William Ouchi, "A Rejoinder," in Andrew Van de Ven and William Joyce, eds., *Perspectives on Organization Design and Behavior* (New York: Wiley Interscience, 1981), 390.

17. Paul J. DiMaggio and Walter W. Powell, "The Iron Cage Revisited: Institutional Isomorphism and Collective Rationality in Organizational Fields," *American Sociological Review* 48 (1983): 147–60.

18. Charles Perrow, "Markets, Hierarchies, and Hegemony: A Critique of Chandler and Williamson," in Van de Ven and Joyce, *Perspectives*, 371–86, 403–04.

19. Williamson, *Markets and Hierarchies*, chap. 7. In *The Economic Institutions of Capitalism* he emphasizes this even more. Because transaction costs have not been operationalized, which would make measurement possible, the fundamental issue of whether they are higher between firms or higher within them will probably never be settled. See my comments on this issue in "Markets, Hierarchies, and Hegemony: A Critique of Chandler and Williamson," in Van de Ven and Joyce, *Perspectives*, 371–86.

20. Horvat, *Political Economy.*

21. Charles Perrow, *Normal Accidents: Living with High Risk Technologies* (New York: Basic Books, 1984), chaps. 3, 9.

22. Perrow, *Complex Organizations*, chap. 6.

23. See the discussion in Perrow, "Markets, Hierarchies, and Hegemony" in Van de Ven and Joyce, *Perspectives.*

24. J. H. Bridges, *The Inside History of the Carnegie Steel Company* (New York: Aldine Press, 1903), 135, 168, passim. For a survey of industries and their history of aggressive market control written by industrial economists – a breed apart from the "new institutional economists" we are dealing with and ignored by the latter – see Walter Adams and Frederick Scherer, *Industrial Market Structure and Economic Performance*, 2d ed. (Chicago: Rand-McNally, 1980), especially chap. 6.

25. Glen Yago. *The Decline of Transit*, (Cambridge, Mass.: Cambridge University Press, 1983).

26. While it is not conclusive, the evidence on the performance of acquired units should induce skepticism regarding the efficiency of acquisition policies. Birch followed 6,400 firms that were acquired during 1972–1974, and compared their before and after growth rates with the 1.3 million firms that were not acquired. He found that, in Rothschild-Witt's summary, "conglomerates tend to acquire fast-growing, profitable, well-managed businesses, contrary to the theory that they seek out poorly-managed, inefficient firms," that is, those that might have, among other things, high transaction costs internally or with the environment. However, growth is not speeded up after the acquisition; in fact, "firms that remain independent grow faster than acquired firms." A Congressional study found that firms that were acquired subsequently had lower rates of job creation, productivity, and innovation. David Birch, "The Job Creation Process," (Cambridge, Mass.: MIT Program on Neighborhood Regional Change, 1979). See also Committee on Small Business, U.S. House Representatives, "Conglomerate Mergers – Their Effects on Small Business and Local Communities" (Washington D.C.: U.S. Government Printing Office [House Document No. 96–343], Oct. 2, 1980). Both are discussed in Joyce Rothschild-Whitt, "Worker Ownership: Collective Response to an Elite-Generated Crisis," *Research in Social Movements, Conflict and Change* 6 (1984), JAI Press: 67–94, a sobering, informative review of worker-ownership developments.

27. Seymour Melman, *Pentagon Capitalism: The Political Economy of War,* (New York: McGraw Hill Book Co., 1970).

28. Kenneth McNeil and Richard Miller, "The Profitability of Consumer Practices Warranty Policies in the Auto Industry," *Administrative Science Quarterly* 25 (1980): 407–26; J. Patrick Wright, *On A Clear Day You Can See General Motors*, (New York: Avon Books, 1979); Harvey Farberman, "Criminogenic Market Structures: The Auto Industry," *Sociological Quarterly* 16 (1975): 438–57.

29. There are other criticisms of Williamson's work, and the related work of Alfred Chandler. Williamson explored the early history of capitalism, arguing that hierarchies proved to be more efficient than cooperatives and inside contracting, but the economic historian S. R. H. Jones wrote a devastating critique of Williamson's evidence

and interpretation. Richard DuBoff, a historian, and Edward Herman, an economist, reviewed the work of Chandler very critically, presenting evidence that the emergence of several of the hierarchies Chandler described had much more to do with market power than coordinating efficiencies (and I have made a similar criticism with more modest evidence). In a volume devoted to Williamson's work, Arthur Francis has a perceptive essay on the issue of efficiency versus market power. See S. R. H. Jones, "The Organization of Work; A Historical Dimension," *Journal of Economic Behavior and Organization* 3, nos. 2–3 (1982): 117–37, replying to Oliver Williamson, "The Organization of Work: A Comparative Institutional Assessment," *Journal of Economic Behavior and Organization* 1 (1980): 5–38 (with a further exchange in vol. 4, 57–68). Richard B. DuBoff and Edward S. Herman, "Alfred Chandler's New Business History: A Review," *Politics and Society* 10, no. 1 (1980): 87–110; Perrow, "Markets, Hierarchies, and Hegemony," in Van de Ven and Joyce, *Perspectives;* Arthur Francis, "Markets and Hierarchies: Efficiency or Domination?" in Arthur Francis, Jeremy Turk, and Paul Willman, eds., *Power, Efficiency, and Institutions,* (London: Heinemann, 1983), 105–16.

30. Ronald Dore, "Goodwill and the Spirit of Market Capitalism," *British Journal of Sociology* 34 (Dec. 1983); 459–82; Harvey Liebenstein, *Beyond Economic Man: A New Foundation for Microeconomics* (Cambridge, Mass.: Harvard University Press, 1976).

31. Arthur Stinchcombe, "Contracts as Hierarchical Documents," Work Report 65, Institute of Industrial Economics (Bergen, Norway, 1984).

32. Harrison White, "Agency As Control," unpublished (Cambridge, Mass.: Harvard University, 1983); Robert G. Eccles and Harrison White, "Firm and Market Interfaces of Profit Center Control," unpublished (Cambridge, Mass.: Harvard University, Feb. 1984). See also, for an industry study, W. Graham Astley and Charles J. Fombrun, "Technological Innovation and Industrial Structure: The Case of Tele-Communications," in *Advances in Strategic Management* 1 (1983), JAI Press: 205–29. See also the interesting discussion of industrial markets in Sweden, developing the notion of heterogeneous markets, in contrast to homogenous ones found in neoclassical economic theory, and of "nets," those parts of the industrial "network" where strong complementary prevails, in Ingemund Hagg and Jan Johanson, *Firms in Networks: New Perspectives on Competitive Power* (Stockholm, Sweden: Business and Social Research Institute, Sept. 1983).

6

The growth of public and private bureaucracies

MARSHALL W. MEYER

Bureaucratization is a pervasive fact of modern life. Not only have strong central governments emerged over the last century (and more recently in the United States), but large centrally administered firms have become the dominant economic actors in modern societies. The facts of bureaucratic growth are indisputable. By any measure, the size and influence of government have increased almost continuously to the present time. And, whether measured by the intensity of supervision or the intensity of administration, bureaucratic growth in private enterprises has also occurred, in some instances more rapidly than in government.[1] These developments are hardly surprising, and they have not passed unnoticed. Governmental bureaucracy is regularly disparaged by the political right. The left has been more sensitive to increased concentration of productive capacity in giant corporate bureaucracies. Rhetoric aside, however, the causes of bureaucratic growth have not been sufficiently understood, and its consequences have not been sufficiently anticipated. One of the most fundamental social transformations of the last century, and one fraught with economic as well as political consequences, has been all but ignored by the social sciences.

Several themes will be pursued simultaneously in this chapter. To begin, I will argue that organizations generally and bureaucracies in particular are best understood in terms of what I call their rationality rather than their efficiency properties. The literature is rife with efficiency models of organizations. Some efficiency models insist that the persistence and growth of organizations depend upon their efficiency advantages over alternative means of coordinating activity, whereas others insist that bureaucratic organizations are endemically inefficient. For this reason, efficiency models do not offer a coherent explanation for bureaucratic growth. Rationality models of organizations, by contrast, consider efficiency outcomes to be secondary to the capacity of organizations to order and to make sense of complicated environments. The arguments concerning the rationality properties of organizations appear to be much more consistent with one another than the arguments concerning efficiency. But these arguments do not, in their present form, constitute a theory of bureaucratic growth.

A second theme is that many of the assumptions made conventionally in the literature on organizations must be modified to transform the rationality model of organizations into a theory of bureaucratic growth. The hypothesis of environmental determination of organizations, to begin, is replaced by choice on the side of organizations and endemic uncertainty – problems not admitting of definitive solutions or whose solutions create more problems – in environments. Organizing – constructing organizations – is understood as nearly synonymous with rational conduct under uncertainty rather than as an outcome of external forces pressing for further rationalization of action. Organizations are not construed as fixed units whose properties are variable; instead, the quantity of formal organization is treated as variable. And bureaucratic growth, although reflected in staff and budgets, is understood principally as an outcome of organizing processes yielding increased quantities of formal organization. Bureaucratic growth, thus, is neither aberrant nor driven in any simple way by environmental constraints, but is instead an outcome of continuous organizing under uncertainty.

A third theme is that bureaucratic growth can yield organizations that are understood as extremely rational yet at the same time are extremely inefficient, a possibility not admitted in efficiency models. For this reason, bureaucratic growth cannot be explained by simple utility maximization on the part of individual bureaucrats, and bureaucratic growth – again, increased formal organization – is not necessarily relieved by privatization of enterprises. The fundamental question remains: What sustains institutions, such as modern bureaucracy, that tend toward complexity and growth? The answer, suggested repeatedly throughout this essay, is that, under uncertainty, continuous organizing is understood as reasonable and rational conduct in modern societies.

Two models of bureaucratic growth

The efficiency and rationality models of organizations will now be outlined. The efficiency model poses more difficulties than the rationality model because its assessment of organizations is inconsistent. The reader is asked to bear with these inconsistencies.

The efficiency model

The efficiency model appears in three forms in the organizational literature. One is in Weber's account of bureaucracy and subsequent studies addressing issues raised by Weber. Another is in the work of the conservative Austrian school of economists. A third form of the efficiency model has appeared relatively recently, in what is now known as the new institutional economics.

Weber's Theory. Although often quoted, Weber's statements concerning the efficiency properties of bureaucracy bear repetition:

The fully developed bureaucratic mechanism compares with other organizations exactly as does the machine with the non-mechanical modes of production.

Precision, speed, unambiguity, knowledge of the files, continuity, discretion, unity, strict subordination, reduction of friction and of material and personal costs – these are raised to the optimum point in the strictly bureaucratic administration, and especially in its monocratic form.[2]

It should be noted that efficiency is only one of several hypotheses explaining bureaucratization proffered by Weber. Furthermore, the efficiency hypothesis is in some respects inconsistent with the premises of Weber's own methodology insofar as his ideal-typical constructs are not intended as hypotheses.[3]

Weber's claims for the superior efficiency of bureaucracy have been questioned severely by sociologists, particularly those conducting first-hand observations in organizations. While the positive functions of bureaucratic organizations are acknowledged, many dysfunctional patterns have been identified. To be sure, Weber and contemporary social scientists have tended to make different kinds of comparisons in evaluating the efficiency of bureaucratic administration, Weber of bureaucratic with pre-bureaucratic forms of administration, contemporary social scientists of actual bureaucracies with organizations less encumbered by hierarchy and formal procedures. Nonetheless, many elements central to the bureaucratic model are today viewed as tending toward inefficiency rather than efficiency. What discussion exists concerns whether bureaucratic dysfunctions are endemic or merely incidental. Robert K. Merton and his students treat dysfunctions as incidental: while bureaucracies are generally efficient, they may be inefficient in specific instances.[4] Michel Crozier, by contrast, views dysfunctions as endemic, indeed as the defining characteristic of bureaucratic organization: bureaucracy is organization that cannot correct its own errors due to a "vicious circle" of unenforceable rules, centralization, ineffectual authority, and nonhierarchical power relations.[5] On balance, these studies emphasizing the dysfunctional aspects of bureaucracy provide little basis for the claim that superior efficiency accounts for bureaucratic growth.[6] They do indicate, however, that certain aspects of bureaucratic organizations may be self-reinforcing and thus not readily changed.

The Austrian School. Orthodox neoclassical economic theory has remained largely inattentive to organizational concerns by assuming organizations to behave like solo entrepreneurs endowed with hyperrationality, subject to market constraints demanding maximally efficient conduct. The conservative Austrian school of economics has, by contrast, been attentive to bureaucracy, which it considers to be endemically inefficient. For this reason, bureaucratic growth is considered aberrant. The argument treating bureaucracy as inefficient organization can be summarized succinctly: bureaucracy replaces voluntary quid pro quo transactions with compulsory obedience to authority.[7] Inefficiencies result mainly because individual persons are not permitted to seek maximally efficient alternatives. (The Austrian school also claims bureaucracy to be anti-democratic because individual persons are not permitted to resist authority.) A variant on the Austrian model assumes bureaucrats to be budget maximizers rather than utility maximizers, and derives from this assumption large bureaucratic size or bureaucratic overproduction of outputs compared to the private sector.[8] This argument, it should be noted, remains controversial: many orthodox economists reject the assumption of budget maximization on the grounds that the marginal costs of production of bureaucratic outputs must at some point increase beyond their value to customers or sponsors. Bureaucracies, in the orthodox view, behave little differently from monopoly firms engaging in price discrimination.[9]

The contemporary literature on public choice is rife with models and research studies showing bureaucracies to operate suboptimally. Derived from the Austrian school, this work distinguishes bureaucracies from organizations seeking profit. Only a sample of the public-choice literature can be reviewed here. To begin, bureaucrats are alleged to extract large "rents" or above-normal compensation from their employers, to distort the intent of policymakers and to resist changes in policy, and to trim outputs rather than "fat" when budgets are reduced.[10] Moreover, bureaucracies are alleged to expand employment in response to demands of interest groups[11] and to suffer from entropy or a "natural running down of an institution's efficiency" over time.[12]

The New Institutional Economists.[13] Very much in contrast to the Austrian school, the new institutionalists have developed a number of economic arguments asserting organizational hierarchy – note again that the term bureaucracy is not used affirmatively by economists – to contribute to efficiency. Their theories take several forms. In one form, hierarchy is asserted to solve the problem of shirking, which occurs when the contributions of individual workers to outputs cannot be ascertained.[14] Another form of this argument asserts that transaction costs –

e.g., the costs of writing and enforcing contracts – may (or may not) render organizational hierarchies more efficient than market alternatives.[15] The transactional argument, interestingly, can be extended to explain other bureaucratic features of organizations, particularly internal labor markets characterized by frequent performance reviews, long-term wage and salary agreements, and career ladders.[16] A third form of the argument that organizational hierarchy engenders efficiency asserts agency costs – that is, costs of ensuring that managers will in fact act in the interest of owners – to be less than costs of day-to-day decision management on the part of owners.[17]

All of the new institutional arguments favoring hierarchy on efficiency grounds share a common logic. Existing economic patterns, whether organizational or nonorganizational, are assumed Pareto-efficient. In the imaginary world of orthodox neoclassical economics fraught with perfect information and limitless as well as costless computational capacity, economic exchange would take place among individual actors, and organizations would not exist. The new institutional school recognizes the reality of imperfect information and limited, costly computational capacity; and argues that these imperfections and frictions may render organizational hierarchies (as well as other institutions, such as law) more efficient than individual exchange. Shirking, for example, is not problematic so long as shirkers are discovered and paid their just desserts. But shirking is often concealed. When two men or women together lift a rock, the relative contribution of each is not readily discerned. Moreover, as rational utility-maximizers, each person may seek to minimize his or her effort and, as a result, the rock may often fall. Some form of organizational coordination may prove more efficient than individual exchange under these circumstances. Transaction costs are trivial so long as contracts can be written and enforced easily. But uncertainties as to both language and future events can render contracting very costly; and organizational coordination, again, may prove more efficient. Agency costs would not arise in a world where owners (or residual claimants) had unlimited decision-making capacity. But, given limited capacity, owners must delegate less important operational decisions to managers, whose actions are supervised and rewarded through organizational mechanisms.

Comment. Although the disparate assessments of the efficiency properties of bureaucracy may reflect differences between market and nonmarket organizations, it is by no means certain that this is the case. Weber, for example, insisted private and public organizations are similarly bureaucratized, which was probably the case at the time he was writing.[18] The Austrian school did define bureaucracy as nonmarket exchange, but it ignored the fact, recognized by the new institutionalists, that nonmarket coordination exists within firms as well as in public bureaucracies.

Empirical evidence further clouds efficiency models of bureaucracy. A number of studies indicate that private firms delivering the same routine services as public bureaucracies may do so more efficiently, and private-public differences appear to hold even where organizational structures are identical.[19] However, nonroutine services are sometimes delivered more efficiently by nonprofit organizations than by private firms.[20] Relatively few studies have addressed the issues raised by the new institutionalists. For the most part, attention has been focused on the relative efficiency of multi-unit and conglomerate forms of organization compared to simpler forms, and empirical results have been mixed.[21] Costs arising from shirking, transaction costs, and agency costs have not been measured, and hence their impact on organizations has not been directly estimated. One recent study suggests transfer pricing within firms, upon which the alleged efficiency advantages of multi-unit and conglomerate firms depend, to be determined arbitrarily rather than as a result of economic or mathematical calculation.[22]

In summary, the inexorable trend toward bureaucratization of society has been matched by neither consistent theorizing nor consistent empirical results showing bureaucratization or extension of organizational hierarchies to be inexorably efficient. It may be that new theories or research will yet yield evidence showing bureaucracy always to offer efficiency advantages over alternative organizational forms, but until such time the explanation for bureaucratic growth must be sought elsewhere.

The rationality model

The rationality model has also appeared in several distinct forms in the organizational literature. Initially, rationality and efficiency properties of bureaucracy were considered to be similar and have remained so in most economic theories, but noneconomic theories have clearly separated the two. The positive contributions of bureaucratic structures to rationality were first noted by Weber and later elaborated by Herbert Simon. Recently, sociologists have begun thinking of organizations as embodying ideas about rational conduct, whether or not these ideas are consistent and whether or not they, in fact, contribute to efficient and effective performance.

Reprise on Weber's Theory. Although Weber viewed bureaucracy as having superior efficiency compared to earlier administrative forms, he viewed bureaucratic efficiency largely as a function of bureaucratic rationality. Bureaucratization, in Weber's view, is part of a historical trend toward rationalization of institutions of all kinds, including law, economic exchange, and, of course, science. Bureaucratization rationalizes large-scale activities by making actions predictable, by making costs and benefits calculable, and by severely limiting the possibility of arbitrary action on the part of any single official. Almost any comparison of traditional with bureaucratic patterns of administration shows the former to yield less orderly and consistent outcomes than the latter, even though traditional administration strongly favored ruling elites.[23] Despite the close connection of bureaucratization with rationalization, Weber's theory describes mainly the displacement of traditional by bureaucratic administration and is not a causal theory of bureaucratic growth. While the historical trend toward rationalization and a parallel historical trend in the direction of bureaucratization are noted, neither antecedent conditions promoting rationalization nor specific consequences of rationalization, in bureaucracies or elsewhere, are indicated.

Bounded Rationality and Bureaucratization. A more concrete argument connecting bureaucratization with rationalization has been developed by Herbert Simon. Simon's theory is well known. Limited human rationality, or bounded rationality, compels construction of organizations to accomplish complex tasks. The structure of organizations is like a decision tree. Large decisions are successively divided into subdecisions, sub-subdecisions, and the like to the point where choices can take place within bounded rationality limits. This division of decisions is accomplished by transforming, at each level of hierarchy, ends determined by higher levels into means to be pursued by lower-level units.[24]

Several comments about Simon's theory are important in this context. The first concerns Simon's use of rationality. Rationality is not equated with efficiency. It is defined instead as the selection of the preferred means, which may be the most efficient but which may not be, given one's ends. Rationality so understood is embedded in organizations: "The rational individual is, and must be, an organized and institutionalized individual."[25] More clearly than Weber, then, Simon separates organizational rationality from efficiency. Also more clearly than Weber, Simon insists that the principal advantage of bureaucratic organization lies in its rationality as opposed to its efficiency properties. A second comment is that Simon's theory presumes organizations isomorphic to environments. Unlike conventional economic thinking treating organizational forms as an outcome of efficiency properties, Simon treats organizational form as a function of the complexity of problems addressed. Problems or tasks determine organizations directly; more complicated problems demand more complicated organizational structures. Equilibrium within organizations is achieved when routines not exceeding bounded rationality limits yet appropriate to problems or tasks are in place. Isomorphism with environments, importantly, implies that bureaucratic growth is environmentally determined. The contrast with Weber's model is instructive: whereas Weber points to general historical trends in the direction of rationalization and bureaucratization, Simon, by implication, ties bureaucratic growth to growth in the complexity of tasks demanded of organizations.

   The New Institutional Sociologists. Despite the overwhelming emphasis on efficiency models of organizations, there has been renewed interest in rationalization as a source of bureaucratization in recent years. This has occurred mainly due to the radical separation of rationalization from efficiency arguments in the work of John W. Meyer and his colleagues.[26] Meyer and others have argued that there are both instrumental and noninstrumental advantages of large-scale formal organization; among the latter, legitimation arises from shared or institutionalized *beliefs* that organizations constructed along the lines of the bureaucratic model are in fact rational. Beliefs are emphasized here. In John Meyer's formulation, rationality has little external referent save for the fact that action believed rational has legitimacy and therefore is not scrutinized closely. But precisely because bureaucratic structures endow action with the appearance of rationality and hence legitimacy, and because the appearance of rationality is demanded by institutions controlling crucial resources, the extensiveness of formal organization tends to increase with modernization.

   Several observations about this theory are in order. First, the rationality argument stands apart from the efficiency argument here as in Weber's and Simon's work. But the difference between the two is extreme: rationality, which is a social construction, may bear little relation to efficiency, which remains a concrete outcome of organizational action. Importantly, this extreme separation of rationality from efficiency may give rise to highly rationalized conduct that is endemically inefficient. Second, as in Simon's theory, organizations are hypothesized to reflect external elements. But these elements are amorphous, consisting mainly of beliefs as to how organizations ought rationally to be constructed rather than of task characteristics. Presumably, bureaucratic growth occurs as new arenas of action fall within the purview of institutionalized beliefs concerning rationality. But whether environments remain truly independent of organizations remains unclear: given that they consist mainly of beliefs, there is the risk that environments are but mirror images of the organizations they purport to explain.

   Comment. Whatever their weaknesses and inconsistencies, diverse arguments converge on the proposition that bureaucratic organizations have superior rationality properties compared to nonorganizational forms of action. Some empirical evidence, which will be reviewed presently, is consistent with these arguments. This result is in marked contrast to the arguments concerning the efficiency properties of organizations, where there is no convergence at all. One conclusion, therefore, is that we must begin thinking of efficiency and rationality as separable and possibly independent properties of organizations. A second conclusion is that the sources of bureaucratic growth are more likely to lie in the capacity of organizations to order, make sense of, and otherwise rationalize complex environments than in their capacity to perform efficiently. Although rationality models of organizations do not, in their present form, anticipate bureaucratic growth, these models become theories of growth once some of their assumptions are reconsidered.

Toward a new synthesis

The efficiency and rationality models of bureaucratization sketched above yield few consistent conclusions. With respect to the efficiency advantages of bureaucracy, there are disparate assessments in both sociological and economic theorizing. With respect to the rationality advantages of bureaucracy, there is greater agreement. Bureaucracy appears to offer substantial rationality advantages compared to alternatives, but there is disagreement as to why this is so. To recapitulate: Weber viewed bureaucracy as an outcome of historical forces tending in the direction of rationalization; Simon treats bureaucratic structures as maximizing rationality, the capacity to link means to ends, which is most easily achieved when complex tasks are successively divided and subdivided in organizational hierarchies; and recent sociological work radically separates rationality from efficiency by understanding the former as a set of beliefs or values as to how organizations ought to be constructed, which are sought and are embodied in bureaucratic structures and procedures and which thereby legitimate organizations.

The problem to be addressed here is whether a theory of bureaucratic growth can be derived from the rationality advantages of bureaucracy over nonorganizational forms of action. Previously, these advantages have not been connected to bureaucratic growth. Quite the opposite, uncontrolled growth has not been thought characteristic of reasonable and rational organizations. The argument developed below is that bureaucratic growth is the outcome of continuous construction of formal organization, which is understood as a reasonable and rational response to uncertainties arising externally. I describe this elsewhere as a problem-organization-problem-more-organization cycle of bureaucratic growth.[27] The argument rests on several unconventional assumptions. One concerns environments, which are considered to be unbounded rather than finite and to pose limitless uncertainty for organizations. Another concerns organizations themselves, which are understood as enhancing peoples' capacity for rational conduct rather than as products of external forces demanding rationalization. A third assumption is that the capacity of bureaucracy to enhance rationality yields pressures in the direction of increased formal organization, and, in turn, larger staffs and expenditures. These three assumptions and research evidence pertaining to them will be reviewed seriatim.

Environments and organizations

The conventional hypothesis, still echoed throughout the literature, is that environments determine organizations.[28] Given this hypothesis and the notion that bureaucratic administration offers powerful rationality advantages compared to nonbureaucratic forms, one might argue that bureaucratic growth is an outcome of increased demands for rationalization arising in the environment. Indeed, there is some evidence that this is the case. For example, changes in local government personnel practices appear to be the result of shifts in federal policy.[29] However, most research studies merely impute external demands for increased rationalization from patterns of organizational change that cannot be explained by more readily measured variables. The *absence* of close correspondences between principals' and teachers' perceptions of school operations is taken as evidence that institutionalized beliefs account for the organization of schools;[30] the *absence* of correlations between urban reform and other city characteristics such as percentage foreign born, literacy, and the like is interpreted as evidence consistent with the argument that reform beliefs have become institutionalized and an independent force in the environment.[31]

Null correlations cannot sustain the hypothesis that environmental demands for rationalization determine bureaucratic growth. Indeed, null correlations, which are rife in the literature,[32] sustain poorly the more general hypothesis that environments determine organizations. In place of theories of environmental determination of organizations, a theory of environmental nondetermination is needed to explain why, in general, simple correspondences between environmental and organizational properties are not to be expected. Such a theory arises from two behavioral postulates. One is that considerable latitude for choice exists within organizations. A large literature on choice makes two points: first, that organizations consciously adopt strategies intended to overcome environmental constraints;[33] and, second, that processes of enactment within organizations determine which environmental elements are attended to and which are ignored.[34] A second postulate is that many environments, once chosen or enacted, may still pose substantial uncertainty for organizations. Sometimes there is relative certainty, particularly when the tasks undertaken by organizations are tied to technologies that are well understood. But often there is uncertainty, particularly where optimal solutions to problems do not exist or have not been discovered. Such uncertainty holds for both physical and administrative tasks. There is no such thing as a problem-free nuclear plant or a municipal budget that takes account of all possible contingencies.[35] *Choice and enactment on the part of organizations in conjunction with uncertainty in environments render most correspondences between environmental and organizational states weak.* Bureaucratic growth, therefore, need not be an outcome of specific environmental forces demanding higher levels of outputs or greater rationalization of administrative processes.

Organizations and rationality

Having cast doubt on the hypothesis of environmental determination, I now want to turn the tables, so to speak, and suggest that organizations are constructed to make sense of or to rationalize environments that otherwise pose problems not admitting of solutions. While this hypothesis is broadly consistent with the rationality models outlined above, it shifts subtly but significantly one of their key premises. Above, external forces demanding rationalization – whether historical change in Weber's model, task complexity in Simon's model, or expectations as to how organizations ought rationally to be constructed in the work of John W. Meyer and others – were viewed as causing organizations to be formed and elaborated. Here, rationality is understood as embedded within organizations, as creating solutions to problems that are otherwise intractable and therefore as synonymous with organizing.

Both historical evidence and contemporary research support the notion that rationality is embedded within modern organizations. The historical argument linking organizing to conceptions of rational conduct is made elsewhere and cannot be reproduced in its details here.[36] Suffice it to note that the idea of rational administration was invented shortly after the beginning of this century, that this idea was derived from organizational patterns that had proved successful in industrial administration and were believed to be the key to solving many of the problems of government, and that organizing patterns consistent with this idea have since been understood as reasonable and rational. Today, " . . . the idea of rational administration as synonymous with creation of rules and formal structures is so deeply embedded in modern cultures that few people can imagine alternatives. Academic theorizing and bureaucratic practice, furthermore, have emphasized that managerial intentions are best made concrete and communicated to individuals through formal procedures and structures. To formalize an activity is to make it visible, external, and apparently stable."[37]

Two sets of contemporary research results also suggest a close connection between modern conceptions of rationality and organizing processes. One set of studies, conducted mainly in the early 1970s, attempted to assess the impact of environmental uncertainty on organizations and yielded decidedly anomalous results. Objective measures describing the amount of variability and volatility in the environment bore little or no relation to either organizational patterns or, more importantly, the amount of uncertainty experienced by people in organizations.[38] Perceived uncertainty, to be sure, was a function of *perceived* variability, unpredictability, and unanalyzability of problems.[39] Perceived uncertainty was also a function of certain organizational characteristics, mainly the level of organizational performance or "situational favorability,"[40] and the extent to which work routines were structured or formalized.[41] Organizational properties, particularly the extensiveness of formal organizational structure, appeared to determine how environments were perceived rather than the reverse, an outcome wholly unexpected given the hypothesis of environmental determination of organizations. The hypothesis that rationality is embedded in organizations anticipates that organizations themselves determine how environments are experienced and therefore renders these research results more plausible.

Research on other sociopsychological concomitants of working conditions also support the hypothesis that formal organization contributes to the capacity for rational conduct. The most extensive of these studies have been conducted by Melvin L. Kohn and his associates.[42] One of their early studies explored the impact of bureaucratization on values and intellectual functioning.[43] Kohn's measure of bureaucratization was conventional, a combination of size and the number of supervisory levels in an organization. Employees working in bureaucratized settings were found to value self-direction and to be more accepting of change than their counterparts in nonbureaucratized organizations. Moreover, bureaucrats scored consistently higher than nonbureaucrats on various indexes of intellectual functioning, even when education and other background variables were controlled. Of particular significance were differences between bureaucrats and others in "ideational flexibility," a measure of problem-solving capacity. Individuals working in large multi-tier organizations appeared to interviewers to be more intelligent and adept at solving abstract problems than others. The effects of bureaucratization, Kohn found, were due largely to the substantive complexity of work as well as the higher salaries and greater job security characteristic of bureaucratic settings. For white-collar employees, the complexity of work was of greatest significance for values and intellectual functioning, whereas for blue-collar workers income and job protections were most important.

The inference to be drawn from research on uncertainty and intellectual functioning is that bureaucratization diminishes the former and augments the latter such that the capacity for rational conduct, the selection of means appropriate to one's ends, is enhanced. While it may be the case that external forces demanding rationalization account to some extent for bureaucratization, empirical evidence also demonstrates that bureaucratization contributes independently to rationalization by increasing people's problem-solving capacity and by decreasing the amount of uncertainty they experience, external conditions held constant. These research results in conjunction with historical evidence describing the origins of modern administration suggest that bureaucratization is closely associated, indeed synonymous, with rationalization rather than a manifestation of external forces imposing the form if not the substance of rationality upon organizations.

Organizing processes and bureaucratic growth
To the extent that environments pose problems not admitting of definitive solutions and to the extent that bureaucratization helps to make sense of or helps to rationalize environments posing such problems, formal organization will be constructed continuously. The continuous construction of organization results in bureaucratic growth.

The notion that formal organization may be constructed continuously carries several implications that, while consistent with casual observation, are somewhat unusual in research. One is that the quantity of formal organization is variable and tends to increase over time. Almost all historical evidence confirms, in fact, that the quantity or population of organizations has increased markedly during the last century.[44] Quantitative research on organizations, however, has been somewhat insensitive to this development, focusing instead on fixed populations of units whose internal properties (e.g., size, structural differentiation, longevity, etc.) are assumed variable, presumably in response to changes in the environment. In this article, environments are considered to pose uncertainties, problems that do not admit of definitive solutions, in response to which new organizations are formed continually. A second implication is that units that are themselves organizations may create new units that are also by any reasonable definition organizations or may, alternatively, be subordinated to units that also have most of the properties of organizations. These properties include identity, purpose, structure, membership (and nonmembership), and exchanges with environments, and are present for the largest and most inclusive organizational units (such as the federal government) as well as for the smallest and least inclusive units (such as the National Science Foundation sociology program, which is a subunit of the Division of Social and Economic Sciences, which is in turn a subunit of the Directorate for Biological, Behavioral, and Social Sciences, which is in turn a subunit of the foundation, which is a unit of the U.S. Government). Abstractly, the idea that organizing processes may give rise to new organizations within or superordinate to existing organizations poses no difficulty.[45] In quantitative research, however, there has been a strong tendency to ignore organizing processes and to treat organizations statically, as more or less fixed units with permanent boundaries. To be sure, the concomitants of reorganization have been identified in some studies, and in other studies the causes of organizational mortality or dissolution have been explored.[46] But the possibility that bureaucratic complexity and growth are outcomes of increased formal organization, specifically the creation within or superordinate to existing organizational structures of new organizational units, has only recently been considered.

There is not at this point an adequate number of sufficiently detailed studies of the evolution of bureaucratic structures to confirm the hypothesis that bureaucratic growth is the outcome of continuous organizing under uncertainty. However, continuous creation of new units is characteristic of most administrative organizations systems during their lifetimes.[47] The creation of subordinate organizational units contributes to the longevity of bureaus at all levels of organizational hierarchy, suggesting a generalized preference for increased formal organization.[48] The hypothesis that bureaucratic growth is an outcome of continuous organizing under uncertainty may account for the historical increase in the ratio of administrative to production workers, the conventional measure of bureaucratization in industry:[49] relative certainty in the technical activities of firms at the production level in comparison to the greater uncertainty of administrative tasks at the managerial and institutional levels would be expected to yield much more organizing activity in the latter than in the former and hence increased A/P ratios over time.[50] More generally, continuous organizing processes may yield the commonly observed ratchet or "bumperjack" effect in administration, whereby administration fails to decrease in periods of declining workload.[51] And continuous organizing under uncertainty may also account for the bureaucratization within specific institutional sectors. Medical practice, for example, is increasingly conducted within bureaucratic hierarchies.[52]

The general proposition that uncertainty promotes continuous organizing and hence bureaucratic growth yields two predictions. One is that, over time, as problems admitting of definitive solutions are solved leaving mainly problems without solutions, rates of bureaucratic growth will increase. In fact, the rate of bureaucratization appears to have accelerated, at least until very recently, in most modern societies.[53] The second prediction is that bureaucratic growth cannot continue without limit. Whereas organizing may be understood as a reasonable and rational response to uncertainty, the organizational structures that are the outcome of continuous organizing may be so unwieldy as to defy reason and rationality. The paradox of bureaucratic growth, then, is this: growth adds to problem-solving capacity, but it does so ultimately by building into organizations complexity equal to or greater than the complexity of problems the organizations were intended to solve in the first place. At this point, the limits to bureaucratic growth may be encountered. Alternatively, bureaucratic systems of administration embodying modern concepts of rational action may prove so resistant to change that they can be displaced only by catastrophic societal failure.[54]

Efficiency reconsidered

In conclusion, I turn to the question of whether the rationality properties of bureaucratic systems of administration are at odds with their efficiency (or inefficiency) properties. Few in the discipline of economics would wish to raise this issue. For the Austrian school and public-choice economists, bureaucracies are inefficient, and, therefore, non-rational instrumentalities of administration. For the new institutional economists, organizational hierarchies may contribute to efficiency and, therefore, have attractive rationality properties. Sociologists have by contrast tended increasingly to separate efficiency from rationality properties of organizations, due mainly to their observation that highly rationalized organizational systems are often inefficient and, sometimes, chaotic. Here, I have added slightly to the distinction between efficiency and rationality by suggesting that organizing – constructing organizations – is often understood as rational action regardless of its consequences for efficiency, and that this is particularly the case under uncertainty where problems do not admit of definitive solutions. Two conditions combine, then, to produce bureaucratic growth. One is the belief in rational administration, that is, in organizing as rational problem-solving activity. The other is uncertainty, again, problems without known solutions. Together, these conditions can give rise to increased administration in face of constant or even declining demand for the activities or outputs of an organization. Bureaucratic growth as an outcome of organizing under uncertainty is ubiquitous in the public sector because problems without solutions, or problems whose solutions yield further problems, tend to flow to government. Bureaucratic growth in the administrative or supervisory component of the private sector occurs for similar reasons: managerial problems involving interchanges with uncertain environments are less likely to admit of definite solutions than are technical problems of production.

Several implications arise from the observation that rationality and efficiency may be separate properties and that, under uncertainty, continuous construction of formal organization may be understood as rational regardless of its consequences for efficiency. One implication is that bureaucratic growth cannot be understood merely as an outcome of utility maximization on the part of individual bureaucrats, officials, or workers. Instead, bureaucratic growth must be understood as a product of institutional structures permitting conduct that is apparently rational to yield inefficient outcomes. Another implication is that bureaucratic growth cannot always be curbed by removing activities from the purview of government and placing them in private sector. The same processes giving rise to bureaucratization, organizing under uncertainty, may operate whether or not a profit motive exists. As noted above, while privatization can lower costs of certain routine services provided by government, privatization may actually increase costs of nonroutine services where outcomes are essentially indeterminate.

If the rationality properties of bureaucratic organizations take precedence over and do not necessarily contribute to efficiency outcomes, then we must ask whether we are condemned to a world of organizations of ever-increasing complexity and ever-declining efficiency. I think not, but not because the market automatically corrects inefficiency. I anticipate, rather, that the rationality or legitimacy of present organizational patterns will be called into question. Confidence in governmental and business organizations has declined sharply in recent years.[55] Whether this erosion of confidence will cause bureaucratic structures to be displaced by wholly different organizational forms cannot be foreseen, but some changes are inevitable. Even so, it must be kept in mind that many people have a substantial stake in maintaining present organizational patterns. The world of bureaucratic organizations is, from most peoples' perspective, a world of relatively simple rules and structures and therefore a world that is predictable and understandable. From the perspective of the organizational theorist, of course, the world of bureaucracy has grown inordinately complex, but it is precisely this complexity that has preserved simplicity and hence rationality for the individual. A world absent of permanent bureaucratic structures would pose much, greater challenges to understanding, for it would force people to comprehend extremely dense and varied sets of interdependencies, and it would render many working relations transient. But the overall structure of such a world would at any given time be much simpler than modern bureaucracy, and its simplicity would be its decisive advantage. Thus, just as early bureaucracy reduced much of the complexity and inertia of traditional administration, new organizational forms reducing much of the complexity and inertia that have accumulated in modern bureaucracy can be expected to emerge. The new organizational forms, no doubt, will eventually be understood as rational, but their rationality advantage will lie not so much in how they order and simplify the world for individual people as in how they manage complicated tasks in uncertain and changing environments without incurring long-term bureaucratic growth.

Acknowledgment

Comments on an earlier draft by Lee Clarke, Randall Collins, Paul DiMaggio, and Sharon Zukin are gratefully acknowledged.

Notes

1. See Marshall W. Meyer, "Debureaucratization?" *Social Science Quarterly* 20 (1979): 15–25; and Marshall W. Meyer, William Stevenson, and Stephen Webster, *Limits to Bureaucratic Growth* (Berlin and New York: de Gruyter, 1985), chap. 2.
2. Max Weber, "Bureaucracy," in H. Gerth and C. W. Mills, eds., *From Max Weber: Essays in Sociology* (New York: Oxford University Press, 1946), 214.
3. See Max Weber, *The Methodology of the Social Sciences* (Glencoe, Ill.: The Free Press, 1949); and Peter M. Blau and W. Richard Scott, *Formal Organizations* (San Francisco: Chandler, 1962), 33–36.
4. Robert K. Merton, "Bureaucratic Structure and Personality," *Social Forces* 18 (1940): 560–68.
5. Michel Crozier, *The Bureaucratic Phenomenon* (Chicago: University of Chicago Press, 1964).
6. Needless to say, many studies of organizational structure and of organization-environment relations have assumed efficiency constraints to operate on organizations. See, for example, James D. Thompson, *Organizations in Action* (New York: McGraw-Hill, 1967); and Peter M. Blau and Richard A. Schoenherr, *The Structure of Organizations* (New York: Basic Books, 1971).
7. Ludwig von Mises, *Bureaucracy* (New Haven: Yale University Press, 1944); Anthony Downs, *Inside Bureaucracy* (Boston: Little Brown, 1967).
8. William A. Niskanen, *Bureaucracy and Democratic Governance* (Chicago: Aldine, 1971).
9. Jean-Luc Migué and Gerard Belanger, "Toward a General Theory of Managerial Discretion," *Public Choice* 17 (1974): 27–43; William A. Niskanen, Jr., "Bureaucrats and Politicians," *Journal of Law and Economics* 18 (1975): 617–43.

10. Migué and Belanger, "Toward a General Theory of Managerial Discretion"; A. Congleton, "A Model of Asymmetric Bureaucratic Inertia and Bias," *Public Choice* 39 (1982): 421–25; David A. Laband, "Federal Budget Cuts: Bureaucrats Trim the Meat, Not the Fat," *Public Choice* 40 (1983): 311–14.

11. David C. L. Nellor, "Public Bureau Budgets and Jurisdiction Size," *Public Choice* 44 (1984): 175–83.

12. R. D. Auster, "The GPITPC and Institutional Entropy," *Public Choice* 19 (1974): 82; R. D. Auster and M. Silver, *The State As a Firm* (Hingham, Mass.: Martinus Nijhoff, 1979).

13. For a detailed review and critique of this approach to organizations, see C. Perrow's chapter in this volume.

14. Armen A. Alchian and Harold Demsetz, "Production, Information Costs, and Economic Organization," *American Economic Review* 62 (1972): 777–95.

15. Oliver E. Williamson, *Markets and Hierarchies* (New York: The Free Press, 1975).

16. Ibid., chap. 4.

17. The costs of decision management on the part of owners (as opposed to ultimate decision control, which is retained by owners) are largely opportunity costs incurred when owners' attention is diverted from long-term investment and portfolio management to operational questions. See Eugene F. Fama, "Agency Problems and the Theory of the Firm," *Journal of Political Economy* 88 (1980): 288–307; Eugene F. Fama and Michael C. Jensen, "Separation of Ownership and Control," *Journal of Law and Economics* 26 (1983): 301–26; Eugene F. Fama and Michael C. Jensen, "Agency Problems and Residual Claims," *Journal of Law and Economics* 26 (1983): 327–49; Michael E. Jensen, "Organization Theory and Methodology," *Accounting Review* 8 (1983): 319–37; and Michael E. Jensen and William Meckling, "Theory of the Firm: Managerial Behavior, Agency Costs, and Ownership Structure," *Journal of Financial Economics* 3 (1976): 305–60.

18. This is discussed in Meyer et al., *Limits*, chap. 1.

19. See D. Davies, "The Efficiency of Public versus Private Firms: The Case of Australia's Two Airlines," *Journal of Law and Economics* 16 (1971): 149–65, which compares two identical Australian airlines, one publicly owned, the other private.

20. Paul Starr, *The Social Transformation of American Medicine* (New York: Basic Books, 1982), chap. 5, notes that corporate medicine appears to offer few economies compared to nonprofit providers; Marshall W. Meyer, "Growth and Complexity in Services for the Developmentally Disabled: The Case of California," unpublished manuscript (University of California, Riverside, 1985).

21. Henry O. Armour and David J. Teece, "Organization Structure and Economic Performance: A Test of the Multidivisional Hypothesis," *Bell Journal of Economics* 9 (1978): 106–22; David J. Teece, "Internal Organization and Economic Performance: An Empirical Analysis of Principal Firms," *Journal of Industrial Economics* 30 (1981): 173–99.

22. Robert Eccles, *The Transfer Pricing Problem* (Lexington, Mass.: Lexington Books, 1985).

23. Vernon Dibble, "The Organization of Traditional Authority," chap. 21 in James G. March, ed., *Handbook of Organizations* (Chicago: Rand-McNally, 1965).

24. Herbert A. Simon, *Administrative Behavior* (New York: Macmillan, 1947).

25. Ibid., 102.

26. John W. Meyer and Brian Rowan, "Institutional Organizations: Formal Structure As Myth and Ceremony," *American Journal of Sociology* 83 (1977): 340–63; John W. Meyer and W. Richard Scott, *Organizational Environments: Ritual and Rationality* (Beverly Hills: Sage, 1983).

27. Meyer et al., *Limits*, 49.

28. See, for example, Howard E. Aldrich, *Organizations and Environments* (Englewood Cliffs, N.J.: Prentice-Hall, 1979).

29. Marshall W. Meyer and M. Craig Brown, "The Process of Bureaucratization," *American Journal of Sociology* 83 (1977): 364–85.

30. John W. Meyer, W. Richard Scott, Sally Cole, and Jo-Ann K. Intilli, "Instructional Dissensus and Institutional Consensus in Schools," chap. 9 in M. W. Meyer, ed., *Environments and Organizations* (San Francisco: Jossey-Bass, 1978).

31. Pamela S. Tolbert and Lynne G. Zucker, "Institutionalized Sources of Change in the Formal Structure of Organizations," *Administrative Science Quarterly* 28 (1983): 22–39. City characteristics predicted reform until 1914 but not thereafter; the null correlations in the post-1914 era were taken as evidence of institutionalization of reform.

32. The literature on environmental effects on organizations is summarized in Peter M. Blau and Marshall W. Meyer, *Bureaucracy in Modern Society*, 3d ed. (New York: Random House, 1986), chap. 6.

33. John Child, "Organizational Structure, Environment, and Performance: The Role of Strategic Choice," *Sociology* 6 (1972): 2–22.

34. Karl E. Weick, *The Social Psychology of Organizing* (Reading, Mass.: Addison-Wesley, 1969).

35. Charles Perrow, *Normal Accidents* (New York: Basic Books, 1983); Meyer et al., *Limits*.

36. Meyer et al., *Limits*, chaps. 1, 3, and 9.

37. Ibid., 200.

38. Henry Tosi, Ramon Aldag, and Ronald Storey, "On the Measurement of the Environment: An Assessment of the Lawrence and Lorsch Environmental Uncertainty Subscale," *Administrative Science Quarterly* 18 (1973): 27–36; H. Kirk Downey, Don Hellriegel, and John W. Slocum, Jr., "Environmental Uncertainty: The Construct and Its Application," *Administrative Science Quarterly* 20 (1975): 613–29.

39. Robert B. Duncan, "Characteristics of Organizational Environments and Perceived Environmental Uncertainty," *Administrative Science Quarterly* 17 (1972): 313–27.

40. Delbert M. Nebeker, "Situational Favorability and Perceived Environmental Uncertainty: An Integrative Approach," *Administrative Science Quarterly* 20 (1975): 281–94; H. Kirk Downey and John W. Slocum, Jr., "Managerial Uncertainty and Performance," *Social Science Quarterly* 62 (1982): 195–207.

41. George Huber, Michael J. O'Connell, and Larry L. Cummings, "Perceived Environmental Uncertainty: Effects of Information and Structure," *Academy of Management Journal* 18 (1975): 725–40; Richard Leifer and George Huber, "Relations among Perceived Environmental Uncertainty, Organizational Structure, and Boundary-Spanning Behavior," *Administrative Science Quarterly* 22 (1977): 235–47.

42. Kohn's work appears in numerous scholarly articles, some of which are reproduced in Melvin L. Kohn and Carmi Schooler, *Work and Personality: An Inquiry into the Impact of Social Stratification* (Norwood, N.J.: Ablex Publishers, 1983).

43. Melvin L. Kohn, "Bureaucratic Man: A Portrait and Interpretation," *American Sociological Review* 36 (1971): 461–74. This article also appears in Kohn and Schooler, *Work and Personality*, chap. 2.

44. See, for example, Howard E. Aldrich, *Organizations and Environments*; and Udo Staber and Howard E. Aldrich, "Government Regulation and the Expansion of Trade Associations," paper presented at the European Group for Organizational Studies 7th Colloquium, Saltsjobaden, Sweden, June 1985.

45. The notion that organizational units exist within other organizational units is not uncommon in the anthropological literature. See Michael G. Smith, "On Segmen-

tary Lineage Systems," chap. 1 in *Corporations and Society* (London: Gerald Duckworth & Co., 1974).

46. Concerning reorganization, see Meyer and Brown, "The Process of Bureaucratization;" concerning organizational mortality, see, for example, Glenn R. Carroll and Jacques Delacroix, "Organizational Mortality in the Newspaper Industries of Argentina and Ireland," *Administrative Science Quarterly* 27 (1982): 169–98; and John H. Freeman, Glenn R. Carroll, and Michael T. Hannan, "The Liability of Newness: Age-Dependence in Organizational Death Rates," *American Sociological Review* 48 (1983): 692–710.

47. Herbert Kaufman, *Time, Chance, and Organizations* (Chatham, N.J.: Chatham House Publishers, 1985), 103–05.

48. Meyer et al., *Limits*, chap. 5.

49. Reinhard Bendix, *Work and Authority in Industry* (New York: Wiley, 1956), chap. 4; Meyer et al., *Limits*, chap. 2.

50. James D. Thompson, *Organizations in Action* (New York: McGraw-Hill, 1967), chap. 1, argues that greater uncertainty characterizes managerial and institutional compared to technical levels of organizations.

51. John J. Freeman and Michael T. Hannan, "Growth and Decline Processes in Organizations," *American Sociological Review* 40 (1975): 215–28; John H. Freeman and Michael T. Hannan, "Internal Politics of Growth and Decline," chap. 7 in Meyer, ed., *Environments and Organizations*; Edward A. Holdaway and Thomas A. Blowers, "Administrative Ratios and Organizational Size: A Longitudinal Examination," *American Sociological Review* 36 (1971): 278–86; Richard L. Daft and Patricia J. Bradshaw, "The Process of Horizontal Differentiation: Two Models," *Administrative Science Quarterly* 25 (1980): 441–46.

52. David Mechanic, *The Growth of Bureaucratic Medicine* (New York: Wiley, 1976); Starr, *The Social Transformation*, chap. 5, argues that the advantage of large firms lies in their ability to deal with the complexities of regulation, financing, and reimbursement rather than in superior operating efficiency.

53. Michele Fratianni and Franco Spinnelli, "The Growth of Government in Italy: Evidence from 1861 to 1979," *Public Choice* 39 (1982): 226.

54. Mancur Olsen, *The Rise and Decline of Nations* (New Haven: Yale University Press, 1982), observes that catastrophic change has the function of removing special-interest groups, the accumulation of which otherwise blocks economic growth. In a review of the book (*Public Choice* 40 [1983]: 111–16), Gordon Tullock criticizes Olsen for failing to explain long-term persistence of interest groups and suggests, consistent with the public-choice school and inconsistent with the above argument, that this is due mainly to the self-interest of professional bureaucrats who staff these groups.

55. Seymour Martin Lipset and William Schneider, *The Confidence Gap* (New York: The Free Press, 1983).

Part III
Finance capital

7
Capital market effects on external control of corporations

LINDA BREWSTER STEARNS

For years, sociologists and economists have argued over who controls corporations as though corporate control did not change from one period of time to another. These arguments focus on whether corporations are controlled internally, by their managers, or from outside, by financial institutions. Generally, arguments ignore the importance of capital markets in determining how and when corporations became dependent on financial institutions. Consequently, they assume rather than demonstrate the potential of financial institutions to influence corporate policies and behavior.

This chapter introduces the capital market as the resource environment in which corporations meet their capital needs. The capital market is also the social context in which the power relations between financial institutions and corporate management evolve within a capitalist economy. Variations in this context therefore change the relation between these actors. In particular, the extent of new capital required, the supply of capital, and the structure of the lending institutions vary over time. However, the present discussion does not directly measure the capital environment surrounding a particular set of corporations, or assess the degree of financial control to which conditions in this environment may be related. First, I explore the theoretical position that capital market conditions play a key role in determining the potential of financial institutions to control corporations. Second, I offer empirical evidence of specific changes in corporate capital needs and capital market conditions that were related to different levels of corporate financial dependence between 1945 and 1980. The pattern of change suggests that managerialists may have been correct in the 1950s while financial control arguments may be more persuasive in the contemporary period.

Theories of financial control

Three major perspectives – resource dependence, class cohesion, and financial control[1] – have been suggested to explain intercorporate control relationships.[2] Recently, some theorists have attempted to partially integrate the resource dependence and class cohesion models.[3] This article pursues the trend toward synthesis by combining elements of the financial control and resource dependence models.

One tenet of all financial control theories is that because capital is an uncertain but crucial resource, control over capital flows provides financial institutions – in particular, commercial banks and life-insurance companies[4] – a means of exerting control over corporations. Major decisions in which corporate control is exercised typically require, and are therefore conditional upon, the availability of investment capital. Financial institutions, the primary depository of society's capital resources, are elevated to a position of power because of their discretion over this essential resource.

Writings on financial control date back to the early twentieth century,[5] when financiers such as J. P. Morgan were universally acknowledged to exercise a great deal of power within the business community. Investment bankers played an important role in the formation and merger of corporations because of their central position in the issuance and sale of new securities.[6] As the major provider of capital in a period of intense competition, bankers were able to appropriate large promoters' profits and to exercise a voice in corporate policy.[7]

Between the 1920s and the 1970s, financial control more or less disappeared from writings about business and the economy.[8] Managerialism became the dominant theory of corporate control from the 1930s through the 1960s. This theory emphasized the power and autonomy of inside managers. By generating internal capital resources, large corporations protected their inside managers from the influence of financial institutions. It is important to note that, although managerialists did not believe financial control existed at the time, they agreed with the premise of financial control theories that dependence on outside capital increases corporations' vulnerability to external control. For example, Baran and Sweezy wrote: "Each corporation aims at and normally achieves financial independence through the internal generation of funds which remain at the disposal of management. The corporation may still, as a matter of policy, borrow from or through financial institutions, *but it is not normally forced to do so and hence is able to avoid the kind of subjection to financial control* which was so common in the world of Big Business fifty years ago [emphasis added]."[9]

Similarly Galbraith maintained: " . . . the corporation accords a much more specific protection to the technostructure. That is by providing it with a source of capital, derived from its own earnings, that is *wholly under its own control. No banker can attach conditions as to how retained earnings are to be used.* . . . It is hard to over-estimate the importance of such a source of capital. Few other developments can have more fundamentally altered the character of capitalism [emphasis added]."[10]

Zeitlin's 1974[11] pioneering and convincing critique of managerialism provided a new impetus for research into the question of "Who controls the corporation?" Zeitlin noted that the increase in corporations' reliance on external financing, the presence of larger stockholdings by financial institutions, and the high incidences of interlocks between the directorates of nonfinancial and financial corporations all gave financial institutions the potential to exert control over corporations. The wealth of research on interlocks[12] and stock ownership[13] following Zeitlin's work empirically documented financial institutions' central position within the business community. Stockholding studies have shown that the dispersal of stock ownership noted by managerialists has been accompanied by centralization of stock management in the hands of financial institutions. These investors account for as much as 70 percent of all stock traded. In addition, studies of interlocking directorates have consistently shown banks and insurance companies to be among the most central corporations in any network of regional or national corporate ties.

Although the amount of external funding corporations obtain from financial institutions is generally agreed to be a significant determinant of financial control, it has not been subject to further research. For example, when discussing external financing, financial control theorists rely solely on the two studies Zeitlin used, i.e., Lintner 1959, and Fitch and Oppenheimer 1970.[14] Glasberg and Schwartz note that, because large corporations' need for outside financing has such great theoretical importance, "it is surprising that this proposition has been subjected to little precise measurement."[15]

However, it is also crucial to know about the structure of the resource environment in which corporations obtained their external funds. Was capital in scarce or plentiful supply? Was there a high or low degree of concentration and coordination among financial institutions? These factors limit the options available to corporations and affect the power of financial institutions to exercise control. Resource dependence theory is useful for developing a framework that accounts for such environmental variables.

Resource dependence theory

Resource dependence theorists analyze how corporations manage and control environmental uncertainty.[16] Because organizations are neither self-contained nor self-sufficient, they must rely on the environment to supply the resources required for organizational survival. It is organizations' reliance on their environment for critical resources that makes some degree of external constraint and control of organizational behavior possible and almost inevitable. Organizations become dependent on and vulnerable to external control when they must rely on other organizations for a crucial resource that is in scarce supply or controlled by one or a few organizations within the resource environment.

The resource environment, however, does not remain static. New organizations enter as others exit, and the supply of resources expands and contracts. As changes occur in the structural characteristics of the environment – mainly concentration (the extent to which power and authority over the resource is dispersed) and munificence (the availability or scarcity of the resource) – the degree of dependency and power within the exchange relation shifts.

Toward a synthesis

The resource environment in which capital flows is the capital market. It consists of three groups of actors: suppliers, financial intermediaries, and users of capital. Suppliers of capital, such as individuals, corporations, and governments, can provide capital directly to users or through financial intermediaries. Financial intermediaries, such as commercial banks, insurance companies, mutual funds, savings and loan associations, finance companies, and credit unions, collect capital from suppliers and distribute capital to users through investments in stocks, bonds, and loans. Users of capital are corporations, governments, and individuals. The interaction among these three groups determines supply, demand, and control over capital resources.

Industries and firms vary over time in their sensitivity to market conditions. However, all corporations seeking outside funds or publicly trading their stock will be affected by general market conditions. As the resource environment in which capital flows, the capital market places structural constraints on decision-makers in individual corporations.

While resource dependence theories do not acknowledge any hierarchy of resource needs, financial control theories view capital as the most important resource. Capital is the motor driving all corporate activity. Capital supplies the physical resources (i.e., raw materials, supplies, plants, and machinery) and human resources (i.e., management, technicians, workers) necessary for production. The flow of capital determines when and where production takes place. With capital, corporations have the resources to adapt to environmental demands and changes (e.g., diversify, automate) and to manipulate the environment to ensure their survival (e.g., political lobbying, advertising). Without capital, corporations cease to exist. As a result, when corporations require outside funds, power gravitates to financial institutions that control the flow of capital resources.

Financial institutions use the leverage that accompanies corporations' dependence on external funds to protect and promote their own interests. To limit the uncertainty surrounding their investment, they may ask to have one of their executives placed on the board of directors of the debtor corporation. This gives the financial institution direct or participatory control in the corporation's decision-making structure. In addition, financial institutions may stipulate that restrictive covenants be included in the loan agreement. These controls have the practical consequences of limiting a firm's strategic options. For example, if financial institutions restrict a firm from incurring any new debt, the firm cannot produce additional outside funds even for product enlargement or technical innovation. Other restrictive covenants give financial institutions veto power over top personnel changes, and provide them a say in how a corporation's profits will be allocated (i.e., the financial institution may limit the amount paid out in dividends and require a set sum retained as working capital). Although restrictive covenants seldom apply to all the corporation's important strategic decisions, they nonetheless have important consequences for corporate behavior. As Herman notes: "It may be argued that if the system of constraints forces managers to choose policies within a narrow range of profit opportunities compatible with stockholders or creditor interests, the constraints may be as, or more important than, the specific discretionary choices of managers in determining corporate objectives and actions."[17]

In addition, financial institutions may use their discretion over capital flows to promote their own business interests. They may directly demand that corporations do other business with them as a condition for extending credit.[18] They may also structure corporations' opportunities indirectly through their investment decisions. For example, they can funnel or deny loans to industries and geographical regions in accordance with their own investment interests.

Finally, conditions of uncertainty concerning the availability of capital put corporations on their best behavior vis-à-vis financial institutions. In this situation, a form of constraint control exists although financial institutions do not directly intervene in corporate decision-making.[19]

Conditions in the U.S. capital market, 1945–1980

A framework for analysis

Resource dependence theorists outline two major conditions within the environment that influence dependence: resource availability (i.e., supply) and the degree of concentration among suppliers. A third element affecting dependence is corporate demand for external funds. Therefore, the extent of aggregate corporate dependence on financial institutions is determined by three conditions: corporate demand for external funds, capital supply, and degree of concentration among financial institutions. The remainder of this paper examines each of these conditions for the 1946–1980 period and discusses their implication for financial control of corporations.

Most of the data presented here have been obtained from the Federal Reserve, Flow of Funds Accounts. The Flow of Funds Accounts provide aggregate measures that can be used to identify the influence of household, corporate, and government spending, saving, and investment behaviors on the capital market and the reciprocal influence of the capital market on the efforts of these sectors to generate income and production. In addition, the accounts provide an empirical base for exploring such questions as the sensitivity of borrowing to interest rates, and the relation of levels of assets and liabilities to demands for goods and services, for credit, and for investment in financial claims.[20]

Corporate demand for external funds

Figure 7.1 illustrates the total funds used by nonfinancial corporations from 1946 through 1980 by external and internal sources. With inflation controlled (using constant 1967 dollars), the demand for external funds increased steadily during this period, from $18 billion in 1946 to $54.2 billion in 1980. More important than the actual dollar increase, however, is the rise in the proportion of funds corporations obtained from external sources. Between 1946 and 1964,[21] corporations obtained approximately one third of their total funds from external sources, whereas between 1965 and 1980, external funds constituted almost half of corporations' total funds. The increase in the proportion of capital resources from external sources was accompanied by significant changes in the conditions surrounding corporations' demand for capital. First, the general financial stability of the corporate sector declined. Table 7.1 lists the average current ratios and debt ratios of nonfinancial corporations from 1900 through 1980. The current ratio equals current assets divided by current liabilities and is commonly used to measure corporations' short-run solvency. It indicates whether corporations can raise the funds necessary to meet their short-term obliga-

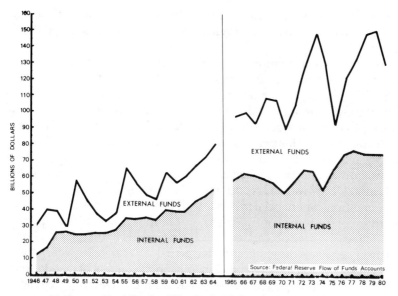

Figure 7.1. Total Funds of Nonfinancial Corporations, 1946–1980.
(Constant Dollars in 1967 = 100)
Source: Federal Reserve Flow of Funds Accounts.

tions (i.e., debt due within the year). While what is acceptable varies by industry, a current ratio of 2 (i.e., $2 of current assets to $1 of current liabilities) is frequently cited as desirable.[22]

The debt ratio equals total debt divided by total assets. It measures the extent of the total debt burden of corporations and reflects their ability to meet their short- and long-term debt obligations. Financial institutions prefer low-to-moderate debt ratios because the lower the ratio, the greater the cushion against losses in the event of liquidation. In addition, financial institutions believe debt ratios that are too high en-

Table 7.1. *Currents and debt ratios, 1900–1980*

Period	Current ratio	Debt ratio
1900–1912	n.a.	0.46
1922–1929	n.a.	0.42
1933–1944	1.8	0.42
1946–1964	1.9	0.33
1965–1980	1.6	0.43

Sources: Federal Reserve Bulletins; Statistical Abstract, 1981; Goldsmith, Lipsey, and Mendelson, *National Balance Sheet.*

courage irresponsibility on the part of corporations because the corporations' stake in a speculative activity becomes small relative to that of their creditors.

From a financial institution's point of view, a high current ratio and a low debt ratio bode well for investment, while a low current ratio and a high debt ratio signal a risky investment. Table 7.1 shows that the current ratio was higher and the debt ratio lower for the period from 1946 to 1964 than for any other time for which data are available. This suggests that, during this period, nonfinancial corporations entered the exchange relation with financial institutions from a strong credit position. Between 1965 and 1980, when corporations were more reliant on external capital, they were a less desirable outlet for investment capital. Under conditions of financial instability, financial institutions are motivated to increase their control over corporations and can demand that restrictive covenants be added to corporate loans and bonds: "The severity of negative covenants and their actual or potential encroachments on managerial discretion depend mainly on the quality of credit (financial stability and expected ability to pay off the borrower), the relative strength of lender and borrower, and lender policies."[23]

A second aspect of demand affecting corporations' dependence on financial institutions is how critical or nondiscretionary borrowing is for corporations. Between 1946 and 1964, corporations borrowed mostly to finance growth. The availability of substantial amounts of internal funds gave them the autonomy to enter or leave the capital market on their own terms. Between 1965 and 1980, borrowing became less discretionary and more critical as the proportion of internal funds to total funds declined and corporations borrowed more to survive than to grow.

Figure 7.2 documents these changes. Between 1946 and 1964, nonfinancial corporations generally decreased their borrowing during the troughs of the business cycle. An increase in short-term debt[24] followed recessions as corporations borrowed to replenish their inventories. As the expansion phase continued, long-term borrowing[25] increased and short-term borrowing subsided as corporations enlarged production facilities to take advantage of the increased demand for their products. When new recessions appeared, corporations reduced borrowing and relied on their own internal funds to cover costs, as demonstrated by the fact that during the four recessions between 1946 and 1964 the ratio of internal funds to capital expenditure was 99 percent.

Between 1965 and 1980 the picture was very different. Corporations increased both their short-term and long-term borrowing in the expansion phase of the business cycle. However, corporations did not exit from the capital market at the onset of a recession as they had done in

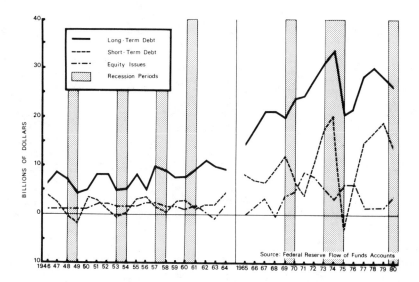

Figure 7.2. Capital Market Funds of Nonfinancial Corporations, 1946–1980
(Constant Dollars in 1967 = 100)
Source: Federal Reserve Flow of Funds Accounts.

the past. Laden with short-term debt, they were forced to increase their long-term borrowing in order to pay off their current obligations and provide themselves a margin of safety should corporate earnings decrease during the recession. (For example, the ratio of internal funds to capital expenditures dropped to 75 percent during the three recessions between 1965 and 1980 despite the fact that corporations trimmed back their capital expenditures.) This strategy increased their dependence on financial institutions as corporations were forced to pay higher costs (both in dollars and control concessions) for long-term funds.

Capital supply

From 1946 to 1980, the single most important condition within the capital market affecting financial institutions' potential to control corporations was the availability of investment capital. Between 1946 and 1964, the unprecedented boom in production and income produced an equal boom in the dollar volume of savings. Gross savings increased from approximately $30 billion a year in 1946 to $150 billion a year in 1964 (or from approximately $51 billion to $160 billion in constant 1967 dollars). Equally important was the growth of intermediation during this period. Intermediation is the process whereby savers deposit funds with financial institutions rather than directly buying bonds or mortgages; and financial institutions, in turn, lend to the ul-

Table 7.2. *Interest rates, 1890–1980*

Period	Prime commercial paper Average	(Range)	AA bond[a] Average	(Range)
1890–1915	5.7	(4.0– 7.6)	4.2	(3.8– 4.6)
1916–1929	5.1	(3.8– 7.5)	5.1	(4.5– 6.1)
1930–1945	1.2	(0.5– 3.6)	3.5	(2.6– 4.6)
1946–1964	2.5	(0.8– 4.0)	3.7	(2.5– 4.4)
1965–1980	7.0	(4.4–12.3)	7.6	(4.5–11.9)

[a]American railroad bonds from 1890 to 1918.
Sources: *Historical Statistics, Colonial Times to 1970; Statistical Abstract, 1981; Federal Reserve Statistical Digest, 1970–1979; U.S. Bureau of Economic Analysis, Long-Term Economic Growth 1860–1970.*

timate borrowers. By the early 1960s, 97 percent of all household financial assets flowed through financial institutions (as compared to 70 percent at the beginning of the period) in the form of demand and time deposits, savings accounts, life-insurance reserves, and pension-fund reserves. The result of intermediation was that the financial assets of financial institutions grew from about $250 billion in 1946 to $850 billion in 1964 (or $430 billion to $920 billion in constant 1967 dollars).

Although intermediation increased the concentration of investment capital in financial institutions, its net effects between 1946 and 1964 for corporations were positive. First, the newly institutionalized funds were distributed so as to increase competition and decrease concentration between financial sectors. Second, more funds were available at lower rates of interest than would have been possible without intermediation.[26] Table 7.2 shows the interest rates for prime commercial paper (short-term funds) and AA bonds (long-term funds) from 1890 to 1980. Interest rates were low between 1946 and 1964, but higher between 1965 and 1980 than at any other time. While interest rates reflect the demand for credit as well as its supply, the fact that interest rates between 1946 and 1964 were below average at a time when demand was up and debt rapidly rising [total outstanding debt went from approximately $300 billion in 1946 to $1,000 billion in 1964 ($513 billion to $1,080 billion in constant 1967 dollars)] demonstrates the ample availability of capital during that period.[27] Between 1964 and 1980, by contrast, there was little real growth in gross savings, and interest rates were higher. When inflation is controlled (constant 1967 dollars), annual gross savings grew from about $190 billion a year in 1965 to $250 billion a year in 1980, or about 30 percent, as compared to about 210 percent growth in gross savings between 1946 and 1964.

There was also a reversal of the trend toward intermediation. Between 1965 and 1980, the average percentage of household financial assets flowing through financial institutions dropped to 87 percent. The decline was partly the result of four periods of disintermediation. In each of these periods (i.e., 1966, 1969, 1973–1974, and 1979) the percent of household financial assets held by financial institutions dropped below 80 percent.[28] For corporate borrowers, disintermediation meant temporary capital shortages and increased uncertainty. Small and marginal businesses were required to pay high control costs (i.e., more restrictive covenants) or were pushed out of the capital market altogether. Large and financially sound corporations went to the public market to meet their capital needs, but these corporations incurred a one-year lag in organizing and implementing their public offerings. Meanwhile, their dependence increased while the discretionary and bargaining powers of financial institutions expanded. The *Federal Reserve Bulletin* noted that "non-price lending terms and standards of creditworthiness were tightened, with banks becoming more reluctant to lend to new customers and more strict about compensating-balance requirements."[29] Another means of measuring the availability of capital is to look at the dollar growth in capital market instruments (i.e., government securities; corporate stock, bonds, and loans; mortgages; and consumer loans). Table 7.3 shows the distribution of these financial assets in 1949, 1965, and 1979.

Four significant changes occurred in the distribution of financial assets within the capital market between 1946 and 1965. First, federal debt decreased dramatically from 43 percent to 15 percent of all capital market debt. Second, the value of corporate stock increased sharply from 23 percent to 41 percent of the value of all capital market instruments. Third, corporate borrowing (in the form of bonds, loans, and commercial mortgages)[30] increased from about 18 percent to 21 percent of credit market transactions; and finally, household debt (in the form of home mortgages and consumer credit) increased from 11 percent to 18 percent.

Together these facts tell the following story. Capital available for investment increased by 258 percent or from $511 billion to $1,827 billion ($715 billion to $1937 billion in constant 1967 dollars). However, the demand for credit capital from all users (i.e., households, businesses, and governments) did not grow at the rate that financial assets did. Because a large proportion of capital market funds were in the hands of institutions (due to the process of intermediation), these funds needed to seek

Table 7.3. *1949, 1965, 1979 total credit-market instruments outstanding* (billions of $) (constant dollars, 1967 = 100)

Instruments	1949		1965		1979	
	Amount	Percent	Amount	Percent	Amount	Percent
U.S. gov. securities	$306.7	43%	$ 291.8	15%	$ 394.2	18%
State & local sec.	29.4	4	106.3	5	134.5	6
Corp. & forgn.						
bonds	53.8	8	129.3	7	195.9	9
Corporate stock	168.0	23	793.9	41	535.1	24
Bank loans[a]	59.1	8	213.3	11	345.6	15
Commercial						
mortgages	16.5	2	58.8	3	103.2	4
Home mortgages	52.6	7	233.7	12	373.4	17
Consumer credit	29.1	4	109.4	6	164.4	7
Total	$715.2	100%[b]	$1,936.5	100%	$2,246.3	100%

[a]Short- and medium-term business loans make up approximately 75% of bank loans.
[b]Figures do not add to 100% due to rounding error.
Source: Federal Reserve, Flow of Funds Accounts.

investment. The presence of the secondary market for stocks kept the capital market in equilibrium.[31] Capital moved into this market because, unlike debt instruments, no demander of capital was required. However, as the demand for stocks within the secondary market increased, stock prices rose. The value of stock increased 5 1/4-fold, or from $120 billion to $749 billion ($205 billion to $809 billion in constant 1967 dollars). Because less than $30 billion of this amount came from the sale of new shares, about $600 billion of the dollar growth was attributable to the higher sale prices of already issued stock.

Ironically, financial institutions seeking investment outlets through stock purchases played a central role in increasing corporations' financial independence. Higher stock prices enabled corporations to reduce their dividend payouts because, in addition to a small dividend, stockholders' return on investment included the increase in the sale price of their stock. Since the income generated from a price increase was taxed as capital gains (i.e., at half the rate of income received from dividends), most stockholders were happy with this arrangement. Lower dividend payouts enabled corporations to keep more of their profits as retained earnings (internal funds), hence decreasing their dependence on financial institutions for external funds.

Between 1965 and 1979, total financial assets outstanding within the capital market grew from about $1,800 billion to approximately $5,200 billion. Controlling for inflation, the figures change from $1,937 billion to $2,246 billion (constant 1967 dollars). Between 1965 and 1979, the important changes that occurred included: first, a reversal in the percent of federal debt from a steadily decreasing proportion to a slowly increasing share – from 15 percent to 18 percent; second, an increase in corporate borrowing from 21 percent to 28 percent of total capital market debt; third, an increase in household debt from 18 percent to 24 percent; and fourth, a sharp decrease in the share of corporate stock in the total value of all capital market instruments from 41 percent to 24 percent.

The dollar amounts borrowed by governments, businesses, and households increased from three to fourfold during this period, ahead of the rate of inflation. Only the dollar value of corporate stock failed to increase at the rate of inflation. The difference between the performance of stock and other capital market instruments is partly due to the fact that other debt issues consisted mainly of primary market transactions, thereby representing relatively new debt at inflated prices. Only $71 billion of the increase in corporate stock resulted from new issues sold in the primary market between 1965 and 1979. Therefore, the difference ($242 billion) is due to increases in stock prices within the secondary market. However, controlling for inflation and deducting new issues, the value of stock outstanding actually declined by 33 percent in this fifteen-year period.

All these factors together suggest that governments, businesses, and households placed heavy demands on the capital market. However, the growth rate of funds to be invested in credit instruments did not keep pace with demand. Suppliers of investment capital (except pension funds) moved their capital to those capital market instruments they believed provided higher or safer returns. Money left the secondary stock market to be invested in primary debt issues at higher interest rates. In addition, the attachment of restrictive covenants to loans and bonds gave financial institutions an effective means of influencing and constraining corporate behavior.

The movement of capital out of the stock market meant, however, that corporations could no longer depend on the demand for their stock to increase their stock prices. Instead, to keep stockholders from selling their stock (and hence lowering stock prices), dividends had to be competitive with the high interest rates obtainable in the capital market. This situation simultaneously decreased the internal funds of corporations while increasing their dependence on financial institutions for external capital resources.

Table 7.4. *Financial assets of selected financial intermediaries 1949, 1965, and 1979 (billions of $) (constant dollars, 1967 = 100)*

	Amount			Distribution			Change in %	
Sector	1949	1965	1979	1949	1965	1979	1949– 1965	1965– 1979
Commercial banks	$197	$ 361	$ 539	39%	30%	32%	− 9	+ 2%
Personal trust[a]	56[b]	122	82[c]	11	10	5	− 1	− 5
Life ins. cos.	81	163	181	16	14	11	− 2	− 3
Mutual savings	31	63	71	6	5	4	− 1	− 1
Svg. & loan assns.	21	138	249	4	11	15	+ 7	+ 4
Priv. pens. funds[d]	7	78	102	1	7	6	+ 6	− 1
St/loc retirement	6	36	77	1	3	5	+ 2	+ 2
Prop./cas. ins. cos.	16	39	67	3	3	4	−	+ 1
Finance cos.	11	48	73	2	4	5	+ 2	+ 1
Mutual funds	4	37	20	1	3	1	+ 2	− 2
Credit unions	1	12	27	0	1	2	+ 1	+ 1
Gov. lending inst.	4	20	70	1	2	4	+ 1	+ 2
Fed. res. bk.	67	68	72	13	6	4	− 7	− 2
Other fin. inst.	6	11	35	1	1	2	−	+ 1
Total	$508	$1196	$1665	100%[e]	100%	100%		

[a]Personal trusts are handled primarily within the trust departments of commercial banks.
[b]Figure is for 1951.
[c]Figure is for 1977.
[d]Private Pension Funds listed here are uninsured pension funds. There funds are administered externally by commercial banks and independent investment counselors or internally by employers.
[e]Figures do not add to 100% due to rounding error.
Source: Federal Reserve. Flow of Funds Accounts.

Concentration of capital resources

Financial institutions' potential for mobilizing influence is determined by the concentration of capital resources within the financial industry and by the amount of coordination that exists among financial institutions. Further, as corporations' alternatives decrease, financial institutions' power increases.

The financial assets of financial institutions expanded from about $250 billion in 1946 to $850 billion in 1964 ($428 billion to $918 billion in constant 1967 dollars), due in large part to the increase in the growth of intermediation of capital funds. However, not all financial institutions grew at the same pace. Table 7.4 shows that, in 1949, commercial banks, personal trusts, and life-insurance companies were the giants among financial intermediaries. By 1965, the share of commercial banks and life-insurance companies, 39 percent and 16 percent in 1949, had dropped to 30 percent and 14 percent. Personal trusts and mutual savings banks lost 1 percent of their proportion of the market, while savings and loan associations increased their share of the capital market from 4 percent to 11 percent to become the third largest intermediary. Meanwhile, private pension funds, mutual funds, and finance companies grew at amazing rates. Krooss and Blyn note that, in less than two decades, the "gap between the giants and the pygmies had diminished considerably."[32] As a result, concentration of capital resources between financial sectors in the capital market decreased.[33] The growth of savings and loan associations provided corporations with an alternative source for obtaining commercial mortgages. In addition, the expansion of private pension funds, mutual funds, and property/casualty insurance assets provided new outlets for the sale of corporate bonds and stock. Between 1946 and 1964, the percent of stock (based on dollar market value) held by institutional investors increased from 3.9 percent to 12.6 percent.

Between 1965 and 1979, the financial assets of financial institutions increased from $1,128 billion to $3,871 billion ($1,196 billion to $1,665 billion in constant 1967 dollars). While there were no radical changes in the market shares of the different financial institutions,[34] not all financial intermediaries fared equally well under conditions of limited growth. Those who gained a larger share of the capital market were savings and loan associations (+ 4 percent); commercial banks, state and local retirement funds, and government lending institutions (all + 2 percent); property and casualty insurance companies, finance companies, other financial institutions (i.e., REIT, money market funds, security dealers and brokers), and credit unions (all + 1 percent). The losers were personal trusts (− 5 percent), life-insurance companies (− 3 percent), mutual funds (− 2 percent), and private pension funds and mutual savings (− 1 percent).

These changes, however, had important consequences for corporate borrowers. While the growth of savings and loan associations provided corporations with an alternative source of commercial mortgages (19 percent of corporate commercial mortgages were placed with these thrift institutions), it also meant that money was located in institutions to which corporations had only limited access. Regulations during this period restricted the investment activity of savings and loan associations primarily to home mortgages.

Life-insurance companies and mutual savings had traditionally been large investors in corporate bonds. A decline in the market share of these institutions decreased corporations' access to long-term funds. However, the expansion of the market share of commercial banks, finance companies, and other financial institutions (in particular money market funds) reflected the growth of financial institutions dealing in short-term credit. In fact, money market funds grew in direct response to the high interest rates and the growing demand of corporations for short-term funds. Money market funds, nonexistent in the early 1970s, equaled $74.4 billion in 1980.

While the decline in the market share of personal trusts, private pension funds, and mutual funds decreased the proportion of capital market resources potentially available to be invested in corporate stock, it did not result in a decline in the percent of stock held by institutional investors. The share of institutional stockholdings increased from 12.6 percent to 24.5 percent. As a result, nonfinancial corporations often found sizable blocks of their stock held by financial institutions. In 1979 the average number of institutional investors was 99, and the average percent of stock they held in 880 large corporations was 22 percent.[35] While financial institutions do not always have the right to vote these stocks, concentrated holdings provide them with a negative form of control. Corporations must consider the possibility that, if they fail to satisfy one or more financial institutions, these institutions may discipline them by dumping large blocks of their stock.[36]

Within financial sectors key to corporate borrowers, i.e., life-insurance companies and commercial banks, the degree of concentration changed little between 1946 and 1980. Both sectors remained highly concentrated, having pyramid-shaped size distributions with a few giants and a preponderance of small firms. Life-insurance companies operate nationwide, with the fifty largest owning 88 percent of the industry's total assets in 1960, and 82 percent in 1980. These fifty companies made up 3.5 percent (1960) and 2.6 percent (1980) of all life-insurance companies.[37] Commercial banks operate primarily through a system of branches located within a state. The states have varying laws that determine the geographic area where branches can be located. Five-firm concentration ratios (based on the percentage of total domestic deposits of commercial banking operations in a state accounted for by the five largest firms) equaled 52.1 in 1960 and 53.1 in 1977.[38] At the national level, a small number of money center banks[39] dominate the banking industry. In 1972, 1/10 of 1 percent (or 16 banks) held 33 percent of all domestic deposits while 90 percent (or 12,290 banks) held only 25 percent.[40]

The unevenness in these size distributions is important because the amount one commercial bank or life-insurance company can lend to one borrower is regulated. The lending limits are based on a fixed percentage of a financial institution's capital supply. As a result, corporations that need large loans have fewer alternatives and are forced to deal with the small number of banks or insurance companies large enough to offer such loans.

The presence or absence of coordination among financial institutions also affects their potential to influence corporations. Syndicate loans all but disappeared between 1946 and 1964. Their absence was due in part to the fact that corporations requested amounts within financial institutions' lending limits, and financial institutions had the capital available to lend to those limits.[41] For example, in 1954 as a single lender, Prudential Insurance agreed to loan Chrysler $250 million for one hundred years at 3¾ percent interest. Original terms were that Chrysler had only to pay the interest during that one hundred year period, paying off the balance in a lump sum in the year 2054.[42]

However, with capital scarcer, a shaky economy, and more corporations in trouble and requiring larger sums, financial institutions became more averse to risk between 1965 and 1980. Syndicate activity increased as lenders sought to cooperate in an effort to reduce the uncertainties surrounding their lending relationships. Because only a few financial lenders can make large loans, large syndicates impose upon the financial community a united policy vis-à-vis any particular corporation. Dealing with syndicates limits corporations' future options. When corporations require additional capital, they may not be in a position to shop around for the best lending agreement, as they are already obligated to all financial institutions large enough to make a loan. (This was Chrysler's fate in 1979 when the company was forced to secure government loan guarantees before it could obtain additional capital.)[43] In addition to depending on one another to participate in syndicate arrangements, the ongoing working arrangements involved in the extension of such loans decrease competition between financial institutions and increase the degree of cooperation and unity among them.

International capital flows

The preceding analysis has been restricted to domestic capital markets because the Flow of Funds Accounts, the primary data source, only covers financial transactions with U.S. borders. For the 1946–1980 period, this does not represent a serious limitation on the validity of the analysis. However, it is interesting to point out why the international capital market at the time did not operate in a substantially different way.[44]

During the 1940s and 1950s, the international capital market was small and existed primarily for foreign exchange transactions. It played an unimportant role in the relation between corporations and financial institutions because: first, U.S. corporations' direct investments abroad were generally financed internally or through the U.S. capital market; and second, nearly all American financial institutions' assets and capital reserves originated in the United States.

Throughout the 1960s and 1970s the international capital market expanded to reflect activity in the Eurocurrency[45] and Eurobond[46] markets. These markets did not exist in 1956. However, in 1979 approximately $1,139 billion flowed through these markets.[47] In addition, U.S. overseas direct investment expanded from $11.8 billion in 1950 to $52 billion in 1966 and $148.8 billion in 1977 (or $16.3, $53.6, and $81.8 billion respectively, in constant 1967 dollars). Similarly, U.S. commercial banks enlarged their participation in the international capital market. In 1966, thirteen U.S. banks operated 211 foreign branches and held $12.4 million in assets; in 1978, 137 U.S. banks operated 761 branches with assets totalling over $305 million ($155.6 million in constant 1967 dollars).[48]

The overall net effect of these changes on the relation between corporations and financial institutions was to strengthen the position of the money center banks. Although the development of an international capital market has the potential for decreasing corporations' dependence on financial institutions by enlarging corporations' borrowing alternatives, in reality it did not. First, Eurocurrency loans are made in large amounts ($500,000 and up) on an unsecured basis; therefore, access to this market is restricted to only those corporations large and financially secure enough to be labeled "prime borrowers" (the very borrowers who do well in the U.S. capital market in terms of cost and control concessions). As a result, the limited data available show that U.S. corporations made only minor use of the international bond market. Between 1965 and 1980 less than 7 percent of U.S. corporate bonds originated in either the Eurobond or other foreign bond markets.[49] Similarly, between 1977 and 1981 less than 4 percent of corporate short-term credit came from foreign institutions.[50]

Second, it was the large money center banks that moved the fastest into the international capital market. As these banks expanded their operations, they established their dominance in this market over U.S. banks. Twelve money center banks owned 76.8 percent of all U.S. foreign branch offices and held 74.8 percent of all U.S. foreign branch assets in 1974. The top four banks alone accounted for 58 percent of the total foreign branch assets of U.S. banks. Moreover, U.S. money center banks quickly established their dominance over foreign banks. By 1979, U.S. banks accounted for 40 percent of London's Eurocurrency market, which in turn accounted for the majority of all Eurocurrency transactions throughout the world.[51] In addition, these large money center banks benefitted substantially from their access to new sources of cap-

Table 7.5. *Effects of corporate demand and capital market conditions on dependency relationship between nonfinancial corporations and financial institutions*

Period	Corporate demand for external funds	Capital market conditions	Dependency between corporations and financial institutions
1946–1964	High; borrowing discretionary and based in growth	Supply: abundant; concentration: competitive with little coordination.	Mutual interdependence
1965–1980	High; borrowing necessary and based in survival	Supply: limited; concentration: becoming less competitive through coordination	Asymmetrical–with financial institutions generally in a strong position due to increased resource importance, limited supply, and increased coordination between financial institutions.

Source: See text.

ital within the Euromarket, especially during the four periods between 1966 and 1980 when money in the U.S. was relatively tight. This supply allowed them to transfer money home whenever necessary, to control the flow of capital to the smaller U.S. banks, and to be among the limited number of financial institutions who could lend U.S. multinationals the large sums they needed. Finally, the U.S. banks' presence in the international capital market provided them with numerous new investment opportunities (e.g., large loans to LDCs and foreign-based multinationals), thereby expanding their investment alternatives.

Capital markets and financial control

These data suggest that, during the 1946–1980 period, changes in the capital market as well as in corporate capital needs increased the ability of financial institutions to control corporations. However conditions were somewhat different in 1946–1964 and 1965–1980. Table 7.5 shows the variation between these two periods in terms of the demand of nonfinancial institutions for external funds, capital market conditions, and

Table 7.6. *Capital resources of nonfinancial corporations, 1956 and 1979.* (billions of $) (constant dollars, 1967 = 100)

Source	1956			1979		
	$	%	%ª	$	%	%ª
Internal funds	$35.3	65%		$ 75.5	49%	
Deprec. allow.	22.8		(64%)	56.7		(75%)
Retain. earng.	12.5		(36%)	18.8		(25%)
			(100%)			(100%)
External funds	18.8	35%		79.4	51%	
Short-trm. lns.	1.6		(8%)	19.0		(24%)
Long-trm debt	8.9		(47%)	28.6		$36%)
Stock issues	2.8		(15%)	1.5		(2%)
Trade debt	5.3		(28%)	26.1		(33%)
Other	0.2		(1%)	4.2		(5%)
			(100%)ᵇ			(100%)
Total	$54.1	100%		$154.9	100%	

ªWithin category.
ᵇFigures do not add to 100% due to rounding error.
Source: Federal Reserve, Flow of Funds Accounts.

the growing dependence of nonfinancial corporations on financial institutions.

The break along these dimensions during the mid-1960s suggests why theories of managerial autonomy predominated until that point. Managerialists emphasized the importance of sizable internal funds for protecting corporations from the interference of financial institutions. The evidence on corporate demand for external funds supports their claim that corporations were financially independent during the earlier period.

However, managerial autonomy reflected factors outside corporate organizations, specifically, the expansion of resources in the capital market. Large pools of investment capital served to keep demand for stocks high and interest rates low. These factors, in turn, enabled corporations to decrease dividends and increase internal funds. Further, a larger capital supply helped to decrease the degree of concentration within the market. Thus corporations seeking funds had a broad spectrum of alternatives available.

Nonfinancial corporations became more vulnerable to financial control after the mid-1960s as a result of corporations' increased dependence on financial institutions to supply their capital needs. Table 7.6

compares corporate capital resources in 1956 and 1979.[52] What is most striking is the difference in reliance on internal versus external funds. In 1956 internal funds supplied approximately two-thirds of corporations' capital resources. In 1979 internal funds provided less than half, indicating a much greater reliance on external financing. In addition, the proportion of external funds provided through short-term loans increased while the percentage provided through long-term debt decreased. The greater use of short-term financing, coupled with low current ratios, increased the financial instability of many corporations. In particular, the low share of equity in total capitalization (67 percent in 1950 versus 53 percent in 1973) meant that relatively high contractual interest payments had to be paid even if there were downturns in sales and incomes (as in the recessions of 1970, 1974–1975, and 1980). These factors increased the dependence of corporations on financial institutions.

Changes in the capital market after 1965 provided the real basis for challenging the concept of managerial autonomy in the 1970s. On one hand, resource dependence theorists argued that managers were restricted by their firms' dependence on other companies for critical resources. Corporate policy, therefore, was not strictly an expression of managerial choices, but rather the outcome of the interplay between management and significant actors in their environment. On the other hand, financial control theorists argued that managerialists underestimated the power of financial institutions. Banks and insurance companies could influence corporate decision-making as a result of their control of huge pools of investment capital, their substantial stockholdings, and their centrality in the network of interlocking directorates.

Most important, the decrease in the general availability of capital (intensified during periods of capital shortages) enabled financial institutions to exercise greater discretion over the allocation of capital. As a result, financial institutions could demand higher prices and more control concessions. Furthermore increased coordination among financial institutions in the form of lending syndicates meant that corporations had to secure their external financing in a less competitive resource environment.

Corporate dependence on financial institutions obviously varies over time. Historical research[53] and individual case studies[54] have shown that financial institutions use their power to shape corporate structure and behavior. For example, Chandler shows that the centralized organizational structure adopted by most railroads in the late nineteenth century was the result of financial influence: "In their railroad reorganizations Morgan and other financiers did much more than merely appoint presidents and members of boards of directors. They instituted financial and administrative reforms within the systems they refinanced."[55]

More recently, Mintz and Schwartz found forty-four incidents of bank intervention involving Fortune 500 firms between 1976 and 1980. Nearly all of these cases occurred when banks perceived their investment threatened. Utilizing the power that accompanies capital resource control, financial institutions directed and redirected corporate policy to best serve their own interests.

Finally, the increased influence of financial institutions can also affect the social relations of production. Using restrictive loan covenants, financial institutions can prevent corporations from risk-taking ventures as a means of increasing profits. As a result, corporations may be forced independently, or through direct lender pressures, to maximize profits by lowering labor costs. A case in point is the International Harvester Company. In an effort to improve its capital position, IHC postponed plans to construct an engine plant in Spain, sold off its 50 percent interest in a Japanese construction and farm equipment venture, and negotiated plant closings and plant sales in every major European country. IHC also slashed employment as much as 40 percent and cut back salaries in the hopes of saving of $300 million by the end of 1982. *Business Week* reported, however, that in spite of these efforts, "If Harvester does request revision of the loan terms, bankers will attempt to tighten the screws on its operations further by pushing for speeded-up cost cutting efforts. At the top of the list will be intensified demands that Harvester wring concessions out of the United Auto Workers. 'They will have to take the UAW to the table for the banks to give much more,' warns one banker."[56]

Conclusions and Suggestions

This article has addressed the question of whether external control by financial institutions is possible due to corporations' dependence on external financing. The paper documented aggregate corporate capital needs, and in addition argued that capital market conditions were a causal factor affecting corporate dependence on financial institutions. The findings suggest that between 1945 and 1980 changes in these factors increased corporations' vulnerability to financial control. However, three qualifying statements need to be made, each suggesting an area for future research.

First, this research has provided a framework for analyzing financial dependence, which can be used to examine how actual control has changed. At the aggregate level, researchers should analyze the relation between changes in market conditions and the prevalence of such control mechanisms as loan covenants. At the firm level, assuming that certain decision-making outcomes reflect the self-interest of financial institutions rather than inside managers, researchers should analyze the relation between financial dependence and corporate behavior (e.g., increases or decreases in dividends, top management firings, plant closings, wage cuts, etc.)

Second, this research has been limited to the 1945–1980 period. Because corporate capital needs and market conditions vary over time, it cannot be assumed that the types of financial dependence noted in this article existed prior to 1946 or exist in the 1980s. Each period requires investigation. Furthermore, as research is conducted on other periods, it should be possible to identify overall patterns of change within the capital market. Are changes cyclic, random, or linear? And what factors in the economy and in social institutions account for them?

Finally, this article has examined the possibilities for financial control as generated by aggregate conditions of corporate capital dependence. However, as Zeitlin has noted, financial control may derive from other factors, especially institutional stockholdings and interlocking directorates. Further research is necessary to examine the relation among aggregate changes in all three of these factors. While most analyses of institutional stockholdings and interlocking directorates have looked at specific corporations at one point in time, a few studies have focused on the aggregate characteristics of institutional stockholdings and interlocking directorates across periods. For instance, Mizruchi has demonstrated that within directorate networks the centrality of banks, insurance companies, and investment banks (each suppliers of different kinds of capital funds) has changed significantly over time. Stockholding studies[57] have shown a clear linear trend of greater holdings by financial institutions. Do these trends correlate with aggregate shifts in corporate capital dependence over the last century? What are the causal or functional relations among them? And finally, are their joint effects on actual control additive or interactive? For example, interlocks may mean different things for different levels of capital dependence: in periods of high capital dependence, director interlocks may represent lines of control, whereas during periods of low dependence they may serve as channels for information.

Acknowledgment

This article is a revision of a paper presented at the 78th Annual Meeting of the American Sociological Association, Detroit, 1983. I would like to thank Mark Granovetter, Charles Perrow, Michael

198   STRUCTURES OF CAPITAL

Schwartz, K. Jill Kiecolt, Gerald Zeitz, William Falk, and John Logan, all of whom provided valuable suggestions and criticisms of earlier versions of the paper. In addition, the exceedingly helpful comments of the editors are gratefully acknowledged.

Notes

1. Financial control as used here includes both bank control and bank hegemony models. Here I focus on their common element: the potential of financial institutions to exercise control over nonfinancial corporations. For a discussion of the differences in the two perspectives, see Davita Silfen Glasberg and Michael Schwartz, "Ownership and Control of Corporations," *Annual Review of Sociology* 9 (1983): 22–32.

2. For a fuller statement, see Thomas Koenig, Robert Gogel, and John Sonquist, "Models of the Significance of Interlocking Corporate Directorates," *American Journal of Economics and Sociology* 38 (1979): 173–186; and Glasberg and Schwartz, "Ownership and Control of Corporations."

3. See, for example, Michael Useem, "Corporations and the Corporate Elite," *Annual Review of Sociology* 6 (1980): 41–77; Donald Palmer, "Interpreting Corporate Interlocks from Broken Ties," *Social Science History* (1983): 217–31; and William G. Roy, "The Unfolding of the Interlocking Directorate Structure of the United States," *American Sociological Review* 48 (1983): 248–57.

4. For the period under study, commercial banks and life-insurance companies were corporations' primary source of external financing. Between 1946 and 1980, commercial banks provided approximately 30 percent, and life-insurance companies approximately 25 percent, of such funds. In addition, most of the 20 percent received from pension-fund investments were channelled through the trust departments of commercial banks.

5. Rudolf Hilferding, *Das Finanzkapital* (Frankfurt: Europäische Verlagsanstalt, 1910); U.S. House of Representatives, Committee on Banking and Currency, "Investigation of Concentration of Control of Money and Credit," (Washington, D.C.: U.S. Government Printing Office, 1913); Louis D. Brandeis, *Other People's Money* (New York: Frederick A. Stokes Company, 1914); V. I. Lenin, *Imperialism: The Highest Stage of Capitalism* (New York: International Publishers, 1917).

6. For details of the key position that investment banks played in the process of capital formation at this time, see Thomas R. Navin and Marian V. Sears, "The Rise of a Market for Industrial Securities, 1877–1902," *Business History Review* 29 (1955); 105–38; and Vincent Carosso, *Investment Banking in America* (Cambridge, Mass.: Harvard University Press, 1970).

7. The power of investment bankers at the turn of the century has been well documented. For a general summary, see William J. Shultz and M. R. Caine, *Financial Development of the United States* (New York: Prentice-Hall, 1937), 430–66; for a more detailed look at their involvement in railroad affairs, see Alfred D. Chandler, *The Visible Hand: The Managerial Revolution in American Business* (Cambridge, Mass.: Belknap Press, 1977), 79–205; and for a biography of the most powerful investment banker, see Stanley Jackson, *J. P. Morgan* (New York: Stein & Day, 1984).

8. Exceptions are Anna Rochester, *Rulers of America: A Study of Finance Capital* (New York: International Publishers, 1936), and Victor Perlo, *The Empire of High Finance* (New York: International Publishers, 1957).

9. Paul A. Baran and Paul M. Sweezy, *Monopoly Capital* (New York: Monthly Review Press, 1966), 15–16.

10. John Kenneth Galbraith, *The New Industrial State* (Boston: Houghton Mifflin, 1967), 92–93.

11. Maurice Zeitlin, "Corporate Ownership and Control: The Large Corporation and the Capitalist Class," *American Journal of Sociology* 79 (1974): 1073–1119.

12. See especially Mark Mizruchi, *The Structure of the American Corporate Network: 1904–1974* (Beverly Hills: Sage, 1982); Richard E. Ratcliff, "Banks and Corporate Lending: An Analysis of the Impact of the Internal Structure of Capital Class on the Lending Behavior on Banks," *American Sociological Review* 45 (1980): 543–70; and Beth Mintz and Michael Schwartz, *The Power Structure of American Business* (Chicago: University of Chicago Press, 1985).

13. For example, David M. Kotz, *Bank Control of Large Corporations in the United States* (Berkeley: University of California Press, 1978), and Edward S. Herman, *Corporate Control, Corporate Power* (Cambridge, Eng.: Cambridge University Press, 1981).

14. Lintner thoroughly discusses corporations' sources and uses of capital. However, the data end in 1953 and therefore cannot be used to analyze corporate dependence *after that time*. Fitch and Oppenheimer's study provides only limited data through 1969. One purpose of the present study is to introduce sociologists to data from the Federal Reserve Flow of Funds Accounts, which can inform future research on the *current* financing patterns of nonfinancial corporations.

15. Glasberg and Schwartz, "Ownership and Control of Corporations," 321.

16. A full understanding of this perspective can be obtained from reading Jeffrey Pfeffer and Gerald R. Salancik, *The External Control of Organizations: A Resource Dependence Perspective* (New York: Harper & Row, 1978), who develop the view that corporate survival depends on corporations controlling their environment to ensure a steady flow of necessary resources, and Howard E. Aldrich, *Organizations and Environments* (Englewood Cliffs: Prentice-Hall, 1979), who argues that corporate survival depends upon corporations' successful adaptation to the uncertainty surrounding the acquisition of necessary resources.

17. Herman, *Corporate Control, Corporate Power*, 20.

18. For examples of direct bank intervention in corporate decision-making, see Robert Fitch and Mary Oppenheimer, "Who Rules the Corporations?" *Socialist Review* (1970): 4: 73–108, 5: 61–114, 6: 33–94.

19. A forceful elaboration of the indirect power of banks can be found in Mintz and Schwartz, *The Power Structure of American Business*.

20. For more detail on the Flow of Funds Accounts, see *Introduction to Flow of Funds*, Board of Governors of the Federal Reserve System (1980).

21. The trends discussed in this article are long term in nature. The year 1964 was selected as a cutoff point for analytical purposes; as shown in Figures 7.1 and 7.2, 1964 is the midpoint in a period of fairly rapid change (1962 to 1966).

22. Lewis E. Davids, *Dictionary of Banking and Finance* (Totowa, N.J.: Littlefield, Adams & Co., 1980).

23. Herman, *Corporate Control, Corporate Power*, 126.

24. Short-term debt is generally payable within one year from date of issue. It includes bank loans, commercial paper, bankers' acceptances, bond and tax anticipation notes, and warrants.

25. Long-term debt has a maturity of more than one year and includes corporate bonds, commercial mortgages, and bank loans.

26. For an explanation of the connections among interest rates, stock and bond prices, and intermediation, see Lawrence S. Ritter and William L. Silber, *Principles of Money, Banking, and Financial Markets* (New York: Basic Books, 1974), 12, 320.

27. Stability over time in the prime interest rate is also an indicator of the degree of certainty that exists within the market as to the availability of capital. Between 1946 and 1964 the prime rate changed only 19 times as compared with 184 times between 1965 and 1980, when supply was less certain and the environment more volatile.

28. Household financial assets left financial institutions primarily to take advantage of the higher interest rates offered by U.S. Government securities. Two factors prevented financial institutions from adjusting their deposit rates to a competitive level. First, they felt they could not afford to raise rates. The assets of most intermediaries were mainly in long-term debt bought some time ago at considerably lower yields. Second, the legal ceilings imposed by the Federal Reserve, the Federal Home Loan Board, and other regulatory agencies prevented them from raising deposit rates once the maximum ceilings were reached.

29. "Recent Corporate Financing Patterns," *Federal Reserve Bulletin* (Sept. 1980), 683–90.

30. A commercial mortgage is a pledge given by a corporation on business property as security for a loan (i.e., it is similar to a home mortgage except that it is on business property).

31. The capital market consists of a primary and a secondary market. In the primary market, capital users demand capital or credit for their own use. Corporations do this by issuing new stock, floating new bonds, or acquiring new loans. In the secondary market, there are no users of capital. Instead, already issued credit instruments (i.e., stocks and bonds) are traded by investors interested in liquidating their assets or increasing their portfolios.

32. Herman E. Krooss and Martin R. Blyn, *A History of Financial Intermediaries* (New York: Random House, 1971), 216.

33. Using sectors rather than firms to calculate Herfindahl indexes shows that concentration decreased as the index fell from .214 in 1949 to .148 in 1965.

34. The Herfindahl index changed only slightly, rising to .155 in 1979.

35. Calculated from data provided in the Dec. 13, 1979, issue of *Business Week*.

36. A dramatic example of financial institutions' power to lower the price of a corporation's stock can be found in Davita Silfen Glasberg, "Corporate Power and Control: The Case of Leasco Corporation versus Chemical Bank," *Social Problems* 29 (1981): 104–16.

37. *Moody's Bank & Finance Manual* (New York: Moody's Investors Service, Inc., 1961 and 1982); *Life Insurance Fact Book* (Washington, D.C.: American Council of Life Insurance, 1984).

38. *The Bank Holding Company Movement to 1978: A Compendium* (Washington, D.C.: Board of Governors of the Federal Reserve System, 1978).

39. "Money center banks consist of about 20 giant banks located in centers of diverse financial activities such as New York, Chicago, San Francisco and Los Angeles. These banks have significantly greater power than other banks. In fact, money center banks are an essentially different type of institution because of their role as pacesetters for the cost of loans, their partial control over the money supply, their correspondent relationships with thousands of other banks and their access to huge pools of unregulated international funds." *Banking & Finance: The Hidden Cost* (New York: Corporate Data Exchange, Inc., 1980), 19.

40. Lawrence S. Ritter and William L. Silber, *Principles of Money, Banking, and Financial Markets*, 378.

41. The laws that limit banks to lending no more than 10 percent of their capital or surplus to any one borrower causes banks to invite other banks to join them in a syndicate agreement for the purpose of handling a very large loan. Several banks each

lend a portion of the amount to the corporation. The participating banks agree on the bank that will serve as lead bank, or syndicate manager (this is generally the bank that initiated the loan), the restrictive covenants that will be attached to the loan, and the manner in which the loan will be liquidated (i.e., some of the banks may wish to be paid off ahead of other banks).

42. Fortunately for Prudential, the loan included a provision that after ten years either party could convert the loan to a twenty-year annual-payment loan. In 1964, when market conditions brought higher interest rates, Prudential took advantage of this option.

43. For more detail on financial institutions' role in Chrysler's financial crisis, see Davita Silfen Glasberg, "Reconceptualizing Marxist Class Categories: Case Studies in the Importance of Finance Capital in Class Formation," paper presented at the ASA Annual Meetings, San Antonio, Tex., 1984.

44. It is not the aim of this section to provide a thorough treatment of the development and workings of the international capital market. Rather its purpose is to relate what went on in this market to the overall question of what effect market conditions had on corporations' dependence on financial institutions. For a more detailed analysis of the international capital market, see Jonathan David Aronson, *Money and Power* (Beverley Hills: Sage, 1977); Sarkis J. Khoury, *Dynamics of International Banking* (New York: Praeger Publishers, 1980); and Eugene L. Versluysen, *The Political Economy of International Finance* (New York: St. Martin's Press, 1981).

45. In the Eurocurrency market, commercial banks accept deposits and make loans in foreign currencies. Between 1970 and 1979 Eurodollars accounted for approximately 75 percent of the gross market size.

46. In the Eurobond market, bonds are underwritten by an international syndicate and sold mostly outside the country of the currency in which it is denominated.

47. Eugene L. Versluysen, *The Political Economy of International Finance*, 38, 213.

48. Sarkis J. Khoury, *Dynamics of International Banking*, 6, 10, 12.

49. Michael Melvin, *International Money and Finance* (New York: Harper & Row, 1985), 184–85; *Flow of Funds Accounts*, Boards of Governors of the Federal Reserve System, 1979 and 1981.

50. *Business Week*, Mar. 1, 1982, 42.

51. Sarkis J. Khoury, *Dynamics of International Banking*, 45.

52. Table 7.6 presents annual flows and shows how corporations aggregately financed their operations and investments in each year. Although these figures vary somewhat from year to year according to the business cycle, they reflect the average of each period as well as the changes that took place between periods.

53. See, for example, Shepard B. Clough, *A Century of American Life Insurance: A History of the Mutual Life Insurance Company of New York, 1843–1943* (New York: Columbia University Press, 1946); and Chandler, *The Visible Hand*.

54. See, for example, Davita Silfen Glasberg, "Corporations in Crisis: Institutional Decision-Making and the Role of Finance Capital," PhD thesis, Department of Sociology, State University of New York at Stony Brook; and Beth Mintz and Michael Schwartz, *The Power Structure of American Business*.

55. Chandler, *The Visible Hand*, 184.

56. "Harvester May Need a New Debt Deal," *Business Week* (Mar. 8, 1982), 29.

57. Robert M. Soldofsky, *Institutional Holdings of Common Stock 1900–2000* (Ann Arbor: University of Michigan Press, 1971); Raymond W. Goldsmith, *Institutional Investors and Corporate Stock* (New York: Columbia University Press, 1973).

8
Capital flows and the process of financial hegemony

BETH MINTZ AND MICHAEL SCHWARTZ

While the importance of capital has been recognized historically in the sociological literature, the precise role which capital plays in an advanced industrial society has recently become an intriguing question in a wide range of investigations.

The following chapter is part of the developing literature which stresses the social base of economic institutions and analyzes the role of capital in that framework. Implicit is the assumption that the economic and the social are intertwined, and that economic relationships can be understood only when considered in the context of the social structure in which they develop. Specifically, this chapter explores the relationship between capital formation and the exercise of power. We investigate relations allocating financial capital among major financial and nonfinancial corporations. A central assumption is that relationships among, rather than within, firms constrain and structure the activities of large economic organizations. This field of power relations is the system within which intercorporate interactions are embedded. Capital allocation plays a key role in this process, for control of financial capital provides a major source of power.

Although few would question the idea that the investment decisions of economic actors can have serious consequences for the larger society, a more controversial notion is that this decision-making is highly centralized. This, of course, affects both public and private economic and social policy. If centralized corporate action is not assumed, the social consequences of economic actions will be viewed as scattered, independent, and unpredictable.

Because many people tend to ignore the collective interests that move individual firms, one of the most controversial issues in the study of intercorporate relations has been the existence of mechanisms for the systematic resolution of conflict among corporate actors. In this chapter, we argue that mechanisms for conflict resolution do, in fact, exist.

Research shows that (1) these mechanisms are a product of differential power; (2) control of capital is the source of this power; (3) the centralization of the financial sector provides the institutional framework for coordinated control over capital allocation; and (4) the exercise of this power is tantamount to making economic and social policy.

The emphasis on intercorporate relations has developed, most recently, under the rubric of either organizational theory or political sociology, but the emphasis on the broader context in which economic relations are established and maintained belongs in the tradition of economic sociology. Rooted in the writings of both Marx and Weber, investigations of intercorporate affairs take as problematic the relationship between social and economic institutions. Marx and Weber also draw attention to questions of power, especially the capacity to exercise differential power. While Weberian analysis emphasizes institutional power and Marxist analysis tends to assume the primacy of capital, virtually all studies in economic sociology take institutional structures as a framework for the analysis of social power.

Like those of Marx and Weber, our investigations of the economic order are framed by assumptions about the social order. Like Parsons and Smelser, moreover, we are still exploring these assumptions. Yet, unlike Parsons and Smelser, we assume a tendency toward cleavage rather than consensus in intercorporate affairs. How to establish cooperation in this framework is viewed as problematic.[1]

We frame our investigation, then, within the traditional field of economy and society. At the same time, we trace our orientation to more recent developments in the study of economic relationships. We take seriously theoretical discussions about the capacity of the state to coordinate economic affairs, but we find an alternative vehicle of coordination – and a more fundamental one in our opinion – in financial markets. To resolve the problem of intercorporate coordination, a theory of financial hegemony is essential.

Business unity

Among the most vexed issues in the sociology of business has been the identification of the conditions under which conflict has been resolved or unity established. Managerialists since Berle and Means have asserted the autonomy of the modern large corporation and this is the foundation for their assumption that capitalist class unity is impossible to achieve.[2] Critics of this view, both Marxist[3] and non-Marxist[4], have challenged the idea of business disunity without questioning the premise of corporate autonomy. They argue that united action is possible either through consensus of interest among firms, or by the imposition of common policy through state action.

Recent work, however, has questioned the assumption of corporate autonomy itself.[5] Based on the notion that intercorporate relations are characterized by potentially coercive structural leverage, this new perspective argues that one firm or group of firms can impose united action upon others, even when such action is not in the narrow self-interest of the complying institutions.

Crucial to this view is the empirical proposition that the centralization of the financial sector (banks, insurance companies, and investment companies) allows for coordinated decision-making over the disposition of investment capital.[6] Because of the importance of outside funding in fueling economic expansion and weathering ongoing economic crisis, such centralized decision-making over capital flows confers upon financial leadership the intermittent capacity to coordinate activity among a wide range of economic actors. They, thus, achieve the capability of planning and executing economic and social policies that depend upon the compliance of other corporations (and even governments), even when such actions do not directly benefit all institutional participants. We have argued elsewhere[7] that this phenomenon is properly understood as financial hegemony, using hegemony in the structural sense developed by Gramsci.[8]

The importance of financial hegemony is found in its implications for economic and political policy formation. In large part, economic theorists have ignored the issue of planning, defending their inattention with the managerial assumption that autonomy makes explicit intercorporate coordination problematic and short-lived. Markets, therefore, are viewed as the capitalist proxy for planning.

In most political sociology, insofar as economic policy formation is studied, it is done so with the pluralist assumption that the government has the mandate to regulate corporate activity and the power to impose its will on business, if necessary. Economic planning, therefore, occurs only when the government initiates it; it is never a consequence of independent action by business.[9]

The theory of financial hegemony undermines this argument by focusing on those occasions when banks and insurance companies are able to impose policy upon resistant nonfinancial firms or actors. These decisions demonstrate the inadequacy of the assumption of autonomy and the corresponding weakness of any analysis that relies exclusively on the notion of a competitive market system.

Moreover, the structural leverage resulting from the concentration of investment capital can sometimes be applied to a broad spectrum of companies simultaneously, thus providing the power to implement economic policies without the intervention of the state. The theory of financial hegemony, therefore, provides the basis for a broad reorganization of our understanding of economic and political policies. To understand this process, we offer examples of the imposition of financial decision-making on three types of business units: individual firms, industrial sectors, and national economies.

Sources of financial cohesion

Although commercial banks and insurance companies independently strive to maximize their profits, structural interdependencies have developed among them that tend to mute competition and contribute to a united financial community. While this unity is at times quite fragile, the long-run tendencies are toward similarity of interest; and these firms, therefore, often constitute a cohesive unit in determining the direction of capital flows.

The cohesion within the financial world is the result of the high concentration levels of investment capital. In the early 1970s, for example, the fifty largest banks in the United States held over two-thirds of lendable funds held by commercial banks; seven New York and Chicago money market banks controlled about 20 percent of all bank assets.[10] The second major source of commercial loan capital, life-insurance companies, is even more concentrated.

This concentration of capital is translated into unity by a developing set of interdependencies among financial institutions. Short-term interbank borrowing creates a consonance of interest among banks because each firm has a stake in the others' economic health. Loan consortia – the typical method for organizing large loans – are another mechanism for unity; they allow banks to share the risk inherent in very large loans while forcing a united financial posture toward the borrowing industrial firm. Concentration, interbank borrowing, and consortia all contribute to another unifying mechanism: similarity of investment portfolios both in terms of loans and stock. Although the details of a particular institution's holdings may vary, the overall profiles of the major institutions' investments are quite similar, thus creating an ongoing community of interests among major financials. While at times competitive tendencies override forces for cohesion, the long-term result is a rough consonance of interest among the largest creditors.

The participation of major financial institutions in all industrial sectors and the consonance of interest among them provides the foundation for the financial hegemony that characterizes intercorporate relations. We explore these processes below.

Capital flows and the imposition of corporate policy by lenders

Although ultimately the impact of financial hegemony can be analyzed in terms of worldwide economic relations, the building block of the hegemonic process is found on the level of the individual corporation. It is on that level that financial institutions periodically attempt – not always successfully – to regulate corporate behavior. While this regulation is sporadic, it is frequently the only force within the business arena capable of constructing imposed coordination.

Financial leverage typically rests on two major mechanisms: the control of loan capital and the stockholding of financial trust departments. While these work in different ways, both potentially affect the behavior of nonfinancial corporations in profoundly important ways.

The most visible examples of bank influence over individual firms involve the intervention of lenders into the internal affairs of borrowers. A survey of the business press during the five-year period of 1 January 1977 to 31 December 1981 revealed reports of interventions in about 5 percent of the one thousand largest American companies, including such firms as Braniff Airlines, Gulf Oil, Lockheed, and Mattel.[11] Although outcomes of the intervention process are often unpredictable, the mechanism can be quite effective under appropriate circumstances.

This point is nicely illustrated by the Hunt brothers' attempt to corner the silver market in the late 1970s.[12] Commodity futures markets are fragile structures, easily upset by a small number of participants with large resources.[13] Futures contracts involve a promise to deliver a commodity at a precise future date at a particular price. When the date arrives, the buyer and seller typically settle accounts by comparing the agreed-upon price with the market price of that day. If the actual price is lower, the buyer pays the seller the difference; if the actual price is higher, the seller pays the buyer. No merchandise changes hands.

The Hunts began buying silver in 1973 and by early 1980 had accumulated over 100 million ounces. They had entered the futures market only as buyers and when due dates arrived, instead of negotiating the differences, they insisted upon delivery. Since sellers were forced to seek out silver to cover their contracts, scarcity created by the hoarding forced up prices. Essentially, the sellers were forced to buy silver from the brothers at very high prices and sell it back to them at the much lower contract price. The Hunts made a great deal of money on each transaction and continued to accumulate silver, thus pushing up the price still further.

In response, the other silver traders united and changed the rules of the futures market. Potential buyers were forced to post a substantial proportion of the purchase price when the contract was signed. This drove many buyers out of the market (at least temporarily) causing a drop in the price of silver. When the Hunts' contracts came due, the sellers could find silver at much below the contract prices, so the Hunts were faced with a serious dilemma. If they kept their silver and tried to buy their way out of the contracts, they needed close to $1 billion in cash. If they tried to sell to pay for the contracts, they would be dumping huge amounts of silver onto a depressed market, depressing it still further and producing even worse losses when the next contracts came due.

Their best option, they decided, was to borrow money, cover their losses, and hope to push the price up again when the market adjusted to the new rules. The Hunts had sufficient collateral for the billion-dollar loan they sought. Placid Oil, the family company, was worth $8 billion with very little debt. Nevertheless, the lenders at first refused a rescue loan, largely because "bankers just weren't in the mood to bail the Hunts out."[14] The bankers did not approve of the Hunts' effort to upset the silver market.

When the rescue loan was finally negotiated, it contained specific provisions that forbade futures trading by the Hunts. The agreement stipulated the "gradual and orderly liquidation" of their silver holdings and prohibited further "speculation in silver and other commodities."[15] A spokesperson for Morgan Guaranty, the lead lender, promised close policing of the agreement, assuring the press that the banks would "throw the loan into default" and foreclose on Placid Oil if the Hunts engaged in further commodity speculation.[16] Paul A. Volcker, Federal Reserve chairman, was particularly gratified by the loan condition. Speaking just before the agreement was finalized, he pointed to its import in protecting the integrity of the futures market: "Mr. Volcker said that if the refinancing – with its restrictive clauses – went through, the public will be far better protected from further Hunt speculation. The restrictive clauses would hold during the life of the loan which, sources said, would be for a number of years."[17]

This example illustrates several important features that make lender intervention one of the most important disciplinary devices in the corporate world. First, loan leverage is capable of altering the economic strategy of corporations or individuals. This leverage derives from the urgent needs of borrowers and the structural unity of lenders. The Hunts needed money quickly. They could not shop around for lenders because of time pressure. They could not rely on interlender competition because almost all major loans are handled by consortia involving all of the major money market banks capable of organizing such large transactions (see above).

Second, lenders often have a great deal of discretion in organizing rescue loans. In the Hunt case, they did not have to lend the money. Or, because Placid Oil was worth many times the loan value, the banks could impose stringent conditions – even those that hindered profitability – without fear of losing their investment. Of course, many rescue loans are negotiated in more constrained circumstances. When a company is already heavily in debt, loan refusal might jeopardize the banks' original investment; stringent loan conditions might force bankruptcy. Lender discretion, therefore, is constrained by the particular circumstances at hand.

Finally, lenders can impose policies extraneous to their narrow concerns for repayment. The major conditions on the Hunt loan had little to do with guaranteeing repayment; they were designed to protect the integrity of the silver market. At least some of the time, therefore, banks enforce system needs upon recalcitrant firms or capitalists. As Paul Volcker suggested during the Hunt episode, the government was unable to control their speculation; only the lenders could rescue the market from "collapse."[18]

Institutional stockholding has developed into a second mechanism by which banks influence the policies of nonfinancial corporations. As of 1979, institutional investors – banks, insurance companies, and investment houses – accounted for about 70 percent of the stock traded on the New York Stock Exchange.[19] And, although accurate figures are difficult to obtain, these same institutions are thought to hold about 40 percent of the outstanding stock in the largest American corporations.[20]

Institutional stockholding is highly concentrated. In 1974 the top seven money market banks (Chase Manhattan, Chemical, Citicorp, Bankers Trust, Manufacturers Hanover, First Chicago and Continental Illinois) – the same banks which dominate corporate lending – accounted for 40 percent of pension money and 25 percent of all trust department holdings. The top sixty bank trust departments held over two-thirds of bank trust assets.[21] Fifty insurance companies held 34 percent of insurance assets, and thirty-five mutual funds accounted for 65 percent of that industry's capital.[22]

Like lenders, institutional investors often coordinate their buying and selling of stocks. The business press refers to the "herd effect"[23] in which institutions "tend to follow a few of the very biggest and best-named firms."[24] This unified buying and selling is the foundation upon which the power of institutional stockholders is constructed.

If corporate prospects and policies please major institutions, they buy huge amounts of the stock, boost prices, and create a favorable financial climate for the firm. If corporate policy displeases them, or financial performance lags, they may dump stock, causing large declines in price, and thus hamstring corporate activities.

The most celebrated stock dumping incident in history was precipitated in 1969 by an attempt on the part of Leasco, a relatively small Long Island-based conglomerate, to acquire Chemical Bank of New York.[25] Leasco proposed to exchange a share of its stock, worth $140, for 1.25 shares of Chemical stock, worth about $100. This was an attractive offer for Chemical stockholders, but the acquisition was thwarted when institutions began dumping Leasco shares. As a result, the conglomerate's price dropped to $106 in two weeks and to a low of $7 by the next year. This frustrated Leasco's acquisition attempt and limited its other expansion. Saul Steinberg, the head of the company, commented to *Business Week*, "I always knew there was an Establishment ... I just used to think I was part of it."[26]

Perhaps the most important consequence of this relatively infrequent exhibition of institutional power is its deterrent effect: *Business Week* concluded that "some corporate managements tend to pander to institutional preferences and thus adopt whatever policies are favored by the money managers in large investment institutions."[27] This confers upon major financials considerable power in setting or altering the policies of nonfinancial firms to conform to their interpretation of corporate health or broader system needs. The breadth of this process can be seen in the treatment of the "Nifty-Fifty."[28]

Between 1965 and 1974 the institutional proportion of all stocks traded on the New York exchange increased from 39.3 percent to 58.9 percent.[29] Much of this increase went into a handful of growth stocks known as the Nifty-Fifty, which included Avon, Coca-Cola, Eastman Kodak, IBM, McDonald's, and Xerox.[30] As the prices of these stocks soared, the price-earnings ratios of many reached thirty-to-one. This meant that dividends paid only about 4 percent on investment; a viable profit was made by stockholders only if prices continued to rise.

By the middle of the 1970s, stock prices had leveled off, even among this group. Between 1972 and 1978, twenty of these favorites had declined an average of 39 percent.[31] These losses, combined with low dividend payouts, were a key factor in the poor performance of institutional investors during the period. At the same time, many of these companies had accumulated large amounts of retained earnings, partly because of their enormous growth and partly because of their low dividend payouts. IBM, Ford, and General Motors, for example, each held over $2 billion in unspent earnings.

While bank trust departments were showing poor returns because of the flat market, bank loan departments were caught in a lending bind. The retained earnings among Nifty-Fifty firms represented a capital surplus that removed the banks' best customers from the lending market, both because they were not borrowing as much and because they borrowed from each other on the commercial paper market.[32]

To escape this double bind, bank trust departments abandoned their policy of investing in growth stocks and called for dividend increases. The business press announced the news: "The litany of advice emerging from Wall Street emphasizes low price earnings multiples and high current dividends."[33]

The immediate result of this change was a further drop in Nifty-Fifty prices because institutional stock dumping concentrated upon these low dividend stocks. But soon this decline was halted by a surge of dividend increases: "Today growth is out among big investors, total return is in, and so not only MacDonalds but Kresge, Johnson and Johnson, and American Hospital Supply have all hiked their dividends."[34]

The responsiveness of companies to the stock purchasing policies of major institutional investors allowed financial firms to organize a shift in dividend payout policy across the economy. This shift did more than improve portfolio performance in bank trust departments; it also contributed to a growing dependence of major industrials on bank loans. IBM, which dissipated much of its retained earnings in higher dividends and purchases of its own stock (designed to maintain stock prices), was forced to borrow nearly a billion dollars in 1979. Both Ford and GM found themselves short of the capital needed to finance the construction of fuel-efficient small cars that could compete with imports. Texas Instruments – despite its record as one of the most profitable American firms in the late 1970s – was pressed to borrow money in order to maintain its leadership in the high-tech field.[35]

Ultimately, higher dividend payouts generated by institutional investors may have made a considerable contribution to the stagnation of the American economy in the early 1980s:

A number of analysts worry that companies may be undermining their financial health by pursuing too generous dividend policies. "In many cases, dividends are being increased even though earnings do not support or justify those increases," says Arnold M. Kaufman, editor of Standard and Poor's Corporation's The Outlook. . . . Clinging to set policies (of high dividend pay-out) in times of lagging earnings could prevent a company from investing in needed capital projects and force it to seek costly external financing.[36]

These sketches suggest that institutional stockholders can exercise significant leverage over corporate policy. The Leasco example illustrates the impact of stock dumping on the level of the individual company while the increased dividend payouts of the Nifty-Fifty demonstrates the effectiveness of this strategy on groups of firms. The *Business Week* article quoted above suggests important implications for the economy as a whole: the increased dividends demanded by the institutional investors may have been implicated in fueling the 1979–1982 recession.

At the same time, these examples illustrate that even extremely healthy firms can be subject to the demands of financial decision-making. The entry of Texas Instruments and IBM into the capital market in the late 1970s illustrates this point, and it also illustrates the interconnection between stock dumping and loan intervention, both of which create corporate responsiveness to the financial community.

These mechanisms, of course, are situationally contingent. Occidental Oil's stock was dumped in the early 1970s and its price remained depressed throughout the decade because institutional investors disapproved of executive turnover produced by Armand Hammer's apparently capricious leadership. Hammer's large personal block of Occidental prevented an unfriendly takeover, a major consequence of deflated stock prices; and the oil boom kept Occidental out of the loan market. The firm, therefore, escaped corrective reform by disapproving bankers.[37]

Such successful resistance is not uncommon, and it encourages further resistance among nonfinancial companies. The discipline imposed by financial institutions is, therefore, problematic and episodic. When many firms compete for scarce loan capital, and when maintaining stock prices is crucial, the discipline increases. When demand for funds is low and loan capital is plentiful – or when mergers are infrequent – the discipline loosens. At any moment, different companies, industries, and even governments have different degrees of dependency on capital flows; and therefore they differ in responsiveness to the cues and dictates of financial firms.[38]

Stock dumping and loan intervention are two interrelated mechanisms that create and enforce corporate responsiveness to financial decision-making. Though the process of policy enforcement is contingent, it is an important phenomenon in the business world because financial leverage is often the major constraint upon the autonomy of the largest corporate actors.

Financial impact on industrial sectors

As distributors of investment capital, financial institutions are forced to judge the viability of a wide range of projects proposed by prospective borrowers. Often these judgments reach beyond the level of the firm and influence the trajectory of entire industries.

Such judgments are certainly subject to larger forces in the economy – notably the discipline of the capital markets – and thus even money market institutions are not autonomous actors in their own right. They are further limited by their inability to predict an uncertain future, a limitation that is endemic in all investment decision-making. Nevertheless, the critical role of capital as a resource and the potential for unity among major financial firms distinguish their actions – even when they are compelled by market forces – from those predicted by the traditional market model of the economist. These differences can be usefully analyzed in the context of industry-wide consequences of financial decision-making. We consider the development of the nuclear-power industry in this context.

The first nuclear-power plant opened in 1959, with the number of new plants increasing steadily in the 1960s, spurred by the drastic increases in demand for electricity and by the capital intensity of the method.[39] Compared to other ways of producing electricity, nuclear power involves enormous initial capital investment and very low fuel and operation expenses. This mix was particularly attractive to the industry because regulatory laws allow a guaranteed profit on the cost of construction of electrical plants but not on fuel and other operating expenses. The promise of a guaranteed return on investment also meant that utilities had little difficulty obtaining the massive loans necessary to finance nuclear power.

By 1974, however, the economic and energy crises of the period reduced the expansion of energy use drastically: the 7 percent annual increase that prevailed for two decades declined to 0.4 percent and remained under 4 percent thereafter. This flattening of demand meant lower than expected revenues, making it difficult to meet loan payments for projects under construction. (Costs of construction can be charged to rate payers only after a plant begins operation.)

At about the same time, the public became aware of the financial and environmental problems associated with nuclear power. Protests in New Hampshire and elsewhere contributed to this growing concern, and led to more diligent enforcement of safety requirements. This added to the already massive cost of the plants and lengthened the already considerable delays in construction.

Inflation exacerbated these problems, and by the mid-1970s escalating costs became the focal problem of nuclear construction. Few plants were completed at less than 200 percent of their original cost estimates. Lilco's Shoreham plant on Long Island, originally projected to open in 1975 at a cost of $271 million, surpassed $1.1 billion early in 1979.[40] By 1985, the still unopened plant was projected at $4.2 billion.[41] Other projects had similar fates. Estimates of the capital costs of one kilowatt hour of nuclear power increased from $185 in 1970 to $1861 for plants in the early phases of construction in 1979.[42] By 1985, the estimates were as high as $5,192.[43]

These problems destroyed the nuclear-power plant market; after 1975, cancellations outnumbered new orders for the industry as a whole, and after 1977 there were no new orders at all.

The Three Mile Island accident alarmed the public by crystallizing fears that nuclear power was a safety hazard. It alarmed the financial community because of fears that the massive construction costs would produce rates so high that consumers would reduce usage and therefore deprive utilities of the revenues necessary to repay loans. Two months after the accident, *Business Week* announced the new posture of the financial community toward electrical utilities and nuclear power in particular: " 'The industry is standing at a bare-bones level of financial integrity,' frets Charles A. Benore, utilities analyst with Paine Webber Mitchell Hutchins, Inc. . . . 'their continuing ability to attract money is now in jeopardy. Lenders and investors are growing increasingly troubled by the industry's inability to boost profits.' "[44]

In the two months after Three Mile Island, the stocks of nuclear-power utilities dropped 8.6 percent, and new stock issues were underpriced by as much as 15 percent. General Public Utilities, the owner of Three Mile Island, headed toward bankruptcy.[45]

Stock prices continued to decline in 1979, and loans became more and more difficult to obtain. In May, Bank of America announced a policy of refusing all future loans for nuclear plants.[46] Other banks were less militant in their posture because they were constrained by existing investment in projects that might fail without further cash infusions. Nevertheless, nuclear plants experienced broad declines in credit ratings and increases in interest rates. Before the end of 1979, eleven plants – more than 10 percent of those on order – had been canceled. Seventy-two others had experienced costly new delays.[47]

In 1980 the crisis deepened further. Many utilities were unable to obtain funding and therefore canceled construction contracts, sometimes after spending hundreds of millions of dollars. Even almost completed plants were vulnerable. The Seabrook, New Hampshire, facility, site of the most celebrated protests, was virtually finished by 1979. It then experienced new delays while the member utilities sought rate increases, sold new stock issues, and recruited new partners in an attempt to cover withdrawn bank financing.[48] In 1985 it remained unopened. A consortium of 88 investors essentially halted trading in a Pacific Northwest Utilities investment because investors' portfolios were "glutted" and their bonds were downgraded. Lenders had made it clear that, without stopping construction of those plants, money would not be available for three other sites that were closer to completion.[49] Ultimately, construction of the other three plants was also halted, and the agency in charge of construction was forced into bankruptcy.

These events illustrate both the broad-ranging impact of financial decision-making on industrial sectors and the limitations of financial power. The withdrawal of capital from nuclear plant construction – through the mechanism of loan refusal – announced the end of domestic nuclear projects and the reorientation of the utility industry toward other sources of electricity. The details of the reorientation were loosely or-chestrated by the withdrawal of capital and, therefore, financial deci-sions were crucial components of the process.

The collapse of the industry, however, appears to have been beyond the control of the financial community. It was forced to act lest it "throw good money after bad" and lose an even larger investment later on. Similarly, the initial participation of financials in nuclear-plant con-struction may have been based on an equally forceful imperative: the appearance of an apparently viable and highly profitable opportunity. Both of these conditions were, at first glance, consistent with a tradi-tional market model of corporate behavior. In first financing nuclear power, they were attracted to an industry that had an excellent credit rating, a promising construction program, rising demand, and govern-ment-guaranteed profit. This was a very impressive profile compared to other potential borrowers. In discontinuing their commitment, they were repelled by high debt ratios, low demand, and poor prospects for repayment. Nuclear power no longer compared favorably with other possible investments.

The market was therefore an important constraint in defining the choices of major financial institutions. But it was not the only force at work. Consider, for example, the timing of the withdrawal of funding. Had lenders chosen to withdraw their support earlier, several billion dollars would have been saved; had the decision come later, several ad-ditional plants would have been completed. Moreover, each plant under construction has now been subjected to an individual judgment by lenders: whether to fund its completion or discontinue support. These choices are conditioned, but not determined, by the market. No one, including the most informed analysts, could tell the exact moment when nuclear power became economically nonviable. In many cases, no one can be sure whether a particular plant is economically feasible (leaving safety issues aside). In many cases, "incorrect" judgments were clearly made – in the case of the Shoreham, Long Island, plant, even Lilco now concedes that it was an unwise original commitment though they argue that it is now logical to complete it. There was, there-fore, a large element of discretion co-existing with market forces in the decisions to discontinue nuclear-power plants and there was an equally large component of discretion in the earlier decisions to commit a large portion of the nation's investment capital to the development of nuclear power.

This discretion was, by and large, exercised by the leadership of ma-jor lending institutions. The decisions were not made by the heads of utilities, who might be seen as technical experts; by government officials, who are the designated representatives of the public interest; or by any of a number of other groups that have some official claim to authority over nuclear power. Ironically, utility executives and almost every government official and agency (including three Republican and one Democratic president) fought to rescue the industry. Their efforts not only failed to prevent the failure of nuclear power, but they did little to alter the timing and the particularities of its demise. In case after case, the specific decisions were made by financial institutions in the context of judging financial viability. The responses of financial companies to investment opportunities are therefore conditioned by much more than traditional market mechanisms. The need for investment capital in all industrial sectors, the centralization of that capital, and the necessity for discretionary decision-making by the lenders means that banks and insurance companies do not simply react to market conditions, even in constrained circumstances like those connected to nuclear power. Instead, they become important actors in the creation of conditions.

In some circumstances, financial institutions are faced with fewer market constraints and they, therefore, have wider levels of discretion and more input into the creation of market forces. These occasions are nicely illustrated by events in the shipbuilding industry during the 1970s, when banks first selected it as a promising investment outlet, and later changed their mind, with very costly consequences.[50]

In 1967 Citibank issued a ten-year prospectus that advocated a great many of the financial developments of the 1970s. Based on this document, the bank formed a holding company (Citicorp) which owned Citibank as well as other nonbanking subsidiaries. This allowed expansion into previously prohibited enterprises, and facilitated the institutional flexibility that Citicorp exploited during the 1970s to become the preeminent banking institution of the world.

The most important investment policy that flowed from this prospectus was Citibank's program of expansion into the Third World, which we discuss below. A less central, but highly influential, innovation was the introduction of leasing as a lucrative device for managing new capital construction projects. This idea was applied with great vigor in the shipbuilding industry; Citicorp announced its intention to become "the principal bank of the world's major shipowners."[51] By 1978, shipping represented 4.6 percent of Citicorp's loan portfolio, and other money market banks had made similar commitments. In that year, the top ten American banks held over $7 billion in outstanding shipping loans.

In negotiating these loans, the banks insisted that the builders lease the completed ships, rather than sell them or run them themselves. They insisted on signed leasing contracts before construction began, thus guaranteeing at least five years of revenues after completion. And they often demanded equity for themselves in the ships, in exchange for extremely favorable loan packages.

The infusion of bank capital stimulated the shipbuilding industry, and by the early 1970s tanker capacity was growing at a very rapid rate. By 1973, however, world oil usage began to decline as a result of the oil crisis and shipping volume leveled off. At that time, approximately 100 million tons of shipping capacity were under construction, and even the cancellation of many of these projects could not prevent an industry-wide recession. In 1978, with 20 million tons still being built, 15 percent of existing capacity lay idle. Long-term leases signed in the early 1970s began to expire without being renewed, and many ship owners could not repay bank loans.

The banks were forced to reassess their commitment to shipbuilding. Peter Douglas, the chief economist at Chase Manhattan Bank, told a meeting of ship owners that they would henceforth be treated "more like borrowers and less like co-owners than they [were] in the past."[52] The major banks scrutinized each loan and each corporation, deciding on rescue or abandonment. The rescue terms were sometimes very generous – a British banker told *Business Week*: "We had to help out a few of our friends by giving moratoriums or rewriting loans."[53] But abandonment also occurred: a French firm was forced to sell a four-year-old, $30 million supertanker for $10 million; two others sold three supertankers for scrap. Two American corporations were sold at distress prices; and another, Pacific Far Eastern Lines, declared bankruptcy, leaving the United States government with $98 million in loan guarantees.

These events illustrate the relation between capital suppliers and industrial sectors. In the late 1960s Citibank and other major lenders were searching for investment opportunity and they selected tanker construction as a promising outlet for investment capital. This choice – one of many they might have selected – transformed the circumstances of builders, owners, and leaseholders in the shipping industry. When the economic tide turned and the industry fell into recession, the lenders made a second set of decisions aimed at protecting their own investment. They selected firms for rescue – based both on their economic standing and on their relation to the banks – and others for abandonment. The abandoned companies were forced to find repayment funds – even if it meant wasteful liquidation – or to declare bankruptcy.

While market conditions played a role in this process, the decision to select shipping out of many possible investment outlets had a discretionary component. Moreover, the decision-makers were the same set of actors who chose nuclear power for development, who lavishly funded aircraft manufacturers in the mid-1950s, who chose to lend to the Hunt brothers, and who redefined dividend rates of the Nifty-Fifty. And the discretion implicit in withdrawal from a sector – choosing which corporations are rescued under what conditions – is in the hands of these same institutions. The centralized nature of this decision-making, then, presents itself as the loose ability to coordinate industrial activity. Though their effects are problematic and contingent, they are nevertheless a source for many general trends in economic development and changes in industrial profiles. And, as the above examples demonstrate, selection of investments and the evaluation of loan renewals can have profound effects on industrial sectors.

Financial decision-making and the shape of national economic policies

As the world economy becomes increasingly integrated, the investment opportunities of American companies have broadened tremendously, reaching every corner of the globe. As offshore investment continues to expand, direct relations between banks and foreign governments have developed. The processes of bank hegemony that influence firms and industrial sectors have now begun to apply to whole countries as well.

This development can be traced in Citibank's ten-year prospectus, mentioned above, which marked the beginning of a new era in international banking.[54] During the 1970s, Citibank invested aggressively in overseas activities with a strong concentration in loans to the Third World – known in the business community as less developed countries (LDCs). Loan criteria were based on outlines in the original Citibank prospectus. First, lending limits for each country would be set in accordance with internal political and economic conditions, thus limiting overinvestment in a particular area.[55] Second, to protect its investment against expropriation, Citibank, whenever possible, lent money to multinationals operating in these countries rather than directly to LDC governments or to indigenous industrial firms.[56] By 1974, LDCs had accumulated $14.7 billion in loans, many of which were channeled through multinationals, just as Citibank had suggested.[57]

The tremendous input of capital into Third World development was an act of hegemonic leadership by financial firms. It encouraged multinational companies to undertake previously inaccessible projects; and it induced Third World governments to act as hosts to multinational subsidiaries as the condition for economic development. Without any overt intervention or coercion, decisions about capital flows determined subsequent decisions by companies and nations.

The energy crisis of 1973–1974 significantly altered the climate of LDC investment. The energy needs accompanying industrial development placed local economies at the mercy of skyrocketing oil prices, and severely limited their ability to meet their loan obligations. These countries were forced to try to refinance existing debt and seek new loans to finance their survival. Their deep financial involvement compelled the major banks to remain involved, lest they lose their entire investment. They were thus left with a choice between immediate losses or even greater financial involvement.

In choosing the latter course, they committed themselves to an ongoing reevaluation of each company and each country. They were forced to make frequent decisions about new loans, about refinancing, and about the changing profile of LDC economies. Each decision influenced the investment environment of other companies and thus reverberated through the international economy.

This situation has the same asymmetrical quality as the examples discussed earlier. The worldwide recession guaranteed markets for lenders and competition among borrowers. The economic crises that accompanied loan negotiations gave lenders tremendous leverage. The compulsions of the drive for maximum return on investment impelled the banks to use this leverage, even when this involved substantial intrusion into the sovereignty of borrowing countries.

The "first public showdown with the international banking community"[58] occurred in Peru, and involved both a loan renegotiation with the government and a $54 million loan to Southern Peru Copper Corporation (53 percent owned by the American mining company Asarco). Until the Peruvian central government agreed to revise the country's tax structure, the banks refused to lend the money necessary to complete a $750 million copper-mining development (designed to increase copper production for export). The government has been taxing the exports of the company to subsidize the purchase of food for poor people. The lenders, led by Chase Manhattan Bank, forced the elimination of the tax so that all proceeds from copper sales could be used for debt financing. Ultimately, food subsidies were eliminated, wage controls instituted, and three left-wing cabinet members were expelled from the government.

Although U.S. banks denied responsibility for changes in Peruvian internal policy, *Business Week* noted that the banks' "passing judgment on Peru's economic performance raises troublesome questions about foreign business interference in the affairs of a sovereign state."[59]

Since then, banks have become more comfortable in their role as policymakers in the Third World. While forced to renegotiate LDC loans, they have become adept at extracting desired concessions. The government of Brazil, for example, agreed both to reduce growth and to honor bank-defined fiscal discipline. As a reaction to political instability in South Korea, all new loans were refused until the financial community developed a set of guidelines for the country. The refusal of the Manley government in Jamaica to accept loan conditions contributed to its downfall since the withdrawal of investment capital deepened the ongoing economic and political crisis that brought down the administration. And, in Poland, tension between government subsidies for food production and Western capital's pressure for debt repayment placed United States banks in the middle of the Polish workers' crisis.[60]

In general, bank intervention in the late 1970s sought two basic policy changes: "fiscal discipline" and "increased exports."[61] Fiscal discipline implied maximizing debt repayment, even at the expense of food imports or subsidies to living standards. Increased exports implied development of extractive and plantation economies, thus increasing dependency on the world market and distorting economic development.[62] In short, the banks' policies for these countries became a force for increasing poverty and aggravating an already desperate economic dependency.

U.S. banks thus became a major determinant in Third World economic policy. The processes of financial hegemony that operate within the American economy have come to apply in this realm as well. Bank decision-making over capital flows stimulated economic development in the Third World in the 1970s and set the initial focus on multinational subsidiaries. As the decade proceeded, Third World countries responded to the ebb and flow of financing by responding to the cues of bank leadership. As the economic climate changed, banks intervened into the internal affairs of these nations with the intention of redirecting economic policy, thus completing the development of hegemonic domination. Banks have long been participants in the creation of corporate policies. The 1980s is a decade of bank partnership in the economic policies of developing countries as well.

Discussion

We are now in a position to offer a rough outline of the mechanisms and processes that condition financial hegemony. First and foremost, financial power rests on three unique qualities of capital as a resource. First, capital is the universal commodity of the business world. Unlike iron, coal, and machine tools, which are important for some firms but not for others, capital is needed by all corporations. It is necessary both in the narrow sense to pay employees and suppliers, and in the broad sense to fuel the replacement and expansion of industrial plants.

Capital may be internally generated by individual corporations. However, this form of self-sufficiency is quite variable: in recent years, companies did well if they produced 50 percent of their capital construction needs internally.[63] This suggests, then, that suppliers of capital, unlike suppliers of other resources, deal with the entire economy; and, unlike members of other industrial sectors, are central units in the system of power and influence created by the network of resource dependencies.

Moreover, this is complemented by the highly elastic nature of the demand for capital. Even at very low prices, most commodities have upper limits on sales, at least in the short run. If electricity rates began to fall, usage would at first increase. Eventually, however, the market would be saturated and usage would stabilize, even if rates continued to decline. With investment capital, however, a decline in interest rates means that projects with lower profit margins become viable. As rates decline, more customers enter the market and the types of projects funded become broader and broader. Although this asymmetry exists in other buyer-seller relationships, normally a firm is highly dependent on one set of suppliers, while the role is reversed in other of its resource relationships. Only in capital markets is there a continuing asymmetry, unbalanced by countervailing leverage.

Finally, suppliers of capital, unlike other suppliers, become temporary or permanent partners in the enterprise they serve. A normal supplier-customer relationship, even in highly convoluted circumstances like the silver futures market, essentially involves an exchange of money for a product. In the financial markets, money is exchanged for stocks – which creates an explicit and quasi-permanent partnership – or for bonds or notes that represent a temporary partnership until the money is repaid at a future date.

These unique aspects of financial relationships force banks and other financial institutions into a unique stance toward their customers. They must make constant choices about the relative merits of competing investment opportunities. The choices made by financials to support one firm or industry – or even a country – over another, or to enter or depart from one area of investment, often represent the crucial, determining reality within which nonfinancial corporations operate.

Essentially there are four mechanisms through which financial decisions over capital flows are transformed into coherent economic profiles. First, lenders or institutional investors may decide to encourage development of a promising area. The availability of investment capital attracts operating companies with the expertise to develop the sector's potential. This occurred during the shipbuilding boom in the early 1970s.

Second, lenders or institutional investors may de-escalate economic commitment in a declining or threatened sector. The withdrawal of capital may constrain further development and force contraction of the industry. This occurred in both the nuclear-power and shipbuilding industries in the mid-1970s.

Third, financial institutions may decrease their commitment to a sector or a company or a country as a signal of declining confidence in its economic viability. In these circumstances, industrial leaders must solve their problems to regain investor confidence, but they are not necessarily constrained by the disinvestment. Stock dumping is often used in this manner, though loan refusal in nonurgent circumstances can also operate this way. It acts as a warning that a continuation of current policy will result in future difficulties in obtaining capital, a circumstance that most chief executives will seek to avoid. The abandonment of the Nifty-Fifty illustrates this process.

Fourth, capital withdrawal or refusal can be used to intervene in the internal workings of a company or an economy. In these instances, economic strategy usually must be altered as a prerequisite for capital investment, even when the objectionable strategies are unrelated to the terms of the investment. Conditions were set on the loan to Placid Oil that had nothing to do with the company's ability to repay; it was used as a device for driving the Hunt brothers from the futures market. Dumping of Leasco's stock had little to do with the status of the firm as an investment; it was a device to defeat the Chemical takeover attempt.

Only the fourth possibility, which might be called disciplinary action, resembles control in the traditional sense in which the term has been used. The other three modes of influence involve a degree of structural distance and a set of processes unfamiliar to students of intercorporate power. The key element in this domination is structural constraint. Because the actions of individual companies, sectors, and even whole economies depend upon the availability of outside capital, their options are substantially altered by expansion or contraction of access to such resources. In some circumstances, this variable alone determines the viability of a project; and, therefore, even the promise or threat of alterations in capital availability is sufficient to force changes in policy. Clearly, sufficient internally generated funds (which, for example, oil companies had accumulated in the late 1970s) lessens the degree of responsiveness to financial decision-making. On the other hand, corporate crisis heightens responsiveness. Different firms, sectors or economies are, therefore, differentially constrained. And the whole system's responsiveness to financial decision-making varies with the degree to which financial corporations are unified in judgment and action.

The mechanisms that produce financial unity and the structural position of capital suppliers in an economy, fueled by the availability of investment funds, place financial institutions outside of the traditional market model studied by economists. Their impact on investment possibilities on the level of the firm, the industry, and even whole countries produces a broad coordination that undermines the image of autonomous corporations. And their impact on, and relation to, the entire spectrum of economic activity places them in the center of an interconnected system of investment opportunities.

In some circumstances, financial leadership acts as a mere agent of a deterministic market system; in other circumstances, financial decisions constrain the large market. Anywhere along this continuum, the financial elite exerts a dominance over the world of business that is unmatched by other leadership groups. Herbert Patterson, who left the presidency of Chase Manhattan in the early 1970s, expressed this importance when he was asked if he missed the world of the money market: "If you are interested in prestige and power and you want to play God with people's lives, you obviously are going to miss it."[64]

Acknowledgment

The authors thank Donna Di Donato, Harry Makler, Lynne Zucker, and the editors of *Theory and Society* for comments and the National Science Foundation for research support.

Notes

1. Talcott Parsons and Neil Smelser, *Economy and Society: A Study in the Integration of Economics and Social Theory* (London: Routledge & Kegan Paul, 1956); Neil Smelser, *The Sociology of Economic Life* (Englewood Cliffs, N.J.: Prentice-Hall, 1963); see also Arthur Stinchcombe, *Economic Sociology* (New York: Academic Press, 1983).

2. Adolph Berle and Gardiner Means, *The Modern Corporation and Private Property* (New York: Harcourt, Brace and World, 1932); Robert Dahl, *Who Governs?* (New Haven: Yale University Press, 1961); Arnold Rose, *The Power Structure* (New York: Oxford University Press, 1967).

3. Paul Baran and Paul Sweezy, *Monopoly Capital* (New York: Monthly Review Press, 1966); Edward Herman, *Corporate Control, Corporate Power* (New York: Cambridge University Press, 1981).

4. Howard Aldrich, *Organizations and Environments* (Englewood Cliffs, N.J.: Prentice-Hall, 1979); Jeffrey Pfeffer and Gerald Salancik, *The External Control of Organizations: A Resource Dependence Perspective* (New York: Harper and Row, 1978).

5. James Bearden, "The Board of Directors in Large U.S. Companies," Ph.D. thesis, SUNY at Stony Brook, 1982; James Bearden, William Atwood, Peter Freitag, Carol Hendricks, Beth Mintz, and Michael Schwartz, "The Nature and Extent of Bank Centrality in Corporate Networks," paper presented at the meetings of the American Sociological Association, 1975; S. D. Berkowitz, Peter Carrington, Yehuda Kotowitz, and Leonard Waverman, "The Determination of Enterprise Groupings through Combined Ownership and Directorship Ties," *Social Networks* 1 (1979): 414–35; David Bunting, "Corporate Interlocking," *Journal of Corporate Action* 1: 6–15, 1976, 2: 27–37, 3: 4–11, 4: 39–47, 1977; Philip Burch Jr., *The Managerial Revolution Reassessed* (Lexington: D. C. Heath, 1972); G. William Domhoff, *The Higher Circles* (New York: Random House, 1970), *Who Really Rules?* (New Brunswick, N.J.: Transaction, 1978), *Who Rules America*

Now? (Englewood Cliffs, N.J.: Prentice-Hall, 1983); Meindert Fennema, *International Networks of Banks and Industry* (Boston: Martinus Nijhoff, 1982); Robert Fitch and Mary Oppenheimer, "Who Rules the Corporations?" *Socialist Revolution* 4: 73–108, 5: 61–114, 6: 33–94, 1970; Davita Glasberg, "Corporate Power and Control: The Case of Leasco Corporation versus Chemical Bank," *Social Problems* 29 (1981): 104–16; Robert Gogel and Thomas Koenig, "Commercial Banks, Interlocking Directorates and Economic Power: An Analysis of the Primary Metals Industry," *Social Problems* 29 (1981): 117–28; Thomas Koenig, Robert Gogel, and John Sonquist, "Models of the Significance of Interlocking Corporate Directorates," *American Journal of Economics and Sociology* 38 (1979): 173–83; David Kotz, *Bank Control of Large Corporations in the United States* (Berkley: University of California Press, 1978); Joel Levine, "The Sphere of Influence," *American Sociological Review* 37 (1972): 14–27, "The Theory of Bank Control: Comment on Mariolis' Test of the Theory," *Social Science Quarterly* 58 (1977): 506–10; Peter Mariolis, "Interlocking Directorates and the Control of Corporations," *Social Science Quarterly* 56 (1975): 425–39, "Type of Corporation, Size of Firms and Interlocking Directorates: A Reply to Levine," *Social Science Quarterly* 58 (1977): 511–13; Beth Mintz and Michael Schwartz, "Interlocking Directorates and Interest Group Formation," *American Sociological Review* 46 (1981): 851–69; idem., "The Structure of Intercorporate Unity in American Business," *Social Problems* 29 (1981): 87–103; idem., *The Power Structure of American Business* (Chicago: University of Chicago Press, 1985); Mark Mizruchi, *The American Corporate Network, 1904–1974* (Beverly Hills: Sage, 1982); idem., "The Structure of Relations among Large American Corporations," *Social Science History* 7 (1983): 165–82; Mark Mizruchi and David Bunting, "Influence in Corporate Networks: An Examination of Four Measures," *Administrative Science Quarterly* 26 (1981): 475–89; Robert Mokken and Frans Stokman, "Interlocking Directorates between Large Corporations, Banks, and Other Financial Companies and Institutions in the Netherlands in 1969," paper presented at the Meetings of the European Consortium for Political Research, 1974; idem., "Corporate Government Networks in the Netherlands," *Social Networks* 1 (1979): 333–58; Donald Palmer, "Broken Ties: Interlocking Directorates and Intercorporate Coordination," *Administrative Science Quarterly* 28 (1983): 40–55; "On the Significance of Interlocking Directorates," *Social Science History* 7 (1983): 217–31; Richard Ratcliff, "Capitalist Class Structure and the Decline of Older Industrial Cities," *Insurgent Sociologist* 9 (1979–1980): 60–74, "Banks and Corporate Lending: An Analysis of the Impact of the Internal Structure of the Capitalist Class," *American Sociological Review* 45 (1980): 553–70; John Scott, *Corporations, Classes, and Capitalism* (London: Hutchinson University Library, 1979); Michael Useem, *The Inner Circle: Large Corporations and Business Politics in the U.S. and U.K.* (New York: Oxford University Press, 1983); J. Allen Whitt, *Urban Elites and Mass Transportation* (Princeton: Princeton University Press, 1982); Maurice Zeitlin, "Corporate Ownership and Control: The Large Corporation and the Capitalist Class," *American Journal of Sociology* 79 (1975): 1073–1119.

6. For discussions of this assumption, see Robert Gogel, *Interlocking Directorships and the American Corporate Network,* Ph.D. thesis, University of California, Santa Barbara, 1977; and Mintz and Schwartz, *The Power Structure of American Business.*

7. Mintz and Schwartz, *The Power Structure of American Business.*

8. Antonio Gramsci, *Selections From the Prison Notebooks* (New York: International Publishers, 1971); Tim Patterson, "Notes on the Historical Application of Marxist Cultural Theory," *Science and Society* 39 (1975): 257–91.

9. See, for example, Arnold Rose, *The Power Structure.*

10. *Business Week,* July 25, 1970.

11. The search concentrated on *Business Week, Fortune,* and *The N.Y. Times* financial section. For supplemental information on particular cases, *The Wall Street Journal* and

Forbes were consulted. See Mintz and Schwartz, *The Power Structure of American Business*, for details on data collection.

12. This chronology of overseas banking is taken from: *Business Week*, Aug. 7, 1977: 62; Nov. 7, 1977: 64–70; Apr. 7, 1980: 29–30; Sept. 22, 1980: 34; June 23, 1980: 120–121; Oct. 6, 1980: 38–40; *Fortune*, Sept. 22, 1980: 125; *N.Y. Times*, Aug. 29, 1976: 3.1; Mar. 6, 1977: F5; Sept. 15, 1977: D1; June 5, 1980: D4; May 31, 1978: D11; Apr. 14, 1980: A1; Apr. 21, 1980: D1; May 5, 1980: D1; Sept. 9, 1980: D1; Sept. 22, 1980: D1; Sept. 23, 1980: D1; Nov. 19, 1980: D1; Apr. 4, 1981: D5; *Forbes*, May 15, 1978: 96.

13. Mitchel Abolafia, "Taming the Market: Bases of Control in Commodity Futures Markets," Ph.D. thesis, SUNY at Stony Brook, 1981.

14. *Fortune*, May 19, 1980.

15. *N.Y. Times*, May 1, 1980: D1.

16. *N.Y. Times*, May 1, 1980: D1.

17. *N.Y. Times*, May 2, 1980: D1.

18. *N.Y. Times*, May 1, 1980: D1.

19. *N.Y. Times*, Oct. 11, 1979: D11; see also Apr. 2, 1975: 55.

20. *Newsday*, Aug. 7, 1977: 56.

21. Roy Schotland, *Testimony on Pension Simplification and Investment Rules at Joint Hearing Before the Subcommittee on Private Pension Plans and Employee Fringe Benefits of the Committee on Finance and the Select Committee on Small Business*. U.S. Senate, May 10– July 17, 1977.

22. *Business Week*, July 24, 1980: 51.

23. *Business Week*, July 25, 1980: 51.

24. Lewis Young, "The Claimants for Influence Within the Corporation," in American Assembly, ed., *Running the American Corporation* (Englewood Cliffs, N.J.: Prentice-Hall, 1978), 45.

25. This account is taken from Glasberg, *"Corporate Power and Control"* and *"Corporations in Crisis: The Significance of Interlocking Directorates,"* Ph.D. thesis, SUNY at Stony Brook, 1982.

26. Apr. 26, 1969: 144.

27. July 25, 1970: 54.

28. This discussion of the Nifty-Fifty is based on accounts from *N.Y. Times*, May 8, 1977: 4; May 21, 1977: 31; Oct. 26, 1980: 8; *Business Week*, Apr. 4, 1977: 110; May 23, 1977: 89; July 13, 1981: 80; *Fortune*, July 31, 1978: 72; *Forbes*, Mar. 15, 1977: 113; Apr. 3, 1978: 69.

29. *N.Y. Times*, Apr. 2, 1975: 55.

30. *N.Y. Times*, Oct. 26, 1980: D8.

31. *Fortune*, July 31, 1978: 72.

32. For information on the commercial paper market, see *Business Week*, Oct. 30, 1978: 164; Mar. 19, 1980: 109–12.

33. *N.Y. Times*, May 8, 1977.

34. *Business Week*, May 23, 1977: 89.

35. For information on IBM, see *Business Week*, Dec. 5, 1977: 62, Mar. 27, 1978: 46; Oct. 8, 1979: 103; Jan. 28, 1980: 34; *N.Y. Times*, Oct. 11, 1979: D10; Sept. 30, 1979: 3.1; for GM and Ford, see *Forbes*, Mar. 20, 1978:80; *Business Week*, June 1, 1981: 55–100; for Texas Instruments, see *Business Week*, Sept. 18, 1978: 66–76; June 1, 1981: 55–100.

36. *Business Week*, July 13, 1981.

37. On Occidental's stock prices, see *N.Y. Times*, Aug. 10, 1980: F15; *Fortune*, Sept. 8, 1980: 47–48; *Business Week*, Jan. 10, 1977: 36–37.

38. See Linda Stearns, "Corporate Dependency and the Structure of the Capital Market," Ph.D. thesis, SUNY at Stony Brook, 1983.

39. This account of the financial problems of the nuclear-power industry is based on the following sources. For general information, see Karl Grossman, *Cover Up: What You Are Not Supposed to Know About Nuclear Power* (New York: Permanent Press, 1980); *Business Week*, May 28, 1979: 108–24; Sept. 17, 1979: 35; Nov. 19, 1979: 43–44; Sept. 22, 1980: 37; June 22, 1981: 23, *N.Y. Times*, May 1, 1979: D6; Nov. 14, 1979; *Newsday*, Jan. 30, 1980: 30. On General Public Utilities and Three Mile Island, see *N.Y. Times*, Nov. 16, 1979: D1; Nov. 29, 1979: D4; May 9, 1980: D7; Sept. 1, 1980: D4; Jan. 13, 1981: D1; *Business Week*, Oct. 22, 1979: 75. On Seabrook, see *N.Y. Times*, Nov. 14, 1979: D2; Mar. 25, 1980: D4; Apr. 4, 1980: D5. On Lilco, see *Newsday*, June 1, 1979: 4; Aug. 21, 1979: 3; Apr. 16, 1980: 5; *N.Y. Times*, June 8, 1980: D1. On Washington Public Power, see *Business Week*, June 4, 1979: 86; *N.Y. Times*, June 16, 1981: D1; Jan. 15, 1982: D1. On Consumer's Power, see *N.Y. Times*, Jan. 19, 1975: 3; Mar. 7, 1980: D4. On Commonwealth Edison, see *Business Week*, Oct. 1, 1979: 49. On Detroit Edison, see *N.Y. Times*, Mar. 25,1980: D6. On Central Area Power, see *N.Y. Times*, Jan. 28, 1980: A13.

40. *Newsday*, June 1, 1979.

41. *Forbes*, Feb. 11, 1985: 85.

42. *Business Week*, May 28, 1979: 109.

43. *Forbes*, Feb. 11, 1985.

44. May 28, 1979: 111.

45. *N.Y. Times*, Nov. 16, 1979: D1.

46. *N.Y. Times*, May 11, 1979.

47. *Newsday*, Jan. 30, 1980: 3.

48. *N.Y. Times*, March 25, 1980: D4; Apr. 10, 1980: D5; *Business Week*, Dec. 10, 1979.

49. *Business Week*, June 9, 1979: 86; *N.Y. Times*, June 16, 1981: D1; Jan. 15, 1982: D1.

50. This discussion of the shipbuilding industry is based on material from *Business Week*, Feb. 10, 1975: 36; May 1, 1978: 80–81; Oct. 6,

51. *N.Y. Times*, July 4, 1980: 3, 11.

52. *N.Y. Times*, July 9, 1978: 3, 11.

53. May 1, 1980: 81.

54. This chronology of overseas banking is taken from: *Business Week*, Aug. 7, 1977: 62; Nov. 7, 1977: 64–70; Apr. 7, 1980: 29–30; Sept. 22, 1980: 34; June 23, 1980: 120–21; Oct. 6, 1980: 38–40; *Fortune*, Sept. 22, 1980: 125; *N.Y. Times*, Aug. 29, 1976: 3.1; Mar. 6, 1977: F5; Sept. 15, 1977: D1; June 5, 1980: D1; Sept. 22, 190: D1; Nov. 19, 1980: D1; Apr. 4, 1981: D5; *Forbes*, May 15, 1978: 96; *New York Magazine,*, Dec. 1980: 31–38.

55. Group of Thirty, "How Bankers See the World Financial Market" (New York: Group of Thirty, 1982.)

56. *Business Week*, Nov. 7, 1977: 66.

57. R. Hancock, "The Social Life of the Modern Corporation: Changing Resources and Forms," *Journal of Applied Behavioral Science* 16 (1980): 279–98.

58. *N.Y. Times*, May 31, 1978: D11.

59. Mar. 27, 1977: 117.

60. *Fortune*, Sept. 22, 1980: 128; Mintz and Schwartz, *The Power Structure of American Business*.

61. *N.Y. Times*, Apr. 21, 1980: D7.

62. A. Gunder Frank, *Capitalism and Underdevelopment in Latin America* (New York: Monthly Review Press, 1967); Peter Evans, *Dependent Development: The Alliance of Multinational, State, and Local Capital in Brazil* (Princeton: Princeton University Press, 1970).

63. *Business Week*, May 28, 1979: 111.

64. *Forbes*, May 15, 1978: 96.

9

Accounting rationality and financial legitimation

PAUL MONTAGNA

The quantitative measurement of value is a central requirement in capitalist production and exchange relations. A major role in this measurement has been played by public accounting since its establishment as a profession in the United States and Great Britain at the turn of the century. Public accountants see themselves as the monitors of world economic order. Their metaphor is the system, in which rationality and unity are assumed and all accounts are monetary and quantitatively measurable in precise, constant terms. Their method is positivist. Uncertainty in financial markets is reducible through objective analysis of the relations of capital in a value-free environment. Their mandate is to provide to the public a periodic independent examination of corporate financial accounts in the form of an annual audit. These audits were instituted by governments following violent fluctuations in the business cycle, particularly the world depression of the 1930s, largely in response to public demand for more comprehensive information. However, despite this charge, public accountants serve primarily the interests of their clients. Not only do they monitor actual expenditures of capital, but they are also gatekeepers of capitalist ideology. The social organization of their work, the organizational and career structures they inhabit, and the body of knowledge they control all serve to legitimate political, economic, and social arrangements.

Their gatekeeping is not a covert operation. Public accountants are aware of their function in protecting the faith. They actively engage in aiding the survival and prosperity of business enterprises. But they also believe they are capable of providing a wholly objective analysis of financial and finance-related transactions of corporations. This belief extends to a large and growing nonbusiness clientele, which includes government agencies, health-care institutions, colleges and universities, churches, research institutes, unions, and occupational associations.

The first part of this chapter examines the occupational and organizational elements in public accounting which create, support, and enhance a distinctive accounting rationality.[1] The most important of these elements are the large public accounting firms. In the context of their annual audit, public accountants in the largest multinational accounting firms advise their clients on capital formation, spending, and reinvestment. The extent of this advice and the degree of concentration within the profession into nine giant firms raise the question of how independent accountants can be from client influence when they conduct their audits. The struggle between the profession and the federal government since the 1970s is examined with regard to the government's charges of a conflict-of-interest within public accounting between accurate and fair reporting to the public and favoritism toward the client. Ideological disputation about accounting theory in journals and at academic conferences is the surface manifestation of an underlying struggle between members of the profession and between the profession and the federal government on the responsibilities of accountants to the public as opposed to those to the client.

The focus of the second part of the chapter is an examination of the ideological base of public accounting and how it serves as a symbolic framework for decisions concerning capital investment and borrowing. Although accountants claim that their theoretical knowledge and its underlying presuppositions make them independent of client and third-party influence,[2] these elements of accounting in fact justify the limiting of interference from the state and from other nonbusiness organizations in capital transactions. Their emphasis on neoclassical principles of economic behavior and their conviction that accounting is a description of what really happens – the real truth – support that justification. These elements also support the belief that economic efficiency can best be improved by centralizing and integrating financial and related information systems in large-scale multinational corporations. All this facilitates a significant degree of financial control over capital flow in nearly every industry by a few giant companies.

In political democracies, extensive financial control requires legitimation. Accountants provide that legitimation through theory and practice. They apply "generally accepted accounting principles," rules which define what is a fair presentation of financial transactions to shareholders and the public, as agreed upon by both accountants and the business community. Bank loans to support Third World development, inventory stockpiling to prepare for anticipated market surges, new capital investment in plant and equipment, distribution of profits to shareholders – all these and other financial management decisions fall under the auditor's review of capital planning and use.

By controlling the development and uses of their technical knowledge, public accountants are able to mediate the market between consumers and providers of capital. There is in general a *mutual sponsorship* between client and professional:[3] a market dependency of corporations on the accountant auditor for good advice and a clean bill of health on their financial statements, and a reverse dependency of the auditor for comfortable fees and support against excessive state regulation.

Beginning in the 1970s, a small group of accounting theorists broke with this tradition to form a political-economy theory of accounting. This theory treats value as a contested concept and interprets accounting reports as representations of class interests. But it is also an example of the political economy of a professional occupation, where ideological conflicts expose hegemony as more complicated than the simple mechanical transfer of the ideas of the dominant classes to the subordinate classes. The political economy of accounting represents an element of contradictory consciousness within the accounting profession. It constitutes the only critical movement in the discipline. Of the two major paradigms in accounting – private value accounting and social value accounting – it is the "radical" arm of the latter.

Analysis of these paradigms emphasizes how most accounting theory supports the commodification of labor by concentrating on the quantifying of values and the standardizing of human behavior in organizations into interrelated, and often interdependent, information control systems. In explaining the costs of financial transactions, accountants treat people as things adapting (private value) rather than as individuals struggling for power in a system of unequal relations to the means of production (social value). Like professionals in general, public accountants espouse the idea that performing a service to the public requires maintaining independence from client influence. Like most other professionals, they are far from achieving this goal. Instead, they directly help clients to maintain control over financial capital throughout the world.

Auditing and advising multinational clients

To accommodate the growing needs of their rapidly expanding corporate clients, some of the more enterprising public accounting firms have grown through a combination of merger, acquisition, and internal expansion. In the early 1900s, these firms were small organizations of ten to twenty partners with a few hundred employees located in a few offices in the major cities of the United States and England. They have evolved into large-scale partnerships, each comprising twenty thousand plus persons, over two thousand of whom are partners. Internationally, they are very highly concentrated into nine firms (formerly eight),[4] which together audit most of the world's largest industrial and financial corporations.[5] The average member of the "Big Nine," as they are known in financial circles, has 340 offices in 70 countries, about 90 of which are located in the United States. The total number of clients is around 50,000 and total average billings are $825 million, with three firms topping $1 billion a year.[6] Half of their revenues is derived from operations in countries other than the United States.[7]

Because they dominate the auditing and related financial services of multinational corporations (MNCs) and because of their influence in all aspects of their profession's development, the Big Nine are the focus for this empirical analysis. Interviews were conducted with public accountants in Western Europe and the United States, and questionnaires were distributed to a representative sample of the U.S. offices of three of the nine firms. In addition, a number of multinational bankers from West European countries and the United States were interviewed to obtain a broad picture of areas of competition and coordination in areas where financial services overlap.[8]

Previous studies have examined the types and extent of financial services large accounting firms provide for their clients.[9] The major function of the firms is to conduct yearly audits of clients. The audit is a systematic investigation and appraisal of an organization's operations as determined by examination of its accounting records and internal control systems of management and administration. It has been and remains the raison d'etre of public accounting firms. However, as much as one-half the Big Nine firm's work is spent in activities only indirectly related to accounting and auditing. Each firm maintains large tax and management consulting operations to supplement the audit or as distinct services with or without an accompanying audit.[10] Since the 1960s, the firms have come to play an increasingly important role in providing financial advice across a broad range of services to the managements of major companies.

Decision-making affecting international capital flows is highly integrated among MNC managements and international financial service firms. The latter include commercial, investment, merchant, and "universal" banks, accounting firms, law firms, and management consulting firms. In their dual function as deposit takers and lenders, banks act as funnels to pool savings of diverse capital sources and as distributors of funds to the most lucrative markets. In addition to their audit services, public accountants are called upon by client MNCs and governments to identify capital-related problems and to determine which financial services are needed to solve those problems. According to the director of international services of a Big Nine firm, "When the client wants to invest in a foreign country operation, he needs advice on tax structures, restrictions on capital investment, and the like. He comes to the public accountant and not the investment banker. Taxes play a very important part in this role. There is a lot of work relating to new tax treaties. Just yesterday I had a West German client sitting right where you are who needed advice on how to structure sales to get the best tax advantages so as to not hinder his company's overall operations in other countries. Very frequently clients will ask us, 'Can you recommend bankers?' Or, 'Can you recommend lawyers?' We suggest several and let them make the final choice. Very frequently we have to tell even the largest MNCs they need them, especially attorneys."

This is a typical response of partners-in-charge of multinational corporate audits to questions concerning interprofessional competition. MNCs have to deal with problems unique to the scale and the scope of their operations: considerations of transfer pricing; a multitude of tax regulations; and cultural variations that require different approaches to labor relations, sales promotion, advertising, marketing, and finance. Even with their own large staffs, MNCs are unable to match the quality of the accounting firms' knowledge acquired in the audit of financial and related information systems of thousands of organizations in hundreds of industries. Partners quite commonly spend three or four hours in conversation every few weeks with senior executives regarding general business trends and capital-allocation strategies. They often describe their role as constructing scenarios for management to help in the decision-making. An executive partner in an American office of one of the Big Nine reports: "We must know the various ways a corporation can structure itself in different countries to take advantage of tax regulations, economies of scale, investment opportunities. We review legal agreements, buy-sell agreements, loan agreements, and others. We present the alternative possibilities and then we suggest one of the alternatives." Says another, "Our services flow with multinational investments. Sometimes we'll give a foreign client an overview of where to invest and how to invest and what the banking arrangements are like." And an audit manager of another firm: "Sometimes the client will come to you and say 'We're at an impasse. We don't know what to do.' That kind of question does occur often."

Beginning in the mid-1970s, many of the largest MNCs created new internal specialist positions and even entire departments to deal with the emerging complex problems of international finance. However, this presented no serious competition to the accounting firms. As employees of MNCs, internal experts do not have access to the entire international field of industry operations from the vantage point of the auditor-as-confidant. Also, auditors have their firm's depth of financial experience in other industries in which the MNC has little or no knowledge. Of course, there is nothing to prevent clients from raiding the accounting firms for these broadly trained auditors and tax and consulting experts. However, as employees, they lose the organizational knowledge base that is a central part of these advisors' services. Consequently, most MNCs pay the Big Nine the $500-an-hour fee for quick, top-level, in-and-out advising and do most of the lower-level preparation and detail work themselves.

In the highly lucrative field of corporate mergers and acquisitions, each of the service firms has its defined role. Investment banks originate and underwrite loans and write prospectuses. Law firms prepare the necessary briefs and act as counsel on all major and most minor stock and bond issues. Accounting firms assist clients in choosing investment and disinvestment programs by providing alternatives and discussing the advantages and disadvantages of each. The accounting firm acts as a catalyst for the client in a way that no law firm, consulting firm, or bank can. As a Peat, Marwick partner noted, "We have ten tax partners who work on the insurance industry full-time. But the investment bank might have only one of its vice presidents work on it part-time." Because of its size and geographical diversity Touche Ross & Co. (and most other Big Nine firms) has more lawyers in its "management advisory services" division (a euphemism for management consulting) than the total number of lawyers in the largest law firm. Arthur Andersen houses the world's largest computer consulting staff of six thousand consultants in a globally integrated network within its firm. As accountants scrutinize capital transactions during their audit, the corporate client frequently asks them to summarize and evaluate the merger/acquisition work of its bankers and lawyers in financial and cost/benefit terms. The banks and law firms, in turn, use these evaluations to write prospectuses for their clients.

Other financial service firms also engage accounting firms to do their own internal reviews. The largest law firms contract Price Waterhouse & Co. yearly to review their administrative and financial operations. Peat, Marwick provides audit, tax, or consulting services to sixty of the hundred largest international banks and to more than one thousand domestic banks. American banks are subject to four different audits every year: an internal audit by their own accounting staffs, the Federal Reserve audit by national bank examiners, an audit by the comptroller of the currency, and a private audit by CPAs. Every banker interviewed said that the most comprehensive, most competent, and most valuable audit is the private audit.

As accountants monitor the movement of capital, they provide global services for corporate penetration into new markets and development of new production centers around the world. For example, a brochure from Touche Ross & Co. describes how the firm can serve a Tokyo-based bank client who wants to open a branch in New York: "Our . . . Program will help the bank through the entire process of setting up a subsidiary here. We'll introduce them to the U.S. market, help scout for office space, find qualified employees, arrange for the necessary legal clearances – just about everything. Once the client gets established, we hope to provide auditing, tax, and other services in this country. Our New York office alone has fifteen Japanese accountants serving the U.S. arm of a Japanese client."[11]

When, in 1979, the U.S. Treasury Department had to determine for Congress whether the nearly bankrupt Chrysler Corporation had developed a recovery plan adequate for government bailout funds to be given, it called on three of the Big Eight (the other five had potential conflicts of interest) to submit proposals for evaluating the proposed $1.5 billion loan. Ernst & Whinney won the assignment and immediately a team of twenty-seven experts in various fields was assembled from fourteen of its offices around the United States. In three weeks this group produced an in-depth detailed report of Chrysler's plan. The equivalent of this project took place in the Untied Kingdom when Coopers & Lybrand was hired by the British government to complete a review of the DeLorean Motor Company in Belfast, Ireland. On the basis of the Coopers' report the government refused any further capital aid, and the company subsequently declared bankruptcy.

Size and its correlates of specialization, geographic diversity, and comprehensiveness of financial services permit the development of highly structured career ladders within the firms. There are four major formal levels of authority – junior staff, senior staff, manager, partner – and several less formalized levels in between. The firms recruit the top college graduates from the highest-ranked accounting departments. Each firm hires approximately 2,000 persons every year and maintains its own internal training program. The firms' internal educational costs are immense, adding up to tens of millions of dollars yearly per firm for extensive formal programs which span a period of several years. They in effect take the place of professional schools of accountancy.

Once in the firm, individuals either move up the career ladder at specified times or they are asked to leave. In this highly competitive atmosphere, one moves (or does not move) from entry-level to partner in an average of nine years. The chances of making partnership are one in seventeen, i.e., of every seventeen hired only one will be chosen for partnership. When matching position by age, the effect of this up-or-out policy is evident. There are no juniors or seniors older than thirty-five, and by age forty few managers remain.[12]

One obvious advantage of this Big Nine personnel policy is that it produces a large number of alumni who thereby become good contacts for expanding the firm's business. Clients are eager to hire the "rejects" because they have technical training unmatched anywhere and have had broad financial exposure in several industries. There is some client hiring of partners as well, although the numbers are much smaller than for nonpartners. The movement from these firms to government, industry, the military, and education ensures that the firms will maintain close connections with the leaders of those institutions.[13]

The problem of independence

The responsibility given to public accountants by the state through the Securities and Exchange Acts of 1933 and 1934 is to protect the public from financial misrepresentations or errors in corporate reporting. Corporations are held responsible to the Securities and Exchange Commission for the accuracy of their financial reporting. Auditors, therefore, must challenge the client (who pays them) on the wisdom of various financial methods used. As external auditors hired by the corporation, public accountants must evaluate whether the accounting principles used are appropriate and whether they have been applied consistently. It is not easy to refuse acceptance of the client's accounting strategy. If it did refuse, the accounting firm's action would be to qualify its opinion – the standardized statement attached to the financial reports of clients that attests to their successful adherence to accounting principles. At the minimum, the opinion is qualified by whatever technique or principle is misapplied. The most severe penalty is a total disclaimer of opinion. Even a qualified opinion is rare and is enough to have a significant negative effect on a corporation's earning power and ability to attract investors.

Auditors are expected to act as adversaries, or at least skeptics, in an accountability situation, i.e., corporations are accountable to their stockholders and accountants will attempt to find a breach in that responsibility. However, they are frequently accused of behaving like lawyers, as advocates for the client in an adversarial situation. In the mid-1970s, a number of government and internal accounting review groups were formed in response to growing public clamor over the seeming inability of auditors to provide adequate analyses of corporate financial operations. The most detailed and most negative of the studies generated by these groups was the report issued by the Senate Subcommittee on Reports, Accounting, and Management.[14] Known as the Metcalf Report, after Senator Lee Metcalf, the chairman of the committee, it concluded that there were serious gaps in accounting controls and audit procedures. It pointed to the excessive concentration of the profession into eight giant international firms, which effectively controlled professional self-regulation in their own interests and the interests of their clients. The report was so strongly condemnatory that it stated that the Big Eight should not be referred to as public accounting firms but only "accounting firms" because the evidence indicated overwhelmingly that they do not serve the pubic nor are they independent from the interests of their clients.[15] It also criticized the SEC for delegating its authority to the profession instead of fulfilling its public responsibility to legislate on accounting matters. It recommended the restructuring of disciplinary procedures and bodies in accounting, the reorganization of state boards of accounting under a national organization, and more direct involvement of the SEC in developing accounting principles and auditing standards.

Another major government report was issued by the House of Representatives' Subcommittee on Interstate and Foreign Commerce, headed by Rep. John E. Moss.[16] The report came to conclusions similar to the Metcalf Report and proposed an accounting review commission of persons from outside the profession who would conduct regular reviews of the firms' work and serve as disciplinarians.

Partly in anticipation of these critical reports, the American Institute of Certified Public Accountants (AICPA), in 1974, established a Committee on Auditors' Responsibilities (known as the Cohen Commission after its chairman) to examine any gap that might exist between public expectations regarding financial statements and what the audit could reasonably expect to accomplish. If such gaps existed, the auditor should provide an answer for disparities. The financial report that was issued in 1978 recommended greater disclosure of audit firm finances and operations information, regular rotation of audit personnel among clients, and more stringent disciplinary methods.[17]

The pressure from investors and the public for increased government regulation was building fast. Already, in 1975, with the passage of the Energy Policy Conservation Act, the SEC was given the responsibility for developing accounting principles for all companies involved in producing crude oil and natural gas. It revoked the profession's own ruling that required a "successful efforts" method for accounting and reporting by oil- and gas-producing companies, and it mandated its own ruling of "reserve recognition accounting." The then chairman of the SEC, Harold M. Williams, assured fearful accountants that it was a unique act on the part of the SEC and did not represent a change in policy to remove the rule-making process from the accounting profession. However, the profession saw this as a threat to its independence.

Then, in 1977, the U.S. Congress passed the Foreign Corrupt Practices Act, which requires all companies subject to the Securities Exchange Act of 1934 to maintain a system of internal controls by which assets can be carefully audited and monitored. This act was the direct result of the uncovering of widespread corporate bribery involving large commissions to foreign agents and politicians. Following the lead of Congress, in 1976 the SEC issued its *SEC Report on Questionable and Illegal Corporate Payments and Practices*, which provides accounting guidelines for determining materiality, i.e., deciding when the value of an item is large enough to warrant inclusion in the financial statements. Construction of these guidelines was formerly the exclusive task of CPAs.

Oligopoly in public accounting

Much of the impetus for the efforts to increase government intervention in public accounting was the result of the rapid expansion of the nine largest firms. Their concentration ratio of personnel is extraordinarily high. Twenty-eight percent of all CPAs who practice public accounting in the U.S. are employed by Big Eight firms; 54 percent of all CPAs who audit public companies work for the Big Eight. Their concentration ratio in the auditing of all major industries is likewise very high.[18] The Metcalf Report also documented the domination of Big Eight CPAs on AIC-PA committees, thereby enabling them to control accounting policy-making. Big Eight CPAs are also active lobbyists for legislation favorable to their clients; engage in severe, covert price-cutting tactics to attract more clients; and experience a much higher growth rate than their smaller counterparts (they averaged a growth rate of 20 percent a year during the 1970s).

Competition among highly concentrated firms has resulted in what accountants refer to as "lowballing," fee wars in which firms lower their bids for services below the break-even point in order to capture the business of clients. As the number of new large clients decreases with the saturation of the Big Nine internationally, the market of auditing services stabilizes and tightens and the field of management consulting services becomes an inviting area for expansion. Multinational consolidations of corporations have opened avenues for consulting in many areas, including tax services, transportation, marketing, and financial forecasting.

Several structural elements of concentration were present in public accounting firms in the 1970s: high concentration rate, barriers to entry of new firms, high net incomes, and a ban on overt price competition.[19] The Metcalf Report covered these elements in its analysis and suggested further that Price Waterhouse & Co. was in a special category all by itself, an elite of the Big Nine elite. In 1974–1975 it audited 24 percent of sales and 28 percent of profits of all companies listed on the New York Stock Exchange and 16 percent of sales and 19 percent of profits of all companies listed on the American Stock Exchange. It audited seventeen of the top fifty U.S. corporations, more than twice the number of the second-ranked firm, Arthur Anderson & Co. It included among its clients six of the ten largest oil companies.[20] Internationally, in 1979, it audited 23 percent of the world's fifty largest industrial corporations. At the time the Metcalf Report was released, the senior partner of Price Waterhouse became president of the Financial Accounting Standards Board (the major rule-making body of U.S. accounting); a former Price Waterhouse partner also was a member of that board; and another Price Waterhouse partner headed the Accounting Standards Executive Committee of the AICPA.[21]

The high rate of concentration in public accounting raises several questions concerning professional independence. In particular, the increase in the number of alumni in client organizations and the overlap of interests among clients served by the same firm are frequently cited as problems of perceived independence, if not actual independence. If Price Waterhouse provides auditing and management consulting services for Morgan Guaranty & Trust Co. and for many of this bank's largest clients and competitors, it is difficult to avoid the question of whether independent professional evaluation can be achieved.

A corporation is interested in presenting its best possible face to outsiders in order to bolster short-term (quarterly) performance reports. The exception occurs when a company knows its stockholders and customers are aware of financial difficulties and will attempt to counter its poor management image by applying stringent regulations that sacrifice early profit-taking. For example, to reduce the effect of several nonpayments of customer loans during 1984, First National Bank of Chicago poured several million dollars into its loss contingency reserve fund that normally would have been assigned as profits. Part of this sum was required by the SEC after performing its own audit of the bank.

Other bans, however, did not follow such conservative procedures. Penn Square Bank, an aggressive Oklahoma bank, loaned over $2.5 billion to local oil and gas companies. The loans were then resold to other banks, including two of its largest buyers, Continental Illinois and Chase Manhattan. Only four months after it received a satisfactory audit report from Peat, Marwick in 1982, Penn Square went bankrupt. Peat, Marwick argued that it had only the information supplied by the bank's management, which it contended was insufficient to disclosure the poor management and falsification of records that were subsequently uncovered. Yet, Peat, Marwick lists over one thousand banks among its clientele, and both Continental Illinois and Chase Manhattan have internal risk-management experts to advise them in investment strategy. The lesson is that the drive for profits can frequently overshadow almost any need for thorough financial evaluation.

Management advisory services

The Metcalf and Moss reports also argued that management advisory services (i.e., those areas of financial management not directly related to accounting: mergers and acquisitions, sales, purchasing, personnel, management science, and actuary) are threatening to independence because they present too many potential conflicts-of-interest. For example, if accountants are to audit a company's financial statement after they recommend to the client that it merge, purchase, or follow any other advice in general administration, they will find it difficult to provide an unbiased view of the financial position of the company. This is, of course, very hard to prove in a court of law. Furthermore, auditors are vociferous in their defense of consulting. One respondent, a Peat, Marwick audit manager, gave a typical answer regarding alleged conflicts-of-interest between the audit and performance of management consulting services: "There are accommodations; the client is paying. But, there are things we don't do. There are SEC cases where we are fired for not following the client's demands for tax shelters, for tax-minimizing opportunities. It's not worth it in the long run to bastardize your practice. There are lots of checks and balances built into the system. We are responsible to many people at many levels. For example, with regard to our banking clients, we are also accountants to regulatory bodies to which banks are responsible. This in itself is a check on independence. It would make no sense to play favorites here. We are not allowed to not be paid and remain independent. If we do free work for somebody in 1983, we cannot charge him for work done in 1984. The idea is that we are not charging the client at one point, so we're showing favoritism."

Moreover, public accountants are responsible not only to their clients (corporate managers – the people who pay the fees) but also to stockholders, credit grantors, government agencies, and potential investors – all of whom at one time or another may have interests directly opposed to management. Therefore, even what is perceived as a threat to independence becomes problematic. The SEC, the government body responsible for overseeing financial reporting, issued several warnings to the profession. Most notably was Release No. AS-264, which emphasized that it was not questioning whether independence was in fact threatened but that performance of nonaudit services could be perceived as a conflict-of-interest, thus negating the value of the accountant's work. During the 1970s, several of the Big Nine firms had large executive placement agencies operating as part of their firm's total client service package. The potential for a conflict-of-interest emerges when the accounting firm places a number of executives in a corporation and then passes judgment in its annual audit on the corporation's ability to handle its financial and related affairs. Through SEC and Congressional pressure, the AICPA ruled that member firms be prohibited from offering executive recruitment services to audit clients in which the auditor makes the actual hiring decision. Given this limitation, several of the Big Nine still decided it was worth continuing with recruitment as part of their firm services. They did this by giving recruiting staff affiliate status, thereby circumventing the ruling. The work of these affiliates has led to greater visibility for the firms, and the firms' partners in turn supply corporate contacts for the executive recruiters.

The overall response of the profession to conflict-of-interest charges was, first, to argue that wider access to information derived from concentration enhanced rather than detracted from professional independence; and second, to institute reforms. Regarding the first, the Cohen Commission report stated that there is no evidence that nonaudit services have actually impaired independence. In its review of alleged cases of conflict-of-interest, the commission stated that performance of other services actually improved the quality of the audit because it provided additional access to client records and thus more information. The response of individual firms varied. Deloitte Haskins & Sells' reply to AS-264 was that it would engage only in activities directly related to "organizational planning, performance measurement, accounting, and reporting aspects of the system for various management functions and the development and analysis of information for management use." They would not engage in psychological testing, public opinion polls, plant layout, merger and acquisition assistance of a finder's fee, and actuarial services.[22] Most firms have announced self-imposed limits similar to Deloitte's but no definite ruling on management consulting parameters has emerged.

Regarding the second response, to institute reforms, the two most important structural changes made were the transferral of rule-making from the AICPA's Accounting Principles Board to the Financial Accounting Standards Board (FASB), a newly created organization outside the formal structure of the AICPA, and the establishment of a peer-review system. The FASB move helped to defuse the Big Nine dominance issue regarding their influence in setting professional standards. The politics of the AICPA, the profession's major association and dominated by the Big Nine, were removed from the scene. Also, several members of the FASB are elected from outside the profession, and CPA members are prohibited from partnership in accounting firms. But the FASB's work of developing standards and defining concepts and principles nevertheless follows the dictates of the profession's dominant accounting paradigm, which, as argued below, does little to help accountants avert potential conflicts-of-interest.

Peer reviews are evaluations of accounting firms' auditing and accounting practice quality controls. Reviews are conducted by other firms at least once every three years. Peer reviews are monitored by a five-member Public Oversight Board. In its first report,[23] the board recommended that, except for certain executive recruiting services and actuarial services that are primary rather than supplementary to the client's operation, there should be no restrictions on consulting services provided by CPAs. It pointed out that consulting is important to everyone concerned: to the auditor because it attracts qualified people to the profession who would otherwise go elsewhere and because it identifies internal control functions and improves the underlying structure of the audit; to the client who needs advice on how to organize complex financial information; and to third parties who need accurate information for investment purposes. The board concluded that "In general . . . the Board is reluctant to support prohibitions against useful services which are based primarily on appearance without an adequate basis in fact."[24]

These arguments become suspect when it is learned that two members of the board are retired chairmen of large corporations and are active on numerous corporate boards and in business associations, that two more are practicing lawyers in large law firms, and that the remaining member is a former SEC chairman. The job of monitoring peer reviews could just as well be accomplished by knowledgeable persons who have not had special interests in audit firm performance. The peer-review program itself lacks any effective rules. Firms can select whichever firms they prefer for peer review, they are able to reject those peer-review quality control measures they object to, and they can deny SEC access to papers used in the preparation of peer reviews.

Harmonisation

When asked whether any successful international standards exist providing investors with fair, accurate, and independent financial reports, most respondents answered positively and cited harmonisation as the example. Harmonisation is the process of supplying comparable information on companies across national boundaries. Its purpose is to permit investors to view the international market as a single market of uniform principles and operations and thus to inspire the investment of risk capital. It also serves to assure the public that the financial transactions of MNCs follow acceptable accounting standards. Harmonisation, however, is a very long way from standardization of information reporting.

The broadest and most detailed reporting requirements for international capital flow are the Directives of the European Economic Council, which cover the 1.5 million European Economic Community private and public companies and all MNCs whose stock is listed on the community's stock exchange.[25] "Derogations" (options) in financial reports are permitted to reflect cultural differences, e.g., West German companies are exempted from inflation accounting and deferred tax standards. The result is a set of weak regulations. Disclosure remains general and vague. There are many rules, but they produce little meaningful information. The Directives fail to assess MNC performance in national economies by not disclosing sales to or purchases from the parent company, sources of capital funding applications, maturities of long-term debts, criteria for diversification of production and other corporate facilities, and the like.[26] The Seventh Directive requires all banks, insurance companies, and other credit institutions in the EEC to publish a full set of annual accounts. However, one requirement that would greatly strengthen the accountability of the international capital markets to investors and the public, the disclosure of secret reserves, is missing. As the managing partner of a Big Nine Zürich office said, "We will always have harmonisation in areas that are not important."

Parts of harmonisation touch upon economic and political matters very sensitive to MNC executives and their financial advisors. Transfer pricing, an accounting method used by MNCs to move costs of goods sold or earnings from one political jurisdiction to another to avoid taxation, is a particularly vexing problem for less-developed countries. Transfers are commonly made between the parent company and its foreign affiliates and among the foreign affiliates themselves. But the accounting profession has not taken the initiative to bring much needed uniformity to the area. MNC managements see their most important objective as the reduction of their assets in more vulnerable jurisdictions. For them, transfer pricing is one of the least conspicuous means of removing assets from a country with higher risk exposure. Because there is no international accounting procedure that reflects all costs of production, allocated overhead, reasonable profit margins, or the related problem of how companies consolidate the earnings of wholly or partially owned affiliates, the Big Nine accounting firms are called on to deal with the multitude of national, state, and local rules and procedures governing MNC operations. Not surprisingly, therefore, in a hands-off policy the International Accounting Standards Committee has chosen to stay clear of transfer pricing. In an interview, one of its directors said, "We are attempting to develop guidelines for basic principles governing the audit. Transfer pricing is not traditional financial information, so we don't deal with it." In addition, the governments of some countries are more interested in developing financial statements that will depict MNCs in a good light in order to advertise the advantages of business operations within their borders. On the other hand, many less-developed countries are tempted to adopt IASC rules, which are patterned after U.S. and U.K. practices, because the bulk of investment monies come from Western bankers and other private investors who prefer Anglo-Saxon accounting standards be used.

Accounting for foreign currency transactions is another area of concern. Some banks are notorious for their circumvention of the loose foreign exchange and tax laws governing various nations. From 1973 to 1980, Citicorp management was able through its own internal accounting department to eliminate $11 million in taxes on foreign currency transactions. The paucity of external accounting controls prevented exposure of this practice in independent audits of the bank during those years. Another serious problem centers on cases where country loans to LDCs are continually rescheduled and there is little hope that the principal will ever be paid off. It is hardly correct to treat these figures in the banks' balance sheets as conventional loans, as in some cases they still are.[27]

The symbolic representation of finance capital

As coordinators of organizational information, professionals in large public accounting firms have formalized, systematized, and standardized – in short, rationalized – economic procedures. The language of accounting, the symbolic representation of these procedures, both reflects and anticipates the needs of capital. Accounting concepts, theories, and assumptions have shaped the rules of accounting, which are a series of generally accepted accounting principles. The application of these principles determines the overall form of the "internal control" environment of an organization. Internal control covers the plan of organization, organizational checks and balances that limit access to assets, separation of key financial functions, and the use of internal (company) audits, and administrative functions, i.e., the delegation of authority, the personnel selection and training process and "all methods and procedures that are concerned mainly with operational efficiency and adherence to managerial policies. . . ."[28] Although corporate management decides which of the generally accepted accounting principles to use, auditors must determine, on the basis of an examination of the systems of internal control, whether management selected the appropriate accounting principles from those available and whether the principles used were applied consistently. This means that auditors must assess managerial decision-making procedures, i.e., whether the decisions were the best ones in the circumstances, as well as the assumptions that lay behind those decisions and the reasons for those assumptions. The comprehensive audit will consequently review the entire sequence of economic and economically related events, from initial production and marketing decisions to the apportionment of earnings. The scope and detail of this review, known as an operational audit, are enough to encourage increasingly frequent requests by clients for reports that require broad financial background such as a financial forecast or a risk analysis dealing with such issues as foreign currency transactions, reorganization and bankruptcy plans, or potential expropriation and nationalization of properties.

Auditor assessments follow accounting principles constructed by the auditors (disproportionately representing Big Nine firms) who make those assessments. As members of a discipline with knowledge-based skills, public accountants have developed competing paradigms – private value accounting and social value accounting – that shape their thinking. These paradigms address what should be studied, what questions should be asked, and what rules should be followed in interpreting the accounting information obtained.[29]

These paradigms are important for public accountants because they underlie capital's response to the question of accountability to shareholders and ultimately to the public. The dominant paradigm – private value accounting – and the theories that follow from it assume that value emanates from consumer utilities rather than worker labor power. This is the preferred mode of thought in the profession because it supports corporate policies. These policies are in turn supported by the state, which controls the mandate and licensure of public accounting. Any attack on conventional accounting theory is therefore an attack on corporations and threatens not only corporate legitimacy but also the very existence of those who are responsible for constructing and applying the rules of legitimation, i.e., public accountants. Therefore, when in 1979 even such a minor accounting change as requiring current value as well as historical cost figures was instituted, many in the profession considered it a dangerous move away from the measurable past and into the uncertain (and, therefore, unmeasurable) future. Accountants who fiddle with indeterminate events are viewed as doing so on weak grounds; they can only injure their image as accurate portrayers of capitalism. Certainly it is understandable that accountants in a capitalist economy will develop paradigms that reflect the interest and norms of dominant economic organizations, but the accounting profession's claims to universality make it important to demonstrate how accountants perceive and reason about reality and how this influences the thinking of finance capital.

Finally, accounting is a "practice" as much as a profession. More of its members are engaged full-time in doing its work rather than thinking about its work than perhaps any other established profession. Consequently, theory does not receive much attention and meta-theory even less. An attempt is made here to sort out paradigms, assumptions, and theories in order to examine the social implications of the relation of accounting theory to practice and in particular how accounting serves as a symbolic system for the legitimating function.

Private value accounting

As with theories of other professions, the theories of accounting are tested in the everyday application of accounting principles, which are symbolic representations of values and commitments shared by a community of practitioners. The values and commitments that presently dominate public accounting are those of private-value accounting. This paradigm has antecedents reaching back to mercantilist and marginalist theories and the origins of modern Western capitalism.[30] Following these antecedents, private value is defined as value based on the subjective utility of individual consumers, whose choices determine the value and price of goods and services. Choices are based on the considered usefulness of "things," i.e., the "factors" of land, labor, and capital. All utility approaches reify the existing social order into "fixed factors."[31] Private value accounting measures costs and not values per se. Value and utility are subjective phenomena and therefore can have no place in accounting. Obtaining information on objective market prices is the focus of accounting. Costs reflect the value placed on expected returns by specific individuals.[32] Private value accounting deals with the *marginal* utility of products; it gives the measure of the value of excess revenue over variable costs.

Although there is some disagreement over the degree to which accounting is governed by convention rather than laws, most accountants agree that accounting is able to measure costs scientifically. They believe that direct observation of data is achievable and data can be presented objectively as long as accounting principles and auditing standards are fully observed.

Table 9.1. *Intellectual sources of major accounting theories*

Background assumption	Paradigm	Theory
Utilitarian rationality	Private value	Historical cost theory
		Decision usefulness theory
Utilitarian rationality	Social value	Cost/benefit theory
Dialectical rationality	Social value	Political-economy theory

Source: See text.

Contrasting these background assumptions of utilitarian rationality, positivism, and possessive individualism with their opposite assumptions of dialectic rationality, subjectivism, and structural factors, major accounting theories can be classified into three types (see Table 9.1).

The two major private value theories of accounting are "historical cost" and "decision usefulness." Historical cost specifies that all unexpired costs of the business entity must be recorded, classified, and matched with revenues. Decision-usefulness theory contains most of the propositions of historical cost but differs in one significant way:[33] because emphasis is placed on the use of accounting data for decision-makers, the current value of transactions must also be recorded.[34] The FASB has been instrumental in the development of this theory, supporting it with a series of conceptual definitions for financial accounting. Advocates of decision usefulness argue that in order to make rational decisions, management, investors, and other interested parties must have appropriate, comprehensive accounting information, both historical and current. One consequence is a controversial regulation issued by the FASB in 1979[35] that requires companies to supplement their regular financial statements with current value figures to show changes in the general level of prices and changes in prices related to specific assets. Decision usefulness states that accounting information cannot be judged only on the grounds of its internal consistency with an assumed model but also must include other, less certain, information. Defenders of historical cost contend that emphasis on decision usefulness places accountants in an untenable position as forecasters. Public accountants must present statements based only on factual data; they are like engineers, who concentrate on the adequacy of the physical structure of a bridge and not whether its use will improve traffic flows, quality of life, or industrial development.[36]

Despite differences in their technical measurement procedures, both theories derive from common antecedents in mercantilism and marginalism. Mercantile economics contributed the notion of commodity pricing, which emphasizes demand-side factors of consumer and owner expectations as the significant determinants of value. In reaction to the Ricardian theory that real value reflected socially necessary labor, the marginalist economists concentrated on the "real" aspect of value, i.e., on the factuality and impartiality of economic data.

In both economics and accounting, the underlying presuppositions of private value theories are: utilitarian rationality, in which self-interest is the regulator of a harmonious society; objective reality, which can be measured to obtain "true" facts; and emphasis on individuals as efficient producers of value.[37] These assumptions permeate the conceptual language of private value accounting. Among the more important accounting concepts derived from these assumptions are materiality, uncertainty reduction, and objective.

Materiality

Ever since the McKesson Robbins case of the 1930s, the courts have held that auditors cannot possibly examine all information items of a client's accounts.[38] Auditors must decide *which* information they will examine, or as the professional code states, which items are material. Materiality occurs when "the magnitude of an omission or misstatement of accounting information that, in the light of *surrounding circumstances*, makes it probable that the *judgment* of a *reasonable* person relying on the information would have been changed or influenced by the omission or misstatement."[39] How do accountants know when an item is material? According to most analyses of actual auditor practice, an item that affects the net income of an organization by at least 5 to 10 percent is a material one.[40] Of course, auditors must decide whether that item, in their judgment, will fall below or above that cutting point. A judgment item is defined by the FASB as "whatever has to be determined to be material or immaterial."[41]

Consequently, auditors must make judgments about judgment items. If these items do not affect the safety of the organization, i.e., profits, then the matter is not a significant one. Again, the FASB: "The more important the judgment item is, the finer the screen should be that will be used to determine whether it is material."[42] Importance is measured by its effect on profitability. A finer screen should be used in a situation where an accounting procedure places a weak business in danger of breach of covenant than if that business' financial condition were very strong. Presumably, the board would not consider social and environmental factors unless corporate violation of government restrictions ended in severe fines affecting corporate health.

Uncertainty reduction

The theory of capital investment uses uncertainty reduction as its central conceptual instrument. The three types of decision situations in capital allocation are certainty, risk, and uncertainty.[43] Risk exists in " . . . [s]ituations in which a probability distribution of the return on a given project can be estimated."[44] In situations of uncertainty, however, there is insufficient knowledge to estimate a probability distribution. But with a normal distribution of outcomes the degree of risk can be directly related to the degree of dispersion of the net income stream. Risk can be measured by "the average standard deviation of the return on assets." The larger the standard deviation, the larger the risk.[45] Risk is a major factor in explaining capital ratios (the proportion of capital to total assets). Increased profits can only be achieved by the firm taking greater risks. The greater the risk, the greater the returns to capital, but as risk increases so too do the possibilities of the loss of returns.[46] In the long run, firms have to settle on the level of risk they are willing to take. Some will raise the risk in one area and lower it in another. Some sort of balance has to be maintained in which the positive factors outweigh the negative.

In the financial forecast review, increasingly performed by auditors for management as a "decision-usefulness" tool, many risk elements must be considered; the uncertainty surrounding the collectibility of accounts receivable, the unpredictability of environmentally produced catastrophic losses, the threat of asset expropriation, and pending litigation. These and many other capital-related factors require that an estimate of risk of loss (or a statement that no estimate can be made) be disclosed by the corporation in its financial statements. The accountant then has to decide on the relevance and reliability of this information to the investor and to the client as well. A highly favorable review of a forecast on the effectiveness of internal management could result in premature company actions such as selling property in order to bolster accounting earnings to meet the forecast. Both investors and clients often anticipate the effects of these and other kinds of accounting information before it is issued. Materiality guidelines often cannot be set because the situation being forecasted is too unpredictable.[47] Such "soft information" generated in financial forecasts is popular with both investors and clients because both can use it to protect their own interests in a situation of mutual distrust. Management uses it to protect itself from legal claims and investors to find something to attach blame to management.

Decision situations of uncertainty are considered too unstable for audit review, and public accountants generally stay clear of them. However, what is considered uncertain by one auditor may be labeled as within the realm of risk estimate by another. The financial forecast review is a good example of these different interpretations. Some critics charge that as competition for clients increases among public accounting firms the line between risk and uncertainty moves further in the direction of the latter, i.e., decisions previously considered uncertain are redefined as risky. This translates into more work for the firms, as previously unmeasurable events become quantifiable.

Most accounting principles are considered to be conventions; they are perceived as less certain and scientific laws as more certain. As one FASB member concludes, conventions aim at uniformity within a "reasonable range of probable error." The least certain of all are social norms that motivate decision-makers to act to further social and economic goals.[48] The assumption is that as one moves from vague social and economic goals to exacting scientific facts (the direction in which accountants should be moving) uncertainty decreases and knowledge increases.[49] The emphasis is on the reduction of ignorance within a given body of information rather than the creation of knowledge by introducing new accounting ideas that are difficult to quantify and often disagree with accepted theory. The social and physical environments are controlled through a steady expansion of organized information, measured by principles objectively ("scientifically") applied.

Objectivity

Accountants argue that facts only ought to be used. Bias is thereby eliminated and the result is objective reality. A 1970 statement of the AICPA emphasizes that the "proper discharge of the [audit] function obviously requires . . . complete objectivity.[50] That is, auditors can separate their beliefs and commitments from what they are examining. The contradiction is that generally accepted accounting principles are applied to determine what the facts are but themselves are not objectively determined. Nor are they necessarily objectively applied. Private value theorists assume individuals are utility maximizers of information, expending effort necessary to maintain the system as it is. When, in a large consulting engagement, a task force from one Big Nine firm reviewed a major poverty program for the city of Detroit, it based its analysis on a not-for-profit poverty "market." Market information, including "data which will satisfy public demand," and thereby ease pressure on government-agency officials, were collected to determine poverty area "performances." Records of performance were: police arrests, welfare relief roles and stamp operations, communicable disease cases, birth and death rates, unemployment rates, etc. The objective of the program, it was agreed, was "to anticipate trouble before it erupts and to make changes and adjustments as required."[51] Accounting assessment becomes a reflection of the needs of capital. No attempt is made to account for external variables with political or social consequences, such as alternate measures of poverty or the effects of other long-term urban redevelopment goals.

Social value accounting

Social value accounting differs from private value accounting in that value is based on socially necessary labor, that is, the assumption that labor effort determines value and price. Labor effort is discussed in general equilibrium economic theory, which analyzes the role of information in the allocation of resources among all or most market participants. Because this information affects the sharing of risks in an economy, it has welfare implications that are cost efficient.[52] The accounting theory that represents this condition of *efficient* social value (the relationship between resources used and outputs achieved) is cost/benefit. Cost/benefit theorists insist that to be accurate and meaningful the measurement of profits and capital allocation must include auditor evaluation of management's socioeconomic decisions that involve ecological, political, and cultural factors. This measurement must use prediction variables, more often than not in a transnational environment. Cost/benefit theory raises several questions, the most obvious and most difficult to answer referring to what variables should be quantified. For example, the stock of knowledge (education) and on-the-job training as investments in human capital can affect the amount and types of capital investments made and resources allocated just as plant and equipment do. Yet the purchase of the latter is treated as an increase in the value of the corporation whereas education, training, and research and development expenses are not. Another question is how to determine whether classes of events are costs or benefits, or both. James Kennedy, a partner in Peat, Marwick, Mitchell & Co., argues that the expense-account meal is a benefit to the corporation (and thus to investors) because it provides uninterrupted time with the client to close a deal.[53] As tax writeoffs, expense-account meals are highly prized management perquisites. Therefore, to support clients, auditors prefer to list these meals as benefits that outweigh the considerable cost involved. The counterargument is that it is a cost that greatly outweighs benefits derived because as an expense account item added to costs of production it is an operation subsidized by consumers. The benefit-side rebuttal is that corporate expense-account meals and services support a labor force of over one million persons, a hotel business of $26 billion a year, and contribute over $50 billion annually to the service industry in expense-account writeoffs alone.

The rules for assigning efficient versus effective values to costs and benefits by accountants are not established. Consequently, in practice, cost/benefit has been used mostly within the framework of efficient values and utility maximization. In the settlement of insurance claims of permanently disabled workers, government economists in the Office of Management and Budget use the "willingness to pay" formula. They calculate from people's behavior what value they place on their lives according to the following theorem: the greater the willingness to risk, the less the value one places on one's life.[54] The monetary value assigned to different occupations with approximately equal incomes varies considerably: the risk jobs are given less value and the safe jobs more. Bartenders and firefighters are worth $500,000 in the full term of their work lives, whereas most clerical workers are estimated at around $7 million. The premise is one of individual choice in a rational market. Its correlates are that individuals place value on their lives according to the occupation they choose; and, second, that individuals receive the jobs they want. There is no consideration of such limiting external factors as race, sex, ethnicity, age, and parents' socioeconomic background in influencing occupational attainment.

Measuring *effectiveness* (the relation between the outputs achieved and the satisfying of societal needs and expectations) in cost/benefit accounting terms requires that social-welfare variables be considered as part of the analysis.[55] However, measures of effectiveness have been extremely sparse in public accounting. In their own planning, corporations generally avoid cost/benefit programs that are effective measures of social value. The inclusion of elements external to the market (e.g., contributions to community development funds, voluntary pollution-control devices) in the short term usually requires more costs expended than benefits received, and long-term benefits are uncertain. Public accounting consultants prefer to limit cost/benefit analyses to those aspects that can show immediate results in increased profits for clients. They use one or more variants of information economics, which better fit the preferences of business and the basic assumptions of marginal utility.[56]

Public accounting practitioners cite the social audit as the new accounting mechanism for dealing with social costs and benefits. It is defined as a procedure that systematically identifies, analyzes, measures (through social indicators), evaluates, and monitors the effects of an organization's operations on social groups and the public's well-being.[57] The social audit was during the 1970s still another response of the profession to the scathing criticism of government. However, even in the in-depth social audits actually performed, the myth of value freedom persists. One of the best known social-audit programs, often mentioned by leaders of the profession as a good example of the genre, states that there is a common monetary measure for different social values.[58] Some of these values ("shadow prices") are derived from outside the business entity's market, for example, the value to a firm of its production input as compared to the market price the firm paid for the input. All values, social and nonsocial, market and nonmarket, are objectively measured: "One can measure changes in social utility as expressed in changes in perceived market value in a way just as free from bias as one can measure changes in economic utility as expressed in changes in economic prices. . . . [D]ifferences in motivation generate differences in real or shadow prices and . . . the perceived social utility . . . is a direct and unbiased measure of it that can be expressed in terms of economic market values."[59] Thus, by measuring actual consumer preferences and behaviors the social audit avoids subjective judgments. This assumes that auditors can directly absorb the information received from other people, the environment, reports, etc., without interpretation, without any symbolic content, without metaphor.

In sum, cost/benefit theory really clothes the old model of utilitarian rationality in the new symbols of social value accounting. Despite the acknowledgment that events produce uncertainty and the acceptance of open-system and natural models of organization,[60] the norm of cost/benefit accounting theory is objective, quantitative measurement of individuals in predictable systems.

Political economy theory

The radical critique of private value accounting and its role in the social reproduction of capital states that the public accounting profession exists primarily to reaffirm capital's position of dominance.[61] Accounting information provided by the internal accounting staffs of corporations is often an after-the-fact justification of decisions that were taken by management for nonlogical reasons in the first place.[62] Critics also argue that, in practice, accountants undertake as many audits of a firm as necessary until one acceptable to the client appears – data are not taken seriously until they conform to the needs of the enterprise, a process of "systematic disinformation."[63]

Few accounting practitioners acknowledge this criticism. Only one very small group, comprised primarily of accounting academicians, has followed through with a critical social value accounting theory: political-economy theory.[64] This political economy of accounting is labor-based rather than consumer-based; it states that labor effort, not consumer demand, determines value and price, that value is based on socially necessary labor (production-side valuation) instead of subjective utility (demand-side valuation).[65] It argues that, rather than emphasize a unitary logic of transactional efficiency, accounting must use causal analysis in a historical setting. The accounting process is dialectical: i.e., it is dynamic, internal systems of control are in constant conflict, and financial analysis requires a review of processes and events over the longer term.

Political-economy theory also suggests that uncertainty may be an inherent characteristic of a market environment in which the potential exists for fragmentation, rupture, and alternative frameworks. The concept of unlimited choices of individuals in markets is replaced by its opposite: choices are limited by sex, age, race, ethnicity, and the structural factors of socioeconomic status and organizational setting. The idea that accountants work independently of the interaction they measure is replaced by the understanding that accountants are part of the dynamics of the social and economic organizations they are measuring.[66]

Political-economy adherents emphasize the necessity of valuing effects external to the immediate production process. They define these valuations as ethically based. Imperfect competition, imperfect knowledge, and factor divisibility characterize markets. Most importantly, perfect measurement of values is not possible.[67] The political economy of public accounting recognizes the *public* nature of the capitalist economy as a system of exchange because there exists the "socially consequential exercise of power."[68] Wage labor violates a person's liberty by the conferring of effective command over the use of labor to the satisfaction of the private ends of capitalists. The same exercise of power takes place in socialist economies as well, where bureaucratic control of labor in the interests of the state – and its bureaucrats – also uses the system of functional rationality found in modern capitalist accounting and auditing techniques.[69]

A full political economy of accounting has yet to be practiced. It presently exists only in bits and pieces, one large piece being the cost-benefit framework. But there will have to be a greatly expanded examination of social and political elements that are presently considered to be outside the accounting system of discourse. Among the important "transactions" that would be given financial import are the value of products in terms of their effects on local or regional employment, the quality of life afforded in the workplace (i.e., health and safety factors), worker participation movements, and the effects of measurers' values on the measurement process.

Political-economy theory has a long tradition, reaching back to the principles of social surplus and labor value of Smith and Ricardo and the labor theory of value of Marx. However, except for the mildly critical work of the accountant D. R. Scott,[70] a student of Thorstein Veblen, there has until quite recently been no activity in this area. The principles and assumptions of political-economy theory are unacceptable to the dominant paradigm, so it does not have access to the large audience that its opposition does. It is a small movement and more theoretical development is needed. However, its very existence provides the basis for a dialectic with private value theories.

Homogenization and accountability

The comprehensiveness and depth of the financial and related services of the giant public accounting firms are a new phenomenon. The coordination of vast amounts of information gathered from multinational organizations and government bodies, and not only from their financial control systems but also from their administrative, communications, transportation, and other related systems of internal control, can only be accomplished efficiently by groups that can mobilize human and technical resources quickly. Such coordination requires access to the financial records and internal information systems of the largest organizations in the industries in which these firms operate. Clearly, the Big Nine are part of the process of what DiMaggio and Powell call "normative isomorphism," a process of homogenization emerging among business, state, and professional organizations. Each of these organizations acts to rationalize and bureaucratize society and each operate through professional networks that span a range of organizations across industries with a pool of almost interchangeable individuals with similar values, dispositions, and orientations[71] – a description that fits the Big Nine partnerships and their members.

Homogenization extends beyond the firms as well through the interchange of personnel with clients. This leaves little room for auditor independence. The theories of the profession's dominant paradigm represent the ideology of finance capital. They prevent the kind of analysis of financial transactions that would permit a reflexive view of events. Dialectical rationality exists only among a small segment of accountants; it has no anchor in private value accounting and little support in social value accounting, except among political-economy theorists.

Public accountants are the experts assigned the task of providing business accountability to the public, but their role of mediation favors their clients. The mutual sponsorship of expert and client rarely uncovers the mistakes and misrepresentations of management. In an attempt to mitigate the worst excesses of this relationship, the state periodically intervenes. This was the case in the mid-1970s, and the accountants' response – self-regulatory mechanisms – effectively quieted the critics. The election of a conservative administration in the Untied States in 1980 ended all serious efforts at further regulation of the profession. However, numerous financial crises erupted in the early 1980s, some with system-threatening potential. The failed Penn Square and Continental Illinois banks, numerous bankrupt corporations in Europe, and the multinational banks involved in the international debt crisis were all audited by Big Nine firms. As a result, once again the state has intervened to investigate the accounting firms[72] and once again it is likely that there will be the ritual slap on the wrists with the admonishment to behave independently.

The main concern of state authorities is the investing public and not the public-at-large. Unless adequate information exists to provide reasonable risk for financial ventures, investors and potential investors will hesitate to commit funds to the market. Accountability is to finance capital – banks, corporations, governments, institutional investors, and wealthy individuals – all accounting firm clients. How much of the thrust of regulation is also due to the encroachment of accounting firms into the professional work of others – management consulting firms, law firms, banks – is uncertain. But the resulting competition has created an additional dynamic between public accounting and the state that will be played out in the continuing homogenization of the institutions of finance capital.

There is some limited opposition within public accounting to the dominant theory of the forces of social reproduction. However, as the illustration of the social audit in social value accounting demonstrates, some of that behavior may not be a clear-cut response to dominant theory and, in fact, may reproduce "the most powerful grammar of domination."[73] Given these serious limitations, there seems little chance that the public accounting profession will overcome its client dependency soon.

Notes

1. Research for this article was supported by a German Marshall Fund fellowship and by grants from The City University of New York PSC-CUNY Research Award Program. Special thanks are owed to Robert M. Maynard of Price Waterhouse & Co. and Dr. Heinrich Meng of Wettingen, Switzerland, for their help in obtaining initial interview contacts and to the students of the 1984 class stratification seminar in the Department of Sociology at The City University of New York Graduate Center for their critique of finance capital.

2. Public accountants are accountants who have received state authority to conduct independent (no conflict-of-interest) audits of industrial, and in some countries,

financial corporations. Accounting is the generic term that encompasses any and all recording, summarizing, and reporting of financial and other economic transactions. Most fully developed capitalist nations have some equivalent of the American certified public accountant.

3. Charles Derber, "Sponsorship and the Control of Physicians," *Theory and Society* 12 (Sept. 1983); 561–602. As Derber establishes for physicians (and as applied to large-firm accountants as well), it is not a precise form of market sponsorship because professional mediation is not based on "command of material resources" but only on "cultural authority" over clients.

4. The firms are: Arthur Andersen & Co.; Coopers & Lybrand; Deloitte Haskins & Sells; Ernst & Whinney; Klynveld, Main, Goerdeler; Peat, Marwick, Mitchell & Co.; Price Waterhouse & Co.; Touche, Ross & Co.; Arthur Young & Co. In 1979 a number of European firms merged with the U.S. firm of Main, Hurdman & Cranstoun to form Klynveld, Main, Goerdeler, a ninth firm comparable in size to the original eight. There is a large gap between these nine, approximately equal in size and earnings, and the tenth and succeeding firms, the tenth with less than one-quarter the size/earnings of the ninth. In public accounting, reference is more frequently to the Big Nine since 1981, especially when discussing the international accounting network.

5. Together the nine firms audit 88 percent of the 50 largest industrial companies in the world, 80 percent of the 200 largest, and 56 percent of the 10,786 largest. Summarized from: *The Fortune Directory* (1980); *Poor's Register of Corporation, Directors, and Executives* (New York: Standard & Poor's Corporation, 1980); unpublished statistics from two of the nine multinational accounting firms; Michael Lafferty and David Cairns, *Financial Times World Survey of Annual Reports, 1980* (London: The Financial Times Business Information Ltd., 1980); and Vinod B. Bavishi and Harold E. Wyman, *Who Audits the World: Trends in the Worldwide Accounting Profession* (Storrs, Conn.: Center for Transnational Accounting and Financial Research, School of Business Administration, University of Connecticut, 1983).

6. Averaged from the 1982 and 1983 annual reports, brochures, and directories of the nine firms.

7. Statistics for 1980 received from five of the nine firms averaged out at 48 percent.

8. Interviews were conducted with twenty-one accountants and fourteen executive bankers in four European countries: England, France, Switzerland, and West Germany. The accounting firms represented are: Coopers & Lybrand; Deloitte Haskins & Sells; Klynveld, Main, Goerdeler; Peat, Marwick, Mitchell & Co.; Price Waterhouse & Co.; and Touche, Ross & Co. The banks included; Deutsche Bank; Crédit Suisse; Union Bank of Switzerland; National Westminster; B. Metzler seel Sohn & Co. In the United States, forty-five accountants from all levels of their firms were interviewed, as well as twelve executive bankers. The U.S. sample includes the same accounting firms visited in Europe. The banks are: Chase Manhattan; Citibank; Merrill Lynch; Morgan Guaranty & Trust Co. The questionnaire N = 179, which represents an 86 percent return.

9. Paul Montagna, *Certified Public Accounting: A Sociological Analysis of a Profession in Change* (Houston: Scholars Books, 1974); John W. Buckley and Marlene H. Buckley, *The Accounting Profession* (New York: Wiley, 1974).

10. In such large firms there is a need for a separate hierarchy of authority and division of labor for nonaccounting specialists, who include economists, mathematicians, computer systems analysts, political scientists, and others. Montagna, *Certified Public Accounting*, chaps. 2 and 5.

11. Mark Stevens, *The Big Eight* (New York: Macmillan Co., 1981), 51.

12. Based on questionnaire results; see note 8 above.

13. To cite a few examples: L. William Seidman, former managing partner of Seidman & Seidman, became special assistant for financial affairs for Governor George Romney of Michigan, then assistant for economic affairs in the White House under Gerald Ford, then vice-chairman of Phelps Dodge Corporation, and then, in 1982, dean of the College of Business Administration at Arizona State University. John C. ("Sandy") Burton, a former member of Arthur Young & Co. and active in AICPA councils, was for many years chief accountant for the Securities and Exchange Commission and then moved to the deanship of Columbia University's Graduate School of Business Administration.

14. Committee on Government Operations, United States Senate, *The Accounting Establishment* (Washington, D.C.: U.S. Government Printing Office, 1976).

15. Ibid., 4.

16. Committee on Interstate and Foreign Commerce, U.S. House of Representatives, *Report by the Subcommittee on Oversight and Investigations* (Washington, D.C.: U.S. Government Printing Office, 1976).

17. *Committee on Auditors' Responsibilities: Report, Conclusions, and Recommendations* (New York: Committee on Auditors' Responsibilities, 1977). The question of stock ownership by public accountants in corporations they audit is covered in an AICPA regulation that prohibits ownership in any corporation audited by the accountant or the accountant's firm. This prohibition includes the accountant's spouse and dependent family members and, in certain circumstances, close relatives.

18. John W. Buckley and Peter O'Sullivan, "Regulation and Public Accounting: What Are the Issues?" in John W. Buckley and J. Fred Weston, eds., *Regulation and the Accounting Profession* (Belmont, Calif.: Wadsworth, 1980), 3 – 53. Also, Bavishi and Wyman, *Who Audits the World*, 63, 65.

19. Michael E. Granfield, "Structural Theory and the Accounting Profession," in Buckley and Weston, eds., *The Accounting Profession*, 54–74.

20. *The Accounting Establishment*, 424–44.

21. The next FASB president, Donald J. Kirk, was the former Price Waterhouse partner who was already a member of the board. Also, in late 1984, Price Waterhouse and Deloitte Haskins & Sells reached a tentative agreement to merge. Only the negative vote of the recalcitrant English partners of the two firms prevented a consummation.

22. Stevens, *The Big Eight*, 209–10.

23. American Institute of Certified Public Accountants, Public Oversight Board, *Scope of Services by CPA Firms* (New York: American Institute of Certified Public Accountants, 1979).

24. Ibid., 20. In March 1985, in testimony to the House Energy Subcommittee on Oversight and Investigations, the chairman and vice-chairman of the Public Oversight Board reemphasized that executive recruitment does not impair independence, even when an audit client is involved.

25. The European Economic Council (EEC) is a supra-national organization responsible for creating corporate laws of financial reporting for member states of the European Economic Community. Individual member states have discretionary power regarding how the council's laws are to be incorporated into national law. The council is led by a Council of Ministers, with one representative from each members state. The Council of Ministers has issued eight directives, of which the fourth is the most important, specifying the detailed requirements for disclosure in annual financial statements of all companies of limited liability through share capital. See Coopers & Lybrand, *Europe: The EEC Directives* (London: Coopers & Lybrand, 1980); and Whinney Murray Ernst & Ernst, *The Fourth Directive* (London: Kluwer Publishing Co, 1978).

26. Vinod B. Bavishi and Harold E. Wyman, "Foreign Operations Disclosure by U.S. Based Multinational Corporations: Are They Adequate?" *International Journal of*

Accounting, 16 (Fall 1980): 153–168; Hanns-Martin W. Schoenfeld, "Harmonization in Accounting," in Dhia AlHashim and James W. Robertson, eds., *Accounting for Multinational Enterprises* (New Brunswick, N.J.: Bobbs-Merrill, 1980), 192–93.

27. The FASB has issued a ruling (Rule 15) on "Troubled Debt Restructuring," which states that interest received on rescheduled loans should not be recorded as income and that such loans should be listed separately in the creditor's financial statements. Multinational banks frequently ignored this rule until the SEC issued its own rules on foreign loans in 1983 to strengthen disclosure regulations on foreign and domestic loans. A survey of the audited reports of the world's one hundred largest banks disclosed that neither the banks nor their auditors satisfied basic international accounting requirements for general information needs of shareholders, third parties, and the general public. Seventy percent of the audited banks were clients of the Big Nine. Michael Lafferty, David Andrews, and Martyn Taylor, *Bank Annual Reports: Financial Times 1982 World Survey* (London: Financial Times Business Information Ltd., 1982), 217.

28. American Institute of Certified Public Accountants, *Reports of the Special Advisory Committee on Internal Accounting Control* (New York: American Institute of Certified Public Accountants, 1979); International Federation of Accountants, *Study and Evaluation of the Accounting System and Internal Control in Connection With an Audit, Exposure Draft* (New York: International Federation of Accountants, June 1, 1980). The latter source notes that the internal accounting system is separate from the internal control system, which is the responsibility of management. However, the intent is clearly that the auditor must evaluate the systems as a whole in order to provide reasonable assurance that the objectives of accounting control and audit procedures are being followed.

29. Following the definition by Margaret Masterman, "The Nature of a Paradigm," in Imre Lakatos and Alan Musgrave, eds., *Criticism and the Growth of Knowledge* (Cambridge, Eng.: Cambridge University Press, 1970), 59–89.

30. The analytic framework used to explain the paradigmatic structure of the accounting profession relies heavily on the recent work of a number of accounting researchers summarized in two articles: Anthony M. Tinker, Barbara D. Merino, and Marilyn Dale Neimark, "The Normative Origins of Positive Theories: Ideology and Accounting Thought," *Accounting, Organizations and Society* 7, no. 2 (1982): 167–200; and David J. Cooper and Michael J. Sherer, "The Value of Corporate Accounting Reports: Arguments for a Political Economy of Accounting," *Accounting, Organizations and Society* 9, nos. 3/4 (1984): 207–32.

31. Tinker, Merino, and Neimark, "Normative Origins," 174.

32. Ibid., 188.

33. There is much confusion in the accounting literature (as much as there is in other disciplines) over the differences between paradigms, theories, and assumptions. Because historical cost and decision usefulness are the two major contending theories in accounting today, some analysts define them as paradigms, e.g., M.C. Wells, "A Revolution in Accounting Thought?" *Accounting Review* 51 (July 1976): 471–82. However, they are treated here as theories within the framework of a single paradigm. Also, clear distinctions between theories often sacrifice some of the subtle connections between them. The American Accounting Association, in a *Statement on Accounting Theory and Theory Acceptance* (Sarasota, Fla., 1977), 47, points out that a weak amalgamation of historical and current costing theory was achieved by William Paton and A. C. Littleton in 1940 in their co-authored work, *An Introduction to Corporate Accounting Standards* (Columbus, Ohio: American Accounting Association, 1940). The two theories are even given different names by different researchers. Historical cost is also called income measurement, and decision usefulness has been referred to as cash-flow theory, current valuation theory, and current cost theory.

34. A benchmark for decision-usefulness theory is Maurice Moonitz and Robert T. Sprouse, *A Tentative Set of Broad Accounting Principles for Business Enterprises* (New York: American Institute of Certified Public Accountants, 1962).

35. Financial Accounting Standard Board, *Statement No. 33: Financial Reporting and Changing Price* (Stanford, Conn.: Financial Accounting Standards Board, 1979).

36. This is the argument of Richard S. Hickok, retired senior partner of KMG, in an editorial in *The CPA Journal* 52 (Dec. 1982): 75–77. It represents the position of a large group of public accountants. The initial statements describing historical cost are by William Paton, *Accounting Theory* (New York: Ronald Press, 1922), and A. C. Littleton, "Value and Price in Accounting," *Accounting Review* 4 (Sept. 1929): 278–88.

37. The distinction between efficient and effective producers or values is that efficiency is a measure of the satisfying of the needs of individuals and effectiveness is a measure of the success of achieving some desired end based on the satisfaction of those needs. These terms were first defined by Chester I. Barnard, *The Functions of the Executive* (Cambridge, Mass.: Harvard University Press, 1938), 19–20. The accounting definition fits closely to this model. Efficiency has to do with the relation between resources used and outputs achieved by individuals and effectiveness with the relation between outputs achieved and the attainment of the needs and expectations of the system. See Cooper and Sherer, "Value of Corporate Accounting Reports," 214.

38. In 1938 the auditors of McKesson & Robbins, Inc., were taken to federal court on charges of improper audit of the company's finances. Investors argued that documents forged by management totaling $19 million in inventory and accounts receivable accounting were not discovered by Price Waterhouse & Co. in the audit. The auditors argued, and the court agreed, that auditors must rely on the information supplied by management, subject to the reviews made from this information. The unstated assumption was that to uncover misrepresentations of management would require that so many transactions be examined and in such detail that the cost of the audit would be prohibitive.

39. Financial Accounting Standards Board, *Statement of Financial Accounting Concepts No. 2: Qualitative Characteristics of Accounting Information* (Stanford, Conn.: Financial Accounting Standards Board, 1980), xv.

40. James W. Pattillo, *The Concept of Materiality in Financial Reporting* (New York: Financial Executive Research Foundation, 1976). The international accounting community agrees to the same limits. See Accountants International Study Group, *Materiality in Accounting* (1974), 30.

41. Financial Accounting Standards Board, *Statement of Financial Accounting Concepts No. 2* . . . , 52.

42. Ibid.

43. James C. Van Horne, *Financial Management and Policy,* 4th ed. (Englewood Cliffs, N.J.: Prentice-Hall, 1977), 115.

44. J. Fred Weston and Eugene F. Brigham, *Essentials of Managerial Finance,* 4th ed. (Hinsdale, Ill.: Dryden Press, 1977), 250.

45. R. R. Dince and J. C. Fortson, "Bank Examination, Capital Adequacy and Risk," *The Bankers Magazine* 163 (May–June 1980): 53–54.

46. Paul M. Van Adsdell, *Corporation Finance: Policy, Planning, Administration* (New York: Ronald Press, 1968), 34–35; J. Fred. Weston, "A Generalized Uncertainty Theory of Profit," *American Economic Review* (Mar. 1950): 40–60; Ezra Solomon, *The Theory of Financial Management* (New York: Columbia University Press, 1963), 31.

47. Financial Accounting Standard Board, *Statement of Financial Accounting Concepts No. 2* . . . , 73. Another related problem is "whether the way a transaction is accounted for is going to affect the decision made about whether to enter that transaction." Philip

B. Chenok, Douglas Carmichael, and Thomas P. Kelly, "Accounting and Auditing: The Technical Challenges Ahead," *Journal of Accountancy* 150 (Nov. 1980): 68.

48. David Masso, "Regulation and the Accounting Profession: An FASB Member's View," in Buckley and Weston, *Regulation*, 128–41. In the celebrated Tarnower-Harris "Scarsdale Diet" trial, the jury was instructed that if "reasonable doubt" were found the defendent could not be found guilty of murder. Reasonable doubt, it was pointed out by the court, is by law defined as "more than an uncertainty but less than mathematical perfection." It is a doubt for which the person stating it can give a reason.

49. Masso, "Regulation."

50. American Institute of Certified Public Accountants, "AICPA Brief in Continental Vending," *Journal of Accountancy* 129 (May 1970): 69–73.

51. J. A. Ruff, "Poverty Programs: A Business Management Approach," *The Quarterly Touche, Ross, Bailey & Smart* 12 (June 1966): 24–25; Robert Beyer, "The Modern Management Approach to a Program of Social Improvement," *Journal of Accountancy* 127 (Mar. 1969); 40.

52. Cooper and Sherer, "Value of Corporate Accounting Reports," 213–14.

53. From a report by William Serrin in *The New York Times*, 29 Mar., 1981.

54. From a report by Bill Keller in *The New York Times*, 26 Oct., 1984.

55. The history of the measurement of efficiency shows that efficiency is given different emphases, depending on the historical situation. As a valuation system for measurement, it therefore is value-laden. Cooper and Sherer, "Value of Corporate Accounting Reports," 214.

56. Three approaches of information economics, each with a different emphasis on marginal utility, are contingency theory, transaction cost, and agency theory. For a review and critique of these theories based on information economics, see David Cooper, "Tidiness, Muddle and Things: Communalities and Divergencies in Two Approaches to Management Accounting Research, *Accounting, Organizations and Society* 8, nos. 2/3 (1983): 269–86; and Charles Perrow, "The Invasion of the Body Snatchers: Economic Theories of Organizations," paper presented at the Annual Meeting of the American Sociological Association, San Diego, Calif., Aug. 1984.

57. David H. Blake, William C. Frederick, and Mildred S. Meyers, *Social Auditing: Evaluating the Impact of Corporate Programs* (New York: Praeger, 1976), 3.

58. Clark C. Abt, *The Social Audit for Management* (New York: American Management Associations, 1977), 26.

59. Ibid., 191.

60. See the comparison by Richard J. Boland, Jr., and Louis R. Pondy, "Accounting in Organizations: A Union of Natural and Rational Perspectives," *Accounting, Organizations and Society* 8, nos. 2/3 (1983): 223–34.

61. The key statements are found in two articles: Tinker, Merino, and Neimark, "Normative Origins"; and Cooper and Sherer, "Value of Corporate Accounting Reports."

62. This point is discussed by Geert Hofstede, *Culture's Consequences: International Differences in Work-Related Values* (Beverly Hills: Sage, 1980), 160.

63. A criticism emphasized by John W. Meyer, "On the Celebration of Rationality: Some Comments on Boland and Pondy," *Accounting, Organizations and Society* 8, nos. 2/3 (1983): 237. Why can't accountants get at the truth? Meyer answers that it is because accounting structures are myths, subject to their own requirements in which the organization is given a mythic unity as a single rational production system.

64. Tinker, Merino, and Neimark, "Normative Origins"; Cooper and Sherer, "Value of Corporate Accounting Reports."

65. Tinker, Merino, and Neimark, "Normative Origins," 173, 185, call these the subjectivist (labor-based) and absolutist (consumer-based) *theories* of value.

66. Cooper, "Tidiness."

67. Hein Schreuder and Kavasseri V. Ramanathan, "Accounting and Corporate Accountability: An Extended Comment," and "Accounting and Corporate Accountability: A Postscript," *Accounting, Organizations and Society* 9, nos. 3/4 (1984): 409–15, 421–23.

68. The rationale for accepting the economy as a public as well as private institution is presented by Samuel Bowles and Herbert Gintis, "The Power of Capital: On the Inadequacy of the Conception of the Capitalist Economy as 'Private,' " *The Philosophical Forum* 14 (Spring-Summer 1983): 225–45. This raises the question of accountability to the public, which requires the accountant/auditor to interpret and articulate social value, to adjudicate social struggles, and thus act as an instrument of social change. Tinker, Merino, and Neimark, "Normative Origins," 192.

69. In socialist societies, emphasis is on maximizing products rather than profits, through control of costs and expenditures. The accounting questions become: How is value-added to be measured? How much and what kind of value is to be measured for the money capitalized? Do auditors add value to an organization by inspiring trust in its finances and internal control systems? These questions are being asked as the Big Nine have become actively involved in the Chinese and East European markets by measuring and evaluating programs of investment either internally or in joint-venture cooperation with capitalist institutions. One firm, Coopers & Lybrand, has for some time been training Yugoslavian state auditors in the application of accounting principles and auditing techniques.

70. D. R. Scott, *The Cultural Significance of Accounts* (New York: Henry Holt & Co., 1931).

71. Paul J. DiMaggio and Walter W. Powell, "The Iron Cage Revisits: Institutional Isomorphism and Collective Rationality in Organizational Fields," *American Sociological Review* 48 (Apr. 1983): 147–160.

72. Starting in February 1985, the House Energy and Commerce Subcommittee on Oversight and Investigations began hearings into the integrity of the largest firms.

73. Henry A. Giroux, "Theories of Reproduction and resistance in the New Sociology of Education: A Critical Analysis," *Harvard Educational Review* 53 (Aug. 1983): 285.

Part IV
Capitalist states

10

Business and politics in the United States and United Kingdom

MICHAEL USEEM

The start of the 1980s was a period of extraordinary political transformation in the United States and United Kingdom. In both countries, governments came to power committed to radical reductions in state social services and traditional safety nets. "Supply-side economics" was the guiding American ideology; "there is no alternative" was the British slogan for the way it was applied. To be supplied without alternative was business: its revival was viewed as the precursor for any social renewal.

Both the Reagan administration and Thatcher government came into office firmly and unabashedly pro-business. They continued to rule under the dual banners of shrinking social spending and expanding free enterprise. The reinvigoration of private capitalism, according to the philosophy of both governments, required nothing less than the dismantling of state welfarism. "Higher public expenditure," stated the Conservative government, "cannot any longer be allowed to precede, and thus prevent, growth in the private sector."[1]

The rise of these governments and their historic redefinition of the role of the state and free enterprise are the subject of this article. I will suggest that the origins are to be found in part in an economic transformation under way in both countries, and in new forms of social organization linking the large corporations of each. This thesis is developed with materials gathered as part of a broader study of business politics in the United States and Great Britain. These materials included intensive interviews with approximately 150 business leaders in London, New York, and Boston; the analysis of several large-scale data sets on large corporations and their managers in both countries; and other information drawn from a range of secondary and analytic sources.[2]

263

The social organization of the corporate community

This analysis is predicated on the broader thesis that the internal social organization of the corporate community requires direct study if we are to more fully understand business relations with government. By internal social organization is meant the enduring informal and formal networks among large corporations, senior managers and directors of these companies, and the associations that represent them to the public. It is this social organization that filters and shapes the policies that business comes to promote.

The existing literature on business political activity has not addressed the issue of internal social organization in depth, but it has focused attention on one central question: To what extent is the business community cognizant of its classwide interests and prepared for concerted action in the political arena? On this general question, theorists have been intensely divided. Pluralist thought and Marxist structuralism alike have generally argued that the parochial concerns of individual firms receive far greater expression in the political process than does the collective welfare of capital. Competition among firms, sectoral cleavages, and executives' and directors' primary identification with their own enterprise all inhibit the formation of even class-wide awareness, let alone an organizational vehicle for promoting the shared concerns. Business disorganization, it is argued, prevails. Pluralism and structural Marxism radically diverge, however, in the implications they draw from the presumed disunity. For pluralism, the corporate elite is far too divided to be any more effective than any other interest group in imposing its views on the government, thus enabling the state to avoid "capture" by business. But, for structural Marxism, it is precisely because of this disorganization that the sate can and does (for other reasons) assume the role of protecting the class-wide interests of major corporations.

Counterposed to both of these theoretical perspectives is the familiar thesis advanced by instrumentalist Marxists and many non-Marxists as well that the government is more responsive to the outlook of big business than of any other sector or class, certainly of labor. The responsiveness is the result in part, according to these theories, of the social unity and political integration of the corporate community. With such cohesion and coordination, business is able to identify and successfully promote those public policies that reflect long-term priorities shared by most large companies.[3]

Studies of the politics of big business are equally divided on whether the corporate community is socially unified, cognizant of its class-wide interests, and capable of concerted action in the political arena. In a number of original investigations, for instance, William Domhoff finds "persuasive evidence for the existence of a socially cohesive national upper class."[4] These "higher circles," composed chiefly of corporate executives, primary owners, and their descendants, constitute, in this view, "the governing class in America," for these business people and their families dominate the top positions of government agencies, the political parties, and the governing boards of nonprofit organizations. Drawing on studies of the United States, Great Britain, and elsewhere, Ralph Miliband reaches a similar conclusion, finding that " 'elite pluralism' does not . . . prevent the separate elites in capitalist society from constituting a dominant economic class, possessed of a high degree of cohesion and solidarity, with common interests and common purposes which far transcend their specific differences and disagreements."[5]

Yet other analysts have arrived at nearly opposite conclusions. In an extensive review of studies of business, Ivar Berg and Mayer Zald argue that "businessmen are decreasingly a coherent and self-sufficient autonomous elite; increasingly business leaders are differentiated by their heterogeneous interests and find it difficult to weld themselves into a solidified group."[6] Similarly, Daniel Bell contends that the disintegration of family capitalism in America has thwarted the emergence of a national "ruling class," and, as a result, "there are relatively few political issues on which the managerial elite is united."[7] And Leonard Silk and David Vogel, drawing on their observations of private discussion among industrial managers, find that the "enormous size and diversity of corporate enterprise today makes it virtually impossible for an individual group to speak to the public or government with authority on behalf of the entire business community."[8]

Observers of the British corporate community have reached equally disparate conclusions, though the center of gravity is closer to that of discerning cohesion than disorganization. Drawing on their own study of British business leaders during the past century, Philip Stanworth and Anthony Giddens conclude that "we may correctly speak of the emergence, towards the turn of the century, of a consolidated and unitary 'upper class' in industrial Britain."[9] More recently, according to John Westergaard and Henrietta Resler, "the core" of the privileged and powerful is "those who own and those who control capital on a large scale: whether top business executives or rentiers make no difference in this context. Whatever divergences of interests there may be among them on this score and others, latent as well as manifest, they have a common stake in one overriding cause: to keep the working rule of the society capitalist."[10] The solidity is underpinned by a unique latticework of old school ties, exclusive urban haunts, and aristocratic traditions that are without real counterpart in American life. Thus, "a common background and pattern of socialization, reinforced through intermarriage, club memberships, etc. generated a community. feeling among the members of the propertied class," writes another researcher, John Scott, and "this feeling could be articulated into a class awareness by the most active members of the class."[11]

Yet, even if the concept of "the Establishment" originated in British attempts to characterize the seamless web at the top that seemed so obvious to many observers, other analysts still discern little in British business on which to pin such a label. Scanning the corporate landscape in the early 1960s, for instance, J. P. Nettle reported in 1965 that the "business community" is in "a state of remarkable weakness and diffuseness – compared, say, to organized labour or the professions," for British businessmen lack "a firm sense of their distinct identity, and belief in their distinct purpose." The years since have brought little consolidation: according to Wyn Grant in 1980, business is still "neither homogeneous in its economic composition nor united on the appropriate strategy and tactics to advance its interests." Thus, "businessmen in Britain are not bound by a strong sense of common political purpose."

Both theoretical and empirical contributions to the debate about the corporate community have thus offered highly conflicting claims about the degree of social organization in Britain and America. Resolution of these opposing visions is essential if we are to understand how and with what effect business enters the politicⁿl process, or, in Anthony Giddens's more abstract framing, "the modes in which . . . economic hegemony is translated into political domination."[12] But the resolution offered here is not one of establishing which of the competing views is more "correct," for either answer would be incorrect. In their own limited and specific fashions, both descriptions are partly true. Yet neither, for reasons detailed below, provides an adequately detailed and developed characterization of the inner structure of the business communities.

The inner structure shapes corporate political activity, but it does so in combination with the political environment of business. The interaction between internal social organization and environmental pressures must be examined as well if corporate political behavior is to be accurately characterized. Thus, study of the rise of business political activity in America and Britain during the past decade is used here as an opportunity to further identify the reciprocal impact of the corporate community's social organization and environment on its political behavior.

The unprecedented reversal of public-sector social spending in America and Britain can be traced in substantial part to a rise in the political capacities and activism of large business corporations in both countries. The new political engagement of business by no means ensured the success of the Reagan and Thatcher campaigns, nor did it fix their policies. But it was an important ingredient. At the foundation of this new activism was the joining of two developments during the 1970s that we detail below: the fortunes of large corporations were in general decline at just the time when their capacities to respond collectively to adversity were on the incline. The interaction of these events led to the movement of major corporations into politics with a force and class-wide coherence not recently seen in the political life of either country. Moreover, the emergence of the class-wide capacity was itself a product of a broader shift in the locus of control of large corporations. The new system of control, here termed institutional capitalism, has recently emerged alongside that of managerial capitalism, the latter having already largely displaced the system of control associated with family capitalism. The growing business capacity to respond will be described first, followed by assessment of the special adversities it has faced. The rise of institutional capitalism will then be briefly described.

Concentration and diversification

A small number of corporate units facilitates the formation of a common culture and social organization among those directing corporate activities. The inexorable trend in both Great Britain and the United States has been for fewer companies to orchestrate ever greater fractions of total economic activity, even as the economies themselves have vastly expanded.

In 1909 the hundred largest British manufacturers accounted for only 15 percent of the net output of all such companies, but the fraction steadily climbs to 23 percent by 1939, 33 percent by 1958, and 45 percent by 1970.[13] Even greater concentration is apparent if net assets are considered instead: the share of all publicly traded companies' assets held by the hundred largest British firms stood at 47 percent in 1948, but had reached 68 percent only two decades later.[14] Financial concentration is even more advanced. The commercial banking sector has undergone vast consolidation, with just four London clearing banks – Barclays, Lloyds, Midland, and National Westminster – now accounting for virtually all retail banking in the country. These four banks alone are responsible for nearly half of all employment in the entire financial sector.[15]

Though there is still less overall concentration in the U.S., American companies are following much the same path. The share of total manufacturing assets held by the 200 largest manufacturing firms has been increasing by approximately one-half of 1 percent per year since the turn of the century, and there is no sign of any slackening of the pace in recent decades. The top 200 are now in control of approximately three-fifths of all manufacturing assets. Finance is still far less concentrated than in the U.K., but U.S. banking activity is also controlled by ever fewer hands: the 200 largest financial institutions now account for over half of all financial activity.[16] Indicative of the overall level of concentration and the opportunities it can present for political coordination, a single business association with fewer than 200 members – the Business Roundtable – brings together those who are responsible for corporate decisions affecting a large proportion of the economy. The 196 chief executive officers who participate in Roundtable deliberations on public policy are collectively responsible for firms whose annual revenues are in the aggregate equivalent to nearly half of the U.S. gross national product.[17] Thus, the great bulk of the private economy in both countries is now overseen by those managers and directors of fewer than a thousand large companies.

Accompanying concentration, particularly in recent years, has been product diversification, paced by the so-called "conglomerates" but pursued to varying degrees by most large firms as well.[18] Not only are large enterprises in control of a dominant and still expanding share of all economic activity, but most are also increasingly familiar with a range of disparate market conditions, labor forces, and business climates. The extent of this diversification is illustrated by changes in a sample of more than 270 *Fortune 500* firms between 1949 and 1974. The percentage of companies in a largely single line of business declined from 42 to 14. Conversely, the percentage of corporations involved in several related or unrelated lines of manufacturing grew over the same period from 30 to 63. Only 1 in 20 of the companies could be considered conglomerates in 1949; 1 in 4 could be so classified by 1974.[19] Diversification has meant that firms now have better appreciation for one another's problems and policy needs, for they face more similar market circumstances than ever before.

Corporate interdependence

At the same time, networks of economic relations among the largest firms are becoming more inclusive. Among the most significant trends is the rise of intercorporate ownership. Once again the U.K. is ahead of the U.S., but the developments are very much the same. The proportion of the market value of U.K. company stock held by financial institutions, the primary source of intercorporate ownership, stood at 21 percent in 1957 for ordinary shares and 36 percent for preference shares. But individual shareholding is being rapidly displaced by company holding in the years since, with financial institutions' share rising to 33 and 59 percent for the two types of shares by 1967, and to 50 and 76 percent by 1978. Over the same period, ordinary shares held by persons declined from 66 to 32 percent.[20]

The analogous figures for U.S. holdings, in this case for the share of all outstanding corporate shares owned by financial institutions, are 23 percent for 1958, 24 percent for 1968, and 33 percent for 1974.[21] Although corporate shareholding in American companies is still a minority in the aggregate, the high degree of concentration of corporate investments has meant that the top stockholders of most large companies are other, primarily financial, corporations. Typical of the present-day ownership profile is that of Mobil Oil Corporation, the fourth largest American industrial firm. Of the top ten shareholders in 1973, possessing in the aggregate some 20 percent of the voting rights for Mobil, nine are other corporations, all but one banks or insurance companies.[22] This transformation in stockholder composition is evident in the shareholder profile of virtually all major firms.[23] The orphans and the widows have been swept away by the institutions.

The intercorporate ownership network now incorporates nearly all large companies, and it is little based on purely particularistic ties between pairs or small cliques of firms. Some intercorporate ownership does reflect an interest on the part of one corporation in pressuring, co-opting, controlling, or even acquiring another company or set of firms. But the bulk of such shareholding is the product of investment strategies that treat large blocs of companies as largely equivalent; the acquisition of stock in one enterprise rather than another is most typically the product of a return-on-investment decision and does not reflect an anticipated exchange of products or some other specific relationship between the firms. The structure of the intercorporate network of ownership, in short, is both inclusive and diffuse. Diffuse signifies the network is spread widely rather than concentrated within small cliques. The rise of this net in the past few decades has created a context in which decisions taken by large companies are necessarily of concern to many other large corporations. The same is true for political factors that may retard the growth of company profits. Corporations not directly affected by a problem confronting a single firm or sector nonetheless may have their own prospects dimmed by virtue of the indirect dependency. Political challenges to one become, in attenuated but real ways, of concern to all.

To this ownership interdependency is added a managerial interdependency. The most important strand is the network of shared directorships, often called the interlocking directorate. This network is constituted of those company directors who simultaneously serve on the boards of two or more large companies. It is not a network, however, whose members are detached from the practice of running business. Approximately three-quarters of the outside or nonexecutive directors of a typical large firm are themselves top managers, often chief executives of still other large companies.[24] As in the case of the economic network, this network encompasses nearly all important corporations and it does so in a dispersed fashion favorable to collective political action.

The interlocking directorate draws together nearly all important corporations. Though the British network has had greater division between the manufacturing and financial sectors than its American counterpart, recent decades have witnessed the formation of shared directorships directly or indirectly linking nearly every important company. This is evident, for instance, in time-series data compiled on the 85 largest British manufacturing and financial companies from 1906 to 1970. At the start of this period, fewer than half of the firms were united by shared directorships; by the end, better than four-fifths were so joined.[25] Moreover, bridges across the great divide between industry and finance (the "City") have grown as well. Directorship links between similar samples of large manufacturing firms and banks increased nearly seven-fold between 1906 and 1970.[26] The resulting network is now highly inclusive. Directorship ties among 40 large industrial and 27 large financial companies in 1970, for instance, were examined in one study: 56 of 67 firms are linked to at least one other company in the set; and, if indirect connections through other corporations are taken into consideration, 62 of 67 companies are ultimately linked.[27] A more recent study of the directors of 235 of the largest manufacturing and financial firms for 1976 reveals comparable levels of network spread.[28]

Network density has not grown in the U.S. during this sample period, but the present level of inclusiveness is much the same as for the U.K. According to an investigation of the interlocking directorate among the 167 largest American firms at seven time points between 1904 and 1974, no secular trend appears in the overall frequency of shared directorships. There is, however, progressive equalization of the number of interlocks per firm, signifying the entry of nearly all large firms into the network.[29] Geographic concentration adds a modest cliquing structure to the network, and the higher rates of shared directorships displayed by the boards of larger commercial banks add some hierarchy to the system. Still, geographic boundaries have been diminishing over time and are now only faintly discernible;[30] and, although banks add disproportionately to the overall connectedness of the interlocking directorate, inclusiveness of the network does not intrinsically depend on banks. Their removal from the network does not significantly reduce its breadth of spread. As a result, nine-tenths of America's 1,131 largest companies were directly or indirectly linked in 1962, according to one study; another reports that better than nine-tenths of the 797 largest firms were joined in 1969.[31]

Like the ownership network, the directorship network is not only inclusive but diffusely structured as well. In previous work on the interlocking directorate, it has generally been viewed as not diffuse at all. Rather, shared directorships have been seen as an instrument for cementing ties between specific pairs or cliques of firms. Sharing a director is a device to ensure cooperation as firms buy and sell products or extend credit to one another.[32] Studies of changes in the directorship network, however, suggest that this is not the main reason they are formed. When ties in the network are broken accidentally, as when a multiple director dies or retires, they are rarely repaired in the same way. New ties do form, but not between the same pairs or cliques of firms.[33] If the ties had been intended to coordinate small groups of firms, their accidental severance should have instead been followed by quick repair.

The results of the interviews with top British and American executives reveal that the interlocking directorate is indeed not reducible to a set of particularistic ties between firms. Rather, most ties are the product of an entirely different corporate consideration. Companies are anxious to place their senior managers on the boards of other firms not to secure some exchange with those firms, but rather to ensure that their managers remain fully abreast of the changing corporate environment and practices of other corporations.[34] These are not the ties that bind, but that inform. Diffuseness is their hallmark.

The unplanned consequence of the inclusive and diffusely structured interlocking directorates is the formation of a communication network with special political capacities. This network, termed here the "inner circle," consists of the limited number of senior managers of the nation's largest firms who are also involved in the affairs of other large corporations. It is propitiously situated. Its foundation on economic and social networks diffusely transcending the major companies ensures that its members comprehend problems faced by all of large enterprise. Its members are more unified than other business leaders, for the inner circle shares a special culture, informal acquaintanceship, and common tradition more developed than anywhere else within the business community. It is rooted in interests that go far beyond the parochial concerns of individual firms or industrial sectors.[35] These characteristics enable the inner circle to act, albeit in a highly imperfect fashion, as a politicized leading edge for all large corporations as a bloc.

Business political leadership

The political leadership of the inner circle takes various forms. Its members are disproportionately found on the numerous councils and boards that provide formal counsel to the national government; among the top ranks of the major business associations most directly involved in the promotion of public policies on behalf of all large business; and among the front ranks of contributors to national political parties and candidates. In 1976, for instance, only 3 percent of the mangers of large American corporations served on an advisory committee to a U.S. government agency (such as the National Industrial Energy Council of the U.S. Department of Commerce), whereas 11 percent of those in the inner circle held such appointment. The parallel figures for British managers serving on U.K. public boards in 1978 or 1979 (such as the National Enterprise Board of the U.K. Department of Industry) are 3 and 12 percent. Similar participation ratios are also obtained for leadership positions in the preeminent business associations, notably the Confederation of British Industry and the British Institute of Management in Great Britain, and the Business Roundtable, Business Council, Committee for Economic Development, and Council on Foreign Relations in the United States. In the case of the Confederation of British Industry, for instance, the undisputed voice of business in Britain and of organizations intimately involved in the shaping of virtually all legislation and policies of interest to business, fully half of the members of the main decision-making bodies are drawn from the ranks of the inner circle. The inner circle has a similar presence in the leadership of the major American associations.[36]

The business activists who travel the class-wide networks on behalf of the corporate community share views distinct from their fellow directors and managers. They are different in two respects. First, members of the inner circle have a better understanding of the aggregate opinion of large corporations on matters of contemporary economic policy. Second, they have a stronger understanding of the complexities and intricacies of the political environment in which business operates. As a result, those most active in the major policy associations and in representing business to the government often share centrist opinions that transcend their own company's immediate welfare, and their perceptions reflect a deeper sense of how the political process works. Members of the inner circle are not necessarily cognizant of the policies that could ultimately best serve the collective welfare of large corporations. But they do hold views that reflect the broader thinking of the business community. They are the cosmopolitans, their single-company brethren the locals.[37]

The inner circle constitutes a leadership cadre for the entire business community. By virtue of the intercorporate networks in which it rests, it has the informal organizational ties, the formal organizational capacities, and the general vision of business needs to serve as a vehicle for class-wide political mobilization. It did not initially form to do this, but it does so as an unanticipated consequence nonetheless. And it became better prepared to do so in the 1970s.

The challenges confronting business

The business communities in both countries faced new challenges in the 1970s, challenges that strengthened both the capacity of business to respond politically and the sense of urgency that it must do so. The challenges derived from two fundamentally different sources. One was economic, the other political. The economic problem was the broad decline of company profitability, a problem endemic to most business sectors in both countries. The economic threat was the same on both sides of the Atlantic, but the political challenge could not have had more different origins. In Britain, it was the resurgence of labor socialism; in America, the spread of government interventionism. Trade union and Labour Party threats became the rallying cry of British business, while consumer activism and federal regulation became the hostile forces around which the ranks of American business closed.

Declining company profits

Few events discipline the corporate mind as fast as a drop in earnings. Work-force and administrative changes inevitably follow: officers are replaced, staffing pared, divisions reorganized, unprofitable units sold. Corners are cut as well, as Marshall Clinard and Peter Yeager found in a study of 582 of the largest U.S. companies in 1975 and 1976. They compiled records of legal action taken by 24 U.S. agencies against the companies – to answer this question: Why do some firms violate environmental, labor, anti-trust and other federal laws and regulations, while others do not? They discovered that declining financial performance was among the best predictors of illegal corporate behavior.[38] When the profit line is threatened, dramatic actions often follow, not all within the law.

Private solutions necessarily had their limits in the 1970s, for the problem was too widespread and fundamental for anything short of collective response. Profit margins were in general retreat, with virtually all sectors affected. The eclipse of profits was not necessarily an extension of some longer cycle or trend. The evidence is yet equivocal on whether British and American capitalism are subject to some law of fall-

Table 10.1. *Annual rates of return on assets of U.K. industrial and commercial companies. 1963–1980*[a]

	Pre-tax real rate of return (%)	
Year	Annual	Period average
1963	11.4	
1964	11.9	11.7
1965	11.2	
1966	9.9	
1967	10.0	10.2
1968	10.1	
1969	9.9	
1970	8.6	
1971	8.8	
1972	9.3	8.2
1973	9.1	
1974	5.2	
1975	5.3	
1976	5.4	
1977	6.2	5.5
1978	6.2	
1979	4.3	
1980	2.9	2.9

[a]Excludes North Sea activity.
Source: Bank of England, 1981.

ing profits.[39] But what is certain is that the 1970s were a decade of shrinking returns for most major businesses.

The profitability of U.K. industry had been in decline since the mid-1960s, reaching extremely low levels by the late 1970s. This conclusion stands whether profit is measured before or after taxes, as a rate of return on investments or share of income. And it describes both aggregate trends and profit pictures of major industrial sectors taken separately.[40] The decline of pre-tax inflation-corrected rates of return on U.K. industrial and commercial assets is shown in Table 10.1. In 1963 and 1964, the profit rate averaged 11.7 percent; during the last half of the 1960s, it dropped to 10.2; for the first five years of the 1970s, it further declined to an average 8.2; and for the 1975–79 period, it stood at only 5.5 percent. By 1980, it had sunk below 3 percent.

Trends in U.S. industrial profits in the postwar period are on a less precipitous downward slope, but the 1970s were a sluggish period for American business as well.[41] Martin Feldstein and Lawrence Summers, for example, examined pre-tax rates of return for nonfinancial U.S.

Table 10.2. *Annual rates of return on U.S. nonfinancial corporate capital.*
1948–1976[a]

| Year | Pre-tax net rate of return (%) | |
	Annual	Period average
1948–49	11.6 to 13.3	12.5
1950–54	10.3 to 13.2	11.8
1955–59	8.5 to 12.4	10.4
1960	9.9	
1961	9.8	
1962	11.2	11.2
1963	11.9	
1964	12.8	
1965	13.7	
1966	13.4	
1967	11.9	12.2
1968	11.7	
1969	10.2	
1970	8.1	
1971	8.4	
1972	9.2	8.1
1973	8.6	
1974	6.4	
1975	6.9	
1976	7.9	7.4

[a]Excludes earnings and assets abroad.
Source: Feldstein and Summers, 1977.

companies, examining the ratios of domestic profits to assets, adjusted for trends in depreciation, interest payments, and other factors. The annual corporate profit rate averaged 12.5 percent at the end of the 1940s, 11.8 percent in the early 1950s, and 10.4 percent in the late 1950s. The movement in the 1960s was modestly upward, peaking in the middle of the decade, as can be seen in Table 10.2. Thereafter it declines, however, reaching unusually low levels in the mid-1970s. Indeed, lower profit rates were recorded than in any other period since the Second World War. The average annual rate for the first half of the 1960s was 11.2 percent; the second half, 12.2 percent. But performance for the first five years of the 1970s declined to 8.1 percent, and for the next two years to an average 7.4 percent. Extending the estimates to 1979, Feldstein and two colleagues find the profit rate in 1979 to be the lowest in two decades save the recession years of 1974–75.[42] Similar trends appear if various alternative measures of profit levels are used instead.[43]

The challenge of labor in Great Britain

To the adversity of bleak profit pictures was added new political challenge. British business came under increasing pressure from labor, while American business felt the growing encroachment of government. The challenges confronted virtually all business; few companies were unaffected. But equally few could achieve individual solutions, and of necessity the response became one of collective combat. Out of common adversity emerged new strength of organization and purpose.

Relations between labor and management are far more strained in Britain than America. Though there are important exceptions, in recent years large British companies have generally been confronted by a labor movement that is better organized and more able to affect public policy than has been the case in the United States. Half of the British work force is represented in unions, compared to a quarter of the American work force, a difference that has been widening in the past decade. Shop stewards are given to greater militancy than their American counterparts. National bargaining is conducted on a more centralized basis and traditional socialist programs, such as public ownership of key industries, are important on the British labor agenda but find only weakest expression in the American labor movement.[44] Moreover, though the significance of American unions to the Democratic Party should not be underestimated, the attachment of British unions to the Labour Party is far more extensive and organic.[45]

The specter of labor challenge and the "socialist threat" pervaded the personal interviews with company executives in London; rarely did either emerge in the parallel discussions in Boston and New York. There were repeated expressions of concern in London, for example, about eventual government takeover of major financial institutions. Much of this anxiety stemmed from a Labour party proposal in the early 1970s to seize the major clearing (commercial) banks and insurance houses.[46] Fears were worsened by another Labour proposal, this to give employees a voice on corporate boards. Under the Labour government, the Department of Trade established a "Committee of Inquiry on Industrial Democracy," and its final report in 1977 called for a restructuring of large companies to include worker participation in corporate governance.[47]

Both proposals were resisted at many levels. At the forefront was the inner circle. It rallied its forces within the financial community to defeat the movement toward nationalization. Informally and through its main organization, the Confederation of British Industry, it also stopped the plan to place employee representatives on company boards. While the labor proposals were thus ultimately turned back, the challenge had the unintended effect of mobilizing large numbers of companies and managers into political participation. It also had the consequence of strengthening the organizational and ideological preparedness of the inner circle to promote the cause of business, to be ready for the next challenge.

The challenge of government regulation in the United States

The political challenge to American business had a different origin. Far more important than labor as an adversary was government. Industry-specific regulation in the past had often served to fragment American business, but regulatory agencies and programs developed in the 1970s achieved much the opposite effect because of their universal impact. At the forefront of general business regulation were the Occupational Safety and Health Administration, the Equal Employment Opportunity Commission, and, above all, the Environmental Protection Agency. Federal expenditures by major regulatory agencies more than doubled between 1974 and 1979, a rate substantially exceeding that of overall government spending and business growth. The most rapidly expanding activity was by agencies responsible for general cross-industry regulation. By the end of the decade, the great majority of federal expenditures were by general, rather than industry-specific, regulatory agencies.[48]

Executives of the large American corporations reported the growth of an awareness that all were experiencing increasingly burdensome federal demands and that a joint counteroffensive was overdue. Some had taken action themselves, while others backed the actions that the Business Roundtable and other associations were taking in the regulatory field. All asserted that the continued expansion of regulation required concerted political counteraction. During the decade, the level of regulation had accelerated far more rapidly than in the U.K.; and the change had engendered a mood of open rebellion in the U.S. business community.[49]

Political mobilization of business

The consequence of the heightened capacity of business to act – and heightened reason to do so – was a general political mobilization. Corporate ranks were disciplined and resolve heightened. Both the Business Roundtable and Confederation of British Industry improved their power and capacity for political action. And, at the urging of these organizations and individuals in the inner circle, many firms began to devote company resources to political ends. Company advertising space was given to issue promotion rather than product claims; top managers increasingly accepted invitations to defend business in the electronic

278   STRUCTURES OF CAPITAL

and print media; and corporations set out to cultivate better relations with journalists, academics, and other influential opinion makers. Business money also increasingly flowed directly into political campaigns and organizations devoted to fostering a political climate more favorable to business.

Corporate political contributions in Britain are direct, while in America they are necessarily indirect. U.K. corporations are permitted to donate *company* money to parties and candidates they favor; U.S. corporations by law cannot. Managers of American companies may give, however, either personally or through a new social invention of the 1970s: the political action committee. Whatever the channel, in both countries the flow of corporate money in the 1970s was transformed from a trickle to a torrent. The scale of increase is so great that corporate money has now become a fundamental force in both British and American politics.

The rise of company financing of British politics can be seen in trend figures for 196 large companies whose activities were tracked as part of the broader study from which this chapter is drawn.[50] The bulk of the companies' donations went to the Conservative Party, but four other business-oriented organizations received significant backing as well. These were British United Industrialists (a conduit in part for money destined for the Tories); the Economic League, an anti-labor organization; Aims, an ardent defender of the principle that "freedom means free enterprise"; and the Centre for Policy Studies, established by Margaret Thatcher and Sir Keith Joseph in 1974 to provide research services to the Conservative Party reflective of their own brand of monetarism.[51]

Total company political contributions grew strongly in the 1970s, especially those directed to the Conservative Party (Table 10.3). The average company donation more than doubled during this period, from £1,761 in 1974 to £3,320 in 1975, £3,707 in 1978 and £4,551 in 1979. The composition changed as well, with the share going to the Conservative Party rising from 52 percent in 1975 to 60 percent in 1979. British Industrialists also became a more favored recipient, while the Economic League held constant and the other advocates of free enterprise lost ground.

The U.S. ban on direct corporate financing of political campaigns has generated two alternative avenues of support. Officers of large firms generously give of their personal funds, with an understanding both within the firm and the receiving organization that the contributions are in effect company, not private. In addition, a substantial number of large corporations have established political action committees which collect funds from management and channel them to candidates deemed friendly to business or the company. Business-related funds

Table 10.3. *Annual average political donations of 196 large British companies,*
1974–1979 (in pounds sterling)

Recipient of company donation	Year of donation					
	1974	1975	1976	1977	1978	1979
Conservative Party	11	1,724	1,420	1,715	1,867	2,748
British Industrialists United	855	1,063	1,180	1,132	1,330	1,378
Economic League	302	370	349	386	382	353
Aims[a]	327	119	24	91	62	41
Centre for Policy Studies	266	44	33	49	66	31
Total political contributions	1,761	3,320	3,006	3,373	3,707	4,551

[a]Formerly Aims of Industry.
Source: Useem, 1984.

flowing through the latter conduit exhibited explosive growth during
the 1970s. Fewer than 100 corporate PACs were in operation during the
1972 election; by 1980 the number exceeded 1,100 (Table 10.4). By contrast, the number of labor political action committees exhibited only
modest growth, rising from 200 to under 300 by the end of the decade.

The divergent growth curves for corporate and labor PACs are evident as well in their aggregate funding level. In 1968 corporate and business-related committees are estimated to have spent $1.4 million on
candidates for national office, while national labor committees distributed $7.6 million to House and Senate candidates. A decade later, busi-
ness committees contributed more than $17 million to federal candi-
dates (another $20 million went to other campaigns); but labor

Table 10.4. *Number of American corporate and labor political action*
committees, 1972–1980

Type of political action committee	Year[a]				
	1972	1974	1976	1978	1980
Corporate	87	89	433	784	1153
Labor	n.a.	201	224	218	290

[a]The 1972 figure is for November; the 1974, 1976, and 1978 figures are for December;
and the 1980 figures are for June.
Source: Epstein (1979, 1980a, 1980b).

spending on federal campaigns had risen to only $10 million (an additional $8 million was spent on other candidates). While political action committee underwriting of Democratic candidates rose two-fold between 1972 and 1979, support of Republican candidates more than tripled. Since the parties themselves decreasingly financed the campaigns of their own candidates during this same period, PACs acquired special salience for aspiring politicians. During the 1978 campaign, for instance, the two parties directly and indirectly provided $11 million to candidates for national office, while PACs gave $35 million. In 1980 the PAC contribution to House and Senate campaigns rose to $55 million, approaching a quarter of the total Congressional campaign receipts of $252 million. In 1982 PAC contributions to Congressional races are estimated to have reached $80 million, a jump of nearly two-thirds over 1980.

The importance of corporate PACs relative to labor committees can be seen in the findings of a study of the leadership of the 97th Congress. Using data compiled by Common Cause, the analyst examined the contributions received from PACs by the majority and minority leaders, whips, and committees chairs in 1981–1982. The House leaders were elected or reelected in 1980, and the Senate leaders in 1976, 1978, or 1980. Of the 24 Senate leaders, the median percentage of PAC contributions relative to all contributions stood near 23; for the 29 House leaders, the median percentage was near 49. In other words, half of the Senate leaders obtained more than a fifth of their campaign contribution income from PACs, and half of the House leaders received near half of their campaign funds from such committees.[52]

In Robert Dole's (R.-Kansas) successful bid for reelection to the Senate in 1980, for instance, $324,000 was raised from PACs, an amount that was 27 percent of his total campaign contributions of $1.2 million. Of this, 97 percent came from PACs affiliated with corporations. When the Republican Party took majority control of the Senate in 1981, Dole assumed the chairmanship of the Senate Finance Committee. Representative Jim Wright (D.-Texas), majority leader of the House, received a third of his 1980 campaign contributions of $807,000 from PACs, of which three-quarters came from corporate PACs (slightly under one-quarter came from labor PACs). The chairman of the House Budget Committee, Jim Jones (D.-Oklahoma), raised 42 percent of his total campaign contributions of $286,000 from PACs, of which 20 percent was contributed by labor PACs and 78 percent by company committees.[53]

Corporate PAC activity is highly concentrated among the nation's largest companies. Nearly half (45 percent) of the 821 corporate committees active in the 1978 election campaign were of firms among *For-*

tune's list of the 1,300 largest enterprises. And it is among the very largest that the committees are most often found: of the manufacturing firms ranked in size between 501 and 1000, 34 had formed a PAC; but, of the 500 top manufacturers, 202 had an operative PAC. And, of the 100 largest, 70 sponsored a PAC. Moreover, PAC expenditures were far greater at the top of the *Fortune* list: the committees of firms in the second 500 industrials disbursed under $2,000 on average; those near the bottom of the top 500, contributed $6,000 each; the PACs of the ten largest industrials provided $70,000 each.[54] By 1982, some corporate PAC expenditures for Congressional candidates reached well into six figures. Citicorp spent $223,000, Grumman Corporation distributed $225,000, and Tenneco, Inc., gave $425,000.

The rise of institutional capitalism

The surge of business political activism may prove a passing phenomenon. The mobilization of both British and American business in the 1970s and early 1980s could be a largely transient response to momentary adversity. The decline of corporate profits and labor as well as government successes in making free enterprise feel less free put large corporations on the defensive. But the downward slope of corporate profits may have been more clinical than secular. And the upward demands of British labor and American regulation may also have represented more a temporary advance than a new stage of industrial development from which there is no turning back.

Yet, while these triggers of the political mobilization of business could be momentary, the organizational foundation on which the mobilization was mounted and through which it received focus has been growing progressively stronger, and this is an irreversible change. The central cornerstones of the foundation are the increasingly inclusive and diffuse networks of intercorporate ownership and directorship, and the establishment and deepening consolidation of the explicitly classwide business associations, most notably the Confederation of British Industry and the Business Roundtable. These elements of classwide organization are certain to remain; and they represent a new stage of corporate development, not economically but organizationally. The triple crises of corporate profits, labor power, and government intervention may subside, and business political activism may be demobilized. But, as business-government relations return to normalcy, the corporate side of the equation will not resume its pre-crisis form, as classwide organization remains irrevocably stronger. When business encounters its next crisis, whether economic or political, it will be better prepared to meet the challenge, to offer class-wide answers. And, if recent experience is any guide, one effect again would be to consolidate further the class-wide system of organization. This is not to suggest that business will necessarily emerge as more powerful than other interest groups, nor that its influence on public policies will be any greater. Indeed, it is arguable that the recent corporate stirrings are in fact a product of greater weakness, not strength. But it is to suggest that the way the business community expresses its views on matters of public importance will be different.

The difference in the way the voice of business is expressed is a product of a broader transformation in the internal social organization of the American and British business communities. Organizational features associated with *family capitalism* have largely given way to those of managerial capitalism, and both are being now eclipsed by the rise of the class-wide organization of what can be termed *institutional capitalism*. All three forms of organization still simultaneously structure the ways in which business attempts to shape its political environment. The salience of the first two, however, is a product of earlier stages of business development, eras whose traditions and conventions remain powerfully with us but whose generative powers are lessening compared to those of institutional capitalism.

The foundation of the great family enterprises during the latter part of the nineteenth century marks the rise of family capitalism. It was an era in which entrepreneurs managed their firms as an extension of themselves, when kinship, ownership, and control were synonymous, and where dynastic marriage was a means of corporate merger. Swift ascent in the company hierarchy was assured those of proper descent.

As family fortunes compounded, and kinship multiplied within the enterprise and crossed into others, the American "business aristocracy" came of age.[55] This business-based upper class in time evolved the many institutions necessary to lend a distinct collective identity, define its parameters, preserve its culture, and socialize its young. Metropolitan clubs were established to acquaint its members, symphony orchestras to exhibit its tastes, preparatory schools to educate its heirs, and Social Registers to demarcate its membership. But above all, the interests of the founding families occupied a primacy in company decisionmaking, overriding when in conflict even with company interests. While the American business aristocracy was self-made, many British business families, especially in finance but often in industry as well, were already established by birth.[56] The move of the British aristocracy into commerce, necessitated by political and financial reality, was not initially at the price of assimilation. The upper class moved to rule business with the same self-assured sense of mission with which it had long overseen land, politics, and the empire.[57] Capitalism was its new mission, but the primacy of the family remained intact.

But the real power of family capitalism has long since given way to corporate rule, most fully in the U.S. as Daniel Bell has detailed, but in the U.K. as well.[58] The slow but irreversible displacement of upper-class dominance by corporate interests in business politics is a product of the historic transformation of the firm from an extension of the founding family to an organization with an internal logic entirely of its own. This transformation is characterized by the emergence of very large firms, a corresponding creation of multidivisional structures demanding new forms of administrative coordination, the formation of a professional management and complex career hierarchy within the firm, and the movement of both daily and final decision-making power from the founding family to trained managers.

The divorce of ownership from control, the "managerial revolution" of Adolf Berle and Gardiner Means, was a leading feature of this transformation, but only one feature. The nature of the business corporation was undergoing change with far more profound implications for business politics than only the emergence of control without appreciable ownership. Family capitalism was giving way to the "visible hand," the economy of the modern business enterprise in which administrative coordination displaced market power as a guiding mechanism of resource allocation. Market exchanges among the nation's numerous small, family-run firms became internally incorporated within a greatly diminished set of large, management-guided firms. Administrative calculus replaced the invisible hand of the market, as Alfred Chandler has described it, though of course the market still determined the allocation of resources among the larger firms. At the top of the new enterprise appeared a "new subspecies of economic man," observed Chandler: the salaried manager. His appearance was a signpost of a far broader transformation in American capitalism. This was the replacement of family rule of the company by the supremacy of the company itself. "In many industries and sectors of the American economy," concludes Chandler, "managerial capitalism soon replaced family or financial capitalism."[59] By the 1970s, many had become most, with the managerial revolution virtually complete among the largest companies in all industries and sectors. Evidence compiled by Edward Herman on this point is compelling.[60] In attenuated but similar form, the visible hand of corporate organization became ascendant in Britain as well.[61]

Yet, as equally compelling data gathered by Herman and others have also shown,[62] the rise of managerial capitalism is still a rise of capitalism, only now even more efficiently pursued by a professional cadre of managers whose organizational role leaves them no choice but to place growth in profits at the front of the corporate agenda. The transition from family capitalism to managerial capitalism is thus not one in which the fundamental guiding principle of free enterprise is altered or downgraded. But it is a transition in which the priorities of the firm come to take precedence over the interests of the founding family. As the principal officers of large corporations enter the political process and direct company resources into the same, the guiding concern is no longer preservation of the fortunes of the upper-class families who once built and controlled the firms, but preservation of the profits of the enterprises which now control the families' economic destinies. Rather than the firm serving as an instrument for accumulation of family wealth, the manager came to be the instrument for accumulation of company wealth. Class was replaced by organization as the fulcrum of decision-making.

The transition from family to managerial capitalism is evident in the rules of succession for top management. In family-controlled firms, the owning family exercised the major voice in who became the chief executive, often a member of the family itself, and how long he remained in office. In the large firm managed by a cadre of professional executives, however, the voice over this decision was assumed by management itself. Control of executive appointment and dismissal slipped from the owning family into management hands. This difference can be seen in the longevity of chief executives of more than two hundred large industrial firms studied by Michael Allen. The average tenure of the principal officers of management-controlled firms was near nine years, while the tenure for those running family controlled firms was over seventeen years. When companies are in the hands of professional managers, they are thus quicker to replace faltering leadership than when the companies are still controlled by an owning family. The firm's interests take precedence in the first instance, the owner's interests in the latter. When companies begin to show poor profits, finds Allen, family-controlled firms do not move to replace their chief executive, but management-controlled corporations are swift to do so.[63]

The transfer of power from family to firm required many decades to complete, but had largely run its course by the 1970s. Yet, just as organization overpowered family in the conduct of company business, in recent years the dominance of the company itself has been giving way to the power of class-wide social organization. Although family rule has been largely replaced by corporate dominance, the rise of class-wide organization has not yet, and probably never will, eclipse the autonomous power of the individual business firm. Yet a class-wide logic has come to co-exist alongside a corporate logic in the making of many company decisions, and it adds a fundamentally new dimension to the way in which business politics are orchestrated.

If the professionalization of corporate management is the driving force in the rise of corporate over upper-class politics, it is the formation of an intercorporate management network that is the engine behind the rise of class-wide principles. In both instances, the transition to the new stage is the unintended byproduct of other forces. For the managerial revolution, the dispersion of ownership and the superior capacities of managerial hierarchies in large organizations propelled the transformation. For the emergence of class-wide organization, the creation of transcorporate networks of ownership and directorships as extensions of individual corporate strategies generated the transformation. Both transitions were thus rooted in changes in corporate organization necessitated by evolving market and bureaucratic conditions. But the consequences of these transitions have extended far beyond economic and administrative questions into the many ways that large firms enter and affect the political process.

Conclusion

A central objective of the business mobilization of the late 1970s and early 1980s in both the United States and Great Britain was to restore company profits to levels of an earlier decade. In the name of "reindustrialization" and "recapitalizing capitalism," government spending was targeted as the chief impediment to such prosperity.[64] In the American case, government restraint on business decisions has also been named as a critical target. And, in Britain, government failure to resist and control organized labor has been identified by business as a first priority as well. All point toward government reductions in social spending, the dismantling of programs that regulate business, and the scaling down of programs that benefit labor.

The political thrust, electoral success, and continued commitment in office of the Thatcher and Reagan governments were in no small part a product of this business rush into politics. Both governments sharply reduced controllable social spending, lifted controls on business, and cut back unemployment, welfare, and other programs of special interest to labor. The squeeze on the private sector was thus translated into a shrinking public sector, with the exception of military spending. The decline of the welfare state, the slowing of social spending, and the end of activist government in the U.S. and U.K. were thus not simply, and indeed not largely, a product of spontaneous disaffection with the socially interventionist state. Nor were they the product of an unarticulated, inchoate response to the chronic stagnation of the "British disease" and its American strain.

Rather, the rise of new conservative forces that were among the pillars of the Conservative and Republican governments was importantly a product of the formation on both sides of the Atlantic of informal and formal organizational networks linking together most large corporations. These networks facilitated the political mobilization of business – by helping business to identify the public policies most needed for its aggregate welfare, and by helping business to express these preferences in electoral campaigns, government lobbying, and other forms of intervention. There was, however, no certainty of outcome. Although both the Reagan administration and Thatcher government ruled in part because of their corporate allies, neither was particularly responsive to the changing calculus of business, nor of the economy for that matter. In power, these governments were guided by their own agendas, coincident only in part with what large corporations and the inner circle would have liked to see achieved.

The formation of a class-wide system of organization within the corporate community is rooted in the rise of institutional capitalism, and this system is generically akin to that expected by instrumentalist analysis. But the class-wide organization has emerged alongside the far more atomized system based in managerial capitalism and expected by pluralist and structuralist analysis. Thus, both schools of theory and analysis are partly right. Pluralism and structuralism have tended to read the organizational patterns associated with managerial capitalism, while instrumentalism has more often read the patterns associated with institutional capitalism. But both portrayals are partly wrong if overextended in application. And both miss much of the diversity and complexity in the social organization of the corporate community that is fundamental to corporate political behavior.

Accordingly, we should revise our thinking about how the corporate community is organized and how it enters the political process. With emergence of class-wide organization, more overall planning initiative is assumed by business, less by government. Rather than having to sift through the disparate demands of a thousand chief executives, government officials are presented with an integrated vision already developed by those members of the corporate community best positioned to reconcile the competing demands. Of course, government decision-makers are subjected to numerous other constraints and pressures, and there is no certainty that any given business position will prevail. Indeed, many are certainly rejected. The Confederation of British Industry and the Business Roundtable were frequently at odds with the

Thatcher and Reagan governments. Still, the class-wide foundation of the inner circle makes its position more authoritative and less easily ignored.

We also need revision in our thinking about the nature of the firm. Under managerial capitalism, corporate principles prevail, and the firm is the primary unit of action. Professional management is fully in charge, the company's profits are the first and final order of business, and a Hobbesian competition of all against all is the environment. The thrust of corporate decisions and politics under managerial capitalism are quite different from those during the era of family capitalism, when upper-class principles prevailed, and family was the central unit of action. The founding entrepreneur and kin held control, family fortunes were of guiding concern, and intermarriage produced alliance and reduced competition.

But the emergence of institutional capitalism and classwide principles of organization have introduced still different rules. The firm remains a primary unit of action, but the transcorporate network becomes a quasi-autonomous actor in its own right. Company management is now less than fully in charge; class-wide issues intrude into company decisions; and competition is less pitched. Management decisions to underwrite political candidates, devote company resources to charitable causes, give advertising space to matters of public moment, and assume more socially responsible attitudes derive in part from company calculus, but also in part from a class-wide calculus.

Structuralist analysts emphasize the "relative autonomy" of the state, signifying that the government's partial independence from business permits it to more effectively formulate policies facilitating the profitable growth of all large companies.[65] We find relative autonomy too, but in a different location. The network of the inner circle arises from a corporate base – but at the same time enjoys a degree of autonomy from it. Yet it is also a limited autonomy, for it is structured in a way that closely channels inner circle actions toward improving the political climate for the entire corporate community. The state may well add further shaping to the policies that emerge from the corporate community, but the relative autonomy of the inner circle now ensures that a significant part of the process of interest aggregation is achieved within the business community itself.

Notes

1. The Government's Expenditure Plans, 1980–81; see Alan Walker, "Right Turn for the British Welfare State?," *Social Policy* 10 (Mar.–Apr. 1980): 47–51.
2. Michael Useem, "Classwide Rationality in the Politics of Managers and Directors of Large Corporations in the United States and Great Britain," *Administrative Sci-*

ence Quarterly 27 (1982): 199–226, and *The Inner Circle: Large Corporations and the Rise of Business Political Activity in the U.S. and U.K.*, (New York: Oxford University Press, 1984).

3. Robert Alford, "Paradigms of Relations between State and Society," in *Stress and Contradiction in Modern Capitalism*, Leon Lindberg et al., eds., (Lexington, Mass.: Heath, 1975); David A. Gold, Clarence Y. H. Lo, and Erik Olin Wright, "Recent Developments in Marxist Theories of the Capitalist State," *Monthly Review* 27 (Oct. 1975): 29–43; Fred Block, "The Ruling Class Does Not Rule," *Socialist Review* 33 (May–June 1977): 6–28; Theda Skocpol, "Political Response to Capitalist Crisis. Neo-Marxist Theories of the State and the Case of the New Deal," *Politics and Society* 10 (1980): 155–201; J. Allen Whitt, "Can Capitalists Organize Themselves?" in *Power Structure Research*, G. William Domhoff, ed., (Beverly Hills: Sage, 1980).

4. G. William Domhoff, *The Bohemian Grove and Other Retreats*, (New York: Harper and Row, 1974), 109.

5. Ralph Miliband, *The State in Capitalist Society* (New York: Basic Books, 1969), 47.

6. Ivar Berg and Mayer N. Zald, "Business and Society," *Annual Review of Sociology* 4 (1978): 137.

7. Daniel Bell, *The End of Ideology* (New York: Free Press, 1962), 62–63.

8. Leonard Silk and David Vogel, *Ethics and Profits* (New York: Simon and Schuster, 1976), 181.

9. Philip Stanworth and Anthony Giddens, "An Economic Elite: A Demographic Profile of Company Chairmen," in *Elites and Power in British Society*, Stanworth and Giddens, eds., (London: Cambridge University Press, 1974), 100.

10. John Westergaard and Henrietta Resler, *Class in Capitalist Society* (London: Heinemann, 1975), 346.

11. John Scott, *Corporations, Classes, and Capitalism* (London: Hutchinson, 1979), 125–26.

12. Giddens, "Preface," in *Elites and Power*, xi.

13. Leslie Hannah, *The Rise of the Corporate Economy* (London: Methuen, 1976), 216.

14. G. Whittington, "Changes in the Top 100 Quoted Manufacturing Companies in the United Kingdom 1948 to 1968," *Journal of Industrial Economics* 21 (1972): 17, 34; William G. Shepherd, "Structure and Behavior in British Industries, with U.S. Comparisons," *Journal of Industrial Economics* 21 (1972): 35–54; Geoffrey Meeks and Geoffrey Whittington, "Giant Companies in the United Kingdom 1948–69," *The Economic Journal* 85 (1975): 824–43.

15. Committee to Review the Functioning of Financial Institutions, 1980 Report (London: H. M. Stationery Office), 407–08, 598.

16. R. Marris, *Theory and Future of the Corporate Economy and Society:* (Amsterdam: North-Holland, 1979).

17. Organization for Economic Co-Operation and Development, *Concentration and Competition Policy* (Paris: Organization for Economic Co-Operation and Development, 1979), 86.

18. Mark Green and Andrew Buchsbaum, *The Corporate Lobbies* (Washington, D.C.: Public Citizen: 1980), 68.

19. R. P. Rumelt, *Strategy: Structure, and Economic Performance* (Cambridge, Mass.: Harvard University Press, 1974).

20. Committee to Review the Functioning of Financial Institutions, 1980 Report (London: H. M. Stationery Office), 496–500; Mervyn King, *Public Policy and the Corporation* (London: Chapman and Hall, 1977), 36; Royal Commission on the Distribution of Income and Wealth, 1975, 6–19.

21. David M. Kotz, *Bank Control of Large Corporations in the United States* (Berkeley, University of California Press, 1978), 65; U.S. Senate Committee on Government Operations 1974, *Disclosure of Corporate Ownership* (Washington, D.C.: U.S. Government Printing Office, 1974), 243, 161.

22. Corporate Data Exchange, *CDE Stock Ownership Directory: Transportation* (New York: Corporate Data Exchange, 1977), 224–25. The importance of financial institutions is evident, but their presence among the top shareholders does not imply financial "control" (discussion of financial dominance of nonfinancial firms, the "finance capital" thesis, can be found in Kotz, *Bank Control of Large Corporations in the United States*). While banks clearly have important influence on the decisions of some firms under certain circumstances (see, for instance, Davita Silfen Glasberg, "Corporate Power and Control," *Social Problems* 29 (1981): 104–16), the thesis of this chapter is that no single sector or group of firms exercises singular power within the corporate community.

23. Corporate Data Exchange, *Stock Ownership Directory: Transportation*, 1977; *Agribusiness*, 1978; *Banking and Finance*, 1980.

24. Jeremy Bacon and James K. Brown, *The Board of Directors: Perspectives and Practices in Nine Countries* (New York: Conference Board: 1977); Committee of Inquiry on Industrial Democracy, Report (London: H. M. Stationery Office, 1977); Louis Harris and Associates, *A Survey of Outside Directors of Major Publicly Owned Corporations* (New York: Louis Harris, 1977); Bank of England, "Composition of Company Boards," *Bank of England Quarterly Bulletin* 19 (1979): 392–93.

25. Anthony Giddens and Philip Stanworth, "Elites and Privilege," in Philip Abrams, ed., *Work, Urbanism, and Inequality* (London: Weidenfeld and Nicolson, 1978).

26. Philip Stanworth and Anthony Giddens, "The Modern Corporate Economy: Interlocking Directorships in Britain, 1906–1970," *Sociological Review* 23 (1975): 5–28.

27. Richard Whitley, "The City and Industry," in Stanworth and Giddens, eds., *Elites and Power*, 73.

28. P. S. Johnson and R. Apps, "Interlocking Directorates among the UK's Largest Companies," *Antitrust Bulletin* 24 (1979): 357–69.

29. Mark S. Mizruchi, *The American Corporate Network* (Beverly Hills: Sage, 1982).

30. Michael P. Allen, "The Structure of Interorganizational Elite Cooptation," *American Sociological Review* 39 (1974): 393–406.

31. James Bearden, William Atwood, Peter Freitag, Carol Hendricks, Beth Mintz, and Michael Schwartz, "The Nature and Extent of Bank Centrality in Corporate Networks," paper presented at the Annual Meeting of the American Sociological Association, 1975; Peter Mariolis, "Interlocking Directorates and Control of Corporations," *Social Science Quarterly* 56 (1975): 425–39.

32. Allen, "Structure of Interorganizational Elite Cooptation"; Jeffrey Pfeffer and Gerald R. Salancik, *The External Control of Organizations* (New York: Harper and Row, 1978).

33. Thomas Koenig, Robert Gogel, and John Sonquist, "Models of the Significance of Interlocking Corporate Directorates," *American Journal of Economics and Sociology* 38 (1979): 173–86; Donald Palmer, "Broken Ties," paper presented at the annual meeting of the American Sociological Association.

34. Useem, "Classwide Rationality," and *The Inner Circle*.

35. Michael Useem, "The Inner Group of the American Capitalist Class," *Social Problems* 25 (1978): 225–40; Useem, "Business Segments and Corporate Relations with American Universities," *Social Problems* 29 (1981): 129–41.

36. Useem, "The Inner Group," and "The Social Organization of the American Business Elite and Participation of Corporation Directors in the Governance of American Institutions," *American Sociological Review*, 44 (1979): 553–72; and *The Inner Circle*.

37. Useem, *The Inner Circle.*

38. Marshall B. Clinard and Peter C. Yeager, *Corporate Crime* (New York: Free Press, 1980).

39. A. Glyn and B. Sutcliffe, *British Capitalism, Workers, and the Profits Squeeze* (Harmondsworth: Penguin, 1972); David Gordon, "Recession is Capitalism as Usual," *The New York Times Magazine*, Apr. 25, 1975; M. A. King, "The United Kingdom Profits Crisis," *Economic Journal* 85 (1975): 33–54.

40. Bank of England, "Composition of Company Boards," *Bank of England Quarterly Bulletin* 19 (1979): 392–93, 1981; N. P. Williams, "Influences on the Profitability of Twenty-Two Industrial Sectors," Discussion Paper No. 15, (London: Bank of England, 1981).

41. William D. Nordhaus, "The Falling Share of Profits," in Arthur M. Okun and George L. Perry, eds., *Brookings Papers on Economic Activity*, No. 1 (Washington, D.C.: The Brookings Institution, 1974); Martin Feldstein and Lawrence Summers, "Is the Rate of Profit Falling?" in Arthur M. Okun and George L. Perry, eds., *Brookings Papers on Economic Activity*, No. 1, (Washington, D.C.: The Brookings Institution, 1977).

42. M. Feldstein, James Poterba, and Louis Dicks-Mireaux, "The Effective Tax Rate and the Pretax Rate of Return," (Cambridge, Mass.: National Bureau of Economic Research, 1982).

43. Feldstein and Summers, "Is the Rate of Profit Falling?"

44. David C. Smith, "Trade Union Growth and Industrial Disputes," in Richard E. Caves and Lawrence B. Krause, eds., *Britain's Economic Performance*, (Washington, D.C.: The Brookings Institution), 1980.

45. Robert Alford, "Paradigms of Relations between State and Society," in *Stress and Contradiction in Modern Capitalism*, Leon Lindberg et al., eds. (Lexington, Mass.: Heath, 1975); J. David Greenstone, *Labor in American Politics* (New York: Knopf, 1969).

46. Labour Party Study Group on Banking and Insurance, *Banking and Insurance Green Paper* (London: The Labour Party 1973).

47. Committee of Inquiry on Industrial Democracy, 1977 Report, (London: H. M. Stationery Office).

48. Murray L. Weidenbaum, *The Impact of Government Regulation* (St. Louis, Mo.: Center for the Study of Business, Washington University, 1978).

49. Useem, "Classwide Rationality in the Politics of Mangers and Directors of Large Corporations in the United States and Great Britain"; Useem, *The Inner Circle.*

50. Useem, *The Inner Circle.*

51. Edwin M. Epstein, "The Emergence of Political Action Committees," in *Political Finance*, Herbert E. Alexander, ed., (Beverly Hills: Sage, 1979); Epstein, "Business and Labor under the Federal Campaign Act of 1971," in *Parties, Interest Groups, and Campaign Finance Laws*, Michael J. Malbin ed., (Washington, D.C.: American Enterprise Institute, 1980); Epstein, "The PAC Phenomenon: An Overview," *Arizona Law Review* 22 (1980): 355–72.

52. Tracey Boyce, "Corporate PACs and the Delicate Balance," Dept. of Sociology, Northeastern University, 1982.

53. Boyce, "Corporate PACs and the Delicate Balance."

54. Epstein, "The Emergence of Political Action Committees"; "Business and Labor under the Federal Campaign Act of 1971"; and The PAC Phenomenon: An Overview"; Herbert E. Alexander, "Corporate Political Behavior," in *Corporations and Their Critics*, Thornton Bradshaw and David Vogel, eds., (New York: McGraw-Hill, 1981); John R. Mulkern, Edward Handler, and Lawrence Godtfredsen, "Corporate PACs as Fundraisers," *California Management Review* 23 (Spring 1981): 49–55.

55. E. Digby Baltzell, *The Protestant Establishment: Aristocracy and Caste in America*, (New York: Random House, 1964).

56. Useem, *The Inner Circle*.

57. Francois Bedardia, *A Social History of England, 1851–1975*, A. S. Foster trans. (London: Methuen, 1979).

58. Daniel Bell, *The End of Ideology*, (New York: Free Press, 1962), chap. 2.

59. Alfred D. Chandler, *The Visible Hand: The Managerial Revolution in America*, (Cambridge, Mass.: Harvard University Press, 1977), 10.

60. Edward S. Herman, *Corporate Control, Corporate Power*, (New York: Cambridge University Press, 1981).

61. Derek F. Channon, *The Strategy and Structure of British Enterprise*, (Boston: Harvard University Graduate School of Business Administration, 1973).

62. Herman, *Corporate Control, Corporate Power*; Michael Useem, "Corporations and the Corporate Elite," in *Annual Review of Sociology* 6 (1980).

63. Michael P. Allen, "Managerial Power and Tenure in the Large Corporation," *Social Forces* 60 (1981): 482–94; M. Allen and Sharon K. Panian, "Power, Performance, and Succession in the Large Corporation," Washington State University, 1982.

64. S. M. Miller and Donald Tomaskovic-Devey, *The Recapitalization of Capitalism*, (London: Routledge & Kegan Paul, 1983).

65. Fred Block, "Beyond Relative Autonomy: State Managers as Historical Subjects," *Socialist Register* (1980): 227–42.

11

Political choice and the multiple "logics" of capital

FRED BLOCK

The perspective of economic sociology has important implications for the analysis of politics, and particularly for understanding the relationship between the state and capital. For the past fifteen years, many key contributions to political sociology have centered on the idea that capitalist states are torn between the conflicting imperatives of legitimation and accumulation.[1] According to this perspective, when legitimation pressures force the state to go "too far" in granting concessions to subordinate groups, the accumulation process is impaired. The problem with this familiar formulation is that it is built on the same image of the economy as an autonomous entity that the perspective of economic sociology calls into question.[2] The consequence has been extremely serious in that theorists of the conflict between legitimation and accumulation have inadvertently legitimated the political demands of the business community.

The nature of the economic

The legitimation versus accumulation argument is very much a mirror image of conservative arguments about interference with free markets.[3] With growing intensity during the 1970s and early 1980s, conservative economists and publicists advanced the argument that problems of high inflation and slowing productivity growth were the inevitable consequence of excessive growth of government – too much regulation, tax rates pegged so high as to discourage initiative, and the proliferation of social programs that insulated individuals from the discipline of the labor market. They insisted that deregulation, tax cuts, and the reduction of social spending were necessary to restore the integrity of the free market, so that the conditions for stable economic growth could be restored.[4]

293

In fact, analysts on the left frequently cited these conservative arguments as evidence for their claim that capitalism and democracy were in conflict.[5] They suggested that, if the various forms of state regulation and state social-welfare spending that had been won through popular struggles did actually interfere with the "logic of capitalism," then this would constitute proof of the necessity and desirability of a transition to socialism. For adherents of this position, a transition to socialism represented the only way to preserve the gains that had come through democratic struggles within capitalism.

Yet the persuasiveness of both leftist and rightist arguments that posited a conflict between democracy and state action on the one hand and the logic of the economy on the other depended on developments in the world economy. After all, it had been the conventional wisdom for the previous twenty years that the "mixed economy" – a combination of private ownership and state intervention – was the optimal institutional form for achieving economic efficiency and social welfare. It took a series of international economic shocks to undermine this conventional wisdom.

In the 1970s with growing international economic competition, the demise of the Bretton Woods international monetary order, and OPEC's oil price rises, American citizens and politicians were suddenly confronted with the reality of international economic interdependence. The scholarly community reflected this shift by rediscovering the constraints placed on national societies by the discipline of the world economy. During the 1970s, American academics elaborated both "world system theory" and "international political economy," both of which had at their core the analysis of the pressures placed on national societies by the world economy.

The international economy that American academics rediscovered had changed from the self-regulating gold standard of the nineteenth century, but the international currency markets continued to operate as constraints on national policymakers. If, for example, a particular country were following expansionary policies when those around it were contracting, it would likely face a balance of payments crisis and severe downward pressure on its currency. Moreover, citizens in country after country were told during the 1970s by politicians and business leaders that they could not afford various types of social-policy measures because of their potential damage to the country's international competitive position in a context of increased conflicts over markets. And in periods of economic contraction, such as 1974–1975 and 1980–1983, existing redistributive policies came under attack on the grounds that they prevented the readjustments that were necessary for improved performance in world markets.[6]

These pressures were highlighted by the efforts of the Mitterrand government in France to go against the tide of the world economy in the early 1980s. The French Socialist government pursued redistributive and expansionary policies while the rest of the major economies were still in recession. The results were higher rates of inflation and mounting balance of payments difficulties for France. The currency markets forced a series of devaluations of the franc, and ultimately the Mitterrand government was forced to reverse many of its policies and pursue a program of austerity.

These experiences provided persuasive support for the idea of a fundamental conflict between government policies designed to increase legitimation and the logic of capitalist accumulation. The evidence appeared overwhelming that, in the context of a highly competitive capitalist world economy, there exist strict limits to the types of governmental policies that are possible in any particular country. Moreover, as competition mounts within that world economy, there are powerful pressures to reduce the level of taxes and social welfare in any particular country toward the lowest international common denominator.

To be sure, leftist and free-market theorists use different concepts to describe the tension between politics and the logic of the economy. Where one would discuss "the logic of accumulation," the other would refer to "the logic of the market." Yet the difference in language conceals an analytic similarity. The two sets of theorists share two central ideas in common. The first is a rejection of optimistic, Keynesian ideas about the mixed economy in favor of the view that there is no "free lunch" – efforts to improve social welfare through government action interfere with either the logic of the market or the imperatives of accumulation.

The second common idea is that there is such a thing as an economy that is autonomous and that has a single logic. This assumption, which can be called the economistic fallacy, was sharply critiqued in a book published more than forty years ago, *The Great Transformation*.[7] In that book, Karl Polanyi challenged the idea that the economy is autonomous and obeys a single logic. While there has been increased interest in Polanyi's work in recent years, this core argument of his is worth elaborating at some length because his position has still not been assimilated by economic analysts of either the right or the left.

Polanyi develops his argument about the autonomy of the economy by directly challenging economic liberalism's account of the evolution of capitalism. Adam Smith and others argued that capitalism evolved out of an innate human desire to truck and barter. While archaic social institutions had placed limits on the market, a process began in the late Middle Ages through which the market gained increasing strength and autonomy, until political institutions finally evolved that maximized market freedom. As one would expect, this history rests on the idea of an autonomous economy that needs only to be given its freedom; the process is one of natural evolution from restrictions on the human desire to trade to a society organized around that desire.

In contrast, Polanyi highlights the unnaturalness and discontinuity in the historical changes that gave rise to capitalism. The traditional account asserts that the growth of both local and international trade in the late Middle Ages resulted naturally in the development of integrated national markets. But Polanyi insists that both local and international trade could flourish indefinitely without the creation of integrated national markets. Under mercantilism, local and international markets were subordinated to political control, so there was no natural dynamic leading to integrated markets.

Polanyi emphasizes instead the importance of political intervention for the rise of modern capitalism. The emergence of national markets was not the result of spontaneous evolution but of the deliberate political interventions of the Crown.[8] Later on, the development of a market economy also depended on action by the state. The particular example that he analyzed most extensively was the role of the English Poor Law Reform in creating a modern labor market. He described in detail the consequences of the Speenhamland Act – a system of welfare relief instituted in 1795 by rural squires to maintain order in the countryside. By providing relief in supplement to wages, the act had the effect of lowering wages and productivity in the countryside, while also discouraging migration to the urban areas. Hence, Speenhamland became a significant obstacle to the full development of capitalism. Only the imposition of the Poor Law Reform created the mobile and driven labor force that allowed industrial capitalism to flourish.[9]

In the analysis of Speenhamland, Polanyi rejects the view that welfare policies are external or supplementary to the economy; rather, he sees them as fundamentally constitutive of the market economy. The emphasis on the importance of Crown policies in creating national markets or on the centrality of welfare policies for creating labor markets is aimed at demonstrating that the economy is not an autonomous entity but that it has always been profoundly shaped by state action.

As to the logic of the economy, Polanyi's analysis is more implicit than explicit. Polanyi did insist that the nineteenth-century ideal of a self-regulating market was utopian, in the sense of being unachievable. He argued that, if markets were left to themselves, they would quickly destroy human society and the natural environment. In pursuit of short-term gains, entrepreneurs would exploit the labor force so brutally that it would not be able to reproduce itself, they would devastate the environment, and they would destroy the trust necessary for a system of contracts to survive. While longer-term considerations might lead individual capitalists to oppose such actions, the pressures of a competitive market would quickly force even the most enlightened either to engage in such destructive practices or to risk bankruptcy. The only alternative is the imposition of regulations by the state that would place legal limits binding on all entrepreneurs.[10] For Polanyi, the classical example of such regulations were the Factory Acts that were passed very soon after the Poor Law Reform.[11] The Factory Acts were the first step of what Polanyi terms the protective countermovement – the movement to preserve human society from the devastation caused by the self-regulating market.

The implicit argument is that the behaviors of economic actors do not – by themselves – aggregate into a whole that is either rational or sustainable; and it is, therefore, only state action that assures a reasonable outcome. One might say that the economy has a logic that is shaped by individual pursuit of profits, but it is a semantic error to assume that this logic produces a rational or coherent outcome at the aggregate level. For example, individual employers struggle to expand output while limiting wage increases, but the result is an expansion in output without sufficient demand and the economy slips into severe depression. Only state action can redirect these economic patterns into a coherent whole.

It must be stressed that this type of argument is not the same as classical Marxist formulations. While Marx stresses the irrationality of capitalism and its tendency toward periodic crises, he emphasizes the purifying nature of those crises, reflecting his fundamental respect for the capitalist economy's capacity to regulate itself. Even in the discussion in *Capital*[12] of the importance of the Factory Acts in placing a limit on the working day and forcing employers to shift toward technological innovation, he fails to address this critical state intervention in theoretical terms. In brief, Marx was a product of his time in perceiving economic logic as aggregating into a coherent – albeit irrational – whole without the need for state action.[13]

Recognition that economic logics by themselves do not aggregate into coherent wholes deepens the importance of the insight that the economy is never fully autonomous. It suggests that what we generally call "the economy" is always the product of a combination of state action and the logic of individual or institutional economic actors. It follows, as well, that crises or dysfunctions in "the economy" cannot be traced solely to interference with economic logics because those economic logics have never – by themselves – produced a coherently functioning whole. Rather, one would expect to find the root of economic crises in the particular fit between economic logics and state action. In brief, instead of assuming, as does the conservative wisdom, that the problem is too much state intervention, this Polanyian view suggests that the issue is the specific structure of state intervention, with the distinct possibility that more intervention might be necessary to overcome crises.

In this view, government policies – including redistributive social policies – are not superstructures built on top of some economic base. Rather, they are constitutive of the capitalist economy – without them, there would be no functioning capitalist society. Hence, it no longer makes sense to speak of a contradiction between government policies and some essential logic of accumulation because the latter is a meaningless abstraction. Some government economic policies are more effective than others, but the explanation for the less effective ones has to be sought at a more concrete level of analysis than interference with the basic logic of the economy.

Analyzing the diversity of capitalist institutional arrangements

The diversity of the conditions under which capitalism has flourished provides considerable support for this line of argument. If the economy were autonomous and had a single logic, one would expect that there would be a very narrow range of difference in governmental policies and institutional arrangements among capitalist countries. But the reality is that capitalism flourishes in such diverse settings as Social Democratic Sweden and authoritarian South Korea. The extent of government regulation, the rates of taxation, and the nature of social policies varies across different capitalist countries far more than can be explained by different levels of development or different positions within the world economy.

The explanation for this diversity is not difficult to see. Individual capitalists tend to be opportunistic and pragmatic. While they might have a tendency to prefer the minimal state of laissez-faire ideology, they also tend to adapt to the political realities that they face. If their efforts to shape the political environment to their liking are unsuccessful, they will generally figure out ways to make profits in the new circumstances. It is precisely this adaptability of capital that makes it understandable how capitalism has flourished despite the enormous growth of the state in the twentieth century.

But, while private ownership of capital is consistent with a broad range of different governmental policies, any particular set of policies must have some coherence if stable growth is to be achieved. If, for example, policies that encouraged production of consumer goods were combined with policies that restricted the growth of domestic and international markets, then one would anticipate serious problems and little growth. This idea of the need for some coherence in the institutional environment in which capitalists operate is captured in the concept of "social structures of accumulation."[14]

According to Gordon et al., each long period of capitalist expansion involves a particular set of social arrangements to sustain the dynamic of capitalist accumulation. The "social structure of accumulation" comprises particular configurations of urban growth, particular types of financial and governmental mechanisms for structuring demand, and specific ways of organizing the relations between workers and employers. It is the social structures of accumulation that assure that economic logics aggregate into a coherent and sustainable whole. As long as we remember that there is not one unique social structure of accumulation at a given moment, but multiple possibilities, then this conceptualization reinforces the Polanyian idea that one cannot simply separate out economic development from the political-economic context that makes it possible.

If, for example, we consider the experience of the 1930s depression in the United States, it becomes clear that a host of government policies laid the basis for a new period of capitalist expansion after World War II. The combination of social insurance programs and the extensive federal role in subsidizing suburbanization played a key role in supporting aggregate demand. Similarly, social insurance provisions and the recognition of industrial unions created the conditions for a relatively successful period of labor management relations in basic industry.

That the specific social structures of accumulation that were put in place in the 1930s and 1940s ultimately came to grief in the 1960s and 1970s is not evidence that there was too much interference in the free market. Rather, social structures of accumulation are always time-limited in their effectiveness. As with the development of organisms, there is a process of growth and decay shaped by several factors. Particular patterns of social and economic development will face a law of diminishing returns – as, for example, when suburban development becomes increasingly problematic because available empty land is so far from the central city. And, over an extended period of time, people will also become dissatisfied with some of the institutional arrangements that are part of particular social structures of accumulation. Industrial employees might grow restive with particular ways of organizing the workplace or a feminist movement might emerge that challenges the established place of women in the society. Finally, some of the positive synergies that occurred during the phase of expansion can turn negative under changing historical circumstances, as when a structure of accumulation that relied heavily on cheap energy faces systematic oil price rises.[15] Through these dynamics, particular social structures of accumulation become dysfunctional – they produce slower growth and more political-economic difficulties. The combination of vested interests and a general resistance to change makes it unlikely that decaying social structures of accumulation will be effectively reformed. Usually, dramatic political-economic deterioration is necessary before forces are mobilized to establish new social structures of accumulation.

In short, the political-economic difficulties that both leftists and rightists have identified as a product of the conflict between state intervention and the logic of the economy can better be understood as the result of decaying social structures of accumulation. This latter diagnosis leads to very different prescriptions. Whereas the conventional view sees the necessity of a reduction in the government's role in the economy, and particularly a sharp reduction in its efforts to redistribute income, a focus on decaying social structures of accumulation suggests that an expanded role of the state, and particularly an increased role of the state in redistributing income to the less well off, could be part of the new social structures of accumulation. Whereas redistributive social policies were central to the last period of expansion because of the tendency of the society's capacity to produce to outstrip market-generated demand, it seems logical to suggest that they could be even more central to new social structures of accumulation in a period when computerization has the potential to expand output far faster than employment.[16]

The international dimension

However, any argument that stresses the multiplicity of possibilities for organizing particular capitalist societies must deal with the issue of the world economy. As was noted earlier, the rediscovery of the ways in which the international economy constrains national choices played a key role in the revival of the economistic fallacy. These constraints have been seen as part of the fundamental economic structure of capitalism; according to this view, they cannot be altered without significant costs in reduced efficiency. I argue to the contrary that these constraints are actually political and ideological; they have little to do with efficiency and they can be altered without significant efficiency costs.

The pressures of the world economy fall into two categories: the impact of competition in international trade and the impact of international capital movements. While there are obvious interactions between these dimensions, they can be discussed separately.

The standard argument that is made about international trade is simply an extension of the argument that wage levels are critical to international competitiveness. It is argued that a country that has more generous social policies will be forced to have higher tax rates to finance these benefits. If these higher taxes fall on firms that produce products that are internationally traded, the firms will be at a competitive disadvantage in relation to firms from countries with lower taxes and less generous social policies.

One problem with this argument, as with many popular economic ideas, is that it traces out only one side of a causal sequence. The positive effects on economic efficiency of social polices are completely neglected, even though it is well known that higher levels of health, education, and general welfare are associated with higher levels of output per employee in manufacturing.[17] Sweden, for example, was able to "afford" more developed social-welfare spending through most of the post-World War II period while maintaining a very strong position in international trade. The reason was that Swedish industry was able to use the high quality "human capital" in the society to produce goods that were internationally competitive by virtue of their technological sophistication and quality.

Furthermore, the experience of the United States in terms of medical care suggests that the failure of the government to take an active role in delivering social services can be even more damaging to international competitiveness. It is well known that health-care costs for employees is one of the largest expense items for American automobile firms.[18] It seems highly likely that, had the United States instead created a system of national health insurance, the burden on industries in international competition would be less great than it is now.

The conventional argument also forgets that productivity gains in internationally competitive production are closely linked to overall rates of economic growth.[19] If redistributive social policies contribute to rapid economic growth in a particular country, it is possible that that country's industries will improve their international competitiveness more rapidly than firms in another country that remains bogged down in slow growth.[20]

Above all, this conventional wisdom vastly exaggerates the importance of wage costs – both direct and indirect – in determining international competitiveness. Tyson and Zysman stress the possibility that comparative advantage in modern mass-production sectors will hinge not on wage rates but on the operational control of complex systems that reduce per-unit labor costs substantially. In this regard, comparing Japanese labor requirements with U.S. labor requirements for production in a wide range of sectors is quite sobering. Also sobering is the fact that in technology-intensive products, the U.S. trade deficit with Japan increased from $2 billion in 1970 to $13.5 billion by the end of the 1970's.[21]

In short, in advanced economies, the international competitiveness of a country's products is influenced by many factors, including a broad range of government policies. And, in the face of adversity, there are strategies to pursue for improved trade performance other than reductions in wages, benefits, and government welfare expenditures.

Arguments about capital movements tend to play a more central role in the conventional wisdom because the impact of capital movements can be much more immediate and dramatic than changes in a country's competitiveness in international trade. For example, a country that institutes generous social policies that require higher taxes on business or that imposes stricter regulations on business than its neighbors will likely experience significant capital flight. Not only will international capital be less likely to invest in such a country, but domestic capital is likely to seek safer and more lucrative opportunities abroad. In its mild form, such net capital outflows can lead to a domestic economic slowdown, a negative balance of payments, and a deterioration in the value of the country's currency. This devalued currency, in turn, means a relative reduction in the citizenry's standard of living. When capital outflows accelerate, the result can be even more serious economic turmoil that usually can force either a change of government or a change of governmental policy.

For adherents of the economistic fallacy, these consequences flow directly from the negative efficiency consequences of the original governmental actions. The increase in taxes or the increase in regulations will impose such burdens on firms that they will not be able to achieve adequate profit levels, so that they have no choice but to shift to foreign investments. It is here, also, that the trade arguments are invoked. Because it is assumed that the government moves will assure a deterioration in the international competitiveness of domestic industry, it would make little sense for a shrewd businessperson to invest there rather than abroad.

But with investments, as with trade, the actual effects of any particular set of governmental initiatives are extremely difficult to predict. Again, redistributive policies might strengthen the domestic market and create all kinds of new investment opportunities. Forms of regulation might spawn new industries, as in pollution control, and even contribute to greater consumer and business confidence. One thinks, for example, of the negative investment climate created by proximity to toxic waste dumps.

The classic example of this unpredictability was Franklin Roosevelt's New Deal reforms. While the business community was almost unanimous in its condemnation of Roosevelt's initiatives on the grounds that he was destroying the conditions for an efficient capitalist order, the reality was that the reforms created the conditions for the great post-World War II economic expansion. There was, to say the least, a large gap between what was perceived to be efficient in the short term and what was efficient over the long term.

The point, however, is that the actual effects of more generous social policies on the country's international trade and investment position are basically irrelevant. Usually domestic and international business will not wait to see whether the policies strengthen or weaken the balance of payments; they will proceed immediately as though the impact of the policies will be negative. In most circumstances, they are then able to make the prediction into a self-fulfilling prophecy. If producers have predicted that higher taxes will be inflationary, they can then prove the accuracy of this forecast by accelerating the pace of price rises. If they have warned of negative effects on the trade balance, these too can be produced by "leads and lags" in payments that are justified through the imminence of a devaluation. If business has warned of an outflow of capital and a reduction in international investment, these too can be arranged by signaling that the business climate has turned bad under the new government.

The claim, however, is that each of these prophecies is soundly based in an economic theory that emphasizes the international trade and capital constraints on domestic economic actions. The reality is that both the self-fulfilling prophecies and the economic theory must be understood for what they are: stratagems in an ongoing political struggle. The business community tends to oppose redistributive social policies and higher taxes for very simple reasons. Redistributive policies can improve the bargaining power of certain sectors of the labor force with a possible negative effect on profit levels. Similarly, higher taxes appear to threaten profit levels and the income of the wealthy. For any particular firm, the impact on profits is not inevitable – it simply means that greater effort might be necessary to generate the same amount of profit. But an inconvenience for particular capitalists is not the same as impairing the logic of capitalism. The gap between system logic and short-term self-interest emerges when capitalists who are "inconvenienced" by various types of government intervention are forced to be more aggressive and imaginative in finding ways to turn a profit, thus contributing to the efficiency with which the society produces.[22]

But, in opposing these types of measures, the business community uses its two complementary weapons: the self-fulfilling prophecy and the claims of economic theory. If business simply warned on the basis of theory that a particular policy would have disastrous consequences without being able to confirm its own predictions, it would not be taken seriously. Alternatively, if the business community fulfilled its own prophecies without the support of a persuasive theory that explained why those outcomes were inevitable, its maneuvers would likely be seen as obvious power plays. And there would be the opportunity to respond to such power plays in the realm of politics. In short, the special potency of economic theory is that it gives business arguments that appear to lie outside of politics and that preclude, in advance, political responses.

To be sure, even if the veil of economic ideology were stripped away, governments would be able to respond effectively to some, but not all, of the self-fulfilling prophecies. If business raises prices to fulfill a prediction of inflation, price controls could be imposed or a tax-incentive scheme could be enacted that rewarded those firms that limited their price increases. Through such measures a government could gain time to demonstrate that the actual economic effects of its policies are positive. However, if capital flight and massive disinvestment are predicted, it is difficult – in most cases – for a single government, acting alone, to respond effectively. Even if capital controls are imposed to slow the flight of domestic capital, it is fairly certain that there will be a net and sizable loss of international capital, which can represent a crippling blow to a government's prospects.

However, much depends at this point on which government is involved. If we are discussing the United States government, it is difficult to foresee conditions under which it would be unable to pursue alternative policy directions because of the pressures of flight capital. Even in a period of significant domestic reforms, the United States would still appear a safer haven for international capital than most other places in the world. In addition, the U.S. has the capacity to mobilize its allies and international institutions such as the IMF to help it resist speculative pressures against the dollar. Moreover, the U.S. has on earlier occasions successfully controlled the outflow of capital by its own international banks and multinational corporations.[23]

The real problem comes with less powerful countries who find their domestic plans foiled by international capital movements. But it is in these cases that most analysts make the mistake of assuming that the free movement of international capital is a fundamental and necessary part of a capitalist world economy. Even without returning to the age of mercantilism, it must be recalled that capitalism flourished at the domestic level through the two world wars despite substantial controls over international capital movements. Moreover, the early plans of J. M. Keynes and Harry Dexter White for the postwar international monetary order contemplated substantial controls over international capital mobility. White, in particular, feared that the free movement of capital could doom efforts within particular countries to pursue full employment policies, so he proposed international arrangements through which other countries would agree to repatriate flight capital that left a country in violation of its domestic capital controls.[24] While these plans were not implemented, their demise reflected the political balance of forces at the time – particularly, the power of internationally oriented business in the United States – rather than the fundamental logic of the system. Moreover, despite the triumph of those forces favoring the free movement of capital, it was not until 1958 that most European countries restored the convertibility of their currencies. Hence, much of the postwar recovery of European capitalism occurred under a system of controls over the outflow of capital.

In fact, the experience of the past twenty years suggests that too much freedom for international capital movements is irrational even on capitalist terms. The huge quantities of "stateless" capital in the Eurodollar market that quickly shift from one currency to another have created turmoil in the currency markets and have repeatedly interfered with the effectiveness of national economic policies. And on numerous occasions, major countries have found it necessary to peg interest rates at excessively high rates – with the resulting slowdown in growth and increases in unemployment – simply because of the pressures of international capital markets. While it was once hoped that the shift in the 1970s from fixed exchange rates to flexible rates would make possible international monetary stability even with these massive pools of speculative capital, the experience of the past ten years has demonstrated that floating rates have not solved the problem.

Moreover, the free movement of international capital has also created significant problems of instability in international banking. During the 1970s, the international banks fell over each other making excessive loans to Third World countries, creating the present debt crisis. And there is continuing fear of a spreading international financial crisis resulting from the failure of a subsidiary or offshore bank that is subject to little or no regulation by national banking authorities.

These problems have created strong pressures for increased regulation of international banking, and even some establishment figures have made policy proposals designed to discourage speculative capital flows.[25] The point is that the degree to which the international economic order regulates and restricts international capital flows is itself a matter of political choice, and the efficiency arguments for complete freedom of capital movement are deeply flawed.[26] Hence, it is a political possibility that the international monetary order be reformed to limit speculative capital flows or to establish means to offset such flows.[27] Such reforms would result in a reduction in the political leverage that comes from the threat or reality of massive capital flight. Governments would then have expanded possibilities for pursuing alternative domestic policies.

In sum, the international argument has the same flaws as the domestic one: it mistakes the political preferences of an extremely powerful interest group for the fundamental logic of an economic system. In doing so, it simply reinforces the political strength of business by denying the real political choices that are available for organizing the international economic order and national political economies.

Conclusion

What this analysis points to is the central role of economic ideologies in shaping the development of the relation between state and capital. Ideologies serve to make certain institutional arrangements or policy choices appear natural or normal, and claims about the economy as an autonomous entity with a single logic are extremely important in placing limits on what state actors can do in particular historical circumstances. Moreover, as we have seen, the business community's capacity to use ideology to make self-fulfilling predictions about the consequences of certain policy measures is an invaluable resource in its effort to constrain and limit state action.

However, it is also important to emphasize that the persuasiveness of economic ideologies does vary over time. In the 1930s, for example, the collapse of the world economy dramatically undermined the vision of the economy as a self-regulating mechanism and left the business community with few resources to resist an expansion in the state's regulatory role. However, economic difficulties do not always produce this same result. Capitalism's problems with inflation and unemployment in the 1970s generally had the opposite effect from the crisis of the 1930s – the ideology of market self-regulation was reinforced and the bargaining position of the business community was greatly strengthened.

We have at this point only the most rudimentary understanding of the dynamics that influence the persuasiveness or lack of persuasiveness of economic ideology over time, but it does not seem farfetched to imagine that economic sociology itself might come to play a role in this drama. When it challenges the idea of the autonomy of the economy, economic sociology is potentially subversive of the power of the business community. Such a stance represents a sharp break from the legitimation versus accumulation perspective that has had the ironic effect of reinforcing the return to "free-market" policies.

When one accepts the position that such reforms as the expansion of social welfare actually interfere with the fundamental logic of a capitalist order, it becomes very difficult to defend those reforms from conservative attack. One can argue that over the long term the only way to protect reforms is through a break with the capitalist system, but this does not provide much strategic guidance in the short term. On the contrary, since the left agrees that these reforms contribute to the problems of the economy – inflation, slow growth, unemployment – it follows that the citizenry is acting rationally when it supports the right-wing attacks on the reforms. In a context in which the immediate transition to socialism is not possible, it follows that the best way to enhance the collective welfare is by trading away reforms for the promise of faster growth.

This is, I would argue, what has happened in the past decade in the United States. While one can easily exaggerate the influence of leftist ideas, the wide dissemination of the accumulation versus legitimation perspective within academia and activist circles has had the effect of persuading key groups that it is futile to resist Reaganite attacks on the all-too-limited American welfare state. The very notion that Ronald Reagan's polices were necessary for American capitalism had the effect of disempowering those who were in a position to resist those policies.

The perspective of economic sociology, in contrast, opens up political possibilities by stressing the multiplicity of different ways that the economy can be organized. Moreover, it provides a basis for challenging many of the central arguments that have been used to justify conservative economic solutions.[28] It could also facilitate the development of alternative policies around which broad political coalitions could coalesce. While these possibilities are only potential, the point is that the way in which we conceptualize "the economy" has extremely important political consequences.

Acknowledgment

Some of the arguments in this chapter were first developed in "Social Policy and Accumulation: A Critique of the New Consensus," in *Stagnation and Renewal in Social Policy*, edited by Gosta Esping-Anderson, Lee Rainwater, and Martin Rein. I am also indebted to Erik Olin Wright, Karl Klare, David Plotke, and the editors of *Theory and Society* for suggestions that were incorporated at various stages of this chapter's evolution.

Notes

1. Key works include Jurgen Habermas, *Legitimation Crisis* (Boston: Beacon, 1975); James O'Connor, *The Fiscal Crisis of the State* (New York: St. Martin's, 1973); Alan Wolfe, *The Limits of Legitimacy* (New York: Free Press, 1978); Samuel Bowles and Herbert Gintis, "The Crisis of Liberal Democratic Capitalism," *Politics and Society* 11, no. 1 (1982): 51–93; and some of the essays included in Claus Offe, *Contradictions of the Welfare State* (Cambridge, Mass.: MIT Press, 1984).

2. Richard Swedberg, Ulf Himmelstrand, and Göran Brulin, "The Paradigm of Economic Sociology," in this volume.

3. This convergence has also been noted by Michael Piore and Charles Sabel, *The Second Industrial Divide* (New York: Basic Books, 1984); and by Robert Kuttner, *The Economic Illusion: False Choices between Prosperity and Social Justice* (Boston: Houghton Mifflin, 1984).

4. See R. Bacon and W. Eltis, *Britain's Economic Problems: Too Few Producers* (London: Mcmillan, 1978); Organization for Economic Cooperation and Development, *Towards Full Employment and Price Stability* (Paris: OECD, 1977); George Gilder, *Wealth and Poverty* (New York: Basic, 1981).

5. See, particularly, Wolfe, *Limits of Legitimacy*, chap. 10.

6. For an influential statement of these arguments, see Barry Bluestone and Bennett Harrison, *The Deindustrialization of America* (New York: Basic, 1982), especially, chap. 6.

7. The original publication was in 1944, but references are to the Beacon Press edition, Boston, 1957. For an extended discussion of Polanyi's thought, see Fred Block and Margaret Somers, "Beyond the Economistic Fallacy: The Holistic Social Science of Karl Polanyi," in *Vision and Method in Historical Sociology*, edited by Theda Skocpol (New York: Cambridge University Press, 1984).

8. Polanyi, *The Great Transformation*, 63–67.

9. Ibid., 77–85.

10. Ibid., 73.

11. Ibid., 165–66.

12. Volume 1, chaps. 8, 15.

13. See Adam Przeworski, "The Ethical Materialism of John Roemer," *Politics and Society* 11, no. 3 (1982): 289–313, for a critique of the Marxist tendency to see the economy as a self-operating automaton.

14. See David Gordon, Richard Edwards, and Michael Reich, *Segmented Work, Divided Workers* (New York: Cambridge University Press, 1982). While I make use of their concept, there is much in their argument with which I disagree.

15. This list of factors is far from complete; it is meant only to be illustrative.

16. The argument is that, if computerization reduces the demand for labor while output rises, there could be a significant shortfall in demand. While such an outcome is not inevitable, a weakening of the labor market from technological displacement can reduce employee bargaining power so that wage gains fail to keep pace with the growth of output. On problems of employment generation in advanced capitalism, see Fred Block, "The Myth of Reindustrialization," *Socialist Review* (Jan.–Feb. 1984), and "Technological Change and Employment: New Perspectives on an Old Controversy," *Economia & Lavoro* (Aug.–Sept. 1984).

17. See Denison's classic work in growth accounting: Edward F. Denison, *Accounting for United States Economic Growth, 1929–1969* (Washington, D.C.: Brookings, 1974).

18. In 1984 Chrysler Corporation budgeted $460 million for health-insurance premiums. This amounts to $5,000 per employee or $275 per vehicle. "Chrysler Program Saves Millions in Health Costs," *New York Times*, Apr. 29, 1985.

19. "In general, there is a logical correlation between increases in production and in productivity, with productivity speeding up as production accelerates and slowing down as production is retarded." Harry Magdoff and Paul Sweezy, "Productivity Slowdown: A False Alarm," *Monthly Review* 31, no. 2 (June 1979): 11.

20. The actual outcome depends, of course, on other variables such as the rate of inflation, exchange rates, and the propensity to import. But my point is that the impact of social policies on international competitiveness is indeterminate and depends on other variables, some of which can be effectively manipulated by governments.

21. Laura Tyson and John Zysman, "American Industry in International Competition," in *American Industry in International Competition: Government Policies and Corporate Strategies*, edited by Zysman and Tyson, (Ithaca: Cornell University Press, 1983), 33.

22. This now neglected line of argument has a distinguished lineage in the economics literature. For example, in his classic study of manufacturing employment, Fabricant argues that reductions in the length of the working day imposed by government or unions can have the effect of inducing greater entrepreneurial efforts by the employer. Solomon Fabricant, *Employment in Manufacturing, 1899–1939* (New York: NBER, 1942), 13.

23. The system of capital controls imposed during the Vietnam war is described briefly in Fred Block, *The Origins of International Economic Disorder* (Berkeley: University of California Press, 1977), 182–84.

24. Block, *Origins*, 42–46.

25. While the Reagan administration's obstinate commitment to free markets and deregulation has discouraged initiatives in this direction, steps were being taken in the late 1970s towards greater international cooperation to regulate banking. See Hugo Colje, "Bank Supervision on a Consolidated Basis," *The Banker* (June 1980): 29–34. Robert Dunn writes that "Prohibitions or limitations on capital flows have been widely discussed as a possible route to a less volatile exchange market . . . ," and he reports a proposal by James Tobin to discourage speculative capital flows by taxing exchange market transactions. Robert M. Dunn Jr., *The Many Disappointments of Flexible Exchange Rates*, Princeton Essays in International Finance, no. 154, Dec. 1983, 24–26.

26. The argument that the new technologies of capital transfer make controls impossible is clearly specious. The reality is that such electronic transfers leave more traces than traditional currency transactions.

27. The natural coalition for such reforms would bring together progressive social forces in Western Europe and the United States with Third World nations that are currently suffering from their indebtedness to international banks.

28. See Fred Block, "Rethinking the Political Economy of the Welfare State," in Fred Block, Richard Cloward, Barbara Ehrenreich, and Frances Fox Piven, *The Mean Season: The Attack on the Welfare State* (New York: Pantheon, 1987).

12

Private and social wage expansion in the advanced market economies

ROGER FRIEDLAND AND JIMY SANDERS

The sources of family income in advanced market economies have become increasingly complex. A family's real income depends not only on the money wages its members receive in the labor market, but also on the extent to which those wage are taxed and the public services and transfer payments it receives from the state. The income and services households receive from the state constitute a social wage, which is growing in importance relative to the private wage. Growth in state support of living standards has added a new institutional locus of conflict over the distribution of income.

Because of the institutional autonomy of capitalism and the democratic state, the growth of private and social wages are presumed to be governed by different logics.[1] While the allocation of private money wages is presumed to be governed by market forces, that of social wages is regulated by politics. If the first moves in response to marginal productivity, to the contribution workers make to profitability, the second responds to the political power of the beneficiaries, and the contribution citizens make to electoral support and regime stability.

Politics and wages

To many, the movements of private and social wages appear to be on a collision course. Rooted in the institutional autonomy of market and democracy, their contradiction threatens the growth and adaptability of the capitalist economies. Conservative theorists increasingly argue that, through the welfare state, politics has gone beyond its appropriate institutional role of correcting the inadequacies of the marketplace, providing succor to those unfortunates who cannot find work and assuring that all will have an equal opportunity to compete in the labor market. The expansion of the social wage, it is argued, has eroded the incentive to work and to save, and thereby reinforced dependence on still more state support. High levels of social wages contribute to rigidities in the labor market by raising the price that employers must pay to induce able-bodied men and women to work at onerous, low-paid jobs that must be done. They thereby contribute to wage inflation.

Whereas Keynesians stressed the impact of welfare state spending on demand under conditions of unused resources, conservatives emphasize the perverse investment, or supply, consequences of public-sector growth. The increased tax burden that such redistributive policies make necessary undercuts the return to investment and savings, and the subsequent decline in profitability slows investment and growth. This leads to higher levels of unemployment and lower levels of private wages, both of which result in more dependence upon the state for income support. Private wage movements should ultimately be regulated by the market, unfettered by politics. Otherwise economic growth will slow, and government support for household incomes will expand inexorably. If only the state were to disengage itself from the labor market, the propulsive forces of entrepreneurship and competition would generate high levels of economic growth and private wage growth.[2]

The connection between the welfare state and private labor markets has also been analyzed by those who do not believe in the benign self-regulating nature of markets, particularly labor markets. The historical origin of state support for wages derives from the interdependent organization of laborers in unions and left political parties.[3] For left parties to gain power, they had to garner support from ex-workers, non-workers, and nonunionized workers. To obtain this support, programs were designed to build alliances between groups that would otherwise be divided by the market. Universalistic provision of social wages was one way to build these alliances. Full employment was another.

From a Kaleckian political business cycle perspective, profitability and growth are regulated by the movement of private wages. Economic downturns are the natural result of tight labor markets that put upward pressure on private wages. Partisan politics and class conflict in the labor market politicize the distribution of the national product through their impacts on the level of welfare state spending. High levels of social wages operate as a "floor" below which private wages cannot fall, and thus are assumed to support private wage growth as well as working-class resistance to poor working conditions. Disability, retirement, and unemployment benefits are supposed to moderate downward wage pressure and provide a buffer for the unemployed to resist poor working conditions.[4] They thus contribute to private wage growth and the resultant incursions on firm profitability. The existence of powerful left political parties and the labor unions that support them also affect the balance of political power in the private marketplace. This is reflected in economic policies favoring low unemployment at the cost of high inflation. Recessions are necessary to discipline labor and restore profitability.[5]

While conservative critics and social democratic defenders of the welfare state differ in their evaluation of the welfare state, they nonetheless share some of the same empirical assumptions about the relationship between the welfare state and the workings of the market economy. Both believe that politics has shaped the growth of the welfare state independently of the operation of the private economy. Both argue that the welfare state has contributed to the upward movement of private wages in a manner that would not have been produced by the labor market alone. Piven and Cloward, for example, explain the Reagan administration's attempt to cut back the welfare state for households as an effort to expand the supply of low-wage labor under conditions of declining profitability.[6] Both see unemployment as a mechanism to induce wage restraint.

However, there is reason to doubt the empirical assumptions shared by analysts on the right and the left. High levels of social wages need not be a source of private wage increases, such that those states that generously support the incomes of their citizens through transfers and public services price their labor out of the international marketplace, slowing growth and increasing unemployment. A number of researchers have pointed to the role of the welfare state in reducing working-class resistance to technological change and smoothing structural change in the economy as a whole.[7] If employers displace high-wage workers who have achieved their privileged labor-market position through the market power of their employers and their unions rather than through increased productivity, high levels of welfare state spending may facilitate their displacement and thereby lower the average level of wages in the economy.

Workers are members of families, with children and parents for whom they care. It is reasonable to assume that they judge the adequacy of their private wages relative to the requirements of providing food, housing, education, and health care for their entire family. They also must judge the current adequacy of their private wages against the eventuality that they may one day not receive them. From this private point of view, we might expect high levels of social wages – the fact that the essentials of life for one's family do not depend entirely on private wages – would constrain wage growth. Trade-offs between private and social wages have frequently been consciously made through collective bargaining. Through incomes policies, labor unions have sometimes agreed to restrain private wages in exchange for growth in the welfare state for households, particularly where they faced intense international wage competition and the prospect of growing unemployment.[8]

Similarly, recent empirical work has also challenged the supposed trade-off between high levels of unemployment and wage-based inflation. First, the relationship is historically variable. In the North American case, for example, there has been a continuous decline in the ability of increased unemployment to restrain the upward movement of either nominal or real wages. In the 1957–1958, 1960–1961, 1969–1970, and 1973–1975 downturns, real wages remained either unchanged or actually went up.[9] Second, the relationship is nationally variable. Thus in time-series analyses of wage inflation in Italy, France, and the United States, Hibbs found that neither levels nor changes in unemployment had significant effects on hourly manufacturing wages between 1951 and 1972, once price inflation and union militancy are taken into account. Only in Great Britain did the level of unemployment depress the upward movement of nominal wages.[10] In Cameron's analysis of eighteen nations between 1965 and 1982, there was a strong bivariate positive relationship between average unemployment and price inflation.[11] Price inflation, in turn, was strongly associated with increases in nominal earnings. Where the working class was organizationally powerful, they exchanged private wage restraint for full employment.

International markets and wages

When the state intervenes in the national economy, it does so partially in response to international pressures over which it has little control. Analysts of national economic policies argue that it is not possible to examine the determinants of national economic policy, in which private and social wages are central, without understanding a nation's position in the international economy.[12] This is clear in Western Europe, where tariff barriers have been reduced. If the cost of labor in one country accelerates relative to its trading partners, it is likely to lose its international market share and face rising trade deficits. Under such conditions, domestic demand must be reduced through restrictive monetary or fiscal policy. While increasing foreign debt or currency devaluations are possible stalling tactics, they have increasingly lost their utility. Currency devaluations in Western Europe, for example, have tended to increase domestic inflation due to higher priced imports faster than they have shifted balances of payments.[13] Because of the state's inability to control the movement of capital across national borders and the declining usefulness of traditional monetary and fiscal instruments in highly open economies, unions have sometimes been willing to limit their demands for wage increases in response to the comparative cost constraints of international trade. Thus we might expect economies that are highly vulnerable to the international market to have more restrained private and social wage growth.

In economies that are highly vulnerable to trade constraints, it is difficult for national policymakers to control inflation, profitability or unemployment.[14] In his study of eighteen OECD nations, Cameron found that the extent of integration into international markets was the most important determinant of public-sector expansion.[15] Cameron argued that open economies tend to produce industrial concentration, which facilitates strong unions, powerful left parties, and economy-wide collective bargaining. All of these factors increase state support for household incomes, particularly in compensation for wage restraint and structural unemployment. Cameron never directly measured the mechanism by which this was purported to occur. There was no measure of private wage restraint or unemployment, no structural model of the processes, nor any measure of expenditure directly in support of household incomes. Only total government revenues were analyzed. Like other cross-sectional studies, Cameron's analysis provides a snapshot that may accurately reflect the gross historical patterning of welfare state expansion. However, it is not clear that it accounts for the contemporary dynamics of welfare state expansion.

Capital formation and wages

International economic interdependence frequently involves the displacement of relatively inefficient domestic industries by imported goods, and the concentration of national economic growth in higher productivity, capital-intensive sectors with lower national employment growth. In many cases, such as France, Germany, and Sweden, the concentration and capital-deepening of leading export sectors has been facilitated by government policy. Whereas incomes policies politically integrated the determination of private and social wages, structural change policies have increasingly forced government to integrate politically the determination of wage and capital formation.

For example, in the post-World War II period, the French state has not only orchestrated a merger movement among key sectors, but has increasingly negotiated planning agreements with the largest, most technically advanced firms in leading export industries: aeronautics, electronics, petrochemicals, and pharmaceuticals.[16] To make its policies politically palatable to the union movement, the government has been forced to maintain the incomes of displaced workers and to finance their retraining.

The Swedes have gone furthest in linking wage and capital formation, and using social wage expansion to facilitate structural change in the economy. The Swedish case literally turns all of the accepted economic truths on their head.[17] The Swedes achieved high levels of economic growth while enormously powerful labor unions representing almost all blue-collar workers successfully bargained for a generous welfare state for households. Until the 1980s, the Swedish public sector grew almost twice as fast as the GNP. High levels of economic growth were achieved with relatively low inflation despite the fact that real wages were comparatively high and unemployment comparatively low (typically below 2 percent). They simultaneously expanded household incomes and profitable corporate investment. This was possible because a strong labor union movement allied to a governing Social Democratic party integrated the politics of consumption with the politics of production.

In the post-World War II period, the Swedish economy faced tight labor markets, high wage-push inflation, and declining profitability. In response to these conditions, the union movement (the LO) – which is both inclusive of most workers and centralized – bargained intensively for equalization of wage differentials between industries and regions. This solidaristic wage politics had the effect of bankrupting less competitive firms and industries, and increasing the incentive for the remaining firms to substitute capital for labor and thereby increase productivity. The politics of wage solidarity thus facilitated structural change in the economy. These policies not only reduced wage differentials in Sweden, they also led to rapid increases in productivity, almost double the American rate. In addition, corporate capital became increasingly concentrated.

To reduce resistance to the inevitable unemployment that such a policy would produce, and reduce the inflationary labor bottlenecks that structural change in the economy produces, the Social Democrats developed an active labor-market policy, called the Rehn model after the union economist of the same name, based upon a national system of localized labor-market boards empowered to train redundant workers for expanding industries, or to provide alternative employment for those who were unwilling or unable to retrain for or relocate to a new industry. These boards were organized on a local corporatist basis, with both union and employer association participation. The AMS boards, which spend about 7 percent of the government's budget, have kept unemployment below 3 percent, even in the 1980s, when unemployment rates above 10 percent were not uncommon elsewhere. If not for government measures, the Swedish unemployment rate would probably double.

Structural change in the economy generated a rapid process of urbanization and a severe shortage of housing. If workers could not find housing where employers wished to expand production, the entire labor-market policy would founder. If housing costs rose rapidly because of insufficient supply, there would be considerable upward pressure on private wages. If the housing sector was highly profitable, private capital would be diverted from investment in expanding export sectors. For all these reasons, the Social Democrats socialized housing finance. Using tax revenues and funds derived from union pension funds, the state provided finance for massive housing construction, coordinated with labor market and economic structural change policies, with preferential terms given to cooperatives and para-state builders.[18]

Finally, the unions and the Social Democrats increasingly used the nation's pension system to directly socialize the investment of capital. Faced with anticipated increases in tax burdens necessary to finance future social-security payments, policies were adopted that created a new pension fund, financed by employer payroll taxes, to be controlled by the public sector. The pension system, graduated according to earnings, won the support of the white-collar workers' union, the TCO. Originally the funds were used to provide housing finance. But due to high interest rates and slackening investment, a state investment bank, integrated with the labor-market boards, was created in 1967, designed to lend or directly invest the pension capital in industrial firms. In the 1970s, increased international competition and high interest rates combined to increase unemployment, reduce profitability, cut down on the level of capital investment, and increase the deficit to almost 10 percent of the GNP. Particularly after the election of the Conservatives in 1976–1978, the government began to subsidize relatively unprofitable firms, in part to prevent unemployment. The government-financed corporate inventories provided tax credits and grants.

However in 1983, after the return of the Social Democrats to power, socialization of investment took yet another step forward with the Meidner plan, over the strenuous opposition of the business community. In return for wage restraint, large corporations were required to set aside 20 percent of their profits each year in "wage earner's funds." These collectively controlled funds were to be used for reinvestment both inside the firm and in other firms. This plan was designed not only to increase the savings rate, but to channel them into productive investments. It also undercut the enormous wage pressures that build up, often ending in wildcat strikes, when Swedish firms accumulate historically high profit levels, profits that would now be directed into the funds.

While the Swedish case is not typical, it indicates the ways in which private capital and social wage formation may be linked. Thus in order to speed the rate and efficacy of capital investment, governments have increasingly made use of social wage programs both to make the costs of such economic policy politically feasible, and now increasingly to tie the financing of social wages to productive capital investment. We might expect capital investment to be directly related to the expansion of the social wage.

Central governments and the welfare state

Since World War II, central governments have increasingly based their legitimacy on their ability to stimulate economic growth. State intervention has moved from the universalistic and macroeconomic to the particularistic and microeconomic, centering on the performance of particular industries and even firms.[19] This shift toward instrumental legitimacy and the particularistic means through which it is often achieved have risen in tandem with claims on the central state for public resources by those who are not advantaged by economic change and may even be its victims. Central governments have financed a rising share of these expenditures, even if central funds are ultimately spent by subnational governments.

Thus there have evolved two welfare states, one that supports household income, or the social wage, and another that supports corporate profitability, or social capital. This "other" welfare state for business has received considerably less attention. Welfare states for business and for households have grown in concert. In 1980, in the United States, for example, government support for private firms – including subsidies, tax expenditures, loan guarantees, and low-interest financing – amounted to almost 14 percent of the GNP.[20] In the same year, transfers to households amounted to 10 percent of the GNP. Today, however, it is the welfare state for households that is maligned as an unproductive use of resources, as a source of rising tax burdens and a deterrent to consumption and investment, and as a source of upward pressure on private wages, for those who, but for public support, would be compelled to accept lower-paying jobs.[21]

Faced with the gargantuan task of reducing the claims that rise thunderously at the center, many states are beginning to decentralize authority to spend, and some, like the United States, even the responsibility to raise revenues. Beneath the rhetoric of democracy, there is a widespread belief that subnational units will tax and spend in a more restrained manner, slowing the growth of the welfare state.[22]

According to this view, the connection between decisions to spend and decisions to tax are more apparent at the subnational level. The opportunity costs of spending are more politically visible. Importantly, the interregional mobility of capital constantly constrains expenditure and taxation decisions that impinge upon local profitability. It will only be those communities or cities that can afford it that will be generous to their disadvantaged residents.[23] Standards of provision will not be centrally mandated, providing a standard against which all groups can make their claims. From these arguments, we would expect *decentralized* governmental structures to have slower-growing welfare states.

However, we argue that decentralized states might have more rapidly growing welfare states.[24] The construction of a government at the subnational level depends more on the satisfaction of particularistic individual and neighborhood claims, as opposed to functional group claims organized at the national level. Lacking authority or power to solve fundamental social problems that give rise to these claims, subnational elites face greater uncertainty in electoral contests. They are also closer and more accessible to their constituents. Spending money is a strategy to manage group conflicts that cannot be adjudicated at the subnational level and a way to garner electoral support by vulnerable political elites, particularly where a few thousand votes can change electoral outcomes.

Central political elites are both less accessible and more likely to have the authority to solve problems rather than spend money to secure electoral support. In addition, they have greater capacity to control subnational spending. In Britain, where the raising of revenue is highly centralized, the central government has sought to control local council spending through the setting of "cash limits" on what they may spend. When local councils attempted to adjust to reduced central funding by increasing their own taxes, particularly property taxes, the central government established rates beyond which councils could not go. The French government had also instituted a similar practice before Mitterrand came to power. Although central solutions to group problems may be costly, the cumulation of band-aid and pork-barrel local politics may be even more expensive and less effective. In most of the advanced market economies, subnational expenditures have risen much more rapidly than those at the national level.[25]

It is only in centralized structures that group, and especially class, conflicts can be managed so that welfare state spending does not rise faster than the societal product out of which it is financed. At the central level, social wages can be negotiated in concert with private wages and unemployment, not to mention capital formation. This is particularly the case where unitary, centralized union movements negotiate national wage contracts within the context of corporatist structures.[26] Such social contracts, like incomes policies, can only be negotiated in centralized systems. For all these reasons, we might expect *centralized* governmental structures to have slower-growing welfare states.

Modeling the movement of wages

Governments support household incomes under several circumstances. First, they do so where families are unable to support themselves due to injury, unemployment, sickness, or old age. Government programs socialize such risks. Second, they do so where it is believed that commodity markets will not produce a sufficient quantity of some good deemed necessary to economic growth. Third, they do so where they do not wish the production and distribution of a good or service to be regulated by ability to pay.

There are three mechanisms by which each of these functions can be executed. First, they rely upon transfer payments in various forms such as welfare, assistance payments to buy medical care or housing, and social security. These payments are either direct payments to households or transfers to provide organizations like hospitals that furnish services to households. Eligibility for transfers is regulated by statute and their expansion is difficult to control. For example, in Sweden, housing allowances are paid to almost 40 percent of all households based on income, number of children, and age.[27]

Second, the state actually produces goods and services, such as schools, universities, hospitals, libraries, housing, police, and mass transit. These are subject to the often well-organized demands of public-sector workers. Governmental taxing and spending have generally had redistributive effects on the final distribution of income, especially where personal income taxes provide a major source of government revenue.[28]

Third, the state may be instrumental in getting employers to finance both transfer payments and public services paid to those who have worked for their firms. Such payments, whether paid into private pension or social-security funds, or paid directly to the employees, constitute a significant portion of wage income in a number of countries, such as France. They also are subject to government regulation and mandating. For example, the first Thatcher government in Britain required employers to provide sick pay for employees in order to eliminate national insurance benefits for sickness.[29] Corporate financing may be a strategy of business and organized labor to segregate the social wages of a high-profitability and productivity sector from those in the lower-productivity, nonunionized sector. We might also expect left political parties to have less impact on this form of corporate spending than on public services or transfer payments. We consider them here as a component of the private wage.

The two forms of social wages considered here – transfer payments to households and government services – have different characteristics.

Transfer payments tend to expand automatically by statute in response to shifts in private incomes and employment. Public-service expansion requires more explicit political decisions. Transfers tend to be more redistributive in their incidence, while public services tend to be less so. Transfer payments do not involve high levels of public employment, while public services do and are therefore subject to the demands of well-organized public-sector workers, with links to the general labor movement. Given these differences, and the difference in constituencies that support them, we might expect a trade-off between their expansion. We might also expect politics to have a greater impact on the movement of public services in comparison with transfer payments.

According to those who see social wages as a floor under private wages, high levels of social wages should stimulate the growth of both real and money wages. High levels of private wages should lead unions and left parties to increase social wages in order to solidify those private wage gains. But it is also possible that contrary to those who see social wages as a source of upward pressure on private wages, there is a trade-off between private wages, on the one hand, and transfer payments and public services on the other. If the collective logic upon which incomes policies operate has any impact, low levels of private wages should lead to more rapidly increasing social wages, and high levels of social wages should slow the growth of private wages. But, even if incomes policies are not operative, private wages are regulated not only by needs for current consumption, but for future consumption. Thus if future consumption requirements for oneself and one's family are assured by government programs, then private wage increases may be more modest.

Social and private wages are also probably a function of their level at an earlier point in time. For both parliaments and unions, previous levels of spending for social and private wages provide a base point against which current bargaining takes place. In both the political (social wages) and economic (private wages) markets, we might expect to find incrementalist growth in household incomes.

We do not assume that wage-earners are necessarily the only consumers of state transfers or public services. For instance, nonworkers receive social-security payments and social-assistance grants. It is desirable to include public incomes consumed by nonworkers for several reasons. First, social wages are directed toward individuals who would otherwise depend upon those who earn private wages or upon entrance into the labor market themselves. Therefore social-security and other income-maintenance payments reduce the cost of retirement on younger families whose members continue to work. They also affect the volume of persons who compete for available employment. Second, social wages are a measure of income outside the private wage system. As such they are a pool of politically manipulable resources available for buffering the incomes of those who cannot find sufficient work or wages to survive.

Economists would expect the movement of nominal wages to be most affected by the political power of the working class, whereas that of real wages would depend more on the productivity of labor. Yet the political processes determining private and social wage expansion over the last twenty years are complex. Strong left political parties, given the material interests and political preferences of their constituencies, should generate faster growth of social wages.[30] On the other hand, because of their greater capacity to negotiate incomes policies and legitimate wage restraint on the part of their unionized constituents, left parties may be more effective in containing real and nominal wage increases in the interest of full employment.[31]

The labor market is subject to political conflict both within the state, and in the labor market itself. As the state has increasingly intervened to regulate class conflict and the distribution of income, strike activity has declined.[32] Nonetheless, cross-national difference in the movement of wages, both private and social, may be responsive to the level of working-class organization in the labor market.[33]

Within the United States, for example, highly unionized industrial sectors have experienced more rapid growth in labor costs per worker. And, over the course of the twentieth century, American unionization has been associated with increases in money wages.[34] In most formulations, it is assumed that unemployment reduces private wage growth by intensifying worker competition for scarce jobs. Political business-cycle theorists assume that tight labor markets generate large wage increases, resulting in reduced profitability, lower investment rates, and hence increased unemployment.[35] However, research indicates that those countries with the lowest levels of unemployment have had lower levels of wage-push inflation.[36] Since the 1930s, rising joblessness automatically sets in motion institutionalized transfer payments for which the unemployed are eligible, and creates electoral demands for welfare state expansion both to support income and the use of state spending as a stabilization policy. Unemployment growth should stimulate social wage growth.

Given the trade constraints of international competition, we would expect relatively open economies to have slower-growing private wage levels, but to have higher levels of growth in social wages as an adaptation to those competitive constraints. However, economies that perform poorly in the international economy would not only be pressured to restrain wage increases in order to preserve employment, but would be required to dampen demand to prevent rapid import expansion. Thus poor performance in the international economy should restrain both private and social wage expansion.

We expect countries with high rates of economic growth to have higher private wage gains due to the expansion of demand and the desire of employers to increase product and market share, and thus their willingness to tolerate real wage increases to attain these ends.[37] This effect would be net of changes due to shifts in unemployment that accompany higher rates of growth. Increases in capital investment, a corollary of economic growth, should be associated with high levels of social wages, to the extent that such government programs expand to facilitate labor displacement associated with capital substitution for labor, while increases in capital investment should be associated with increased productivity, especially where new technologies require new capital goods, and thus increased wages. So too, capital can most easily be substituted for low-wage, unskilled labor performing routine tasks, thereby reshaping the composition of the labor force in an upward direction.[38]

Expenditures have increased much faster at subnational levels of government than at the national level. Whether this is due to greater public accessibility at the local level, the superior power of interest groups at the subnational level, or the inefficiencies of fragmented local governments, is unclear.[39] Because centralized systems may be better able to control expenditures, resist client pressures, coordinate programs, and integrate social wage programs into macroeconomic policy, we would expect centralized systems to have slower-growing social wage programs. This expectation is contrary to findings in past research.[40]

Explanations of the tax revolt have centered not on the progressiveness of taxation, but on its visibility. Because indirect taxes are less visible than direct ones, they conceal the true costs of public spending. Wilensky thus found that tax revolts were more likely in those countries that relied heavily on direct forms of taxation.[41] If, on the other hand, the populace reacted more positively to progressivity than negatively to visibility, we would expect social spending to increase more rapidly in revenue structures that rely more on indirect taxation.

A number of analysts have argued that the welfare state grows in response to need and subsequent political demands for state intervention. The age structure of a society, especially the proportion of its population considered too old to work, is perhaps the best indicator of need.

Measurement and methods

We conducted an empirical analysis of the movement of private and social wages in a dozen advanced market economies between 1962 and
1980. Data were collected for Austria, Belgium, Finland, France, Germany, Italy, the Netherlands, Sweden, Switzerland, Great Britain, Canada, and the United States. The data are organized into six panels. The
equations discussed below are specified in each of the six panels, each
of which spans three years. For example, the last panel begins in 1977
and ends in 1980. Thus there are 72 data points, 12 countries times 6
panels. By pooling the panels, both cross-national and time-wise variation are taken into account. The GLS pooled cross-sectional and longitudinal estimation procedures employed here correct for heterosce-
dasticity, serial correlation, and contemporaneously correlated
residuals.[42] The relative desirability of generalized least squares solutions in small sample pooled cross-sectional and time-series applications has been demonstrated through Monte Carlo simulation.[43] Our
approach has the benefit of considering cross-sectional tendencies
among countries while simultaneously taking into account dynamics of
the model across time. The model assumes that the true effects operate
similarly across countries and and across time.

The four dependent variables – government transfers, government
services, and real and nominal private compensation including both
money wages and benefits – are measured in 1965, 1968, 1971, 1977,
and 1980. Their levels are also controlled for three years earlier within
each panel. This lagged endogenous variable procedure has the advantage of controlling for omitted variables operating at both points in
time, and in not assuming a determinate functional form, as does a
growth rate, for example.[44] All fiscal variables are standardized to U.S.
dollars and deflated to 1963 price levels.[45]

Government transfers are composed of social-security benefits, social-assistance grants, and transfers to nonprofit institutions serving
households. These data are taken from the income and outlay transactions of general government. Transfers are measured as a ratio to constant GDP. Government services are measured as general government
final consumption expenditure, net of defense spending. This is the
value of government output subtracting the value of government production sold in the market. It is primarily a measure of the value of public employment for nonmarketed goods and services. The largest out-
lays are usually for education and health care. Public services are also
measured relative to GDP. Private compensation is measured as the
sum of wages and salaries and employer contributions to private pen-

sion plans and to social-security programs in thousands of dollars.[46] All variables are gathered from OECD, unless otherwise stated.

The strength of organized labor is measured as the ratio of the total trade-union membership to the size of the civilian labor force. The political power of left parties in European nations is measured as the proportion of parliamentary seats held by social democrats, socialists, communists, and labor party members, if at least one of these parties is included in the cabinet. For Canada, the proportion of seats held by Liberals and New Democrats (when one or both parties are represented in the cabinet) is used. For the United States, the proportion of Democrats in Congress if a Democratic president is in office is used. The proportion of Democrats in Congress divided by two is controlled for when a Republican president is in office.[47] This variable is based upon partisan alignments stemming from the most contemporary general election (presidential election in the United States) that took place at least one year prior to the year in which the dependent variable is measured in each panel.[48] For example, if elections occurred in 1980, the political alignment prior to that election is measured for the panel stretching from 1977 to 1980. We measure this variable at least one year prior to the dependent variable in order to take into account the lag-time between the establishment of a government and the implementation of its policies.

The level of openness of the economy is measured as a three-year average of the proportion of the total value of imports and exports relative to GDP. Economic growth is measured as the percentage change in GDP over the three-year time period between the lagged and current measures of the dependent variables. Unemployment growth is measured as the three-year change in the percentage of the civilian labor force that is unemployed.[49] Thus the metric is a simple arithmetic difference between unemployment rates at two points in time. The change in capital investment is measured as the percentage change in the percentage of capital investment in new plant and equipment relative to GDP. The proportion of the population that is sixty-five years of age or older at the initial year covered by each panel is measured to control for the impact of need.

Government centralization is measured as the ratio of central government expenditure relative to general government expenditure. This includes intergovernmental transfers and is thus a measure of central extraction. The revenue structure is measured as the ratio of central government tax revenues that are levied indirectly. Direct taxes are primarily taxes on profits, incomes, and capital gains. Indirect taxes are primarily value added and use taxes.

Table 12.1. *The determinants of social wage growth, 1962–1980.*

Item	Transfers to households		Public services	
	b	t	b	t
Intercept	0.220	0.88	0.006	0.22
Transfers, lagged	1.134	17.10	− 0.052	1.06
Public services, lagged	− 0.035	0.55	0.893	16.55
Total compensation, lagged	− 0.004	1.47	0.002	1.73
Change in unemployment	0.005	4.77	0.003	4.59
Economic growth	− 0.029	6.06	0.013	1.85
Left political influence	0.015	2.07	− 0.002	1.30
Unionization	− 0.025	1.78	0.016	1.36
Openness of economy	0.023	2.53	− 0.011	1.42
Balance of payments	− 0.021	0.38	− 0.025	0.43
Growth in capital investment	0.011	1.09	− 0.004	0.27
Indirect taxation	− 0.014	0.59	0.013	0.62
Government centralization	− 0.031	1.60	0.022	1.04
Percent elderly	0.063	0.57	− 0.054	0.82

Source: See text.

Empirical results

What shapes the movement of social and private wages? Parameter estimates for the determinants of the two forms of social wages and private compensation are reported in Tables 12.1 and 12.2.

Looking first at the two forms of social wages, the movement of both transfers and public services are shaped by their level at an earlier point in time. The higher the extent of spending for either form of social wage three years earlier, the more they are likely to grow over the next three years. The two forms of social wage do not constrain each other's growth. There do not seem to be powerful trade-offs between the growth of public transfers and public services, even though they serve different constituencies.

Neither form of social wage growth is much affected by the partisan coloration of the government. When left parties are powerful, public provision does not increase significantly faster. However, transfers do increase significantly when left parties are strong. While the relationship is positive, it is small in real terms. A 10 percent increase in left parliamentary strength is directly associated with a less than .2 percent increase in transfer payments. Strong labor unions have no appreciable

Table 12.2. *The determinants of private wage growth, 1962–1980*

Item	Real Wages[a]		Money Wages	
	b	t	b	t
Intercept	63.65	.82	− 1,180.92	− 1.05
Transfers, lagged	− 3,258.97	− 2.91	− 10,190.8	− 2.59
Public services, lagged	− 3,575.31	− 4.45	8,834.58	1.06
Total compensation, lagged	1.28	21.09	1.35	21.46
Change in unemployment	63.03	3.36	329.11	9.41
Economic growth	2,143.32	13.84	4,147.98	24.40
Left political influence	245.01	2.39	− 70.61	− .26
Unionization	128.71	.32	541.97	.82
Openness of economy	81.65	.46	1,192.43	3.15
Balance of payments	3,624.14	2.18	6,294.49	2.31
Growth in capital investment	1,055.43	4.34	210.98	.43

[a]The metric of the GLS coefficients (b) for the real-wage equation are 1963 U.S. dollars.

Source: See text.

impact on the growth of either form of social wage. Although unionization is positively related to the growth of public services, the form of social wage most likely to benefit unionized workers and their families, the relationship is small and statistically insignificant. The stronger negative relationship between unionization and transfer growth, a form of social wage less likely to benefit their core constituency, is also statistically not significant.

Both forms of social wage expansion are highly sensitive to economic performance, but in different ways. Countries that have higher rates of economic growth are able to reduce the share that transfer payments take out of the societal product, but increase the share of resources allocated to public services. The latter result is statistically significant at only the .07 level. Declines in the share of transfers are more responsive to shifts in economic growth than are increases in the share of public services. Countries whose economies are highly vulnerable to international trade pressures have more rapidly growing transfer payments, but not public services. Performing poorly in the international market place does not lead to more slowly growing social wages. Countries do not slow the growth of either form of social wage in response to negative balances of payments. Further, the growth of social wages does not appear to be affected by growth in capital investment. In those countries where unemployment is increasing, both forms of social wages grow as a result, although transfers rise more rapidly in response than do public services. A 2 percent increase in unemployment over three years is directly associated with a 1 percent increase in transfers relative to GDP over three years. The effect of changes in unemployment on public services is also substantial, although smaller. Finally, we find that high private wages have little impact on the growth of social wages. While high levels of compensation lead to higher growth rates in public services, the substantive effect is quite small and borders on statistical insignificance (p = .09).

Thus the two forms of social wages – transfer payments that are geared to income maintenance programs at the bottom end of the social spectrum and public services that are more universally consumed – do not respond similarly to economic changes. Transfer-payment growth is a response to economic decline, rising unemployment, and to international trade pressures. Public-service growth is a response to economic growth, high wages, as well as unemployment. Transfer payments grow as a way to compensate the victims of economic decline and trade constraints, while public services grow as a way to complement the incomes of the beneficiaries of growth. While both forms of social wage grow in response to rising unemployment, their other determinants differ. Transfer payments substitute for private wealth, while public services complement it.

The "new federalists" assume that decentralized structures will slow the growth of the welfare state. Contrary to their assumptions, we find no evidence that centralized governments, those whose expenditures account for a larger proportion of total government expenditure, have more rapidly growing welfare states. Centralized structures have neither more rapidly growing transfer payments nor more rapidly growing levels of public services. This is inconsistent with past work.[50]

Contrary to those who believe that hiding the true burden of taxation is a way to allow for expansion of the welfare state, we find that the extent of government reliance on indirect taxation – the least visible kind – has no impact on the growth of either form of social wage. And the movement of neither form of social wage was responsive to the relative size of the elderly population.

Now let us examine how these two forms of social wage affect the movement of real and nominal private wages. We measured wages as the total level of wages and salaries, including employer contributions to private pensions and social-security schemes, per worker in the entire economy. Contrary to those on the right and left, we find no evidence that high levels of social wages put upward pressure on private compensation whether real or money wages. High levels of transfer payments, those which are most responsive to shifts in unemployment rates, lead to slower growth in compensation per worker.[51]

On average, a 5 percent increase in government transfer payments to households relative to GDP is related to more than a $160 real (1963 U.S. dollars) or $509 nominal annual decrease per worker in private compensation. Similarly, high levels of public services constrain private wage growth. What is striking about these results is that neither form of social wage has been found to be highly politically manipulable, yet both act as sources of private wage restraint. These results cast doubt on the thesis that rising welfare expenditures have undermined corporate profitability and growth through their real or nominal wage-push effects in the labor market.

Like social wages, private wages are also highly responsive to economic performance. Contrary to the conventional wisdom, higher levels of unemployment do not slow real or nominal wage growth. Rather, increases in unemployment are associated with modest gains in the real and nominal level of workers' private compensation. Virtually the same results are obtained when hourly wage rates in manufacturing are analyzed.[52] This contradicts what we might expect based upon neoclassical models of the labor market, as well as Kalecki's analysis of the business cycle.[53] Slack labor markets should produce slower wage growth, if not decline. These results suggest that induced recessions are not necessarily an effective strategy to halt wage inflation.

But how to explain this result? There are four possibilities. The first is the operation of dual labor markets. According to this perspective, economies are divided into two relatively isolated labor markets: one with high productivity, high-wage jobs, with internal, firm-specific career ladders; and the other with low productivity, low-wage jobs, based on open, competitive labor markets.[54] It is in the core, rather than the periphery, that job security is greatest. Thus under conditions of high unemployment, increases in unemployment will be concentrated among those jobs that are relatively low paid, leading to higher *average* wages.[55] This does not contradict the possibility that those workers who are subject to unemployment moderate their wage demands. It also suggests the need for sector-specific, cross-national models.

A second possibility, reviewed above, is suggested by Cameron's work on the business cycle, in his analysis of unemployment, wage inflation, and the organizational strength of the working class. A weak working class, to compensate for its inability to achieve secure employment and an adequate social wage not conditional upon employment, engages in efforts to push private wages up as much as possible. Thus private wage increases are an adaptation to an economy where workers face high levels of insecurity due both to a poorly developed welfare state and periodically high levels of unemployment. In addition, we might expect that where the working class is either poorly organized or excluded from macroeconomic decision-making, the state would be more likely to use the political business cycle to try to discipline wage behavior. Our results, consistent with recent work on wage behavior in the classic case of such exclusion – the United States – suggests that contra-cyclical wage constraint does not affect the average industrial wage, although it may affect wage behavior at the margins.

As a third possibility, our findings are also consistent with a neo-classical model, if countries with comparatively high minimum wages – a legal floor under private wages – account for this result. In this case, high minimum wages would lead to higher levels of unemployment as employers are not allowed to bid the cost of labor down to clear the market, as well as high-wage growth. If this is so, the relationship between growth in unemployment and private wage growth may be spurious.

There is, finally, a fourth possibility. Employers may respond to increased wage costs by substituting capital for labor. Capital substitution increases productivity, which in turn can be passed on in higher wages. In his study of the impact of unionism on profitability across industrial sectors in the United States, Freeman found that unionization both increased labor costs, but also produced a counteracting increase in capital and consequently value added per worker. But capital substitution may also tend to produce higher short-term unemployment. If this is the process, then again the positive relationship between increased unemployment and real and nominal wages is not correctly specified.[56]

Private compensation is also highly responsive to economic performance in a manner anticipated by macroeconomic theory. High levels of economic growth and increases in capital investment both lead to higher real private wages. Workers traditionally make the greatest wage gains during business-cycle upswings when growth rates are high. And capital investment, by increasing productivity, contributes to real wage growth. However, while money wage growth also is greater when the economy is growing, neither the movement of money nor real wages is affected by rates of capital formation. Both real and nominal wages tend to increase more rapidly in economies characterized by a favorable balance of payments. Failure to compete successfully in the international market appears to result in wage constraint at home. While economic openness per se has no impact on the movement of private wages, it does tend to be associated with upward movements in nominal wages, presumably through the importation of inflation.

If anything, we would expect that politics might have an impact on the movement of nominal wages. Indeed, some economists have argued that unions bargain in terms of movement of monetary, as opposed to real wages, and thereby suffer from a monetary illusion. Certainly, governments and employers can adapt more easily to extra-market driven increases in nominal wages than in real wages. Our findings suggest that, net of economic conditions, politics has little effect on the movement of private wages. Real wages do rise more rapidly where the left is politically powerful, but the effect is quite small in substantive terms. Unionization has no impact on the movement of total compensation. Thus, over the two decades studied here, high levels of working-class power, whether organized through left political parties or labor unions, were not directly responsible for rising real or nominal wages. Whether this is due to the autonomy of the labor market from political direction or, on the contrary, the efficacy of incomes policies where the working class is powerful, or to labor's success in protecting a bifurcated wage structure wherein the growth of low-paid, nonunionized labor increasingly pulled down the average wage in the economy as a whole, requires further analysis.

Discussion

There are significant trade-offs between private and social wages. Contrary to those on the left and right who contend that cutbacks in income maintenance and government provision will force down private wages, our results suggest the opposite.[57] High levels of transfer payments and public services lead to more slowly growing private wages. Whether this is due to incomes policy trade-offs, or simply the private logic of workers trying to maximize their earnings in anticipation of a rainy day, we cannot say. Given the lower reaches of the income distribution at which many forms of social wages are directed, it may be that the trade-off between private and social wages operates most forcefully for those workers who have low-paying jobs in secondary labor markets rather than for better-paid workers in primary labor markets. Future research will be required on these relations within different sectors of the economy.

The evidence above also suggests that the movement of social wages is largely unaffected by politics, whether in the state or the labor market. Where left parties were powerful, neither form of social wage increased markedly. This is inconsistent with the results of others.[58] These results may be fairly criticized because only changes in the relative size of the welfare state are measured, rather than its content or connection to private labor-market criteria.[59] Nonetheless, they suggest that change in the relative magnitude of the welfare state for households is not as politically manipulable as cross-sectional studies have led us to believe.[60]

Wilensky explained the populist tax backlash not by the size of the welfare state, and hence the level of taxation necessary to support it, but by the visibility of resource extraction.[61] Our findings do not support this thesis. At those times when nations make greater use of indirect taxes – the less visible kind – their welfare states do not grow more rapidly. Indirect taxes are not simply less visible, they tend also to be less progressive. Consequently, where the population must finance welfare state expansion through greater regressive tax burdens, there may also be resistance to welfare expansion. This would be consistent with the greater level of hostility to local tax burdens when compared to national ones. Subnational governments have to rely on more regressive forms of taxation because of the high mobility of investment.[62]

Previous analysts have argued that centralized governmental structures tend to create faster-growing welfare states.[63] From this point of view, efforts to decentralize government structures, such as the Reagan administration's "New Federalism," are strategies that will slow the growth of the welfare state. While it may be so at the cross-sectional aggregate and over longer periods of time, it is not true at the margin for shorter time periods. Neither form of social wage appears to grow more rapidly in centralized states.

Our analysis of the market determinants of wage expansion suggests that the dynamics are both domestic and international. High rates of economic growth reduce the product share of transfer payments, contrary to those who argue that growth increasingly entails high levels of social costs that must be absorbed by the state.[64] More open economies have more rapidly growing transfer payments to households, but not more rapidly growing public services. This suggests that Cameron's argument that states with open economies engage in more interventionist labor-market policies, both to reallocate labor and absorb the social costs of structural unemployment, applies only to transfer payments, and not to public employment as a whole. On the other hand, poor performance in the international economy, as opposed to vulnerability, has no impact on either form of social wages. Private wages do not grow more or less rapidly in more open economies. It is performance in the international arena, and not openness to it, that affects the movement of private wages.

Labor markets do not operate efficiently. Unemployment does not lead to lower real-wage gains, at least over the period of time studied here. Wages are indeed "sticky" on the downward side. But if unemployment does not push down real or money private wages, it does stimulate social wage expansion. Perhaps it is this expansion in social wages in response to unemployment that helps explain why private wages do not decline in response to unemployment. Labor markets have been sufficiently politicized in all countries such that unemployment has increasingly lost its efficacy as a tool for wage restraint, particularly in the context of national wage-bargaining and segregated labor markets. The determinants of private wage expansion are not so much located in the labor markets and the unions that organize there, as in the dynamics of national investment and international trade.

Decentralization for what?

Projects to decentralize the state will not do much to slow the growth of the welfare state. Why then the simultaneous efforts to decentralize across the market economies of the West, usually involving only expenditure responsibility, sometimes including the raising of revenues as in the United States? The results presented here suggest that decentralization will not affect *aggregate* resource-allocation patterns.

A number of answers can be ventured. First, decentralization is a strategy to reduce the political pressures that have accumulated at the center for all forms of income support. Central governments, which have taken responsibility for economic performance, wish to disengage from the related responsibility for the social costs of economic growth. With the rise of persistent structural unemployment, where unemployment persists in spite of relatively high rates of economic growth, devolution of the welfare state has appeared increasingly attractive. The result will be to structurally segregate the political management of growth from that of its social costs.

Second, and related, is that decentralization will reinforce the inter-urban and interregional inequities in tax base and service provision that are rooted in the growing mobility of capital. Slow-growing productivity, rising international competitiveness, massive central deficits, and slow economic growth have all eroded the possibility of managing distributional conflicts at the central level of government. Central governments have been unable to deliver full employment and high rates of growth, or to protect real working-class wages, particularly with the increasing policy emphasis on microeconomic intervention directed at modernizing particular industries. Decentralization is a way to substitute spatial inequality, which can be politically managed, for income inequality, which cannot. Decentralization will reinforce territorial forms of political organization, including the blocs of corporations and unions that are concentrated in particular industries like automobiles, steel, and coal-mining. Such areal worker-corporate interest groups have become increasingly important in the auto industry in the United States and in the steel industry in France, for example. In more decentralized structures, territorial competition for growth and central state protection will substitute for class conflict over the distribution of the social product.

Third, decentralization will allow for quicker, place-specific adaptation to the ever-increasing speed of capital mobility. Decentralized structures can adapt their public policies more quickly to shifts in investment than can centralized structures, given the Byzantine politics of compromise and potential stalemate operating there. On the one hand, labor markets are increasingly segmented, with core/periphery wage differentials increasing over time. These segments frequently correspond to specific places or regions. Decentralized structures will allow public policies to be adapted to the specific requirements of those labor markets. On the other hand, governments are increasingly turning to areally-specific, microeconomic interventions. Decentralized structures are more consistent with the movement away from macroeconomic policymaking.

The poverty of public policy

Around the Western world, there is growing anxiety that wage gains in excess of productivity increases push up inflation, cut into profits, and slow economic growth. It is argued that the expansion of income-maintenance programs and public services have undermined the incentive to work, and the taxes to pay for them have reduced the incentive to save and invest. Under this banner, private and social wages are being pushed down.

Our results suggest that decreased social wages will not help hold down private wages, that increased unemployment will be relatively ineffective at slowing the growth of private wages, and that the best way to hold back private wage increases is to have a better, not a worse, welfare state. If we want to increase private wages and reduce the relative size of the welfare state, the point is to develop an effective strategy to stimulate investment and growth. Welfare cutbacks only blame the victims of decline.

Acknowledgment

The authors would be like to thank Michael O'Higgins, Gosta Esping-Andersen, Alex Hicks, and the editors of *Theory and Society* for their criticisms of earlier drafts. We also acknowledge the support of the German Marshall Fund; the Academic Senate of the University of California, Santa Barbara; and of our wives, who provide us the saving intimation that there is more to life than unbiased estimators.

Notes

1. See Robert Alford and Roger Friedland, *Powers of Theory: State, Capitalism, and Democracy* (New York and Cambridge: Cambridge University Press, 1985), for an explication of contradictory institutional logics.

2. Conservative economic analyses are developed by George Gilder, *The Spirit of Enterprise* (New York: Simon and Schuster, 1984); idem., *Wealth and Poverty* (New York:

Basic Books, 1981); Jack Kemp, *The American Renaissance: A Strategy for the 1980's* (New York: Harper and Row, 1979); Richard W. Rahn, "Supply-Side Economics: The U.S. Experience," in William Craig Stubblebine and Thomas D. Willet, eds., *Reaganomics: A Midterm Report* (San Francisco: Institute for Contemporary Studies, 1983); J. Wanniski, "Taxes, Revenues, and the 'Laffer Curve,' " in A. B. Laffer and J. P. Seymour, eds., *The Economics of the Tax Revolt* (New York: Harcourt Brace and Yovanovich, 1979); and idem., *The Way the World Works* (New York: Simon and Schuster, 1979).

3. A number of statistical analyses support this social democratic portrait. See, for example, K. Armingeon, "Determining the Level of Wages: The Role of Parties and Trade Unions," in F. Castles, ed., *The Impact of Parties* (London: Sage, 1982); Douglas Hibbs, "Political Parties and Macro Economic Policies," *American Political Science Review* 71 (1977): 467–87; idem., "Industrial Conflict in Advanced Industrial Societies," *American Political Science Review* 70 (1976): 1033–58; Walter Korpi, *The Democratic Class Struggle* (London: Routledge & Kegan Paul, 1983), idem., *The Working Class in Welfare Capitalism* (London: Routledge & Kegan Paul, 1978); and John Stephens, *The Transition from Capitalism to Socialism* (London: Macmillan, 1979).

4. See especially the work of Gosta Esping-Andersen, *Politics against Markets: The Social Democratic Road to Power* (Princeton: Princeton University Press, 1985).

5. Hibbs, "Political Parties"; David C. Cameron, "The Politics and Economics of the Business Cycle," in Thomas Ferguson and Joel Rogers, *The Political Economy* (Armonk, N.Y.: M. E. Sharpe, 1984); Raford Boddy and James Crotty, "Class Conflict and Macro-Policy: The Political Business Cycle," *The Review of Radical Political Economics* 7 (1975): 1–19.

6. Frances Fox Piven and Richard Cloward, *The New Class War* (New York: Pantheon, 1982).

7. The work of James O'Connor, *The Fiscal Crisis of the State* (New York: St. Martin's, 1973), and Robert B. Reich, *The Next American Frontier* (New York: Penguin, 1983) converge on this point.

8. I. McDonald and R. Solow, "Wage Bargaining and Employment," *American Economic Review* 71 (1981): 869–908; Leo Panitch, *Social Democracy and Industrial Militancy: The Labour Party, the Trade Unions, and Incomes Policy, 1945–1974* (Cambridge, Eng.: Cambridge University Press, 1976); Gosta Esping-Andersen and Roger Friedland, "Class Coalitions in the Making of West European Economies," *Political Power and Social Theory* 3 (1982): 1–52.

9. Samuel Bowles and Herbert Gintis, "The Crisis of Liberal Democratic Capitalism: The Case of the United States," *Politics and Society* 11, No. 1 (1982): 51–94.

10. Douglas A. Hibbs, Jr., *The Political Economy of Industrial Democracies* (Cambridge, Mass.: Harvard University Press, 1987).

11. David Cameron, "The Politics and Economics of the Business Cycle."

12. David Cameron, "The Expansion of the Public Economy: A Comparative Analysis," *The American Political Science Review* 72 (1978): 1243–61; Peter Katzenstein, "International Relations and Domestic Structures: Foreign Economic Policies of Advanced Industrial States," *International Organization* 30 (1976), 4–13; and Robert Keohane and Joseph Nye, *Power and Interdependence: World Politics in Transition* (Boston: Little, Brown, 1977), are but examples.

13. W. Robinson, T. Webb, and M. Townsend, "The Influence of Exchange Rate Changes on Prices: A Study of 18 Industrial Countries," *Economica* 46 (1979): 27–50; John Papantoniou, "Growth and Recession in Western Europe," *Political Power and Social Theory* 3 (1982): 309–26.

14. Assar Lindbeck, "Economic Dependence and Independence in the Industrialized World," (Stockholm: Institute for International Economic Studies, 1977); idem., "Business Cycles, Politics, and International Economic Dependence," *Skandinaviska Enskilden Bank Quarterly Review* 2 (1975): 53–68.

15. Cameron, "Expansion."

16. Peter Hall, "Economic Planning and the State: The Evolution of Economic Challenge and Political Response in France," *Political Power and Social Theory* 3 (1982); 175–214.

17. This thumbnail sketch of the Swedish political economy is based on a series of works, especially those by Gosta Esping-Andersen. See especially his *Politics against Markets*, as well as Gosta Esping-Andersen and Roger Friedland, "Class Coalitions"; Gosta Esping-Andersen, "Social Class, Social Democracy, and the State," *Comparative Politics* 11, no. 1 (1978); Gosta Esping-Andersen, "From Welfare State to Economic Democracy," *Political Power and Social Theory* 2 (1981); Rudolph Meidner, *Employee Investment Funds* (London: Allen and Unwin, 1978); Robert Kuttner, *The Economic Illusion* (Boston: Houghton Mifflin, 1984); Philip Revzin, "Swedes Gain Leisure, Not Jobs, By Cutting Hours," *The Wall Street Journal*, Jan. 7, 1985, 20; and John Stephens, *Transition.*

18. Esping-Andersen, "Welfare State."

19. Hall, "Economic Planning."

20. Reich, *American Frontier.*

21. In our analysis of the growth rates of advanced market economies between 1962 and 1983, we found that direct subsidies to firms tended to depress rates of economic growth. In addition, we found that transfers to households contribute to higher rates of growth, while public services constrain national growth rates over this period. See Roger Friedland and Jimy Sanders, "The Public Economy and Economic Growth in Western Market Economies," *American Sociological Review*, 50 (1985): 421–37.

22. See for example, Cameron, "Expansion"; Manfred Schmidt, "The Role of Parties in Shaping Macroeconomic Policy," in Castles, *The Impact of Parties*, 97–176; and Harold Wilensky, *The Welfare State and Equality* (Berkeley: University of California Press, 1975).

23. Paul Peterson, *City Limits* (Chicago: University of Chicago Press, 1981). For a critique of Peterson's position, see Frances Fox Piven and Roger Friedland, "Public Choice and Private Power: A Theory of Fiscal Crisis," in Andrew Kirby, Paul Knox, and Steven Pinch, eds., *Public Service Provision and Urban Development* (New York: St. Martin's Press, 1984), 390–420.

24. Piven and Friedland, "Public Choice"; Roger Friedland, Frances Piven, and Robert Alford, "Political Conflict, Urban Structure, and the Fiscal Crisis," in Douglas Ashford, ed., *Comparing Public Policies* (Beverly Hills: Sage, 1977).

25. Arnold Heidenheimer, *Comparative Public Policy* (New York: St. Martin's Press, 1975).

26. Cameron, "Politics"; Philippe C. Schmitter, "Interest Intermediation and Regime Governability in Contemporary Western Europe and North America," in Suzanne Berger, ed., *Organizing Interests in Western Europe* (Cambridge, Eng.: Cambridge University Press, 1981), 287–330.

27. Richard Appelbaum, "Housing Policy in Sweden," *Urban Affairs Quarterly* (1984).

28. Claudio J. Katz, Vincent A. Mahler, and Michael G. Franz, "The Impact of Taxes on Growth and Distribution in Developed Capitalist Countries: A Cross-National Study," *American Political Science Review* 77 (1983): 871–86; Robert Jackman, "Socialist Parties and Income Inequality in Western Industrial Societies," *Journal of Politics* 42 (1980): 135–49; S. Stack, "The Effect of Direct Government Involvement in the Economy on the Degree of Income Inequality: A Cross-National Study," *American Sociological Review* 43 (1978): 880–88.

29. See the work of Michael O'Higgins, "Privisation and Social Security," *Political Quarterly* 55 (1984): 129–39, and "Income during Initial Sickness: An Analysis and Evaluation of a New Strategy for Social Security," *Policy and Politics* 9 (1981): 151–71.

30. Stephens, *Transition*; Francis G. Castles, "The Impact of Parties on Public Expenditure," in Castles, *The Impact of Parties*; Schmidt, "Role."

31. Armingeon, "Determining the Level of Wages."

32. Hibbs, "Political Parties and Macro Economic Policies."

33. Alexander Hicks and Duane Swank, "On the Political Economy of Welfare Expansion: A Comparative Analysis of 18 Advanced Capitalist Democracies, 1960–1971," *Comparative Political Studies* 17 (1984): 81–119; Larry J. Griffin, Joel A. Devine, and Michael Wallace. "On the Economic and Political Determinants of Welfare Spending in the Post–World War II Era," *Politics and Society* 12 (1983); 331–72; Stephens, *Transition*; Schmidt, "Role"; Castles, *Impact*.

34. Richard B. Freeman, "Unionism, Price-Cost Margins and the Return to Capital," unpublished paper, National Bureau of Economic Research, Jan. 1983.

35. Boddy and Crotty, "Class Conflict and Macro-Policy."

36. Cameron, "The Politics and Economics of the Business Cycle."

37. This view has been developed by Adam Przeworski and Michael Wallerstein, "The Structure of Class Conflict in Democratic Capitalist Societies," *American Political Science Review* 76 (1982): 215–38; and "Democratic Capitalism at the Cross-roads," *Democracy* 2 (1982): 52–68.

38. On the other hand, capital may be substituted for high-wage workers. See, for instance, Barry Bluestone and Bennett Harrison, *The Deindustrialization of America* (New York: Basic Books, 1982). While technological changes are embodied in capital investment, there is no determinate relationship between investment or capital-labor ratios and productivity growth. Nominal wage movements are, both by collective agreement and market behavior, linked to rates of inflation, whose inclusion as a regressor did not change any of the results.

39. Piven and Friedland, "Public Choice;" Friedland et al., "Political Conflict;" see also Roger Friedland, *Power and Crisis in the City* (New York: Schocken, 1983).

40. Cameron, "Expansion;" Wilensky, *Welfare State*; Schmidt, "Role."

41. Wilensky, *The Welfare State and Equality.*

42. R. Parks, "Efficient Estimation of a System of Regression Equations When Disturbances Are Both Serially and Contemporaneously Correlated," *Journal of the American Statistical Association* 62 (1967): 500–509; J. Kmenta, *Elements of Econometrics* (New York: Macmillan, 1971). For a more technical explication of the assumptions and statistical procedures, readers should consult Friedland and Sanders, "The Public Economy and Economic Growth in Western Market Economies."

43. See M. Hannan and A. Young, "Estimation in Panel Models: Results on Pooling Cross-Sections and Time Series," in D. Heise, ed., *Sociological Methodology* (San Francisco: Jossey-Bass, 1977), 52–83.

44. While our reason for modeling lagged endogenous variables is theoretical, this methodology is widely used in attempting to control for nonspecified variables. There are possible advantages and disadvantages to such a strategy. See, for example, A. Boardman and R. Murnane, "Using Panel Data to Improve Estimates of the Determinants of Educational Achievement," *Sociology of Education* 52 (1979): 113–21; K. Alexander, A. Pallas, and M. Cook, "Measure for Measure: On the Use of Endogenous Ability Data in School-Process Research," *American Sociological Review* 46 (1981): 619–31; and George Bohnstedt, "Observations on the Measurement of Change," in F. Borgatta, ed., *Sociological Methodology* (San Francisco: Jossey-Bass, 1969), 113–33. It is also plausible that the hypothesized trade-offs between the three sources of household income may occur simultaneously. This seems most probable for the relationship between the two forms of the social wage. However, the specification of our model does

not meet the order condition of identification necessary for meaningful estimation of nonrecursive relationships. Hence, estimation of the potentially reciprocal causal paths must await future study. In addition, it is possible that the effects of the variables we study operate differently than at time lags other than the one specified in our equations. Further, in the future, we intend to collect adequate information that will allow us to estimate instrumental variables to substitute for the lagged dependent variables. An instrumental variable is a proxy independent variable estimated in such a way as to be uncorrelated with the residual of an equation. In principle, an indirect least squares approach would be preferable to our present strategy. In practice, however, the bias in parameter estimates that could result from a nonzero covariance between an observed lagged dependent variable and the residual of an equation often is slight. Consequently, the use of observed lagged dependent variables (our current strategy) rather than instrumental lagged dependent variables is an accepted practice. As a crude check on whether our results appear to be influenced by covariation between the lagged and predicted dependent variables, we estimated equations with the difference or "change" between Y_t and Y_{t-1} as the dependent variable and omitted Y_{t-1} as a regressor. An undesirable assumption imposed by this strategy is that the direct metric relationship between Y_t and Y_{t-1} is constrained to equal 1.0. Sometimes this constraint may be reasonable but it is a hypothesis that can and should be tested rather than assumed. This assumption is not that inconsistent with our results (see Table 12.1). Thus we reestimated each equation with Y_t-Y_{t-1} as the dependent variable and deleted Y_{t-1} as a regressor. There were no sign changes nor meaningful differences in the parameter estimates among statistically significant variables in either equation. One or two substantively trivial and statistically nonsignificant estimates reversed signs in each equation. However, in every case these estimates remained nonsignificant substantively and statistically. The uniformity of each equation's estimates across the two specifications also indicates that the direct influences of the remaining regressors operate independently of the lagged dependent variable in each equation. This means that removing Y_{t-1} as a regressor in our "change" equations did not compromise the comparisons made between the alternative specifications. Hence it would appear to be reasonable to conclude that our specification of observed rather than instrumental lagged dependent variables does not bias the findings. In terms of the mean squared error, the equations reported in Table 12.1 are preferable to all alternatives we examined.

45.   Pooling across countries and across time entails the difficult choice of metric. We chose current U.S. exchange rates and 1963 prices. As a result, our measures of government spending and economic activity may be different from deflated series derived from national currency estimates. This is because of the cross-national and temporal variation in exchange rates. This is particularly problematic in the post-1971 period of floating exchange rates. Our results, therefore, might be contingent upon the choice of metric. To assess this possibility, an analysis using another currency or weighted basket of currencies could be conducted. Also, if the data were not so limited, it would be possible to reanalyze the data weighted by purchasing power parities.

46.   Sources include *National Accounts of OECD Countries,* Volumes 1 and 2, *Main Aggregates and Detailed Tables* (Paris: Organization for Economic Corporation and Development, 1950–1982); also *Main Economic Indicators, Historical Statistics* (1960–1979); *Europa Yearbook,* Volumes 1 and 2 (London: Europa Publications, 1962–1982); *Yearbook of Labor Statistics* (Geneva: International Labor Office, 1962–1982); *Statistical Yearbook* (New York: United Nations, 1962–1981); and *Demographic Yearbook* (New York: United Nations, 1961–1981). We also measured wages as the hourly earnings of female and male full-time workers in manufacturing (United Nations, 1962–1981) in order to as-

sess whether average compensation per worker operated similarly to measures of hourly compensation. We found that the determinants of the two were more or less identical.

47. A number of readers have pointed to the potential noncomparability of left parties in the United States and Canada with those in Europe. We chose to control for these parties because they do represent the left-of-center alternative. Our measurements of the potential political power of Democrats in the U.S. government differs from that employed for other countries due to the unique form of government in the United States. Because Democrats held majority control of both Houses of Congress throughout the period we studied, to consider Democrats as being out of the government during Republican presidencies would clearly be unwarranted. While our weighting procedure is somewhat arbitrary, we feel that it is reasonable. Further, our results are not sensitive to alternative weightings.

48. A reader pointed out that the left parties measured in Canada and the United States have limited comparability to those in Western Europe. We reestimated the model with Canada and the United States omitted. The only significant result affected by their exclusion was the attenuation of the impact of growth on public services. This also casts doubts on the supposed exceptionalism of North America.

49. OECD; *United Nations.*

50. Cameron, "Expansion"; Castles, *The Impact of Parties.*

51. To check the sensitivity of this result to our measurement of compensation, we reran the same equation using hourly wage rates for male and female workers in manufacturing in constant 1963 U.S. dollars. Again transfers depress the growth in hourly wage rates, but the level of public service has no effect. This is only one of two findings that do not replicate between the two equations (see Table 12.2).

52. To check the sensitivity of this result to our measurement of compensation, we reestimated the same real wage equation using hourly wage rates for male and female workers in manufacturing in constant U.S. dollars. Again, transfers depress the growth in hourly wage rates, but the net association between hourly wage rates and public services is not statistically significant. In this time series analyses, Hibbs also found a positive effect of unemployment growth on nominal wages.

53. Michael Kalecki, "Political Aspects of Full Employment," in Ferguson and Rogers, *The Political Economy.* Gosta Esping-Andersen has criticized expenditure studies of the welfare state for neglecting the structure of welfare state regimes. "Social policy," he writes, "is not just a battle over money and rights, but also over principles of stratification." In his cross-national correlation study, he found that left party power had a negative impact on the use of means-tested public assistance and of stratified social insurance during the 1970s in eighteen capitalist nations. See "Power and Distributional Regimes," *Politics and Society* 14, no. 2 (1985): 223–56. The impact of social wages upon private wage behavior is probably conditional upon the structure of the welfare state.

54. Robert Althauser and Arne L. Kalleberg, "Firms, Occupations, and the Structure of Labor Markets: A Conceptual Analysis," in Ivar Berg, ed., *Sociological Perspectives on Labor Markets and Manpower Analysis* (Lexington, Mass.: Heath, 1971); James N. Baron and William T. Bielby, "Bringing the Firm Back In: Stratification, Segmentation, and the Organization of Work," *American Sociological Review* 45 (1980): 737–65; Peter B. Doeringer and Michael J. Piore, *Internal Labor Markets and Manpower Analysis,* (Lexington, Mass.: Heath, 1971).

55. This interpretation is not consistent with analyses of the U.S. labor market which show the differential between primary and secondary market wage rates going down under conditions of higher unemployment. See Michael Reich, "Segmented Labor: Time Series, Hypothesis, and Evidence," *Cambridge Journal of Economics* 8, no. 1 (1984): 63–82.

56. Freeman, "Unionism." Because labor costs tend to be fixed in the short-run in high-wage, highly unionized sectors, large firms in these highly concentrated sectors tend to react by cutting output and laying off workers. Thus real wages and unemployment can be increasing simultaneously. See Martin L. Weitzman, *The Share Economy: Conquering Stagflation* (Cambridge, Mass.: Harvard University Press, 1984).

57. Piven and Cloward, *The New Class War.*

58. See Gosta Esping-Andersen and Walter Korpi, "From Poor Relief to Institutional Welfare States," in R. Eriksson et al., eds., *Welfare Research and Welfare Society* (New York: M. E. Sharpe, 1984); Castles, *Impact*; Schmidt, "Role"; Stephens, "Transition"; Cameron, "Expansion"; and S. Borg and F. Castles, "The Influence of the Political Right on Public Income Maintenance Expenditure and Equality," *Political Studies* 29 (1981): 604–21.

59. See Gosta Esping-Andersen, "Politics against Markets: De-commodification in Social Policy," paper presented at the Arne Ryde Symposium on the Economics of Social Security (Lund: 1981).

60. Some have argued that military spending puts a constraint on civilian expenditure in the advanced market economies. See, for example, Wilensky, *Welfare State.* Recent work on the United States finds no trade-off. See Bruce Russett, "Defense Expenditures and National Well-Being," *American Political Science Review* 76 (1982): 767–77. We have not considered it here, but will do so in future research.

61. Wilensky, *The Welfare State and Equality.*

62. See the work of Peterson, *City Limits.* Max Weber made the same argument long ago.

63. Cameron, "Expansion"; Castles, "The Impact of Parties."

64. O'Connor, *The Fiscal Crisis of the State.*

Part V

Entrepreneurship

13

Visions of American management in postwar France

LUC BOLTANSKI

Historical studies of Franco-American relations in the years following World War II, whether French or American, scholarly reports or personal accounts, have until now mainly dealt with diplomatic, military, and financial relations.[1] Always politically colored and controversial, the French debate on "Americanization," especially in the mid-1960s when France left the Atlantic Alliance and de Gaulle opposed the purchase of certain French companies by American firms, and then in the May 1968 period and during the Vietnam war, acted as a sort of projective test in which the different groups devised a partial – in both senses of the term – image of the United States implicitly defined with respect to their respective positions in the French social structure and their related interests. To each his own "good" and "bad" America; it could be demonstrated, for example, that criticism of the Vietnam war and of "imperialism" also contributed, through the exaltation of the hippie movement, sit-ins, and protest songs, to the diffusion of an enchanted image of the U.S.A.

In this ambiguous debate, a period of recent cultural history seems to have been somewhat forgotten or repressed, the period from the Liberation to the beginning of the 1960s. Yet the "discovery" of America dominates French social and intellectual life as of 1945, and the interrogations accompanying it concern far more than just the military alliance or economic aid. Or, to be more precise, the economic and military questions are quite explicitly subordinated to the more fundamental question of the "nature" of "French society" compared to "American society," that is, indissociably, the nature of its political regime and its social structure, its economic management techniques, and its methods of social control and of solving social conflicts. How can American dominance be explained? What can be learned from the United States? What should be rejected? What should be adopted or imported?

At the heart of these questions lie the social problematics which arise in the immediate postwar period concerning the nature of company management. What should the *cadres* be? Whom should they be? How can they be recruited, trained, and supervised so that they are both "efficient" and tolerated by the working class? Social technologies (such as group psychology) were first imported from the U.S. in order to reform the traditional bosses (*patrons*) and to train middle-management personnel. Their diffusion toward other fields (social work, even school systems or the Church) later contributed to generalizing these new forms of social control.

The following analysis is an attempt to re-create the intellectual and political atmosphere in which, from 1945 to about 1955, a new industrial ideology and a new image of the social space took shape (and was to become dominant in the 1960s), by reviewing documents and personal accounts in relatively different fields, from the managerial press to "role-playing seminars," bearing in mind the risks that such a thematic collection implies, the greatest of which is certainly to suggest the existence of an "invisible hand": the "foreign hand." While it is necessary to recall the obvious relation between, for instance, the action taken on the initiative of international administrations which arose from the Marshall Plan and certain changes – ideological in particular – which affected France in the 1950s, it can be taken for granted that official speeches and programs would have remained without effect had they not found the means to become efficient within the historical context and in existing social structures. And it could be endlessly debated as to whether postwar society would have changed in the same way and as strongly in the absence of a concerted, organized effort.[2]

Productivity missions in the United States

Human engineering and American-style management were introduced into France during the economic changes which, latent in the first Monnet Plan (and, before, in the Economic and Social Plan of the National Resistance Committee), developed mainly around the 1950s with the Marshall Plan and the grouping and reorganization operations which marked the period from 1948 to 1953, even before the creation of the European Coal and Steel Community.[3] Undertaking to modernize the economy was not merely a matter of technology. Its application was not just in material objects, blast furnaces, or rolling mills. Partly inspired by the American economic authorities who required training of a group of economically competent and politically sure native "managers" in order to obtain funds[4] (as well as, in general, the establishment of a stable social order capable of restraining the rise of the French Communist

Party, particularly after the big strikes of 1947),[5] it was presented quite plainly as an attempt to transform French society in its whole, stressing action on men and women, on their "mentality" and "structures," and on intergroup and interclass relations.

In 1948 the Commissariat Général au Plan was created, with a subcommittee on productivity presided over by Jean Fourastié, who established the "French program for productivity." The program included "establishing documents and statistics on productivity, dispatching experienced managers to the U.S., and training men capable of teaching productivity." Subsequently, the Comité Provisoire de la Productivité (Provisional Productivity Committee) was created in 1949; then in 1950, the Association Française pour l'Accroissement de la Productivité or "AFAP"; and finally, in 1953, the Commissariat Général à la Productivité, directed by Gabriel Ardant (who was a close associate of Pierre Mendès-France). One of the main duties of AFAP, which was awarded substantial American funds on its creation, was to organize productivity missions to the United States. In 1949 the head of the Bureau of Technology and Productivity of the U.S. Department of Labor was sent to France, where he investigated 120 companies and contributed to the elaboration of the French productivity program. From about 1950 to 1953, AFAP organized more than 450 productivity missions to the U.S. involving over 4,000 members, bosses, engineers, managers (approximately 45 percent of the "missionaries"), trade union representatives (approximately 25 percent, excluding representatives of the CGT, as they did not approve the AFAP program), top executives, economists, psychologists, and sociologists (approximately 30 percent), etc.[6] The effort to rationalize enterprises, which inspired the productivity missions to the U.S., was not limited to technology nor even to organization and methods. As noted by the first "missionaries," "France's lag in productivity . . . is not due to technological backwardness," since French technology "is similar to and sometimes better than" American technology: "On the whole, American equipment was no surprise to the French technicians."[7] The "slow" French economy was not due to any technological deficiency or incompetence on the part of French engineers.[8]

The wonder-struck discovery of the American "productivity spirit," of "psychological factors," of the "new concept of human factors in industry"[9] can be found in most reports. The productivity missions were intended by their promoters mainly to transform in depth the "spirit," the way of "being" and "thinking" of economic agents. A brief review of the reports by the different missions suffices to show that importing social technology had priority over transferring material technology. Priority imports were to be the "scientific" management models and "rational" company management, in order to promote the "climate" of American companies in French firms. This climate was the product of technology, but of a new technology, which depended not only on engineering know-how, but also, above all, on social sciences, psychology, and sociology.

Thus, all the reports on productivity include, with a practically ritual frequency, an appeal to "staff cooperation in firms."[10] The inauguration of a "climate" of productivity, of a "spirit" of productivity, is to accomplish what corporatism could not, but through other means. It is to succeed, where corporatism failed, at the cost of sacrifices and self-denial, changes and mutations which are the condition for survival. The Americans showed how to substitute flexibility for toughness, "communication" for secrecy, "dialogue" for authority, "generosity," the most fruitful of investments, for greed. First, relations with trade unions should be changed, "for their role in current American management seems increasingly important." Acknowledge them, make them "participate" and "cooperate." At least, that is what was attempted with the "free union confederations," whose representatives participated in the productivity missions to the United States and which associated in 1951 to create the Interunion Center of Productivity Studies and Research.

Once the "climate of trust" is established, redistribution of productivity profits, which should be partially recycled into wages (a considerable innovation with respect to the 1920s and 1930s when the very large profits from increased productivity had had practically no effect on the evolution of wages, thus contributing to triggering the crisis of 1929 and making "recovery" very difficult), will contribute to maintaining "cooperation between employers and workers."[11] Again, the example of the United States is to be followed because "American productivity" "is partly due to the fact that American workers have generally become aware of the influence of productivity on their standard of living and on the standard of living of the entire nation."[12]

The American "experts" sent to France within the framework of the Marshall Plan concentrated their criticism on French company managers and bosses. Pointing out that the "constructive attitude shown by workers" in the U.S. depended mainly on the "constructive attitude of the management," they condemned French managers in particular for "being opposed to any constructive change," "not taking into account the future when making plans," "not giving enough responsibility and authority to their subordinates," not paying enough attention to "human factors" and to "respect of worker dignity": they encouraged them to "adopt an attitude of realistic optimism, enthusiasm and self-confidence, confidence in their subordinates and in the future of their firm," to "make communication between management and labor easier in

both directions," to "apply sound methods regarding human relations," and finally to "give workers the feeling that they are participating in the company" (which does not necessarily mean, the report specifies, "their participation in company profits or the management").
Above all, said the "experts," French firms should find devoted and efficient "middle-management" personnel and first of all learn how to
train them: "The Americans were quite surprised to note the complete
absence of any university training for industrial management." In particular, there was no business administration training, which is the
only type which could "make Europe admit the principle that industrial
business administration is a profession," but neither were there any
courses on marketing or sales; companies were "often assured of the
collaboration of the most competent engineers in the production units,
but were hardly preoccupied by the aptitudes and training of their sales
managers." "The recruitment and training of sales managers must be
improved" and "dynamic, methodical prospection of new markets"
promoted by "reinforcement of marketing research and studies." Training of new managers and the creation of business administration
schools, as well as "perfecting the skills of current managers," thus
constituted "fundamental duties." "Meetings, conferences and study
sessions" should be developed, "more works concerning industrial
business administration, books, handbooks and journals should be
published in the native language"; "study groups, conferences, evening and weekend classes" should be multiplied; "regular visits of lec-
turers and animators" should be organized, particularly "American experts in Europe to participate in that type of project"; "French teams"
should be sent "to the United States to follow study courses of about a
year"; "a program should be elaborated in order to encourage the creation of specialized associations" capable of "spurring progress in
know-how in the many fields of scientific work organization," etc. But,
in addition, the "attitude of the management" and of the managers
should also "be changed": "The most delicate project is to develop
techniques and methods which will help this change take place."[13]

The productivity campaign, with "productivity actions" and "productivity missions" to the U.S., was one of the consequences of the
Marshall Plan. This was not particular to France. Organized by the
OEEC, the "missions" were organized all over Western Europe.[14]
Nevertheless, the mediations through which the missions took effect
cannot be grasped without abandoning the mechanistic diffusion
models which they invoke, a universal determinism of an economic and
technical nature (which is often the case among the engineers in companies undergoing reorganization who introduced American business
administration techniques into France) or "imperialist violence." This

is necessary in order to analyze, on the one hand, the collision of the American model and the older French image; and, on the other hand, the struggles within the French bourgeoisie concerning the introduction and diffusion of the American model. In these struggles, the *cadres* hold a central position, in more than one way: they are both the privileged agents (in particular through their organizations) and one of the main stakes, their conversion to the new economic ideology being one of the top priority goals set for the productivity missions.

America: youth, success, beauty, the future[15]

For the image of the modern *cadre* to emerge in the postwar period as being "skilled in handling management techniques," it is paradoxically necessary to set aside "managerial movements" and turn our attention to those who seem more like their adversaries: Catholic or socialist government officials from the Resistance, newly salaried bosses of nationalized firms, and the ensuing planners, economists, organizers, sociologists, psychologists, etc. At the service of the state, attached to defending the public domain, hostile toward the *patronat* and in general toward the private sector which they suspected of individualism and egotism, sensitive to "working-class" problems, "exploitation," and "poverty," they were the main sources and company spokesmen of modernization of French society. They demanded modernization for both progressive and nationalistic reasons: first, to block the road to "totalitarianism," that is to stop communism from growing further and to make any return to fascism impossible; and, second, to restore national power on the international scene, with respect to the United States in particular. Modernization of the economy and of society was mainly the expression of a will and political line which demanded, in order to be instituted, either the liquidation or the transformation of two potentially dangerous classes: the "red" one, or working class; and the "black" one, or traditional petty bourgeoisie, where the various forms of fascism found their most solid bases.

The American models could not have been diffused so extensively or so rapidly if the Marshall Plan administration had not decided on actions in the interests of this reformist avant-garde. The latter did not identify itself with any association or party, it was free of any formal organization or instruments of representation, it had neither emblem nor clear-cut contours, but its members were related to one another by a chain of personal contacts, in a network-like structure which prolonged the armed network of the Resistance through peace and in the logical sequence of selective affinities. By reconstructing chains of cross references (in oral or written accounts), by going up the streams of interrelations, of ideological heritage, of political allegiance or alliance, two main characters can be found at the intersection of the different networks: on the one hand, Jean Monnet, who orchestrated the productivity campaign;[16] and, on the other hand, Pierre Mendès-France, whom the reformers saw, according to numerous accounts,[17] as the "only" politician capable of carrying out "modernization" and "democratization" of French society. Pierre Mendès-France had close ties with Pierre Dreyfus, Georges Boris, Alfred Sauvy, and with the young progressive economists of the Plan: Hirsch, Marjolin, Ripert, Massé, Dumontier, and above all Pierre Uri, along with Gabriel Ardant, who was commissioner of productivity, François Block-Lainé and the SEEF economists who created the instruments of national accounting, Claude Gruson (to whom Bock-Lainé entrusted creation of the SEEF) and his collaborate Simon Nora, with whom he had special ties since Nora was Jean-Jacques Servan-Schreiber's "best friend" (according to various sources). Servan-Schreiber mobilized his family, his clientele and his paper around Pierre Mendès-France: the history of *L'Express*, says Françoise Giroud (see below), is "the history of a group of people who wanted with all their might to make France take off: the idea was to put Mendès-France and his ideas in power, in action, for the best [interests] of France."

The strategic position of the Schreiber family in the progressive, modernistic avant-garde of the 1950s is due less to their directly political stands and actions than to their talent combining agents and groups previously quite separate, even socially opposed (top executives, intellectuals, bosses, etc.), and at appropriating the sometimes antagonistic values attached to such agents and groups. They thus contributed toward designing and imposing a relatively new type of culture.

The relevant characteristics dispersed among the members of the economic and political vanguard were highly concentrated among the Schreibers, who were undoubtedly predisposed – paradigmatically – to incarnate the values of the "new bourgeoisie." The family had only recently risen to bourgeois status, was of Jewish origin, and, as is often the case in Jewish families (and, to a lesser extent, in Protestant families), where the minority situation tends to maintain group cohesion by attenuating divisions between fractions, it included several overlapping social circles: journalists, businessmen, civil servants, politicians, and university scholars. The Jewish bourgeoisie, or what was left of it after the war, was quite present in the 1950s avant-garde. Its members seem to have been ahead of their time, though this had nothing to do with the Jewish culture or religion as such (Jewish intellectuals found their political roots in republican universalism or *radical* – in the French sense – or socialist inspiration). Their "lucidity" was the result of the collective exclusion that the practically unanimous anti-Semitism on the part of the dominant factions of the French ruling class had imposed on them during the 1930s and the German Occupation. Anti-Semitism contributed toward driving them "left," away from Vichy, from the fascist illusion and corporatist utopia. It made them feel closer to Great Britain and the United States, where they sometimes took refuge. Nationalistic – often passionately – having for the most part fought in the Resistance, these survivors attained positions of power or symbolic authority in 1945 at an age when, in the previous generation, the young bourgeois entered society. They were predisposed to embody "youth" not only because they were young but also because the war had cut them off from their past, their roots, their class. The Liberation gave them a future by acknowledging their merits, rewarding them with military medals and scholarly titles. Against the "established bourgeoisie," against the "old values" and the "old families," whose decline had been somewhat accelerated by the fall of Vichy, they embodied the "new values" and could validly deny their belonging to the ruling class, with which they also had personal scores to settle.

Their difference was mainly expressed in "personal values" (intelligence, efficiency, competence, "professional" work – as opposed to amateurism) but also in a special life-style, a combination of aggressive asceticism and American-style informalism: contempt for food and French "gastronomy" (the well known "lunches" at L'Express magazine with sandwiches and airline-like lunch trays), for alcohol, for high society, for "bourgeois" mannerisms, for sexual hypocrisy, and for traditional education. They were also avant-garde feminists, and in particular, through Françoise Giroud, the founders of the Family Planning Movement. What was meant by the term "new wave," coined by Françoise Giroud in 1955 to designate L'Express readers ("the young people's paper"), was an original, informal, dynamic way of being bourgeois, a way of living which had not yet become an art of living, in conformity with the stereotyped images of the United States and a value system which was relatively original, at least for France. It was at the crossroads of the quality principles on which capitalist enterprise is based and the civil servant spirit including the values of the entrepreneur taking risks and following the work ethic as well as being a good business administrator and an honest executive; a sense of "service," of "democracy," and collective responsibility (as opposed to profit-seeking for profit's sake and exclusive attachment to private interests).

The second alternative: from corporatism to the New Deal

The sort of fascination America exerted on the French avant-garde in the 1950s was identical with the criticism of the traditional right, of bosses intent on defending "caste interests" and "bourgeois elites" which had "failed to accomplish their misssions."[18] The social image of the America of the 1950s, even in the midst of the cold war and Mc-Carthyism, was that of the New Deal, economic planning, and the anti-fascist struggle.

It is impossible to understand the relationship that the French avant-garde entertained with the United States in the 1950s, particularly the former Resistance members, without briefly reviewing the image of the U.S. in France in the 1930s, at the time when most of the avant-garde constituted their intellectual and political concepts of the social world and perceived the political significance of those images. At the end of the 1920s and in the 1930s, anti-Americanism grew in the French ruling class, especially among intellectuals; and critical studies, "theoretical" essays as well as travelers' accounts, became increasingly numerous until the end of the decade. Most of the authors were not of Marxist, socialist, or communist persuasion since leftists were absorbed mainly by the evolution of Soviet Russia, and through internationalism, were insensitive to arguments about growing American power being a threat to Europe and France. Even before the New Deal, they tended to view the development of American capitalism as "positive": according to most observers during the period between the wars, it was character-ized by economic concentration, mechanization, and mass production.

Anti-Americanism developed from the right, and to be precise, from the young right, Ordre Nouveau, the upholders of traditional Catholi-cism who, since the end of the nineteenth century, had associated "lib-eral Catholicism" with American Catholicism.[19] Many of the most vio-lent critics of American society were to become associated, a few years later, with fascist movements or become active supporters of Vichy (this was the case, for example, of Lucien Romier, one of the most well-known critics of American "materialism,"[20] as well as Alfred Fabre-Luce,[21] Paul Morand, and Henri Massis).

For these critics, anti-Americanism was not founded merely on the diplomatic conflicts which opposed France to the United States after World War I, concerning, for instance, war reparations or disarma-ment.[22] Neither could it be reduced to nationalism, which is neverthe-less what inspired the first criticism of "American imperialism" as "fi-nancial imperialism"[23] (different from, though in a way as "dangerous" as, military imperialism), and also the first debates on American in-vestments in Europe, the latter having increased considerably between the two World Wars, especially in the electronic industry (with the im-plantation of ITT) and in the oil business.[24]

More profoundly, anti-Americanism was aimed at what had become symbols of the U.S.: mass production, Taylorism, the assembly line, mass consumption – multiplying uniform objects – advertising which "violated" consciences, in short, "mass society," and with it, at least implicitly, a form of society considered since the nineteenth century to be the archetype of democracy. The assembly line, for example, which travelers of the early 1920s hailed, had become, ten years later, no longer the symbol of efficiency and progress, but of American "materialism," of mass society, even a special form of collectivism which the most extremist critics, such as Alfred Fabre-Luce or Lucien Romier, considered a variety of Communist Bolshevism: "Neither Ford nor Lenin." These are some of the themes of personalism, which, particularly as interpreted by Ordre Nouveau, are based on a series of oppositions between the "material" and the "spiritual," the "individual" and the "person," "public opinion" and "consciousness," etc.[25] In contrast to the "standardized" man of American mass society (the term *babettisation* was used in the 1930s), writers of the Young Right (or of Social Catholicism) endorsed the peasant or artisan, the individual entrepreneur, the responsible company owner, holding a patrimony, uniting in one man both capital and labor, both manager and worker, in the worker's sense of the term.

Corporatism is not only opposed to Soviet Bolshevism but also to mass society as exemplified by the United States. The rhetoric of the "alternative way" (*troisième voie*) is not completely intelligible if it is not understood that it superimposes references to political regimes (communism vs. liberal democracy), social classes (proletariat vs. plutocratic oligarchy), and national cultures (American materialism vs. Soviet materialism). In this system of oppositions, there is a homology between corporatism (or fascism), the middle class and "Europe" (anti-Americanism and the trend supporting the "European idea" develop in parallel, at least until the beginnings of World War II). These collective persons, of different sizes and natures, are characterized by identical properties and values: ancient roots in the land, spiritualism, refinement and culture, respect of the individual, and richness of "personal" relations. Europe opposes its "civilization" to the "masses" in both East and West, to the "hordes." In certain respects, the "alternative" discourse constitutes a transformation of the binary schema (masses vs. elites) which, at least since the beginning of the nineteenth century, had dominated conservative thought.

Opposing the apocalyptic visions of America conveyed by the prefascist right is the often benign conception of the "modernists," whether reformist liberals or socialists. The former, such as Hyacinthe Dubreuil[26] or Emile Schreiber,[27] considered automation and rational industrial engineering instruments of collective enrichment and, at least eventually, of worker emancipation. Like certain socialists – for instance, George Boris or Robert Margolin[28] – they were passionately interested in the New Deal, though interpretations varied according to the political and social positions of the interpreters. For the liberals with close business ties (such as Emile Schreiber), the New Deal was supposed to reestablish the free enterprise system on a more sound basis; for the socialists, particularly interested in "code" policy, the New Deal could lead to an original form of socialism.

However, while Emile Schreiber's vision of America – Taylorism and capitalistic industrial rationalization – hardly corresponds to Georges Boris's or Pierre Mendès-France's image of a pre-socialist America, the progressive democrats at least agreed on considering the New Deal not only an alternative to capitalism and Bolshevism, but above all an alternative to corporatism and fascism, which were defined by the same oppositions. The New Deal was an intermediary solution between old private capitalism and state-run socialism which, contrary to fascism, respected democracy. With the historical defeat of fascism (which had been presented as an "original" response to the 1930s economic crisis), the second "alternative" became the only ideology available with a solution to the crisis. An ideology and a substitute social technology were being sought, an association of planning, reformism, and liberalism, such as the New Deal, or at least the New Deal as presented by the progressive factions of the French bourgeoisie, rejecting the solutions to the class problem (particularly the problem of the middle classes) fascism had planned, and taking into account the reversal of the political situation following the fall of Vichy. That made it necessary to create or adopt a relatively new image of the political and social space, a "circular" political system in which the extreme right connects with the extreme left, and a social system based on a time vector, with on the one hand, the declining groups, that is, the traditionalist middle classes, and on the other hand, the rising future-oriented groups in which the salaried bourgeoisie (that is, the *cadres*) dominate.[29]

This second "alternative" no longer required an authoritarian organization of class relations because it implied the progressive disappearance of class divisions while economic growth continued. Following the "discovery" of America, the ideological undertaking of defining the common denominator between *cadres* and bosses, the relevant feature capable of justifying the appeal to their union, was not only to be rejected, but reversed. The *cadres* became identified as the opposite of small employers, of the traditionalist, Malthusian, Poujadist middle classes, that is, those destined to vanish; and along with the *cadres* were the new middle classes whom the *cadres* represented, the only group capable of conveying the fantasy of the "third choice," the "third party." The rise of the *cadres* meant the birth of a social order in which the opposition between the bosses and the proletariat was to be transcended both by the dissolution of property (the "bosses" became salaried workers), which makes the basic Marxist criterion obsolete – the position in production relations – and by the expected disappearance of the opposition between manual and mental work through the progress of automation.

In corporatism, social order was viewed as a construction of solids; it now became analogous rather to a liquid state undergoing "currents," slightly different from a "flow," or a gas, a stochastic aggregate of independent molecules (high government officials, engineering school graduates, use – and misuse – images borrowed from thermodynamics). Although certain strata or layers can still be distinguished within this "mass," they remain unstable and tend to fade and fuse. They all converge on a new focus, the new center of gravity around which society revolves: the middle class. But the term is no longer understood in the corporatist sense (heritage and family). Instead, it refers to the American middle class, the enormous aggregate of people working in the tertiary sector, having a comfortable, average standard of living, uniform values, integrated in large "organizations," individualistic, dominated by the spirit of competition and the pursuit of a successful career. The transformation of the "traditional" middle class into an American-style middle class was to provide the most turbulent Western European countries (Germany and the Latin countries) with access to political stability.

In a well-known article reviewing the changes in European politics and the causes of the decline of ideologies, Seymour Martin Lipset sees these changes as converging toward the emergence of a "new middle class" consisting of technicians and *cadres* who stabilize the tensions between classes by rewarding moderate parties and penalizing extremist parties. They encourage the policy of collective bargaining; they favor increased productivity, which by allowing a juster distribution of consumer goods and education, reduces social tension and consequently discourages resort to extremist ideologies. They acknowledge scientific thought, professionalism, and expert authority in those fields which are at the root of political controversy; they thus constitute the most representative group of post-industrial or post-bourgeois society in which achievement overrides ascription and universalism rules over particularism, and whose ultimate form is the most technologically advanced society, the United States, representing the future of Western Europe.[30]

It was also in the 1950s that the term "new middle classes" became more widely used to designate those factions of the salaried middle classes who worked in large companies, were technically competent, and had a high level of education – that is, mainly, technicians and *cadres* – as opposed to the artisans, shopkeepers, and entrepreneurs, who comprised the "traditional" middle classes.[31]

L'Express: the magazine for cadres

This new social image was not accepted immediately without any reactions or conflicts; most of the traditional right mobilized against it. In the 1950s, opposition to both communism and fascism was not just a figure of ideological rhetoric, but the objective position of Mendès's followers in that area of the political spectrum between the Communist Party and the Pétain-inspired or fascist right. The latter was represented by Maurice Gingembre and the Confédération Générale des Petites et Moyennes Entreprises, or "CGPME," which, in association with the Confédération Générale des Cadres, the CGC, supported Pinay and Laniel,[32] and as of 1954 by Pierre Poujade's Union de Défense des Commerçants et Artisans, the "UDCA." Poujade, although in conflict with Gingembre, shared his main enemy, "Mendès and his clique," and also used the slogan "Mendès in Jerusalem."[33] The opposition between Pierre Mendès-France and Antoine Pinay was highly symbolic for the fascist right-wingers: it was the reincarnation of an archetype (France, common sense, and the Land versus the stateless Jews, intellectuals, and demagogues) – a paradigmatic expression of which can be found in *Mendès ou Piney* by Alfred Fabre-Luce (who published the book under the pseudonym of Sapiens).[34]

The reactionary forces, among which CGC played an important part, as seen above, struggled both for the survival of the traditional *petit partonat* (owners of small businesses), small farmers, and shopkeepers, and to maintain the immediate interests of the *cadres* in the private sector (maintenance of the hierarchy in wages, lower taxes, and increased authority), as well as for continued colonial occupation of Indochina and North Africa.

Conversely, Servan-Schreiber repeatedly stated that the struggle for decolonization and for modernization of the economy were inseparably linked, the former being given priority only because it conditioned the latter. At the end of the Algerian war, Servan-Schreiber changed *L'Express* from a political paper into an American-style news magazine. His response (as well as that of Françoise Giroud) to criticism of this was that *L'Express* had not changed and that the 1964 weekly was in accord with the original project, which had simply been postponed by the colonial wars ("such a waste of time," said Servan-Schreiber to Roger Priouret in 1968). As early as 1954, *L'Express* – which was later to call itself the magazine for *cadres* – demanded certain changes characteristic of the 1960s such as company concentration, industrial engineering, increased productivity, higher wages, increased consumption, and better managerial training. *L'Express* was also to contribute to training competent managers and *cadres*, and, in general, to a vulgarization of economics.

Faith in the virtues of "economic information" was shared by management pioneers and the enlightened government officials of the Plan or the Ministry of Finance, who all believed that France's "economic lag" was mainly due to the policy on the part of employers of keeping business operations secret and to the ignorance of the *cadres*, whether salaried or independent: prejudice and *a priori* views were considered "obstacles to the harmonious development of the economy. . . . Modern democracy requires widespread knowledge of economics. . . . " Thus, for example, only "education of public opinion" could "make income policy operative."[35] Rational management of the economy required informed – and therefore rational – producers and consumers, whose economic behavior was consistent with the laws of economics and who were at least willing to acknowledge the rationale of the decisions made in their names by experts.[36]

The Schreiber family is again responsible for the emergence of the *cadre*-oriented press, whose growing influence in the mid-1960s contributed greatly to constituting, defining, and diffusing the Schreiber image popularized in the 1960s. The history of the Schreiber family press summarizes the development of the economic press in France as a whole. In the first third of the century, Emile Schreiber founded *Les Echos*, originally a journal for announcements, which until the 1950s and 1960s constituted the stronghold of the Schreibers' growing political influence. In 1953 *L'Express* was published (in its first few months as a weekly supplement to *Les Echos*) and then in 1967, the business magazine *L'Expansion*, directed by the youngest Servan-Schreiber brother, Jean-Louis. *Les Echos*, which had approximately 40,000 subscribers in the 1950s, was mainly geared to employers. In the postwar years, only financial and stock market journals existed, such as *La Côte Desfossés* or *La Vie Française*, a financial weekly founded in 1945 with a circulation of 150,000. On the whole, the financial press was tightly controlled by employers (a journalist claimed that a telephone call from the Centre National du Patronat Français, the CNPF, could have an article changed or deleted).

At the end of the 1950s, a new type of economic press appeared, consisting of monthly papers with circulations of often less than 25,000: *Direction, L'Economie, Economie Contemporaine, La France Industrielle*, and, above all, *Enterprise*, which had the highest circulation (40,000) and whose editor-in-chief, Michel Drancourt, was a popular spokesman of progressive employers and modern managers.[37] Journals for *cadres* mainly developed in the mid-1960s with the creation by Jean-Louis Servan-Schreiber of the bimonthly *L'Expansion,* whose editor-in-chief was Jean Boissonnat (a progressive Catholic who had worked at *Esprit*). Founded on an American model (*Fortune*), *L'Expansion,* with a circulation of 150,000, was explicitly geared toward the *cadres* in general. It taught them how to manage their careers (in particular by publishing a yearly survey on wage scales or the "price" of *cadres*), provided information on large corporation operations and interviews with their managers, and served in general as a guide for "young" or "junior" *cadres* to make their way through the business world. It was also used (just as the new *L'Express*) as a sort of *savoir-vivre* manual: the portraits of the leaders, the advertising images, the career analyses, and the interviews all supplied the newcomer with identification patterns and quality scales. (This is quite comparable to the role of the weekly *Le Nouvel Observateur* among intellectuals.) For *L'Expansion,* the policy was quite clear: the journal, said one of its editors, is for *cadres* "the mirror that reflects their image and cultivates their narcissism." Jean-Jacques Servan-Schreiber himself is now one of the most successful incarnations of the "American-style" French manager his elders ever dreamed of.

The management industry

However, the *cadres* press could not have had a homogenizing effect on values and life-styles if it had not been preceded by the creation of institutions to reform the business bourgeoisie and petty bourgeoisie by instilling the values of the American middle-class stereotype. According to Michel Beaud, in order to understand how "concentration and heavy accumulation of capital to the benefit of monopolies" had occurred, "without any strong protest on the part of the classes and fractions of classes submitted to liquidation and submission,[38] it is important to examine the institutional instruments for readaptation created mainly with the framework of the Marshall Plan or in relation to it. Their main function was to assist the purely economic undertaking of restructuring industry: mainly intended to organize *cadres* management, they also helped members of the traditional factions of the petty bourgeoisie to convert their identity. Increasingly, the latter were to define themselves as *cadres,* but, although they may have claimed the title, they had neither the privileges nor the properties associated with it in the paradigmatic image.

The list of organisms, groups, seminars, and sessions, devoted to *cadres* and also to employers, created from approximately 1950 to 1965, is endless. The first such institutions seem to have been founded under the direct impulse of AFAP, which incited management consultants, trade unions, and professional associations to create or develop training programs for management, human relations, sales, and marketing.

That was the case, for instance, of the Commission Nationale d'Organisation Française, or CNOP, which developed the Ecole d'Organisation Scientifique du Travail, the EOST, and set up various training programs for cadres,[39] as well as for the Paris Chamber of Commerce which founded the Centre de Préparation aux Affaires, the CPA. During the same period, the Lille Chamber of Commerce created the Centre d'Etudes des Problèmes Industriels. The Centre de Formation et de Perfectionnement in association with the Association Nationale des Chefs du Personnel created a system of study groups in plants, a French adaptation of the American "Training Within Industry" (TWI) method. It also organized "dinner-debates" and invited public figures involved in labor relations (such as Hyacinthe Dubreuil and André Siegfried). The Centre Français du Patronat Chrétien, CFPC, founded a school called "Ecole des Chefs d'Entreprise et des Cadres Supérieurs," and as early as 1950 the Centre des Jeunes Patrons organized three-day full-time sessions on industrial management problems. Until the late 1960s when large American offices settled in France, CEGOS, founded by major French corporations (see below), was the largest French management council and had an especially active training policy. Finally, in 1954, CNPF created the Centre de Recherche et d'Etudes des Chefs d'Enterprise, which organized ten yearly sessions to teach modern management methods to managers and executives (approximately 2,500 sessions from 1955 to 1963).[40] In 1960 there were 150 bodies in France specialized in cadres training, twenty-five of which offered a "general refresher course on management methods."[41]

It was not until later that management schools proper, designed for students and not working cadres, were developed, business administration and management courses introduced in universities, and the social sciences and human relations taught in professional schools. In 1953 the Catholic Faculty of Lille created pioneering courses on human relations in its Institute of Economic Research. This initiative was followed by the creation of the Institut des Sciences Sociales du Travail, ISST, in 1954 by the Ministry of Labor, later to become part of the University of Paris (ISST alumni mainly found jobs in personnel management and company social services, in particular as advisers for comités d'entreprise)[42]; then the Instituts d'Administration des Affaires, founded in 1955 in the Faculties of Law and Economics, created a degree in business administration.

But university management training did not really develop until the late 1960s in the faculties of law and economics (even later in the professional engineering schools, partially thanks to Bertrand Schwartz, head of the Ecole des Mines of Nancy).[43] In 1968 the Foundation Nationale pour l'Enseignement de la Gestion des Enterprises,

FNEGE, created by CNPF, the association of Chambers of Commerce, and the Ministry of Industry, began to coordinate business administration training, which had been dispersed among a wide variety of schools: faculties, Instituts Universitaires de Technologie, known as IUTs, professional trade schools (such as Ecole des Hautes Etudes Commerciales and Ecole Supérieures de Commerce), and the Ecoles Supérieures de Commerce et d'Administration des Entreprises, ESCAE, which since the mid-1960s had assembled eighteen average-size schools of commerce (one per educational district). Moreover, from 1950 to 1970 a great number of private schools specializing in management training were founded: out of the thirty private management schools in the Paris area in 1972, twenty-five had not existed before 1950 (nine were founded in the 1950s and sixteen in the 1960s).[44]

The creation of the first management schools was supported by the European Productivity Agency, which in 1956 started organizing year-long training courses in American universities for future professors of management (with approximately 225 participants from 1956 to 1958), as well as summer courses open to practicing professors who wished to study the "contents of and teaching methods used for American manager training." In addition, the Ford Foundation provided French business administration schools with American professors.

Another characteristic of the 1950s was rapid development of management councils in charge of reforming already existing agencies, which accompanied and often preceded establishment of a management teaching system. These management councils and organization and methods were not initiated in France by the productivity missions. Taylor found his first followers during the period preceding World War I and his ideas spread during the war, particularly in the arms industry under the pressure of reformists, while the beginnings of economic planning were being set up.[45] However, the number and size of the councils remained modest until productivity efforts opened a new market for them. The management consultants themselves, inspired as much by local tradition as by Taylorism,[46] appeared just before World War II.

On the initiative of the *grand patronat* (large corporation heads), the Commission d'Etudes Générales des Organisations, CEGOS, was founded, and presided over by Auguste DeBoeuf (but was not very active until 1945), as well as the Comité National de l'Organisation Française, CNOF, and the Bureau des Temps Elémentaires, BTE, directed by Bedeau, who applied timing techniques rigorously and schematically. But BICRA, founded by Jean Coutrot in the late 1930s, was probably the closest to modern councils. Set up in collaboration with two management specialists, a Dutchman, Hernst Hysman, and a German, Heinz Oppenheimer, BICRA's most original principle was to develop new labor management techniques inspired by the social sciences, along with the "rationalization techniques" already used by Bedeau or Paul Planus. Coutrot was probably the first French businessman to perceive the possible use of psychology and sociology in business, and was passionately interested in these fields. His friend Gérard Bardet was to follow. Inspired by corporatism, in 1936 he had instituted, in the plant he managed, "shop delegates" and "corporative commissions" each including a manager, shop steward, foreman, and delegate. After the death of Coutrot in 1942, he created his own council, COFROR, with two ex-BICRA consultants.

Jean Coutrot had organized a meeting in 1934 at Paul Desjardins's home in the Pontigny Abbey to "expand the concrete knowledge we already have of the universe to human problems, both individual and social." He called for a gathering of specialists in the social and natural sciences: biologists, physiologists, doctors, philosophers, sociologists, businessmen, and political economists. This was the spirit in which he created the Centre d'Etude des Problèmes Humains, CEPH, in association with the writer Aldous Huxley, the archeologist Robert Francillon, and the economist Georges Guillaume. Hyacinthe Dubreuil, Jean Ullmo, Alfred Sauvy, Teilhard de Chardin (a close friend of Coutrot's), Tchakotine, and others participated in the CEPH meetings, which included eight commissions: economic humanism, applied psychology, rational and humane limitation of inequality, propaganda, industrial decentralization, psychobiology, history and analysis of Marxism. The commission reports were published in the Center's journal, *Humanisme Economique*. Jean Coutrot was one of the masters of management training in the 1950s, who taught new management techniques and social psychology – of American origin – the oldest of whom had often participated in BICRA. They were thus prepared to follow the road from corporatism to human relations.[47]

In the 1950s AFAP supported – with some reticence – such groups as the Bedeau council which had been created between the wars and were still active. The councils were criticized for having ignored the "human factor" and, in the 1950s, praising "American-style productivity" often implied criticizing French management councils. The new generation of engineering consultants which emerged in the 1950s, mainly around a group of Ecole Centrale (engineering school) graduates from CEGOS who had worked in BICRA, such as Noël Pouderoux or Gilbert Bloch, broke off – or at least claimed to – from the "authoritarian" and "rigid" instrumentalism which had until then dominated the councils. Mangement was no longer conceived in a strictly technical, flatly Taylorist view, and rationalization of the material process of production, the breakdown and restructuring of manual tasks, was no longer considered sufficient to increase productivity or turnover. The two main trends dominating management science had to fuse: the technical tradition centered on mechanical organization of the work process and the human relations and group dynamics movement. Open to psychology, even psychiatry and sociology, the new managers wanted to take into account the human factor and analyse the motivations buried deep inside managers, at the very heart of the spirit of capitalism glorified by Octave Gélinier, director of CEGOS in the 1960s, another Ecole Centrale alumnus trained by Pouderoux who for twenty years was to be one of the main importers of American management techniques.

But above all – and this is the fundamental difference from the prewar period – management councils no longer geared their work only or even in priority to rationalization of manual labor or the concrete arrangement of workshops. A large part of their activity became devoted to the new tasks of screening, socializing, and training the management, sales, technical, and administrative staffs. This change in purpose was decisive in the change of methods: the technical focus and authoritarian rationalism applied until then by the Ecole Centrale graduate engineers to worker management could not be used as such for reforming engineers, and even less so for the self-taught managers who showed little tolerance for brutal forms of authority, and who, themselves having attained positions of relative power, had to be spared.

The "authority crisis" theme recurs frequently in manager consultant writings in the late 1950s. On the one hand, the myth of the *chef* (supervisor), as honored by the Catholic engineers at the height of the Vichy period, had to be destroyed; and, on the other hand, hierarchical relations had to be founded on new principles of legitimacy. "Problems of authority are now being raised in quite a new way in all fields. In the family as well as in education, industry or politics, an authority crisis has appeared," said the report on the 1958 CEGOS seminar on "*cadres* and the exercise of authority." "What is it that justifies a man's authority, that is, the fact that he has a certain power over others? How can his position as superior be acknowledged, attributed and valorized? Are the traditional justifications of authority still valid today . . . ? In a period of transition, such as nowadays, there is a certain gap between the development of material techniques and the development of the social sciences. Human problems, particularly in a country with very old structures, are often tackled with outdated methods. Thus we are still haunted by the 'myth of the supervisor.' First, it should be acknowledged that there is no absolute distinction between supervisors and people who are not supervisors. It is impossible to speak of 'supervisors' in themselves, of supervisors isolated from the entire network of human relations which makes them supervisors."[48]

Nothing could justify the appearance of new control methods better than this report, written during the "transition period" in which the industrial concentration following the opening of the Common Market had begun. The myth of the supervisor corresponds quite well to the experience of engineers and even junior executives during the 1930s and again in the immediate postwar period, in which the division of authority among the so-called *collaborateurs* (that is, the "associates" of the employer) was connected to the concrete division of production units rather than to specialization of tasks. "Engineers" were involved in concrete production techniques and even carried out research and supervised equipment maintenance and manual labor, in addition to performing so-called social activities, which in many cases were not covered by independent personnel management. This division of labor and the absence of instruments of representation available to *cadres* to define themselves as a specific group, contributed, along with other factors (such as their training in engineering schools and in particular at the Ecole Centrale) to mold the social identity of employees in positions of relative authority in companies. They borrowed identification patterns from the model of the military officer conscious of his "social role" (especially if they were Catholic, came from bourgeois families, were engineering school graduates, or were interested in the armed forces or public service), as well as from the role of the "individual boss," the rigorous, absolute master of isolated units, responsible for both product quality and production costs.

Such images were no longer adapted to the changes in business which accelerated in the early 1960s. Instead of the old pattern, the one-dimensional, univocal hierarchical relationship, a new pattern had to be substituted, that of the network of human relations, miraculously adjusted to the structural properties now a part of industry, with its intermingling financial ties and its complex domination structures through which the power of groups with unclear limits was exercised. The invention of a new way of controlling the new petty business bourgeoisie thus seems very closely related to the intensified bureaucratization of industry and the progressive integration of small units into group structures.

The value the managerial avant-garde attached to the new social technology inspired by psychology was at least partially due to the fact that such technology seemed capable of conciliating demands hitherto considered relatively contradictory because they referred to different types of methods and rhetoric, and ultimately to different social groups. On the one hand, there was efficiency, rationalization, company discipline, the respect of the hierarchy demanded by industrial imperatives; on the other hand, imagination, intelligence, initiative, and above all flexibility, in the relationships with both higher and lower-ranking employees, a restrained type of permissiveness which excluded "blind" obedience as much as open conflict. New psychology had to make *cadres* more flexible in their professional relations, make them bow to company discipline (but without any excessive rigidity) and, above all, make them understand that the authority they have is relative and has been "delegated" to them, while supporting their efforts in carrying out their assignments, stimulating their zeal in their work and their alertness at monitoring the performance of their subordinates. New psychology was thus supposed to make *cadres* "happy," one way among others to acknowledge their belonging to the bourgeoisie and to keep them from joining workers' unions. Contrary to the administrative or even military methods of control which had hitherto dominated industry, "soft" techniques had the advantage of respecting bourgeois manners, thereby contributing toward maintaining "good feelings" between *cadres* and employers and especially toward promoting internalization of the new values based on which the company was to operate. "Stationed" workers could be managed in an authoritarian manner because application of Taylor's techniques of division of labor made it possible to transfer a large portion of worker know-how to the technical system of industrial management and which, through this act of dispossession, produced interchangeable manual labor. But the *cadres* managing companies and supervising subordinates had to be the object of another type of action capable of instilling not only compartmental rules but also patterns for the reproduction of the operations through which the patterns had been acquired, capable of orienting identification by providing models and promoting both cognitive and emotional investment.

Restructuring of industry and production as well as training and reeducation of *cadres* all contributed, during this period, to make management a booming industry. CEGOS, which had approximately forty associates in the 1950s, when Octave Gélinier became director, grew during the following years at a yearly rate of 20 percent. It created new departments (marketing, personnel management, administration, financial control, management, data processing, and *cadre* training), specialized in merger and purchase operations, and opened branches in various European countries. By the mid-1960s, CEGOS employed six hundred persons in several countries. Its board of directors included university scholars (such as Dean Capelle), financiers (Banque Nationale de Paris, Banque d'Indochine, etc.), and senior executives.

In the late 1960s, Noël Pouderoux, president of CEGOS, met Jean Stoetzel, professor of social psychology at the Sorbonne, and with him embarked upon an association which led to the creation of ETMAR ("Etudes de Marché") and to recognition of the Institute Français d'Opinion Public (the French polling institute known as IFOP).[49] CEGOS thus created a branch in a new niche – marketing studies and public opinion polls – competing with the Société d'Economie et de Mathématique Appliquée (known as SEMA), which directed SOFRES (the other main polling institute). Connected to Banque de Paris et des Pays-Bas, and founded in the late 1950s by an Ecole Polytechnique graduate, Jacques Lesourne, and a handful of engineers, SEMA had 120 associates in 1960 before its implantation in the main Common Market countries. By 1969 it had over two thousand employees. The new company specialized in the most modern forms of management, decision-making, applied economics, and above all, operational research, inspired by systems theory, not to mention "softer" sciences, with psychosociological studies, staff screening, and evaluation and training contributing to the boom of a new industry: the "brain" industry.[50]

As of 1960, management and advisory counsels flourished: the Chambre Syndical des Sociétés d'Etudes et de Conseil, or SYNTEC, founded in 1969, included, in just the "management and training" section, over thirty large councils, practically all located in Paris.[51] Growth was particularly rapid in the field of "sales management," sales promotion, training of sales staff, and in *cadre* recruiting. In the late 1960s there were two hundred *cadre* recruiting councils, eighty of which were located in the Paris area, where the ten largest councils earned 80 percent of the income of the entire profession.[52]

Group dynamics, politics, and culture

To understand the interest the "progressive" businessmen and the "modern managers" had in the human sciences and particularly in the modern techniques derived from industrial psychology, which was invented in the U.S. in the 1930s and spread rapidly in France in the 1950s, it should be noted that it was a reaction against the bureaucratization of business. Group techniques, psychosociology, brain-storming and creativity, educational or training cells, and role-playing were first applied to the *cadres* and particularly to the *petits cadres*. They were used as a sort of "social orthopedics" through which the participants "would understand themselves in relation to others" and "experience their conflicts" in the context of restricted, artificial groups and would thus acquire the ability to transfer the informal, efficient "rational style" in accord with the new economic ethics to their actual jobs, in their relations with their co-workers, both higher and lower ranking.

The large nationalized enterprises, directed by progressive employers (e.g., Renault and Electricité de France) in the forefront of the battle for productivity, for the modernization of the economy and for the reeducation of the old "reactionary" *patronat*, were also the first to take the "human relations" movement seriously, to welcome psychologists among their executives, to establish services for the screening and management of personnel inspired by the new methods, and to open their doors to the *sociologues du travail*. They were followed, in the mid-1950s, by the progressive employers, directors of the large modern firms already heavily bureaucratized (e.g., Télémécanique, Alsthom, Péchiney, and Ciments Lafaye) often belonging to Catholic movements and to ACADI (Association de Cadres Dirigeants de l'Industrie pour le progrès social et économique), which in 1948 set up a group for the study of "industrial relations."[53] "Americans," declared a Catholic employer, "ultimately concur with our philosophical and moral conceptions since they consider that an employee who does not feel free, who has the impression of being frustrated, who is placed in an unfavorable work atmosphere, will only bring the company a small part of his possibilities."[54]

Everything happened as if, from the mid-1950s, the innovative avant-garde of the *grand patronat* (often tied to Social Catholicism) had, in turn, reinvested the hopes formerly placed in corporatism in the social sciences, social psychology techniques, and industrial sociology imported from the U.S. Thus, a mixed discourse can be seen to be forming in which the words and expressions borrowed from the spiritualist and personalist vocabulary (community, person, man, liberty, dialogue) are blended with terms used for technical efficiency and psychoanalysis. The switch to human relations and the social sciences by the heirs of Social Catholicism after the *aggiornamento* of corporatism, contributed to a large extent to making it possible for a closely woven instrument of *cadre* management to be created.

The diffusion in France of industrial psychology and particularly of "group techniques" owes much to the efforts of members of the French Psychotechnical Mission to the United States, organized by the French Association for the Growth of Productivity (AFOP) in 1952, which included, in addition to Paul Fraisse, head of the mission, Jean Bonnaire (head of the psychotechnical service of Renault), Jean-Marie Faverge (who belonged to the Center of Psychoanalytic Studies and Research of the Ministry of Labor), and Suzanne Pacaud (*maître de recherche* at the Centre National des Recherches Scientifiques (CNRS) and head of the

Psychotechnical Laboratory of the SNCF (national railroad)). The mission reports were the object of a special issue of *Revue de Psychologie Appliquée* (vol. 4, no. 1, January 1953). One article was devoted to the *cadres* and their selection, which must be founded upon the experimental study of "leadership," their promotion, which must be "rationally organized," and the "grading systems" and "training"; another discussed their education in psychology.

A new generation of psychosociologists followed the importing of group techniques by both legitimizing them in the universities and diffusing them in business. Claude Facheux, Jacques Ardoino, Guy Palmade, Max Pagès, Robert Pagès, Didier Anzieu, Jean Maisonneuve, and Roger Muchielli were all born between 1920 and 1925. Most received, after their university studies, a complementary education in the United States from the "masters" of American social psychology (in particular Carl Rogers); all were active in universities or in research in the CNRS and worked in numerous organisms, usually private – management, selection, or training councils – which were created or developed during the 1950s. Sometimes they also founded their own "consulting" business in the form of a nonprofit association. Thus, Guy Serraf, who was to become in 1960 the main associate of Bernard Krief, owner of one of the most important recruitment agencies, founded with Didier Anzieu and Jacques Ardoino the National Association for the Development of the Human Sciences (ANSHA), "an association of a small number of high-ranking academics who already had consulting activities. Thanks to the association," said Bernard Krief, "in 1959, I discovered the techniques of group animation, transmission of information, comprehension of human relations, etc., techniques which business was not to apply until several years later."[55]

This intermediate position between the university and business and sometimes political power (specialists in the social sciences were welcomed in the technical sections of ministries or the Plan)[56] predisposed the masters of industrial psychology to incarnate the new model of the intellectual manager, directly involved in "action." More generally, the interest which the government officials and employers had for psychology and sociology contributed to a large extent to the development of the social sciences in the 1950s and 1960s.

"The Conversion of the Whole World"

But the introduction of management, human relations, group dynamics, marketing, and, no doubt more profoundly, the representation of economic agents as free subjects invested with the deep-seated desire to "succeed and to consume," also helped to impose, particularly among the middle management, the high standards, knowledge, and objects rightly or wrongly associated with the culture of the United States (which was one of the conditions for the opening of the financial market to American capital). It also made it seem inevitable that France develop a social order similar to "American society."

Octave Gélinier, one of the most ardent proselytizers of the new belief, wrote in 1965:

Today, we can have a clearer view. First, the political and economic system of traditional Europe has shown its failure. This strange amalgam of medieval conceptions and modern techniques was able to hold the stage for three centuries, by virtue of its initial advance and the weakness of competition, but its collapse, which has nothing to do with chance, is definite. . . . As imperfect as it may be, the American model constitutes the principle of unification of industrial civilization. It had demonstrated its effectiveness in creating wealth and power, proved its flexibility and its adaptive faculties. Those who intelligently adapt this model to their particular case soon receive the same fruits: and they are increasingly numerous. It is reasonable to believe that this movement is going to continue. . . . The puritan ethic, now the science of management, has acquired a new force. It is no longer taught in Sunday school but in business schools. To propagate it throughout the world, missionaries have been replaced by the 'institutes of productivity' created in each country with the support of subsidies and American experts. And each year the leaders of the whole world come on pilgrimage (which they call a 'productivity mission') to see and hear first hand the latest revelations. The puritan ethic of good management in the modern version of the Science of Management, is now rapidly converting the entire world, including France and the U.S.S.R.[57]

The partial homogeneity of the value systems and behavior style due in part to the management industry clarifies in particular one of the remarkable aspects of the functioning of multinational corporations. This is the aptitude of these companies to find or establish in countries with relatively different social structures and cultural traditions a sufficiently homogeneous staff, especially the management staff, to make it possible to orchestrate the internal policies and rules of personnel management and even professional habits.[58] (This occurs despite the increase, in this period of economic strife, in the authority of the parent company over its national subsidiaries.) The analysis of the effects of cultural dependence, which economic dependence also induces, shows to what extent the multinationalization, that is, the Americanization, of the managerial frame of reference for *cadres* constitutes an important aspect of the rising factions of the middle classes.

However, to avoid overinterpreting this discourse as triumphant and unchallenged, its banality should be stressed. It only expressed in a rigid fashion (the celebration of America sometimes particularly dogmatic) a conviction that was almost unanimous, at least in the dominant class at the beginning of the 1950s. T. A. Wilson was not wrong when he noted that if "in Europe it later became more fashionable to jeer at those who imitated American cultural models and American business and to accuse the United States of practicing 'Coca-Cola imperialism' during the Marshall Plan years, the United States still constituted a generally acknowledged model: some Europeans were passionately attracted by everything that America represented."

Yet the fascination of America could be expressed in a language which, if taken at face value, often appeared interchangeable, but carried very different senses depending on the social position and the political projects of the agents and groups who generated it. A more profound analysis would show the difference between those for whom the adoption of American models was justified by the goals of increasing national independence (notably vis-à-vis the U.S.A.) and redistributing the wealth created by economic growth (as was often the case in Pierre Mendès-France's circle), and those who, only interested in interpreting the "lessons of history" in their positive aspects, found in the archetypal representation of "American democracy" an instrument for rediscovering conservatism in more enlightened form. The latter were prepared to accept concessions in order to avoid subversion of the establishment. In the submission to American enterprise, they saw a means to increase the prosperity of private industry and, above all, to maintain its independence from the state.

Of these different, though sometimes apparently interrelated political projects, the attitudes toward the Plan undoubtedly constitute a privileged indicator because they refer to the opposition, fundamental in France since the end of the nineteenth century, between the public and the private sectors, between the groups and the classes whose interests are tied either to the reinforcement of the institutions placed under state control or to the development of free enterprise. It is often difficult to separate these two types of interests, for the political conjuncture imposed blame on the Vichyite *grand patronat*, and the Plan seemed to be the indispensable instrument of growth policy favorable to private industry. But these two types of interests tended to oppose each other more clearly as, with the reinforcement of industrial and financial groups and the unanimous conversion of the upper business bourgeoisie to the ideology of management toward the mid-1960s, the "Plan appeared a vestige of a leftist thought now out of date."[59]

Notes

1. This text is a chapter of a book published in 1982 on the formation and evolution of the category of *cadres* in France from 1936 to 1975. A different French version was

published in *Actes de la Recherche en Sciences Sociales 38* (May 1981). This English translation was prepared by Alexandra Russell and subsequently edited.

2. Sociology has not been included in this analysis, in particular the *sociologie du travail* which developed during that period outside the French intellectual traditions (the Durkheim school), mainly by importing methods, problematics, and concepts derived from American sociology, not only because such an analysis would necessarily have been construed as polemical, but also insofar as, unlike psychosociologists, sociologists, who are often influenced by Marxism, often critical of employers, often *ouvriéristes* (and tending to confuse "field work" with "going to the masses"), generally did not act directly in firms to carry out reorganization.

3. See F. Braudel and E. Labrousse, *Histoire Economique et Sociale de la France*, 4, vol. 2, (Paris: PUF, 1980), 785–86. After 1952, reorganization became more frequent: only twenty-six of the fifty largest firms in 1952 were listed under the same name in the 1962 list of the fifty largest firms. P. Bourdieu and M. de Saint Martin, "Le Patronat," *Actes de la Recherche en Sciences Sociales* 20-21 (Mar./Apr. 1978), 3–82.

4. M. Elgozy, *L'Aide Economique des Etats-Unis à la France, Plan Marshall et "Defense Support,"* Documentation Française (Paris: 1953), 37.

5. J. Gimbel, *The Origins of the Marshall Plan* (Stanford University Press, 1976), in particular 228 *et seq.*

6. Cf. *Actions des Problèmes de Productivité*, First Report for the Comité National de Productivité, 1950–1953 (Paris: 1953).

7. P. L. Mathieu, *La Politique Française de Productivité Depuis la Guerre*, I.E.P. thesis, under the direction of Jean Fourastié (Paris, 1961).

8. For example, the April 14, 1949, report for the Plan Commission by the electrical construction team upon returning from the United States: *Notes et Etudes Documentaires* (no. 1296). Mar. 15, 1950, 15.

9. OEEC, *Les Problèmes de Gestion des Entreprises. Opinions Américains, Opinions Européennes,* (Paris, Oct. 1954), 13.

10. European Productivity Agency, *Notes et Etudes Documentaires* (No. 2604), (Dec. 1959), 10.

11. European Productivity Agency, *Notes et Etudes.*

12. *Recueil de documents sur la productivité*, 16.

13. OEEC, *Les Problèmes*, 14 *et seq.*

14. T. A. Wilson, *The Marshall Plan*, Headline Series (New York, 1977), 43–44.

15. J. L. Servan-Schreiber said, "It was normal to identify oneself with John Kennedy, who incarnated the central concepts of my age: America: youth, success, beauty, the future," in *A Mi-Vie: L'Entrée en Quarantine* (Paris: Stock), 137.

16. J. Monnet, *Mémoires* (Paris: Fayard, 1976), 276–77.

17. Many sources of precise information on Pierre Mendès-France, his associates, and above all on the Servan-Schreiber family are now available. In addition to interviews, the following were consulted: Pierre Mendès-France, *Choisir* (Paris: Stock, 1974) and *La Vérité Guidait Leurs Pas* (Paris: Gallimard, 1976) (in particular, the chapter on Georges Boris, 231–48); C. Gruson, *Programmer L'Esperance*, (Paris: Stock, 1976); F. Bloch-Lainé, *Profession: Fonctionnaire* (Paris: Le Seuil, 1976); P. Dreyfus; and, above all, the fundamental work by François Fourquet, *Les Comptes de la puissance* (Paris, 1980), 76. For the Schreiber family and *L'Express*, the following were consulted: E. Schreiber, *Raconte Encore* (Paris: Presses de la Cité, 1968); J. C. Servan-Schreiber, *Le Huron de la Famille* (Paris: Calmann-Levy, 1979); Jean-Jacques Servan-Schreiber, interview with Roger Priouret, in R. Priouret, *La France et le Management* (Paris: Stock, 1972); S. Siritzky and F. Roth, *Le Roman de L'Express, 1953–1978* (Paris: M. Jullian, 1979); M. Jaumet, *L'Express de Jean-Jacques Servan-Schreiber*, doctoral thesis (Paris, 1979).

18. G. Boris, *Servir la République*, presentation by P. Mendès-France (Paris: Julliard, 1936), 181.

19. For the religious traditionalists, who are known to have contributed more than any other group to the creation and diffusion of the "social doctrine of the Church," liberal Catholics who favored adaptation of the church to the liberal society stemming from 1789, the "modern world" as it stands, were dubbed "Americans." D. Strauss, *Menace in the West, the Rise of Anti-Americanism in Modern Times* (Westport: Greenwood Press, 1978), 11.

20. L. Romier, *L'Homme Nouveau: Esquisse des Conséquences du Progrès*, (Paris: Hachette, 1929). L. Romier, journalist for *Le Figaro*, was connected to the Action Catholique circle. He was to become one of Pétain's advisers.

21. A. Fabre-Luce, *A Quoi Rêve le Monde*, (Paris: Grasset, 1931). The first part ("Crise à Wall Street, 9–10) contains most of the stereotypes about the "materialism" of American society."

22. On Franco-American conflicts during the interwar period over debt, reparations, and disarmament, see M. R. Zahniser, *Uncertain Friendship: American-French Diplomatic Relations Through the Cold War* (New York: J. Wiley, 1975), 219–39.

23. See, for instance, C. Pomaret, *L'Amérique à la Conquête de l'Europe* (Paris: A. Colin, 1931). Charles Pomaret, who was a businessman, held a position that diverged from that of the "young right" in that he suggested that in order to fight against "American imperialism" European business should adopt the main innovations American capitalism had used to become wealthy.

24. On American investments in Europe during the interwar years, see M. Wilkins, *The Maturing of Multinational Enterprise: American Business Abroad from 1914 to 1970* (Cambridge, Mass.: Harvard University Press, 1974), particularly 70 *et seq.* (electric industry) and 211 *et seq.* (oil industry).

25. Cf. R. Aron and A. Dandieu, *Décadence de la Nation Française* (Paris: Ed. Rieder, 1931); and R. Aron, *Le Cancer Américain* (Paris: Ed. Rieder, 1931).

26. In the late 1920s, Hyacinthe Dubreuil spent fifteen months in the United States, where he worked in large metallurgical plants. He wrote a book on his experience showing a very favorable attitude toward the new methods of rationalizing labor (see H. Dubreuil: *Standards: Le Travail Américain Vu par un Ouvrier Français*, preface by H. Le Chatelier [Paris: Grasset, 1929]). A few years later, H. Dubreuil wrote a book on the New Deal, *Les Codes de Roosevelt et les Perspectives de la Vie Sociale* (Paris: Grasset, 1934). He saw organization and methods as "the essential tools of true socialism . . ." (*Standards*, 422) and viewed the National Recovery Act, which "induced the creation of fair competition laws," as an extension of Taylor's works, *Les Codes de Roosevelt*, 58–60, and the "code" policy as an "attempted transition from the old individualism to the coming forms of organized democracy," 82.

27. Emile Schreiber published two reports on the United States: the first, during his youth, in 1917, to "carry out useful, gripping propaganda in favor of the ideas which–more than ever–should rule after the war," *L'Exemple Américain, Le Prix du Temps aux Etats-Unis* (Paris: Payot, 1917)), xix; the other book, *L'Amérique Réagit* (Paris: Plon, 1934) concerned the New Deal and the administration stemming from the National Recovery Act, which, for Emile Schreiber, should also be an example for the European ruling classes.

28. R. Marjolin, *Les Expériences Roosevelt* (Paris: Librairie Populaire, 1933).

29. See P. Bourdieu and L. Boltanski, "La Production de l'Idéologie Dominante," *Actes de la Recherche en Sciences Sociales* 2, nos. 5–6 (1976): 3–73.

30. S. M. Lipset, "The Changing Class Structure and Contemporary European Politics," *Daedalus* (winter 1964): 271–303. These ideas were vulgarized at the same time by Michel Crozier (see, for example, "Classes san Conscience ou Préfiguration de la Société sans Classes," *Archives Européennes de Sociologie* 1, no. 2 (1960): 233–47.

31. This opposition between the "old" middle classes and the "new" middle classes originated in German social democracy. Already mentioned in texts by Bernstein and Kautsky, it recurred during the interwar period through German university scholars in sociology. However, it is rarely used in France except in studies, usually by Germanists, on the rise of National Socialism in Germany and is based on the untranslated work of Theodor Geiger. Henri de Man, who worked in Frankfurt and wrote in German, used it, "Le Socialisme et le Nationalisme Fasciste," *Le Socialisme Constructif*, (Paris: Alcan, 1933), 199–249. This is also the case for H. Laufenburger, who taught at the Strasbourg faculty of law, "Classes Moyennes et National-Socialisme en Allemagne," *Revue Politique et Parlementaire*, 40 (461), 1933, 46–60. For the definition of classes, see T. Geiger, *On Social Order and Mass Society* (Chacago: University of Chicago Press, 1969), 10–11; and P. Ayçoberry, *La Question Nazie–Les Interprétations du National-Socialisme, 1922–1975* (Paris: Seuil, 1979), 103–7.

32. On the role of CGPME in the advent of the Pinay government, the ties between Gingembre and Laniel, and the CGPME hostility toward Mendès-France, as well as the overall role of the government officials working on the Plan, see G. Lavau, "La CGPME," *Revue Française de Science Politique* 5, no. 2 (1955): 370–84.

33. J. Touchard, "Bibliographie et Chronologie du Poujadisme," *Revue Française de Science Politique* 6, no. 1 (1956): 18–43.

34 Sapiens, *Mendès ou Pinay* (Paris: Grasset, 1953).

35. See R. Salmon, *L'Information Economique, Clef de la Prospérité* (Paris: Hachette, 1963), 24–30.

36. This is one of the functions of industrial journals, which numbered twenty in 1939 and five hundred in 1962, with an overall circulation of 1,500,000 (as opposed to, for example, 600,000 in 1952).

37. M. Drancourt, *Les Clefs du Pouvoir*, conclusion by Louis Armand (Paris: Fayard, 1964).

38. M. Beaud, A. M. Levy, and S. Liénard, *Dictionnaire des Groupes Industriels et Financiers en France* (Paris: Seuil, 1978), 19.

39. In 1950 twenty thousand engineers and foremen had taken evening classes organized by CNOF. *Revue Internationale de Travail*, July 1950.

40. See "Le CRC, Dix Ans d'Activité," *Direction du Personnel* 76 (Dec. 1963): 15–17.

41. "Evolution de la Formation à l'Administration des Entreprises,"*Direction du Personnel* 73 (July 1964): 17–24.

42. L'Institut des Sciences Sociales du Travail," *Direction du Personnel* 88 (June 1964): 38–40.

43. Until the 1950s, economics was of only secondary importance in engineering school curricula, with the exception perhaps of the Ecole des Mines of Paris, where Maurice Allais taught as of 1943. In this respect, the Conservatoire National des Arts et Métiers was a precursor (François Simiand, for instance, began teaching there in 1923). F. Etner, "Note sur la formation économique des ingénieurs," communication at the Le Creusot Colloquium, Oct. 1980.

44. Calculation based on *Précis de l'Enseignement Gestion* (Paris: FNEGE, 1972).

45. A. Moutet, "Les Origines du Système Taylor en France, le Point de Vue Patronal, 1907–1914," *Mouvement Social* 93 (Oct.–Dec. 1975): 15–49.

46. As shown by Judith A. Merkle, *Management and Ideology* (Berkeley: University of California Press, 1980) in her chapter on France (130–171), the influence of Fayol on the scientific management movement in France was deep and long-lasting, stressing less the technical division of labor than the administrative abilities of the management, the quality of the *cadres*; underlining less organization of production and appropriation of worker skills than rationalization of management and authority.

47. The information used here was drawn from two unpublished notes written respectively by Marie Coutrot Toulouse and Gilbert Bloch, a CEGOS engineer, ex-BICRA assocate, as well as from various documents courteously loaned to the author by Mme. Aline Coutrot.

48. CEGOS, "Les Cadres et l'Exercise du Commandement," *Hommes et Techniques*, Jan. 1958.

49. Interview with Noël Pouderoux in Priouret, *La France et le Management*, 397.

50. R. Armand, R. Lattes, and J. Lesourne, *Matière Gris, Année Zéro* (Paris: Denoël, 1970), 206.

51. In 1976, 205 firms belonged to SYNTEC, representing over forty thousand people, out of whom close to sixteen thousand were engineers and *cadres*. Their overall turnover for 1975 was over four billion francs, 30 percent from exports (source: brochure on engineering professions published by SYNTEC in 1976).

52. "Les Cabinets de Conseil en Recrutement de Cadres," *Hommes et Techniques* 325 (Nov. 1971): 841–76.

53. H. W. Ehrmann, *La Politique du Patronat Française* (Paris: A. Colin, 1959), 387. Founded in 1946 by a group of Catholic Ecole Polytechnique graduates, some of whom worked in the nationalized sector, ACADI assembled the reformist and progressive employers of the 1950s.

54. *Actions et Problèmes*, 412.

55. B. Krief, *Le Médecin Chinois, Pour un Politique de la Santé de l'Entreprise* (Paris: Presses de la Cité, 1979), 30.

56. M. Pollack, "La Planification des Sciences Sociales," *Actes de la Recherche en Sciences Sociales*, June 1976 (2–3): 105–121; M. Pollack, "Paul F. Lazarsfeld, fondateur d'une multinationale scientifique," *Actes de la recherche en Sciences Sociales* 25 (Feb. 1979): 45–60.

57. O. Gélinier, *Morale de l'Entrepise et Destin de la Nation* (Paris: Plon, 1965), 155.

58. On the strategies developed by American multinationals in the organization of foreign subsidiaries, the recruitment and training of local managers, personnel management, see M. Z. Brooke and H. L. Remmers, *The Strategy of Multinational Enterprises* (London: Longman, 1970), particularly the first part, chaps. 2 and 5.

59. C. Gruson, *Programmer*, 92.

14
Markets, managers, and technical autonomy in British plants

PETER WHALLEY

The first century and a half of industrialization has been marked by the seemingly inevitable rise of large organizations as the "anarchy" of the market was replaced by the internal planning and controls of the large corporation.[1] A consequence of this growth was the emergence of a class of technical experts and skilled managers deploying their talents within corporations and governmental bureaucracies; this new class has replaced the old petty bourgeoisie as the problematic "middle class" of industrial capitalism.[2]

Recent developments in Western economies, however, have cast doubt on the inevitability of this concentration of employment in large corporations. There has been a revival of interest in small firms, and a growth in the practice of subcontracting.[3] Instead of organizational loyalty, the entrepreneurial ethic is back in fashion, even within the increasingly decentralized structures of large organizations.

These developments have had consequences, as yet only partially understood, for the positions of new middle-class labor. Some have already joined the ranks of the self-employed, still more have reassessed the possibilities of self-employment as an alternative to the corporate career. For others, while their employment position has remained constant, the nature of their relationship to the market has changed as corporations have restructured. As a consequence, many professional and managerial workers, technical staff among them, have found themselves relating to capital in a new way. This chapter examines the impact of one new organizational form, the internalization of market forces within corporations, on the way technical and business goals are integrated in the work of technical professionals.

Professionalism, deskilling, and trust

The growth of the "new middle class" seemed to solve one problem for capital–how to secure direct control over the labor process carried out by manual labor–only to create a potential new one: how to integrate these new employees, especially those with professional and technical skills, into the capitalist firm. Indeed, much of the literature on the new middle class has focused on the problematic success of this integration.[4] Given that capital needs the expertise of technical employees to transform the forces of production, but dependence on that knowledge threatens employers' ultimate control over the labor process, how can such employees be integrated into the corporation?

Social scientists, for whom this situation has often seemed more problematic than for employers, have argued that the tension is inherently unstable and have predicted two different resolutions of the problem. "Post-industrial" theorists emphasize the transformative functions of technical professionals, and see their scientific knowledge as a power base to challenge both managerial authority and, ultimately, the ends of capitalist accumulation itself. The demands of profit will be replaced by professional goals as technically involved employees demand to expand the control they possess over their immediate tasks to include the overall strategy and structure of the company.[5] In the neo-Marxist version, such experts will lead a "new working class" in rebellion against the subordination of their knowledge and skills to capitalist goals.[6] The alternate solution predicts that employers will complete the subordination of technical employees by deskilling and rationalizing their work. The professional autonomy that threatens employers' control of the labor process could be reduced; critical knowledge of design and planning further centralized: and the work of many technical professionals routinized and divided in a manner similar to the strategy pursued against skilled artisans in an earlier time.[7] In this case, professional autonomy would only be transitional, the product of the early stages of new technologies, or the remnant of an earlier mode of production.

There is in fact little evidence to suggest that either process has proceeded very far.[8] Some lower-level technical and administrative positions *have* suffered deskilling and narrow specialization, but in many cases "deskilling" is as much a function of occupational title inflation for lesser skilled workers as a genuine routinization of positions filled by professional labor. Even the narrowing down of specific jobs does not necessarily entail the deskilling of their occupants since routine careers for many technical workers pass through "deskilled" positions on the way to much more autonomous work.[9] Engineers continue to play a critical role in modern production and carry it out with a fair degree of autonomy. Nor is there much evidence that technical employees seek to "professionalize" their companies. There have been occasional outbreaks of professional unionization, but much of this is in the public sector where the logic of capital accumulation is mediated by the state.[10] The strains between technical advance and commercial profitability remain central to the role of technical staff, but, overall, they have remained remarkably well integrated into capitalist firms.[11]

This integration has two dimensions: the securing of technical professionals' consent to a managerial authority rooted in bureaucratic position rather than technical expertise; and the securing of their consent to the subordination of technical goals per se to capital's goal of profit maximization.[12] In part, of course, both types of consent are secured by the "production" of the right kind of employee. Professional technical staff are socialized and selected from the *beginning* to accept the legitimacy of both bureaucratic authority and the dominance of business values.[13] Engineers, like cost accountants, personal management, sales and marketing professionals, even general management, owe their existence as an occupation to capital's need to have a trusted labor force carry out certain functions.[14] Indeed, without the availability of a labor force *already* willing to accept capitalist hegemony by virtue of its class background or education – early American engineers were recruited from the children of the old petty bourgeoisie – there would have been no possibility of employers developing real control over the labor process. Without alternate employees in which to vest conception and design, the deskilling of craftsmen would have had little point.[15]

The production of this trustworthy labor force is now largely a function of the educational system. American professional engineering schools have long seen socializing their graduates into business values as one of their primary functions.[16] In England, many engineers are recruited via apprenticeship programs controlled by employers and designed to intertwine technical and business values in the engineers' professional self-definitions. This selection and socialization process continues, however, through the early years of employment. Promotion to more autonomous positions is only available to those judged "responsible." In fact, the various grades of technical work are more accurately characterized as being levels of organizational *trustworthiness* than of technical skill, each grade of responsibility carrying with it greater intrinsic and extrinsic incentives for allegiance to managerial and corporate goals.[17] This is particularly so in England, where there is no separate occupation of technician and where all technical staff, whatever their educational background, start their careers at the bottom of the technical scale, leaving ample room for selection for trust-worthiness.

Such selection and socialization processes are important since they provide a general basis for treating engineers as trusted employees, eliminating much of the incentive for deskilling or other external control strategies. Nonetheless, the tension between technical expertise and profit maximization, inherent in the definition of the engineering profession, is continuously generated *within* the structure of the capitalist firm. It emerges from the potential contradiction between the pressures to develop new technology and the need to maintain profitability, and is not solved by simply recruiting an appropriate work force. The relationship between technical advance and commercial constraints needs to be actively *managed*.

This chapter examines two organizational strategies – here called "insulation" and "exposure" strategies – which function to integrate technical specialists into a profit-oriented company. The first mode *insulates* professionals from direct exposure to business constraints so that they are free to practice their technical skills. Decisions about project costs and capital allocation are set according to managerial assumptions about long-run profitable returns, and engineers and scientists are "loosely-coupled" from short-run market demands. If they are given adequate funding to pursue projects of sufficient complexity, engineers develop little interest in financial matters and no concern to participate in company business matters outside their technical fields.

The insulation strategy causes problems, however, when corporate priorities change and employers want technical staffs to limit their technical practice. To deal with this, employers have another option, that of *exposing* their professional staffs to market constraints directly, with minimal managerial intervention. By providing their staffs with detailed financial information about the company's competitive situation, employers can deliberately encourage a managerial perspective and reward commercial interest. Most directly they can "internalize the market," i.e., use a market-based pricing mechanism to structure intraorganizational decision-making. In so doing, constraints placed on the pursuit of technical excellence are depersonalized and depoliticized. Engineers in such situations have, of necessity, to be involved in budgetary matters and become increasingly interested in the financial and commercial affairs of the company from a managerial, even entrepreneurial, perspective.

This latter strategy, which I will examine in more detail below, suggests that the boundary between firms and markets has been broken down by the growth of the divisionalization of company structures, and the corresponding growth in the use of profit centers between which transfers take place at prices equivalent to those on the "outside."[18] Internalizing the commodity market tends to substitute direct customer pressure for low costs and speedy delivery for managerial control,[19] while the use of unit profitability as an investment criterion by corporate headquarters – i.e. the internalization of the credit market – simulates the relationship of the small business to the bank. Such systems, which are widespread in industry and growing in importance, have the effect of locating the staff subject to them in simulated markets that mimic the pressures on the self-employed entrepreneur.

The contrasting effects of these organizational strategies on engineers' integration into the firm will be illustrated with material from research carried out in two British engineering companies, part of an investigation into the class location of technical workers in advanced capitalist societies.[20] One plant, Computergraph, makes electronics and laser equipment for the printing industry. It is a typical high-tech company operating in a relatively favorable product market and employing a high percentage of engineers. The other, Metalco, manufactures basic metal components for the automobile industry and employs far fewer engineers in relation to its size. It is also struggling to maintain its share of the business. Both companies in their different ways are fairly typical of their respective industries in Britain.[21]

Managerial legitimation

Whatever the system for producing trustworthy employees, the aim was to provide a staff that can carry out its work largely without direct supervision. Engineers had their work allocated to them in relatively large clumps, or organized their work in "rounds" spent largely out of sight of supervisors. Only rarely were they subject to the close supervision common in manual and clerical occupations.[22] Only about a quarter of the engineers at Computergraph and Metalco even *mentioned* supervision as one managerial role amongst others, and even then saw it in benign terms:

He's here to ensure that I am doing my work correctly, to give me my work, supervise it, and then evaluate it. To give technical advice and a mutual generation of ideas with the details left to me. Everybody needs some kind of guidance. People rarely function on their own. You need some sort of stimulation. (Tony Stevens, R&D engineer, Computergraph)

For most engineers, "bad work" is discovered only by results: when machines fail to work or designs are not produced on time. When asked how their work was checked, only a quarter of the engineers reported that their bosses directly observed them working, and these were concentrated in a few departments where working conditions in general were characterized by relatively low autonomy.[23]

Engineers thus do not experience managers as the hostile disciplinarians that many manual workers do. In British factories at least, technical staff personnel are differentiated from management by a number of status distinctions, but, nonetheless, both are "staff," differentiated from manual workers by hours and conditions of work, educational experiences, and career structures. The social organization of work encourages the perception that managers are not the hostile representatives of the employer but rather colleagues performing a specialized function in a complex division of labor. Instead of being perceived primarily as supervisors, managers are seen as experts in linking technical work to commercial and organizational ends, either by coordinating the different technical specialties or as a source of organizational or commercial information. This is seen as a distinctive and rare expertise, what Perrow has called "administrative-technical competence."[24] "I'm not sure I could do his job" was a common remark by engineers, particularly junior ones, and it was said with a degree of admiration:

It's not the technical skills. I can do that. It's keeping everything in the air at once that I admire; the technical specs., the organizational politics, and he seems to have a nose for what will sell in the market, or at least for what he can convince top management will sell. That takes real expertise and I admire him for it. (Simpson)

Coordination in particular, was mentioned by at least half the engineers, particularly in those departments with high levels of technical autonomy. At Metalco, where autonomy was handed out sparsely, the more successful engineers were more likely to mention coordination (70 percent of the most successful compared to 30 percent of the least), and so were the more highly qualified.[25] Three-quarters of Computergraph's staff engineers and half of Metalco's emphasized this function. As one R&D engineer put it:

He coordinates projects together, allocates time and doesn't allow personal interests to dominate all one's time. He's necessary, the department wouldn't run as well without him, and people would pull in all directions. (Crawford)

Although not allowing "personal interests to dominate all one's time" might sound like supervision, it is a recognition of the need to coordinate the division of labor in a collective project. The greater the degree of insulation that engineers have from the direct line authority, the greater the need for coordination by management. When engineers are left alone, someone is necessary to pull all the separate pieces together.

Where the bureaucratic organizational structure was more visible, as at Metalco, engineers emphasized management's role in the articulation of organizational structures.[26] Management set policy, channeled policy down from higher positions, or, in the reverse direction, acted as the departmental representative to the rest of the company. As one Metalco draftsman put it graphically: "The boss is there to join up the organizational tree, at the point of the join of the branches and ladders." The organization exists and managers hold the bits together; because of their position they can get things done:

It's a position of power. He has access to high places where there is a greater chance of getting things done. I have to invoke him to get things done over someone else. There are certain levels above which I cannot go. I can go up to the line superintendent level, and possibly up to manager level to put my case, but not above that. I have to take it to the boss, and he'll take it above. (Cready)

He can see how the pattern fits into the overall sub-group position. For example the overall use of manpower in this department. He's a heavyweight prod when the units are slow. He has an overall view, and can develop new markets. And he has a directional role, he takes a broad view and sets overall policy. (Berry)

These organizational linkages are so taken for granted that, when they are absent, engineers feel so isolated from the organizational structure they complain about it:

I feel so undermanaged. I should be given more direction. You need someone to sort out longer term priorities. It's not done. I'm not in a position to reject demands. (Green)

Management engineers, as the most organizationally involved of all, were particularly likely to see *their* bosses functioning on both these organizational roles.

Engineers, of course, are not entirely unaware that a boss is a boss is a boss. Even the role of technical adviser still contains elements of hierarchy since the distinctive feature of a boss's advice is its authoritative nature:

I don't know exactly was his function is, he keeps the administration away from me and gives advice if needed. It's nice to know he's there. When he gives advice it's authoritative advice. He can take the responsibility. (Head)

Some degree of authority is seen as necessary for the coordination function to work, but it is facilitative rather than coercive. Thus managers are seen as experts in organizational knowledge. The control function seems largely invisible. Even explicit control functions are seen as organizational necessities. Much of the supposed conflict between technical expertise and managerial authority is absent because of the organizational embeddedness of the engineers' work. Given the organizational structure of the firm, the engineer cannot function alone and therefore needs coordination. The ratio of coordination to supervision is very high for such workers; and, as long as they continue to accept the goals of the company, the position of the manager is fully legitimated, both as a special kind of expert and as one performing a necessary role in the organizational division of labor.

Organizational legitimation

Under normal circumstances, managers do not have to exert the kind of direct control that would place their authority in question. The critical issue, therefore, is not the legitimation of direct managerial authority but the legitimation of the goals and interests of the organization itself, the legitimation of the capitalist firm in whose interests managers are assumed to operate. In part, of course, this is secured by the socialization and selection processes we have already discussed, but they are not enough. The tension between technical expertise and profit maximization is continuously generated within the structure of capitalist firms since it is one expression of the contradiction between the development of the forces of production and the attempts to maximize capital accumulation. Both the "insulation" and "exposure" strategies in place at Computergraph and Metalco succeeded, in their very different ways, in dealing with this problem.

Insulation

At Computergraph, and in most high-tech industries, engineers are generally given considerable freedom of maneuver. Such companies want to free the creative talent of their technical staff by "loose-coupling" them from the controls which govern other personnel, and *insulate* them from commercial pressures so that they can engage in technical innovation.[27] The most visible form of this is carried out in basic research units such as Bell Labs or IBM research centers, where research scientists and engineers are given a good deal of autonomy to pursue their own technical interests within broad guidelines and relatively generous budget constraints.

In Computergraph's R&D department, parameters of new projects were decided at meetings of senior management; and, once technical and market feasibility studies were done, new projects were allocated to R&D with cost and time constraints already laid down. By the time the project reaches the development engineers, commercial constraints have already been built into the product as part of the technical requirements. Costs, like performance "specs," are just part of the design parameters. As long as the final product meets these initial specifications, any criticisms of the technical design is considered illegitimate. The "elegance" of proposed solutions is what excited the engineers most, and they defended strongly their right to solve problems in their own way. But then, as management is the first to admit, that's what they are paid for. Though strongest in the R&D lab, this attitude toward technical activity extended throughout most of the high-tech company.

Such a strategy was made easier by Computergraph's favorable product market position,[28] but the company's whole existence depended upon the ingenuity of its engineers and its technical products had a high value added in production. The critical feature was that Computergraph's top management saw technical innovation as the core of the company's future, recognized that long-run profit maximization depended on such innovation, and that returns would be somewhat risky and long term. They were also very aware that a certain degree of autonomy for technical staff was an efficient strategy for encouraging technical innovation.[29] Therefore, they insulated long-term design from short-term commercial pressure.

The consequence was that most Computergraph engineers were content to practice their expertise and leave the commercial and organizational matters to others. They became "ideologically desensitized" to the ultimate goals to which their work was put.[30] Less than a quarter of Computergraph's technical staff thought that financial knowledge was relevant for engineering practice. The engineers did not have to deal with the company's market situation in their everyday work; cost constraints were not critical; and long-term development work was a regular possibility. When such engineers did deal with financial pressures, they focused narrowly on their own product cost:

I've not got the time to be involved in company finance. It's my job to be concerned with product cost but not with overall profit, that's someone else's job. (Martin Wood, Senior Designer)

Similarly, Computergraph engineers showed little interest in participating in company policy outside their specialty:[31]

I don't want to be involved in more decisions. I'm not trained in other subjects and I prefer not to be involved if I don't know anything about the subject. That's a trait common to engineers. (Altherton, R&D engineer)

I don't think it's the responsibility of people like me to make other decisions. If I'm left alone to do the job, that's O.K. (Williams, production engineer)

Computergraph's engineers rejected participation because it was not their business, and they did not think they had the expertise to deal with it.

There are two potential disadvantages for companies practicing this insulation strategy. The first is that engineers become too wrapped up in technical matters to show any interest at all in business affairs. There are limits, even in high-tech companies, to the amount of business disinterest permitted engineers. This is partly counteracted, however, by reserving the highest rewards for managers, and managers *do* have to be involved in business concerns. Thus at Computergraph only managers made comments such as this:

It's the name of the game to make money, not serve as a social service. All managers need to know and not leave it to the Accountants. (Neville Evans)

Those staff engineers who did show an interest in financial affairs saw it as being helpful for promotion:

If you want to go up the ladder, you have to be concerned. I'd like to know policy and ideas for the future. Particularly on the commercial and sales side. I see myself as management potential. (Tim Simmons, service engineer)

In fact, managerial ambition was strongly correlated with both the perception that financial information was central to technical work and the desire for more such information.[32] Computergraph's insulation strategy, however, encouraged an orientation to technical specialization rather than management, and only 11 percent of the engineers were actually interested in pursuing a high-level managerial career.

The second problem is potentially more serious, and stems from the way constraints on technical practice are perceived in such an organizational structure. Because the engineers are largely insulated from the worlds of finance and commerce, all constraints are liable to be seen as organizational ones, stemming from pressure from other departments of management.

There is always the constraint that we are never given enough time. We are the last in line and therefore our time gets cut. Management thinks it's better to meet deadlines and get cash flow than to maximize profit by doing a good production engineering job. It doesn't bother me personally but professionally it does. My professional vanity takes a minor knock. (Padget)

While it is Computergraph's commercial success that created the pressure to keep up with sales demand, the strategy of deliberately insulating engineers from the outside market meant that such commercial pressures were seen as being imposed on engineers by managerial orders. Although technical and organizational constraints were far fewer than at Metalco, those that did exist were much more likely to be seen as extraneous and as interfering with proper technical practice. Whereas at Metalco such constraints were seen as "inevitable" or "part of the job," at Computergraph they were seen as decisions made by some manager or some department within the company and thus, in the widest sense, *political* decisions.[33]

As long as the number of such constraints remains small, their politicization is of little concern since they do not challenge engineers' sense of being free from managerial domination. But, should a changed market strategy or increased cost constraints lead management to restrict technical autonomy, then engineers are likely to place the blame for this directly on management's shoulders.

Exposure

Extensive cost constraints were already in evidence at Metalco. The division where research was focused faced a deteriorating product market position. The British automobile industry to which it was a major supplier had been rapidly losing its share of the market to overseas competition, weakening demand for Metalco's own products. The latter were also facing direct competition from Far Eastern imports. This weakening of segments of its product market had been plaguing the larger Metalco corporation for a number of years, and a variety of strategies had been developed to deal with it.

At the division under discussion here, a previous chief executive had attempted a high-tech response by encouraging technical innovation in both methods and products in order to open new markets and increase the value added of the basic product. But for reasons about which there is considerable dispute, the strategy, which had required considerable capital investment from the main corporation board, had been abandoned. In the period of retrenchment that followed, this division, along with a number of others, retreated from its high-tech experiments to the mass production of its standard items. In Gorz's imagery, long-term research lost ground to the "manufacture of saucepans."[34] This inevitably created the problem of how to divert the interests of the engineers – previously encouraged by block grants to pursue technical innovation – to more routine technical activities.

One solution was to encourage an orientation to general managerial careers, something that has been relatively rare for British engineers in the past. Metalco was very successful in this: fewer than 20 percent of the company's engineers had no managerial ambitions. This was partly the result of self-selection, but was also generated by the patterns of motivation that Metalco had built into its organizational reward structure; not only pay and status, but also much technical responsibility was increasingly being concentrated into managerial hands. Such careers were not available to everyone, however, and the company was still left with the problem of constraining technical activity without the straightforward imposition of close managerial supervision.

A major part of its strategy involved organizational changes. Instead of channeling commercial pressure through managerial hierarchies, Metalco had begun to provide its technical staff with increased financial information tied directly to their unit, and to impose cost constraints on them by "internalizing the market." This strategy involved a radical extension of the company's long-term policy of divisionalization.

Historically, a divisionalized structure had developed at Metalco because of the company's growth by the amalgamation of a series of family-owned firms. Corporate headquarters saw its role primarily as a financial holding company. In public, the company extolled the efficiency of small-scale organizational units; in private, senior executives were likely to point to two more tangible virtues: the avoidance of group-wide bargaining by the company's trade unions, and the "discipline" that such divisionalization placed on middle-level management and technical staff. In both cases, corporate management liked to place considerable distance between itself and the day-to-day operations of the local divisions, judging them only on their profitability and being willing, where necessary, to abandon them to their fate if more profitable investments should appear.

This principle had, however, been carried much further in the division under study, and one of the prime reasons for this was to secure the control advantages of internal market pricing at a much lower level in the company than was the case elsewhere. Shortly before the research was conducted, a formerly large plant had been divided into three separate operating divisions, one for each of the main product lines. In addition, there was now a separate technical methods unit; a tooling unit; a unit dealing with site-maintenance, security, power, and personnel matters; and a product-finishing unit. Each of these operated under a separate management, was responsible for its own financial well-being as a profit center, and was expected to trade with all the other units only on open-market terms, competing with non-Metalco companies even for intracorporate business. The links of these units with Metalco corporate headquarters were therefore not dissimilar to those that many small companies have with their banks. New investment depended on the division making a profit and therefore on dealing with the other units as *customers*. The evaluation of successful performance by managers and engineers alike had come to directly depend on the profitability of the assets which they used.

The consequences for engineers were most visible in the methods development unit which had previously been most closely associated with long-range development plans. Under the old system, it had been insulated from commercial pressure by the provision of block grants from group funds designed to encourage new technical developments. Under the new system, however, in order to receive money to develop new machinery the unit – and this often meant the team leader or the designer himself – had to sell the concept to one of the production units or to an outside firm. Costs, therefore, became of direct relevance to the individual designer without the continued intervention of higher management. If projects could not be undertaken, it could be blamed directly on market competition. If costs had to be cut, it was the customer not the manager who was to blame. In contrast to Computergraph, where such decisions only reached the engineers via a series of managerial intermediaries, the structure of Metalco was set up so as to maximize the direct impact of such market pressures on as many staff as possible. In doing so, it had a significant impact on its engineers' attitudes.

Metalco engineers were much more likely than those at Computergraph to feel they possessed knowledge of the financial position of the firm and, more importantly, that financial and commercial knowledge of the company was directly relevant to their jobs as engineers (69 percent at Metalco, 22 percent at Computergraph). Tom Stockbridge, an active trade unionist and a technical specialist without managerial ambitions, expressed a typical Metalco attitude about the relevance of financial knowledge to the engineer's job.

Now we get quite a bit of financial information. In the last two or three years in any case. . . . It's part of any person's job to be interested in the financial structure of the company. I have a vested interest in the success of the company. I may help find ways of decreasing its problems. It's the prime object of the company to make money.

This financial interest was not a hostile one but shared the basic managerial perspective. Thus, Arthur White – like all the staff engineers, a union member – was critical of a number of decisions that had been made not to develop new technology and wished to be more involved, but he didn't criticize the firm's goals:

Engineers have got to be in on the discussion. All successful companies make a product, something that others cannot make as well or at all. X division depended on its own new technology back in 1926 [sic], for example. I'd like to be involved in policy questions over financial decisions. For example over selling our technology.

Nearly half of Metalco staff engineers were eager to participate in general policy decisions in their company, compared to only 12 percent of their Computergraph equivalents. The type of participation they supported, however, was not the radical kind that Gorz and Mallet, or even Freidson and Bell, had in mind. Engineers did not want to take over the company and run it on radically different principles. Even someone like Stockbridge, whose extensive union activism made him a radical by most engineers' standards, discussed the issue in these moderate terms:

I do like to be involved earlier in meetings, in projects or other technical involvements. The situation is changing, we used to have separate trade union negotiations with managers and we have a site Works Council, and Methods Unit Works Council which has a wider scope to discuss policy. It's not fully utilized by management but I hope that management will come at an early stage and discuss policy with the reps. I hope it will deal with really important discussions.

Engineers wanted to participate in the management of their companies, not to radically change its direction, but because they had something to contribute to its success.

The most practical result of Metalco's strategy was that most of the serious constraints on technical practice were treated as simply part of the job:

Yes, sales and business considerations always get in the way of doing the best technical job, they always have done. But it doesn't bother me. It's part of the job. You can always spend more money but you have to finish a project at the point at which you can sell it for a profit. I accept the fact that we are in it for the money. You can only design things that sell. (Greenstone)

The only time business constraints were seen as a problem was when they were perceived as "political," rather than being grounded in external "reality."

Business constraints only bother me if I don't know the reason. If it's purely political then it's a bit frustrating. For example, on a machine purchase, if they don't accept my recommendation for non-economic reasons that can be frustrating and they don't tell you why. Basically it boils down to things that aren't explained. (Smith)

By wanting to know "the reason," Smith was seeking a justification for the decision in commercial terms. By "political," he refers to decisions which are *not* justified on directly economic grounds, but on bureaucratic or other principles. This latter, of course, is just what management was trying to avoid by its use of market factors to impose constraints.

Even those engineers who had doubts about the financial material the company provided its staff – calling it "Mickey Mouse" material and the like – did not reject the basic relevance of such information for the practice of the engineer's craft. Still fewer challenged the artificiality of the market to which the divisions were being exposed. Metalco was able to defend itself successfully from being seen as a single corporate group, allocating resources to its varying divisions according to corporate management's conception of potential profitability. Instead each division, each unit, was perceived as operating in an open-market environment, dependent on its own market success.

In the Marxist and neo-Marxist literature, it has been conventional to make a sharp distinction between managerial authority and the authority of the market, but, as this example illustrates, they are to a degree *substitutable* for each other. In the highly decentralized corporate structure of Metalco, the pressures on engineers' technical concerns came from customers rather than higher management. In this respect, the engineers, though employed, were in a very similar position to that they would have faced as self-employed artisans or entrepreneurs, but with one critical difference: the extent of that exposure to customers stemmed from deliberate corporate decision making. Metalco is sufficiently large that, if it wished to follow Computergraph's example, it could have continued to insulate its technical staff from such pressures by granting them block development grants as part of a future investment strategy. It had done so in the past, and continued to do so with other units in the corporation. But having decided to restrict long-term investment in technical innovation in this division, and hence the technical autonomy of its staff, the method it chose to use was one that substituted market discipline for direct bureaucratic control. Metalco was able to use the market as a control mechanism just because market allocation was not rejected by the engineers. In fact, the engineers' basic criticism of the functioning of British nationalized industries was that they were run inefficiently because they lacked the necessary discipline that market information provided and were insulated from "realities" by political "intervention."

Labor strategy as a means

In the renewed interest in the labor process generated by Braverman's work, it has sometimes been forgotten that the prime focus of capital's interest is accumulation, not direct control of all aspects of the labor process for its own sake. If labor power can be translated into labor by means other than close supervision, then there is no *a priori* reason to assume that deskilling and routinization will be the preferred strategy. In fact, the existence of a "Service Class" of trusted occupations is predicated on the existence of alterative modes of securing labor. These means need not be narrowly focused on the production process – the education system, for example, especially its vocational and professional components plays a particularly important role – but the "production" of trusted labor continues inside the company via career structures that serve selection, socialization, and motivation functions.

Nonetheless, there are issues of organizational integration which continue to need to be managed at the point of production: most particularly for technical professionals who – whatever commitment they may have developed to business values – have also acquired, of necessity if they are to be useful, a commitment to technical innovation and excellence. Such integration does not, however, turn out to be as problematic as is sometimes suggested.

"Insulation" has come to be a well-recognized strategy for providing technical professionals with appropriate conditions for pursuing their technical goals. They can be insulated not only from direct market pressures, but even from the bureaucratic hierarchies which may organize other aspects of the parent firm. But at some point the limits to such a strategy are reached. If technical departments become too divorced from the profit requirements of the company, or the company seeks to control its expenditures on technical investments more tightly, then internal market arrangements provide an alterative to the closer imposition of direct managerial domination.

At Metalco the two sources of compulsion in the modern capitalist firm – management's control of employees and market constraints on the firm – become inextricably interrelated in engineers' eyes because managers are only seen to exert constraints that stem directly from market exigencies. As long as management decisions are shown to be reasonable given the market conditions under which the company is operating or – and this is critical – is *seen* to be operating, then this is a sufficient grounding for their decision. Their decisions are accepted because they are thought to be correct.

However, the extent to which the market determines managerial decisions at the subunit level is a *variable* over which corporate management itself has a good deal of control. By "insulating" technical staff, and granting them the necessary capital to pursue their research, management can free them to pursue technical excellence. By deliberately "exposing" engineers to the market and demanding that they show short-run operating profits, decisions that have an unfavorable impact can be "depoliticized." The market is a legitimating tool of great power since it seems to place the source of any constraints on the engineers' work beyond the reach of managerial decision-making. The constraints of the market are seen as being as "natural" as the constraints provided by any of the physical materials the engineers have to deal with in their own jobs.

In a system such as Metalco's even a desire for increased involvement in decision-making is not particularly problematic for capital. Because both the organizational structure of the firm and the ultimate rationality of profit-seeking are imbued with such facticity, most engineers see greater involvement in company policy as just another form of job satisfaction. For Computergraph engineers, such participation seemed unnecessary – as extra business that would interfere with their pursuit of technical satisfaction. Only managers were, or had to be, interested in such things. For Metalco engineers, largely deprived of technical involvement, encouraged to see their careers in organizational terms and to be concerned with the company's commercial position, such involvement was desired, but represented only a wish for further participation in the business decisions of the firm.

What, then, could lead to challenges to managerial authority? A sense that decisions that directly affect engineers are somehow arbitrary or "political" – when, in other words, things "could be otherwise." This is one of the reasons why state involvement often generates increased protest. If a decision to close off a project is made in a nationalized or state-related industry, then that decision is clearly "political" in its widest sense, and not legitimated by the "facticity" of the market. It is significant that whatever struggles British engineers have been involved in have involved either nationalized aerospace companies or companies where the major customer was the government – in other words, have involved cases where the criteria for investment or success have not been clearly measurable in market terms but have been subject to negotiation. For an interest in participation to be threatening to the legitimacy of the system requires a sense that the world can be somehow other than it is, i.e., it requires an ideological critique of the operations of the capitalist market. The strategy of decentralization and internalizing the market was one way of ensuring that corporate decision-making was seen as "nonpolitical" and hence more resistant to challenge.

If Tayloristic control strategies and Fordist organizational practices are going out of style, and post-industrial society is seeing a greater reliance on strategies that grant employees – including an increasing number of manual workers – greater autonomy on the job, then even more than before employees need to be convinced that their material interests can best be secured by the maintenance of the system.[35] This hegemony has to be secured at two levels: at the level of the firm, where allegiance has to be sought to managerial authority; and at the level of the system of market capitalism itself. I have argued in this chapter that acceptance of the facticity, if not necessarily the desirability, of the latter can be used as powerful strategy for the reinforcement of the former, and indeed may permit the relaxation of direct control over the labor process without weakening the system as a whole, as long as the commitment to market allocation remains.

Marketplace and factory

Most writing on the relationship of markets to hierarchical firms has assumed the long term supersession of the former by the latter. Indeed, a central component of the Marxist analysis is the gradual replacement of the "anarchy" of the market by the rationality of planning, first within the capitalist firm and then by the state, and the direct domination of the labor process within the factory has been seen as necessary for capital accumulation.[36] Similar conclusions have been drawn by non-Marxists who have pointed to the minimization of uncertainty and the reduction of transaction costs that result from the growth of the firm.[37]

However, the prevalence of internal market arrangements and the growth of subcontracting, representing as they do the decreasing strength of the boundary between firms and markets, suggests that this assumption needs to be reassessed.

The deliberate use of market incentives has long been recognized as a strategy for motivating and controlling senior management. Since Sloan's reorganization of General Motors, the idea that divisionalization – breaking down the corporation into series of (quasi-)autonomous and competing units – might be more profitable than functional differentiation as a way of managing very large companies has received wide currency.[38] Increasingly, however, the system is being used to bring market discipline to smaller and smaller units of the firm, and hence to lower and lower levels of employees. It is true that there are technical inefficiencies built into a fully developed internal market system, where transfers between units of the same corporation take place at market prices rather than marginal costs.[39] Economies of scale and the advantages of centralized planning are also sacrificed. But there are a number of benefits to central management as well. Incentives can better be tied to measurable performance. Customer feedback can be provided directly to employees in ways that have visible consequences. Risks can be minimized by reducing the dependence of the whole corporation on one particular unit, thus making it potentially expendable. And, most importantly for the issues under discussion here, market conditions can take the blame for cutbacks, even failure.

These are advantages which have appealed to central planners in a number of planned economies, such as China and Yugoslavia, as well as to the central managements of capitalist corporations. In some cases, such arguments have persuaded corporations to rely on external subcontracting for a larger share of their needs, thus increasing the size of the small-business sector without noticeably weakening the control that the core corporation can exert on the subordinate suppliers. In many more cases, such market systems can be simulated inside the corporation itself.

This is not the place to attempt a general theory of when firms will choose to rely on market systems of control. Indeed, if modern organization theory tells us anything, it is that we need to allow considerable room for managerial choice in deciding corporate strategy. Metalco's reliance on internal market arrangements was only an extension, however radical, of its traditional pattern of divisionalization and – as the saga of centralization and decentralization at British Leyland has shown – such strategies may be as much a function of executive style as of some rational drive to profit maximization. There are certainly significant international variations in the distribution of such arrangements.[40]

What I do want to suggest, however, is that corporations are not unaware of some of the consequences I have discussed above and that in examining control structures we need to look at the whole relationship of the unit to its commodity and capital markets instead of focusing our attention solely on the internal organizational structure of the firm or operating unit. In particular we need to look at the strategy of reinserting employees more directly into the marketplace. We may even need to raise the question of how much direct control of the labor process is actually necessary to maintain capitalist exploitation in a world where control over investment capital and credit is so centralized.[41] Certainly, the boundaries between the factory and the marketplace are diminishing.

Acknowledgments

Research for this chapter was conducted under a grant from the Ford Foundation. The author thanks Allan Silver, Stephen Crawford, and Robert Zussman for many discussions of the organization of technical work, and Ross Scherer, Judy Wittner, and the editors of *Theory and Society* for their comments on an earlier draft.

Notes

1. This is the essential argument of the classical tradition in social science. See Michael J. Piore and Charles F. Sabel, *The Second Industrial Divide* (New York: Basic Books, 1984).

2. The story is best reviewed in R. Carter, *Capitalism, Class Conflict, and the New Middle Class* (London: Routledge & Kegan Paul, 1985).

3. See Piore and Sabel, chaps. 10 and 11.

4. Though their arguments differ radically in the implications that are drawn from them, all of the following works point to a tension between the demands and needs of technical workers and those of the bureaucratically organized command systems of industrial capitalism: J. K. Galbraith, *The New Industrial State* (Boston: Houghton Mifflin, 1967); Andre Gorz, *Strategy for Labor* (Boston: Beacon Press, 1967); Serge Mallet, *The New Working Class* (Nottingham, Eng.: Spokesman Press, 1975); Elliot Freidson, "Professionalism and the Organization of Middle Class Labour in Post Industrial Society." in P. Halmos , ed., *Professionalism and Social Change*, Sociological Review Monograph no. 20 (Keele, Eng.: University of Keele, 1973); Daniel Bell, *The Coming of Post-Industrial Society* (New York: Basic Books, 1973); and Alain Touraine, *The Post-Industrial Society* (New York: Random House, 1971).

5. The best statements of the post-industrial thesis as it relates to technical professionals remain Bell's *The Coming of Post-Industrial Society* and Freidson's "Professionalism and the Organization of Middle Class Labour," but see also Warren Bennis, *Beyond Bureaucracy* (New York: McGraw-Hill, 1973).

6. Mallet, *The New Working Class*; Andre Gorz, *Strategy for Labour*

7. The proletarianization model has periodically dominated discussions of technical professionals on the left, but, for relatively early statements of the theme in this

round of the debate, see Harry Braverman, *Labor and Monopoly Capital* (New York: Monthly Review Press, 1974); and Martin Oppenheimer, "The Proletarianization of the Professional," in Halmos, ed., *Professionalization and Social Change*. See also Magali Larson, "Proletarianization and Educated Labor," *Theory and Society* 9 (1980): 131–75.

8. The deskilling thesis dates back to classical Marxism, while Saint-Simon and Veblen are only the most famous of those writers who predicted a revolt of the professionals. Henri de Saint-Simon, *Selected Writings* (New York: Macmillan, 1952 [1859]); Thorstein Veblen, *The Engineers and the Price System*. (New York: Harcourt, Brace and World, 1963). See also Krishan Kumar, *Prophecy and Progress: The Sociology of Industrial and Post-Industrial Society* (Harmondsworth, Eng.: Penguin Books, 1978).

9. For an illustration of the deskilling of one technical occupation, see Philip Kraft's *Programmers and Managers: The Routinization of Computer Programmers in the U.S.* (New York: Springer Verlag, 1977). For a more extended argument about title inflation and the central importance of career structures, see my "Deskilling Engineers? The Labor Process, Labor Markets, and Labor Segmentation," *Social Problems* 32, no. 2 (1984): 117–32. While we must be rightly suspicious of occupational census categories, even a preliminary inspection of modern companies suggests that engineers and other technical staff play an increasingly important role in production. See Harry Braverman, *Labor and Monopoly Capital*, and Stanley Udy "The Configuration of Occupational Structure," in Hubert Blalock, Jr., ed., *Sociological Theory and Research* (Glencoe, Ill.: Free Press, 1980).

10. In Britain, the growth of engineering unionization has as much to do with state industrial relations policies and the growth of centralized pay policies in the nineteen seventies, as with a specific transformation of engineers' position in the labor process. For a discussion of American engineering unions, see Bernard Goldstein, "Some Aspects of the Nature of Unionism among Salaried in Industry," *American Sociological Review* 20, no. 2 (1955); and James Kuhn, "Engineers and their Unions" in Albert A. Blum, ed., *White Collar Workers* (New York: Random House, 1971). For England, see R. Carter, "Class Militancy and Union Character," *Sociological Review* 27, no. 2 (1979). Some French engineers did take part in the events of May 1968, but there is little evidence that this was other than a temporary, and specifically French, occurrence. See John Low-Beer, *Protest and Participation* (Cambridge, Eng.: Cambridge University Press, 1978), chap. 7.

11. There is always a problem in talking about "capitalist" firms specifically, in the absence of direct comparisons with the position of technical experts in other kinds of economic and social systems. In the absence of such comparisons, "capitalist" remains largely a descriptive rather than an analytic term.

12. See Charles Derber, "Managing Professionals: Ideological Proletarianization and Post-Industrial Labor," *Theory and Society* 12 (1983): 309–341; and Michael Burawoy, *Manufacturing Consent* (Chicago: University of Chicago Press, 1979).

13. For interesting discussions of the use of the education system as an important socializing mechanism from the point of view of employers, see Rosabeth Kanter, *Men and Women of the Corporation* (New York: Basic Books, 1977); and Richard Edwards, *Contested Terrain* (New York: Basic Books, 1979); as well, of course, as the discussion of the role of education in the system of reproduction in such works as Samuel Bowles and Herb Gintis, *Schooling in Capitalist America* (New York: Basic Books, 1973); and Michael W. Apple, "Reproduction and Contradiction in Education," in Apple, ed., *Cultural and Economic Reproduction in Education* (London: Routledge & Kegan Paul, 1982).

14. It is important to recognize the essential discontinuity in mode of organization between pre-industrial civil engineering and the modern industrial engineer in this respect. The former often had the status and freedom of either the pre-industrial self-

employed professional (in the U.K. and the U.S.), or the state bureaucrat (Germany and France); and, while the emergent occupation of industrial engineers often sought to assimilate themselves to these civil and military engineering traditions, they were rarely successful, and often met with explicit rejection just because they were seen to lack the requisite independence. On the U.S., see David Noble, *America By Design* (New York: Alfred Knopf, 1977); for France, see Stephen Crawford, *Technical Workers in an Advanced Society: The Work, Careers and Politics of French Engineers* (Cambridge, Eng.: Cambridge University Press, 1989).

15. For an extended discussion of this point, see Peter Whalley, *The Social Production of Technical Work: The Case of British Engineers* (Albany, N.Y.: State University of New York Press, 1986, and London: Macmillan, 1986). See also Peter Whalley and Stephen Crawford, "Locating Technical Workers in the Class Structure," *Politics and Society* 13, no. 3 (1984): 235–48.

16. See Noble, *America by Design.*

17. Thus, in Computergraph's elaborate and "scientific" job evaluation scheme, the scores given the various grades of technical staff differed only on "accountability" rather than "know-how"; while at Metalco job descriptions for junior and senior engineers differed only in degree of technical responsibility. The description of senior engineers reads: "Decisions and recommendations are usually accepted as technically accurate and feasible, but are reviewed to ensure adherence to policies and objectives." That for junior engineers reads: "Main decisions and recommendations are based on independent study but difficult, complex or unusual matters are usually referred to a higher authority."

18. See the discussions in Alfred D. Chandler, Jr., *Strategy and Structure: Chapters in the History of the American Industrial Enterprise* (Cambridge, Mass.: MIT Press, 1962); David Granick, *Managerial Comparisons of Four Developed Countries: France, Britain, United States, and Russia* (Cambridge, Mass.: MIT Press, 1972); and Oliver E. Williamson, *Markets and Hierarchies: Analysis and Antitrust Implications* (New York: The Free Press, 1975). See also Robert G. Eccles, *The Transfer Pricing Problem: A Theory for Practice* (Boston: Lexington Books, 1984).

19. See Dominique Pignon and Jean Querzola, "Dictatorship and Democracy in Production," in Andre Gorz, ed., *The Division of Labor* (Atlantic Highlands, N.J.: Humanities Press, 1976).

20. In Britain, three months of field work was spent in each company, and approximately fifty engineers at each site were extensively interviewed.

21. Though generalizing from limited case studies is always difficult, extensive preliminary visits to a variety of companies prior to the selection of the two research sites provided considerable confidence that the *processes* reported on here were not atypical of the industries concerned.

22. See Peter Whalley, *The Social Production of Technical Work,* chaps. 2 and 4, for further discussion of engineers' daily workloads. See also Peter F. Meiksins, "Science in the Labor Process: Engineers as Workers," in Charles Derber, ed., *Professionals As Workers: Mental Labor in Advanced Capitalism* (Boston: G. K. Hall and Co., 1982); and Robert Zussman, *Mechanics of the Middle Class* (Berkeley: University of California Press, 1985).

23. By comparison with manual workers, all the technical departments were relatively autonomous, and here we discuss the management and control of such semiautonomous employees. Nonetheless there were variations, both between companies and between departments within companies.

24. Charles Perrow, *Complex Organizations: A Critical Essay,* 2d ed. (Glenview, Ill.: Scott, Foresman and Co., 1979), 55.

25. Eighty-three percent of the graduates, compared to 45 percent of those with

Higher National Certificates – a credential best approximated, in status if not in knowledge, by an American two-year associate degree.

26. Nearly half of Metalco engineers emphasized managers' role as linkages in the organizational structure, compared to only 20 percent of Computergraph engineers (10 percent of the staff engineers).

27. For a review of the literature on coupling, loose and tight, see W. Richard Scott, *Organizations: Rational, Natural, and Open Systems* (Englewood Cliffs, N.J.: Prentice-Hall, 1981).

28. For a discussion of the importance of the market position of the firm for the granting of "responsible autonomy" to employees, see Andrew Friedman, *Industry and Labour* (London: Macmillan, 1977). Friedman errs, however, in seeing "monopoly" profits as the essential prerequisite for such arrangements.

29. In early discussions with the company about access, senior management indicated considerable awareness of the organizational literature on managing professionals and the desirability of granting autonomous work conditions.

30. Derber, "Managing Professionals," 325–30.

31. Only 12 percent of Computergraph's staff engineers wanted to participate in business and commercial decisions, compared to the 47 percent of Metalco engineers who expressed such an interest.

32. The two correlations were $r = .29$ sig $= .02$ and $r = .40$, sig. $= .001$, respectively.

33. Sixty-six percent of Computergraph's engineers complained of unnecessary organizational or business constraints that interfered with their technical work, compared to 37 percent of Metalco's. On the other hand, 44 percent of Metalco's engineers considered such constraints "part of the job." Overall, Metalco engineers experienced, and perceived, far more constraints on their work than did Computergraph's, but they were more accepting of them as inevitable.

34. Gorz, *Strategy for Labour*, 104.

35. See Adam Przeworski, "Material Bases of Consent: Economics and Politics in a Hegemonic System," *Political Power and Social Theory* 1 (1980): 21–66.

36. See Stephen Marglins's classic discussion in "What Do Bosses Do?" in Gorz, ed., *The Division of Labour*.

37. See, for example, Galbraith's *New Industrial State* and the extended theoretical discussion in Williamson's *Markets and Hierarchies*.

38. See Chandler, *Strategy and Structure*.

39. See Williamson, *Hierarchies and Markets*, 138–39. Indeed, such inefficiencies were noted by one engineer at Metalco, who noted that the production divisions were often doing technical development in-house rather than pay the full costs that the technical unit would have to charge when: "We have people to spare. We should charge them the costs it takes to do the job and not charge them overhead since that's already paid for. From Metalco's perspective overall, it doesn't make sense." But this was a minority opinion of one.

40. See J. Child, "Culture Contingency and Capitalism in the Cross-National Study of Organizations," in L. L. Cummings and B. M. Shaw, eds., *Research in Organizational Behavior*, vol. 3 (Greenwich, Conn.: JAI Press, 1979); and David Granick, *Managerial Comparisons*.

41. See John Roemer, *A General Theory of Exploitation and Class* (Cambridge, Mass: Harvard University Press, 1982).

15

Immigrant enterprise in the United States

ROGER WALDINGER

In the prevailing models of modern society, there is little room and precious little time left for the small firm and the independent entrepreneur. Marx argued that the lower strata of the middle class would gradually sink into the proletariat and, whatever the reception of his other views on the development of capitalist society, these particular prognostications were seconded by most subsequent observers. The conventional view is that working for oneself has been reduced to a marginal phenomenon and that small businesses persist either because market size has not yet permitted sufficient economies of scale, or because some residual need for specialization or a hankering after personalized services has postponed the advent of standardization.

If the prevalence of self-employment and the importance of small business have declined for the population at large, they continue to be poles of attraction for immigrants and their descendants. Historically, immigrants have gravitated toward small business: in turn of the century New York, it was not only in the petty trades of peddling and huckstering that the foreign-born were overrepresented, but also among "manufacturers and officials," "merchants and dealers," and other proprietary occupations. Small enterprise played an important role in the economic progress of a variety of immigrant groups that implanted themselves in business then – Jews, Italians, Greeks, and others – and their proportionally higher involvement in entrepreneurial activities continues to differentiate these groups from much of the native population.[1]

The renewal of mass immigration to the United States since 1965 has brought an infusion of new immigrant owners to the ranks of petty proprietors. Miami, for example, has a flourishing sector of Cuban-owned businesses that includes more than 150 manufacturing firms, 230 restaurants, 30 furniture factories, a shoe factory employing 3,000 people, and 30 transplanted cigar factories.[2] In New York, Chinese immigrants operate more than 500 garment factories employing over 20,000 Chinese workers; newcomers from Asia and Latin America operate 60 percent of the city's restaurants; and Koreans have made great inroads into the grocery store industry, much to the consternation of their competitors among the supermarket chains. Just as immigrants were overrepresented among the self-employed at the turn of the century, so they are today. In New York, 12.2 percent of employed foreign-born males were self-employed in 1980 as opposed to 9.2 percent for the native-born. For these immigrants, small business appears to be an important part of the settlement process. Only the most recent newcomers are self-employed at a rate below that of the native-born; after ten years in the United States, self-employed rates exceed those for the native-born and continue to climb with length of stay.[3]

In contrast to small business, immigrant enterprise in both its historical and contemporary manifestations has attracted considerable research interest. There is now a variety of explanations for the overrepresentation of immigrants in small business. These various accounts have considerable merits, but, as I shall show in the critique that follows, they fall short in several key respects. In some instances, the problems are of an empirical nature; in other instances, the issue is one of not adequately specifying the particularities of the ethnic firm; in yet other cases, the objection is that the explanatory factors are necessary but insufficient conditions of immigrant entrepreneurial success. The alternative that I will develop in this chapter is an argument about the interaction between the opportunity structure of the host society and the social structure of the immigrant group. Presented in summary form, my contention is that ethnic business growth depends on: (1) a niche in which the small firm can viably function; (2) access to ownership positions; (3) a pre-disposition toward small-business activities; and (4) a group's ability to mobilize information resources in organizing the firm.

Theories of ethnic enterprise

Among the explanations for ethnic business success offered in the literature, cultural and "middleman minority" theories are the most important. This section will offer a critical assessment of these theories.

Cultural analysis focuses on two arguments. One hypothesis is that immigrant groups import individualistic traits and behaviors that override initial placement in low-level jobs and catapult them instead into small-business positions.[4] The alternative argument, currently more popular in ethnic and immigration research, was offered by Ivan Light in his now classic book, *Ethnic Enterprise in America*; this was an imaginative variation of the Weber thesis, showing how ethnic solidarism helped immigrant groups organize those collective resources needed to exploit small-business opportunities, thus providing an "elective affinity" with the requirements of small business.[5] In a later adumbration of the original argument, Light has proposed that these solidaristic traditions might be classified as either "orthodox" or "reactive." Traditions in the first category would include those present in the group prior to migration; those in the latter would encompass patterns arising in response to the specificities of the immigration situation. For Asian immigrants, whose economic behavior is seen as exemplifying the influence of group solidarity, rotating credit associations would fall into the orthodox category while clan and family groups, which propped up the Chinese immigrant subeconomy during the early twentieth century, would be classified as reactive.[6]

Although cultural theories are suggestive for the importance that they attribute to predisposing factors, they are open to criticism on several counts. The entrepreneurial-values approach can be thought of in a "hard" and a "soft" form: the hard form would ascribe entrepreneurial values to a belief system distinctive from a group's economic role; the "soft" form would see those values as an adaptation to the original conditions in which a group lived prior to emigration. One strike against the hard form is simply that groups noted for their entrepreneurial bent also seem remarkably adaptive and their tendency is to become more like the native labor force over time, shifting from self-employment to salaried employment over the course of two to three generations – an issue discussed at greater length below. A more important criticism of the "hard" form is that its conditions are difficult to meet because what one needs is evidence of business-relevant values that are not ultimately reducible to a group's pre-migration experience. Some groups do indeed seem inclined toward entrepreneurship thanks to the influence of a particular belief system: such is the case of Koreans immigrating to the United States, many of whom are Protestants but still maintain Confucian values; the value systems common to both religions emphasize self-abnegation and self-control and thereby reinforce the qualities needed for small business gain. But, as Illsoo Kim has shown, the character structure of Korean immigrants also has its source in the after-effects of state centralism and the fluid class structure of pre-industrial Korea – both of which bred marginality and individualism.[7] Thus, whatever the origins of the initial thrust toward competitiveness, entrepreneurial values were thoroughly reinforced by the character of Korean society and consequently internalized prior to their immigration to the U.S., which lends support to the soft, rather than the hard, form of the entrepreneurial-values approach. But, if a value system is adaptive, the issue then becomes why the behavioral traits acquired in one society are rewarded in another. To that question, Werner Cahnmann's comments on the historical experience of Jews offer an instructive response: " . . . the era of liberalism . . . unleashed the energies of the Jews and gave them a free reign. The Jews had been conditioned to competitive risk-taking for a long time. Now, the rules which had governed their conduct under specific circumstances, found wide application."[8] Thus, the entrepreneurial-values approach presupposes the existence of opportunity structures congruent with acquired behavioral patters. This in turn begs the questions of the source of opportunities as well as their variation over time and space.

The collective-resource perspective also elides the relationship between culture and the environment. Analysts such as Light and Modell base their case on Asian-American subeconomies of the pre-World War II period, when nepotistic trade guilds and marketing organizations set prices, regulated output, and rationed entries to new firms.[9] Undoubtedly, these economic activities sprung up out of pre-existing cultural forms. But, if culture is to serve as a predictor of ethnic business success, then the limiting case is the constraining power attributed to cultural norms: that is to say, to what extent will cultural traditions influence economic behavior (as in the case of clan groupings that restrict competition) when nontraditional, individualistic actions elicit environmental rewards?

Reconsider, in this light, the evolution of those solidaristic organizations among Chinese- and Japanese-American business owners that served to set prices and regulate competition. These activities can be construed as rational responses to highly constricted market situations in which unimpeded business activity would have quickly exceeded the demand for ethnic products. Moreover, cultural consensus seems likely to have been less important in organizing the ethnic subeconomy than control mechanisms because, at the time, these immigrants were institutionally segregated from the mainstream labor market. Confinement to the ethnic subeconomy made the threat of exclusion a potent weapon of associational control. Among the Chinese, in particular, collective economic organizations were instruments of elite organization[10] whose efficacy derived from the autonomy that local authorities granted to Chinatown elites.[11]

If this reading is correct, then such organizations are likely to diminish in importance if the environmental constraints lose force. The reason is that more expansive market opportunities should reduce the need for associational controls while at the same time increasing the tension between guild-like regulation and economic growth. Indeed, ethnic economic associations occupy a greatly attenuated place in the Asian subeconomies that have arisen in the wake of the new immigration. In New York's Chinatown, for example, the proliferation of garment factories from twenty in 1965 to close to five hundred in 1985 has helped fuel the growth of the entire subeconomy. Yet, in contrast to the pre-war situation, when guilds and family groups controlled business transactions and guarded against saturating Chinatown's limited market, the Chinatown garment industry is now racked by the pains of overexpansion, with price wars and labor shortages forcing 20 percent of the businesses to change hands every year. Similarly, the ease with which Korean immigrants have been able to enter New York's fruit and grocery business has promoted intense intraethnic competition, completely overwhelming the ability of organizations like the Korean Produce Retailers Association to limit the entry of new Korean-owned stores.[12]

Another body of research identifies the business success of contemporary ethnic or immigrant groups as a "middleman-minority" phenomenon. Traditionally, middleman-minorities have been associated with pre-capitalist situations, where their role has been ascribed to the possession of valued skills or status considerations.[13] However, Edna Bonacich has argued that the middleman-minority role persists into advanced capitalist societies despite the attenuation or disappearance of original contextual factors. The initial hypothesis suggested that middleman-minorities begin as sojourners, enduring short-term deprivations for the long-term goal of return and choosing portable and liquifiable livelihoods. This orientation elicits a hostile reaction from the host society; that antagonism, in turn, strengthens solidaristic behaviors and in-group economic ties.[14] In a case study of Japanese immigrants in the United States in the first half of the twentieth century, co-authored with John Modell, Bonacich has argued that the Japanese's rapid penetration of small-scale, speculative lines in California agriculture and food retailing and wholesaling exemplifies the middleman-minority phenomenon.[15]

But in this, the most recent formulation of the "middleman-minority" approach, the theoretical status of the initial hypothesis has been altered and obscured. Attempts to order or specify the causal variables of context (in economic terms, demand), culture, and antagonism have been abandoned, and the middleman-minority approach now seems designed to elaborate an ideal type exemplified by a variety of characteristics. Thus, middleman-minorities are those ethnic business groups whose firms are concentrated in marginal business lines; recruit from a labor force encapsulated within the ethnic economy; integrate activities with one another so as to compete collectively with majority-owned firms; maintain "petit bourgeois" and familistic management norms; and contend with a "somewhat" antagonistic relationship to the host society.[16]

Exception to the middleman-minority approach can be taken on several grounds. First, it fails to specify the grounds for inclusion or exclusion with respect to both businesses and minorities. Any and all small-business activities undertaken by immigrants are classified as middleman-minority phenomena; similarly, the defining traits of the minorities are stated in such diluted form as to encompass almost any range of behavior. Secondly, the interpretive and factual bases for the middleman-minority hypothesis are at variance with its fundamental claims. For example, the middleman-minority approach posits a simple interaction between minority solidarity and host society antagonism. But this hypothesis is very difficult to reconcile with the historical record of middleman-minority responses to host-society hostility as well as the reactions of host societies to middleman-minority activities. Similarly, the relation between sojourning and self-employment is at best ambiguous and certainly not validated by the American experience. There is little evidence and numerous counterexamples to the hypothesis that ethnic solidarity bars the route to either business expansion or the employment of outsiders. The hardly representative instances of Japanese- and Chinese-American entrepreneurs apart, immigrant groups active in small business have tended toward high levels of internal competition, dooming efforts toward self-regulation.[17]

Most importantly, the argument that ethnic enterprise in modern societies is a carryover of earlier middleman-minority situations is unfounded. If concentration in peripheral, low-status activities defines the contemporary small-business class, the position of traditional middleman-minorities encompassed a much wider range of pursuits circumscribed by their relationship to state power. The symbiosis between middleman-minorities and traditional elites was the condition of all middleman activities. The freedom of peddlers and petty traders hinged on the services that middleman elites rendered to the emerging state through banking, tax-collecting, estate management, and later, industrial development. Thus, the economic ambit to which middleman-minorities had access grew up under patterned social relationships; hence, their historical role cannot be conceptualized without reference to the structure of their host societies and to the ways in which that structure created a demand for middleman pursuits.

These disparities in contexts and functions suggest a qualitative distinction: traditional economies in which middleman-minorities act as the engine of exchange relationships; and market economies, with peripheral, if still dynamic, ethnic enclaves. But, once we drop the assumption that immigrant business owners in capitalist societies are identical to the middleman-minorities of the pre-industrial past, then we can appreciate the importance of strictly market-based factors as pre-conditions of ethnic enterprise in the very case that Bonacich and Modell discuss. Land in Los Angeles was available to Japanese farmers because the city encroached on large holdings as it grew, and growth made extensive investments too costly and too uncertain for capital-intensive farming. As large-scale agriculture receded, land was bought by real estate investors who sought to rent out small parcels until higher yielding uses could be realized – speculative practices that coincidentally lowered the costs of capitalization for would-be Japanese truck farmers. In contrast to pre-capitalist or developing societies, in which middleman-minorities interject market relations into nonmonetized sectors, thereby undermining traditional producers, the role of Japanese farmers never altered the fundamental structure of truck farming. Nor did their basic orientation toward the market vary from that of their non-Japanese competitors since both sought to maximize profits.

A theory of immigrant enterprise

The cultural and middleman-minority approaches are not so much wrong as they are incomplete. A penchant for risk-taking, a preference for independence, the existence of ethnic economic organizations – all of these culturally-bound phenomena will facilitate the setting up of a new firm and making it a success. But setting up a new firm is neither a trivial nor a random event. Industries vary considerably in the degree to which they breed new-business births. For example, services made up the largest share (38 percent) of the 1,031,000 net new business formed in the United States between 1976 and 1982, followed by the finance, insurance and real estate and construction sectors (accounting for 14 percent and 13 percent, respectively, of all new firms). By contrast, manufacturing and transportation, communications and technology lagged behind, together producing only 9.3 percent of all net business births.[18] Business births and deaths cannot be tracked by the ethnicity of their owners, but minority self-employment rates (which include black, Asian, and Hispanic immigrants) can be disaggregated by industry: what we find is that minority-business owners are over-represented in trade and services, suggesting that these are the sectors where the bulk of new minority and immigrant businesses are born.[19] The point is that structural barriers – technology, capital needs, the level of competition – define the contours for the emergence of new firms. Hence a culturally-induced propensity for business may be a necessary, but not a sufficient, condition of entrepreneurial success.

In the sections that follow, I will argue that (1) access to ownership positions and (2) a niche in which the small firm can viably function comprise the sufficient conditions of immigrant business development. The first point is a reminder that immigrants usually have fewer resources than natives; if ownership positions are equally coveted by immigrants and nationals, then the former are not likely to win out. But recruitment to ownership may function similarly to those processes of recruiting immigrant labor detailed in Michael Piore's *Birds of Passage*.[20] That is, natives opt out of the supply of potential owners in a particular industry, perhaps because ownership in the industry generates too little status, perhaps because its economic rewards are insufficient to retain them compared to the alternatives available. If this is the case, then there may be a replacement demand and immigrants could then enter the industry to fill the ownership positions vacated by the natives.

But this condition presupposes (a) that the small firm is a viable entity and (b) that the existing small-business industries can be penetrated with the immigrants' limited resources. The literature on industrial organization identifies several barriers to the creation of new firms. Of these impediments, the most important are economy of scale barriers, absolute cost barriers, and product differentiation barriers; as I shall argue in the pages that follow, immigrant businesses proliferate where product market characteristics tend to keep such barriers low.[21]

It is in assessing what will happen in the existence of small-business niches and vacancies for small-business owners, that the cultural and middleman approaches are helpful. Immigrants will be more likely to succeed should they possess a pre-disposition toward business although, as we have argued, that predisposition is likely to be most developed among immigrants whose original environment bears a significant resemblance to their adopted society.

Ethnic resources are another necessary condition of business success, and middleman and cultural approaches are correct in underlining the importance of ethnic solidarity. However, their assessment of these resources is incomplete, in part, because their mode of approach is the ethnic case study. This tells us much about how ethnic businesses operate, but provides little information on how ethnic firms are distinguished from native competitors and therefore makes it difficult to understand whence the advantages of the ethnic businesses stem.

A second, and more important point, is that ethnic resources will generate a competitive edge if they provide a better fit with the environment in which the ethnic business functions. Even in low-barrier industries, there are significant liabilities associated with newness – how to learn and master new roles, how to wean away customers from their old vendors, how to establish trust – and the weight of these liabilities is evidenced by the high death rate among new concerns.[22] Moreover, small businesses, whether new or established, confront an additional set of problems by virtue of their smaller size. One such difficulty is access to finance; how ethnic firms might resolve this problem is handled quite nicely by both cultural and middleman approaches. Not considered by these approaches, however, is the fact that small firm industries tend to have an unstructured labor market in the sense that there are few established institutions by which jobs are matched with workers and skills and maintained and transmitted; hence, a critical problem of the small firm is securing a skilled and attached labor force. I argue that immigrant firms in small-business industries enjoy a competitive advantage because the social structures of the ethnic community provide a mechanism of connecting organizations to individuals and stabilizing these relationships.

The opportunity structure for immigrant enterprise

The first precondition for business development is a need that the immigrant firm can service competitively. Such demands arise first in the immigrant community, which has a special set of wants and preferences that are best served, and sometimes can only be served, by those who share those needs and know them intimately, namely, the members of the immigrant community itself. Generally, those businesses that first develop are purveyors of culinary products – tropical goods among Hispanics, for example, or Oriental specialties among the Asians. Businesses that provide "cultural products" – newspapers, recordings, books, magazines – are also quick to find a niche in the immigrant community. The important point about both types of activities is that they involve a direct connection to the immigrants' homeland and knowledge of tastes and buying preferences – qualities unlikely to be shared by larger, native-owned competitors.[23]

Immigrants also have special problems – caused by the strains of settlement and assimilation and aggravated by their distance from the institutionalized mechanisms of service delivery. Consequently, the business of specializing in the problems of immigrant adjustment is another early avenue of economic activity, and immigrant-owned travel agencies, law firms, realtors, or accountancies are common to most immigrant communities. Such immigrant businesses frequently perform a myriad of functions far above the simple provision of legal aid or travel information and reservations.

To a large extent, these are services that are confidential, unfamiliar, and unintelligible to the newcomer unaccustomed to American bureaucratic procedures. In some cases, they may impinge on the often dubious legal status of the immigrant and his or her family. Whichever the case, trust is an important component of the service, and the need for trust pulls the newcomer toward a business owner of common ethnic background. To this tendency may be added a factor common to many of the societies from which the immigrants come, namely, a preference for personalistic relationships over reliance on impersonal, formal procedures. This further increases the clientele of those businesses that specialize in problems of adjustment.[24]

If immigrant business stays limited to the ethnic market, then its potential for growth is sharply circumscribed, as Howard Aldrich has shown in his studies of white, black, and Puerto Rican businesses in the United States and (in research conducted with Cater, Jones, and McEvoy) of East Indian and white businesses in the United Kingdom. The reason is that the ethnic market can support only a restricted number of businesses both because it is quantitatively small and because the ethnic population is too impoverished to provide sufficient buying power. Moreover, the environment confronting the ethnic entrepreneur is severe: because exclusion from job opportunities leads many immigrants to seek out business opportunities and consequently, business conditions in the ethnic market tend toward a proliferation of small units, overcompetition, and a high failure rate – with the surviving businesses generating scanty returns for their owners.[25]

However, these conclusions may be too pessimistic in at least two respects. First, not all immigrant communities have enjoyed so few economic resources as blacks and Puerto Ricans in the United States and east Indians in the United Kingdom. One case in point is that of New York's Jewish community in the 1920s. As Jews moved into the lower middle and middle classes they also dispersed from the tenement districts of the lower East Side; their search for better housing created a market for Jewish builders who evaded restrictive covenants by constructing new housing and then recruiting Jewish tenants.[26] While the real estate and construction firms that grew up in the 1920s have since extended far beyond the confines of the ethnic market, the initial demand for housing from co-ethnics provided the platform from which later expansion could begin. A similar process is being played out in New York's Asian communities today where the housing needs of the growing Asian middle class have attracted Asian capital and stimulated the emergence of an Asian real estate industry.

The immigrant market may also serve as an export platform from which ethnic firms can expand. For example, Greeks started out in the restaurant trade serving co-ethnics looking for inexpensive meals in a familiar environment. This original clientele provided a base from which the first generation of immigrant restauranteurs could branch out. More importantly, the immigrant trade established a pool of skilled and managerial talent that eventually enabled Greek owners to penetrate beyond the narrow confines of the ethnic market and specialize in the provision of "American food."[27] In the 1980s, Dominican and Colombian immigrants active in the construction contracting business in New York City appear to be playing out a similar development. Most of these immigrant business owners are engaged in additions and alterations work for an immigrant clientele; what leads these immigrant customers to patronize co-ethnics is not so much a search for savings as a preference for reliability, vouchsafed for by the immigrant contractor's reputation in the community to which he is linked.[28] These initial jobs are important in two respects. First, they are small and therefore allow immigrants to start out at a relatively low level. Secondly, the ethnic demand has supported immigrant contractors in assembling a skilled labor force and gaining efficiency and expertise, qualities that are gradually allowing them to edge out into the broader market.

But these examples notwithstanding, Aldrich's strictures still hold: the growth potential of immigrant business hinges on its access to customers beyond the ethnic community. The crucial question, then, concerns the type of market processes that might support neophyte immigrant capitalists.

As noted earlier, the structure of industry is a powerful constraint on the creation of new business organizations. In that part of the economic world dominated by the demand for standardized products, scale economies, high absolute costs, and product differentiation bar the path of entry to new immigrant concerns. But there are certain products or services where the techniques of mass production and mass distribution do not pertain. It is in these markets – most often affected by uncertainty or differentiation or relatively small size – where the immigrant firm is likely to emerge:

(a) *Low economies of scale.* As an industry where the entrepreneur is likely to be his or her own boss and nothing but that, the taxi industry illustrates one path of immigrant entry into small business.[29] The reasons for immigrant concentration in this field lie in the cost structure of the taxi industry and in the barriers it presents to the realization of economies of scale. Economies of scale arise when the fixed costs of any operation can be spread over larger units so that the average cost per unit declines. However, the importance of economies of scale depends, in part, on the ratio of fixed to variable costs.

What is distinctive about the taxi industry is that none of the most crucial cost components – wages, benefits, and gasoline – is fixed; rather, they vary directly with the number of vehicles. Consequently, the ability of the taxi operator to lower costs by building up a fleet of taxis is highly constrained. The owner of two or possibly three taxis achieves the greatest possible scale economies; by contrast, a fleet of, say, twenty to thirty cars operates at essentially the same costs as the owner-operator of a single cab. Though scale economies at the firm level are thus negligible, one can attain sizeable reductions in fixed costs by keeping the vehicle under the wheel for a longer period of time. One possibility is to hire operators to keep the cab busy for two shifts or possibly more. But an alternative exists if there's a supply of owner-operators amenable to self-exploitation, in which case working long hours results in the same economies of scale.[30] Immigrants' restricted opportunities make them more likely to work long hours than natives (see below); hence, the taxi industry is a field in which immigrant business has grown because the characteristics of this industry are congruent with immigrants' economic orientations.

(b) *Instability and uncertainty.* The basic notion of economies of scale, as noted above, associates declining average unit costs with increases in the number of goods produced. However, the length of time over which the flow of output will be maintained is an equally crucial factor. Where demand is unstable, investment in fixed capital and plant is likely to be endangered. And, if product requirements change frequently, the learning curve is low because there is little time for workers to build up specialized proficiencies. Hence, when demand is subject to flux, versatility is preferable to specialization, and smaller units gain advantages over large.[31]

As Michael Piore has argued in his studies of economic dualism, industrial segmentation arises when demand falls into stable and unstable portions and the two components can be separated from one another. Where these conditions hold, we can expect an industry to be segmented into two branches: one, dominated by larger firms, that handles staple products; and a second, comprising small-scale firms, that caters to the unpredictable or fluctuating portion of demand. The consequence of this type of segmentation is that the two branches tend to be noncompeting; hence, where segmentation arises, it offers a sheltered position to small firms of the type that immigrants might establish.[32]

Such is the case in the garment industry, where large firms predominate in the staple-product categories but are kept out of fashion-sensitive markets whose terrain is better suited to small firms that can nimbly respond to the least predictable alterations in consumer taste. Fashion design and merchandising centers like New York, Los Angeles, and Miami also function as spot markets specializing in the production of styled items and overruns of more standardized goods; immigrant garment firms have thrived under these conditions because they favor small firms with flexible work arrangements and simple production-line technologies.[33] Roughly the same pattern characterizes the construction industry, with similar implications for immigrant business. One case in point is Carmenza Gallo's study of construction businesses in New York City, which shows that the building trades have provided the staging ground for new immigrant firms that specialize in residential and renovation work. The reason for this is that competition with larger, native firms for the residential and renovation market is limited. Large construction firms dominate the market for commercial and institutional building, where the projects are large and the lead times long. By contrast, small firms predominate in the highly volatile residential and renovation sectors, where the demand is highly fragmented and the dollar value of contracts is considerably smaller.[34]

(c) *Small or differentiated markets.* Still another environment favorable to small immigrant firms is one in which the market is too small or too differentiated to support the large, centralized structures needed for mass production or distribution. One such example is the retail grocery industry in New York City, where the structure of the market is unfavorable to the large supermarket chains that dominate the industry nationally. One crucial reason for the weakness of the chains is the complexity of the New York market, whose heterogeneous mix makes it a quagmire for national chains with cumbersome and rigid central administrations. While chains reduce distribution costs by carrying only a few basic product lines, servicing the tastes of New York's varied populace is more costly since it requires a much more diversified line than usually carried. Similarly, the chains attain economies of scale in overhead by centralizing administrative functions, but to ensure that ethnic tastes are efficiently serviced – for example, stocking Passover goods in stores located in Jewish neighborhoods, but not in black neighborhoods, or providing West Indian specialties in a Jamaican neighborhood, but not in the nearby Dominican area – a shorter span of control is preferable.

Thus, not only are large firm concentration shares lower in New York than elsewhere but also the national chains that dominate the industry in the rest of the country have ceded place instead to locally based chains whose territory is often limited to one or two of New York City's five boroughs. These local chains are sufficiently small to process information about New York's highly differentiated market segments and then service those needs appropriately. On the other hand, because they are relatively small, these local chains also lack the economies of scale needed to achieve significant market power, with the result that food retailing has been easily penetrated by smaller, ethnic concerns that compete with very considerable success against their larger counterparts.[35]

In conclusion, what distinguishes the variety of processes giving rise to immigrant business is an environment supportive of neophyte capitalists and the small concerns that they establish. Ethnic consumer tastes provide a protected market position, in part because the members of the community may have a (cultural) preference for dealing with co-ethnics, but also because the costs of learning the specific wants and tastes of the immigrant groups are such as to discourage native firms from doing so, especially at an early stage when the community is small and not readily visible to outsiders. If the ethnic market allows the immigrant to maintain a business at somewhat higher than average costs, the other processes outlined above reduce the cost difference between native and immigrant firms. Low capital-to-labor ratios keep entry barriers low, as in the taxi, garment, and construction industries; and we can predict that immigrant businesses will be most common in industries such as these. Where there are problems in substituting capital for labor, because changes in demand might idle expensive machines, immigrant businesses with labor-intensive processes can operate close to the prevailing efficiencies; the same holds true when small markets inhibit the realization of economies of scale.

Access to ownership

Given the existence of markets conducive to small business, the would-be immigrant capitalist still needs access to ownership opportunities. At the turn of the century, rapid economic growth created new industries, allowing immigrants to take up business activities without substantial competition from or displacement of natives. The classic case is that of the garment industry, which became immigrant-dominated because the massive tide of Italian and Jewish immigration to New York occurred just when the demand for factory-made clothing began to surge. But, in the economy of the late twentieth-century United States, growth proceeds more slowly, there are fewer opportunities for self-employment, and until recently the ranks of the self employed have been diminishing. Thus, the conditions of immigrants' access to ownership positions largely depend on the extent to which natives are vying with immigrants for the available entrepreneurial slots. If these positions are coveted by natives and immigrants, then natives should capture a disproportionate share. But, if the supply of native owners is leaking out of a small-business industry, then immigrants may take up ownership activities in response to a replacement demand.[36]

What are the conditions under which a replacement demand might arise for the new immigrants who have arrived in U.S. cities since the liberalization of immigration laws in 1965? In most large cities, the small-business sector has been a concentration of European immigrants and their later generation descendants. The last date for which we have information for both the immigrant and the foreign-stock population is 1970; at that time, the proportion of all self-employed in the five largest SMSA's who were first or second generation European ethnics ranged from a high of 57 percent in New York to a low of 30 percent in Los Angeles. Both immigrants and the foreign stock were overrepresented among the self-employed in all five SMSA's; but, in all five cases, rates of self-employment were lower in the second than in the first generation.[37]

Thus, the initial placement in small business is giving way to a pattern more squarely based on salaried employment; how this evolution is taking place is exemplified by the case of the Jews. Jews migrating from Eastern Europe at the turn of the century moved heavily into small business for a variety of historical reasons. Their arrival coincided with the massive expansion of small-business industries; this made it possible for them to utilize previously acquired entrepreneurial skills and habits and also pursue a culturally and religiously induced preference for independence and separation; finally, the tendency to concentrate in business was reinforced by discrimination, which at the upper white-collar level persisted well into the 1960s.[38] However, assimilation, occupational advancement, and the dwindling of corporate discrimination have diluted the Jewish concentration in small business.

Analysis of the 1965 and 1975 Boston Jewish Community Surveys found that "while almost a quarter (23 percent) of the 1965 heads of households were self-employed outside the professions, only one in seven (14 percent) were so employed in 1975"; moreover, the ratio of business owners was higher for almost all age cohorts in 1965 than was the case in 1975.[39] Similarly, the 1981 New York Area Jewish Population Survey found consistently declining rates of self-employment from first generation to third, with much higher levels of education in the latter generation, suggesting that much of its self-employment was concentrated in the professions rather than in business.[40] Finally, results from a study that examined Jews as well as a variety of Catholic ethnic groups (French Canadians, Irish, Italians, and Portuguese) in Rhode Island in the late 1960s show that "without exception the level of self-employment of fathers was higher than the level of self-employment of sons and the proportion of fathers of the oldest cohort who are self-employed is higher than that of fathers of the youngest cohort."[41]

This tendency toward greater salaried employment as part of a shift toward higher positions in the social structure sets in motion a vacancy chain. Small businesses generally experience a very high rate of failure, and consequently a population must produce large numbers of new owners just to maintain its existing size. But, as I have argued above, the younger cohorts and later generations among European ethnic groups are less likely to be self-employed business owners; hence, opportunities for immigrant business are freed up as older ethnic firms either go out of business or fail to transfer ownership to the next generation.

Two cases illustrate how this process takes place. New York's garment industry has been a province of Jewish and Italian businesses since the industry first grew up at the turn of the century. Historically, the average garment firm enjoyed an abbreviated life expectancy, but the availability of aspiring Jewish and Italian owners kept the supply of new entrepreneurs high. However, new immigrants now account for virtually all of the new business births of garment-contracting firms, which perform jobs to specifications set by larger "manufacturers" that design and sell the goods. By contrast, start-ups of contracting businesses by Jews and Italians have ceased; and, though Jewish and Italian contracting firms are still numerous, they are all long-established businesses, usually run by older owners close to retirement age.[42] A similar set of circumstances favored the proliferation of Korean fruit and vegetable stores in New York City, starting in the early 1970s. As Illsoo Kim explains in his book on *The New Urban Immigrants*:

> The majority of Korean retail shops . . . cater to blacks and other minorities by being located in "transitional areas" where old Jewish, Irish and Italian shopkeepers are moving or dying out and being replaced by an increasing number of the new minorities. . . . Korean immigrants are able to buy shops from white minority shopkeepers, especially Jews, because the second- or third-generation children of these older immigrants have already entered the mainstream of the American occupational structure, and so they are reluctant to take over their parents' business. In fact, established Korean shopkeepers have advised less experienced Korean businessmen that "the prospect is very good if you buy a store in a good location from old Jewish people."[43]

What the garment and retail examples further indicate is that succession takes place in a patterned way: while the most competitive, lower-status fields are abandoned, higher-profit, higher barrier-to-entry lines retain traditional ethnic entrepreneurs. Thus in food retailing, grocery store ownership passes from Jews and Italians to Koreans, but the wholesalers and food processors that supply these new ethnic concerns remain wholly dominated by older entrepreneurial groups.[44] Similarly, in the garment industry, immigrant entrepreneurs play an important role, but they do so as contractors working for manufacturers that are invariably Jewish- or Italian-owned concerns. Thus, complementarity, rather than competition, characterizes the links between new and old small-business groups.[45]

Predispositions toward entrepreneurship

The reasons why immigrants emerge as a replacement group rest on a complex of interacting economic and psychological factors. Blocked mobility is a powerful spur to business activity. Immigrants suffer from a variety of impediments in the labor market: poor English-language facility; inadequate or inappropriate skills; age; and often, discrimination.[46] Lacking the same opportunities for stable career employments as natives, immigrants are more likely to opt for self-employment and to be less averse to the substantial risks entailed. The limited range of job and income-generating activities is also an incentive to skill acquisition. Native workers will tend not to acquire particular skills if the returns to the needed investment in education and training are lower than for comparable jobs. By contrast, the same skills might offer the immigrants the best return, precisely because they lack access to better-remunerated jobs. As Bailey has shown, this is one reason for the prevalence of immigrants in the restaurant industry, where managerial and skilled (cooking) jobs offer lower returns to investment in training than other comparable skilled and managerial jobs.[47] Immigrants' willingness to put in long hours, needed to capitalize a business or maintain economies of scale, is similarly conditioned. For those without access to jobs with high rates of hourly return, such activities as driving a cab or running a store from early morning to late night offer the best available rewards for their work effort.

There are also psychological components to the entry of immigrants into small business. Much of the sociological literature has characterized the small-business owner as an anachronistic type impelled by a need for autonomy and independence.[48] Auster and Aldrich note that this approach assumes that entrepreneurship reflects the decisions of isolated individuals and thus ignores the issue of why certain groups disproportionately channel new recruits into small business.[49] Moreover, the traditional perspective also fails to account for the social pressures that condition groups and individuals for small business activity, among which the immigration process itself should be counted.

Immigration involves a process of self-selection, in which the more able and better-prepared workers enter the immigration stream. In contrast to other groups in the low-wage labor market, where labor-force participation competes with alternative social attachments, immigrants are at once more motivated, more willing to take risks, and better prepared to adjust to change.[50] The original society also conditions them for adaptability to small-business routines. Michael Piore has suggested that immigrants have a more favorable view of low-level work in industrial countries than do natives because the migrants view their job in terms of the much different job hierarchy of their home societies.[51]

Quite the same disparity would give the immigrant a distinctive frame of reference from which to assess the attractiveness of the small business that opens us as previously incumbent groups move on to other pursuits.

Ethnicity as resource

Ethnicity is a resource insofar as the social structures that connect members of an ethnic group to one another can be converted into business assets. These connections lend ethnic businesses a competitive edge against native competitors because (a) they provide a mechanism of organizing an otherwise unstructured labor market; and (b) they provide a mechanism for mediating the strains in the workplace and providing a normative basis on which the rules of the workplace can be established. In the discussion that follows, these two points will be treated separately.

The labor market in small-business industries tends to be unstructured in that it contains "few, if any established institutions by means of which people obtain information, move into and out of jobs, qualify for advances in rank or pay, or identify themselves with any type of organization . . . for purposes of security or support."[52] The reasons why stable labor-market arrangements are undeveloped are various: work contracts are of short and uncertain duration due to sensitivity to seasonal or cyclical factors; the persistence of competition places a limit on firm size (and thereby on the articulation of internal, structured job ladders) and also reduces the profit margins needed to pay for training workers in specific skills; and general skills that can be carried from one firm to another are usually required, which means, however, that one firm is reluctant to make an investment in training that will redound to another firm's gain.[53]

Because small firms therefore rely on the external labor market, a chief problem is how to secure and maintain a trained labor force. One option is to lower skill levels so that the costs of training can be drastically reduced, and this is the path that many small, low-wage employers in the "secondary labor market" have apparently pursued. As Piore has argued, jobs in the secondary sector "are essentially unskilled, either requiring no skill at all, or utilizing basic human skills and capacities shared by virtually all adult workers."[54] One case is that of the fast-food restaurant where the worker has been converted into an assembler and packer whose skills can be learned in a matter of hours.[55]

What the fast-food case also shows is that deskilling is only an alternative when demand is standardized and tasks can then be broken down into repetitive components. However, this is the definition of mass production; and many businesses arise in niches where specialty, not mass production, is required. This is the case in construction, where new buildings are often custom-made jobs and also in the fashion segments of apparel, where only small batches of highly varying products are made. Where specialty work prevails, jobs involve a variety of tasks; the ability to adjust to changing job requirements and perform them with proficiency is precisely what is meant by skill.

Thus, the central issue confronting small firms is how to increase the probability of hiring workers who are capable of learning required skills and will remain with the firm and apply their skills there. One recruitment practice widely favored in industry is to recruit through "word-of-mouth" techniques. Word-of-mouth recruitment appeals to employers for three reasons. Workers hired tend to have the same characteristics as those friends or relatives who recommend them; employees concerned about their future tenure in the plant are unlikely to nominate "bad prospects"; and, finally, new hires recruited through word-of-mouth channels are likely to be subject to the informal control of their associates once they are placed on the job.[56]

Consider now the possibilities in an industry like clothing or restaurants or construction, where nonimmigrants and immigrants both own firms, but the first group recruits a heterogeneous pool of workers, all of different ethnicities, while the second recruits primarily through ethnic networks. The logic of word-of-mouth recruitment is that applicants resemble the existing labor force, but, in the first case, social distance between native employer and immigrant employee makes it difficult to accurately discern the characteristics of the incumbent workers. As an example, many nonimmigrant owners have but the vaguest impressions of the national origins of their workers; thus ask a nonimmigrant factory owner whether his Hispanic workers are Puerto Rican or Dominican and the answer is likely to be: "How do I know? They all speak Spanish. They're from the islands, somewhere." Furthermore, the presumption of trust inherent in the process of assembling a skilled work force through word-of-mouth recruitment is frequently weak or absent under the conditions that seem prevalent in industries that employ large numbers of immigrants and minorities. For example, the principal complaint among personnel managers of supermarkets and department stores whom I interviewed as part of a study of youth employment was about the high level of theft among the largely minority, inner-city youth hired to work in their stores.[57] These comments recall Elliot Liebow's finding that stealing from employers was a prevalent practice among the black streetcornermen whom he studied, but so was the assumption among employers that their workers will steal, resulting in a consequent reduction in the level of remuneration.[58] Trust is further weakened when ethnic differences separate workers from employers.

In some cases, this is due to stereotyping on the part of immigrant labor and native management alike – a matter to which I shall return in greater detail below. But it may also be that the situational constraints provide little room for trust to grow up. For instance, many immigrants in an industry like garments work under assumed names, thus making their very identity uncertain. Similarly, a work force may be prone to high levels of turnover – which may occur because of seasonality or because of frequent travel or return migration to the immigrants' home societies – but, whatever the cause, high turnover will hinder the development of stable relationships on which trust might be based. A firm with high turnover is also apt to be caught in a vicious circle since the costs of constantly hiring make it uneconomical to exercise much discretion over the recruitment process.[59]

Now, take by contrast the immigrant firm. Immigrant owners can mobilize direct connections to the ethnic community from which they come in order to recruit an attached labor force. One means of securing a labor force is to recruit family members; unlike strangers, the characteristics of kin are known and familiar; hence, their behavior is more likely to be predictable, if not reliable; and, futhermore, trust may already inhere in the family relationship. Thus, Korean greengrocers tend to employ family members or other close relatives in the hope of "eradicating 'inside enemies' – non-Korean employees who steal cash and goods or give away goods to their friends or relatives who visit the store as customers."[60]

Of course, while some ethnic businesses may pivot around nuclear or perhaps extended family relationships, the average size of many businesses makes it necessary to extend beyond the family orbit. Still, kin can be used to secure key positions. Moreover, immigrants can also recruit through other closely knit networks that will bring them into contact with other ethnics to whom they are tied by pre-existing social connections. For example, migration chains often link communities in the Dominican Republic to Dominican-owned garment factories in New York City.[61] Similarly, Chinese immigrants may gravitate toward immigrant owners who speak the same dialect as they – and thus a Toisanese-speaking newcomer may opt for a Toisanese-speaking owner as against one who only speaks Cantonese. Moreover, trust may be heightened if an immigrant culture contains mechanisms for transforming friendship relations into fictive kinship relations. For example, *compradazgo* relationships between a child and godparents and between the parents and godparents are common to many Latin American societies and are seen as functional equivalents to kinship relationships. Similar relationships of fictive kinship are constructed among the Chinese.[62]

Ethnicity might also serve as a mechanism for mediating the strains in the workplace and providing the normative basis on which the rules of the workplace might be established. In the literature, there are two conflicting descriptions of the industrial-relations environment of the small firm. On the one hand, researchers working in the dual labor-market framework have argued that the small firm is riven by antagonism: supervision is tyrannical and capricious; there are no formal grievance procedures through which workers can seek redress for their complaints; and management and workers are caught in a vicious circle in which workers respond to the harsh exercise of discipline with further insubordination.[63] On the other hand, research investigating the "size effect" indicates that small firms garner favorable ratings when checked against large concerns on turnover levels, propensity to strike, job satisfaction, and a variety of other indicators.[64]

If size per se is unlikely to yield a particular industrial-relations environment, these contrasting findings suggest that industrial-relations outcomes are the product of the interaction of size with other factors. Compare the small concern to the large business, which is governed, not only by a web of formal rules (promulgated by management or negotiated through collective agreements with unions),but also informal understandings about how tasks are to be performed and jobs are to be allocated. Such understandings originate on the plant floor because workers, if put into stable and constant contact with one another, tend to form communities, with norms, expectations, and rules of their own. These rules are often contested by management; and, in unionized settings, much of the bargaining appears to center on the scope and permanence of these rules. Yet, the tendency is for management to abide by central rules and seek change on the margins. The reasons are two-fold. First, workers have the economic power to punish management for breach of the customary workplace rules. Secondly, management, especially at the lower levels, is socialized into the rules of the workplace as well and, to some extent, belongs to the work group itself.[65] This being said, we can now assess the possible effects of ethnicity on industrial-relations patterns in small firms.

As I argued above, small firms where management and labor are ethnically distinctive have difficulty stabilizing the employment relationship. One consequence of their failure to do so is that turnover tends to be too rapid to permit the formation of social groups in which customary work norms might be embedded. Moreover, even where such groups take cohesive form, social distance between management and immigrant labor tends to preclude managerial acceptance of work-group norms. In part, this is because ethnic behavioral patterns are often so divergent that simple stylistic differences are perceived in deeply threatening ways.[66] The conditions of duress that so often confront small firms (bottlenecks, short delivery deadlines, understaffing, etc.) further contribute to antagonism. Repeated conflict over production quotas, behavioral rules, absenteeism, and instability tends to take on an explicitly racial character as management interprets workers' behavior in racially stereotyped ways. And, when immigrant or minority workers are employed by members of the majority group, the economic disparities between the two groups fuel discontent with wages, personnel policies, and general working conditions, making work just another instance of inequitable treatment.[67]

By contrast, ethnicity provides a common ground on which the rules of the immigrant workplace are negotiated. In the previous section, I argued that the social structures around which the immigrant firm is organized serve to stabilize the employment relationship. However, these social structures are also relations of meaning suffused with the expectations that actors have of one another. One consequence is that authority can be secured on the basis of personal loyalties and ethnic allegiance rather than harsh discipline, driving, and direct control techniques. Furthermore, ethnic commonality provides a repertoire of symbols and customs that can be invoked to underline cultural interests and similarities in the face of a potentially conflictual situation. On the other hand, custom also serves as a constraint on employers' behavior. Immigrant owners who hire kin or hometown friends are expected to show that the employment relationship is more than a purely instrumental exchange, by making a place for workers' newly arrived relatives, by accommodating work rules to employees' personal needs, and by assisting workers with problems that they encounter with the host society. Moreover, it is anticipated that the standards of conduct that prevail in the broader ethnic community will extend to the workplace as well. As Bernard Wong has pointed out, little loyalty is given to the Chinese garment employer who fails to show *"yan ching"* (human feelings) or *"kan chin"* (sentimental feeling); and, if problems arise in keeping a stable work force, the employer stands not only to lose money but to lose "face."[68]

Opportunities and entrepreneurial behavior

Thus immigrant business develops as a result of the interaction between the opportunity structure of the society and the social structure of a particular immigrant group. One advantage of this approach is simply that it offers a more complete explanation than the other research frameworks. The second advantage is that it offers a dynamic perspective in which feedback processes link opportunities to the behavioral patterns and aspirations of the immigrant group.

One way in which this happens is through the accumulation of advantages. Once an immigrant economy is in place, it tends to attract a disproportionate number of new immigrant workers who gravitate toward immigrant firms because this is where jobs can be easiest found and where the working conditions are most comfortable. For example, immigrant-owned clothing firms in New York's garment industry tend to hire the newly arrived friends and relatives of workers already employed in the plant; and, as Bailey has noted, some immigrant restaurants serve as way-stations where recent immigrants who know friends and relatives of the owners can earn a little money and make contacts while they are looking for a job. Thus, if privileged access to the immigrant labor force is an initial condition of business success, that access tends to widen as the immigrant business sector grows.[69]

Secondly, the development of an ethnic economy provides both a catalyst for the entrepreneurial drive and a mechanism for the effective transmission of needed business skills. As the immigrant sector grows, it creates a pool of potential role models whose success reinforces the drive for independence. Interviews with Hispanic and Chinese immigrant owners in the clothing industry, for example, indicated that their perceptions of opportunities were often linked to the experiences of other immigrants within their reference group. As one Chinese garment-factory owner put it: "My boss was making money, so I decided to go into business for myself." Growth takes place through a process of imitation, in which the social structures of the immigrant community serve to diffuse information about a new innovation. Initial business success signals the existence of a supportive environment, thereby encouraging other, less adventurous members of a group to follow suit.

Thirdly, the social arrangements characteristic of the immigrant firm increase the likelihood that immigrant workers can acquire the know-how that the role of ownership will entail. Skills are relatively easy to pick up in the small immigrant firm, where responsibilities are flexibly defined; and, because of understaffing, jobs often include several tasks. Family members, brought in with the expectation that they will help out in various aspects of the business, thereby gain the chance to acquire not simply managerial training but also those contacts to suppliers and customers needed for business success. As I've argued, the immigrant owner creates the basis for trust by recruiting through the immigrant community; this also promotes the delegation of authority to co-ethnic employees as opposed to conditions in the native-owned firm, where prejudice often confines immigrants to low-skilled jobs.

For example, few native-owned restaurants in New York hire immigrants as either managers or waiters, but immigrants are employed in both of these positions throughout the immigrant-restaurant sector.[70]

While the immigrant sector gains new entrants on the basis of imitation, expansion may also have a dynamic effect on the customer base. Economies of agglomeration occur when firms proliferate and attract additional customers drawn by the size and diversity of the physical marketplace – as in the case of stores that draw in passerby traffic from customers patronizing other nearby shops. Such agglomeration economies play a catalytic role for immigrant merchants catering to the distinctive tastes of their co-ethnics since the size of the market provides a scope for specialists whose services would otherwise not be in sufficient demand.

As small ethnic businesses grow in both number and capability, the external environment may also become more supportive. One reason is that the expanded size of the ethnic economy may make it profitable for other businesses (ethnic or not) to specialize in supplying the particular needs of ethnic concerns, which in turn will promote the proliferation of additional, new ethnic businesses. A second reason is that the surplus generated by the "export activities" of ethnic businesses – that is to say, the revenues produced through transactions with nonimmigrant customers – loops back into the ethnic economy, producing multiplier effects. Thus, a certain percentage of the wages earned by immigrant workers in the "export activities" of the immigrant sector will be spent for ethnic products or services supplied by other co-ethnics. Similarly, some portion of profits will be plowed into investments that add to the size of the ethnic economy. In both these cases, ethnicity and opportunity interact: the more distinctive ethnic consumer tastes are, the more likely immigrants are to patronize immigrant-owned firms; the more reliant are immigrant capitalists on their co-ethnics as either customers or employees, the more likely are their investments to flow back into the community rather than gravitate outside. Thus, in a highly self-sufficient community like New York's Chinatown, the expansion of the Chinese garment industry has meant a vast increase in expenditures for local ethnic supplies and services. Similarly, a large proportion of the annual profits generated by the Chinese garment industry – estimated at $11 million in 1981 – is reinvested in other garment factories, Chinese restaurants, real estate, or Chinese fast-food storefronts.[71]

Opportunity and constraint in ethnic business growth

An alternative to the argument developed so far would suggest that immigrant firms are privileged only in their ability to exploit the immigrant work force. By hiring through the ethnic networks, immigrant employers engage their workers in a sponsor/client relation whose claims extend far beyond the cash nexus. Workers entangled in close sponsor/client relationships may be inhibited, not only from pressing for better wage and working standards, but also from setting out into business on their own.

The probability of movement out of the ethnic firm depends on the broader structure of opportunities in which ethnic enterprise emerges. Where immigrants are institutionally segregated from the broader labor market or highly dependent on ethnic trade, as I argued earlier, immigrant employers can effectively use the threat of exclusion or ostracism to effectively maintain control and stability. Mobility may also be hindered if ethnic elites establish formal structures that regulate intraethnic economic activity, such as the trade guilds and marketing organizations that were common among Chinese-Americans and Japanese-Americans in the early twentieth century.[72]

In the current context, several factors, most importantly the reduced level of competition with natives and the growth state of the immigrant economy, diminish the potential for a captive labor force. Efforts to regulate business activity have arisen on occasion among the Chinese and Koreans, but they have foundered against the immigrant entrepreneur's incessant search for individual opportunity. This follows from the argument made above, namely that the growth of an ethnic business tends to increase the rate of ethnic firm formation, by providing a spur to ambition among would-be immigrant capitalists and facilitating their acquisition of needed business skills.[73]

Furthermore, where the immigrant firm services an open market – as is the case for Chinese clothing manufacturers, Greek restaurants, or Korean vegetable and fruit dealers – workers who seek to go out on their own can do so with little punitive threat. Since these businesses involve market relationships to outsiders, trust between sellers and customers is of reduced importance and performance is judged according to abstract criteria. Under these conditions, the demands of patron-client relations can be evaded upon the acquisition of business contacts and managerial skills. Because entry into business is thus unhindered by social control mechanisms, the ethnic business sectors are rife with competition, and turnover rates for new businesses are high.[74]

Finally, the would-be owners' thrust toward independence does not necessarily conflict with the interests of the immigrant employer. From the standpoint of the worker, the opportunity to acquire managerial skills through a stint of employment in the immigrant firm both compensates for low pay and provides the motivation to learn a variety of different jobs. For the employer who hires a co-ethnic, the short-term consideration is access to lower-priced labor. Over the long term, the immigrant owner can act on the assumption that the newcomer will stay on long enough to learn the relevant business skills. Moreover, the new entrant's interest in skill acquisition will reduce the total labor bill and increase the firm's flexibility. Thus, one can trace out a sequence of developments that shape regular labor-market behavior within the ethnic subeconomy: first, the development of a distinct business niche; then a community-wide orientation toward business; finally, an understanding that newcomers will seek to go out on their own.

This chapter has provided an alternative explanation of immigrant enterprise by emphasizing the interaction between the opportunity structure of the host society and the social structure of the immigrant community. The demand for small-business activities emanates from markets whose small size, heterogeneity, or susceptibility to flux and instability limit the potential for mass distribution and mass production. Because such conditions favor small-scale enterprise, they lower the barriers to immigrants with limited capital and technical resources. Opportunities for ownership result from the process of ethnic succession: vacancies for new business owners arise as the older ethnic groups that have previously dominated small-business activities move into higher social positions. On the supply side, two factors promote recruitment into entrepreneurial positions. First, the situational constraints that immigrants confront breed a predisposition toward small business and further encourage immigrants to engage in activities – such as working long hours – that are needed to gain minimal efficiencies. Secondly, immigrant owners can draw on their connections to a supply of family and ethnic labor as well as a set of understandings about the appropriate behavior and expectations with the work setting to gain a competitive resolution to some of the organizational problems of the small firm.

Acknowledgment

Thanks to Tom Bailey and the editors of *Theory and Society* for their helpful comments on earlier drafts of this article. Funding, in part, was provided by a fellowship from the International Labor Organization.

Notes

1. Cf. U.S. Department of Commerce and Labor, Bureau of the Census, *Twelfth Census of the United States, Special Reports, Occupations* (Washington, D.C.: Government Printing Office, 1904).

2. "Hispanic Immigrants: Soon the Biggest Majority," *Time*, Oct. 16, 1978.

3. Self-employment rates for immigrants and natives in New York City calculated from the Public Use Microdata Sample of the 1980 Census of Population.

4. Nathan Glazer, "Social Characteristics of American Jews," *American Jewish Year-book* 55 (New York: American Jewish Committee: 1955): 3–43; William Caudill and George Devos, "Achievement, Culture, and Personality: The Case of the Japanese-Americans," *American Anthropologist* 58 (1956): 1102–26.

5. Ivan Light, *Ethnic Enterprise in America* (Berkeley: University of California Press, 1972).

6. Ivan Light, "Asian Enterprise in America: Chinese, Japanese, and Koreans in Small Business," in Scott Cummings, ed., *Self-Help in Urban America: Patterns of Minority Business Enterprise* (Port Washington, N.Y.: Kennikat, 1980).

7. Illsoo Kim, *The New Urban Immigrants: The Korean Community in New York* (Princeton: Princeton University Press, 1981), 281–304.

8. Werner Cahnman, "Socio-Economic Causes of Anti-Semitism," *Social Problems* 5 (1957): 21–29, quotation on p. 27.

9. Ivan Light, *Ethnic Enterprise in America*; John Modell, *The Economics and Politics of Racial Accommodation* (Urbana, Ill.: University of Illinois Press, 1977).

10. This interpretation leans on the material presented by Stanford Lyman; see his books on *Chinese-Americans* (New York: Random House, 1974) and *Asians in North America* (Santa Barbara: ABC-Clio Press, 1977). In addition, it should be pointed out that elite dominance was related to the migration process itself. Emigration from China was organized by wealthy kinsmen or fellow villagers who lent funds for transportation; control over the indebted emigrants facilitated their organization into elite-dominated economic organizations.

11. In work written subsequent to *Ethnic Enterprise in America*, Light has himself given greater emphasis to social control factors. For example, in a 1975 article, co-authored with Charles C. Wong, Light noted that "the dependence of Chinatowns upon the tourist industry has exerted a strong brake on abrupt change. The conservative force is economic rather than cultural in origin. . . . (Dependence on the tourist industry is the) industrial foundation for the self-sufficiency and hard work which have, in the past, been too glibly attributed to the cultural endowment of Chinese-Americans." "Protest or Work: Dilemmas of the Tourist Industry in American Chinatowns," *American Journal of Sociology* 80 (1975): 1345.

12. The material on immigrant business in the garment industry cited here and elsewhere in the article is more fully discussed in my book, *Through the Eye of the Needle: Immigrants and Enterprise in the New York Garment Industry* (New York: New York University Press, 1986). On competition among the Koreans, Philip K.Y. Young's article, "Family Labor, Sacrifice, and Competition: Korean Greengrocers in New York City," *Amerasia* 10 (1983): 53–71 is particularly informative. Young reports that "the real source of competition for the individual store owner is not from supermarkets or grocery stores but from other Korean owned produce stores located close by" (67).

13. John Armstrong, "Mobilized and Proletarian Diasporas," *American Political Science Review* 70 (1976): 393–408; Walter Zenner, "Middleman Minority Theories: A Critical Review," in Roy S. Bryce-Laporte, ed., *Sourcebook on the New Immigration* (New Brunswick, N.J.: Transaction Books, 1980).

14. Edna Bonacich, "A Theory of Middleman Minorities," *American Sociological Review* 38 (1973): 583–594; "Middleman Minorities and Advanced Capitalism," *Ethnic Groups* 2 (1980): 211–220.

15. Edna Bonacich and John Modell, *The Economic Basis of Ethnic Solidarity* (Berkeley: University of California Press, 1980).

16. Ibid., 20–24, 30–33.

17. A more detailed critique, with further bibliographical references, is developed in Waldinger, *Through the Eye of the Needle*, 9–13.

18. Data calculated from Table 1.30, pp. 65–66, in *The State of Small Business: A Report of the President* (Washington, D.C.: Government Printing Office, 1984).

19. *The State of Small Business*, 382.

20. Michael Piore, *Birds of Passage* (Cambridge, Eng.: Cambridge University Press, 1979).

21. F. M. Scherer, *Industrial Market Structure and Economic Performance*, 2d ed.(Boston: Houghton Mifflin, 1980), 86–150.

22. Arthur Stinchcombe, "Social Structure and the Invention of Organizational Form," in Tom Burns, ed., *Industrial Man* (Harmondsworth, Eng.:Penguin, 1969), 161–63; Howard Aldrich, *Environments and Organizations* (Englewood Cliffs, N.J.: Prentice-Hall, 1979).

23. For the original formulation of the special consumer-tastes argument, see Robert Kinzer and Edward Sagarin, *The Negro in American Business: The Conflict between Separatism and Integration* (New York: Greenburg, 1950); for a recent, quantitative assessment of the effects of culturally based tastes on business opportunities for immigrants and minorities, see Howard Aldrich et al., "Ethnic Residential Concentration and the Protected Market Hypothesis," *Social Forces*, forthcoming.

24. See, for example, Glenn Hendricks, *The Dominican Diaspora* (New York: Teachers College Press, 1974), 123–24.

25. Howard Aldrich, "Ecological Succession in Racially Changing Neighborhoods: A Review of the Literature," *Urban Affairs Quarterly* 10 (1975): 327–48; Howard Aldrich and Albert Reiss, Jr., "Continuities in the Study of Ecological Succession: Changes in the Race Composition of Neighborhoods and their Businesses," *American Journal of Sociology* 81 (1976): 846–66; Howard Aldrich, John Cater, Trevor Jones, and Dave McEvoy, "From Periphery to Peripheral: the South Asian Petite Bourgeoisie in England," in I. H. Simpson and R. Simpson, eds., *Research in the Sociology of Work*, vol. 2 (Greenwich, Conn.: JAI Press, 1982).

26. Deborah Dash Moore, *At Home in America* (New York: Columbia University Press, 1981).

27. Theodore Saloutos, *The Greeks in the United States* (Cambridge, Mass.: Harvard University Press, 1964).

28. Carmenza Gallo, "The Construction Industry in New York: Black and Immigrant Entrepreneurs," Working Paper, Conservation of Human Resources, Columbia University, 1983.

29. Marcia Freedman and Josef Korazim, "Israelis in the New York Area Labor Market," *Contemporary Jewry* 7 (1986): 141–53; Raymond Russell, "Ethnic and Occupational Cultures in the New Taxi Cooperatives of Los Angeles," paper presented at the 77th Annual Meeting of the American Sociological Association, San Francisco, Sept. 8–10, 1982.

30. Gorman Gilbert, "Operating Costs for Medallion Taxicabs in New York City," Report prepared for the Mayor's Committee on Taxicab Regulatory Issues, New York City, Oct. 1981; Edward G. Rogoff, "Regulation of the New York City Taxicab Industry," *City Almanac* 15 (1980): 1–9, 17–19.

31. E. A. G. Robinson, *The Structure of Competitive Industry*, (Cambridge, Eng.: Cambridge University Press, 1931); William Shepherd, *The Economics of Industrial Organization* (Englewood Cliffs, N.J.: Prentice-Hall: 1979).

32. Michael Piore, "The Technological Foundations of Dualism and Discontinuity," in Suzanne Berger and Michael Piore, *Dualism and Discontinuity in Industrial Society* (Cambridge, Eng.: Cambridge University Press, 1980).

33. Roger Waldinger, "Immigration and Industrial Change: A Case Study of the Apparel Industry," 323–349 in Marta Tienda and George Borjas, eds., *Hispanics in the U.S. Economy* (New York: Academic Press, 1985).

34. Carmenza Gallo, "The Construction Industry."

35. This analysis is based on a case study of the grocery store industry prepared as part of a report on youth employment for the New York City Office of Economic Development (Thomas Bailey and Roger Waldinger, "Youth and Jobs in Post-Industrial New York" New York, 1984). For a similar analysis of the effects of population heterogeneity on market size and large-firm shares in the grocery story industry, see Paul Cournoyer, "The New England Retail Grocery Industry," Working Paper 1121–80, Sloan School of Management, MIT, Cambridge, Mass., 1980.

36. For a similar argument based on research conducted in the United Kingdom, see Aldrich, Cater, Jones and McEvoy, "From Periphery to Peripheral." This work has been very helpful in my own thinking on the process and implications of ethnic succession. Aldrich et al., however, were principally concerned with the effects of residential succession on business opportunities for immigrant shopkeepers; they concluded that, as neighborhoods shifted from white to Asian, the proportion of white storekeepers declined and the proportion of Asian storekeepers increased.

37. Data calculated from U.S. Department of Commerce, Bureau of the Census, *1970 Census of Population: National Origin and Language*, PC(2), 1A, Table 16 (Washington, D.C.: Government Printing Office, 1973).

38. For the historical background, see Kessner, *The Golden Door*, and Moses Rischin, *The Promised City* (Cambridge, Mass.: Harvard University Press, 1962); on the persistence of corporate discrimination against Jews, see the studies summarized in Nathan Glazer and Daniel Moynihan, *Beyond the Melting Pot*, 2d ed., (Cambridge, Mass.: MIT Press, 1969), 147-49.

39. Steven M. Cohen, *American Modernity and Jewish Identity*, (New York, Tavistock, 1983), 86–87.

40. Data calculated by me from the 1981 New York Area Jewish Population Survey; I am grateful to my colleague, Paul Ritterband, for making the survey available to me.

41. Calvin Goldscheider and Frances Kobrin, "Ethnic Continuity and the Process of Self-Employment," *Ethnicity* 7 (1980): 262.

42. Waldinger, *Through the Eye of the Needle*, chap. 5.

43. Illsoo Kim, *The New Urban Immigrants*, 111.

44. New York City-City Planning Commission, *City Assistance for Small Manufacturers*, report prepared by the City Planning Commission, 1982; Philip K. Y. Young, "Family Labor, Sacrifice, and Competition," 70.

45. Waldinger, *Through the Eye of the Needle*, chap. 6.

46. Roger Waldinger, "The Occupational and Economic Integration of the New Immigrants," *Law and Contemporary Problems* 45 (1982): 197–222.

47. Thomas Bailey, *Immigrant and Native Workers: Contrasts and Competition* (Boulder, Colo.: Westview, 1987).

48. C. Wright Mills, *White Collar* (New York: Oxford, 1958).

49. Ellen Auster and Howard Aldrich, "Small Business Vulnerability, Ethnic Enclaves and Ethnic Enterprise," in Robin Ward and Richard Jenkins, eds., *Ethnic Communities in Business: Strategies for Survival* (Cambridge, Eng.: Cambridge University Press, 1984), 44.

50. Barry Chiswick, "Immigrants and Immigration Policy," in William Fellner, ed., *Contemporary Economic Problems* (Washington D.C.: American Enterprise Institute, 1978).

51. Michael Piore, *Birds of Passage*.

52. Orme W. Phelps, "A Structural Model of the U.S. Labor Market," *Industrial and Labor Relations Review* 10 (1957): 406.

53. In addition to Phelps, see Peter Doeringer and Michael Piore, *Internal Labor Markets and Manpower Analysis*, (Lexington, Mass.: Heath, 1971).

54. Michael Piore, "An Economic Approach," in Piore and Berger, *Dualism and Discontinuity*, 18.

55. Thomas Bailey, *Immigrant and Native Workers*.

56. Peter Doeringer and Michael Piore, *Internal Labor Markets*; Richard Lester, *Hiring Practices and Labor Competition*, Industrial Relations Section, Princeton University, Research Report 88, 1954.

57. See Thomas Bailey and Roger Waldinger, "Jobs and Youth in Post-Industrial New York City"; and, Waldinger and Bailey, "The Youth Employment Problem in the World City," *Social Policy* 16, 1 (1985): 55–58.

58. Elliot Liebow, *Tally's Corner* (Boston: Little, Brown, 1967). See also Michael Piore, "On-the-Job Training in a Dual Labor Market," in Arnold R. Weber et al., eds., *Public-Private Manpower Policies* (Madison, Wis.: Industrial Relations Research Association, 1969).

59. For further evidence and discussion, see Waldinger, *Through the Eye of the Needle*.

60. Illsoo Kim, *The New Urban Immigrants*, 112.

61. Roger Waldinger, "Immigration and Industrial Change," and "Immigrant Enterprise in the Garment Industry," *Social Problems* 32, 1: 60–72.

62. Hendricks, *Dominican Diaspora*, 31; Bernard Wong, *A Chinese-American Community* (Singapore: Chopmen, 1979).

63. Doeringer and Piore, *Internal Labor Markets*; Richard C. Edwards, *Contested Terrain* (New York: Basic, 1979).

64. Cf. Geoffrey K. Ingham, *Size of Industrial Organization and Worker Behavior* (Cambridge, Eng.: Cambridge University Press, 1970), and references cited therein.

65. Doeringer and Piore, *Internal Labor Markets*, 17–27; William F. Whyte et al., *Money and Motivation* (New York: Harper, 1955).

66. Gerald Suttles, *The Social Order of the Slum* (Chicago: University of Chicago Press, 1968); Thomas Kochman, *Black and White Styles in Conflict*, (Chicago: University of Chicago Press, 1983).

67. See Waldinger, *Through the Eye of the Needle*, chap. 7.

68. See Waldinger, "Immigrant Enterprise"; Bailey, *Immigrant and Native Workers*; Wong, *Chinese-American Community*.

69. See Waldinger, "Immigrant Enterprise"; and Bailey, "Immigrants in the Restaurant Industry."

70. Bailey, "Immigrants in the Restaurant Industry."

71. *Chinatown Garment Industry Study*, 111–42.

72. Ivan Light, *Ethnic Enterprise*; John Modell, *Politics and Economics*; Edna Bonacich and John Modell, *The Economic Basis*.

73. See, Illsoo Kim, *The New Urban Immigrants*; and Waldinger, *Through the Eye of the Needle*.

74. Cf. Kim and Waldinger cited above.

Index